NORTHERN IRELAND

A POLITICAL DIRECTORY

1968·88

W D FLACKES

SYDNEY ELLIOTT

THE

D1331679

First edition published in 1980 by
Gill and Macmillan Limited
Second edition published in 1983 by the
British Broadcasting Corporation

This fully revised and updated edition published in 1989 by
The Blackstaff Press Limited
3 Galway Park, Dundonald, Belfast BT16 0AN, Northern Ireland

Printed by The Guernsey Press Company Limited

British Library Cataloguing in Publication Data
Flackes, W.D.
Northern Ireland: a political directory, 1968–88. –
3rd ed.
1. Northern Ireland. Politics. – Directories
I. Title II. Elliott, Sydney
320'.025'416

ISBN 0-85640-418-7

CONTENTS

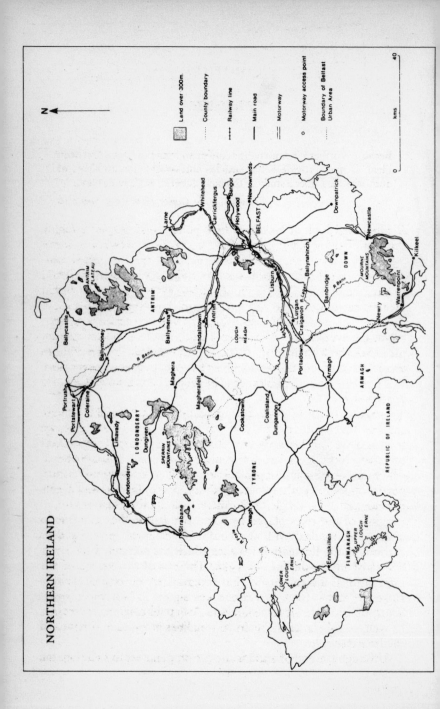

NORTHERN IRELAND

	Land over 300m.
	County boundary
	Railway line
	Main road
	Motorway
	Motorway access point
	Boundary of Belfast Urban Area

N

0   kms   40

PREFACE

> Because Northern Ireland politics differs so from the Anglo-American ideal, it may provide better insights into worldwide problems of authority than does a study of England, America or New Zealand.
>
> Richard Rose, *Governing Without Consensus*

A superficial look at Northern Irish politics may suggest a highly simplistic situation, with monolithic groups lined up on either side of a divided community. The reality is that there are unexpected complexities and subtleties, and the affairs of the region may even be said to have a quicksilver quality that cannot readily be packaged within the neat categories of a directory. None the less, *Northern Ireland: A Political Directory* was published in response to the many enquiries about the availability of a reference guide and this updated version preserves the format of the 1980 and 1983 editions in seeking to record the main participants and the twists and turns of events since 1968 when the Troubles in Northern Ireland caught world headlines.

Reaction to the previous editions from both sides of the Atlantic suggests that the directory is used primarily as a day-to-day reference tool, and the dictionary, plus the chronology and specialised sections on government and security systems, are designed to meet that end. The basic aim remains of providing a quick guide to the politicians, parties, policies, polls, pressure groups, paramilitaries, and events that make up the tangle of Northern Irish affairs. There is also an account of the roles played by successive British Governments in attempting to deal with the conflicting political forces, and in containing the fluctuating violence which has accounted for 2,711 lives lost up to the end of 1988. There is also coverage of the international dimension that has progressively developed, notably since the Anglo-Irish Agreement was signed in November 1985. Thus, the attitudes of some key American public figures are set out, as well, of course, as the main personalities involved in Britain and the Irish Republic.

Although the end of 1988 is the cut-off point for this edition, the

Troubles still continue and events in early 1989 came too late to figure in detail. For example, the secret inter-party discussions, involving Jack Allen (OUP), Peter Robinson (DUP), Austin Currie (SDLP) and Gordon Mawhinney (Alliance), while held in October 1988 in Duisburg, West Germany, only became public in February 1989. In any case, these discussions did not suggest an immediate breakthrough in finding a formula for serious negotiations between Unionists and Nationalists. However, they did indicate strenuous efforts on both sides to get round the Unionist insistence that the Anglo-Irish Agreement must be suspended in advance of such exchanges, and the SDLP's counter-demand that the agreement and its secretariat should remain active and dialogue be held outside the agreement. Above all, the background papers to the Duisburg Talks put the public statements of major politicans in a revealing light and underlined the risks of secret diplomacy in local politics. But it also gave rise to a Government initiative to get dialogue going.

Obviously, the directory cannot be wholly exhaustive, given the sheer range of activity over two decades. There is the ongoing problem of deciding where politics begins and ends in Northern Ireland. Churchmen seem to become ever more active in making political pronouncements. Few economists venture a comment on the local situation without airing some political opinion. The number of marginal political groups grows by the month, and few areas in the world can boast as many amateur politicians per square mile. Also, there has been a vast spin-off in published material about the Troubles since 1968. Robert Bell, supervisor of the Northern Ireland Political Collection in Belfast's Linen Hall Library, claims that this is 'the most documented conflict ever'. As evidence, he points out that the library's own unique collection now runs to more than 40,000 items, including books, reports, pamphlets, periodicals and posters. There are also substantial collections in the Belfast Central Reference Library, the Public Record Office of Northern Ireland, Queen's University library, and the local BBC and newspaper libraries. With gratitude, we have drawn on all these sources, and we wish also to record our thanks to the information offices at the Northern Ireland Office, European Commission, and Royal Ulster Constabulary and army headquarters, *Fortnight* magazine's chronology and *Northern Ireland 1968–74; A Chronology of Events* (3 vols) by Richard Deutsch and Vivien Magowan have also been useful points of reference.

Our difficulties in summarising events since 1968, given such an enormous wealth of source material, have been compounded, ironically, by lack of access to important information contained in Cabinet and other Government papers, for these have yet to be released. However, some interesting insights have been provided by the memoirs of former Northern Ireland Secretary of State Merlyn Rees, and former Northern Ireland Prime Minister, the late Lord Faulkner. And 1989 is expected to yield memoirs from Lord Whitelaw and Dr Garret FitzGerald, which might have given greater certainty to the relevant dictionary entries if they had been available. The same can be said of the eagerly awaited autobiography of Lord Fitt. We have also been very conscious of the fact that current Government policy seems to be pointing to tighter restrictions on the release of information about the security services, while the restrictions aimed at curtailing broadcasting opportunities for supporters of terrorism may even affect archive material dealing with violent politics. In the Northern Ireland context these developments could make future production of books of this kind even more difficult.

We are grateful for suggestions from reviewers and readers, some of which are reflected in this book. Finally, a word of thanks to senior BBC executives, who have been helpful in regard to this and previous editions – most recently, former Northern Ireland controller, Dr James Hawthorne CBE, and current Northern Ireland editor of news and current affairs, John Conway.

W.D. FLACKES AND SYDNEY ELLIOTT
BELFAST, FEBRUARY 1989

LIST OF ABBREVIATIONS

AAOH	American Ancient Order of Hibernians
ACE	Action for Community Employment
ADC	aide-de-camp
AIA	Anglo-Irish Agreement
ALJ	Association for Legal Justice
All.	Alliance Party
AOH	Ancient Order of Hibernians
ABD	Apprentice Boys of Derry
ASU	Active Service Unit
b.	born
BA	Bachelor of Arts
B.Agr.	Bachelor of Agriculture
BAO	Bachelor of Art of Obstetrics
BAOR	British Army of the Rhine
BBC	British Broadcasting Corporation
B.Ch.	Bachelor of Surgery
B.Comm.	Bachelor of Commerce
BDS	Bachelor of Dental Surgery
B.Ed.	Bachelor of Education
BIA	British Irish Association
BIIC	British-Irish Intergovernmental Council
BL	Bachelor of Law
B.Litt.	Bachelor of Letters
BMA	British Medical Association
B.Sc.	Bachelor of Science
B.Sc. (Econ.)	Bachelor of Economic Science
BUDP	British Ulster Dominion Party
Cantab.	Cambridge University
Capt.	Captain
CBI	Confederation of British Industry
CCDC	Central Citizens' Defence Committee
CEC	Campaign for Equal Citizenship
CESA	Catholic Ex-Servicemen's Association
CIA	Central Intelligence Agency
Com.	Communist
Cons.	Conservative Party
CPI	Communist Party of Ireland
CSO	Central Statistical Office
d.	died

DASS	Diploma of Applied Social Services
DCDC	Derry Citizen's Defence Committee
DCL	Doctor of Civil Law
DED	Department of Economic Development
Dip.Ed.	Diploma in Education
Dip.H.E.	Diploma of Higher Education
Dip.Obst.	Diploma in Obstetrics
D.Lit.	Doctor of Literature
D.Litt.	Doctor of Letters
DNA	deoxyribonucleic acid (genetic code)
DOE	Department of the Environment
DPH	Diploma in Public Health
DPP	Director of Public Prosecutions
DULC	Democratic Unionist Loyalist Coalition
DUP	Democratic Unionist Party
E.	east
EC	European Community
ECHR	European Convention on Human Rights
Ecol.	Ecology Party
EDG	European Democratic Group
Elec.	electorate
EOC	Equal Opportunities Commission
EPA	Emergency Provisions Act
ERG	European Right Group
FBI	Federal Bureau of Investigation
FEA	Fair Employment Agency
FF	Fianna Fáil
FG	Fine Gael
FRCS	Fellow of the Royal College of Surgeons
GAA	Gaelic Athletic Association
GB	Great Britain
GDP	Gross Domestic Product
GEC	General Electric Company
Gen.	General
GHQ	general headquarters
GLC	Greater London Council
GOC	General Officer Commanding
HAA	heavy anti-aircraft
HQ	headquarters
IAAG	improvised anti-armour grenade
ICTU	Irish Congress of Trade Unions
IDB	Industrial Development Board
IIP	Irish Independence Party

IMF	International Monetary Fund
INC	Irish National Caucus
Ind.	Independent
Ind. Lab.	Independent Labour
Ind. N.	Independent Nationalist
Ind. Soc.	Independent Socialist
Ind. U.	Independent Unionist
INLA	Irish National Liberation Army
IONA	Islands of North Atlantic
IPLO	Irish People's Liberation Organisation
IRA	Irish Republican Army
IRSP	Irish Republican Socialist Party
ITGWU	Irish Transport and General Workers' Union
ITV	Independent Television
Lab.	Labour Party
Lab. and TU	Labour and Trade Union Group
LAW	Loyalist Association of Workers
LCI	Labour Committee on Ireland
LCU	Loyal Citizens of Ulster
Lib.	Liberal Party
LLB	Bachelor of Laws
LLD	Doctor of Laws
LLM	Master of Laws
LOL	Loyal Orange Lodge
Loy.	Loyalist
Loy. Coal.	Loyalist Coalition
LPNI	Labour Party of Northern Ireland
Lt.	Lieutenant
MA	Master of Arts
MAFF	Ministry of Agriculture, Fisheries, and Food
MB	Bachelor of Medicine
maj.	majority
MEP	Member of European Parliament
MP	Member of Parliament
M.o.D.	Ministry of Defence
MORI	Mass Opinion Research Institute
MPA	Member of Parliamentary Assembly (1982)
MRCGP	Member of the Royal College of General Practitioners
M.Sc.	Master of Science
N.	north
Nat.	Nationalist Party
Nat. Dem.	Nationalist Democratic Party
NATO	North Atlantic Treaty Organisation

NCCL	National Council for Civil Liberties
NCO	non-commissioned officer
NDP	National Democratic Party
NEC	National Executive Committee
NI	Northern Ireland
NICRA	Northern Ireland Civil Rights Association
NICVA	Northern Ireland Council for Voluntary Action
NIE	Northern Ireland Electricity
NIF	New Ireland Forum
NILP	Northern Ireland Labour Party
NIO	Northern Ireland Office
NORAID	Irish Northern Aid Committee
NPF	National Political Front
NUI	National University of Ireland
NUJ	National Union of Journalists
NUM	National Union of Mineworkers
NUM	New Ulster Movement
NUPRG	New Ulster Political Research Group
NUU	New University of Ulster
Off. Rep.	Official Republican
Off.U.	Official Unionist
OIRA	Official Irish Republican Army
OU	Open University
OUP	Official Unionist Party
Oxon.	Oxford University
PLO	Palestine Liberation Army
PC	Privy Councillor
PD	People's Democracy
PESC	Public Expenditure Survey Cycle
Ph.D.	Doctor of Philosophy
PIRA	Provisional Irish Republican Army
PM	Prime Minister
POW	prisoner of war
PP	Peace People
PPP	People's Progressive Party
PPS	Parliamentary Private Secretary
PR	Proportional Representation
PRO	Public Relations Officer
Prog.D.	Progressive Democrats
Prot.U.	Protestant Unionist Party
PSF	Provisional Sinn Féin
PTA	Prevention of Terrorism Act
PTF	Protestant Task Force

PUP	Progressive Unionist Party
QC	Queen's Counsel
QUB	Queen's University Belfast
RECOG	Royal College of Obstetricians and Gynaecologists
Rep. C.	Republican Clubs
Rep. Lab.	Republican Labour Party
RHU	Red Hand Commandos
RSF	Republican Sinn Féin
RTE	Radio Telefís Éireann
RU	Real Unionist
RUC	Royal Ulster Constabulary
RUCR	Royal Ulster Constabulary Reserve Force
S.	south
SACHR	Standing Advisory Commission on Human Rights
SAS	Special Air Service
SDA	Shankill Defence Association
SDLP	Social Democratic and Labour Party
SDP	Social Democratic Party
SLD	Social and Liberal Democrats
Soc.	socialist
STV	single transferable vote
TCD	Trinity College Dublin
TD	Teachta Dáil (member of the Dáil)
U.	Unionist Party
u/a	unavailable
UAC	Ulster Army Council
UCA	Ulster Citizen Army
UCC	University College Cork
UCD	University College Dublin
UCDC	Ulster Constitution Defence Committee
UCG	University College Galway
UDA	Ulster Defence Association
UDI	Unilateral Declaration of Independence
UDR	Ulster Defence Regiment
UFF	Ulster Freedom Fighters
UIP	Ulster Independence Party
UK	United Kingdom
ULA	Ulster Loyalist Association
ULCCC	Ulster Loyalist Central Co-ordinating Committee
ULDP	Ulster Loyalist Democratic Party
U. Lib.	Ulster Liberal Party
ULP	United Labour Party
UN	United Nations

Unoff.	Unofficial
Unoff. U.	Unofficial Unionist
UPNI	Unionist Party of Northern Ireland
U. Pro-A.	Pro-Assembly Unionist
UPUP	Ulster Popular Unionist Party
UPV	Ulster Protestant Volunteers
US	United States
USC	Ulster Special Constabulary (B Specials)
USCA	Ulster Special Constabulary Association
USSR	Union of Soviet Socialist Republics
Utd.	United
Utd. Loy.	United Loyalist
UTV	Ulster Television
UU	University of Ulster
UUAC	United Unionist Action Council
UUUC	United Ulster Unionist Council (or Coalition)
UUUM	United Ulster Unionist Movement
UUUP	United Ulster Unionist Party
UVF	Ulster Volunteer Force
UWC	Ulster Workers' Council
VCR	video cassette recorder
VHF	very high frequency
VPP	Volunteer Political Party
VSC	Vanguard Service Corps
VULC	Vanguard Unionist Loyalist Coalition
VUPP	Vanguard Unionist Progressive Party
W.	west
WBLC	West Belfast Loyalist Coalition
WP	Workers' Party
WPRC	Workers' Party Republican Clubs
WT	Women Together
WUUC	West Ulster Unionist Council
YTP	Youth Training Programme

CHRONOLOGY OF MAJOR EVENTS
1921–88

1921 First NI Parliament opened by George V on 7 June.

1922 Widespread violence in NI, in which 232 people killed and about 1,000 wounded.

1925 Irish Free State Government confirmed the border in the 1920 Act and registered it with the League of Nations.

1931 IRA declared illegal in Irish Free State.

1932 De Valera's Fianna Fáil Party secured power in Irish Free State. In Belfast new Stormont Parliament Buildings opened by Prince of Wales.

1937 New Southern Irish Constitution claimed sovereignty over island of Ireland.

1941 German air raids on Belfast – 949 killed and more than 2,000 injured.

1942 US troops arrived in NI on way to second front in Europe.

1943 Sir Basil Brooke (later Lord Brookeborough) became NI PM, amid demands for more vigorous local war effort.

1949 Southern Ireland became a full Republic and British Government gave new constitutional guarantee to Stormont Parliament.

1956 IRA launched border campaign which led to introduction of internment without trial both in Republic and in NI.

1962 IRA called off its campaign.

1963 Terence O'Neill became NI PM.

1965 Sean Lemass visited Stormont for talks, the first Taoiseach of Republic to do so. The visit and its secrecy was attacked by many Unionists.

1966 UVF declared illegal.

1967 NICRA formed. Republican Clubs declared illegal.

1968 Civil rights marches began with violence at Derry march on 5 October. First government reforms announced but regarded as inadequate by civil rights movement. O'Neill sacked William Craig from Cabinet.

1

1969

30 APRIL O'Neill resigned and was succeeded by James Chichester-Clark.

AUGUST Violence in the Bogside area of Derry led to the army being put on the streets to help the RUC. Severe rioting in Belfast, Derry and other places. Rest of year marked by pressure from Westminster for reforms. RUC reorganised; proposed disbandment of B Specials. New electoral laws. PIRA formed.

1970

1 APRIL UDR inaugurated to replace B Specials.

30 APRIL B Specials disbanded.

19 JUNE Rev. Ian Paisley elected MP for N. Antrim.

26 JUNE Bernadette Devlin MP jailed for part in Bogside disturbances.

21 AUGUST SDLP formed.

1971

10 MARCH Three Scottish soldiers found shot dead at Ligoniel, Belfast.

20 MARCH Chichester-Clark resigned as PM and was succeeded three days later by Brian Faulkner.

16 JULY SDLP withdrew from Stormont after refusal of inquiry into shooting by army of two men in Derry.

9 AUGUST Beginning of internment without trial. Subsequently NICRA launched civil disobedience campaign.

27–8 SEPTEMBER Tripartite talks at Chequers involving Edward Heath, Jack Lynch, and Brian Faulkner. Widespread violence: PIRA apparently growing in strength.

25 NOVEMBER Harold Wilson put forward fifteen-year Irish unity plan.

4 DECEMBER Fifteen people died in explosion at McGurk's bar in Belfast. (Self-confessed UVF man convicted of the explosion.)

1972

30 JANUARY Thirteen men shot dead by army in Derry ('Bloody Sunday').

2 FEBRUARY British Embassy in Dublin burned down.

22 FEBRUARY Seven killed by bomb at Aldershot military barracks; OIRA claimed responsibility.

25 FEBRUARY John Taylor, Minister of State, survived OIRA assassination attempt in Armagh.

4 MARCH Abercorn restaurant bombed; 2 killed, 130 injured.

24 MARCH British Government announced direct rule in NI after Faulkner Government said they would not accept loss of law-and-order powers.

26 MAY SDLP urged those who had withdrawn from public offices to return.

29 MAY In situation of growing violence, OIRA called a ceasefire.

26 JUNE PIRA began what it called a 'bilateral truce'.

1 JULY UDA set up no-go areas in Belfast.

7 JULY William Whitelaw, Secretary of State, met PIRA leaders in secret in London.

9 JULY PIRA claimed that British army had broken ceasefire in Lenadoon area of W. Belfast.

21 JULY Nine people killed when twenty-two bombs exploded in Belfast ('Bloody Friday').

31 JULY Army entered W. Belfast and Bogside no-go areas in 'Operation Motorman'. Eight people killed by car bombs in Claudy, Co. Derry.

24 SEPTEMBER Darlington conference on political options.

30 OCTOBER British Government published discussion paper on NI's political future, repeating guarantee of constitutional position but recognising 'Irish dimension'.

16–17 NOVEMBER Edward Heath visited NI and said that UDI would lead to a 'bloodbath'.

1 DECEMBER Two people killed and eighty injured in Dublin when two bombs exploded while Dáil was debating tougher anti-subversion laws. Both wings of IRA and the UDA denied responsibility.

1973

1 JANUARY NI, like the rest of the UK, became part of the EC.

8 MARCH Voting in border poll. In London two car bombs exploded, one man killed and 180 injured; PIRA later claimed responsibility.

20 MARCH British Government published White Paper, proposing an Assembly elected by PR and with Westminster retaining law-and-order powers.

28 MARCH Shipment of arms for PIRA found on vessel *Claudia*, off Waterford.

30 MAY First elections for the new District Councils – first voting by PR in NI since 1925.

28 JUNE Polling for the new seventy-eight-member Assembly.

31 JULY Noisy scenes at first meeting of new Assembly.

21 NOVEMBER Agreement reached on setting up power-sharing Executive.

6–9 DECEMBER Sunningdale Conference on NI attended by British and Irish Ministers and NI power-sharing parties.

1974

1 JANUARY	NI Executive takes office.
4 JANUARY	Ulster Unionist Council rejected the Council of Ireland proposed in the Sunningdale Agreement.
7 JANUARY	Brian Faulkner (Chief Executive in power-sharing administration) resigned as Unionist Party leader.
16 JANUARY	Brian Faulkner flew to Dublin for talks with Taoiseach Liam Cosgrave.
22 JANUARY	Loyalist disruption of Assembly proceedings led to police forcibly ejecting eighteen members, including the Rev. Ian Paisley. Harry West appointed OUP leader.
1 FEBRUARY	Cosgrave and seven of his Ministers flew to Hillsborough, Co. Down, for a meeting with NI Executive Ministers.
28 FEBRUARY	In Westminster general election eleven seats won by UUUC candidates and SDLP held W. Belfast.
5 MARCH	With Labour forming a Government, Merlyn Rees became NI Secretary of State.
26 APRIL	UUUC, after a conference in Portrush, Co. Antrim, called for a NI regional parliament in a federal UK.
14 MAY	The power-sharing Executive won by forty-four to twenty-eight an Assembly vote on Sunningdale Agreement. The loyalist UWC immediately threatened power cuts in protest.
15 MAY	Power cuts forced the closure of several factories, and many workers, including those in Belfast shipyard, went on strike.
16 MAY	As the stoppage developed, the Secretary of State accused the organisers of intimidation, and said it was a political, not an industrial, strike.
17 MAY	In Dublin twenty-two killed by car bombs which exploded without warning, and five people killed by a car bomb in Monaghan town. Two of three cars used in Dublin bombing had been hi-jacked earlier in Protestant areas of Belfast; UDA and UVF denied responsibility. (Three more people died later from injuries received in the explosions.)
25 MAY	Harold Wilson, in a broadcast, said the strike was being run by 'thugs and bullies'.
28 MAY	In face of the strike, the Unionist members of the Executive resigned and the Executive collapsed. Direct rule resumed.

29 MAY	UWC called off its strike.
31 MAY	Merlyn Rees said that the rise of 'Ulster nationalism' was a major factor which the Government would have to take into account.
4 JULY	British Government announced the setting up of an elected Constitutional Convention to seek a political settlement.
1 AUGUST	Meeting between representatives of SDLP and UDA.
4 SEPTEMBER	Brian Faulkner launched UPNI.
5 OCTOBER	Five people killed and fifty-four injured when bombs exploded without warning in Guildford, Surrey, in two pubs popular with off-duty army personnel.
10 OCTOBER	In Westminster general election, UUUC got ten of the twelve seats, the SDLP retaining W. Belfast and Frank Maguire, Independent, unseating OUP leader Harry West in Fermanagh–S. Tyrone. Enoch Powell returned in S. Down.
15 OCTOBER	Republican convicted prisoners in the Maze Prison set fire to a large number of huts, and troops were brought in to suppress a riot.
16 OCTOBER	Secretary of State Rees revealed that nine Maze prisoners were in hospital after disturbances, while fifteen prison officers had been injured and sixteen soldiers hurt, nine seriously. At Magilligan Prison Republican prisoners burned cookhouse, prison shop and a hut. In Armagh Women's Prison the governor and three women prison officers were held captive overnight in an attic, and were only released after they had got an assurance through clergymen that prisoners in the Maze were safe.
21 OCTOBER	John Hume, deputy leader of SDLP, said Rees had lost all credibility and that they saw little point in talking to him.
22 OCTOBER	UUUC MPs elected James Molyneaux as their leader.
30 OCTOBER	Rees said riot and burnings at Maze Prison had caused £1.5 million of damage, and at Magilligan, £200,000.
6 NOVEMBER	In the early hours of the morning thirty-three Republican prisoners escaped through a tunnel from the Maze Prison; twenty-nine recaptured a few hours later and three in Andersonstown in the evening. During the escape, a twenty-four-year-old detainee was shot dead by a sentry.
9 NOVEMBER	Defence Ministry ruled that names of soldiers killed in NI not to be added to war memorials since it was not classed as war zone.

18 NOVEMBER	Plans announced for £30-million high-security prison at Maghaberry, Co. Antrim.
21 NOVEMBER	Nineteen killed and 182 injured when bombs exploded in two Birmingham pubs.
22 NOVEMBER	PIRA denied responsibility for Birmingham bombings.
25 NOVEMBER	Home Secretary Roy Jenkins announced that IRA was to be declared illegal in GB and tougher anti-terrorist laws would be introduced.
28 NOVEMBER	In Dublin the Government introduced Bill to allow terrorists to be tried for offences committed outside the jurisdiction.
5 DECEMBER	Parliament extended the new Prevention of Terrorism Act to NI, allowing, among other things, persons to be held without charge for up to seven days.
10 DECEMBER	At Feakle, Co. Clare, a group of Protestant Churchmen met members of PSF and PIRA.
18 DECEMBER	Churchmen met Rees to report on their talks in Feakle.
20 DECEMBER	PIRA announced ceasefire from midnight on 22 December to midnight on 2 January 1975.
23 DECEMBER	Edward Heath, during a visit to Stormont, said he believed there was majority support in NI for power-sharing.
29 DECEMBER	PIRA prisoners at Portlaoise, top security prison in the Republic, caused serious damage and held fourteen warders hostage in a bid for better conditions. The officers were freed unhurt when troops stormed the jail.
31 DECEMBER	Rees said Government would not be wanting in its response if 'a genuine and sustained cessation of violence' occurred.

1975

2 JANUARY	PIRA extended its Christmas ceasefire.
16 JANUARY	PIRA called off ceasefire.
9 FEBRUARY	PIRA announced new ceasefire.
12 FEBRUARY	Incident centres, manned by PSF, set up to monitor ceasefire in liaison with Government officials.
18 FEBRUARY	Airey Neave MP appointed Conservative NI spokesman.
18 MARCH	Two Price sisters, Marion and Dolours, convicted for London car bombings in 1973, transferred from Durham Jail to Armagh, following long campaign for their transfer.
25 MARCH	Harold Wilson visited Stormont and announced 1 May as Convention election polling day.
5 APRIL	Secretary of State Rees said loyalist gunman had tried to murder him in 1974.

1 MAY	Convention polling day.
8 MAY	First meeting of Convention.
5 JUNE	Common Market referendum showed narrow majority in NI for membership.
24 JULY	Rees promised to release all detainees by Christmas.
31 JULY	Three members of Miami Showband killed and one seriously injured in UVF gun attack. Two UVF men also died, blowing themselves up during the attack.
8 SEPTEMBER	William Craig cast the only vote for voluntary coalition with SDLP during UUUC meeting at Stormont.
2 OCTOBER	In a series of UVF attacks twelve people killed, including three women and four UVF men, and forty-six injured.
3 OCTOBER	UVF declared illegal.
12 OCTOBER	Split in VUPP after Craig's support for voluntary coalition.
14 NOVEMBER	Conservative leader Margaret Thatcher visited Belfast.
5 DECEMBER	Last detainees released.
18 DECEMBER	Harold Wilson visited Londonderry, where two soldiers were killed by PIRA soon after he left.
22 DECEMBER	US authorities broke up gang of IRA gun-runners.

1976

4 JANUARY	Five Catholics killed in two separate shooting incidents near Whitecross, S. Armagh.
5 JANUARY	Ten Protestant workers shot dead at Kingsmills, S. Armagh. Republican Action Force claimed responsibility.
7 JANUARY	SAS unit moved into S. Armagh.
15 JANUARY	PM Wilson presided at first all-party security meeting on NI, held at 10 Downing Street.
21 JANUARY	Government said 25,000 houses damaged in violence.
3 FEBRUARY	Convention recalled in bid to secure agreement.
12 FEBRUARY	UUUC and SDLP inter-party talks broke down after an hour.
1 MARCH	Persons committing terrorist-type offences no longer entitled to special category status.
3 MARCH	Final sitting of Convention ended in uproar.
9 MARCH	Convention formally dissolved.
18 MARCH	Rees came out against any increase in the number of NI MPs.
30 MARCH	NICRA called off rent and rates strike, originally started in 1971.

7

5 MAY	Nine members of IRSP escaped from Maze Prison through tunnel.
15 MAY	Three RUC men killed in explosion at Belcoo, Co. Fermanagh.
22 MAY	UVF announced three-month ceasefire.
25 MAY	Loyalist vigilante group, Ulster Service Corps, announced that it was mounting patrols in view of 'deteriorating security situation'.
4 JUNE	Rev. Ian Paisley leaked news of private talks between OUP and SDLP.
7 JUNE	UUUC vote opposing OUP–SDLP talks.
3 AUGUST	Extensive damage caused in Portrush, Co. Antrim, by six explosions for which PIRA claimed responsibility.
8 AUGUST	Gerry Fitt fought off, with a gun, Republican demonstrators who broke into his Belfast home.
10 AUGUST	Two Maguire children killed in Andersonstown by a car whose driver had been shot dead by troops.
11 AUGUST	A third child from the Maguire family died as a result of Andersonstown accident.
12 AUGUST	Women demonstrated in favour of peace in Andersonstown and sparked off the women's peace movement (later the Peace People).
18 AUGUST	Brian Faulkner announced his resignation from active politics.
21 AUGUST	Some 20,000 attended peace rally in Belfast.
1 SEPTEMBER	Republic's Government declared a state of emergency which allowed people to be held for seven days without charge.
2 SEPTEMBER	European Commission of Human Rights decided that Britain had a case to answer before the European Court concerning its treatment of internees in 1971.
9 SEPTEMBER	Leaders of main Churches supported women's peace movement.
10 SEPTEMBER	Roy Mason succeeded Merlyn Rees as Secretary of State.
13 SEPTEMBER	Anne Dickson became leader of UPNI.
28 OCTOBER	Maire Drumm, vice-president of PSF, shot dead in Mater Hospital, Belfast, where she was a patient.
11 NOVEMBER	ULCCC put forward plan for NI independence with title 'Ulster Can Survive Unfettered'.
26 NOVEMBER	Mason said NI in danger of being left behind by 'the tide of devolution'.
1 DECEMBER	Fair Employment Act, making it an offence to discriminate in employment on religious or political grounds, became effective.

4 DECEMBER	SDLP annual conference rejected by 158 to 111 a motion calling on Britain to declare its intention to withdraw from NI.
9 DECEMBER	PIRA fire-bombs caused more than £1-million damage to Londonderry shops.
12 DECEMBER	ULCCC claimed that some loyalist politicians, who were not named, had been involved in the past in gun-running, selecting targets for bombs, and in promising money to buy arms and explosives.
25–7 DECEMBER	PIRA had Christmas ceasefire.

1977

19 JANUARY	PIRA in S. Derry claimed it had carried out wave of booby-trap bomb attacks on members of security forces.
15 FEBRUARY	Rhodesia's Ian Smith thanked Portadown DUP for message of support.
21 FEBRUARY	Conservative leader Margaret Thatcher visited Belfast and Derry.
3 MARCH	Lord Faulkner of Downpatrick killed in hunting accident.
8 MARCH	In a Dublin court eight SAS men, who were found on the Republic side of the border, were each fined £100 for carrying guns without a certificate.
11 MARCH	Twenty-six UVF men sentenced to a total of 700 years' imprisonment.
12 MARCH	Mason denied reports that his officials were involved in 'black propaganda'.
29 MARCH	Disclosed that OUP were boycotting UUUC.
1 APRIL	Government backed the idea of NI as one constituency, with three seats, for European direct elections. It also supported PR. OUP and DUP attacked the plan, and SDLP and Alliance supported it.
17 APRIL	Catholic Primate Cardinal William Conway died in Armagh, and there was praise of his efforts for peace and reconciliation.
23 APRIL	UUAC said it would call a loyalist strike in May to protest against security policy and demand a return of majority government.
3 MAY	UUAC strike began, but many factories stayed open, although the port of Larne was closed.
4 MAY	As a result of the stoppage, supported by Rev. Ian Paisley and Ernest Baird, the UUUC Parliamentary Coalition was dissolved.
6 MAY	UUAC failed to get support of Ballylumford power-station workers for strike.

9

9 MAY	Demonstrations and road blocks in many places in support of strike, and Paisley joined farmers who blocked roads in Ballymena, Co. Antrim, with tractors.
13 MAY	UUAC called off its strike, which had failed to stop industry and commerce. Critics of the strike praised the Government for refusing to make concessions, but Paisley claimed the stoppage had been a success.
23 MAY	Mason began a new round of talks with political parties.
25 MAY	In a Labour switch of policy, PM James Callaghan announced that an all-party Speaker's conference would be set up to consider the possibility of more NI MPS.
8 JUNE	Mason announced that more troops would be used on SAS-type activity and that RUC and UDR strength would be increased. UUAC claimed the move was in response to the strike, but OUP, which had opposed strike, said it arose from constitutional politics.
14 JUNE	Lord Melchett announced that the eleven-plus examination would be scrapped and comprehensive education promoted.
16 JUNE	In the Republic, Jack Lynch's Fianna Fáil Party regained power by defeating the Coalition by a record margin of twenty seats.
19 JUNE	New Zealand Premier Robert Muldoon discussed with Peace People leaders in Belfast the possibility of ex-terrorists being permitted to emigrate to New Zealand.
21 JUNE	Unemployment in NI reached 60,000, the highest June total for thirty-seven years.
12 JULY	PIRA threatened disruption during Queen's jubilee visit in August.
16 JULY	SDLP deputy leader John Hume appointed adviser on consumer affairs by EC Commissioner Richard Burke.
27 JULY	Four killed and eighteen injured in Belfast in feud between OIRA and PIRA. US naval communications base in Derry closed.
9–10 AUGUST	Queen's jubilee visit. On second day PIRA caused some minor explosions at edge of campus of NUU, but royal programme unaffected.
30 AUGUST	US President Carter, in a special statement, said that his administration supported a form of government in NI which would have widespread acceptance throughout both parts of the community. He also urged Americans not to support violence and said that if NI people could

resolve their differences, the US would be prepared, with others, to see how additional jobs could be created for the benefit of all the people.

12 SEPTEMBER	Mason, after a year as Secretary of State, said the 'myth of British withdrawal from NI' was now dead for ever.
20 SEPTEMBER	SDLP defined its policy as 'an agreed Ireland'.
28 SEPTEMBER	James Callaghan and Jack Lynch met in Downing Street; cross-border economic co-operation one of main topics.
5 OCTOBER	Seamus Costello, leader of IRSP, shot dead in Dublin.
7 OCTOBER	Irish Independence Party launched.
10 OCTOBER	Betty Williams and Mairead Corrigan, founders of the Peace People, awarded 1976 Nobel Peace Prize.
14 OCTOBER	Dr Tomás Ó Fiaich appointed new Catholic Primate.
18 OCTOBER	William Craig MP, as member of Council of Europe, appointed by Council to carry out research aimed at updating European Convention on Human Rights.
20 OCTOBER	Roy Jenkins, EC president, on a visit to Belfast, confirmed that EC would open NI information office.
6 NOVEMBER	SDLP, at its annual conference, rejected call for British withdrawal from NI.
21 NOVEMBER	Mason suggested the setting up of a Stormont Assembly without legislative powers to run local departments.
26 NOVEMBER	Craig announced that VUPP would cease to be political party.
3 DECEMBER	Seamus Twomey, former PIRA chief of staff, arrested in Dublin.
21 DECEMBER	Five hotels throughout NI damaged by PIRA fire-bombs.
22 DECEMBER	PIRA said there would be no Christmas ceasefire.
1978	
11 JANUARY	Fair Employment Agency report stated that Catholics suffered more from unemployment than Protestants.
18 JANUARY	European Court of Human Rights in Strasbourg held that interrogation techniques used on internees in 1971 did not amount to torture, but had been 'inhuman and degrading'.
17 FEBRUARY	Twelve people killed and twenty-three injured when La Mon House Hotel in Co. Down destroyed by PIRA fire-bombs.
25 FEBRUARY	Standing Committee of Irish Catholic Bishops conference said the overwhelming majority of Irish people wanted the campaign of violence to end immediately.
6 MARCH	OUP turned down idea of talks with the Rev. Ian Paisley and Ernest Baird.

12 MARCH	Comments by Mason about the role of the Republic in terrorism brought angry retorts from Government and opposition in Dublin.
26 MARCH	Speakers at PIRA celebrations of Easter Rising said that their campaign of violence would be stepped up.
7 APRIL	Conservative spokesman Airey Neave said power-sharing was no longer practical politics. James Callaghan and Jack Lynch, at Copenhagen EC summit, had talks which apparently helped to heal the breach between London and Dublin on security issues.
19 APRIL	James Callaghan announced that legislation would be introduced to increase NI's representation to between sixteen and eighteen seats.
2 MAY	Belfast appointed its first non-Unionist Lord Mayor, David Cook (Alliance). Mason had talks in Dublin with Irish Ministers.
1 AUGUST	Catholic Primate, Dr Ó Fiaich, after visit to Maze Prison, said Republican prisoners engaged in 'no wash – no toilet' protest were living in 'inhuman' conditions.
2 AUGUST	Mason announced 2,000-job sports-car factory for W. Belfast, a project hailed as a breakthrough in securing US investment.
28 AUGUST–1 SEPTEMBER	Visit to NI by US Congressmen Joshua Eilberg (Democrat) and Hamilton Fish (Republican), who later urged that the US should seek to assist in a political solution in NI.
21 SEPTEMBER	PIRA bomb attack on Eglinton airfield, Co. Londonderry, destroyed terminal building, two hangars and four planes.
22 SEPTEMBER	Mason and Conservative spokesman Airey Neave issued simultaneous statements attacking calls in GB for British withdrawal from NI.
24 SEPTEMBER	Paisley held his first religious service in Dublin, at the Mansion House.
8 OCTOBER	Sixty-nine RUC men injured in Londonderry when PSF and a number of other organisations held a march to celebrate the 5 October 1968 civil rights march, and the DUP staged a counter-demonstration. Sixty-seven of the police were injured in a clash with loyalists, and two were hurt by Republicans.
14 OCTOBER	DUP march in Derry to protest against Republican march on previous Sunday. Thirty-two RUC men injured when trouble broke out near Guildhall Square, and loyalists caused much damage to property.

4 NOVEMBER	With only two dissenting votes, SDLP annual conference voted that British withdrawal was 'desirable and inevitable', and called for fresh conference involving British and Irish Governments and two communities in NI.
14 NOVEMBER	PIRA bomb attacks caused serious damage in Belfast, Armagh, Dungannon, Enniskillen, Cookstown and Castlederg.
26 NOVEMBER	Albert Miles, deputy governor of Belfast Prison, shot dead by PIRA.
28 NOVEMBER	Commons passed by 350 votes to 49 the Bill to give NI five more MPs.
30 NOVEMBER	PIRA warned that it was 'preparing for a long war', after admitting to setting off explosives and fire bombs in fourteen towns and villages, with the most serious damage in Armagh city.

1979

20 FEBRUARY	Eleven Protestants, known as the 'Shankill butchers', were sentenced to life imprisonment for a wide variety of offences including nineteen murders.
28 MARCH	Votes of NI MPs decisive in defeat of Labour Government by 311 votes to 310, thus precipitating a general election. Eight Unionists voted with Conservative opposition and two OUPs, John Carson and Harold McCusker, voted with the Government. Gerry Fitt (SDLP) and Frank Maguire (Ind.) abstained.
30 MARCH	Conservative NI spokesman Airey Neave killed when bomb exploded in his car at House of Commons car park. INLA claimed responsibility.
17 APRIL	Four RUC men killed by PIRA at Bessbrook, Co. Armagh, when 1,000-lb bomb exploded in a van.
3 MAY	In Westminster general election DUP gained two seats from OUP, E. Belfast and N. Belfast.
5 MAY	Humphrey Atkins (Conservative) succeeded Mason as NI Secretary of State.
7 JUNE	In first European election Rev. Ian Paisley, John Hume and John Taylor elected to fill the three NI seats.
30 JUNE	Dr Ó Fiaich received his cardinal's hat at a ceremony in Rome.
2 JULY	INLA declared illegal throughout the UK.
17 JULY	Rev. Ian Paisley, at opening session of European Parliament in Strasbourg, was first MEP to speak, apart from the acting president, when he protested that the Union flag was flying the wrong way up on the Parliament Buildings.

18 JULY	Paisley shouted down in European Parliament when he sought to interrupt Jack Lynch as European Council president.
21 JULY	Visit of Pope John Paul II to Ireland announced for 29 September, and Paisley and Orange Order warned that NI must not be included in itinerary.
31 JULY	US State Department stopped private arms shipments to NI, including supplies to RUC.
11 AUGUST	Irish National Caucus deputation said in Belfast that it planned to make NI a major issue in 1980 US presidential election.
22 AUGUST	Secretary of State Humphrey Atkins rejected proposal from New York Governor Hugh Carey that he (the Governor) should preside at New York talks involving the NI Secretary of State and Irish Foreign Minister Michael O'Kennedy.
27 AUGUST	PIRA bombers killed eighteen soldiers near Warrenpoint, Co. Down; biggest death toll in a single incident in NI in ten years of violence. Lord Mountbatten of Burma was murdered by PIRA at Mullaghmore, Co. Sligo, when his boat was blown to pieces in a radio-triggered explosion. His fourteen-year-old grandson, Nicholas, and crew member Paul Maxwell, aged fourteen, also died instantly, and the Dowager Lady Brabourne died later from her injuries.
29 AUGUST	PM Margaret Thatcher flew to NI to discuss tightening of security. It was announced in Rome that, because of the recent violence, the Pope would not now visit Armagh.
30 AUGUST	British Cabinet decided to increase RUC by 1,000.
2 SEPTEMBER	UFF threatened to strike back at PIRA.
5 SEPTEMBER	Thatcher and Taoiseach Jack Lynch met in London for security talks.
29 SEPTEMBER	The Pope, speaking in Drogheda, Co. Louth, appealed 'on [his] bended knees' for an end to violence.
2 OCTOBER	PIRA rejected the Pope's appeal and declared that it had widespread support, and that only force could remove the British presence.
5 OCTOBER	British and Irish Governments agreed to tighten up the anti-terrorist drive, British Labour Party conference rejected a call for withdrawal from NI.
15 OCTOBER	Opinion poll published by Dublin-based Economic and Social Research Institute, based on questioning in July–September 1978, showed 21 per cent of people in

Republic giving some degree of support to PIRA activities, with under 3 per cent expressing strong support.

25 OCTOBER   Atkins announced that he was inviting four main parties – OUP, DUP, SDLP and Alliance – to a Stormont conference to discuss a possible political settlement. The OUP immediately rejected the invitation and said the Government should proceed with two-tier local government. PIRA denied that it had planned to assassinate Princess Margaret during her recent US visit.

1 NOVEMBER   Jack Lynch said the NI problem 'continues to be as intractable as at any stage in the last ten years'. One hundred and fifty-six guns, including a powerful M-60 machine gun, seized at Dublin docks. They were believed to have been sent from the US for use by PIRA.

3 NOVEMBER   SDLP, at its annual conference, urged a joint approach by the British and Irish Governments to the NI problem. It also rejected a proposal for talks with PIRA.

22 NOVEMBER   SDLP leader Gerry Fitt MP resigned from the party because of its initial refusal to attend Atkins conference.

28 NOVEMBER   John Hume MEP became SDLP leader.

5 DECEMBER   Jack Lynch resigned as Republic's Taoiseach.

7 DECEMBER   Charles Haughey TD appointed to succeed Lynch by forty-four votes to thirty-eight of Fianna Fáil Parliamentary Party.

15 DECEMBER   SDLP decided to attend Atkins conference.

16 DECEMBER   Four soldiers killed by PIRA landmine in Co. Tyrone and another by a booby-trap bomb in S. Armagh.

1980

7 JANUARY   Constitutional Conference opened at Stormont.

17 JANUARY   Three people killed in terrorist train explosion at Dunmurry, near Belfast.

8 FEBRUARY   Leonard Kaitcer, Belfast antique dealer, murdered after kidnap linked with £1-million ransom demand.

11 FEBRUARY   Serious differences emerge within Peace People.

16 FEBRUARY   Charles Haughey at Fianna Fáil conference in Dublin urged joint British-Irish initiative on NI.

5 MARCH   Cardinal Ó Fiaich and Dr Edward Daly met Secretary of State Atkins to voice concern about conditions within H-Blocks.

11 MARCH   Body of German industrialist Thomas Niedermayer found at Colinglen Road, W. Belfast. He had disappeared December 1973.

24 MARCH   Stormont Constitutional Conference adjourned indefinitely with no sign of agreement.

26 MARCH   Announced that as from 1 April there would be no

entitlement to special category status for terrorist offenders.

15 APRIL	Atkins in Dublin for talks with Haughey Government.
30 APRIL	Marion Price, convicted with sister Dolours for their part in London car bombing in 1973, released from Armagh Prison on humanitarian grounds. She was suffering from anorexia nervosa.
5 MAY	PIRA blew up pylon at Crossmaglen, part of North–South power link, which both Governments were seeking to re-establish.
13 MAY	SDLP leader John Hume met Thatcher at 10 Downing Street.
21 MAY	Thatcher and Haughey had meeting at 10 Downing Street. Communiqué promised closer political co-operation and referred to 'unique relationship' between the two countries.
4 JUNE	John Turnly, Protestant joint chairman of IIP, shot dead in his car at Carnlough, Co. Antrim, in front of his family.
5 JUNE	Presbyterian General Assembly voted 443 to 322 to take Church out of World Council of Churches on the basis that the Council supported terrorist groups.
9 JUNE	Haughey appealed to Britain to accept that withdrawal was in the best interests of UK and Ireland. On BBC *Panorama* programme he also mentioned the possibility of some form of federation and separate social laws for NI.
11 JUNE	PIRA threatened to renew attacks on prison officers, suspended since March.
12 JUNE	Markethill town centre seriously damaged by PIRA car bomb.
19 JUNE	European Commission of Human Rights rejected the case of protesting H-Block prisoners, finding that the debasement arising from the 'dirty protest' was self-inflicted. The Commission also criticised British Government for 'inflexibility'.
25 JUNE	US Democratic Party adopted Senator Edward Kennedy's policy, calling for 'an end to the divisions of the Irish people', and a solution to the conflict based on the consent of all the parties.
26 JUNE	Dr Miriam Daly, prominent Republican member of National H-Block/Armagh Committee, shot dead at her home in Andersonstown.

2 JULY	British Government published two-option document on NI devolution. It produced no agreement – Unionists rejected the option with a large element of power-sharing, and anti-Unionists turned down the option of majority rule.
20 JULY	Car bomb in Lisnaskea, Co. Fermanagh, caused extensive damage.
6 AUGUST	Extra Government spending of £48 million in NI announced after ICTU delegation had met Thatcher to protest at 14.7 per cent unemployment.
8 AUGUST	Three killed and eighteen injured in widespread violence on ninth anniversary of internment.
24 SEPTEMBER	Cardinal Ó Fiaich 'hopeful of progress' on H-Block issue.
27 OCTOBER	Seven H-Block prisoners began hunger strike in support of demand for, among other things, the right to wear their own clothing.
8 DECEMBER	Thatcher, accompanied by three Cabinet Ministers – Lord Carrington (Foreign Secretary), Sir Geoffrey Howe (Chancellor of Exchequer) and Humphrey Atkins – had talks in Dublin with Haughey and senior colleagues. The meeting agreed to joint studies on a wide range of subjects and Haughey called it 'a historic break-through'.
18 DECEMBER	H-Block hunger strike called off with one PIRA prisoner critically ill.

1981

16 JANUARY	Bernadette McAliskey and husband shot and seriously wounded by gunmen at their home near Coalisland, Co. Tyrone.
21 JANUARY	Two leading Unionists – Sir Norman Stronge and son James – shot dead by PIRA gunmen at their home, Tynan Abbey.
6 FEBRUARY	British coal boat, *Nellie M*, sunk by PIRA off Moville, Co. Donegal.
9 FEBRUARY	Paisley launched 'Ulster Declaration' against Anglo-Irish talks.
12 FEBRUARY	Paisley suspended from Commons when he persisted in calling Humphrey Atkins a 'liar'.
19 FEBRUARY	James Molyneaux, OUP leader, described as 'ludicrous' an allegation by Paisley that there was an OUP plot to kill him.
21 FEBRUARY	Eight stores in Belfast and three in Londonderry damaged by PIRA fire bombs.

27 FEBRUARY	Three-hundred-pound van bomb damaged forty premises in Limavady, Co. Derry.
1 MARCH	New H-Block hunger strike in support of political status began when PIRA prisoner Bobby Sands refused food.
3 MARCH	In Commons Humphrey Atkins said there would be no political status for prisoners, regardless of protests inside or outside the prison.
5 MARCH	Frank Maguire, Ind. MP for Fermanagh–S. Tyrone, died. Thatcher, on a visit to NI, again denied that Anglo-Irish talks threatened NI's constitutional position.
21 MARCH	Cardinal Ó Fiaich called on PIRA to end violence.
22 MARCH	Republic's Foreign Minister, Brian Lenihan, said Anglo-Irish talks could lead to Irish unity in ten years.
28 MARCH	Paisley attracted large attendance at Stormont rally against Anglo-Irish talks. RUC estimated 30,000 audience.
1 APRIL	DUP held three late-night rallies on hillsides near Gortin, Newry and Armagh. At Gortin two RUC vehicles were overturned.
9 APRIL	Hunger-striker Bobby Sands won the Fermanagh–S. Tyrone by-election.
11 APRIL	Riots in Belfast, Lurgan and Cookstown after celebrations of Sands's election.
19 APRIL	On fifth successive night of rioting in Derry, two nineteen-year-old youths were killed when struck by army landrover.
22 APRIL	Dolours Price released from Armagh Prison since her life was said to be in danger from anorexia nervosa; her sister Marion had been released in 1980 for the same reason.
28 APRIL	President Reagan said US would not intervene in NI, but he was 'deeply concerned at the tragic situation'.
5 MAY	Bobby Sands MP died on sixty-sixth day of his fast. There was rioting in Belfast and Londonderry, and also in Dublin.
6 MAY	Six hundred extra troops sent to NI as sporadic violence continued.
7 MAY	Massive attendance at Bobby Sands's funeral in Milltown cemetery, Belfast.
9 MAY	PIRA claimed they had planted a bomb at the Sullom Voe oil terminal in the Shetlands to explode during the Queen's visit there.
12 MAY	Hunger-striker Francis Hughes died, and blast and

18

petrol bombs were thrown at security forces during riots in Belfast and Derry.

13 MAY	John Hume met Thatcher and unsuccessfully urged concessions to hunger-strikers on clothing and free association.
19 MAY	Five soldiers killed when their Saracen armoured car was blown up by landmine near Bessbrook, Co. Armagh.
20 MAY	Polling in council elections.
21 MAY	Cardinal Ó Fiaich criticised 'rigid stance' of Government on hunger strike.
26 MAY	Arms found in RUC raid on UDA HQ in Belfast.
11 JUNE	Eight PIRA men awaiting sentence escaped from Belfast Prison. Two H-Block prisoners elected to Dáil in general election which resulted in return to power of Fine Gael–Labour Coalition.
2 JULY	Atkins suggested an advisory council of already-elected representatives; the idea was later dropped because of lack of support.
4 JULY	H-Block hunger-strikers said they would be happy that any concessions granted to them should apply to all prisoners.
14 JULY	Irish Government asked US to intervene with Britain over the hunger strike.
18 JULY	In Dublin over 200 people were injured during a riot when an H-Block march was prevented by Gardaí from passing British Embassy.
2 AUGUST	Hunger-striker Kieran Doherty TD died.
5 AUGUST	Concentrated PIRA car-bomb and incendiary attack in seven centres, including Belfast, Londonderry and Lisburn, caused widespread damage, but no serious injuries.
8 AUGUST	Two people died during violence in Belfast; more than 1,000 petrol bombs were thrown at security forces.
20 AUGUST	Owen Carron won Fermanagh–S. Tyrone by-election.
2 SEPTEMBER	Paisley called for Third Force on lines of former B Specials.
7 SEPTEMBER	Two RUC men killed by PIRA landmine near Pomeroy, Co. Tyrone.
13 SEPTEMBER	James Prior became NI Secretary of State and Humphrey Atkins deputy Foreign Secretary.
17 SEPTEMBER	Prior visited Maze Prison for three hours, with growing signs that the hunger strike was collapsing.

29 SEPTEMBER	British Labour conference voted to 'campaign actively' for united Ireland by consent.
3 OCTOBER	H-Block hunger strike, which had led to deaths of ten Republican prisoners, called off.
6 OCTOBER	Prior announced that all prisoners would now be allowed to wear their own clothes.
8 OCTOBER	Belfast Independent councillor Lawrence Kennedy shot dead in Ardoyne, apparently by loyalist gunman.
10 OCTOBER	PIRA set off remote-controlled nail bomb outside Chelsea Barracks in London. One woman killed and twenty-three soldiers and seventeen civilians injured.
22 OCTOBER	European Court of Human Rights ruled that NI law banning male homosexuality was a breach of European Convention.
6 NOVEMBER	Margaret Thatcher and Irish Taoiseach Dr Garret FitzGerald decided in London talks to set up British-Irish Intergovernmental Council.
14 NOVEMBER	Rev. Robert Bradford MP assassinated by PIRA gunmen at Finaghy, Belfast.
16 NOVEMBER	Three DUP MPs suspended from Commons after protests on security. Third Force march in Enniskillen, Co. Fermanagh.
17 NOVEMBER	Prior faced barrage of verbal abuse at Robert Bradford's funeral at Dundonald near Belfast. RUC leave cancelled.
23 NOVEMBER	Loyalist 'Day of Action' to protest against security policy marked by rallies and stoppages of work in Protestant areas. Both OUP and DUP had separate rallies at Belfast City Hall. Some 5,000 men paraded at a DUP rally in Newtownards, Co. Down, addressed by Paisley.
25 NOVEMBER	INLA bomb exploded at British army camp at Herford, West Germany, but caused no injuries.
30 NOVEMBER	Several Unionist-controlled councils adjourned in protest at the security situation.
3 DECEMBER	Paisley claimed Third Force had 15,000–20,000 members. Prior said private armies would not be tolerated.
21 DECEMBER	Revealed that US State Department had revoked Paisley's visa.

1982

29 JANUARY	A prominent E. Belfast loyalist, John McKeague, shot dead in his shop, apparently by INLA.
1 FEBRUARY	OUP delegation met Prior to tell him they were opposed to his 'rolling devolution' plan and reaffirmed support

for Convention report. Labour leader Michael Foot arrived in NI for three-day visit and said more jobs was the top priority.

8 FEBRUARY   Five Belfast men arrested when they tried to enter US from Canada with lists of firearms.

18 FEBRUARY   General election in Republic returned Fianna Fáil to power when the party secured the backing of WP and Independent TDs. None of the PSF's seven candidates returned.

23 FEBRUARY   PIRA used bombs to sink coal boat *St Bedan* in Lough Foyle. At European security conference in Madrid, Poland alleged Britain was using torture in NI.

24 FEBRUARY   Government said it would bring homosexual laws in NI into line with rest of UK, following European Court of Human Rights ruling against existing laws. Catholic Bishops and DUP opposed reforms.

4 MARCH   Rev. Martin Smyth, OUP, returned in S. Belfast by-election.

6 MARCH   Gerard Tuite, who escaped from prison in London, was charged in Dublin with causing explosions in London. He was the first person charged in Republic with a crime committed in GB.

14 MARCH   SDLP leader John Hume called the new devolution plan 'unworkable'.

16 MARCH   Eleven-year-old boy killed and thirty-four people injured, some seriously, by a bomb which exploded without warning in Banbridge, Co. Down.

17 MARCH   On a St Patrick's Day visit to the US, Taoiseach Charles Haughey said US Government should bring more pressure on Britain to adopt a more positive attitude to Irish unity. President Reagan said any solution must come from NI people themselves.

25 MARCH   Three soldiers killed in PIRA ambush in Crocus Street, W. Belfast. M-60 machine gun used. British Cabinet approved 'rolling devolution' plan.

26 MARCH   PIRA offered 'amnesty' to informers if they retracted their evidence.

28 MARCH   RUC Inspector Norman Duddy shot dead by PIRA in Londonderry.

1 APRIL   Two plain-clothes soldiers killed in Derry in PIRA machine-gun attack.

14 APRIL   Four leading members of UDA arrested after ammunition and some gun parts found in Belfast HQ during police raid.

16 APRIL	Prior said he had no plans to proscribe UDA. He also said Falklands crisis would not delay devolution plans.
17 APRIL	A soldier who rammed 'Free Derry Wall' in a personnel carrier was taken into military custody.
19 APRIL	James Molyneaux MP said the Falklands crisis had vindicated the Unionist position and his suspicion of the Foreign Office.
20 APRIL	Two killed, twelve injured and £1-million damage caused by PIRA bomb attacks in Belfast, Derry, Armagh, Strabane, Ballymena, Bessbrook and Magherafelt.
22 APRIL	WP in Dublin denied a claim in *Magill* magazine that OIRA was still active and involved in murders and armed robberies.
24 APRIL	Alliance leader Oliver Napier told his party's conference that devolution plan might be last chance for NI to solve its own problems.
25 APRIL	Sinn Féin the Workers' Party decided to call itself simply 'The Workers' Party'.
3 MAY	Republic's Defence Minister Paddy Power described Britain as the 'aggressor' over the Falklands.
10 MAY	Haughey appointed Seamus Mallon, SDLP deputy leader, and John Robb of New Ireland Group to Republic's Senate.
13 MAY	European Parliament called for ban on use of plastic bullets throughout EC.
20 MAY	INLA bomb defused at home of Rev. William Beattie, DUP.
24 MAY	Closure of de Lorean car plant at Dunmurry announced, with loss of 1,500 jobs.
28 MAY	British and Irish Governments said NI would get natural gas from Republic in about two years' time.
29 MAY	Friends of Ireland Group in US Congress on fact-finding visit to NI.
18 JUNE	Ex-RUC Inspector Albert White shot dead near his home in Newry, Co. Down.
21 JUNE	FBI arrested four men in New York who were said to have tried to buy 'Redeye' surface-to-air missiles for PIRA.
25 JUNE	Devolution Bill amended to ensure that both Commons and Lords must be satisfied about 'cross-community support' before transfer of powers.
1 JULY	Gardaí found large cache of bombs at Castlefin, Co. Donegal.

19 JULY	Prior on short visit to US to explain his devolution scheme.
20 JULY	Eight soldiers died and fifty-one people were injured by two PIRA bombs in London – one near the Household Cavalry barracks at Knightsbridge and the other at the Regent's Park bandstand, where an army band was playing. Three people died later.
27 JULY	Disclosed that British Government had told Irish ambassador in London that it was under no obligation to consult Republic about NI matters.
8 AUGUST	Representatives of NORAID and PLO spoke at internment anniversary demonstrations in W. Belfast.
15 AUGUST	In the US Rev. Martin Smyth MP claimed that he knew who killed the Rev. Robert Bradford, and he alleged that CIA was involved in NI.
25 AUGUST	SDLP decided to contest Assembly elections, but not to take seats.
28 AUGUST	PIRA was believed to have suffered one of its biggest setbacks through seizures of arms and explosives. The RUC found about one and a half tons of gelignite hidden in a lorry near Banbridge, Co. Down; the Gardaí seized a smaller quantity of gelignite and 10,000 rounds of ammunition at Glencree, Co. Wicklow.
1 SEPTEMBER	Merger of departments of Commerce and Manpower took effect to create new Department of Economic Development. Belfast DUP councillor Billy Dickson wounded in INLA gun attack at his home.
16 SEPTEMBER	INLA bomb at Divis Flats in W. Belfast killed a soldier and two boys of eleven and fourteen.
20 SEPTEMBER	INLA blew up radar station at Schull, Co. Cork.
23 SEPTEMBER	RUC Chief Constable Sir John Hermon said PIRA and INLA 'reeling' from arrests arising from evidence of informers.
2 OCTOBER	British Labour Party conference called for ban on use of plastic bullets throughout UK.
20 OCTOBER	Polling day in Assembly election. John de Lorean charged in California with drug-smuggling offences.
27 OCTOBER	Three RUC men killed in booby-trap landmine explosion near Lurgan, Co. Armagh.
2 NOVEMBER	SDLP delegation told Prior they would continue their boycott of the Assembly.
3 NOVEMBER	Queen's Speech at opening of Parliament reaffirmed Government's intention to carry on with Assembly.

9 NOVEMBER	RUC constable and woman leisure-centre worker died in Enniskillen, Co. Fermanagh, in booby-trapped car.
11 NOVEMBER	At Assembly's first session James Kilfedder MP was elected Speaker. Three PIRA men shot dead by RUC when they were alleged to have driven through checkpoint near Lurgan, Co. Armagh.
16 NOVEMBER	Two RUC Reserve constables shot dead in Markethill, Co. Armagh. Leonard Murphy, reputed to have been leader of the notorious 'Shankill butcher gang', shot dead.
25 NOVEMBER	In Republic's general election Fine Gael and Labour secured overall majority, paving the way for a coalition.
30 NOVEMBER	Prior addressed Assembly, and announced increase in RUC strength.
6 DECEMBER	Seventeen people, including eleven soldiers, died in INLA bombing of the 'Droppin' Well' pub disco in Ballykelly, Co. Londonderry.
16 DECEMBER	Election Petition Court in Armagh deprived SDLP deputy leader Seamus Mallon of his Assembly seat on the grounds that he was a member of the Republic's Senate.
23 DECEMBER	Thatcher made one-day visit to NI, mainly to meet members of security forces.

1983

5 JANUARY	INLA declared illegal in Irish Republic.
6 JANUARY	Two RUC men shot dead by PIRA in Rostrevor, Co. Down.
16 JANUARY	County Court judge William Doyle shot dead by PIRA as he left Catholic church in S. Belfast.
28 JANUARY	Republic's Government announced that it would give full voting rights to 20,000 British citizens.
30 JANUARY	SDLP annual conference reaffirmed Assembly boycott.
1 FEBRUARY	Irish Foreign Minister Peter Barry met Prior in London and expressed doubts as to whether the Assembly had a useful future.
17 FEBRUARY	At Westminster Labour Party decided to oppose Prevention of Terrorism Act in its present form.
23 FEBRUARY	European Parliament's political committee voted for an inquiry as to whether EC could help solve NI's economic and political problems, despite opposition by British Government and Conservative and Unionist MEPs.
26 FEBRUARY	GLC leader Ken Livingstone flew to Belfast for two-day

visit at the invitation of PSF – a visit strongly attacked by Unionists.

27 FEBRUARY   Haughey at Fianna Fáil conference in Dublin urged British and Irish Governments to organise a constitutional conference as a prelude to final British withdrawal from NI.

2 MARCH   NI Assembly voted unanimously for a halt to European Parliament inquiry.

7 MARCH   Home Secretary announced new anti-terrorism Bill with five-year life, subject to annual renewal.

11 MARCH   Republic's Government announced it would set up all-Ireland Forum on lines suggested by SDLP.

17 MARCH   President Reagan said those who supported terrorism were no friends of Ireland. Senator Edward Kennedy called for Irish unity in a Senate motion.

21 MARCH   Thatcher's meeting with Garret FitzGerald at Brussels EC summit was her first with an Irish Taoiseach for nearly sixteen months.

24 MARCH   OUP, DUP and Alliance Party rejected Garret FitzGerald's invitation to take part in all-Ireland Forum.

3 APRIL   Statements at Republican Easter Rising celebrations indicated that PIRA was dropping punishment shootings commonly known as 'kneecappings'.

8 APRIL   Prior announced an inquiry into working of Emergency Provisions Act.

11 APRIL   Fourteen UVF men jailed, two for life, on evidence of supergrass Joseph Bennett, former UVF battalion commander, who had been granted immunity in respect of two murders and other terrorist offences.

25 APRIL   Republic's Coalition Government suffered first Parliamentary defeat when its proposed wording for anti-abortion referendum was defeated by twenty-two votes.

5 MAY   Prior in Dublin for talks with the Government. But occasion overshadowed by Irish Government protest to London about remarks in NI by Defence Secretary Michael Heseltine that small neutral countries allowed NATO 'to carry responsibility for the whole area'.

10–11 MAY   NI Assembly had all-night sitting on devolution, but failed to agree on any clear-cut approach.

24 MAY   1,000-lb PIRA bomb outside Andersonstown police station in W. Belfast caused £1-million damage.

30 MAY   New Ireland Forum held initial meeting in Dublin.

9 JUNE   In Westminster election Unionists took fifteen of the

seventeen NI seats, with SDLP and PSF getting one each.

11 JUNE   Prior reappointed NI Secretary of State in Thatcher's new Cabinet.

28 JUNE   SDLP leader John Hume in maiden Commons' speech spoke of Britain's 'psychological withdrawal' from NI.

3 JULY   Unoccupied Belfast home of ex-MP Gerry Fitt set alight by youths from nearby New Lodge Road.

4 JULY   Catholic Bishops in NI warned against reintroduction of death penalty and called for ban on use of plastic bullets.

8 JULY   NI Assembly voted thirty-five to eleven for death penalty for terrorist murders.

10 JULY   Prior said return of capital punishment would increase terrorism and lead to 'violent disorders' in NI.

13 JULY   Commons rejected death penalty for terrorist murders by majority of 116. Four UDR soldiers killed by PIRA landmine in Co. Tyrone – the regiment's heaviest loss in a single incident.

17 JULY   Former NI Secretary of State Merlyn Rees said a Cabinet subcommittee had considered withdrawal from NI between 1974 and 1976 but no Minister had favoured it.

21 JULY   Ex-MP Gerry Fitt became life peer; former NI Secretary of State Humphrey Atkins was knighted; and OUP leader James Molyneaux was appointed Privy Councillor.

26 JULY   Irish Foreign Minister Peter Barry told MPs at Westminster that democracy in NI was being undermined by increased PSF vote. Gerry Adams, PSF MP for W. Belfast, in London as guest of GLC leader Ken Livingstone, said Britain had erected 'wall of misinformation' around NI.

5 AUGUST   One-hundred-and-twenty-day trial of thirty-eight people implicated in terrorism by PIRA supergrass Christopher Black ended in Belfast. Mr Justice Kelly jailed twenty-two of the accused, with sentences totalling more than 4,000 years. Four were acquitted and the others got mainly suspended sentences. (In 1986 eighteen of the twenty-two jailed had their convictions quashed by Court of Appeal.)

25 AUGUST   Elizabeth Kirkpatrick, wife of an informer, freed in Belfast after being held captive for two months by INLA.

8 SEPTEMBER   Unionists said 67 per cent vote for pro-life amendment

in Republic's Constitution underlined the sectarian nature of Southern society.

13 SEPTEMBER Prior defended use of supergrasses.

23 SEPTEMBER FEA said it would be monitoring recruitment at Short Brothers aircraft factory after allegations of anti-Catholic bias.

25 SEPTEMBER Thirty-eight PIRA prisoners escaped from Maze Prison – the biggest escape in British prison history. During the escape a prison officer was stabbed and died. Within a few days nineteen had been recaptured, but the others got away.

26 SEPTEMBER A NIF group on a visit to Derry was attacked by DUP demonstrators.

6 OCTOBER Two RUC Reservists shot dead by PIRA in Downpatrick, Co. Down.

28 OCTOBER Sir George Terry (former Sussex Chief Constable), in report on Kincora boys' home sex allegations, said he had found no evidence that civil servants, RUC or military intelligence were involved in homosexual activities at the home or had tried to suppress information about them.

4 NOVEMBER PIRA bomb at Ulster Polytechnic at Jordanstown, Co. Antrim, killed RUC inspector and a sergeant and injured thirty-three others.

10 NOVEMBER Prior said a PSF takeover in NI could lead to the whole of Ireland becoming another Cuba.

13 NOVEMBER Big changes in PSF leadership, with Gerry Adams MP being elected president at Ard Fheis.

21 NOVEMBER Three elders shot dead during service in Darkley Pentecostal Church, Co. Armagh. Seven others were injured. Shooting claimed by 'Catholic Reaction Force'.

27 NOVEMBER Dominic McGlinchey, said to be INLA chief of staff, admitted his organisation had been indirectly involved in Darkley killings.

4 DECEMBER SAS undercover soldiers shot dead two PIRA members near Coalisland, Co. Tyrone.

7 DECEMBER OUP Assembly member Edgar Graham shot dead by PIRA at Queen's University Belfast.

8 DECEMBER FEA found Catholics under-represented at policy-making levels in NI civil service.

16 DECEMBER Irish soldier and a Garda cadet killed in gun battle with PIRA when Dublin supermarket executive Don Tidey, kidnapped three weeks earlier, was rescued at Ballinamore, Co. Leitrim.

| 17 DECEMBER | Five people killed and eighty injured when PIRA car bomb exploded outside Harrods in London. |
| 24 DECEMBER | Thatcher made six-hour NI tour, including meeting with Christmas shoppers in Newtownards, Co. Down, and visit to security forces in counties Armagh and Tyrone. |

1984

15 JANUARY	Cardinal Ó Fiaich described Thatcher's visit to Armagh UDR base, where several UDR men were accused of murder of Catholics, as 'disgusting'. He also said that, because of its work on housing and other community issues, it was not morally wrong to join PSF.
16 JANUARY	Irish Government said it could not identify with Cardinal Ó Fiaich's remarks.
25 FEBRUARY	Two thousand loyalists staged protest at Stormont against proposal to change Londonderry District Council's name to 'Derry'.
29 FEBRUARY	NI Assembly voted twenty to one against extending 1967 Abortion Act to NI.
6 MARCH	PIRA shot Maze Prison assistant governor outside his E. Belfast home.
14 MARCH	PSF president Gerry Adams shot and wounded in Belfast; UFF admitted responsibility.
15 MARCH	Garret FitzGerald, addressing US Congress, urged US politicians to call for British acceptance of NIF proposals.
17 MARCH	Alleged INLA leader Dominic McGlinchey, extradited from Republic to NI to face murder charge, was claimed as first in North–South extradition of a member of Republican paramilitary organisation.
22 MARCH	PIRA bombed three buildings in Belfast city centre.
29 MARCH	RUC Constable John Robinson, on trial for murdering Armagh INLA man Seamus Grew in December 1982 (he was later acquitted), claimed senior RUC officers had ordered him to tell lies about events leading to the shooting so as to protect Special Branch officers and an RUC informer operating inside the Republic.
4 APRIL	British Government apologised to Irish Government for RUC undercover action in Republic in December 1982.
7 APRIL	RUC Chief Constable denied a cover-up in Armagh killing of two INLA men, but said two unarmed RUC men had gone into Republic for observation purposes in December 1982.
8 APRIL	PIRA shot dead Mary Travers, and seriously wounded her

father, Magistrate Tom Travers, as they left Mass in
S. Belfast.

19 APRIL   FEA chairman said Belfast shipyard, Harland and Wolff
plc, had agreed to recruit more Catholic workers.

26 APRIL   OUP proposed NI should have regional council with
strictly administrative powers.

2 MAY   NIF report issued.

6 MAY   Riots in Belfast and several towns on third anniversary
of death of hunger-striker Bobby Sands.

17 MAY   *Sunday World* Northern editor Jim Campbell shot and
seriously injured by UVF at his N. Belfast home.

18 MAY   Two RUC men killed and another seriously injured in
PIRA landmine explosion at Camlough, S. Armagh.

25 MAY   Security forces made large hauls of explosives at
Carrickmore, Co. Tyrone, and Castlewellan in S. Down.
Both Houses of US Congress unanimously backed NIF
report.

1 JUNE   President Reagan began four-day visit to Republic.

4 JUNE   President Reagan told Dáil and Senate in Dublin that
current US policy was not to interfere in Irish matters.
But he praised the NIF and strongly criticised violence
in NI.

5 JUNE   Assembly member George Seawright lost DUP Whip after
commenting at a meeting of Belfast Education and
Library Board that Catholics and their priests should be
incinerated.

14 JUNE   European election poll.

18 JUNE   In European election count Ian Paisley, John Taylor and
John Hume retained seats.

20 JUNE   British Labour leader Neil Kinnock voiced support for
NIF report and united Ireland by consent.

2 JULY   Prior, speaking in Commons, rejected the unitary state,
federal Ireland, and joint authority options of the NIF
report.

12 JULY   Orange Order demonstration resolutions condemned
NIF report. Violence after parades included attacks on
security forces and shops in Londonderry, and on
Catholic families in Limavady, Ballymena and
Ballynahinch.

14 JULY   Two UDR soldiers killed by PIRA landmine at Castlederg,
Co. Tyrone.

18 JULY   Public Accounts Committee at Westminster said loss of
£77-million public money in de Lorean project was 'one
of the gravest cases of misuse of public resources in
recent years'.

9 AUGUST	NORAID leader Martin Galvin, banned from UK, appeared in Derry.
12 AUGUST	Sean Downes of Andersonstown died when hit by plastic bullet as RUC tried to arrest Martin Galvin at a W. Belfast rally.
13 AUGUST	W. Belfast march in honour of Sean Downes was followed by serious rioting in area.
14 AUGUST	Prior admitted ban on Galvin was 'a bad mistake'.
16 AUGUST	RUC came under sniper fire in riots on Belfast's Shankill Road.
22 AUGUST	Armagh coroner Gerry Curran resigned after finding 'grave irregularities' in RUC files relating to shooting by RUC of two INLA men in 1982.
10 SEPTEMBER	Douglas Hurd appointed NI Secretary of State in succession to James Prior, who left the Government. Rhodes Boyson became NI Minister of State.
20 SEPTEMBER	DUP suggested devolution scheme involving majority cabinet government with a Bill of Rights and minority having strong role in departmental committees.
24 SEPTEMBER	Oliver Napier resigned as Alliance Party leader; succeeded by party Chief Whip John Cushnahan.
27 SEPTEMBER	Eight Maze Prison officers and five prisoners injured in clash between loyalist and Republican prisoners.
29 SEPTEMBER	Seven tons of arms and ammunition intended for PIRA seized on trawler *Marita Ann* off Kerry coast. Five men arrested. It was biggest capture of PIRA arms since *Claudia* was intercepted off Waterford coast in 1973.
5 OCTOBER	British Labour Party conference in Blackpool opposed Diplock courts, and the use of supergrass evidence, and also called for ban on plastic bullets and an end to strip-searching of prisoners.
12 OCTOBER	PIRA set off bomb inside Grand Hotel, Brighton, HQ of the Conservative conference, in a bid to kill Margaret Thatcher and senior Government figures. No member of the Government died, but the four killed (a fifth died later) included Sir Anthony Berry MP and Roberta Wakeham, wife of Government Chief Whip Robert Wakeham, and Secretary for Trade and Industry Norman Tebbitt and his wife were among the thirty-four injured.
16 OCTOBER	Thatcher rejected idea of any 'sudden new initiative' on NI.
17 OCTOBER	In Boston, US, trawler *Valhalla* seized on suspicion of

being ship which transferred arms to trawler *Marita Ann* off Kerry coast eighteen days earlier.

22 OCTOBER   European Commission of Human Rights held that use of plastic bullets was justified in riot situation.

25 OCTOBER   Nineteen Maze prisoners, recaptured after the 1983 escape, appeared in court on charge of murdering a prison officer and firearms charges.

1 NOVEMBER   Kilbrandon report published; the unofficial committee, set up by British Irish Association, suggested in majority report that NI should be run by five-member executive, including an Irish Government Minister.

6 NOVEMBER   New anti-personation measures announced for NI elections.

19 NOVEMBER   Thatcher, after Anglo-Irish summit at Chequers, ruled out three options of NIF report.

21 NOVEMBER   Garret FitzGerald reported to have told his backbenchers that Thatcher's behaviour after the summit had been 'gratuitously offensive'.

2 DECEMBER   SAS soldier and a PIRA member died in exchange of shots at Drumrush, Co. Fermanagh.

4 DECEMBER   Hurd warned NI Assembly that Unionists would have to make a significant move to accommodate Nationalists. Thatcher, in Dublin for EC summit, suggested that misunderstandings after the London summit had been due to her weakness 'for giving a direct answer at a press conference to a direct question'.

6 DECEMBER   Two PIRA members shot dead by SAS in Derry.

14 DECEMBER   Private Ian Thain became first soldier to be convicted for murdering a civilian while on duty in NI.

18 DECEMBER   In Derry thirty-five local people held on 180 charges were cleared by Lord Chief Justice Lord Lowry in the Raymond Gilmour informer trial.

23 DECEMBER   Cardinal Ó Fiaich said alienation among NI Catholics was at an 'unprecedented level'.

24 DECEMBER   Court of Appeal quashed convictions of fourteen men jailed on evidence of UVF supergrass Joseph Bennett.

1985

30 JANUARY   Hurd rejected Nationalist demands for disbandment of UDR.

1 FEBRUARY   John Hume accepted PIRA invitation to talks, but said he would be urging them to end their campaign of violence. Unionists said such a meeting would be an obstacle to SDLP–Unionist dialogue.

3 FEBRUARY   Garret FitzGerald said SDLP–PIRA meeting could be used by PIRA for propaganda purposes, but Charles

Haughey supported the exchange. Hurd said it could only give credibility to PIRA.

16 FEBRUARY   US State Department refused PSF president Gerry Adams a visa to address meeting of Congressmen.

19 FEBRUARY   Republic's Government pushed through legislation to freeze £1.75 million in bank account said to be held by PIRA nominees.

20 FEBRUARY   Thatcher, in address to US Congress, asked Americans not to give money to NORAID.

23 FEBRUARY   Meeting between SDLP leader John Hume and PIRA at secret venue lasted only a few minutes because Hume refused to have part of meeting recorded on video.

Three members of PIRA shot dead by soldiers in Strabane, Co. Tyrone.

27 FEBRUARY   INLA threatened lives of visiting British sports teams after leaving bomb near Windsor Park, Belfast, during World Cup match between England and NI.

28 FEBRUARY   Nine RUC members killed in PIRA mortar attack on Newry, Co. Down, RUC station.

23 MARCH   At DUP conference Paisley accused Irish Government, SDLP and Catholic hierarchy of having vested interest in PIRA atrocities.

5 APRIL   Government announced it was not prepared to put up funds to save NI's gas industry and some 1,000 jobs.

11 APRIL   Hurd announced new RUC complaints procedure.

20 APRIL   Four senior PIRA men expelled after internal row.

15 MAY   District Council elections—PSF took fifty-nine seats.

20 MAY   Four RUC officers killed by PIRA bomb at Killeen on the border.

26 MAY   US Lear Fan aircraft company announced closure of its NI plant with loss of £57 million in Government grants.

23 JUNE   Scotland Yard said it had uncovered a PIRA plan to bomb English seaside resorts.

3 JULY   Thousands of loyalists demonstrated in Portadown, Co. Armagh, against any ban on Orangemen walking through Catholic areas.

7 JULY   Clashes in Portadown between Nationalist protesters and RUC after police allowed Orange Church parade through Catholic Obins Street.

12–13 JULY   Sporadic rioting in Portadown as police prevented Orange and Royal Black Institution parades passing through Obins Street/'Tunnel' area, with fifty-two RUC men injured and extensive damage to property.

21 JULY   Cardinal Ó Fiaich, in interview with the *Universe* news-

paper, said he believed 90 per cent of religious bigotry in NI was found among Protestants.

29 JULY   Belfast Magistrates' Court among buildings damaged by PIRA van bomb.

30 JULY   BBC governors stopped transmission, after Government representations, of a TV documentary which featured PSF Assembly member Martin McGuinness of Derry. (It was later broadcast, with slight amendments, after protest strikes by BBC and ITV journalists and a threat of resignation by the BBC's NI controller, James Hawthorne.)

16 AUGUST   Some shops in Portadown, Co. Armagh, looted and set alight in disturbances which followed a band parade.

30 AUGUST   Two Unionist leaders, James Molyneaux and Ian Paisley, met Margaret Thatcher at Downing Street to protest at continuing Anglo-Irish talks.

2 SEPTEMBER   Tom King succeeded Douglas Hurd as NI Secretary of State.

4 SEPTEMBER   RUC training depot in Enniskillen, Co. Fermanagh, seriously damaged in PIRA mortar attack.

8 SEPTEMBER   PIRA shot dead husband and wife, Gerard and Catherine Mahon, in E. Belfast, claiming they were RUC informers.

5 OCTOBER   Charles Haughey said Fianna Fáil would not stand for any departure from the principle of Irish unity set out in NIF report and enshrined in 1937 Constitution.

8 OCTOBER   NI Court of Appeal quashed a murder conviction against former INLA leader Dominic McGlinchey. (Three days later he was re-extradited to the Republic.)

14 OCTOBER   Study by Irish Information Partnership said more than half the 2,400 killings in NI since 1969 were carried out by Republican paramilitaries, and that more than a quarter of their victims were Catholic civilians.

30 OCTOBER   Paisley and Molyneaux met Thatcher and warned that a consultative role for Republic in NI affairs would result in loyalist backlash.

2 NOVEMBER   Campaign launched to set up loyalist 'Ulster Clubs' in every District Council area.

15 NOVEMBER   Margaret Thatcher and Irish Taoiseach Garret FitzGerald signed AIA at Hillsborough, Co. Down.

16 NOVEMBER   NI Assembly called for a referendum on the AIA, and Unionists disclosed that all fifteen OUP and DUP MPs would resign their seats in protest at the agreement, and so create by-elections on the issue.

20 NOVEMBER   Tom King attacked by angry loyalists as he arrived at Belfast City Hall.

21 NOVEMBER	Dáil approved AIA by eighty-eight votes to seventy-five, with Fianna Fáil opposing, although its leader, Charles Haughey, said they would not oppose developments which would benefit Northern Nationalists.
23 NOVEMBER	Massive loyalist demonstration against AIA in Belfast city centre.
25 NOVEMBER	High Court in London refused leave to Unionists to challenge the legality of AIA.
27 NOVEMBER	Commons backed AIA by 473 votes to 47, with Thatcher declaring that her Government would not give way to threats or violence.
3 DECEMBER	King expressed regret for a speech in Brussels in which he said he believed that the Irish Government now accepted that there would never be a united Ireland – a remark which embarrassed Thatcher and brought protests from Dublin.

1986

14 JANUARY	King said coming by-election results would not change Westminster support for the AIA, and Unionist attitude to it was misconceived and negative.
16 JANUARY	Police who raided an Amsterdam flat arrested Maze escapees Brendan McFarlane and Gerard Kelly, who were later extradited conditionally to UK.
23 JANUARY	In the fifteen by-elections on the AIA Unionists increased their vote on the 1983 general election, but lost Newry and Armagh to SDLP.
24 JANUARY	King said he was encouraged by swing of 5 per cent in Nationalist vote against PSF.
30 JANUARY	Fianna Fáil welcomed suggestion by OUP deputy leader Harold McCusker MP of a conference of British, Irish and NI politicians to discuss the 'totality of relationships' in the two islands. Unemployment in NI reached 21.6 per cent.
18 FEBRUARY	Republic's Government announced its intention to sign the European Convention on the Suppression of Terrorism.
25 FEBRUARY	Paisley and Molyneaux met Thatcher on the AIA, and said afterwards that they welcomed her promise to consider their ideas for round-table talks on devolution. Later, after talks in Belfast with a variety of Unionist representatives, including spokesmen for power and shipyard workers, they said they would be discharging their electoral mandate and withdrawing consent from

34

the Government and there would be no further discussions with Thatcher unless the AIA was abandoned.

26 FEBRUARY   Unionist leaders announced a general strike on 3 March against the AIA, and urged a peaceful protest without paramilitary involvement.

3 MARCH   The Unionist strike, or 'Day of Action', against the AIA halted most of industry and commerce, disrupted public services and transport, including air travel, and led to extensive power cuts. In many areas masked loyalists manned barricades, and during riots at night in Belfast, shots were fired at the RUC in loyalist districts. The Government and the RUC were criticised for not keeping roads open and failing to prevent intimidation.

4 MARCH   Molyneaux and Paisley, in a joint statement, condemned the violence and intimidation of the previous day and said these were not acts of loyalty. In the Commons King accused Unionist MPs of making common cause with people in paramilitary uniform.

7 MARCH   Garret FitzGerald accused Charles Haughey of trying to sabotage the AIA during a visit to the US. In a New York speech Haughey had suggested that his own opposition to the AIA had been vindicated by King's remarks that the agreement meant that there would not be a united Ireland.

9 MARCH   Chief Constable Sir John Hermon defended the RUC's behaviour during the loyalist strike, but admitted that they had not always been in sufficient strength to deal with particular situations.

10 MARCH   Unionist leaders offered to reopen talks with British Government if AIA suspended, but King ruled out suspension.

11 MARCH   Three DUP Assembly members arrested when they tried to cut through barbed wire surrounding Stormont Castle, where AIA ministerial conference was meeting.

13 MARCH   Extra battalion of troops brought in to support RUC.

17 MARCH   Garret FitzGerald told President Reagan he believed there was a desire among Unionists opposed to the AIA to 'get off the hook' and to begin discussions on devolution.

18 MARCH   Women prisoners from Armagh jail became first occupants of new £30-million prison at Maghaberry.

20 MARCH   NIO, in a press advertisement, denounced the Unionist

35

anti-AIA campaign as one of 'lies, deceit, distortion and half-truths'.

24 MARCH Thatcher, in letter to Unionist leaders, rejected the idea of suspension of AIA as a prelude to devolution talks.

31 MARCH Serious clashes between loyalists and RUC in Portadown, Co. Armagh, after banning of an Apprentice Boys parade. Eleven Catholic homes petrol-bombed in Lisburn, Co. Antrim.

1 APRIL More rioting in Portadown, with a twenty-year-old Protestant fatally wounded by plastic bullet.

3 APRIL SDLP leader John Hume praised RUC action in Portadown.

4 APRIL Main Protestant Churches condemned loyalists involved in attacks on Catholic-owned property and RUC members' homes, fourteen of which were attacked during previous night.

8 APRIL Rioting in Belfast and more petrol-bombing of policemen's homes.

23 APRIL A rates strike was among anti-AIA measures announced by Unionist leaders.

25 APRIL OUP executive voted to end special relationship with Conservative Party, dating from the nineteenth-century Home Rule Crisis.

1 MAY Sir Charles Carter warned Government of further violence without state action to help industry.

2 MAY Chief Constable Sir John Hermon condemned intimidation of police officers and Catholics (fifty RUC and seventy-nine Catholic families were fire-bombed in their homes from 1 to 26 April). He accused politicians of 'consorting with paramilitary elements'.

6 MAY Belfast City Council voted twenty-seven to twenty-three to resume normal business and end adjournment policy imposed in protest at AIA.

11 MAY King recommended release of UVF supergrass William 'Budgie' Allen after serving only two years of fourteen-year sentence.

14 MAY In Assembly several Unionists warned of sectarian 'bloodbath' unless AIA suspended.

15 MAY Six-month anniversary of AIA marked by loyalist demonstration in Hillsborough, Co. Down, DUP takeover of telephone switchboard at Stormont, a short work stoppage at Ballylumford power station and a renewed poster campaign.

16 MAY	At seminar on NI in Amsterdam PSF president Gerry Adams said AIA copper-fastened partition and insulated British Government from international criticism.
21 MAY	Ulster Young Unionist Council advocated integration with a NI Grand Committee.
29 MAY	King tells Commons of decision to dissolve NI Assembly.
2 JUNE	James Molyneaux claimed that AIA beginning to 'totter' and 'crumble'.
4 JUNE	Ian Gow and others launched Friends of the Union Group.
5 JUNE	John Stalker replaced in investigation of RUC alleged 'shoot to kill' policy in 1982.
11 JUNE	Five Irish people, including Patrick Magee (Brighton Hotel bomber), found guilty at the Old Bailey of conspiring to cause explosions in Britain.
12 JUNE	Five people arrested in France after major arms seizure.
13 JUNE	Loyalist Workers Committee '86 warned Southern delegates to ICTU conference in Belfast to 'stay at home'.
17 JUNE	Deputy Libyan leader Ahmed Jalloud told German MEPs that his country planned to resume aid to PIRA.
20 JUNE	Chief Constable Sir John Hermon threatened legal action against accusations by media of his involvement in the removal of John Stalker.
23 JUNE	NI Assembly dissolved. Police baton-charged 200 loyalist protesters outside Stormont. Twenty-two Assembly members, mainly DUP, refused to leave the chamber and were removed physically by the RUC early next day.
30 JUNE	Referendum in Republic rejected divorce.
2 JULY	Loyalist politicians continued their own version of Assembly in Belfast City Hall.
3 JULY	RUC permitted Orange Church parade to pass through the Catholic Obins Street area in Portadown, Co. Armagh, but banned 12–13 July parades.
6 JULY	Rioting as RUC barred George Seawright from 'Tunnel' area of Portadown.
7 JULY	NCCL report opposed prison strip-searching.
10 JULY	Ian Paisley and Peter Robinson and 4,000 loyalists took over Hillsborough, Co. Down, in early morning protest against AIA.
11 JULY	Portadown Orangemen accepted compromise Garvaghy Road route. Later at a bonfire, the RUC fired

over 200 baton rounds to disperse loyalist crowds. The twenty-six-day-old loyalist hunger strike at Magilligan Prison ended after visit by Paisley.

13 JULY   Chief Constable Sir John Hermon suspended two senior officers after investigations into alleged 'shoot to kill' policy in 1982. Weekend violence resulted in 128 police and 66 civilian injuries and 127 arrests; 281 baton rounds fired and 79 reported cases of intimidation.

15 JULY   Peter Barry shared 'deep resentment' of Nationalists about the RUC decision on Garvaghy Road route.

16 JULY   Sixth consecutive night of riots in parts of Belfast and Portadown. RUC said 167 police and 125 civilians injured since 11 July; 300 baton rounds fired and 200 people arrested; 111 cases of intimidation reported, including 11 against the homes of police officers.

17 JULY   Court of Appeal quashed convictions of eighteen sentenced in 1983 on the evidence of Republican supergrass Christopher Black; convictions of four others confirmed.

18 JULY   Orange Order inquiry into rioting in Portadown blamed RUC.

22 JULY   A report on recruitment and promotion trends in the NI civil service revealed more Catholic recruits in the last five years but that Catholics and women were still under-represented in top grades.

5 AUGUST   PIRA issued new warning to contractors servicing the security forces, and extended list of 'legitimate targets'.

7 AUGUST   Peter Robinson arrested when 500 loyalists converged on Clontibret, Co. Monaghan.

15 AUGUST   In Dundalk Robinson remanded to Ballybay; supporters stoned and petrol-bombed.

22 AUGUST   John Stalker cleared of allegations of misconduct and reinstated as deputy Chief Constable in Manchester. Short Brothers management ordered removal of flags and emblems from their premises following claims of intimidation of Catholics.

2 SEPTEMBER   SDLP-controlled Newry and Mourne District Council instructed its workers not to collect refuse from local RUC station.

3 SEPTEMBER   Harold McCusker called for new relationship between Britain and NI, arguing that under the AIA the Union was not worth fighting for, much less dying for.

10 SEPTEMBER   NIO reshuffle. Nicholas Scott promoted to Minister of

State and deputy Secretary of State; Peter Viggers replaced Rhodes Boyson at Industry.

16 SEPTEMBER OUP and DUP politicians attended funeral of UVF member John Bingham.

19 SEPTEMBER Sir Frederick Catherwood MEP (Conservative) at QUB urged a round-table conference of main parties to get devolution under AIA.

23 SEPTEMBER OUP and DUP councillors separately decided to continue anti-AIA protest in council chambers but opposed full-blooded boycott or mass resignations.

24 SEPTEMBER Paisley and Molyneaux advised AIA rate-protesters to pay the amount in full now.

25 SEPTEMBER Molyneaux revealed Department of Environment (NI) confidential document on policy changes on Irish language and use of Irish street names.

29 SEPTEMBER Amnesty International renewed its call for judicial inquiry into disputed killings in NI.

2 OCTOBER George Seawright given nine-month sentence for protest at Belfast City Hall, November 1985, during visit by Tom King.

6 OCTOBER Anglo-Irish Conference's first meeting in Dublin discussed border security and agreed that 'I' (non-NI-born) voters could vote in local elections.

12 OCTOBER Charles Haughey at Bodenstown said position of Northern minority had 'seriously worsened' since AIA; in office his party would seek to renegotiate it.

13 OCTOBER NIO agreed to progressively demolish Divis Flats in Belfast and Rossville Flats in Derry.

16 OCTOBER Unemployment rose to new peak of almost 135,000, 23.1 per cent – up 11,500 on 1985.

24 OCTOBER Richard Needham announced legislation to allow pubs to open on Sundays.

1 NOVEMBER Paisley and Molyneaux launched anti-AIA campaign in Britain at Orange rally in Glasgow.

2 NOVEMBER PSF's Ard Fheis voted to allow successful candidates in future Dáil elections to take their seats. Former PSF leader Ruairí Ó Brádaigh, and a hundred others, walked out.

4 NOVEMBER Thatcher rejected the demand that Diplock court judges be increased from one to three in confidential letter to Taoiseach FitzGerald.

7 NOVEMBER Lord Mayor Sammy Wilson barred NIO Ministers from Remembrance Day service at Belfast City Hall.

8 NOVEMBER	UFF planted four devices in Dublin city centre.
10 NOVEMBER	Ulster Resistance formed to 'take direct action as and when required' to defeat AIA at Ulster Hall closed meeting.
12 NOVEMBER	Queen's Speech reiterated Government's commitment to AIA.
15 NOVEMBER	Huge anti-AIA demonstration outside Belfast City Hall. City-centre shops damaged afterwards when RUC confronted a section of the crowd.
18 NOVEMBER	Paisley and Molyneaux met Labour leader Neil Kinnock in London.
20 NOVEMBER	Sir Geoffrey Howe reaffirmed Government's commitment to AIA and criticised its opponents.
21 NOVEMBER	SDLP annual conference in Newcastle, Co. Down, rejected suspension or abrogation of AIA.
26 NOVEMBER	OUP councillors voted not to resign from District Councils despite party leadership support for the option. SACHR recommended three judges in Diplock courts but rejected return to jury trial of scheduled offences.
28 NOVEMBER	FEA report on geographical distribution of Government-sponsored employment said it did not disadvantage Catholics, even before 1972.
1 DECEMBER	King announced proposed changes in laws affecting demonstrations, incitement and the repeal of the Flags and Emblems Act.
3 DECEMBER	Maze escapees Brendan McFarlane and Gerard Kelly extradited from Netherlands.
9 DECEMBER	Paisley expelled from European Parliament after repeatedly interrupting address by Thatcher, in protest against AIA.
10 DECEMBER	PSF president Gerry Adams, at the launch of his book, *Politics of Irish Freedom,* said he had never been a member of IRA.
16 DECEMBER	Lisburn Road police station in Belfast destroyed by proxy bomb and 700 homes and scores of businesses damaged.
21 DECEMBER	Cardinal Ó Fiaich said on RTE that morale of Nationalists had improved since AIA, but time was not right to join RUC.
23 DECEMBER	Thatcher visited NI and reaffirmed Government's commitment to AIA and stated that a change of Government in the Republic would not alter it.

1987

3 JANUARY	At Belfast City Hall OUP and DUP leaders launched

petition to the Queen for referendum on the AIA.

6 JANUARY   NI Housing Executive revealed it dealt with 1,118 cases of intimidation in 1986.

8 JANUARY   David Calvert (DUP) shot and wounded by INLA gunman at Craigavon shopping centre, Co. Armagh. Molyneaux warned against another 'Day of Action' against AIA.

14 JANUARY   Cardinal Ó Fiaich 'appalled' by Lord Brookeborough's description of him in the Lords as an 'evil prelate'.

16 JANUARY   Peter Robinson pleaded guilty in Dublin to unlawful assembly; freed after paying £17,500 in fines and compensation.

18 JANUARY   Charles Haughey said NI and AIA would not be election issues.

19 JANUARY   Nicholas Scott contradicted Haughey view that article one of AIA might be open to renegotiation.

20 JANUARY   Two members of INLA shot dead in a Drogheda hotel in an internal feud. John Taylor (OUP) MEP left European Democratic Group in European Parliament to join European Right Group.

21 JANUARY   INLA said it would disband in its present form.

24 JANUARY   Neil Kinnock visited border security bases; defended Labour meetings with PSF but said 'not productive' for him to meet PSF in person.

29 JANUARY   UDA published 'Common Sense' proposing constitutional conference, devolved assembly and coalition government based on party strengths.

7 FEBRUARY   UFF planted eighteen incendiary devices in Dublin and Co. Donegal.

10 FEBRUARY   Report of SACHR recommended end of excessive remands and of exclusion orders under PTA, more flexibility on transfer of prisoners from GB, three judges in Diplock courts, and reforms in strip-searching procedures. PTA renewed by Commons. *Daily Express* poll found 61 per cent of British in favour of withdrawal from NI.

12 FEBRUARY   Unionist MPs delivered 400,000-signature petition to Buckingham Palace calling for referendum in NI on AIA.

17 FEBRUARY   Richard Needham announced extra £28 million for projects over three years as part of the Belfast programme.

19 FEBRUARY   In Republic's election Fianna Fáil won eighty-one seats – three short of a majority.

23 FEBRUARY	Outgoing Presbyterian Moderator, Dr John Thompson, described Unionist anti-AIA campaign as 'counter-productive and morally questionable'. Belfast City Council fined £25,000 by High Court for contempt in failing to resume normal business; DOE appointed a commissioner to strike a rate in loyalist-controlled councils.
24 FEBRUARY	US Police Foundation cancelled invitation to Chief Constable Sir John Hermon after INC protests.
26 FEBRUARY	Nicholas Scott rejected Enoch Powell amendment to EPA to proscribe PSF.
2 MARCH	Ulster Clubs announced plan to set up alternative system of government run by Unionist political and paramilitary groups.
9 MARCH	Thirty-one RUC women awarded £240,000-compensation in sex-discrimination case against Chief Constable who later agreed to offer women equal access to all training and employment opportunities.
10 MARCH	Charles Haughey elected Taoiseach on the casting vote of Speaker. NIO approved a £300-million development plan for Lagan Bank in Belfast.
11 MARCH	Garret FitzGerald resigned as Fine Gael leader.
17 MARCH	President Reagan authorised first $50-million grant for International Fund for Ireland.
21 MARCH	Alan Dukes elected leader of Fine Gael.
22 MARCH	Former MI5 agent James Miller claimed British intelligence had helped promote the 1974 UWC strike to destabilise Wilson Government.
23 MARCH	PIRA car bomb at officers' club in joint army/RAF base at Rheindalen, West Germany; thirty-one people, mostly German, injured.
24 MARCH	Molyneaux and Paisley called for 'peaceful' demonstrations on 11 April against new Public Order Order.
25 MARCH	SACHR asked Government to strengthen fair employment law, claiming 'serious problems of inequality' between Catholics and Protestants.
26 MARCH	End of INLA feud announced by two W. Belfast priests.
1 APRIL	RUC statement said 'provocative' flying of Union flag could be illegal under new Public Order Order.
8 APRIL	The Lawrence Marley Republican funeral with around 5,000–6,000 mourners was largest since hunger strike.
10 APRIL	Ten Unionist MPs, including Molyneaux and Paisley,

protested at the new Public Order laws by an illegal
march through Belfast.

11 APRIL Low turnout for loyalist 'Day of Defiance'.

15 APRIL PIRA letter bombs franked 'Students' Union, University
of Ulster' sent to Thatcher's press secretary, a deputy
secretary in the Cabinet Office, and the head of the
Cabinet Office economic secretariat. Colonel Gaddafi
announced that he would open centres for the PIRA
and the PLO.

16 APRIL PIRA said it would no longer fire volleys of shots over
dead members' coffins in Church grounds.

23 APRIL Labour spokesman on NI Peter Archer wrote letter
supporting MacBride Principles circulated in the US by
Fair Employment Trust.

25 APRIL Lord Justice Maurice Gibson and his wife Cecily killed
by PIRA car bomb at Killeen, Co. Down. He was fifth
member of NI judiciary killed by PIRA.

28 APRIL Unionists launched anti-AIA campaign in Britain
with press conference and £15,000-advertisement in
The Times.

30 APRIL SDLP criticised NIO pamphlet, 'Northern Ireland: Fair
Treatment For All' (for distribution in the US), for
implying that the SDLP sided with the NIO against the
MacBride Principles.

1 MAY PSF issued 'Scenario for Peace', demanding British withdrawal and calling for all-Ireland constitutional
conference.

4 MAY SDLP fund-raising poker game in a Cookstown hotel,
Co. Tyrone, robbed of £15,000–£20,000 by
armed gang.

5 MAY Paisley said his party would have no part in power-
sharing arrangement after rumours that Unionist Task
Force might propose a form of devolution with an
executive based on proportions of party support.

6 MAY King announced that several hundred full-time RUC
Reservists would be recruited.

8 MAY Eight PIRA men shot dead by SAS in Loughgall,
Co. Armagh.

9 MAY Chief Constable Sir John Hermon in statement on
paramilitary funerals said RUC would liaise with family
and clergy of the dead.

13 MAY US State Department warned that application of the
MacBride Principles to US companies in NI could

leave them 'possibly contravening UK law, or losing access to the UK market'.

19 MAY	Robert McCartney expelled from OUP because of his presidency of the CEC and comments about OUP leadership.
21 MAY	Molyneaux and Paisley launched joint election manifesto which offered Unionist MPs' 'consent' to a new government for a suspension of AIA.
4 JUNE	Presbyterian General Assembly urged Unionist MPs to return to Westminster.
5 JUNE	RUC figures showed more punishment beatings and shootings by paramilitaries in first four months of 1987 than whole of 1986.
9 JUNE	Lord Fitt attacked SDLP and said that if he had a vote, it would go to the WP.
12 JUNE	Conservatives returned to power with 375 seats. The only change in NI was defeat of Enoch Powell (OUP) by Eddie McGrady (SDLP) in S. Down.
15 JUNE	King returned as Secretary of State for NI. Nicholas Scott replaced by former Armed Forces Minister, John Stanley.
25 JUNE	Queen's Speech at the opening of Parliament expressed a commitment to seeking devolution in NI.
30 JUNE	Three men jailed in Boston for *Marita Ann* (1984) arms smuggling to PIRA.
1 JULY	Short Brothers management threatened closure of sections of plant over display of loyalist flags.
3 JULY	Short Brothers closed three of its main production areas.
5 JULY	Protest march at Glasdrummond, S. Armagh, at takeover of lands, and building of observation posts by army.
6 JULY	Production resumed at the three Short Brothers plants.
7 JULY	Legislation for NI included provisions for Sunday pub opening and the abolition of jurors in civil injury cases.
8 JULY	Paisley and Molyneaux announced they would use the Task Force report in low-level introductory talks with Government.
22 JULY	FEA draft inquiry into Derry City Council cleared it of Unionist allegations of discrimination against Protestants.
1 AUGUST	Fifty-strong NORAID group from the US arrived on a NI 'fact-finding' mission.
2 AUGUST	Jim McAllister (PSF) led march to protest at a 'spy camera' monitoring cross-border traffic at an army base near Crossmaglen, Co. Armagh.

3 AUGUST	SDLP claimed PSF used hundreds of forged medical cards in W. Belfast during June election; PSF dismissed the claim.
4 AUGUST	Planning Appeals Commission refused permission for the 'Belfast Says No' banner at the City Hall.
12 AUGUST	Paisley rejected Archbishop Robin Eames's attempts to set up informal talks between the four main constitutional party leaders.
14 AUGUST	Unionists called for end to cross-border RUC–Garda intelligence co-operation after a Garda memo fell into PIRA hands.
2 SEPTEMBER	John Taylor claimed that PIRA campaign united Protestants and, ironically, benefited their commercial rebuilding plans; he urged Unionists to accept the challenge of devolution and improved links with Dublin.
5 SEPTEMBER	Two men and one woman, with Dublin and Kildare addresses, charged with conspiracy to murder King in Wiltshire (later convicted). Eleven Unionist MPs, including Molyneaux and Paisley, summoned under new Public Order laws for an illegal march on 10 April and the loyalist 'Day of Defiance' on 11 April.
6 SEPTEMBER	Chris Mullin, Labour MP, claimed to have interviewed the 'real' Birmingham pub bombers.
7 SEPTEMBER	John Cushnahan, Alliance leader, announced he was going to resign.
9 SEPTEMBER	Government proposed that electoral candidates be required to 'declare opposition to the use of violence for political ends'.
10 SEPTEMBER	US ambassador to UK Charles Price supported UK Government's stand against the MacBride Principles.
12 SEPTEMBER	WP leader Tomás Mac Giolla announced his resignation. Cardinal Ó Fiaich described the AIA as 'a shot in the arm for Catholics in the North'.
14 SEPTEMBER	Unionist leaders Molyneaux and Paisley ended nineteen-month boycott of Government Ministers to meet Tom King at Stormont for 'talks about talks'.
15 SEPTEMBER	King launched 'Religious Equality of Opportunity in Employment: An Employer's Guide to Fair Employment'.
16 SEPTEMBER	European Commission of Human Rights held that provisions of PTA for seven-day detention breached requirement that suspects be charged 'promptly'.
29 SEPTEMBER	Strabane DUP councillor Ronald Brolly jailed for two years for sectarian arson attacks.

45

3 OCTOBER	Dr John Alderdice elected new Alliance Party leader.
4 OCTOBER	Peter Barry claim of a British undertaking to reform Diplock courts denied by Sir Geoffrey Howe in Denmark.
7 OCTOBER	Peter Robinson resigned as deputy leader of DUP.
8 OCTOBER	Lord Hailsham, former Lord Chancellor, rejected need for reform of Diplock courts.
9 OCTOBER	Chief Constable Sir John Hermon approved new code of conduct.
11 OCTOBER	Charles Haughey at Bodenstown expressed disappointment at AIA results.
15 OCTOBER	DPP Sir Barry Shaw denied Garret FitzGerald's claim that supergrass trials ended in NI due to AIA.
20 OCTOBER	Belfast Unionist councillors agreed to pay £25,000-fine and £11,000 in costs imposed by the High Court over AIA protest.
21 OCTOBER	King met Brian Lenihan for four hours and warned of 'serious implications' if no extradition after 1 December.
22 OCTOBER	Thatcher told MPs: 'The future of courts in NI is a matter for the UK Government and it is not a bargaining point.'
23 OCTOBER	PSF won Belfast City Council by-elections in Upper and Lower Falls.
27 OCTOBER	Republic's Government expressed concern at lobbying of opposition politicians on extradition by senior British Embassy staff in Dublin.
1 NOVEMBER	One hundred and fifty tons of arms and ammunition for PIRA seized on French coaster, *Eksund*.
7 NOVEMBER	OUP conference in Belfast opposed devolved government with minority veto arising from AIA. At SDLP conference John Hume called on Unionists to negotiate.
8 NOVEMBER	Eleven killed and sixty-three injured when PIRA bomb went off at Enniskillen Remembrance Day ceremony.
11 NOVEMBER	Charles Haughey met British Labour leader, Neil Kinnock, to discuss extradition.
12 NOVEMBER	Molyneaux and Paisley led 2,000 Unionists through London to mark their opposition to AIA. Unemployment total fell by 5,283 to 124,707 – 18.2 per cent.
14 NOVEMBER	Paisley and Molyneaux attended Hillsborough rally against AIA.
15 NOVEMBER	Republic observed one minute's silence over Enniskillen bombing.
16 NOVEMBER	AIA Conference met in Dublin and agreed 'a very positive response' to security post-Enniskillen.

17 NOVEMBER	DOE published 'Belfast Urban Area Plan 2001', which met widespread criticism.
18 NOVEMBER	Fianna Fáil backbenchers demanded prima-facie evidence requirement in Extradition Bill.
19 NOVEMBER	George Seawright shot and fatally injured by IPLO.
22 NOVEMBER	Thatcher joined 7,000 for rearranged Remembrance Day service at Enniskillen.
23 NOVEMBER	Massive arms search in Republic and NI after claims of three successful arms runs before the *Eksund*. Republic's Bill published amending 1965 Extradition Act to require the Attorney-General to satisfy himself of a case to answer before endorsing a warrant.
24 NOVEMBER	Forty PSF activists arrested in Belfast, Derry and border counties.
25 NOVEMBER	King disagreed with Republic's proposed extradition safeguards.
30 NOVEMBER	Republic's Extradition Act effective at midnight.
1 DECEMBER	Thatcher claimed Britain was 'least-favoured nation' in new extradition arrangements.
2 DECEMBER	Molyneaux and Paisley met Tom King for fifth of series of 'talks about talks'.
5 DECEMBER	Thatcher met Taoiseach Haughey at EC summit in Copenhagan and re-established 'working relationship'.
12 DECEMBER	Chief Constable Sir John Hermon confirmed cross-border co-operation between bomb disposal teams.
14 DECEMBER	Tony Benn published draft Bill sponsored by Labour Campaign Group setting a date for British withdrawal from NI.
17 DECEMBER	PIRA bomb exploded outside home of Judge Donald Murray.
18 DECEMBER	County Court judge Andrew Donaldson resigned after a dispute with the RUC Chief Constable over his security arrangements.
22 DECEMBER	UDA deputy leader John McMichael killed by PIRA booby-trap car bomb outside his Lisburn home.

1988

1 JANUARY	Chief Constable Sir John Hermon warned that PIRA had SAM-7 missiles.
8 JANUARY	Police intercepted 100 guns and ammunition, destined for loyalists, in cars near Portadown, Co. Armagh. Peter Robinson re-elected as DUP deputy leader at annual meeting.
11 JANUARY	John Hume met Gerry Adams for talks in Belfast at request of a third party; both parties denied PIRA cease-fire on agenda.

14 JANUARY	Unemployment 120,588 (17.6 per cent) – 8,200 fewer than December 1986. Recorder of Belfast upheld FEA decision of discrimination by Ministry of Defence against W. Belfast Catholic.
20 JANUARY	UK opposed inclusion of NI with poorest EC regions to gain increased structural funds. NI MPs united to support David Alton's Bill to reduce the abortion time limit to eighteen weeks.
21 JANUARY	King announced more control by army over border security.
24 JANUARY	SDLP constituency representatives endorsed Hume/Adams talks.
25 JANUARY	Sir Patrick Mayhew (Attorney-General) announced that eleven RUC officers investigated by Stalker/Sampson would not be prosecuted for reasons of 'national security'; Republic expressed 'deep dismay'.
26 JANUARY	Molyneaux and Paisley met King with plan for administrative devolution with committee system and proportionate chairmanships.
27 JANUARY	Gardaí discovered PIRA arms dump at Malin Head, Co. Donegal.
28 JANUARY	Court of Appeal in London rejected plea by Birmingham Six.
5 FEBRUARY	NIO confirmed new draft fair employment legislation.
6 FEBRUARY	Five thousand attended Dublin anti-extradition rally.
7 FEBRUARY	Molyneaux wanted AIA rewritten to cover 'totality of relationships' between Britain and Ireland.
9 FEBRUARY	European Parliament asked Britain to reconsider non-prosecution decision on Stalker/Sampson findings.
13 FEBRUARY	PSF executive permitted Adams to resume talks with SDLP.
14 FEBRUARY	Republic said Britain sent extradition warrants without new evidence requirements.
15 FEBRUARY	Thatcher met Haughey after EC summit in Brussels.
17 FEBRUARY	King announced two disciplinary inquiries into the RUC over Stalker/Sampson investigation.
18 FEBRUARY	Unemployment rose to 121,778. SACHR recommended three-judge Diplock courts.
20 FEBRUARY	Haughey spoke about 'historic inability in Britain to comprehend Irish feelings and sensitivities'; willing to travel North to talk to Unionists.
21 FEBRUARY	Aidan McAnespie shot dead at Aughnacloy, Co. Tyrone, border checkpoint.
23 FEBRUARY	Private Ian Thain released from life sentence after twenty-six months to rejoin his regiment.

24 FEBRUARY	FEA annual report published: Catholic share of public-sector employment increased.
25 FEBRUARY	John Hume accepted King's invitation to talks on devolution.
1 MARCH	John Stanley (NIO), on the PTA renewal debate, said SAM-7 missiles were 'in the island of Ireland'. Belfast City Council refused invitation to Dublin millennium celebrations.
2 MARCH	Haughey said devolution proposals neither 'workable nor beneficial' at present.
6 MARCH	Mairead Farrell, Sean Savage and Daniel McCann (all PIRA) shot dead by SAS in Gibraltar.
8 MARCH	Spanish police found car packed with explosives in Marbella.
10 MARCH	Sixty Labour MPs denounced Gibraltar shootings as 'capital punishment without trial'.
11 MARCH	Andy Tyrie (UDA) resigned as leader after no-confidence motion in inner council of the organisation.
16 MARCH	Loyalist attacked Gibraltar funerals at Milltown cemetery in Belfast, killing three and injuring several.
19 MARCH	Two army corporals killed by mob at W. Belfast funeral.
23 MARCH	After temporary resistance, BBC, ITN and RTE handed over film of killing of two army corporals to RUC.
28 MARCH	Tony Benn published Bill to end British rule in NI by 1990.
29 MARCH	SDLP presented strategy document on political progress to King.
1 APRIL	Colonel Gaddafi of Libya pledged support for PIRA.
12 APRIL	RUC annual report said 1987 worst year for violence since 1981.
16 APRIL	Proinsias de Rossa replaced Tomás Mac Giolla as leader of WP.
21 APRIL	Brian Donnelly (Dem.) introduced Fair Employment Incentives Bill in US Congress.
26 APRIL	King met SDLP delegation at Stormont.
28 APRIL	King said AIA 'an end in itself' not 'part of a process sliding to something else'.
1 MAY	PIRA killed two RAF men at Niew Bergen in Holland and one at Roermond in West Germany.
3 MAY	Nigel Dodds (DUP) elected youngest-ever Lord Mayor of Belfast.
15 MAY	UVF gun attack on Belfast bar kills three. Molyneaux in *Weekend World* interview was prepared for OUP officials to exchange position papers with Haughey.

19 MAY	Unemployment rose by 733, but 8,938 lower than April 1987.
26 MAY	Paisley and Molyneaux met King for last of 'talks about talks'.
27 MAY	Seamus Mallon (SDLP) asked Government not to deploy Royal Irish Rangers in NI.
7 JUNE	Police Federation asked for simultaneous internment in NI and Republic.
10 JUNE	Conservative Association launched in Bangor, Co. Down.
13 JUNE	SDLP and PSF met in Belfast for on-going discussions.
14 JUNE	The McGimpsey brothers' action challenging the AIA began in Dublin High Court.
15 JUNE	Six soldiers killed by bomb at Lisburn, Co. Antrim, fun run.
16 JUNE	King refused to rule out internment as security response.
22 JUNE	Chief Constable Sir John Hermon said he would retire in 1989. Catholic Bishops attacked proposed educational reforms.
23 JUNE	PIRA shot down helicopter at Crossmaglen, Co. Armagh.
27 JUNE	Amnesty International sought judicial inquiry into disputed killings by police and army since 1982.
28 JUNE	Government said Harland and Wolff to be privatised. PM Thatcher and Taoiseach Haughey met at EC Hanover summit and discussed security.
29 JUNE	Police Authority decision (by one vote) not to inquire further into senior officers' role in 'shoot to kill' cases criticised by Republic.
30 JUNE	King said new Police Authority included substantial representation of Catholics. Labour hard-left supporters launched 'Time to Go' campaign for British withdrawal from NI.
1 JULY	DED said Short Brothers would 'ultimately return to the private sector'.
3 JULY	Eddie McGrady, SDLP MP, expressed disquiet at continuation of his party's talks with PSF.
4 JULY	Twenty RUC men to be subject to disciplinary proceedings as result of Kelly inquiry arising from Stalker/Sampson investigations. Belfast City Council meeting abandoned after PSF and Unionists came to blows.
11 JULY	King willing to remain in any reshuffle of Cabinet.
13 JULY	Duisburg (West Germany) British army base damaged by two PIRA bombs.
14 JULY	Harland and Wolff announced loss of £17.3 million,

lowest since 1970s. Criminal Justice Bill permits RUC to take mouth and saliva swabs from suspects.

15 JULY   NIO said NIE would be privatised as a unit.

18 JULY   It was announced that Gerry Adams and John Hume met in private on 11 July. Attorney-General Sir Patrick Mayhew met Dublin counterpart on extradition.

19 JULY   £10-million extra aid for W. Belfast.

20 JULY   Molyneaux rejected Anglo-Irish Inter-Parliamentary tier.

22 JULY   NI trade unionists lobbied Westminster over privatisation of Short Brothers and Harland and Wolff.

23 JULY   Border bomb (1,000-lb), intended for Mr Justice Higgins, killed Robert and Maureen Hanna, and their son David; they were among the seventeen civilians to die in PIRA 'mistakes' since November 1987.

25 JULY   John Stanley replaced by Ian Stewart in Cabinet reshuffle and returned to back benches.

28 JULY   All NI parties opposed privatisation of Short Brothers and Harland and Wolff in Commons debate.

29 JULY   Ed Koch, Mayor of New York, withdrew favourable comments on British army role in NI on his return home.

1 AUGUST   First PIRA bomb in GB since 1984 killed soldier at Inglis barracks, N. London.

4 AUGUST   The McGimpsey brothers decided to appeal the rejection by the High Court in Dublin of their constitutional challenge to AIA.

5 AUGUST   Police Federation and OUP urged reintroduction of internment. PIRA bomb at British army base at Düsseldorf. WP and Prog. D. urged SDLP to end PSF contacts.

8 AUGUST   Mr Justice Brian Hutton succeeded Lord Lowry as Lord Chief Justice.

11 AUGUST   NIO confirmed three helicopter overflights into Republic in past two weeks.

12 AUGUST   IPLO exploded proxy bomb outside Belfast Law Courts. Republic denied overflight agreement.

14 AUGUST   Martin McGuinness (PSF) praised the 'Continental battalion' of PIRA.

15 AUGUST   John Hume defended his latest meeting with Gerry Adams. Charter Group warned Molyneaux of challenge to his leadership.

16 AUGUST   Coopers and Lybrand review of the economy criticised absence of political stability and urged caution on privatisation of Short Brothers and Harland and Wolff.

17 AUGUST	Robert Russell failed to have his extradition order set aside by the Dublin High Court. British and Irish Governments denied overflight agreement. Unemployment rose 2,500 to 118,239.
20 AUGUST	Eight British soldiers killed by bomb attack on service bus at Ballygawley, Co. Tyrone. (Most serious attack since 1979 at Warrenpoint.)
21 AUGUST	King announced major security review.
22 AUGUST	Royal Navy recruiting officer in Belfast killed by bomb attached to his car.
23 AUGUST	Gerard O'Hare became the first extradited from the Republic under the 1987 Act. PIRA exploded massive car bomb in Belfast city centre.
27 AUGUST	Robert Russell transferred by Garda to RUC at border.
30 AUGUST	Three PIRA members shot by SAS near Drumnakilly, Co. Tyrone.
31 AUGUST	Two PIRA suspects arrested by West German police near Dutch border.
1 SEPTEMBER	Committee on Administration of Justice urged a stronger Police Authority.
2 SEPTEMBER	SDLP/PSF talks broke down.
5 SEPTEMBER	SDLP and PSF formally announced end of talks. NIO blocked FEA investigation of NIE contract on grounds of national security.
6 SEPTEMBER	Gibraltar inquest opened into deaths of three PIRA members.
7 SEPTEMBER	IPLO shot dead William Quee (UDA) in Belfast.
8 SEPTEMBER	Marketing Research Consultancy poll for UTV supported requirement that politicians sign an 'anti-violence' declaration. International Fund for Ireland to devote more funds to disadvantaged areas.
9 SEPTEMBER	PIRA shot dead Colin Abernethy, treasurer of Ulster Clubs movement.
13 SEPTEMBER	Seamus Mallon said SDLP would talk to Unionists irrespective of whether the AIA was in operation or not.
19 SEPTEMBER	David Owen (SDP leader) said that the AIA should be 'recast'.
20 SEPTEMBER	Home Secretary Douglas Hurd announced plans to attack funds raised by paramilitary groups.
21 SEPTEMBER	Labour document proposed harmonisation of policies on economy, security, currency, and social security as a prelude to united Ireland by consent.
26 SEPTEMBER	DPP announced he would not proceed with charges in the Aidan McAnespie case.

27 SEPTEMBER	Ian Stewart (NIO) confirmed an agreement on border overflying to 200 metres which had existed for two years.
28 SEPTEMBER	PM Thatcher visited NI.
29 SEPTEMBER	Republic's Foreign Minister Brian Lenihan addressed UN Assembly on AIA.
2 OCTOBER	Molyneaux criticised King for saying that Unionists had made no proposals for political development. BBC postponed *Panorama* documentary on SAS in NI.
3 OCTOBER	Alliance Party urged a devolved government with power-sharing and an input into the Anglo-Irish Conference.
5 OCTOBER	Brian Mawhinney (NIO) published educational reforms for NI, which followed those in GB and boosted integrated education locally.
6 OCTOBER	Trial opened at Winchester of three charged with conspiracy to murder King.
7 OCTOBER	Patrick McVeigh arrested in Dundalk but released by Gardaí despite being wanted in Britain. Tom Hartley (PSF) refuted SDLP claim that Britain was neutral on NI since AIA.
8 OCTOBER	Corrymeela conference at Ballycastle, Co. Antrim, brought Ken Maginnis (OUP) and Eddie McGrady (SDLP) together on devolution. Derry Civil Rights march marked twentieth anniversary.
10 OCTOBER	Molyneaux rejected King's invitation to talks on security. Conservative Party conference opened in Brighton for first time since 1984 PIRA bomb.
11 OCTOBER	Paisley ejected from European Parliament after interrupting an address by Pope John Paul II. King invited general submissions to the review of the workings of the Anglo-Irish Conference.
13 OCTOBER	Unionist joint-policy group formally rejected any involvement in the review of AIA. Monsignor Colm McCaughan said Catholic parents sending children to integrated schools were breaking canon law. Unemployment fell to 115,743 (16.6 per cent).
14 OCTOBER	In Brighton Thatcher praised SAS action in Gibraltar. Taoiseach Haughey admitted to hospital with a respiratory illness. Talks in Duisburg, West Germany, aimed at finding formula for inter-party negotiations in NI.
15 OCTOBER	James Craig (UDA) killed by UFF.
18 OCTOBER	MRBI/*Irish Times* opinion survey in Republic revealed

that support for extradition had fallen from 40 to 31 per cent.

19 OCTOBER   Home Secretary Douglas Hurd announced a ban on 'direct statements' by spokesmen and supporters of paramilitary organisations on radio and television.

20 OCTOBER   King announced that the law would be changed on the right to silence.

22 OCTOBER   RSF Ard Fheis in Dublin condemned extradition from the Republic.

28 OCTOBER   Three Irish defendants in King conspiracy case were sentenced to twenty-five years each after a ten to two verdict.

29 OCTOBER   Molyneaux told a Friends of the Union conference in London that the 1980 British-Irish Intergovernmental Council might be an acceptable alternative to AIA.

1 NOVEMBER   Mr Justice Nicholson called on loyalists to reject the UDA, when he sentenced three of its members for possessing the largest haul of loyalist arms uncovered during the Troubles at Portadown in January 1988.

2 NOVEMBER   Anglo-Irish Conference met at Stormont and decided to widen review of AIA. Public spending of £5,468 million for 1989-90.

4 NOVEMBER   AIA inter-Parliamentary body of fifty members proposed, but Unionists indicated they would not take part while AIA operated.

7 NOVEMBER   British and Irish Foreign Ministers Sir Geoffrey Howe and Brian Lenihan met in Dublin: agreement on continental shelf exploitation and discussion of AIA matters.

8 NOVEMBER   King attacked right to silence in Criminal Evidence (NI) Order debate.

10 NOVEMBER   Conservative National Union rejected application by N. Down Model Conservative Association; political reasons cited: split pro-Union vote, critical of Conservative policies. Settlement of £900,000 for 310 RUC women Reservists in EOC case.

14 NOVEMBER   Inquest opened on three S. Armagh deaths in 1982 – the subject of the Stalker/Sampson inquiries. Five-hundred-job Korean investment in VCR plant for Antrim. Friends of the Union published proposed replacement for AIA. Lagan Valley Model Conservative Association formed.

15 NOVEMBER	Small protests marked third anniversary of AIA. Molyneaux said proposals with King for eight months may be withdrawn. King said he was uncertain of their status.
16 NOVEMBER	President Reagan renewed pledge on AIA and promised extra funds.
17 NOVEMBER	Ulster Independence Committee (leader Rev. Hugh Ross) formed network of eleven branches after fifteen public meetings in NI. Unemployment 110,445 (15.9 per cent).
18 NOVEMBER	Loyalist arms find in Co. Armagh linked with Ulster Resistance.
19 NOVEMBER	Six RUC stations and five police posts close to save £2 million. OUP conference at Portrush, Co. Antrim, called for referendum on AIA. DUP said they had severed all connections with Ulster Resistance some time ago.
22 NOVEMBER	Queen's Speech promised stronger fair employment legislation, anti-violence oath and 'I' votes (non-NI-born voters) in local elections and a new PTA. Princess Royal (Anne) visited NI.
24 NOVEMBER	Bomb explosion at Benburb, Co. Tyrone, RUC station killed two civilians.
25 NOVEMBER	New PTA Bill published.
26 NOVEMBER	SDLP annual conference attacked changes in right to silence and councillors' oath.
28 NOVEMBER	Unionists studied letter from Thatcher on their proposals.
29 NOVEMBER	European Court of Human Rights ruled against detention without charge beyond four days – affects PTA seven-day provision.
30 NOVEMBER	Law officers admitted errors in original Father Patrick Ryan extradition warrant. Thatcher statement strongly critical of Belgium and Republic on Ryan case. E. Londonderry Model Conservative Association set up at Coleraine meeting.
1 DECEMBER	Commons row over Ryan; chronology of crisis set out. Paddy Ashdown (SLD) visited NI.
3 DECEMBER	Irish Attorney-General posed twenty new questions on Ryan extradition. Labour Party split on whether to abstain on second reading of new PTA: Clare Short and Andrew Bennett resigned over abstention policy.
6 DECEMBER	Dáil debate approved Extradition Act 1987 amid public protests. Forty-two Labour backbenchers revolted on PTA.

7 DECEMBER	US ambassador Charles Price urged NI businessmen to get involved in politics.
8 DECEMBER	Joint European approach to extradition suggested. FEA twelfth annual report criticised pivate employers.
10 DECEMBER	EC ordered review of extradition between members. Denmark ended cross-border shopping restrictions on its citizens, leaving Republic isolated with such measures.
12 DECEMBER	Danny Morrison (PSF) left to visit Belgium for four days. Haughey stance on Ryan boosted public support for Taoiseach by 8 per cent to 62 per cent.
13 DECEMBER	Irish Attorney-General rejected British request for extradition of Ryan. Labour '87 published plan for devolution.
14 DECEMBER	AIA Conference meeting at Stormont heard King express dissatisfaction on extradition. Thatcher described Irish decision on Ryan as an 'insult to the British people'. John Taylor (OUP) urged Unionists to apply for funds to the International Fund for Ireland.
15 DECEMBER	Second report of International Fund for Ireland showed 858 projects, supported by £26.5 million, created 4,500 jobs. Unemployment fell 1,400 to 108,981 (15.7 per cent). PLO formally denied any links with PIRA.
16 DECEMBER	Fair Employment Bill published.
17 DECEMBER	Apprentice Boys launched tercentenary celebrations of the Siege of Derry.
19 DECEMBER	Visit by Neil Kinnock, Labour leader, to Fermanagh, army families and trade unionists.
20 DECEMBER	Court of Appeal ruled RUC witnesses were compellable and ordered a fresh inquest into three 1982 deaths in Co. Armagh.
21 DECEMBER	IDB secured biggest inward investment of £90 million and 1,000 jobs by French-owned Montupet company to make aluminium cylinder heads for Ford on former de Lorean site. Police discovered PIRA bomb factory in N. London.
22 DECEMBER	Government decided to retain seven-day detention of suspects despite European Court of Human Rights decision and to seek temporary derogation from European Convention.
27 DECEMBER	It was announced that the Harland and Wolff management buyout was lodged on 23 December.
28 DECEMBER	The *Independent* newspaper revealed that NI judges had informed King of their disquiet over the effects of

changes in the right to silence and a proposed role for them in detention under the PTA.

30 DECEMBER   Ivor Stanbrook, Cons. MP, criticised Christmas parole for 117 life-sentence prisoners as a 'crass and dangerous error of judgement'. PIRA end-of-year message explicitly warned British politicians and the royal family.

DICTIONARY OF NORTHERN IRISH POLITICS

A

ABERCORN, DUKE OF
Unionist MP for Fermanagh–S. Tyrone,
1964–70. Sat in Parliament as
Marquess of Hamilton, succeeding to
Dukedom in June 1979. b. 4 July 1934.
Member, Council of Europe,
1966–70; European Economic and
Social Committee, 1973–8.
Conservative. Served in UDR, 1974–8.
Wide business interests include chair-
manship of North West Exploration, a
mining company exploring in Co.
Tyrone and other sites in Ireland, and
chairmanship of a company set up in
1987 to develop the River Lagan
frontage in Belfast. NI Industrial
Development Board, 1982–. Her
Majesty's Lieutenant for Co. Tyrone,
1986–.

**ABERCORN RESTAURANT
BOMBING**
The explosion of a bomb in the
crowded central Belfast restaurant, the
Abercorn, on 4 March 1972, was one
of the most horrific incidents of the NI
violence. Two women were killed and
some 130 people injured. There was no
warning and the casualties were mainly
women and children having a break
from Saturday afternoon shopping.
Many suffered severe mutilation. Two
sisters out shopping were among the
most seriously affected, each lost both
legs, and one of them, who was buying
her wedding dress, also lost an arm and
an eye.

ACTIVE SERVICE UNIT *see*
Provisional Irish Republican Army

ADAMS, GERARD (GERRY)
PSF MP for W. Belfast, 1983–.

Assembly member for W. Belfast,
1982–6. Vice-president, PSF,
1978–83; president, PSF, 1983–.
b. Belfast, 1949. Barman in Belfast
when he became involved in what
Republicans describe as 'defence work
during the pogroms', and he was
believed by the security forces to be
head of the PIRA in the Ballymurphy
area of W. Belfast when he was
interned in 1971. Released in July 1972
to take part in secret London talks
between PIRA and Secretary of State
William Whitelaw, which gave rise to a
brief ceasefire. In resumed campaign he
was believed by British intelligence
sources to be the Belfast brigade
commander of PIRA, and in 1973 one of
three-man group running PIRA after
arrest of Seán Mac Stiofáin, chief of
staff. After arrest with other leading
Republicans in Belfast in 1973, he tried
to escape from the Maze Prison. For
this, he was sentenced to eighteen
months' imprisonment and released in
1976. Both as an internee and a
convicted prisoner, he was in the PIRA
compound at the Maze, but he has
repeatedly denied that he has been a
member of PIRA. In February 1978 he
was charged with membership of PIRA,
but after being remanded in custody for
seven months, he was freed after the
Lord Chief Justice Lord Lowry ruled
that there was not sufficient evidence
for a conviction. He has on several
occasions stressed the need for
increased political action by Republicans. In June 1979 he told a Wolfe
Tone commemoration ceremony at
Bodenstown, Co. Kildare, that the aims
of the movement could not be achieved
simply by military means, and their

failure to develop an alternative to constitutional politics had to be continually analysed. At the 1980 PSF Ard Fheis he said that the British now realised that there could not be a military victory, and it was time that Republicans realised it too. He had a leading role in deciding policy on the 1981 H-Block hunger strike, and when he topped the poll in W. Belfast in the 1982 Assembly election, he became the dominant NI personality in PSF.

Tim Pat Coogan, an authority on the IRA, called him a 'Shogun-like figure' in Northern republicanism. He is among those who have campaigned for a more socialist approach by PSF, and when the party dropped federalism from its policy in 1982, it was a further triumph for Adams and his supporters and put him at odds with some leading Southern PSF figures such as Dáithí Ó Conaill. In December 1982 he was banned by Home Secretary William Whitelaw, under the Prevention of Terrorism Act, from entering GB to speak to Labour MPs and councillors at the invitation of GLC leader Ken Livingstone. But the ban was lifted by the Home Office in June 1983 when he took W. Belfast in the general election with a majority of more than 5,000, unseating veteran MP Gerry Fitt. In July 1983 he provoked controversy with a visit to London, where he met some Labour MPs, but his efforts to explain his policies in the US and Canada have been frustrated by the denial of a visa. However, within PSF his influence has developed steadily and he became president in a Northern coup in 1983. He moved PSF towards further political participation and the 1986 Ard Fheis took the radical step of dropping abstention from the Dáil. This commitment to politics provoked a split in the movement and division from former associates. Public prominence brought dangers and in March 1984 Adams and three PSF colleagues were shot as they travelled by car through Belfast city centre from the Magistrates' Court. The loyalist gun gang were captured by a UDR patrol. In May 1987 PSF published 'Scenario for Peace', which envisaged a British withdrawal followed by an all-Ireland constitutional conference. Adams retained his W. Belfast constituency in the June 1987 general election despite a determined campaign against him led by the SDLP; he increased his majority and his share of the vote. Early in 1988 he engaged in private talks with SDLP leader John Hume, which were later widened to include other prominent members of both parties. The discussions created some puzzlement in political circles in view of the previous tensions between PSF and SDLP. Most Dublin politicians suppressed their doubts out of regard for Hume; the British Government saw no value in the exchanges, while Unionists declared them an insuperable obstacle to dialogue between themselves and the SDLP. Repeated statements by PSF figures discounted the idea that they could satisfy Hume's hope for an end to the PIRA campaign, even if it were to be the ticket to all-Ireland round-table negotiations. But the exchanges, which broke down after six months with some recriminations, fitted in with an increased trend towards self-examination within PSF, which was reflected in Adams's own mild criticisms of some PIRA killings in 1987 and 1988. In what he himself described as an 'unprecedented' intervention at the PSF Ard Fheis in January 1989, he said accidental killings of civilians by PIRA must stop because they 'retarded' the Republican struggle. But he reiterated support for the PIRA campaign generally. He also supported co-operation with other Nationalist groups in elections.

ADVISORY COMMISSION

An eleven-member body set up by William Whitelaw, Secretary of State soon after direct rule in 1972, to advise him on local legislation and matters generally. It first met on 25 May 1972 and subsequently twenty-five times that year. It continued until the setting up of the Assembly, and was controversial from the start. Both Unionists and the SDLP boycotted it, although the Secretary of State gave an assurance that it would not usurp the functions of MPs. Members: Sir Robin Kinahan, leading local businessman and one-time Unionist MP; Sheelagh Murnaghan, former Liberal MP for QUB; Professor Norman Gibson of NUU; R.D. Rolston, president of the Confederation of British Industry Council in NI; Ada Malone, headmistress of Enniskillen Collegiate School for Girls; Norman Kennedy, trade-union leader; Tom Conaty, businessman and chairman of the Falls Road-based CCDC; R.B. Price of Ballymoney, who had been active in local authority and chamber of commerce affairs; James O'Hara, a member (later chairman) of the Housing Executive and first Catholic appointed to former Housing Trust; A.E. Gibson, former president Ulster Farmers' Union; and John H. Nicholl, vice-chairman of Londonderry County Council, to which he was elected as a Nationalist.

AGNEW, FRASER

OUP Assembly member for S. Antrim, 1982–6. Served on committees on Economic Development and Environment. b. 1942. Newtownabbey Council, 1981–. Chairman, Association of Belfast Orange Unionist Delegates' Association. In the early days of the AIA he appeared to have inside information on the date, place and agenda of the ministerial conference meetings.

ALDERDICE, DR JOHN

Leader of the Alliance Party, 1987–. b. 1955. Educated Ballymena Academy and QUB. Consultant psychiatrist at Belfast City Hospital. Alderdice was an unexpected choice to succeed John Cushnahan. He had joined the party in 1978 and although he had been on the party council since 1979 and had been a vice-chairman, he had never held elected office. He had failed to win a council seat in Lisburn in 1981. But in 1987 he produced the best-ever Alliance showing in a Westminster election by polling 32 per cent against Peter Robinson, DUP MP for E. Belfast. In the leadership election in October he defeated Seamus Close by 117 votes to 77. In January 1988 he began a series of meetings with party leaders in the Republic, GB and NI. On the AIA he expressed the view that Unionist demands for its suspension were unrealistic; he called for a constructive review of its operation in 1988 through wide consultation and efforts to allay Unionist fears. At the Alliance Party conference in April 1988 Alderdice welcomed David Steel (SLD) and Des O'Malley (Prog. D.), and the presence, after a gap of a number of years, of three Fianna Fáil observers. Chosen as candidate for 1989 European election.

ALISON, MICHAEL JAMES HUGH

Minister of State, NIO, 1979–81. b. 27 June 1926. At the NIO he was deputy to Secretary of State Humphrey Atkins, and his most arduous period at Stormont was in 1981 when he was responsible for handling the prison situation during most of the H-Block hunger strike. He left NI, however, a month or so before the protest ended. Conservative MP for Barkston Ash, 1964–83; Selby, 1983–. Conservative Research Department, 1958–64; Parliamentary Under-Secretary, Health and Social Security, 1970–4; Minister of State, Employment, 1981–.

Parliamentary Private Secretary to
Margaret Thatcher, 1983–7.

ALL CHILDREN TOGETHER
An organisation aimed at bringing
together Protestant and Catholic
children in shared schools, with the co-
operation of the Churches and where
parents have expressed a wish to have
their children educated together. It
promoted a parliamentary bill to
achieve this object, which was
introduced in the House of Lords in
June 1977 by the Alliance peer, Lord
Dunleath. In Parliament, the
Government supported its general
aims, but suggested its withdrawal. It
was, however, passed, and got the
royal assent on 26 May 1978.
Education proposals published in 1988
pleased the organisation because they
gave extra encouragement to
integrated schools, five of which,
including the pioneer Lagan College,
were then operating.

ALLEN, DAVID
VUPP Convention member for N.
Antrim, 1975–6. b. 1937. Ballymena
Borough Council, 1973–7. A former
teacher and active educationist, he
became general secretary of the Ulster
Teachers' Union in 1977. In 1982 he
claimed that the closure of State-
controlled schools in border areas was
threatening many Protestant communities, particularly in Co.
Fermanagh.

**ALLEN, JOHN ALEXANDER
(JACK)**
OUP Assembly member for
Londonderry, 1982–6; chaired
committees on Economic Development
and Devolution, member of
Environment Committee. b. 1943.
Londonderry Corporation, 1967–9.
Londonderry City Council, 1973–85.
Mayor, 1974–5. Chairman, NIH
Housing Association, 1983–.

Chairman, OUP executive, 1988–.
Chairman, local government Staff
Commission, 1985–. Participant in
Duisburg Talks, October 1988.

ALLIANCE PARTY
One of NI's main political parties, it
prides itself on giving priority to
attracting support from both sides of
the community. The party was
launched in April 1970, and although
its initial leadership was drawn largely
from people previously unknown in
politics, it quickly gained support from
a section of Unionists who had backed
the PM Terence O'Neill, and who felt
that Alliance, rather than the OUP,
represented their outlook. Although its
main base, to start with, appeared to be
middle class, it also absorbed many
people who had formerly backed the
NILP. It got an early boost in 1972,
when three sitting MPs joined it: Phelim
O'Neill ex-Unionist Minister; pro-
O'Neill member, Bertie McConnell,
and Tom Gormley, Nationalist. In its
first electoral test, the May 1973
district council elections, it got 13.6 per
cent of the vote. This should have
secured it more than seventy seats,
under the newly introduced PR system,
but in fact it got sixty-three. In the
hard-fought Assembly election, which
followed the next month, it secured 9.2
per cent of the total vote and eight
seats. Many of its supporters had
hoped for more, but it went on to take
part in the crucial negotiations on the
power-sharing scheme and in the
Sunningdale Conference. Two of its
members – Oliver Napier, the party
leader, and Bob Cooper, the deputy
leader – were included in the
short-lived Executive Government. In
the 1975 Convention election its share
of the vote rose slightly to 9.8 per cent
and it again got eight seats. In the
Convention campaign it called for a
strong legislative assembly. It said that
both sides of the divided community

must be involved at all levels in the government of NI, although it indicated in the Convention itself that it would not object to majority government eventually if the atmosphere improved. It dropped the idea of a Council of Ireland, as envisaged at Sunningdale, saying that it was unnecessary to have such a formal body to achieve practical co-operation with the Republic. Its main policy contribution in the Convention was to outline a scheme for government by committees, elected in proportion to the strength of parties in the Assembly. In the district council elections in 1977 it improved its poll to 14.4 per cent of the total and secured seventy seats. It benefited from transfers, notably from Official Unionists and SDLP. In the 1979 Westminster election the party fought all twelve seats, but failed to gain a single one, despite its prediction that it would take E. Belfast. Its share of the poll was 11.9 per cent. In the 1979 European election its candidate was Oliver Napier, and his share of first preferences was only 6.8 per cent. In the 1980 Constitutional Conference, it continued to press the case for partnership government. But this did not bring it any dividends in the 1981 council elections when it suffered from the polarisation produced by the H-Block hunger strike. Its 9 per cent vote was more than 5 per cent down on the previous council contests. In 1982 it emerged as the party showing most enthusiasm for the 'rolling devolution' initiative. However, its vote in the October Assembly election stayed at 9 per cent, but PR worked very appreciably to its advantage, so that it took ten Assembly seats – or twice as many as PSF, which had 10 per cent of the vote. But its share of the poll in the 1983 Westminster election fell to 8 per cent, and its hope of taking one or more seats was disappointed. Partly for tactical reasons, it contested only twelve of the seventeen seats. In the

second European election in 1984 David Cook polled only 5 per cent of the vote and lost his deposit. The district council elections of 1985 saw Alliance lose further ground to become largely a party of the Greater Belfast area. It won thirty-four seats, four fewer than in the highly polarised 1981 election, and only 7.1 per cent of the vote compared with 8.9 per cent. The pressure had fallen largely on one section of the party support as SDLP sought to counter-balance losses to PSF. In November 1985 the conditional acceptance of the AIA by Alliance threatened its support from the Protestant section of the community. This was evident in the January 1986 by-elections when it fought its five best seats but lost 17 per cent of its 1983 vote in the same constituencies. In June 1987 Alliance fielded sixteen candidates to capitalise on Unionist discontent with their party leaders' adjournment policy against the AIA. They polled 10 per cent of the vote, recovered their 1983 position and produced good performances in E. Belfast and N. Antrim. In contrast party leader John Cushnahan was pushed into third place in N. Down and in September he resigned from politics for 'family reasons'. He was replaced by Dr John Alderdice in October, who early in 1988 began a round of meetings with the party leaders in the Republic, GB and NI. By March he was not hopeful about devolution. However, the launch of the Social and Liberal Democrats brought the prospect of links between them and the Progressive Democrats in the Republic, and Alliance in NI. The aim was to fight the 1989 European election on the same platform and manifesto. David Steel (SLD) and Des O'Malley (Prog. D.) attended the Alliance Party conference in April 1988. A new policy statement in October 1988 called for devolved power-sharing government which would have equal role with Republic in new tripartite AIA conference.

ALLISTER, JAMES HUGH (JIM)

DUP Assembly Whip and member for N. Antrim, 1982–6. Served on committees on Finance and Personnel, and Devolution. b. 1953. Educated Regent House School, Newtownards; LLB (QUB). Barrister. European Parliament personal assistant to Rev. Ian Paisley and DUP press officer, 1980–2. Joint organiser of OUP–DUP 'Operation USA' publicity campaign in the US, January 1982. In the 1983 Westminster election, he was only 367 votes behind the OUP winner in the new E. Antrim seat. The decision of the two Unionist parties not to oppose one another in the 1987 election in furtherance of their drive against the AIA prevented his standing for the seat, and soon afterwards he announced that he was leaving active politics. Several councillors in the E. Antrim area and elsewhere resigned in protest at the leadership's decision.

ALTON, DAVID PATRICK

Liberal and later SLD spokesman on NI, January 1987–8. b. 1951. MP for Mossley Hill, Liverpool, a constituency with a significant Irish community, 1979–. Britain's youngest councillor (Liverpool) in 1972. As Liberal Chief Whip he sought, during 1987, to increase contacts with Alliance Party in NI and Progressive Democrats in Republic, which resulted in a SLD–All.–Prog. D. common front for 1989 European election. Critical of Unionist MPs' boycott of Westminster in their anti-AIA campaign. Urged SDLP to give full support to RUC. In 1988 promoted parliamentary bill to outlaw abortions after eighteen weeks, which had support of all NI MPs.

AMERICAN ANCIENT ORDER OF HIBERNIANS

This Irish-American organisation claims several hundred thousand members, and it figures largely in the annual New York St Patrick's Day parade. In 1978 spokesmen for the AOH in Ireland stressed that the US organisation was entirely autonomous. This arose from controversy, going back to 1972, about the precise attitude of the US body to NI affairs. In 1972 Judge James Comerford, a former president of the AAOH, declared that it 'unequivocally supports the Provisional IRA campaign'. But this was denied by the US National Secretary, William Bartnett, who said that the organisation neither granted financial aid to PIRA nor maintained goodwill contacts with its leadership. When the AAOH held its annual convention in Killarney in July 1978, a resolution which repudiated violence in NI and praised the Irish Government's stand on the North was ruled out of order. The motion was stated to have been backed by Senator Edward Kennedy. Later a spokesman for AAOH stressed that the conference decision was strictly procedural, since the organisation could not support any foreign government. And the spokesman said it was totally opposed to the use of violence as a solution to the NI problem. Argument also arose from a comment by the then deputy leader of the SDLP, John Hume, that the AAOH had been writing to US firms, opposing the idea of investment in NI. George Clough, a director of the AAOH, said they did not want to stop US investment in NI, but they wanted equal opportunities in employment there. It organised the 1983 St Patrick's Day parade in New York, which provoked controversy because a PIRA supporter, Michael Flannery, founder of NORAID, was chosen to head the parade. By 1985 there were some signs that leaders of the Order were anxious to present a more moderate image. Peter King, the New York parade marshal that year, suggested that the admission of Protestants to the Order could have a positive influence. But in 1988 Nick Murphy, leader of the AAOH, was among Irish-Americans who criticised the Republic's Government for its new extradition arrangements. He also said that a ten-day search for arms was turning the South into 'a banana republic'. Early in 1989 the chairman, M.J. Coogan, lobbied to have Joe Doherty (PIRA), currently held in prison and fighting extradition to GB on murder charges, made grand marshal of the St Patrick's Day parade.

AMNESTY INTERNATIONAL

The London-based human rights body which has taken a close interest in NI issues since the start of the Troubles. Its intervention in the late 1970s persuaded the Labour Government to set up the Bennett inquiry into allegations of ill-treatment of terrorist suspects by the RUC. In 1988 its call for a judicial inquiry into disputed killings by the security forces since 1982 was rejected by the Government, although it attracted support from the Labour opposition, the Irish Government, and the SDLP. It also took up the SAS killings of three unarmed PIRA members in Gibraltar in 1988, and suggested that there was evidence of 'extra-judicial executions'. PM Margaret Thatcher dismissed the claim as 'utterly disgraceful'. The organisation has also criticised the operation of non-jury courts, the supergrass system, and strip-searching.

ANCIENT ORDER OF HIBERNIANS

An organisation often regarded as the Catholic equivalent of the Orange Order. It has always been associated with defence of the Catholic faith and promotion of Irish nationalism. Its

present title dates from the 1830s, but its origins are traceable from the Catholic insurrection of 1641 through the Whiteboys and the Ribbonmen of the eighteenth and nineteenth centuries. A formidable AOH personality was Joe Devlin, the Belfast Nationalist MP who was active in the early years of the twentieth century and became national president. In the 1960s the national vice-president, the late Gerry Lennon of Armagh, a Nationalist Senator, had talks with the then leader of the Orange Order, Sir George Clark, about a possible political settlement. The discussions, known as the 'Orange–Green talks' were unsuccessful. The Order has declined somewhat in recent years, a trend evidently linked with the eclipse of the Nationalist Party. It still has a substantial membership, however, and the AOH hall remains a familiar landmark in many parts of rural Ulster. It is organised in divisions, and its public parades, with bands, banners and sashes, superficially resemble those of the Orange Order. They are held on 15 August (the Feast of the Assumption) and sometimes on St Patrick's Day. The leadership decided not to hold any parades between 1971 and 1974 because of the violence. Its national vice-president, Hugh News of Lurgan, defined its aims in 1976 as 'faith, unity and true Christian charity'. In 1978 he criticised the AAOH, which, he said, had no connection with the Irish organisation. His statement followed claims that the AAOH had been discouraging investment in NI, a claim denied by spokesmen for the US organisation.

ANDERSON, ALBERT WESLEY

Unionist MP for Londonderry at Stormont, 1968–72. b. 23 July 1907; d. 1981. Mayor of Londonderry, 1963–8. Senior Parliamentary Secretary, Home Affairs, 1971–2.

ANDERSONSTOWN

The district on the western fringe of W. Belfast which has been one of the main strongholds of PIRA, and where the Peace People movement was born in 1976. There is a strong Republican tradition, so that it became an area of intense confrontation between the PIRA and the security forces, particularly after the introduction of internment. The area has been heavily scarred by the violence, and troops and police have operated from strongly fortified stations. The former RUC station has become a joint police-and-army centre, and is protected by high walls, steel plates and special netting. There is heavy unemployment, but the Government has set up several factories at Kennedy Way in an effort to provide local employment. The local SDLP Convention member, Vincent McCloskey, wrote in May 1976: 'More than any other area, Andersonstown has suffered all the horrors of this undeclared civil war. There is not a street that has not suffered its own private tragedies. There is not a child that cannot recognise the sound of gunfire or the type of weapon being used. The people have been battered from all sides with the propaganda of the various forces but have managed in spite of all to maintain their civilised standards of behaviour.' Loyalists have tended to see it as the heartland of republicanism. Before the launching of the Peace People, after the incident in which three young children died, there were several moves by women in the area to organise peace meetings, and on some occasions they clashed with women supporting the PIRA. In the 1981 hunger strike it was the venue of many rallies in support of the anti-H-Block cause, and there were emotional scenes as the funerals of hunger-strikers paused on the way to Milltown cemetery. The area became more quiet in the next few years, but in 1988 two incidents put it again in the world spotlight. On 16 March three men, among thousands of mourners at the funeral in Milltown cemetery of three PIRA members shot dead by the security forces in Gibraltar, died in a loyalist gun and grenade attack. (*See also* Gibraltar Shootings.) The RUC, who had come under criticism from Nationalists for their strong presence at PIRA funerals, had kept their distance and a lone attacker created panic by his assault on the mourners. Just three days later, as the cortege of one of the victims of the cemetery shooting moved towards Milltown cemetery, two British soldiers in plain clothes, who had suddenly driven close to the procession, were dragged from their car, beaten and shot dead. The soldiers, Derek Wood and David Howes, both corporals in their early twenties, were said by the army to have been on the scene quite innocently as they were attached to the Royal Signals and returning to their base at Lisburn. With the security forces again absent, apart from having a helicopter overhead, the incident sparked fresh controversy about their tactics. Since the mob attack on the soldiers was projected worldwide on TV, the killings aroused much wider condemnation than is usually attached to deaths in NI. The Nationalist *Irish News* commented: 'While one must make allowances for the understandable initial fear that some kind of repetition of the Milltown cemetery killings was imminent, such concessions do not lessen the sense of collective guilt that all decent citizens in the Nationalist sector are now experiencing.'

ANDREW, SIR ROBERT (JOHN)

Permanent Secretary, NIO, 1984–7. b. 25 October 1928. MA (Oxon.). Served with Intelligence Corps, 1947–9, and joined Civil Service, 1952. Defence counsellor, UK NATO delegation, 1967–

70. Served with three NI Secretaries of State in first twenty-one months at NIO and had crucial role in negotiations leading to AIA.

ANDREWS, SIR JOHN LAWSON ORMROD

Minister and leader, NI Senate, 1964–72, in which capacity he frequently acted as deputy PM. b. Comber, Co. Down, 15 July 1903; d. 1986. Son of second PM of NI, John Miller Andrews. Unionist MP for Mid-Down, 1953–64, holding office successively as Minister of Health and Local Government, Minister of Commerce and Minister of Finance, before being elected to Senate. Took part in Downing Street talks immediately prior to direct rule, 1972. Sided with Faulkner in the 1974 split and went out of politics in the late 1970s.

ANGLO-IRISH AGREEMENT

The AIA, signed at Hillsborough by PM Margaret Thatcher and Taoiseach Garret FitzGerald on 15 November 1985, is arguably the most far-reaching political development since 1920 and the creation of NI. In it the UK and Irish Governments committed themselves to much closer working on NI, and the agreement was later registered at the UN. The communiqué issued after the signing said the aims were to promote peace and stability in NI, the recon-ciliation of the two traditions in Ireland, the creation of a new climate of friendship, and co-operation in combating terrorism. The radical feature of the agreement was that it set up a joint ministerial conference of British and Irish Ministers, backed by a permanent secretariat at Maryfield, close to the Stormont estate, to monitor political, security, legal and other issues of concern to the Nationalist minority. Thus, while the agreement

was not formally a joint authority, since the UK Government had the final word on matters affecting NI, it represented a major change of attitude by the British PM. In July 1982 Thatcher had forcibly pointed out that no commitment existed for her Gov-ernment to consult the Irish Govern-ment on matters affecting NI. The new role of the Irish Government in the Anglo-Irish Conference (which first met in Belfast on 11 December 1985), and the commitment that 'determined efforts shall be made. . . to resolve any differences' meant that in practice it was something more than consultation. The main points of the AIA may be summarised as follows:

ARTICLE 1 on the status of NI, recognised that any change could only occur with the consent of a majority in NI; it further recognised that there was no present wish for change but if there were a swing in the future, legislative change would give it effect.

ARTICLE 2 stated that the Anglo-Irish Conference existed within the frame-work of the 1981 BIIC, and that it was concerned with NI, and relations North and South; that the Irish Government would put forward proposals; that 'determined efforts' would be made to 'resolve any differences', but that there would be no derogation of sovereignty.

ARTICLE 3 said that the conference could meet, regularly and frequently, at ministerial or official level, and that a secretariat would service the conference.

ARTICLE 4 set out the aims for the conference as a framework to accommodate the rights and identities of the two traditions in NI, and to promote peace, stability and prosperity in Ireland. It recognised that Government policy was to devolve power on a 'widespread acceptance' basis; that the conference would be the framework for proposals on the 'modalities' of bringing devolution about and that the Irish Government would propose schemes on behalf of the interests of the minority community.

Articles 5–10 set out the functions and concerns of the conference:

ARTICLE 5 stated that on political matters the Irish Government could put forward proposals on behalf of the minority where major legislation or policy was involved. It listed as examples the protection of human rights and the prevention of discrimination in areas such as cultural heritage, electoral arrangements, flags and emblems; the avoidance of social and economic discrimination; and a possible Bill of Rights.

ARTICLE 6 accepted that the Irish Government could make proposals on the role and composition of various public bodies, including SACHR, FEA, EOC, Policy Authority, and Police Complaints Board.

ARTICLE 7 concerned security and related matters: the conference could consider security policy, the relation- ship of security forces to the community, and prisons policy.

ARTICLE 8 concerned legal matters, including the administration of justice, policy aspects of extradition and the possibility of mixed courts in both jurisdictions (that is, additional judges drawn from the other jurisdiction). (See also Diplock Report.)

ARTICLES 9 AND 10 concerned cross- border co-operation in security and practical economic and social matters.

ARTICLE 11 provided for a review of the

working of the agreement after three years, or earlier, if requested.

ARTICLE 12 reiterated the possibility of an inter-Parliamentary link between London and Dublin, first suggested in 1981.

The response inside NI to the AIA was an immediate welcome by Nationalists on the one hand and on the other, a series of protests by Unionists against the role given to the Republic on the internal affairs of part of the UK. The Unionist protests took the form of mass demonstrations, the simultaneous resignation of fifteen MPs and the subsequent holding of by-elections, protests at Maryfield, and other methods of visibly showing the withdrawal of consent. Indeed, the existence of the NI Assembly as a representative body became itself a platform for protest against the AIA. It suspended its scrutiny function, the Devolution Committee was wound up, and a new Committee on the Govern- ment of NI was set up to examine the effects of the AIA on the government of NI, the 1973 Constitution Act and the 1982 NI Assembly Act. But as a con- sequence of the Assembly neglecting its scrutiny role, the Alliance members withdrew from the Assembly, leaving only forty-nine members attending, and the NIO cut off access to persons and papers in the departments. Even though the committee issued three reports, the Assembly had become preoccupied with its assault on the AIA across a wide front, and around the time when arrange- ments for new elections to the Assembly were due, it was dissolved on 23 June 1986. In the summer of 1988 two brothers, Christopher and Michael McGimpsey, challenged the legality of the AIA in the Dublin High Court. The McGimpseys were members of the OUP, which opened a fund towards legal costs. Although the case was not successful, costs were awarded and the path opened to appeal to the Supreme Court. The belief that devolution would follow once the overarching framework had been established between the UK and the Republic has proved facile. From the summer of 1987 Unionists engaged in 'talks about talks' with Secretary of State Tom King on the principle of suspending the Anglo-Irish Conference to enable inter-party talks to begin – early in 1988 outline proposals were submitted to him but no response was made. King has also held talks with other parties but without any indication of 'widespread acceptance'. In November 1988 the AIA completed three years' operation and a formal review has begun. Altogether some twenty-five meetings of the conference have taken place – eleven in Belfast, nine in London and five in Dublin – and a communiqué was issued after each, giving a very bare outline of the main areas discussed. There were ten meetings in the first year, four in the second and ten in the third.

ANNESLEY, HUGH NORMAN
Chief Constable of RUC, June 1989–. b. 1939. Although he was Assistant Commissioner of the Metropolitan Police when he was appointed by the Police Authority to succeed Sir John Hermon, his appointment came as a surprise and was attributed in some quarters to a more independent stance by the authority. Born and educated in Dublin – his father was from NI and his mother from the Republic – he joined the Metropolitan Police in 1958, and rose through the ranks to Chief Superintendent by 1976, when he became Assistant Chief Constable of Sussex. In 1979 he began an intensive course with the Royal College of Defence Studies, which involved extensive travel in the Far East. In 1981 he returned to the 'Met' as deputy

Assistant Commissioner, and was appointed Assistant Commissioner in 1985. It was his responsibility for specialist operations since 1987, including the Special Branch and anti-terrorist work in GB, which obviously impressed the authority. In this post he was in regular contact with both RUC and Gardaí. He was also on the executive committee of Interpol. Most NI politicians welcomed his appointment, and there were hopes in Dublin Government circles that he would be able to improve relations between the RUC and the Nationalist community. His Irish family background was also seen as an advantage in the context of the AIA.

ANNON, WILLIAM
DUP Convention member for N. Belfast, 1975–6. b. 1912; d. 1983. Before his adoption as DUP candidate for the Convention, he was chairman of the OUP's Sydenham (Belfast) branch and returned to the OUP in 1983. Belfast City Council, 1977–83.

APPRENTICE BOYS OF DERRY
One of the Protestant 'Loyal Orders', which is based on the 'no surrender' action of the thirteen apprentice boys in slamming the gates of Londonderry on the army of King James II at the start of the siege of 1689. Its main parade in the city is held on 12 August to celebrate the relief of the city and the end of the siege, and usually some 10,000 to 12,000 members take part, drawn from all parts of NI and sometimes accompanied by members from GB and overseas. There is a lesser demonstration on 18 December to mark the shutting of the gates. On that occasion an effigy of Colonel Lundy, an officer who tried to negotiate the surrender of the city at the start of the siege, is burned. This is the origin of the term 'Lundy', frequently used by extreme loyalists to describe someone whom

they regard as having betrayed their cause. Members of the ABD can be initiated only within the city walls, and such ceremonies are held in August and December. There were serious riots in the city after the August march in 1969, and parades were banned in 1970 and 1971. In 1972 the ABD's general committee decided to call off its parade when it was limited to the Waterside area – that is, the predominantly Protestant east side of the River Foyle. But many Apprentice Boys rallied on the Waterside and were addressed by one of their number, the Rev. Ian Paisley. The then NI PM Brian Faulkner was expelled from the Order in 1971 for being associated with the parades' ban. Members of the organisation were permitted to parade again within the old walled city in 1975. But they were not allowed to walk round the walls, which had been part of their traditional route, because these overlook the mainly Catholic Bogside. In 1985 the Order dropped two of its main office bearers because, as local councillors, they had refused to support a Unionist boycott of the council over the changing of the council name from Londonderry to Derry. James Guy was replaced as 'Lieut.-Governor' and David Davis as chief marshal. Guy became Mayor of Derry, 1987–8. The Order has planned extensive celebrations in 1989 of the three-hundredth anniversary of the siege.

ARCHER, PETER KINGSLEY
Labour front-bench spokesman on NI, 1983–7. MP for Warley W., 1974–. b. 20 November 1926. QC. Solicitor-General, 1974–9. As Labour spokesman he maintained close touch with parties in the Republic and NI, including PSF. Gave strong support to the AIA, but critical of secrecy surrounding its drafting and held open the possibility that a Labour Government would enter into talks on it

without preconditions. Supported Republic Government's call for three judges in Diplock courts. On Charles Haughey's opposition to article one of AIA – protecting NI's position in UK while it has majority support – he said in Dublin in December 1986 that a Labour Government would be prepared to delete the article, although he pointed out that the guarantee already existed in British legislation. Strong critic of supergrass system. In January 1989 stated that he would not stand at the next election.

ARDILL, CAPTAIN ROBERT AUSTIN
OUP Whip in Assembly, 1974, and in Constitutional Convention, 1975–6. b. 1917. As MP for Carrick, 1965–9, and Secretary of the '66 Committee (Unionist back-bench committee), he was opposed to leadership of Terence O'Neill. He was chairman of the Ulster Loyalist Association in 1971 and deputy leader of the Vanguard movement in 1972. Before Harry West took over as leader of the OUP in 1974 he was Whip of the Unionist Assembly members who did not accept Brian Faulkner as leader. In the Convention he was one of the UUUC team of negotiators with the SDLP, and after the Convention was dissolved he and the Rev. Martin Smyth had private talks with John Hume and Paddy Devlin of the SDLP. The talks did not lead to any agreement. In 1977–8 he was one of the party delegation who met Secretary of State Roy Mason and his officials about the possibility of some form of interim devolution. Joint Honorary Secretary of Ulster Unionist Council, 1978. He has been associated with the strongly devolutionist wing of the OUP and was a leading member of the Charter Group when it was launched in 1986.

ARDOYNE

A mainly Catholic area of N. Belfast, adjoining the upper Crumlin Road. There was serious rioting in the district in August 1969, and there has been considerable burning of homes, many explosions, and a variety of violent incidents in the area over the years. In the early 1970s the PIRA was extremely active in the district. In August 1969 there were clashes between local people and the RUC, and with Protestants from the nearby Shankill area. Some of the initial violence in August 1969 was attributed by the Scarman tribunal to efforts to tie up the RUC, and so prevent police reinforcements being sent to the Bogside in Derry. The Scarman report mentioned that stones, petrol bombs, and explosive devices made from copper tubing had been used in assaults on the police. Scarman also held that Protestants had been responsible for the burning of several Catholic-owned pubs in the area on 15 August and for the burning of about twenty houses in Brookfield Street which had been occupied by Catholics before the riots. On the night of 15–16 August twenty-six civilians suffered gunshot injuries and one man was killed. The army moved into the area on 16 August. The Scarman report rejected suggestions that the Ardoyne monastery had been used as an arsenal and that priests had been handing out bullets. Referring to the RUC's use of the Browning machine gun, Scarman said these incidents illustrated the unsuitability of this weapon for riot control, and that it was a merciful chance that there was no fatal casualty from Browning fire. In October 1981 local city councillor Lawrence Kennedy, thirty-five, an Ind. Republican, was shot dead in a local social club, apparently by loyalist gunmen. PIRA was active in the area during the 1981 hunger strike and there were several shootings and riots. A report produced for the local Flax

Trust in January 1983 said support for PIRA and INLA was high in the area, which had been 'abused and abandoned by Government and industry alike'. The report added that male unemployment was over 54 per cent among the 8,000 residents, with poverty rampant, 28 per cent of families living in overcrowded conditions and 35 per cent of homes lacking basic amenities. In the 1980s considerable deprivation persisted despite local efforts to promote employment.

ARMAGH

Ireland's ecclesiastical capital, which was mentioned as a possible venue for a Council of Ireland if it had come into being after the 1973 Sunningdale Agreement. With fairly well-defined Protestant and Catholic areas, it has always had a reputation for intense political rivalries. One of the major incidents involving loyalists and civil rights supporters occurred here on 30 November 1968. The police had given permission to the civil rights supporters to have a march through the city centre, but at 2 a.m. the Rev. Ian Paisley and his supporters began to arrive in the central area. By the time the civil rights march had moved off from the fringes of the town, the loyalists had effectively occupied the key junction. Many of them carried walking sticks and clubs, and although they were warned by the police that it was an illegal assembly, they were able to prevent the civil rights march getting into the main thoroughfare. Later Paisley and one of his supporters, Major Ronald Bunting, were each sentenced to three months' imprisonment for illegal assembly, but they were released early as part of an amnesty. Armagh's main shopping streets have suffered heavily during the PIRA bombing campaign, and there have been many murders in the area, which has become known, together with adjoining areas of Co. Tyrone, as the 'murder triangle'. In December 1972 an Armagh Unionist councillor and member of the Police Authority, William Johnston, was kidnapped and murdered. In 1982 Cardinal Ó Fiaich and Church of Ireland Archbishop John Armstrong co-operated in promoting a one-day 'at home' festival aimed at improving inter-community relations. Soon afterwards the shooting dead by the RUC of two local INLA members who had driven through a checkpoint provoked angry controversy. In November 1983 council chairman Charles Armstrong (OUP) was killed by PIRA car bomb as he left council meeting. In 1986 the long-established women's prison closed and prisoners moved to new Maghaberry Prison. In 1988 local Drumadd barracks became base of revived 3 Brigade of army given responsibility for border operations.

ARMSTRONG, MICHAEL

OUP Convention member for Armagh, 1975–6. b. France, 1924. Fatally injured in car accident, 1982. LLB (Cantab.). Barrister. With a strong military background (Captain in Irish Guards, 1939–45, and for a time in Allied military Government in West Germany; district commandant in USC at disbandment; commander in Armagh company UDR, 1970–4), he had been OUP spokesman on security and Honorary Secretary of the Ulster Unionist Council.

ARMY see Security System section, pp. 389–98

ASHDOWN, JEREMY JOHN DURHAM (PADDY)

Leader of SLD, July 1988–. MP for Yeovil, 1983–. b. 27 February 1941. Although born in India, he spent his boyhood in NI. In early years of the Troubles he served in NI with Royal Marine commandos and for a period was commander of Special Boat Section; served in Crumlin Road area of Belfast and in Derry, where he arrested John Hume for obstruction in February 1972. Diplomat attached to UN, 1971–6. On his appointment as SLD leader he made it clear that he would further strengthen the party's links with the Alliance Party.

ASSEMBLY see Election Results section, pp. 315–19 and 339–43, and Systems of Government section, pp. 364–70

ASSOCIATION FOR LEGAL JUSTICE

A body set up in 1971, it has been active in investigating allegations of ill-treatment against the security forces and in monitoring the reform programme. In 1971 it published a booklet, *Know Your Legal Rights*, setting out procedures to be adopted by persons if they were arrested, subjected to search, or approached to give evidence. It campaigned for an end to political appointments to the judiciary. It strongly opposed internment, and in 1971 co-operated with NICRA in protesting that detainees had been ill-treated by the security forces. In 1974 it opposed the system of extra-territorial courts in NI and the Republic, and in a report in 1974 accused NI courts of showing an anti-Catholic bias in terms of longer sentences for Catholics. In 1974 it also complained that the RUC was using torture to extract confessions of PIRA membership. In 1982 it complained that shootings by the security forces of suspected terrorists represented 'summary executions'.

ATKINS, HUMPHREY see Colnbrook, Lord

ATKINS CONFERENCE see Colnbrook, Lord and Constitutional Conference

B

BABINGTON, ROBERT JOHN

Unionist MP for N. Down, 1969–72.
b. Dublin, 9 April 1920. QC. County
Court judge, 1974–. In his 1969
election address he called for one man,
one vote, and in 1970 urged the
expulsion from the Unionist Party of
those who refused to support Government policy. He frequently warned
against the dangers of UDI for NI, and
advised Unionists not to get involved in
violence. He complained in 1972 that
the PIRA ceasefire had resulted in
gunmen finding NI a safer haven than
the Republic. In 1973 he resigned from
the Orange Order 'for personal
reasons'. He was a firm backer of Brian
Faulkner as PM, and was closely
associated with him in the period
immediately after direct rule.

BAILIE, ROBIN JOHN

Minister of Commerce, NI, 1971–2.
b. 6 March 1937. Unionist MP for
Newtownabbey, 1969–72. LLB (QUB).
Solicitor, NI Supreme Court, 1961. On
the liberal wing of the Unionist Party,
he gave up active politics and resigned
from Brian Faulkner's 'shadow
cabinet' soon after direct rule in 1972.
As Minister of Commerce he had been
interested in the possibilities offered to
NI by EC membership, and was among
the earliest to urge a cross-border
development plan for the north-west,
with Common Market support. In
1973 he joined the Alliance Party for a
brief period.

BAIRD, ERNEST AUSTIN

Leader of the UUUP, 1977–84.
b. Ballycampsie, Co. Donegal, 1930. A
founder and the first chairman of the
Vanguard movement in 1972, he was
closely associated with William Craig
until 1976, when, as deputy leader of
the VUPP, he disagreed with Craig's

advocacy of voluntary coalition with
the SDLP, and established the UUUM,
dedicated to promoting Unionist unity.
In this it failed, and became the UUUP to
fight the local government elections in
1977. He polled surprisingly strongly
in the Assembly elections in
Fermanagh–S. Tyrone in 1973,
securing more first-preference votes
than either Harry West, who was
shortly to become Unionist leader, or
John D. Taylor, who had been MP for
S. Tyrone in the former Stormont
Parliament. He was also returned there
in the Convention election, but this
time he lagged behind West. He was
extremely active in the UWC strike in
1974, and was associated with the Rev.
Ian Paisley in the UUAC strike in May
1977, which secured much less
support. Unsuccessfully contested
Fermanagh–S. Tyrone in 1979
Westminster election, and the 1982
Assembly election.

BAKER REPORT

Sir George Baker, in a review of
working of Emergency Provisions Act,
recommended in April 1984 the
retention of single-judge Diplock
courts, with the continuing use of
supergrass evidence and the non-
proscription of the UDA. He also
suggested that victims of PIRA violence
should have legal aid so that they could
sue PSF, as its political wing, for
damages.

BALLYGAWLEY BUS BOMBING
see Provisional Irish Republican Army

BALLYKELLY BOMBING *see*
Londonderry/Derry

BALLYMURPHY

The W. Belfast Catholic housing estate
which was the centre of serious rioting
in 1971 and 1972. In January 1971
trouble on a serious scale continued for
five consecutive nights and the NI PM

Major Chichester-Clark declared that the army would not be forced out of its main base there, the Henry Taggart Memorial Hall, by either physical or political pressure. The hall had been repeatedly attacked by crowds with stones and bottles. The security forces claimed that the rioting had been orchestrated by the PIRA, and Dr William Philbin, the Catholic bishop of Down and Connor, said in Ballymurphy that members of secret organisations had no obligation to obey immoral orders. A group of Ballymurphy women demonstrated at the bishop's home in protest against the sermon. In October 1971 an arms' haul by the security forces included seven Thompson sub-machine-guns and a number of rifles and revolvers. Mother Theresa of Calcutta set up a mission in Ballymurphy in late 1971 and stayed there until 1972. In 1988 the area was said to have 86 per cent adult unemployment.

BANNISTER, GRACE
First woman Lord Mayor of Belfast (OUP), 1981–2. b. 1924; d. 1986. Left school at fourteen years of age. Served as deputy Lord Mayor in 1975 and High Sheriff in 1979.

BARNHILL, JOHN (JACK)
OUP member of the NI Senate, 1958–71. b. 1904. Assassinated in his home at Brickfield, near Strabane, Co. Tyrone, on 12 December 1971. He was the first politician to be assassinated in the violence which began in 1969, and his death was claimed by the OIRA. They claimed that they had not intended to kill him, but only to destroy his home 'in reprisal for the destruction of working-class homes by the British army'. The OIRA said they had shot him during a struggle. The NI PM Brian Faulkner blamed an OIRA gang which, he said, had been able to operate from a safe haven in nearby Donegal in the

Republic, and he said this gang might have killed five people in the Strabane area in the previous three months. Jack Barnhill was remembered by his fellow Senators as a speaker who laced his Senate speeches with poetic quotations.

BARR, GLEN
Vanguard Unionist Party. Assembly, 1973–4, and Convention, 1975–6, member for Londonderry. b. Londonderry, 1932. He was in the LAW and the UDA in 1971, and in 1974 he had the key post of chairman of the Co-ordinating Committee which ran the loyalist strike. The committee included loyalist politicians, the UWC and representatives of Protestant paramilitary groups. During the strike he commented that it would have been perfectly possible to set up a provisional government. After the stoppage he led paramilitary spokesmen in talks with Secretary of State Merlyn Rees. In October 1974 he was suspended from the UUUC for three months for supporting the VPP candidate in W. Belfast in the Westminster election. In November 1974, as political adviser to the UDA, he took a UDA deputation to Libya for talks with the Libyan Government. A PSF delegation was there at the same time and there was apparently some contact between them, although both sides denied that there had been any negotiations. Barr said on his return that the possibility of Libyan financial aid to an independent NI, and the prospect of Libyan orders for NI firms, had been discussed. (He was involved later in negotiations for the sale of NI beef to Libya.) A UDA spokesman said they had been trying to stop Libyan aid for the PIRA. The VUPP executive at first decided to expel Glen Barr over the visit, but later changed its mind, and in the end took no action. In the Convention he stood by William Craig when VUPP split over the idea of a

voluntary coalition, and he was joint leader of the VUPP until February 1978, when it reverted to the status of the Vanguard movement, and ceased to be a political party. He did not follow Craig into the OUP, but took up an independent stance. Involved with UDA again in 1978–9 when he took part in a body known as New Ulster Political Research Group, which produced a plan for an independent NI, and he visited the US in 1979 with UDA leaders for talks in Washington with leading politicians. In June 1981 he withdrew from politics when the UDA set up the Ulster Loyalist Democratic Party. He then became head of a Londonderry training centre for unemployed youths drawn from both sides of the community. In 1988 he was associated with a project to attract US investment and the development of leisure and other facilities in Derry as a result of a link-up between the city and Boston.

BARRY, PETER

Foreign Minister of Irish Republic, 1982–7. b. Cork, August 1928. He was deputy leader of Fine Gael, 1979–87, when he took over as Foreign Minister, and shared responsibility with the Taoiseach Dr Garret FitzGerald for NI matters. Formerly served as Transport Minister and Education Minister. TD, 1969–. Alderman, Cork City Council, 1967–73 (Lord Mayor, 1970–1). In January 1983 he visited NI for talks with local political parties. In March 1983 he declared that a long-term British presence in Ireland was a barrier to peace. As Foreign Minister he had a key role in negotiation of the AIA, and became the first co-chairman of the ministerial conference set up in November 1985, a post which he held until the defeat of the FitzGerald Government in 1987. In that year he was briefly Tánaiste (deputy Taoiseach) when Labour pulled out of the coalition. In early 1988 he said Unionists had

been excluded from consultation on the AIA because it was feared they would sabotage it. At the same time he was critical of Charles Haughey's attitude to the agreement and suggested a confederal system in Ireland.

BAXTER, JOHN LAWSON

Head of the Office of Information Service in NI Executive, 1974. b. Coleraine, Co. Derry, 1940. BA (TCD), LLM (Tulane University, New Orleans); qualified as solicitor, 1964 (QUB). He was chairman of N. Antrim Unionist Association, and member of committee which had drawn up Unionist election manifesto, when he was returned from N. Antrim to Assembly in 1973. Strong supporter of Brian Faulkner, and during the lifetime of the Executive pressed for energetic presentation of the administration's case.

BEATTIE, REVEREND WILLIAM JOHN

DUP Assembly member for S. Antrim, 1982–6. Deputy chairman, Economic Development Committee, member, Devolution Committee. b. 1942. Deputy leader of DUP, 1971–80; party secretary, 1980–3. Chairman, party's social/economic research unit. Minister, Dunmurry Free Presbyterian Church. In April 1970, as a Protestant Unionist, he gained the S. Antrim seat at Stormont from the OUP by a majority of 958 votes in a by-election. He headed the poll in S. Antrim in the Assembly election, 1973, with 10,126 first-preference votes. Deputy Chief Whip of the United Unionists in Assembly, 1973–4. Re-elected in S. Antrim in Convention election, 1975, and one of UUUC negotiators in talks with the SDLP in the Convention. Lisburn District Council, 1977–. Candidate, Westminster general elections, for N. Belfast in 1970 and Lagan Valley in 1983. In 1982 INLA placed a bomb at his home near Lisburn but it was discovered in time and defused.

BEGGS, JOHN ROBERT (ROY)
OUP MP for E. Antrim, 1983–. Assembly member for N. Antrim, 1982–6. Larne Council, 1973–. Mayor of Larne, 1977–. b. 20 February 1936. Originally DUP, but joined OUP in 1982 after being suspended by the DUP for visiting the council at Dun Laoghaire in the Republic in 1981 in defiance of DUP policy. First chairman of Assembly's Economic Development Committee, 1983–4. In 1983 his majority in E. Antrim was only 367 over Jim Allister of DUP, but in 1987 he raised it to over 15,000 as agreed Unionist candidate. In 1987 he resigned as chairman of North Eastern Education and Library Board in protest at AIA, and attacked the idea of power-sharing with SDLP.

BELFAST see Andersonstown, Ardoyne, Ballymurphy, Europa Hotel, Falls Road, Markets, New Lodge Road, Peace Line, Sandy Row, Shankill Road, Short Strand, Stormont, Tiger Bay and Population.

BELL, EILEEN
General secretary and information officer of Alliance Party, 1985–. BA Hons, history and politics (NUU). Before becoming general secretary, she was engaged in political organisation as a member of W. Belfast party executive, 1981–4. Spokeswoman on women's affairs, 1988–.

BELL, STUART
Labour spokesman on NI, 1984–7. b. 16 May 1938. MP for Middlesbrough, 1983–. Barrister. In 1986 attended special NI Assembly committee on AIA to give Labour views. In March 1987 his comments on AIA were widely

interpreted as an offer to Unionists to bring forward the review of AIA in return for Unionist support in Parliament, but party chiefs, including Neil Kinnock, denied any change of policy on AIA.

BELL, WILLIAM BRADSHAW
OUP Assembly member for S. Antrim, 1982–6. b. Belfast, 1935. Served as N. Belfast Convention member, 1975–6. Chairman, N. Belfast Unionist Association, 1973–5. Belfast City Council, 1977–85. Lord Mayor of Belfast, 1979–80.

BELL, SIR WILLIAM EWART
Head of the NI civil service, 1979–84. b. 13 November 1924. MA (Oxon.). Joined NI civil service, 1948. Assistant Secretary, Commerce, 1963–70; deputy Secretary, 1970–3. Permanent Secretary, 1973–6. Permanent Secretary, Finance, 1976–9. On retirement from civil service, headed a group aiming to develop locally lignite power. He became a Senator and Honorary Treasurer of QUB. Former Irish rugby international.

BELSTEAD, LORD
Parliamentary Under-Secretary, NIO, 1973–4. b. 30 September 1932. MA (Oxon.) At the NIO he was House of Lords spokesman, and maintained interest in local legislation as Conservative frontbencher, 1974–9. Home Office Under-Secretary, 1979–82. After periods as Minister of State at the Foreign Office and Department of Agriculture, he succeeded Lord Whitelaw as leader of House of Lords in 1988.

BENN, JOHN NEWTON
NI Ombudsman, 1972–4. Commissioner of Complaints, 1968–74. b. Burnley, Lancashire, 16 July 1908. Before becoming Ombudsman (Parliamentary

Commissioner dealing with grievances channelled through MPs about administration) he was Permanent Secretary, NI Ministry of Education.

BENNETT REPORT
The report produced by a three-man committee, headed by Judge Harry Bennett QC, an English Crown Court judge, on the interrogation procedures of the RUC, and the operation of the machinery for dealing with complaints. The committee was set up by NI Secretary of State Roy Mason in June 1978 in response to many demands for an official inquiry after an Amnesty International team had inquired into seventy-eight complaints of ill-treatment by persons who had been held at the Castlereagh interrogation centre in Belfast and other centres. The committee, which reported in 1979, went outside its terms of reference to mention that there had been cases where medical evidence had been produced concerning injuries sustained while in police custody which were not self-inflicted. Two of the main recommendations of the committee – that closed-circuit TV should be installed in interview rooms and that terrorist suspects should have access to a solicitor after forty-eight hours – were accepted by the Labour Government, and virtually all the remaining forty recommendations were endorsed by the Conservative Government. But one Government minister stressed in Parliament in May 1979 that only fifteen cases had fallen into the category of injuries sustained while in police custody, and not self-inflicted, out of a total of some 3,000 people who were detained in 1977–8. The Bennett committee was requested by the Government to make medical evidence in these cases available to the Director of Public Prosecutions so that he could decide whether any prosecutions should be brought against members of

the RUC. The publication of the report was accompanied by angry controversy about the extent of ill-treatment and two doctors involved at the interrogation centres voiced their concern about ill-treatment.

BIAGGI, MARIO
Democratic Congressman for New York and chairman of the *ad hoc* Congressional Committee on Irish affairs, 1978–88. b. New York, 26 October 1917. LLB (New York Law School). First New York policeman elected to US National Police Hall of Fame. Despite an Italian background, he took up the Irish cause in 1970 when he co-signed a letter urging President Nixon to act on claims about the deprivation of human rights and discrimination in NI. He made several visits to Ireland. Biaggi was in Newry for a protest march held after 'Bloody Sunday' in 1972. In 1975 he met British officials and representatives of political parties, including PSF. The *ad hoc* Committee on Irish Affairs in 1978 had the objectives of holding Congressional hearings on Ireland, challenging the State Department refusal of visas to PSF members and generally promoting a 'broader' perspective on Ireland. In the same year he also met leaders of the Republican movement to urge a six-month ceasefire to facilitate a peace forum he proposed to hold in Washington DC. This visit, on behalf of the Irish National Caucus, was criticised by the Taoiseach, Jack Lynch, for associating with men of violence and for misrepresenting the Irish Government's view in the US. The Peace Forum idea, however, was opposed by Senator Edward Kennedy and invitations were declined by political parties and PIRA. Biaggi reportedly showed interest in schemes for independence proposed by the UDA and Ulster Independence Committee. In 1979 Biaggi announced the

suspension of weapon sales to the RUC pending a review of US policy and subsequently campaigned to retain the suspension. In 1980, after the Democratic Party election platform confirmed its support for Irish unity, Biaggi sought a meeting, under the auspices of the UN, to decide the future of NI, to secure from GB a declaration of intent to withdraw in an orderly way and to secure US economic aid. In 1983 he co-sponsored a bill obliging US firms in NI to provide equality of opportunity. In the same year a delegation was sent to examine the employment record of Short Brothers plc and in 1984 he turned his attention to Harland and Wolff plc. In 1987 he was sentenced to two and a half years' imprisonment and fined $500,000 on charges in connection with a Brooklyn ship repairer and in 1988 he was convicted in a corruption scandal involving a New York defence contractor, Wedtech. He was sentenced to eight years' imprisonment for soliciting kickbacks in return for using his influence in the award of defence contracts.

BIGGS-DAVISON, SIR JOHN
Conservative front-bench spokesman on NI, 1976–9, and chairman of party's NI committee, 1979–88. b. 7 June 1918; d. 1988. MA (Oxon.). MP for Chigwell, 1955–74; Epping Forest, 1974–88. He had lengthy association with NI Unionists, and spoke frequently at party meetings. He warned repeatedly of an 'Irish Cuba' on Britain's doorstep. In January 1973 he wrote in the *News Letter*: 'Civil rights have been used as a front by the formenters of civil war; social reform as a stepping stone to social revolution. What civil rights are there in Cuba?' In 1980 he suggested loose linkage of UK, Republic of Ireland, Isle of Man and Channel Islands as Islands of North Atlantic (IONA). Strongly opposed Prior

devolution plan in 1982. A Catholic, he said in 1985 that the lesson of the old Stormont was that Catholics were safer under Westminster. A leading Conservative critic of AIA, but unhappy about Unionist policy of abstention from Westminster in protest against it. In 1986 one of founders of Friends of the Union Group set up to convince people in GB that the union with NI must be maintained. He spoke at a number of CEC meetings. He wrote several books, including *The Cross of St Patrick: the Catholic unionist tradition in Ireland* (1985).

BIRMINGHAM SIX *see* Provisional Irish Republican Army

BLACK, ALISTAIR
Vanguard Unionist (later UUUM) Convention member for Armagh, 1975–6. b. Lanarkshire, 1913. MA, Dip. Ed. (QUB). Headmaster at Lurgan, Co. Armagh. Chairman of Co. Armagh Committee of UWC, 1974. One of the Vanguard Convention members who refused to support William Craig's idea of voluntary coalition, he became a member of UUUM, later UUUP, led by Ernest Baird. Stood unsuccessfully as UUUP candidate in Armagh in the 1982 Assembly election.

BLACK, SIR HAROLD
Last Secretary to NI Cabinet before direct rule. b. 9 April 1914; d. 1981. As Cabinet Secretary, 1965–72, he accompanied three PMs (O'Neill, Chichester-Clark and Faulkner) to London for talks with British Ministers. He had a key role in reform programme after James Callaghan's October 1969 visit, since he was on three-man steering committee which co-ordinated the work of committees on detailed changes. After direct rule, he was deputy Secretary in NIO until his retirement in 1974.

BLACKBURN, RONALD HENRY ALBERT
Clerk of the NI Parliament, 1971–2, of Assembly, 1973–4, and of Constitutional Convention, 1975–6. b. 9 February 1924. LLB (London). Served Foreign Office, 1943–6; Stormont Parliamentary staff, 1946. Planning appeals commissioner, 1980–.

BLANEY, NEIL
MEP for Connaught–Ulster, 1979–84. Independent Fianna Fáil TD for Donegal, 1977–. Earlier, TD for North-East Donegal, 1948–77. b. 1922. Neil Blaney succeeded his father, an old IRA man, in North-East Donegal, and has made it a strong power base. With his Republican background and his closeness to events in NI, he has regarded himself as a voice of NI nationalism in the Republic. He survived politically his expulsion from the Fianna Fáil party in 1970, following his sacking by the Taoiseach Jack Lynch. Soon after his dismissal from the post of Minister of Agriculture, he was accused of conspiring to import arms illegally into the Republic. But a district court found that he had no case to answer. In the Dáil in 1972 he attacked new anti-terrorist legislation and complained that the PIRA was being smeared, although it had arisen from the needs of the time from local defence committees in NI. He has frequently demanded British withdrawal from NI, and has urged that cross-border co-operation should be withheld until this is achieved. Despite his expulsion from Fianna Fáil, he topped the poll in North-East Donegal in 1973, and in 1976 a supporter, Paddy Keaveney, gained a Donegal seat from Fianna Fáil in a by-election, although he lost it again in the 1977 general election. In earlier years Blaney was one of the most influential figures in Fianna Fáil. He was Minister for Posts and Telegraphs and Minister for Local Government before becoming Minister of Agriculture. His capacity for local political organisation in Donegal led to his supporters being dubbed the 'Donegal Mafia' and his appeal in the north-west was confirmed when he easily won a seat in the first directly elected European Parliament. In Strasbourg he was appointed chairman of a group of independent MEPs. In the Fermanagh–S. Tyrone by-elections in 1981 he supported hunger-striker Bobby Sands, and his successor Owen Carron. After he lost his European seat in 1984, he was the centre of much speculation as to whether he would rejoin Fianna Fáil but he was clearly opposed to Fianna Fáil's acceptance of new extradition arrangements in 1987. He said an Irish person could not get a fair trial in GB or NI. He became longest-serving TD in 1987.

BLEAKES, WILLIAM GEORGE
OUP Assembly member for N. Down, 1982–6. b. 1934. Lisburn Council, 1977–, Mayor, 1987–. Chairman, Official Unionist Councillors' Association, 1978–. Member of OUP executive. He defied Unionist critics in his decision to meet Margaret Thatcher when she visited Lisburn in September 1988, saying twenty people had been murdered in the town and he had protested to her about security.

BLEAKLEY, DAVID
Minister of Community Relations, April–October 1971. b. 1926. The only NILP member to serve in a NI Government, he was appointed to the Community Relations post by Brian Faulkner. He was not then an MP, so his tenure of office was limited to six months. Best-known NILP personality. MP for Victoria, Belfast, 1958–65, and served as chairman of Stormont Public Accounts Committee. Elected in E. Belfast to Assembly and Convention, in

both of which he was the only representative of his party. He unsuccessfully contested E. Belfast in the Westminster elections, February and October 1974, and he was also unsuccessful in the 1979 European election, in which he stood as a United Community candidate. Chief Executive, Irish Council of Churches, 1979–. Chairman, Standing Commission on Human Rights, 1981–4.

BLEASE, LORD
Created Labour life peer, 1978. Opposition spokesman on NI in House of Lords and Labour Whip, 1979–83. b. Cromac, Belfast, 1914. Formerly William (better known as Billy) Blease, he was officer of the NI Committee of ICTU, 1959–75. He had a key role in securing recognition of ICTU by Unionist Government for the first time under PM Terence O'Neill. In 1974 he faced an arduous task when ICTU was unable to counter the loyalist strike aimed at bringing down the power-sharing Executive. Associated over many years with NILP, and party candidate in four elections in Belfast. NI member, Independent Broadcasting Authority, 1975–9. Rapporteur, EC cross-border communications study on Londonderry–Donegal, 1978. Hon LLD (QUB) and Hon D.Litt. (NUU).

BLELLOCH, SIR JOHN
Permanent Secretary, NIO, 1988–. b. 1930. In a lengthy civil-service career he served as deputy Secretary at the NIO, 1980–2, before moving to the Defence Ministry, where he became second Permanent Secretary in 1984. Thus he brought a useful mix of experience to Stormont at a time when security issues figured strongly in AIA discussions.

'BLOODY FRIDAY'
Friday 21 July 1972, when PIRA set off twenty-six explosions in Belfast, which

killed eleven people and injured 130. Seven people were killed at the Oxford Street bus station, which had been crowded at the time, and four at a shopping centre on the Cavehill Road. Two soldiers were among the dead. Since this was the most devastating day of violence in Belfast up to that time, and many of the injured suffered serious mutilation, the impact on public opinion was enormous, and many observers regarded it as the point at which PIRA had put itself outside the pale of political negotiation.

'BLOODY SUNDAY'
The incident in Londonderry's Bogside on 30 January 1972, in which thirteen people were shot dead by soldiers of the First Parachute Regiment. The shootings occurred on the occasion of an illegal march organised by the Derry Civil Rights Association, and they gave rise to angry controversy. They were denounced by civil rights leaders as 'another Sharpeville'; the Republic's Taoiseach Jack Lynch (FF) said it was 'an unwarranted attack on unarmed civilians'; the British Embassy in Dublin was burned down by demonstrators, and in the Commons, Bernadette Devlin MP struck the Home Secretary, Reginald Maudling. The PM Edward Heath announced an inquiry into the shootings by the Lord Chief Justice of England, Lord Widgery. That report did not appear until April 1972, but by then the Stormont Parliament had been suspended: and the convulsion caused by the affair was regarded as the decisive factor in the decision to impose direct rule from Westminster. Lord Widgery's verdict was a complex one. He held that there would have been no deaths if there had not been an illegal march, which had created 'a highly dangerous situation'. But he also said that it might well be that if the army had maintained its low-key attitude and had not launched a large-scale

operation to arrest hooligans, the day might have passed off without serious incident. Lord Widgery also found that the soldiers had been fired on first and he said there was no reason to suppose that they would have opened fire otherwise. None of the dead or wounded had been proven to have been shot while handling a firearm or bomb. The verdict was sharply attacked and Jack Lynch said that it showed the need for an international examination of the activities of the British army. Unionist MP Lawrence Orr said it 'exploded some of the myths surrounding the so-called Bloody Sunday'.

BLOOMFIELD, SIR KENNETH (PERCY)

Head of NI civil service, 1984–. Permanent Secretary, Department of Economic Development, 1982–4. Earlier Permanent Secretary of Commerce, 1981–2. Environment, 1976–81 and Housing and Local Government, 1975–6. b. 15 April 1931. MA (Oxon.) As deputy Secretary to the NI Cabinet, 1963–72, he was involved in many of the crucial negotiations linked with the reform programme and the period prior to the abolition of the old Stormont Parliament. Under-Secretary, NIO, 1972–3, and Permanent Secretary to the power-sharing Executive, January–May 1974. With the signing of the AIA, he was heavily engaged in the meetings of the ministerial conference, as well as with political parties in 1987–8. In August 1988, after PIRA issued a threat to senior civil servants, his N. Down home was severely damaged by a bomb, but he and his family escaped injury.

BOAL, DESMOND

Unionist MP for Shankill, 1960–71; DUP MP, 1971–2. b. Londonderry, 1929. LLB (TCD). One of NI's leading barristers (QC, 1973), he is also one of

its most intriguing political figures. As a Unionist MP, he was frequently at odds with the party leadership. He was deprived of the party Whip for criticism of Lord Brookeborough as PM; he was prominent in the backbench revolt against Terence O'Neill as Premier, largely because of O'Neill's decision to invite Sean Lemass, Taoiseach of the Republic, to Stormont, for unannounced talks; and he was highly critical of the law-and-order policies of the Chichester-Clark and Faulkner Governments. In 1966 he lost his post as counsel to the Attorney-General after he had defended the right of Free Presbyterians to protest at the General Assembly of the Irish Presbyterian Church. In 1971 he resigned from the Unionist Party after describing the tripartite talks between Brian Faulkner, Jack Lynch and Edward Heath as 'adding a new dimension of dishonesty' to Unionist politics. Soon afterwards he joined the Rev. Ian Paisley in launching the DUP, of which he became the first chairman. He resigned his Shankill seat immediately following the introduction of direct rule in March 1972, as a protest against Westminster's move. In 1974, after he had given up the chairmanship of DUP, he announced support for a federal scheme in Ireland. He wanted an Irish federal parliament holding the powers reserved to Westminster under the 1920 Act, and the restoration of the Stormont Parliament with its old powers. The idea attracted some interest in Dublin, but was generally rejected by Unionists. Paisley joined in the denunciation. In 1977 Boal was involved with Sean MacBride in a chain of contacts between PIRA and loyalist paramilitaries aimed at securing a PIRA ceasefire. In 1987 be became a senior counsel in the Republic after he had been admitted to the Dublin Bar for the first time to defend Peter Robinson, DUP MP, on charges arising from loyalist 'invasion' of Clontibret, Co. Monaghan.

BOGSIDE *see* Londonderry/Derry

BOLAND, KEVIN
The Minister for Local Government in the Republic, who resigned from the Lynch Government (FF) as a protest against the sacking in 1970 of two Ministers – Charles Haughey and Neil Blaney – on the grounds that they had been implicated in the illegal importation of arms intended for NI. b. 1917. Boland claimed later that he had originally offered his resignation in August 1969, when he said B Specials in Belfast had led loyalist attacks on Catholic areas, but he had been persuaded by President Eamon de Valera to stay in office. After his split with Fianna Fáil he set up Aontacht Éireann (the Republican Unity Party), and claimed that the major parties in the Republic had abandoned their republicanism. But he failed in a series of efforts to return to the Dáil, and decided to quit active politics in 1976, when he got just over 1,000 votes in a Dublin by-election. In 1974 he sought to have the Sunningdale Agreement, reached by the British and Irish Governments, declared unconstitutional. This was the agreement which paved the way for the power-sharing Executive in NI. The paragraph to which he took exception read: 'The Irish government fully accepted and solemnly declared that there could be no change in the status of Northern Ireland until a majority of the people of Northern Ireland desired a change in that status.' But in the High Court, Mr Justice Murnaghan held against Boland. He said that this paragraph did not acknowledge that NI was part of the UK, that it was no more than a statement of policy and that the court should not usurp the functions of the Dáil. Boland's appeal to the Supreme Court was dismissed.

BORDER POLL
The constitutional referendum introduced by Westminster to establish the extent to which support existed for the British link and for a united Ireland. The poll, intended to be taken every ten years, was first held on 8 March 1973. Questions and votes in favour were as follows:

> Do you want NI to remain part of the UK? 591,820
> Do you want NI to be joined with the Republic of Ireland, outside the UK? 6,463

Other figures: total electorate, 1,030,084; percentage poll, 58.7; spoiled votes, 5,973 (1.0 per cent); percentage of valid poll for UK link, 98.9; percentage of valid poll for united Ireland, 1.1; percentage of non-voters, 41.3; percentage of total electorate supporting UK link, 57.5. The SDLP and most Nationalists boycotted the poll. The Secretary of State William Whitelaw said the wishes of the majority would be respected. Unionists welcomed the outcome, and the SDLP said it proved nothing since everyone knew that there was a Protestant majority in NI. The poll could have been repeated in March 1983, but Secretary of State James Prior decided against it. He said it would not tell them anything since recent elections had shown that a large majority wanted to remain within the UK. The AIA did not specify whether the poll would be decisive in gauging the wishes of the people under article one of the agreement.

BOYSON, SIR RHODES
Minister of State and deputy Secretary of State, NIO, 1984–6. b. 11 May 1925. An ex-headmaster on the right wing of the Conservative Party, and with a combative approach to opponents, he hit back at Unionists for their boycott of Ministers and their protests against

the AIA. In March 1986, as Industry Minister, he said: 'Days of inaction, heckling Ministers and generally making a mockery of the political process is deplored by rational people. It is an abuse of the unemployment situation.' The rate of unemployment was particularly high during his tenure of office and he stepped up job-creation measures, put forward plans for the development of tourism, and raised FEA spending by 26 per cent. Shortly before leaving NI, he drew hostile comment with a suggestion that he would try to ease emigration to US and Canada for unemployed people. Moved to GB Department of Environment and left government in 1987.

BRADFORD, REVEREND ROBERT JOHN
The first NI Westminster MP to be assassinated in the Troubles, he had been OUP MP for S. Belfast for seven years when he was shot dead by a five-man PIRA squad at a community centre in Finaghy, in his constituency, on Saturday 14 November 1981. b. 1941. Formerly Methodist minister at Suffolk, close to the Lenadoon estate in W. Belfast, a flashpoint in the early period of the violence. Resigned from Methodist Church, 1974. In the 1973 Assembly election, he stood unsuc-cessfully as a Vanguard candidate in S. Antrim. His maiden speech at West-minster broke with tradition since he attacked the Constitution Act, 1973, as undemocratic, and security policy as inadequate. Keen sportsman and played for House of Commons soccer team. He was industry spokesman of the OUP and made a reputation at Westminster as campaigner against pornography. His murder was widely seen as an attempt by PIRA to provoke a loyalist backlash. Some of his friends also regarded it as a bid to silence an MP who had frequently accused Republican

paramilitary groups of racketeering. PIRA itself accused him of being 'one of the key people responsible for winding up the loyalist paramilitary sectarian machine'. His death provoked a tense situation and calls by Unionists for better security generally, and a greater effort to protect politicians. Secretary of State James Prior (Cons.) got a hostile reception from a section of the congregation when he attended the funeral service. In 1984 his widow Norah wrote an account of his career, *A Sword Bathed in Heaven*.

BRADFORD, ROY HAMILTON
Unionist member for E. Belfast in Assembly, 1973–4, and head of Department of the Environment in Executive, 1974. b. Belfast, 7 July 1920. BA (TCD). Unionist MP for Victoria (Belfast), 1965–72. Parliamentary Secretary, Ministry of Education, 1967. Minister of Commerce, 1969–71; Minister of Development, 1971–2. Strongly criticised British Government's initial handling of direct rule. He came into conflict with some Executive colleagues when he suggested that there should be some contact between the British Government and the UWC during the loyalist strike in 1974. In 1975 he was an unsuccessful candidate in the Convention election in E. Belfast. He speaks French and German fluently and was active as a broadcaster for both BBC and ITV before entering politics. Has had a long-standing interest in EC affairs, and chairman of the European Movement in NI, 1977–87 (president, 1987–). In a novel, *The Last Ditch* (1981), he gave a barely fictionalised account of the inside struggle by NI Cabinet in 1972 against imposition of direct rule.

BRADLEY, PATRICK A.
Chief electoral officer, NI, May 1980–. b. 1935. BA (OU). Has had varied career

in civil service both in London and Belfast, including periods at Air Ministry and Local Enterprise Development Unit in NI, and in private industrial management (Chemstrand and Du Pont). Joined electoral office in NI, 1974.

BRAY, BRIGADIER MICHAEL
Commander of UDR, 1986–8. b. 1937. His family has an unbroken record of military service going back over 300 years. He moved from NATO HQ to UDR post, but had considerable previous experience of NI. He spent first two years of commissioned service with the Duke of Wellington's Regiment at Holywood in the 1950s, and as a Company Commander in the same regiment, spent sixteen months in Londonderry in mid-1970s. In 1978–9 he had a four-month tour in Derry as Commanding Officer of a 'Dukes' regiment and was mentioned in despatches. During his career he served in many parts of the world, and was for a time at the Defence Ministry before going to NATO, where he became Chief of Land Operations. In 1988 he rejected suggestions that the UDR had a problem with links with Protestant paramilitaries. He said an internal review at the end of 1987 had shown that only one soldier had faced dismissal because he had taken part in a UDA parade.

BRIGHTON HOTEL BOMBING
On 12 October 1984 five people, including a Conservative MP Sir Anthony Berry, died in a PIRA explosion at the Grand Hotel, Brighton, where PM Margaret Thatcher and several leading Ministers were staying during the Conservative conference. The PM was not injured. The judge in sentencing top PIRA bomber Patrick Magee, who placed the delayed-action bomb, to eight life sentences told him: 'You intended to wipe out a large part of the Government, and you very nearly did.' Two of Magee's five accomplices were also sentenced to life imprisonment. The bomb, with a long-delay fuse, had been placed in a sixth-floor bathroom, and went off at 2.54 a.m., while Margaret Thatcher, in a room below, was working on her party conference speech. She later described the bombing as 'an indiscriminate attempt to massacre innocent and unsuspecting men and women. . . to cripple Her Majesty's democratically elected Government'. A PIRA statement said: 'Today we were unlucky. . . but remember we have only to be lucky once; you have to be lucky always.'

BRITISH IRISH ASSOCIATION
An organisation which annually brings together top London, Belfast and Dublin politicians, diplomats, security chiefs, officials, journalists and academics to discuss the current situation. The weekend conference is usually held in Oxford, Cambridge or London, and several NI Secretaries of State have spoken at the gatherings as well as leading Irish Ministers. Garret FitzGerald (FG) addressed several meetings as Foreign Minister and Taoiseach. Proceedings are 'off the record', although accounts of interesting developments usually leak out. David Astor has been chairman of the BIA in recent years, and Sir Robin Day has presided at some debates.

BRITISH-IRISH INTERGOVERNMENTAL COUNCIL
The structure for Anglo-Irish consultations which developed from the Thatcher–Haughey summit in Dublin in December 1980. The idea was finally approved at the Downing Street meeting between Margaret Thatcher and Garret FitzGerald in November 1981, although many of the details remained unresolved. The British and

Irish Government officials who drafted the plan envisaged a four-tier structure – ministerial, official, parliamentary, with an advisory committee. The council may be said to have existed since November 1981, at ministerial and official level, and the London meeting in January 1982 between NI Secretary of State James Prior and Irish Foreign Minister James Dooge was the first ministerial get-together under the council. Initially there seemed to be more enthusiasm for the parliamentary tier in Dublin than in London, where it seemed to be considered as simply a formalising of the regular contacts between interested MPs and TDs. There was the possibility, however, that members of a NI Assembly might be involved, although Unionists continued to say that they would have nothing to do with such a body. In July 1983 both Governments agreed to sponsor an 'Encounter Organisation' to organise high-level Anglo-Irish conferences, an arrangement that continued into the era of the AIA. Technically, the BIIC survived the AIA, and the signing ceremony of the AIA at Hillsborough was under its aegis.

BRITISH ULSTER DOMINION PARTY
A small organisation originally launched in 1975 by Professor Kennedy Lindsay under the title Ulster Dominion Group, which changed its name to BUDP in 1977. Professor Lindsay, who was elected to the Convention on the VUPP ticket, submitted a policy document to that body in September 1975, urging that NI should become a self-governing dominion, with the Queen as monarch and with a resident Governor-General. The idea did not attract any support in the Convention, but it seemed to owe something to the scheme promoted in the 1950s and 1960s by the late William F. McCoy QC, Unionist MP for

S. Tyrone. Both Lindsay and McCoy argued that the suspension of the Stormont Parliament in 1972 had demonstrated the weakness of any local devolution system.

BROADHURST, BRIGADIER JOSEPH CALLENDER
Deputy Speaker, Assembly, 1973–4. b. 24 December 1906; d. January 1987. UPNI member of Assembly for S. Down, 1973–4, unsuccessful candidate there for Constitutional Convention, 1975. A strong supporter of Brian Faulkner in Assembly. Had a distinguished military career in Middle East, and was Chief of Staff in Arab Legion. Expert on Middle East affairs.

BROCKWAY, LORD
Labour life peer, who campaigned over many years for more discussion of NI affairs at Westminster. b. Calcutta, 1888; d. 1988. As Archibald Fenner Brockway, Labour MP (latterly for Eton and Slough, 1950–64), he was among the first Labour members to call for reforms in NI. He was involved with the Campaign for Democracy in Ulster, and in 1971 made the first of several unsuccessful attempts in the House of Lords to have a bill passed providing for a Bill of Rights in NI. The measure also suggested PR in elections. He opposed internment without trial, and spoke at one Tyrone anti-internment rally. He was at the centre of the successful campaign to have the Price sisters moved to Armagh Prison.

BROOKEBOROUGH, 2ND VISCOUNT
Son of 1st Viscount Brookeborough, PM of NI, 1943–63, and active as a Conservative peer in the House of Lords and in the old Stormont Commons and Government. b. 9 November 1922; d. March 1987. As Captain John Brooke, he succeeded his father as Unionist MP for Lisnaskea in

1968, and held the seat until the dissolution of the Stormont Parliament in 1972. Parliamentary Secretary, 1969–70, at Ministry of Commerce and to PM James Chichester-Clark, with special responsibility for Government information services, Government Chief Whip, 1971–2. Represented N. Down in Assembly, 1973–4, and Convention, 1975–6. While the UPNI was in existence, he put forward that party's views in the Lords, where he concentrated on security, farming and EC issues. At home in Fermanagh he was deeply involved in the promotion of tourism and in 1985 became president of Fermanagh OUP Association. He was a strong opponent of the AIA, and attracted widespread criticism in January 1987 for a remark in the Lords that Cardinal Ó Fiaich was an 'evil prelate'. His son Alan succeeded to the title.

BROWN, WILLIAM

OUP Assembly member for S. Down, 1982–6. Deputy chairman, Agriculture Committee, 1985–6. b. 1930. Down Council, 1977–. Farmer; active in unionism and Orange Order.

BROWNLOW, WILLIAM STEPHEN

Unionist and later UPNI Assembly member for N. Down, 1973–4. b. Winchester, 1921. Down County Council, 1969–73. Unsuccessfully contested N. Down Westminster seat, October 1974, and Convention election, 1975.

BRUGHA, RUAIRÍ

Fianna Fáil spokesman on NI affairs, 1973–7. b. Dublin, 15 October 1917. Fourth son of veteran Republican Cathal Brugha, who was killed in 1922. Senator, 1969–73 and 1977–81; TD, 1973–7. He has described, in Tim Pat Coogan's *The IRA*, how he joined the IRA at sixteen, was interned during the war, and how he came to realise that IRA activities had not helped to end partition. Frequently visited NI as Fianna Fáil spokesman. In 1975 he called on Britain to disarm the loyalist paramilitaries. In 1976 he claimed that it was unrealistic to expect Ulster Unionists to abandon their 'not an inch' attitude while Britain was guaranteeing their position. In 1977 he suggested a federal Ireland, independent of Britain, with autonomy for NI. In the 1979 European election he was an unsuccessful candidate in Dublin. In 1987 he praised the UDA 'Common Sense' plan which, he said, was a recognition that it was futile to say 'no' to the AIA without providing alternatives.

BRUSH, LIEUTENANT-COLONEL EDWARD JAMES AUGUSTUS HOWARD

OUP Convention member for S. Down, 1975–6. b. Fermoy, Co. Cork, 5 March 1901; d. 1984. Had distinguished army career. Wounded and taken POW during the British evacuation from France in 1940. Spent three years as POW. After the war he took up farming in Co. Down, was a leading figure in the Territorial Army and became deputy Lord Lieutenant for Co. Down. He first attracted public attention in 1973, when it was disclosed that over the previous two years he had built up a loyalist paramilitary group known as Down Orange Welfare, which claimed a membership at that time of about 5,000. In the 1974 loyalist strike he was a member of the organising body – the UWC Co-ordinating Committee. In October 1974 he resigned as deputy Lieutenant for Co. Down. Soon afterwards there were suggestions that he might lead a new loyalist home guard but this did not materialise. In the 1975 Convention he represented S. Down, where he was president of the local OUP Association.

B SPECIALS *see* Security System section, pp. 383–5

BUNTING, MAJOR RONALD
A leading loyalist activist in 1968–70. b. 1924; d. 1984. BA (OU), M.Sc. (Manchester). An ex-regular army officer, he was involved, while a mathematics lecturer, in promoting local government reform. One of his earliest political activities was to help Gerry Fitt in a Belfast election. In 1968 and 1969 he was a leader of the Ulster Protestant Volunteers and the Loyal Citizens of Ulster, and associated with other loyalist groups opposed to the civil rights campaign. In November 1968 he joined the Rev. Ian Paisley in leading a Protestant rally in Armagh which blocked the path of a civil rights march. Like Paisley, he was jailed for this activity, but he was released quickly under the amnesty called by Major Chichester-Clark when he took over as NI PM. Bunting was prominent in harassing the PD march from Belfast to Londonderry in January 1969. He broke with Paisley in 1970. His son, Ronald, who was associated with IRSP, was murdered in Belfast in October 1980.

BURCHILL, JEREMY
OUP Assembly member for E. Belfast, 1982–6. In 1983 resigned from committees on Environment, and Finance and Personnel. Representative of same constituency in Convention, 1975–6. Belfast City Council, 1981–5. b. Dublin, 1951. Barrister. Former Honorary Secretary, Ulster Unionist Council, and chairman of Young Unionist Council. Frequent speaker for the party in NI and GB. Conservative Party executive committee, 1973–4. Stood unsuccessfully against the Rev. Ian Paisley in N. Antrim at 1979 Westminster election.

BURNS, JOSEPH
Parliamentary Secretary, NI Government, 1971–2, and Whip, 1968–9. Unionist MP for N. Derry, 1960–72. b. Belfast, 19 July 1906. Joined USC at fourteen. In the early 1920s he worked on farms in Canada and later as a stocks-and-bonds salesman. Studied at New York University, 1928. Strong traditional loyalist, and prominent in Orange, Black and Apprentice Boys' Orders. Chairman of UUAC which organised the loyalist strike of May 1977.

BURNS, THOMAS EDWARD
DUP Assembly, 1973–4, and Convention, 1975–6; member for S. Belfast. b. Lurgan, Co. Armagh, 1927. Company director, whose firm developed a new building material – rubber concrete – in 1977.

BURNTOLLET
The point in Co. Derry at which the PD Belfast–Derry march was ambushed by militant Protestants on Saturday 4 January 1969. The marchers, then numbering about 70 and accompanied by 80 police, were attacked by about 200 Protestants using sticks and stones. Several of the marchers were injured and some were driven into the nearby river. The marchers included two prominent PD figures – Bernadette Devlin and Michael Farrell. The incident gave rise to criticism of the RUC by civil rights spokesmen, who said the police had failed to provide adequate protection and had not acted strongly enough against the Protestants involved. The police pointed out that the marchers had continued through Burntollet despite police warnings.

BURROUGHS, RONALD ARTHUR
UK Government representative in NI from March 1970 to April 1971. b. 4 June 1917; d. 1980. His period of office covered the growth of both PIRA

87

and loyalist violence and anxious decisions about marches through sensitive areas. He was also concerned in the security arguments between London and Stormont which culminated in the resignation of Major Chichester-Clark as PM in March 1971.

BUSH, GEORGE
President of US, 1989–. b. 12 June 1924. Vice-president, 1981–9. Congressman for Texas, 1966–70. US Permanent Representative, UN, 1971–3. Director, CIA, 1976–7. When he took office, he was expected to follow policies he had endorsed as vice-president – that is, support for AIA and for extradition arrangements affecting PIRA suspects, along with opposition to US contributions to pro-PIRA groups. In 1988 election he made no special effort to attract Irish-American votes, but is believed to have had substantial support from that sector because of emphasis on values likely to appeal to Catholics. One of his first engagements as president-elect was a meeting with PM Margaret Thatcher, and his relations with her were forecast to be almost as close as those she had had with his predecessor, President Reagan. He paid an official visit to Dublin in 1983, and said that while the US adopted a 'non-interventionist' policy towards Irish affairs, it would continue to condemn violence. When in the oil industry in the early 1960s, he paid a brief business visit to NI. A Boston genealogist has claimed that some of the President's ancestors named Halliday came from Rathfriland, Co. Down.

BUTLER, SIR ADAM COURTAULD
Minister of State, NI, January 1981–September 1984. b. 11 October 1931. Son of Lord Butler – R.A. Butler. Pembroke College, Cambridge. Took charge initially of the Departments of

Commerce and Manpower, and in September 1981 of Agriculture as well. With the recession and the image of NI cutting outside investment, in 1982 he set up a new Industrial Development Board to spearhead the drive for new industry. The establishment of the IDB coincided with the merger of the Departments of Commerce and Manpower into the new Economic Development Department for which he took responsibility. In 1982 he negotiated with Republic's Government on plan (later dropped) for bringing natural gas from Kinsale to Belfast. After the 1983 election, he became deputy Secretary of State, and took charge of Finance and Economic Development. Minister of State at Defence until September 1985. Resigned as MP, 1987.

C

CAHILL, JOSEPH
A member of the PSF executive, who was among the founders of the PIRA. b. Belfast, 1920. A former carpenter and construction foreman, he was reprieved in 1942 after being sentenced to death with four other men for the killing of a policeman in Belfast. He was Belfast commander of the PIRA for a time before moving to Dublin in 1972. In 1973 he was sentenced to three years' penal servitude for illegal gun-running and PIRA membership. In a Dublin court Cahill and four other men were convicted of attempting to import arms and explosives which had been captured when the ship *Claudia* was intercepted in Waterford Bay on its way from Libya. When the judge described Cahill as the ring-leader in the operation, he replied from the dock, 'You do me an honour.' He was in ill-health when released from prison, and turned his attention to PSF work.

For a time he handled aid for Republican prisoners and their families, and later became general secretary and treasurer of the party. In July 1984 he was deported from the US for illegal entry.

CALDWELL, THOMAS HADDEN (TOM)

Ind. Unionist MP for Willowfield division of Belfast, 1969–72. b. Uganda, 30 June 1921. He won Willowfield as a pro-O'Neill candidate, and unsuccessfully contested S. Antrim in the 1970 Westminster general election. In 1971 he aroused controversy and criticism from Unionists when he met PIRA leaders in the Republic in a bid 'to stop the killings'. In 1973 he joined the Alliance Party, but resigned a year later.

CALEDON

The Co. Tyrone village where the first protest in the 1968 civil rights campaign occurred. Austin Currie, then a Nationalist MP, took possession of a council house on 20 June which he claimed had been improperly allocated to a Protestant single girl by Dungannon Rural Council. He was ejected by police.

CALLAGHAN, LORD (OF CARDIFF)

As James Callaghan, Labour PM, 1976–9. Responsible for NI affairs as Home Secretary, 1967–70. b. 27 March 1912. He first became interested in NI affairs in the 1950s, when, with other Labour MPs, he was concerned with studying ways of strengthening the local economy. His tenure at the Home Office saw NI move from being a departmental detail to one of the Government's most pressing problems. As the civil rights movement gathered pace in the spring of 1968, he also came under pressure from Labour MPs in the Campaign for Democracy in Ulster.

They not only demanded changes in line with those urged by the civil rights demonstrators, but argued that it was wrong for NI MPs to have equal voting rights in Parliament when NI issues could not be debated effectively at Westminster. In August 1969, after the serious violence in Londonderry, Belfast and other towns, he was involved, with PM Harold Wilson, in the decision to send troops to NI to support the RUC. At the end of August 1969 he visited NI for talks with the Government and a wide variety of interests. This was the first major intervention by the British Government in NI affairs. Although Callaghan sought to give the impression that electoral, housing and other reforms were being taken on Stormont's initiative, the Home Secretary was clearly the driving force. He returned for a second visit in October 1969, when the new-style RUC emerged, and the B Specials were abolished, in line with the Hunt report. Although he had drawn up contingency plans for direct rule, it fell to the Heath Government to implement these. In his book *A House Divided*, which he wrote while in opposition, and which was published in 1973, he made a number of points. He asked why the RUC had not tried to gain control of Derry's Bogside from the rear in August 1969. He also wrote that if the majority made the Assembly and Executive unworkable, then the UK would be entitled to reconsider its position and its pledges on all matters. He also said that the unity of Ireland could only come about through a freely negotiated voluntary agreement. 'So at the end of the day I would like to see Ireland come together again. If and when it does, it will be a signal to the world that the people themselves have entered freely into a new compact because they are at peace and at ease with one another and recognise how much they have in common.' As PM he seemed to be anxious to concentrate on helping the NI economy and gave little priority to political advance, although he stressed on several occasions that there would have to be partnership government. The decision of his Government to back extra MPs for NI pleased Unionists and angered the SDLP, who claimed that he was buying Unionist votes to keep his minority Government in office. In May 1979, in his first speech as leader of the opposition, he indicated that his party would seek to keep a bipartisan policy on NI and he offered to co-operate with the Conservatives in seeking a political initiative. In 1981, after he had given up the party leadership, he called for an independent NI. He has, however, given general support to the AIA.

CALVERT, DAVID NORMAN
DUP Assembly member for Armagh, 1982–6. Served on committees on Education, Environment, Finance and Personnel. b. 1945. Craigavon Council, 1973–. Member, Southern Education and Library Board. He was prominent in the council protest against the AIA, and in January 1987 he was wounded in an assassination attempt by INLA, which claimed it was the start of a campaign against all those 'responsible for the continued oppression of Nationalists'. Candidate, NI Convention, 1975, for Fermanagh–S. Tyrone. Fought Armagh in Westminster general election in 1979.

CAMERON COMMISSION
A three-man commission of inquiry announced by PM Terence O'Neill in January 1969. Its terms of reference were to inquire into the violence since 5 October 1968, to trace the causes of the violence and to examine the bodies involved. The chairman was Lord Cameron, and the other members were Professor Sir John Biggart and James Joseph Campbell. It sat in private, and

the NI Attorney-General gave an assurance that no prosecutions would be brought on the basis of any written or oral evidence to the inquiry. Brian Faulkner, Minister of Commerce, resigned from the Government because he disagreed with the decision to establish the inquiry. The commission's findings were believed to be known to the Home Secretary, James Callaghan, when he visited NI in August 1969, but they were published in early September 1969. The commission declared that there had been a failure of leadership on all sides, and that the Stormont Government had been 'hidebound' and 'complacent'. It gave seven main causes for the disorders:
 1 A rising sense of continuing injustice and grievance among large sections of the Catholic population, particularly because of the inadequacy of the housing provision of some local authorities and 'unfair methods of allocation' of houses to perpetuate Unionist control.
 2 Religious discrimination in appointments by some Unionist-controlled authorities.
 3 Deliberate manipulation of local government electoral boundaries to achieve or maintain Unionist control of some local authorities.
 4 A growing and powerful sense of resentment and frustration among the Catholic population at the failure of the Government to investigate complaints and provide a remedy for them.
 5 Resentment, particularly among Catholics, at the existence of the USC as a partisan paramilitary force recruited exclusively from Protestants.
 6 Widespread resentment, among Catholics in particular, about the Special Powers Act.
 7 Fears and apprehension among Protestants of a threat to Unionist domination and control of government by the increase of the Catholic population. These feelings were

inflamed in particular by the activities of the UCDC and the UPV which had provoked a hostile reaction to civil rights claims as asserted by NICRA and later by the PD. The atmosphere thus created was readily translated into physical violence against civil rights demonstrators. The commission also criticised the RUC, which was said to have been inept on occasions. It said that 'subversive elements' had used the civil rights platform to stir up trouble in the streets.

CAMPAIGN FOR DEMOCRACY IN ULSTER

A London-based group which monitored civil rights in NI and which was especially prominent in pressing for reforms in 1968–9. Although not confined to parliamentarians, it had the support of up to 100 Labour MPs on occasion, and among those who held office in it were Lord Fenner Brockway, and Labour MPs Stanley Orme, Paul Rose and Kevin McNamara. Gerry Fitt, as W. Belfast MP, was a frequent speaker at its meetings, which were normally held either at the House of Commons or at the annual conferences of the Labour Party.

CAMPAIGN FOR DEVOLVED PARLIAMENT

A group launched in March 1988 to campaign for a 'strong devolved Parliament' as an initiative to replace the AIA and command 'extensive cross-community support'. Executive responsibility would be exercised by representatives chosen by an agreed method, such as PR or voluntary coalition, and would have responsibility for policing. There would be both legislative and administrative powers, and considerable financial autonomy. There would also be a Bill of Rights and a cross-border dimension. The proposals were outlined in a pamphlet, *A Better Deal Together*. Among those associated with the group were ex-UPNI Assembly member Peter McLachlan, former OUP leader Harry West, Austin Ardill, James Cooper, Christopher McGimpsey, David McNarry, Alex Boyd, Ken Larmour, James Gorman and David Reid.

CAMPAIGN FOR EQUAL CITIZENSHIP

A pressure group headed by Robert McCartney QC, which has campaigned for the main British parties to organise in NI. McCartney stood unsuccessfully in N. Down in the 1987 Westminster election as a 'Real Unionist'. The CEC has attracted some supporters of integration and has argued that the setting up of devolved government under the AIA would hasten a united Ireland. It also claims backing from outside Unionist ranks, and says that members of the Campaign for Labour Representation, who urge the British Labour Party to be active in NI, have been among its supporters. Some divisions appeared in the organisation in 1988 when McCartney returned as president after a brief absence. In 1988 both the Conservative and Labour parties came out against organisation in NI, but Conservative 'model' associations were launched in several constituencies.

CAMPAIGN FOR SOCIAL JUSTICE

An organisation based in Dungannon, Co. Tyrone, which began in January 1964, and which over the next five years mounted a strong publicity campaign in Britain and abroad. Its declared aims were to collect data on injustices in NI and to fight discrimination, especially in employment, housing, electoral practices and boundaries, and public appointments. Its efforts were particularly effective in building up support for the civil rights movement within the British Labour Party. Councillor Patricia McCluskey and her husband Dr Con McCluskey, of Dungannon, were the members of the twelve-member campaign committee who became best known as speakers for the group.

CAMPBELL, GREGORY LLOYD

DUP Assembly member for Londonderry, 1982–6. Served on committees on Economic Development, Environment, Finance and Personnel, and as deputy chairman of Security Committee. Derry City Council, 1977–. b. 1956. Leads DUP group on council. He featured in the controversial *Real Lives* documentary broadcast by BBC in 1985 despite Government opposition arising from inclusion of Martin McGuinness of PSF. Strong opponent of Government decision to change name of City Council from 'Londonderry' to 'Derry' in 1984 and has also campaigned against the admission of PSF to councils and against the AIA. In December 1984 he and his family survived an INLA murder bid when a bomb fell off their car as they were driving away from church. Has criticised FEA for discriminating against Protestants, and one of founders of loyalist-sponsored Anti-Discrimination Association set up in 1988. Chairman, DUP Councillors' Association. Member, Independent Orange Order.

CAMPBELL, ROBERT VICTOR

Unionist member of Assembly for N. Down, 1973–4, and unsuccessful UPNI Convention candidate for the same constituency. b. Coleraine, Co. Londonderry, 1914; d. 1978. Mayor of Bangor, Co. Down, 1966–70. Member, N. Down District Council, 1973–7.

CANAVAN, MICHAEL

SDLP member for Londonderry in the Assembly, 1973–4, and the Convention, 1975–6. Security spokesman of SDLP, 1974–82. b. Derry, 1924. Prominent in civil rights campaign in Derry. Chairman of Derry Citizens' Central Council in 1970, after holding office in the Derry Citizens' Defence Association and the Derry Citizens' Action Committee. Earlier he was on the executive of the University for Derry Campaign in 1965 and in later years led the successful drive to have full university status for Magee College. He was a founding member of the SDLP, and as security spokesman, paid frequent visits to prisons and opposed the use of plastic bullets or any excessive force by the security forces. He expressed his opposition to the 1982 Assembly by refusing to stand as a candidate in Londonderry. In 1986 he was on the first board of the International Fund for Ireland but resigned for family reasons in 1987.

CARDWELL, JOSHUA

Unionist member, Assembly, 1973–4, and UPNI Convention, 1975–6, member for E. Belfast. b. 1910; d. 1982. Belfast City Council, 1952–82. Unionist MP for Pottinger at Stormont, 1969–72.

CAREY, HUGH

Governor of New York, 1974–83. b. 11 April 1919. Associated with Senator Edward Kennedy and other leading Irish-Americans in encouraging US Government interest in NI, and in discouraging Americans from giving money gifts to organisations associated with violence in Ireland. Member of Friends of Ireland Group. Stayed away from New York dinner for British Labour PM James Callaghan in June 1978 because he wished to protest against British slowness in eradicating violence in NI, and in ending discrimination against Catholics in jobs and housing. In 1979 he tried to set up a

New York meeting between Britain and Irish Republic on NI. The idea was accepted by the Republic but rejected by Britain. On a visit to Ireland in 1981 he said the British Government's attitude to the hunger strike was increasing support for the PIRA in the US.

CARRINGTON, LORD
Closely involved with NI as Defence Secretary in the Conservative Heath Government, 1970–4. Leader of opposition, House of Lords, 1974–9. Foreign Secretary, 1979–82. Resigned in the wake of the Falklands crisis. Secretary-General, NATO, 1984–. b. 6 June 1919. He was responsible for big build-up of UDR, but would not agree to radical changes in security tactics being demanded by NI Government in early 1971. He flew to Stormont in March 1971 in an unsuccessful bid to persuade Major Chichester-Clark to stay as PM. In December 1980 he accompanied Margaret Thatcher at Dublin summit.

CARRON, JOHN
Nationalist MP for S. Fermanagh, 1965–72. b. Kinawley, Co. Fermanagh, 1909. Was Lisnaskea rural councillor when he succeeded veteran Nationalist Cahir Healy in S. Fermanagh in 1965. In 1949 he unsuccessfully contested Lisnaskea, held by the then PM, Lord Brookeborough. During the short-lived opposition alliance at Stormont in 1969, he was spokesman on community relations.

CARRON, OWEN
Republican MP for Fermanagh–S. Tyrone, 1981–3. PSF member of the NI Assembly, 1982–6. b. Macken, Enniskillen, 1953. Trained as teacher at Manchester University and held a variety of teaching posts in Armagh and Fermanagh, 1976–9. Although he had no Republican family background, he was a founder member and chairman of Fermanagh H-Block committee, and was a member of PSF when he acted as election agent for Bobby Sands in the April 1981 by-election in Fermanagh–S. Tyrone. When Sands died Carron was elected as a 'proxy political prisoner' in the August 1981 by-election. He fought on an abstentionist ticket and said he would operate as a full-time constituency MP. In the 1982 Assembly election he stood as a PSF candidate. In January 1982 he was arrested while trying to enter the US from Canada, along with PSF colleague Danny Morrison. He lost his Westminster seat in the 1983 election when SDLP intervened to take nearly 10,000 votes and he was succeeded by an Official Unionist. In 1985 he denied an accusation in the Assembly that he was PIRA commander in Fermanagh. In January 1986 he was in custody on a firearms charge, but was given bail to fight the Westminster by-election in Fermanagh–S. Tyrone. He went on the run, however, and was only recaptured in the Republic in February 1988.

CARSON, JOHN
OUP Assembly member for N. Belfast, 1982–6. Served on Environment, and Finance and Personnel committees. b. 1933. A Belfast shopkeeper, he was elected to Belfast City Council, 1971–; High Sheriff in 1978 and Lord Mayor, 1980–1 and 1985–6. MP for N. Belfast, February 1974–9. Pushed up majority in N. Belfast between two 1974 general elections from 10,000 to more than 18,000. The OUP lost seat to DUP when he retired for health reasons in 1979. Repeatedly called for tougher security measures in N. Belfast, and also specially active on housing issues. Voted with Labour Government on crucial confidence vote which led to 1979 election. His independent line, particularly in City Hall politics, has occasionally put him at odds with

colleagues; recently his criticism of Unionist boycott of councils over the AIA lost him the party Whip.

CARTER, JAMES EARL (JIMMY)
US President (Democrat), 1976–80. b. 1 October 1924. In the final stages of his election campaign in October 1976 Carter was widely reported as saying that there should be an international commission on human rights in NI; that the Democratic Party was committed to the unification of Ireland; and that the US could not stand idle on the NI question. His remarks caused the Irish National Caucus (an umbrella group for Irish-American organisations) to call for support for Carter. But there were protests from Unionists in NI, some MPs at Westminster, and the Peace People. There were also demands for clarification from the Irish Republic's Government. Carter then sent a cable to Dr Garret FitzGerald, Irish Foreign Minister, in which he complained that he had been mis-represented in some reports. He stressed that he did not favour violence as a solution to the Irish Question. He believed in negotiations and peaceful means of finding a just solution which would involve the two communities in NI, and protect human rights which had been threatened. In August 1977 he issued a statement which indicated that there would be economic help for NI if a political settlement could be reached. On 16 March 1978 he had a brief meeting at the White House with Mairead Corrigan of the NI Peace People at which he likened the US Government's efforts for peace to those of the peace movement in NI.

CARTER, RAYMOND JOHN (RAY)
Parliamentary Under-Secretary, NIO, 1976–9. b. 17 September 1935. Labour MP for Northfield (Birmingham), 1970–9, when he lost his seat in the general election – the only member of the Stormont team of Ministers to do so. Initially responsible at Stormont for assisting the Ministers of State in charge of Commerce, Manpower Services and Education. Later took charge of the Environment Department, which covered housing, planning and local government matters. Ran into controversy in 1977 over his unsuccessful attempt to make car seat belts compulsory in NI in advance of GB.

CASTLEREAGH *see* Bennett Report

CATHERWOOD, SIR HENRY FREDERICK ROSS
Conservative MEP, June 1979–. Ulster-born industrialist and chairman, 1975–8, of the British Overseas Trade Board. He had put forward a scheme for a political settlement in NI. b. 30 January 1925. In January 1972 he first suggested a Stormont Parliament in which the minority would have influence through a system of two-thirds majority voting and offers of Government posts to individual members of opposition parties. He repeated the proposal in 1974, when he came out strongly against an independent NI, which he said would be 'catastrophic'. In 1985 he assisted the NI Assembly devolution committee in the preparation of an agreed report, published before the AIA. In 1986 he urged a round-table political con-ference, but the idea foundered because Unionists insisted on the prior sus-pension of the AIA.

CATHOLIC ANTI-DISCRIMINATION
A body active between 1969 and 1974 in opposing prejudice against Catholics in private firms, Government depart-ments, and institutions generally. It was also involved in pressing for reform of the RUC.

CATHOLIC EX-SERVICEMEN'S ASSOCIATION

Catholic paramilitary organisation formed after the introduction of internment without trial in the summer of 1971. Its organiser Phil Curran quickly claimed to have 8,000 registered members, and it was very active during 1972. It was described as a 'people's army' for the defence of Catholic areas, and although it was unarmed, it claimed to be able to get arms if necessary.

CENTRAL CITIZENS' DEFENCE COMMITTEE

This organisation, based on the mainly Catholic Falls Road in Belfast, brought together in 1969 the various W. Belfast defence and community groups operating in Catholic areas. Its first chairman Jim Sullivan was a leading Republican, who was succeeded by businessman Tom Conaty. It also brought together local politicians such as Paddy Devlin MP (NILP) and Paddy Kennedy MP (Rep. Lab.), and the local priest, Canon Pádraig Murphy. Its first major crisis was over the Government demands for removal of the barricades set up during the violent summer of 1969. This entailed talks with the Home Secretary, James Callaghan, and many contacts with the army. There were repeated rows over the RUC and the extent to which the troops could prevent any loyalist attack. In July 1970 the CCDC was engaged in the angry controversy over the thirty-four-hour curfew imposed by the army on a large section of the Lower Falls. It argued that the army operation was unjustified, and particularly criticised the tactics which had led to the deaths of five men during the curfew. It claimed that hundreds of complaints had been filed with the CCDC over the behaviour of the troops, and that any ammunition seized did not begin to compare with arms supplies held in

Protestant areas. The CCDC published a special book, *Law (?) and Orders, 1970*, itemising its case against the army, but official spokesmen denied an excess of force. During 1970 the CCDC took a strong line against violence. It called for a halt to the throwing of missiles at the army, attacked the shooting of RUC men, and said violence could harm the cause of justice. With the introduction of internment in 1971, it became involved in the organising of visits to Long Kesh, and in arranging parcels for internees and prisoners. In June 1973 the committee made a bid to persuade the PIRA to call a ceasefire. The PIRA replied eventually that it could not agree to peace at any price. It set out a series of demands – an amnesty for all imprisoned because of the Troubles, withdrawal of troops from sensitive areas, declaration of intent to withdraw from Ireland, and agreement by Britain that the Irish people should decide their own future. The CCDC replied that PIRA should show maturity and recognise that peace was the first priority. The general theme of CCDC policy was that Catholics had been treated unfairly by the security forces in comparison with Protestants. In 1973 it put out a 'Black Paper' calling for replacement of the RUC by an 'impartial police force'. William Whitelaw, as Secretary of State, retorted that there was little point in looking back and rehearsing old grievances. The CCDC HQ was among Falls Road premises bombed in November 1973. (*See also* Falls Road.)

CHANNON, HENRY PAUL GUINNESS

Minister of State, NIO, 1972. b. 9 October 1935. Has Irish family associations – his mother was a daughter of the 2nd Lord Iveagh, head of the Guinness family. His London home was the venue for the secret meeting between Secretary of State

William Whitelaw and PIRA leaders in July 1972. Conservative MP for Southend W., 1959–. Secretary for Trade and Industry, 1986–7. Secretary for Transport, 1987–.

CHARTER GROUP
Group established in 1986 and drawn from OUP to campaign for the return of devolved government to NI. Headed by ex-OUP leader Harry West. Its policy document issued in 1987 was signed by West, ex-OUP MP Austin Ardill, and David McNarry, who claimed the group had about 200 supporters. But OUP leader James Molyneaux stressed that the group did not speak for the party.

CHICHESTER-CLARK, MAJOR JAMES see Moyola, Lord

CHICHESTER-CLARK, SIR ROBERT (ROBIN)
Unionist MP for Londonderry, 1955–February 1974. Announced decision not to seek renomination in January 1973. Unsuccessful in contesting nomination for Lewes in Sussex. b. 10 January 1928. Brother of Lord Moyola, PM NI, 1969–71. Chief Conservative spokesman, NI, 1964–70. Minister of State, Employment, 1972–4. Chairman of the Unionist MPs at Westminster, 1971–4. He kept closely in touch with his brother as PM, and in January 1971 he voted against the Conservative Government as a protest against what he called the 'ineffectiveness' of the Government's security policy in NI. In July 1971, a few weeks before internment was introduced, he threatened to withdraw support altogether unless there was a tougher anti-terrorist policy. Patron of Friends of the Union, 1986–.

CLARK, SIR GEORGE
President of the OUP council, 1979–. Member of NI Senate, 1951–72. b. 24

January 1914. Grand master, Grand Orange Lodge of Ireland, 1957–67. Chairman of standing committee of Ulster Unionist Council, 1967–72. Sir George, who had started out in politics as Stormont MP for Dock division of Belfast, attracted interest in the early 1960s when he had talks with the late Gerry Lennon, a Nationalist Senator, about the possibility of improving relations between both sections of the community. The discussions, known as the 'Orange–Green talks', did not have any tangible result. As chairman of the Unionist standing committee, he presided at a series of crucial meetings which preceded the resignation of Terence O'Neill from the premiership. He was a member of the party delegation which made clear to Secretary of State James Prior in 1982 its opposition to 'rolling devolution'.

CLOSE, SEAMUS
Alliance Assembly member for S. Antrim, 1982–6. Served on committees on Economic Development, and Finance and Personnel. b. 1948. Lisburn Council, 1973–. Chairman, Alliance Party, 1981, and economic spokesman, 1982–. Member of Alliance deputation at the Atkins conference, 1980. Unsuccessfully fought the Fermanagh–S. Tyrone by-election, August 1981, and the 1983 and 1987 elections in Lagan Valley. In 1986 he was among Alliance councillors who initiated a High Court challenge against the anti-AIA Unionist adjournment policy in councils. Contender for Alliance leadership in 1987.

COALISLAND
A village a few miles from Dungannon, Co. Tyrone, with a mainly Catholic population, and suffering heavily from unemployment, from which the first civil rights march set off for Dungannon on 24 August 1968. The Scarman tribunal mentioned in its

report that it had been told that 400 men were without employment out of a total population of 3,000. 'It is not without significance,' said Scarman, 'that the first of the events of the 1968–9 sequence of disturbances began in this little place.'

COLLINS, JAMES GERARD (GERRY)

Justice Minister of Irish Republic, March 1987–. b. 1938. BA (UCD). Former school teacher, he succeeded his father James as TD for W. Limerick in 1967. First became familiar with cross-border security problems as Justice Minister, 1977–81. As Foreign Minister in short-lived Fianna Fáil administration in 1982, he was strongly critical of British policy on NI. He protested that his Government had not been consulted about James Prior's 'rolling devolution' scheme, which, he said, had no Anglo-Irish dimension and represented a retreat from power-sharing. As Justice Minister since 1987, he has regularly attended AIA conference meetings and was prominent in the varied security discussions which raised intense controversy in late 1987 and early 1988. Minister for Posts and Telegraphs, 1970–3. Council of Europe, 1973–.

COLNBROOK, LORD

As Humphrey Atkins, Secretary of State for NI, May 1979–September 1981. b. 12 August 1922. After service in Royal Navy, 1940–8, he developed an interest in politics, and became Conservative MP for Merton and Morden, 1955–70, and Spelthorne, 1970–. He was Parliamentary Private Secretary to Civil Lord of the Admiralty, 1959–62, and Honorary Secretary of the Conservative Defence Committee, 1965–7. From 1967 to 1979 he served either as an opposition or Government Whip, and was Government Chief Whip, 1973–4. He was

the third former Conservative Chief Whip to become NI Secretary of State, the others being William Whitelaw and Francis Pym. His appointment as NI Secretary was one of the few surprises in Margaret Thatcher's first Cabinet. It became necessary because of the assassination of the party's NI spokesman, Airey Neave. Like Neave, he was a very close adviser of the new PM. The upsurge of PIRA violence in August 1979 led to his policy of increasing RUC strength by 1,000. His most severe test came with the Republican hunger strikes in 1980 and 1981 – the latter resulting in the deaths of ten prisoners, including Bobby Sands MP. He reflected Thatcher's uncompromising opposition to the protest, which was still under way when he left office. He tried two unsuccessful political initiatives. The first was a Constitutional Conference at Stormont, January–March 1980, attended by the DUP, SDLP and Alliance. The Official Unionists boycotted it. And in 1981 he proposed a fifty-member Advisory Council which would consist of nominated members. On leaving NI he became deputy Foreign Secretary, but he resigned along with the Foreign Secretary at the start of the Falklands crisis in 1982. He was knighted in 1983 and created life peer in 1987.

COLVILLE, LORD (OF CULROSS)

Conservative peer appointed by Home Secretary Douglas Hurd to independently review emergency legislation. QC. b. 1933. Lord Colville, who visits NI periodically, had some of his recommendations included in the new PTA brought forward in 1988. The Government accepted that the legislation, formerly limited to five years, should have greater permanence, but it rejected his idea of dropping annual renewal by Parliament. It also failed to adopt his proposal that exclusion orders should be replaced by tighter immigration procedures. This change, Lord Colville argued, would be 'more acceptable than a system of internal exile'. When the European Court of Human Rights ruled in 1988 against seven-day detention under the PTA, he opposed calls for a special tribunal to consider such cases. He said this would raise expectations that reasons for detention would be made public when this could not be done.

COMMISSIONER OF COMPLAINTS
The officer who deals with complaints of maladministration against local authorities and public bodies. First created in 1969. (*See* Hayes, Maurice N.)

COMMITTEE ON THE ADMINISTRATION OF JUSTICE
Broadly based group formed in 1980 to monitor the administration of justice. Has issued frequent comments on legal developments and was particularly critical of the supergrass system. Its chairman, Stephen McBride, in 1988 deplored 'the efforts of sectarian supporters of violence to hi-jack the mantle of successors to the civil rights movement'.

COMMON MARKET *see* European Community

COMMON MARKET REFERENDUM
In the Common Market poll in June 1975 NI recorded a narrow majority in favour of remaining in the EC. The result was a surprise, since there had been a strong lobby against membership, involving a large section of unionism, including MPs like Enoch Powell and the Rev. Ian Paisley. The Northern Ireland Committee of the Irish Congress of Trade Unions had also campaigned against membership. The turnout of 48.2 per cent of the

1,030,534 electors was low by local standards. The figures were:

YES	259,251	52.1 per cent
NO	237,911	47.9 per cent
YES MAJORITY	21,340	4.2 per cent

COMMUNIST PARTY OF IRELAND
The party was originally founded on an all-Ireland basis in 1933, but it split during World War II into the Communist Party of Northern Ireland, and the Irish Workers' Party in the South. In 1970 the party was reunited at a Belfast conference, with separate area committees North and South. The NI executive members at the time of the merger were: Andrew Barr, Hugh Moore, James Graham, Brian Graham, Edwina Stewart, James Stewart, Betty Sinclair, Hugh Murphy, Sean Morrissey, and Bill Somerset. Barr and Graham were leading trade unionists, and Sinclair secretary of Belfast trade-union council and first secretary of NICRA, of which Edwina Stewart later became secretary. Membership of the CPI at the time of the merger was probably between 400 and 500. The CPI has taken the line that there must be a declaration of independence by the whole of Ireland and that 'it is not in the interests of the Irish people to be part of the monopoly capitalist system'. In 1975 the party called on all paramilitary groups to order a cease-fire, and it also urged the withdrawal to barracks of British troops. No Communist candidate has been returned in any Stormont election, although candidates have stood in Belfast on several occasions. In the 1982 Assembly election two CPI candidates appeared in S. Antrim and S. Belfast; they polled about 400 votes between them and lost their deposits. The Communists have been credited, by

some writers, with exercising a large background influence in the Troubles but there is evidence that party members in London, Belfast and Dublin have often been at odds on the NI situation. External broadcasts from Communist countries, notably the USSR, China and Albania, have frequently attacked British policy in Ireland, but Russian authorities have always rejected suggestions that they have supplied arms to the PIRA. In March 1987 CPI had a visit from a member of the Soviet International Department, and later that year rejected suggestions that the Workers' Party was being given more attention in Moscow than the CPI. *Pravda* had mentioned a WP speech at the seventieth anniversary of the October revolution, while ignoring the CPI. The party has been generally critical of the operation of the AIA. In 1988 it put forward a development plan for W. Belfast.

COMPTON REPORT

The report of the committee set up to investigate allegations that men being interrogated after their arrest on 9 August 1971 – the date of the introduction of internment without trial – had been subjected to brutal treatment. The inquiry was conducted by Sir Edmund Compton, Edgar Fay QC, Recorder of Plymouth, and Dr Ronald Gibson, former chairman of the BMA Council. The commission, in its report issued in November 1971, found that there had been physical ill-treatment of detainees, but it dismissed charges of brutality. The methods which had been investigated were hooding, exposure to continuous noise, standing against a wall leaning on fingertips, and deprivation of food and sleep. Apart from one man, the detainees involved refused to give evidence, on the grounds that the commission was sitting in private, and that there would be no opportunity to

cross-examine official witnesses. The report was widely criticised both in Britain and in NI, and Home Secretary Reginald Maudling announced a new inquiry, under Lord Parker, to consider whether interrogation methods should be changed. Most of the cases before the Compton inquiry eventually went to the European Court of Human Rights.

CONATY, THOMAS (TOM)
Chairman of the Central Citizens' Defence Committee (based on Falls Road, Belfast), 1969–74. b. 1930. In 1969, while serving as an ordinary member of the CCDC, he flew to London with a deputation for talks with Home Secretary James Callaghan about plans to protect Catholic areas if the barricades were taken down. He also served on the Peace Committee, a short-lived Government-sponsored body set up in 1969. In 1970 he was highly critical of the army curfew imposed over two days on an area of the Falls Road, and in 1971 he was a leading opponent of internment without trial. His decision to join the Secretary of State's Advisory Commission after direct rule was attacked by Republicans, some of whom demonstrated at his home. In 1974 he issued a strong appeal to the PIRA to call off its campaign of violence. He also called on the Republic to provide a guarantee that it would defend NI Catholics in the event of a doomsday situation. In 1975 he stood unsuccessfully in W. Belfast in the Convention election on the platform that existing public representatives did not accurately reflect the priorities of the Catholic people.

CONCANNON, JOHN DENNIS (DON)
Minister of State, NIO, 1976–9. b. 16 May 1930. After period as branch official of National Union of Mine-

workers, became Labour MP for Mansfield, 1966–87. Labour Whip, 1968–74. Parliamentary Under-Secretary, NIO, 1974–6. As Minister of State, NI, he was responsible for Commerce and Manpower Services. Also acted as deputy Secretary of State. Active in seeking new industrial investment, notably through trips to US, Germany and Scandinavia. When he left NIO with defeat of the Labour Government in May 1979, he was longest-serving Minister ever in NIO – over five years. (Later, Nicholas Scott set new record.) Gave strong backing to Conservative Government during H-Block hunger strikes, 1981, and also encouraged 'rolling devolution' initiative in 1982, although pressing for larger Irish dimension. At the 1982 party conference he was critical of a decision to call for a ban on the use of plastic bullets throughout the UK. He dropped out of politics at the 1987 election because of injuries suffered in a road accident. His support of the breakaway Union of Democratic Mine-workers had already led to conflict with NUM-sponsored colleagues.

CONN, SHENA E.
OUP Assembly, 1973–4, and Convention, 1975–6, member for Londonderry. b. Belfast. BDS (QUB).

CONSERVATIVE PARTY, BRITISH
The British Conservative Party has greatly altered its attitude to NI affairs since 1969. In earlier years the OUP was considered an integral part of the Conservative Party. The link went back to the Home Rule controversies of the nineteenth century when Conservatives aligned themselves with the Unionists against the Liberals and Home Rule. Edward Heath's attitude was decisive in bringing about a change. He veered away from positive defence of the Union above all else, and infuriated Unionists with his suspension of the Stormont Parliament in 1972. The break became all but complete when Heath supported the Sunningdale Agreement and the great majority in the OUP came out against power-sharing. After the February 1974 election, Unionist MPs were not offered the Conservative Whip and they adopted a neutral stance in Parliament. In 1977 OUP MPs used their bargaining power to secure support from the Labour Government for extra NI MPs. Meantime, the Conservatives moved close to Unionist policy by urging that priority should be given to local government reform. Clearly, Margaret Thatcher was initially more appealing to Unionists as Conservative leader than Edward Heath – her frequent references to support for maintenance of the Union were particularly acceptable to Unionists, but the SDLP became highly suspicious of Conservative intentions. In its 1979 election manifesto, the Conservative Party suggested a regional council or councils in the absence of devolved government. But this approach was quickly dropped as first Humphrey Atkins and then James Prior tried to get devolved government established. The right wing of the party strongly opposed Prior's Assembly plan in 1982. In April 1983 the OUP executive voted narrowly to seek restoration of its links with the Conservative Party. The Unionists clearly had in mind the possibility of Tory backing for the return of majority government at Stormont. The Conservative 1983 election manifesto, however, said NI would continue to be offered devolution through the Assembly, but only on the basis of cross-community support. The manifesto also urged a practical working relationship with the Republic without threatening in any way the majority community in NI. But when the AIA was signed in 1985, only a small group of Tory MPs rallied to the

support of the Unionists, and only one Government Minister, Ian Gow, felt strongly enough to resign his post. The firmness of the party in support of the AIA was very welcome, however, to the SDLP and the Irish Government. Serious division seemed to be confined to the Young Tories, whose 1987 conference showed 300 delegates, or 40 per cent, critical of the AIA. In April 1987 Norman Tebbit, then party chairman, disappointed the CEC by turning down the idea of the party organising in NI. In 1988 this refusal was endorsed by the party's National Union, when a 'model' Conservative association set up in N. Down applied for affiliation. Conservative party chairman Peter Brooke, who has family links with the Brookes of Colebrook, also gave his support to the refusal.

CONSTITUTIONAL CONFERENCE
A conference organised by Secretary of State Humphrey Atkins and held at Parliament Buildings, Stormont, between January and March 1980. All four main parties were invited, but the OUP declined the invitation. The DUP, SDLP and Alliance delegates met privately under the chairmanship of the Secretary of State. They agreed that there should be devolved government, but while the SDLP and Alliance maintained their position that there should be power-sharing government, the DUP stuck to its demand for majority rule, although it conceded that the minority should have a 'meaningful role'. From outside the conference, the OUP also supported majority government, with no entrenched powers or privileges for any group. The three parties in the conference were against local government reform without devolved government, and in this they differed from the OUP, who believed that such reform should be pursued in the absence of devolved government – a move to invoke the

Government's general election pledge. Since the conference did not deal with security or relations with the Republic, these matters were examined in a parallel conference. With the conference failing to point to any agreed solution, Atkins, in July 1980, put forward fresh options for study. One involved an executive made up of parties achieving a certain measure of popular support and in proportion to their strength. Another envisaged a majority cabinet balanced by an assembly council which would include opposition parties. Again, there was no common ground, and a further proposal by Atkins for an advisory council composed of already-elected representatives was quickly abandoned in 1981.

CONSTITUTIONAL CONVENTION
The elected Convention of NI parties established by the British Government in 1975 to consider, as the Government White Paper put it, 'What provision for the government of Northern Ireland is likely to command the most widespread acceptance throughout the community there?' It comprised seventy-eight members elected by PR on the same basis as the former Assembly, which had been abolished when the power-sharing Executive fell in 1974. (See Election Results section, pp. 325–9.) The Convention chairman was Sir Robert Lowry, Lord Chief Justice of NI (now Lord Lowry), and he had two special advisers, Dr John A. Oliver and Maurice N. Hayes. The Clerk of the Convention was Ronald Blackburn. The fact that forty-seven of the Convention seats were held by supporters of the UUUC indicated that agreement would prove elusive. They were committed to the rejection of power-sharing on the 1973 model. At the same time, the parties of the former Executive – SDLP, Alliance and UPNI – still pressed for partnership. Although

the public debates simply underlined these facts, an elaborate programme of inter-party discussions was mounted. The UUUC made it clear that they wanted restoration to a new devolved government of the powers conferred on Stormont by the original 1920 Act, including law-and-order powers. They also saw minority participation in Government as something which would be achieved by inclusion in departmental committees rather than the Cabinet. This approach was firmly opposed by the power-sharing parties. The Vanguard Unionist leader William Craig MP made an attempt to break the deadlock by suggesting a voluntary coalition during the emergency – he used the analogy of a wartime coalition at Westminster – but he got no support from his coalition partners and very little within his own party, which split on the issue. Westminster refused to accept the majority report of the Convention as meeting the criteria of the White Paper. But Secretary of State Merlyn Rees MP recalled the Convention for a further month at the start of 1976 to allow it to think again. He also told the Convention that the Government would not agree to extra NI seats at Westminster until a local political settlement had been reached (this attitude was reversed by the Labour Government in 1977). The Government also held that a formal Council of Ireland was not essential to cross-border co-operation, and that any transfer of law-and-order powers from Westminster (excluding judicial appointments and control of courts) would have to be gradual. The Convention ended its sittings in March 1976, without finding any agreement acceptable to Westminster.

COOK, DAVID
Deputy leader of Alliance Party, 1980–4. Assembly member for S. Belfast, 1982–6. Served on committees on Environment and Security. b. 1944. Lord Mayor of Belfast, 1978–9, and first non-Unionist to hold that office. His election as Lord Mayor was a major political surprise and arose because two UPNI councillors opposed the outgoing OUP Lord Mayor James Stewart, and gave Cook a two-vote margin. Leader of Alliance group in Belfast City Council, 1973–80, but lost council seat in 1985. Unsuccessfully contested S. Belfast in the 1974, 1983 and 1987 general elections, and in the 1982 and 1986 by-elections. Lost deposit in 1984 European election. Stood down in 1984 as party deputy leader so as to devote more time to his business as a solicitor. Involved in court action against Unionist adjournment policy in Belfast City Council directed against AIA. Chairman, NICVA.

COONEY, PATRICK MARK
Minister for Justice, Irish Republic, 1973–7, and Defence Minister 1982–6. b. 2 March 1931. BA, LLB (UCD). Solicitor. Cooney was a Fine Gael member of the Dáil, 1970–7, when he lost his seat and was elected to the Senate, where he was Fine Gael leader, 1977–81. As Justice Minister in the Cosgrave administration, he took a strong stand against the IRA, and strengthened cross-border security co-operation, notably by improving communications between the Gardaí and the RUC. He also negotiated with the British Government the reciprocal legislation to enable a person accused of terrorism to be brought to trial on whichever side of the border he was arrested and after the assassination of the British Ambassador to Dublin in 1976, he introduced the power to hold without charge for seven days. He was an unsuccessful candidate in the European election of June 1979. In 1988 he urged the internment of terrorist suspects on both sides of the border.

COOPER, SIR FRANK

Permanent Under-Secretary, NIO, 1973–6. b. 2 December 1922. Head of the civil service in the NIO during a critical period, which extended from the Sunningdale conference through the five-month life of the NI Executive, the loyalist strike of 1974, and over the period of the Convention. He worked under three Secretaries of State – Whitelaw, Pym and Rees. He was no desk-bound administrator, and through a great variety of political and other contacts was usually aware of the smallest intrigue. He knew in advance of the talks at Feakle, Co. Clare, between leading Churchmen and PIRA. In 1976 he moved to the Defence Ministry as Permanent Secretary. When he retired in 1982, he talked of 'organising' the people who had talked to PSF. He also said he did not expect a NI solution for a long time, and commented that the British and the loyalists had never understood each other.

COOPER, IVAN AVERILL

Minister of Community Relations in NI Executive, 1974, SDLP Assembly member, 1973–4, and Convention member, 1975–6, for Mid-Ulster. b. Killaloo, Co. Londonderry, 1944. First experience in politics as a Young Unionist; member NILP, 1965–8; prominent in civil rights movement from earliest days, and president of the Derry Citizens' Action Committee, 1968–9. MP for Mid-Derry at Stormont, 1969–72: Independent until 1970, then SDLP, of which he was a founder member. Unsuccessfully contested Mid-Ulster in both the February and October 1974 Westminster elections.

COOPER, ROBERT GEORGE (BOB)

Head of the Department of Manpower Services in the NI Executive, 1974.

b. Donegal, 24 June 1936. LLB (QUB). Gave up his job in industrial relations to become Alliance Party's first full-time general secretary, and later deputy leader. Elected from W. Belfast to Assembly, 1973–4, and Constitutional Convention, 1975–6. Head of the FEA, set up to investigate allegations of political and religious discrimination in employment, 1976–. In 1987 and 1988 he strongly defended the FEA against a variety of charges, and welcomed the Government's proposals for tougher anti-discrimination laws. In the US he was active in countering the campaign for the rival MacBride Principles. In 1988 he answered Unionists who alleged that the FEA was only interested in anti-Catholic discrimination by saying that the important fact was that Catholics were still two and a half times as likely to be unemployed as Protestants.

CO-OPERATION NORTH

An organisation based in Dublin and aimed at fostering friendship and co-operation with NI. Launched in June 1978 with the support of a large number of voluntary bodies, trade unions, commercial companies, professional organisations and State-sponsored companies. Dr T. K. Whitaker, an Ulsterman who was largely responsible for organising the historic Stormont meeting between Sean Lemass and Terence O'Neill in 1965, presided at the inaugural meeting. The organisation has steadily expanded its activities, notably in promoting North–South sporting events and in working through schools.

CORRIGAN-MAGUIRE, MAIREAD

As Mairead Corrigan, one of the three founders of the Peace People, she was joint recipient, with Betty Williams, of the Nobel Peace Prize for 1976. b. 1944. Aunt of the three Maguire children whose deaths, when they were struck by a gunman's getaway car in W. Belfast, led to the formation of the PP. In September 1981 she married Jackie Maguire, husband of her sister Anne, who 'died of heartbreak' in a suicide in 1980, when she was said to have been seriously depressed by the death of her children and the continuing violence. Has travelled widely in the US and in Europe to advance the movement, and in 1978 she had a brief meeting with President Carter, who later sent her a personal message wishing the movement well. She disclosed in 1977 that she had almost joined the PIRA in 1973 because of the behaviour of troops in W. Belfast. She became chairwoman of the PP in 1980, when it was affected by internal rows, but in 1981 she returned to the role of an executive member. In 1986, when the movement was said to have 200 members, she said in a TV programme that the split had occurred because the German support organisation planned to provide money on condition that they avoided controversy, and they could not do that.

CORRYMEELA

The community centre at Ballycastle, Co. Antrim, set up in 1965 to promote reconciliation by bringing together people of differing backgrounds from both sides of the community. The project was the idea of Rev. Ray Davey as Presbyterian chaplain at QUB, and it now has a complex of buildings on an eight-acre site. In April 1966 PM Terence O'Neill caught attention when he spoke about the need for better community relations to an audience of about fifty leading Protestants and Catholics.

COSGRAVE, LIAM

Taoiseach of the Irish Republic, 1973–7. b. 13 April 1920. Son of William T. Cosgrave, former Taoiseach of Irish Free State. TD, 1943–81. Leader of

Fine Gael, 1965–77. Cosgrave's ministerial career began as a Parliamentary Secretary in the Inter-Party Government of 1948–51, which took the Republic out of the Commonwealth, and he was Minister for External Affairs, 1954–7. Chairman of Council of Ministers, Council of Europe, 1955. Chairman, first Irish delegation, UN General Assembly, 1956. His most crucial involvement with NI affairs was as head of the Irish Government delegation at the Sunningdale Conference in December 1973. His comments afterwards suggested that he believed that this get-together of British and Irish Ministers and representatives of the pro-power-sharing parties in NI would provide the basis for a permanent settlement. He was personally acquainted with the Chief Executive designate of the NI Executive, Brian Faulkner, both as a politician and a lover of horses and hunting. And while Cosgrave did not concede that there was any need for amendment of the Republic's Constitution (unlike some of his Ministers, particularly Garret FitzGerald and Conor Cruise O'Brien), he did agree to the clause in the Sunningdale Agreement which stated that there could be no change in the status of NI unless the people there desired it. Although Britain would have preferred the Republic to agree to straight extradition of suspected terrorists who had entered the Republic, a compromise was reached, with the joint legislation providing that such a person could be tried on whichever side of the border he was arrested. And broadly, the Cosgrave Government's security policies were welcomed by Britain. Cosgrave pressed for British initiatives to secure partnership government in NI, and what he regarded as fair representation of the minority in NI in the new directly elected European Parliament. His proposal that there should be

three NI seats filled on the PR system
was eventually adopted by
Westminster.

COSTELLO, SEAMUS

Leader and founder of the Irish
Republican Socialist Party until he was
shot dead in Dublin in October 1977.
b. Bray, Co. Wicklow, 1939. Active in
his early years in the Republican movement, he was the leader, according to J.
Bowyer Bell, in his history of the IRA,
The Secret Army, of an IRA flying
column which was active in NI during
the 1956 campaign. He was said to
have been responsible for burning
down the courthouse in Magherafelt,
Co. Derry. During the campaign, he
was interned at the Curragh for two
years. He opposed the OIRA ceasefire in
1972, and after his expulsion from the
IRA, he established the IRSP. From 1967
he had been active in council politics in
Co. Wicklow. In 1975, during the feud
between the Official Republicans and
the IRSP, he survived an assassination
bid in Waterford. In 1977 both the
PIRA and OIRA denied that they had
been responsible for his murder. In
1982 INLA accused OIRA of carrying it
out. It was the first assassination of a
party leader in the history of the
Republic.

COULTER, JEAN

OUP Assembly member for W. Belfast,
1973–4, and Convention member for
the same constituency, 1975–6.

COUNCIL FOR THE UNION *see*
Molyneaux, James

COUSLEY, CECIL JAMES

DUP Assembly member for N. Antrim,
1982–6. Served on Agriculture
Committee. Ballymoney Borough
Council, 1981–. b. 1932. One of
several DUP councillors to resign the
Whip in the wake of the James Allister
resignation in 1987. Farmer.

CRAIG, WILLIAM

MP for E. Belfast at Westminster,
February 1974–9. b. 2 December
1924. One of Northern Ireland's most
controversial politicians, he began as
an orthodox Official Unionist, notably
active in the Young Unionist movement. He became MP for Larne in 1960,
and as Government Chief Whip,
1962–3, had a key role in the choice of
Captain Terence O'Neill as PM in
1963. He became Minister of Home
Affairs in the O'Neill Government, and
then Minister of Health and Local
Government in July 1964. When
O'Neill set up a new Ministry of
Development to look after local
government reform and establishment
of the new city of Craigavon in 1965,
Craig took charge of it. He returned to
the post of Minister of Home Affairs in
October 1966. He became the centre of
intense controversy in October 1968,
when he restricted a civil rights march
in Duke Street, Londonderry – a march
which went ahead on 5 October and
led to a bitter clash between police and
civil rights supporters, who included
several Westminster and Stormont
MPs, among them Gerry Fitt MP and
Eddie McAteer, then leader of the
Nationalist Party. Batons and water
cannon were used by the RUC, and the
scenes transmitted on TV focused world
attention on the NI situation. Craig was
sharply attacked by anti-Unionists on
all sides but he defended himself
vigorously. He denied police brutality
and claimed that the IRA had been
involved in the Derry march. He also
accused the British Government of
bringing pressure on the NI
Government to introduce reforms. He
said there had been financial pressure
which amounted to blackmail. In
December 1968 Captain O'Neill
sacked Craig from the Cabinet. He said
Craig had been attracted by ideas of a
UDI nature and a 'go it alone' NI was a
delusion. Craig now hit out strongly at

O'Neill's tactics, and as a backbencher was a steady critic of what he regarded as the 'appeasement' of the enemies of unionism. He also assailed the security policies of Westminster and of the Chichester-Clark and Faulkner Governments. The disbandment of B Specials he considered to be one of the major blunders in this field. Although he was frequently at odds with the Rev. Ian Paisley, they often came together on loyalist platforms. He headed the Ulster Loyalist Association from 1969 to 1972, and on various occasions mentioned that force might have to be used to achieve 'normality'. He led the Unionist pressure group, Ulster Vanguard, which was in the forefront of the opposition to the Heath Government's suspension of Stormont and intro-duction of direct rule in 1972. It helped organise a forty-eight hour loyalist strike against the move. At that period, Craig became familiar as the leading speaker at massive rallies. One of these was held at Parliament Buildings to coincide with the last sitting of the local Parliament and Brian Faulkner, as PM, appeared on the balcony beside Craig – much to Faulkner's embarrassment, it emerged later. In the Assembly election in 1973 he was returned in N. Antrim, some 6,000 votes behind the Rev. Ian Paisley. He forcefully attacked the Sunningdale Agreement, and the power-sharing Executive, and con-verted Vanguard into a full political party (VUPP). In February 1974 he won the E. Belfast seat at Westminster, and with the other two leaders of what had now become the UUUC – the Rev. Ian Paisley and Harry West – he was among the top planners of the May 1974 loyalist strike which brought down the three-party Executive. In the October 1974 Westminster election he strengthened his hold on E. Belfast – his majority was up about 10,000. He headed the poll in E. Belfast in the

Convention election in 1975. In the Convention he caused a major surprise by advocating the idea of a voluntary coalition, including the SDLP, for a limited period. He claimed that this was not power-sharing, which he had attacked in the Assembly. But he got no support from his coalition partners – the OUP and the DUP – and the majority of his own party deserted him on the issue. The breakaway group, under the leadership of Ernest Baird, now called themselves the United Ulster Unionist Movement. When Paisley and Baird backed the loyalist strike in May 1977, Craig stood aside. In 1977 he was appointed to the Council of Europe on the nomination of the British Govern-ment, and as a member of the legal committee he was appointed by the council to report on human rights legislation in Europe – an assignment which was criticised by some of those associated with the original civil rights campaign. Then, in February 1978, the VUPP ceased to exist as a political party. It reverted to the title Ulster Vanguard, as a pressure group, and Craig remained at its head. In more than one sense his career had turned full circle. But in the general election of May 1979, when he stood as OUP, he lost E. Belfast to the DUP by sixty-four votes. Six months after the election, he was threatening to resign from the OUP because of its refusal to attend the Atkins conference, and in 1980 there were hints that Vanguard might reappear as a political party. In July 1981 he urged that James Callaghan's plea for an independent NI should be carefully examined, and soon afterwards he criticised the OUP for failing to respond to Dr Garret FitzGerald's constitutional 'crusade' which he described as 'very significant'. In November 1981 he had talks in Dublin with Dr FitzGerald who, he believed, wanted to be helpful. And the next month he called for a decision to take NI out of the UK by 1983 if the

Convention report was not implemented. But the 1982 Assembly election showed that his power-base in E. Belfast had all but vanished and he failed to secure election. He stood as a Vanguard Unionist. In 1985, on the eve of the AIA, he warned Unionists that Margaret Thatcher was 'sailing close to a policy of condominium'. But he opposed abstention from Westminster by Unionists in face of the agreement. In 1987 he suggested that force would be used ultimately to end the AIA.

CRAIGAVON

The new city in Co. Armagh which embraces the two old-established boroughs of Lurgan and Portadown, both of which have suffered seriously in the PIRA bombing campaign. The Craigavon project was the focus of sharp controversy when it was launched by the O'Neill Government in the early 1960s, with a population target of 100,000 by 1981. The opposition parties accused the Government of neglecting W. Ulster, and especially Londonderry, and providing a new centre for incoming industry at Craigavon, with its mainly Protestant population. In the event it proved difficult to persuade people to move from Greater Belfast to the new city, despite special grants for new occupiers of public authority and private housing. Apart from bombing in the shopping streets, the area has had many attacks on members of the security forces and sectarian assassinations. In July 1979 a plan to have a twinning scheme between Craigavon and Santa Rosa, California, was abandoned after protests by Irish-American groups, including the Irish National Caucus. In the 1981 H-Block hunger strike tension was high in the Lurgan area and there was a row over Republican attempts to rename streets after hunger-strikers. At the end of 1982 three policemen were killed by a

booby-trap landmine near Lurgan, and soon afterwards a row developed over the shooting dead by the RUC of three PIRA members who were said to have driven through a checkpoint. In the 1980s the council was accused by the FEA of anti-Catholic bias. In March–April 1986 there were serious clashes in Portadown between loyalists and RUC after the banning of an Apprentice Boys' parade. A Protestant, Keith White, was fatally wounded by a plastic bullet. OUP and DUP councillors were among the most determined in obstructing council business as a protest against the AIA.

CREASEY, LIEUTENANT-GENERAL SIR TIMOTHY

Army GOC, NI, November 1977–9. b. 1923. After wartime service with Indian troops, he joined the Royal Norfolk Regiment in 1947. His later career included a period as Military Secretary to the Defence Ministry in 1967–8. He acquired special expertise in anti-guerilla operations as commander of the Sultan's forces in Oman, 1972–5. He was Director of Infantry, 1975–7. In December 1977 he commented that the PIRA was being 'suppressed, contained and isolated'. In August 1979 he drew criticism from both Unionists and the SDLP when he called in at the Falls Road, Belfast, shop of PSF with an army patrol. In a BBC programme in January 1980 he said they were faced in NI with an organised revolutionary force of some 500 hardcore terrorists. But he did not subscribe to the view that they could not be defeated – 'given the national will' and using all the resources of a modern state.

CROSSMAGLEN

The S. Armagh village regarded as one of the main strongholds of the PIRA. With a population of about 1,000, and situated six kilometres from the border, it has taken on a legendary quality for Republicans, and is more widely identified as defying authority through the lines, 'From Carrick-macross to Crossmaglen, there are more rogues than honest men.' To natives, it is known simply as 'The Cross'. The area has a long history of support for the Republican cause, and more than thirty British soldiers were killed by local PIRA units in the three years after internment, mainly through culvert bombs and booby traps on the twisting roads which criss-cross the border. There have been several attacks on the RUC and the army post, and the use by the army of part of the Gaelic football pitch as a helicopter landing pad has particularly angered villagers. In August 1979 Margaret Thatcher visited the army base during a border tour following the Mountbatten and Warrenpoint killings. In the same year a memorial to dead Republicans was unveiled in the village and attracted protests from Unionists. On a visit to Crossmaglen in March 1981 Cardinal Ó Fiaich urged PIRA to end violence.

CUBBON, SIR BRIAN CROSSLAND

Permanent Secretary, NIO, 1976–9. b. 9 April 1928. Sir Brian first became familiar with NI problems as Private Secretary to Home Secretary James Callaghan in 1968–9. Soon after taking up his Stormont post, he narrowly escaped death when he was travelling in the same car as the British ambassador to Dublin *en route* to the embassy, when it was blown up by a landmine and the Ambassador and a woman civil servant were killed. Before going to Stormont, he had been deputy Secretary at the Home Office and earlier deputy Secretary to the Cabinet.

CUMANN NA MBAN

The women's section of the IRA, which has always had a significant part in IRA

activities. It is illegal in both NI and the Republic. In the PIRA campaign its members have been used as couriers for the gathering of intelligence, reporting on the movements of army and police, and in finding shelter for PIRA men. Women have also had a role in the placing of fire bombs, particularly during 1977. The exact strength of the section is uncertain, since it has always relied on the support of sympathisers and relatives of PIRA activists.

CUNNINGHAM, LIEUTENANT-COLONEL JAMES GLENCAIRN

Patron of Ulster Unionist Council, governing body of OUP, since 1979 after five years as president. b. 1904. Served in World War II with 8th (Belfast) Regiment, HAA, and with 14th Army in Burma. NI Senate, 1958–72.

CUNNINGHAM, JOSIAS

Chairman of the executive of the OUP, 1976–9. b. 20 January 1934. MA (Cantab.) Member of a family long associated with Ulster unionism, and chairman of S. Antrim Unionist Association, 1974. Irish deputy grand master in Orange Order. Chairman of the Belfast unit of the Stock Exchange.

CURRIE, AUSTIN

SDLP Assembly member for Fermanagh–S. Tyrone, 1982–6. Head of the department of housing, planning and local government in the power-sharing Executive, 1974. b. Coalisland, Co. Tyrone, 11 October 1939. BA (QUB). Youngest MP ever returned to Stormont when he was elected as Nationalist in 1964 by-election in E. Tyrone (a seat he held until 1972), and he was active, in association with Nationalist leader Eddie McAteer, in a bid to give the Nationalist Party a more progressive image and a stronger organisational base. In June 1968 he was engaged in the first direct action of the civil rights campaign, when he staged a sit-in in a council house at Caledon, Co. Tyrone, as a protest against its allocation to an unmarried Protestant woman. He was a regular speaker at civil rights demonstrations and helped organise the first civil rights march at Dungannon, Co. Tyrone, in August 1968. A founder member of the SDLP, he was returned as a member for Fermanagh–S. Tyrone to both the Assembly, 1973–4, and the Convention, 1975–6. Chief Whip of the SDLP from 1974 to 1979, when he resigned the post to fight Fermanagh–S. Tyrone unsuccessfully as Independent SDLP in the 1979 Westminster election. He was defying a party decision not to contest the seat, but he retained his SDLP membership and was the prospective candidate of the party when it again decided to opt out of the 1981 by-elections in the constituency. SDLP North–South spokesman, 1979–82. In the 1986 by-elections he polled some 12,000 votes in Fermanagh–S. Tyrone – one of the constituencies where the results showed a swing away from PSF. In 1987 he argued for a new power-sharing administration with security powers. During the Troubles, his home has been attacked on some thirty occasions, and his wife was injured in one attack. Participant in Duisburg Talks, October 1988.

CUSHNAHAN, JOHN
Leader of Alliance Party, 1984–7. Party Whip in Assembly, 1982–4. Assembly member for N. Down, 1982–6. b. 1948. B.Ed. (QUB). Alliance general secretary, 1974–82. Belfast City Council, 1977–85. Chairman of 1982 Assembly's Education Committee. Member, Devolution Committee. Unsuccessfully contested Westminster elections: N. Belfast, 1979; N. Down, 1983, 1986 by-election, and 1987. As party leader, developed strong contacts with British Liberals and the Liberal–SDP Alliance.

Also kept lines open to major politicians in Britain, including Thatcher, and to Dublin parties. Under his leadership, Alliance gave general support to AIA and initiated court actions against councils adjourning in protest, but he said at one point that he would have preferred the Government to impose power-sharing rather than the agreement. He stood down as leader in 1987 because he saw little prospect of early devolved government and could not support his family as unpaid party leader. Joined Fine Gael in 1989 and sought party nomination in Munster for European election.

D

DÁIL ULADH
The name given to a proposed new nine-county Ulster parliament, which was promoted energetically by PSF and PIRA during 1972. A council was set up to promote the idea, and among those also associated with it were Frank McManus, then Unity MP for Fermanagh–S. Tyrone, and Patrick Kennedy, Republican Labour MP at Stormont, as well as some members of the NICRA.

DALY, THOMAS
SDLP Assembly, 1973–4, and Convention, 1975–6, member for Fermanagh–S. Tyrone. b. Belleek, Co. Fermanagh, 1938. BA (QUB). Irvinestown Rural District Council, 1963–8. Fermanagh County Council, 1968–73. Fermanagh District Council, 1973–9 (chairman, 1975–9). Joined SDLP from Nationalist Party in 1973, and announced resignation from

public life in February 1979. Brother of Dr Edward Daly, Catholic Bishop of Derry.

DARLINGTON CONFERENCE

A three-day conference on NI affairs held at Darlington, 25–7 September 1972. It was called by William Whitelaw, as Secretary of State, in a bid to find inter-party agreement on a future form of government for NI. It achieved very little, since only three parties agreed to attend – OUP, Alliance and NILP. Four other parties – SDLP, Nationalist, DUP and Republican Labour – rejected the invitation for a variety of reasons, and the politicians who did attend could not agree on the form of a top tier of government.

DAVIS, IVAN

DUP Assembly member for S. Antrim, 1982–6. Served on Education Committee. b. 1937. Lisburn Council, 1973–. Joined OUP in 1987.

DEMOCRATIC UNIONIST PARTY

Founded in September 1971 by the Rev. Ian Paisley and the then MP for Shankill, Desmond Boal (a leading barrister), who had been expelled from the Unionist Parliamentary Party. Boal had been a strong opponent of Terence O'Neill as PM, and his views at that time coincided with Paisley's – the new party, said Boal, would be 'right wing in the sense of being strong on the Constitution, but to the left on social policies'. Boal was the first chairman of the party, which took the place of the Protestant Unionist Party, also led by Paisley. The Protestant Unionist Party's first successes were in the two April 1970 by-elections for the NI Commons. Bannside, seat of Terence O'Neill, was won by Paisley, while the Rev. William Beattie gained the S. Antrim seat from an Official Unionist. In the Assembly elections, when it got eight seats (10.8 per cent of first-

preference votes), it opposed power-sharing with the SDLP, and fought both the 1974 Westminster general elections as part of the UUUC. In both elections Paisley retained the N. Antrim seat which he had won in 1970. The DUP also contested the 1975 Convention elections in co-operation with UUUC partners. It secured twelve seats (14.7 per cent of first-preference votes). Again in the Convention, it publicly rejected power-sharing, and firmly denied suggestions that it had on occasion privately toyed with some form of partnership with the SDLP. Paisley strongly attacked William Craig's proposal for a voluntary coalition, which would have included the SDLP. In 1977 the withdrawal of the Official Unionists from the UUUC over the issue of an action council, which organised the abortive loyalist strike in May 1977, created a new situation for the DUP. Paisley and Official Unionist leaders publicly attacked each other. These exchanges came at the same time as the District Council elections, and undoubtedly robbed the DUP of many OUP second-preference votes. None the less, the DUP, which employed the slogan 'the Unionist Party you can trust' to underline its differences with the Official Unionists, got seventy-four seats (12.7 per cent of first-preference votes). In 1978 the DUP tried to get an agreement with the Official Unionists and the UUUP on how candidates could best be deployed in the coming Westminster election, but the Official Unionists pointed out that they had no control over local associations in the selection of candidates. In the May 1979 Westminster election DUP gained two seats from Official Unionists – E. and N. Belfast – by narrow majorities. The successful candidates were Peter Robinson and John McQuade. Its share of the poll in that election was 10.2 per cent (five seats contested). In the 1979 European election Paisley headed the poll with 29.8 per cent of first-preference votes – a triumph which surprised even the most enthusiastic of DUP supporters. The DUP took a firm anti-EC line, and polled strongly even in Fermanagh–S. Tyrone, Mid-Ulster and Londonderry, areas where it had not been active to any extent in previous elections. Its run of success was maintained in the 1981 council elections, when its 142 seats doubled those of the previous council election, and its 26.6 per cent of the vote was even slightly ahead of OUP. But it ran second to OUP in the 1982 Assembly election, getting twenty-one seats and 23 per cent of first preferences. In contrast to the OUP, it welcomed the first stage of the 1982 Assembly with mainly scrutiny powers, and it also angered the OUP by supporting James Kilfedder as Assembly Speaker and not OUP candidate John Carson. In the 1983 Westminster election, its representation remained at three seats in the redrawn constituencies. It held N. Antrim and E. Belfast; lost N. Belfast and gained Mid-Ulster. It took 20 per cent of the votes, after making a limited agreement with the OUP by which the DUP were not opposed by the OUP in Foyle, while OUP got a clear run on the Unionist side in Fermanagh–S. Tyrone, and Newry and Armagh. In the event, its position was weakened relative to the OUP which got 34 per cent of the votes and eleven seats. In the 1985 council elections DUP fared less well than in 1981. It was now 5 per cent behind OUP in first preferences and had forty-eight fewer seats. The AIA, however, ushered in a period of co-operation with the OUP, Glengall Street, in opposing the agreement. In both the Westminster by-elections of 1986, forced in protest at the AIA, and the 1987 general election, the three DUP seats were secure. But in E. Antrim there was dissatisfaction within the DUP that the inter-Unionist pact

prevented it contesting the local seat, which had been narrowly won by OUP in 1983. The runner-up at that time, James Allister, had been anxious to stand again and when this was denied, he withdrew from politics. Several party officials and councillors also resigned. The party faced a further problem in October 1987, when Peter Robinson MP resigned as deputy leader, apparently because he was not satisfied with anti-AIA tactics or the weight given to the OUP–DUP Task Force report which he had helped to draft as the party representative. But in January 1988 he was back in his old post after the party conference.

DE ROSSA, PROINSIAS

Leader of the Workers' Party, 1988–. b. 1940. TD, Dublin North West, 1982–. Dublin City Council, 1985–. Interned in 1950s as a member of Fianna na hÉireann and the IRA. When questioned in 1988 about repeated allegations of WP links with OIRA, he said no organisation could deny its past but WP had no weapons and no paramilitary links.

DERRY *see* Londonderry/Derry

DERRY CITIZENS' ACTION COMMITTEE

A body established on 9 October 1968 and made up of five local groups which had helped to organise the civil rights march in Duke Street, Londonderry, on 5 October 1968. Ivan Cooper was chairman and John Hume deputy chairman. The first move by the committee was a sit-down in the Diamond, Londonderry, on 19 October, and the committee also sponsored a massive parade from the Waterside across Craigavon Bridge on 2 November 1968, and supported the People's Democracy march from Belfast to Derry in January 1969. They were also concerned with organising patrols in the Bogside after complaints about RUC behaviour there. They took a petition to Downing Street, calling for police and other reforms. (*See also* Londonderry/Derry.)

DERRY CITIZENS' DEFENCE ASSOCIATION

The vigilante group set up in the Bogside area of Derry in July 1969, which took a more militant line than the Derry Citizens' Action Committee. It was involved throughout the period of rioting in August 1969, erecting barricades, mounting patrols, providing first-aid, countering CS-gas attacks, and on 24 August it said it had taken control of administration and security behind the barricades of what became known as 'Free Derry'. (*See also* Londonderry/Derry.)

DEVLIN, BERNADETTE *see* McAliskey, Josephine Bernadette

DEVLIN, PATRICK JOSEPH (PADDY)

SDLP member of NI Executive, 1974, as head of the Department of Health and Social Services. b. Belfast, 8 March 1925. M.Sc. (1981). A highly individualistic politician, he has switched party several times. He was in the Republican movement from 1930 until 1950, and was interned in Belfast Prison, 1942–5. In 1950 he joined the Irish Labour Party, but moved to the NILP in 1958 and was chairman, 1967–8. In 1970 he became a founder member of the SDLP, and was Chief Whip in the Assembly and chairman in the Convention. But in 1977 he was expelled from the SDLP after he had complained that the party was departing from its previous approach, and reducing the socialist content of its policy. Belfast City Council, 1956–8 and 1973–85. MP at Stormont for Falls, 1969–72. Elected to Assembly, 1973–4, and Convention, 1975–6,

from W. Belfast, where he had the largest single vote of any candidate in the 1977 District Council election. He was a founder member of NICRA and was closely involved in dealing with the situation in the Falls Road area in the violence of 1969. When the Convention failed, he joined his then SDLP colleague, John Hume, in private talks with the Rev. Martin Smyth and Captain Austin Ardill of the OUP on a possible political settlement. But the effort was unfruitful. He has had a lifelong association with the trade-union movement, and became full-time district secretary of the Irish Transport and General Workers' Union in 1976, but left the post in 1985 to devote himself to writing. In 1978 he was among a small group who launched the United Labour Party, and he stood unsuccessfully as the party's candidate in the 1979 European election, claiming that he was the only candidate backing a socialist policy on Europe. In the 1981 council election he narrowly retained his Belfast City Council seat in the west of the city, but had to leave his home in that area because of threats from Republican extremists. In 1985 he failed to win a council seat in N. Belfast as a candidate of the LPNI, which he had helped to form. In 1987 he was first vice-chairman of Labour '87, which absorbed the LPNI as well as the NILP. In that year he campaigned against the MacBride Principles in the US. Housing Executive, 1983–6. He has written a book on the fall of the NI power-sharing Executive and one on outdoor relief in Belfast in the inter-war years.

DICKSON, ANNE LETITIA

Leader of UPNI, 1976–81. b. London. Elected as Unionist MP for Carrick in 1969 and strong supporter of Terence O'Neill as Premier. Vice-chairman of Newtownabbey Urban Council, 1967–9. In the Assembly election of

1973 she was elected in S. Antrim without the support of Unionist Party HQ. She supported the power-sharing Executive, and was also elected to the Convention from S. Antrim in 1975. When Brian Faulkner gave up the leadership of UPNI in 1976, she succeeded him as the first woman leader of a NI political party. In 1979 she unsuccessfully contested N. Belfast in the Westminster election. In October 1981 she presided at UPNI's final conference, when it was decided to wind up the party after a series of poor election results. Chairwoman, NI Consumer Council, 1985–.

DIPLOCK REPORT

The report of the commission, headed by Lord Diplock, 1985, which reported in December 1972 that non-jury trials should be introduced for a wide range of terrorist offences. It argued that trials should be held before judges sitting alone, because of the risks of intimidation, for the period of the emergency. The commission also held that there should be easier admissibility of confessions. The proposals were adopted by the Government and the courts became known as Diplock courts, with a High Court judge sitting for the more serious cases, and a County Court judge for the less serious. (*See also* Anglo-Irish Agreement.)

DIRECT RULE *see* Systems of Government section, pp. 371–3

DOBSON, JOHN

Government Chief Whip and leader of the Commons at Stormont, 1969–71. b. Lurgan, 7 May 1929. LLB (TCD). Solicitor. Banbridge Urban District Council, 1961–7. Unionist MP for W. Down, 1965–72. He was one of twelve Unionist MPs who signed a statement in February 1969 saying they would like to see Terence O'Neill replaced as party leader.

DONALDSON, LORD (OF KINGSBRIDGE)

Parliamentary Under-Secretary, NIO, (and spokesman of the NIO in the House of Lords), 1974–6. b. 9 October 1907. A Labour life peer, he took charge of three NI departments – Health and Social Services, Agriculture, and Community Relations – after the fall of the NI Executive in May 1974. He was involved in public controversy mainly because he also had responsibility for prison administration.

DONALDSON, JEFFREY

OUP Assembly member for S. Down, 1985–6. b. 1965. Returned in 1985 by-election before Assembly was wound up. Served briefly on Environment, and Health and Social Services committees. Honorary Secretary, OUP council, 1988–. Unsuccessful contender for OUP nomination for 1989 European election.

DONEGAN, PATRICK SARSFIELD

Defence Minister (Fine Gael) in the coalition Government in the Republic, 1973–7. b. 29 October 1923. TD for Louth, 1954–7 and 1961–77. Senator, 1957–61. As Defence Minister, Donegan took a strong line against the PIRA. In April 1974 he declared that he would be 'tightening up everything' to beat the PIRA, and pointed out that the Republic's security forces had reached the highest point for twenty years. There were 11,257 in the defence forces and 7,500 in the Garda Síochána. Under his direction the patrolling of the border was intensified, principally by the use of planes and light armoured cars. Communications were also strengthened between the security forces on either side of the border, although he resisted any direct army-to-army link-up.

DOOGE, JAMES CLEMENT IGNATIUS

Foreign Minister (Fine Gael) of Republic, 1981–2. Appointed to the Senate in 1981 by the Taoiseach, Dr Garret FitzGerald, he was surprise choice as Foreign Minister in the Fine Gael–Labour Coalition which took office in July 1981. Involved with Dr FitzGerald in negotiations with British Government on setting up of British-Irish Intergovernmental Council, and was at first formal meeting of that council in January 1982, when he had talks with NI Secretary of State James Prior. Was successively Professor of Civil Engineering in UCC and UCD before taking office.

DOUGLAS, WILLIAM ALBERT BOYD

OUP Assembly member for Londonderry, 1982–6. Served on Agriculture, Finance and Personnel, and Security committees. Also served in 1973–4 Assembly and 1975–6 Convention. OUP Whip in 1982 Assembly. b. 1921. Farmer. Flight lieutenant, RAF, during World War II. As Limavady district master of the Orange Order, he was prominent in demonstrations against civil rights meetings in S. Derry in 1969, and in staging loyalist demonstrations in Dungiven, where there were clashes between Orangemen and their opponents on several occasions during 1971. Limavady Rural District Council, 1960–73.

DOWN ORANGE WELFARE

Loyalist paramilitary group based in N. Down and linked with membership of the Orange Order. Formed in 1972, and especially active during the loyalist strike in May 1974, under the leadership of Colonel Brush (d. 1984). Its members were involved in road blocks during the stoppage. The organisation also backed the more limited loyalist strike in May 1977.

DRUMM, MAIRE

Vice-president of PSF, 1972–6, who was shot dead while a patient in the Mater Hospital, Belfast, on 28 October 1976. b. 1920. She was assassinated by two gunmen, dressed as doctors, who burst into the ward. An open verdict was returned at the inquest in 1978, and her husband Jimmy Drumm (also a leading figure in PSF) protested after the inquest that the army had put about suggestions that she had been killed by the PIRA. This was denied by the army. (In 1985 an ex-soldier and former security man at the hospital, who said he was in the UVF, admitted having shown the gunmen the ward in which Maire Drumm was a patient, and he was jailed for life.) Maire Drumm had resigned as vice-president of PSF ten days before her death; she said she had done so strictly for health reasons and supported the leadership. She had been acting president of PSF in 1971–2 when Ruairí Ó Brádaigh was in prison in the Republic. She herself had been to prison several times – the first occasion was in 1970 when she was accused of inciting people to join the PIRA in the Bogside area of Londonderry. In a speech in Belfast in 1975 she spoke of Republicans 'pulling down Belfast stone by stone' in defence of political status for prisoners. This led Secretary of State Merlyn Rees to describe her as 'a Madame Defarge sitting by the guillotine'. Roy Mason, Secretary of State at the time of her death, spoke of her murder as 'savage' and there was a message of sympathy from the UDA. In 1978 all sections of the Provisional Republican movement were represented at a ceremony in Milltown cemetery, Belfast, when a memorial to her was unveiled. She had previously requested that she should be buried outside the Republican plot. Her husband, Jimmy Drumm, continued to serve on the executive of PSF.

DUFFY, PATRICK ALOYISIUS
SDLP Assembly, 1973–4, and
Convention, 1975–6, member for
Mid-Ulster. b. Stewartstown, Co.
Tyrone, 1934. BA, LLB (QUB). Solicitor,
with extensive business interests.
Representative, National Political
Front, 1964. Secretary of the Assembly
of the Northern Irish People, 1971–2.
Cookstown District Council, 1973–.
When the NI Executive collapsed in
1974, he urged a joint British-Irish
administration as 'the only means of
providing a satisfactory form of
government in Northern Ireland'.
Unsuccessfully contested Mid-Ulster in
1979 Westminster election. At the
party's annual conference in November 1980 he said he could support the
five individual demands of the H-Block
hunger strikers, but not the idea of
bringing them together as political
status. He caused some surprise when
he declined to be a candidate in Mid-
Ulster in the 1982 Assembly election.

DUISBURG TALKS
Secret talks in Duisburg, West
Germany, on 14–15 October 1988
between Jack Allen (OUP), Peter
Robinson (DUP), Austin Currie (SDLP)
and Gordon Mawhinney (All.) on the
possibility of inter-party negotiations.
Discussion centred on ways of accom-
modating the Unionist demand that the
workings of the AIA should first be
suspended and the insistence of the
SDLP that there should be no suspension
and that discussions should be held
outside the agreement. Disclosure of
the Duisburg exchanges in early 1989
produced a confused reaction, but
encouraged Secretary of State Tom
King to try to set up formal talks, using
junior Minister Brian Mawhinney as
an intermediary.

DUKAKIS, MICHAEL
Democratic candidate for US
presidency, 1988. b. 3 November

1933. Governor of Massachusetts,
1974–8 and 1982–. Of Greek origin,
he made civil rights for minorities a key
issue of his campaign, and was the first
Governor to sign into law the
MacBride Principles on fair employment in NI. His strong attack on British
policy on NI helped him to secure heavy
Irish-American support in the vital
New York primary, and he visited
Gaelic Park in New York in April 1988
to 'throw in the ball'. He was critical of
extradition of PIRA suspects from US,
and also opposed broadcasting
restrictions imposed by UK in 1988.

DUKES, ALAN
Leader of Fine Gael, March 1987–. b.
Dublin, 1945. MA (UCD). As Minister
for Justice, 1986–7, in the FitzGerald
Government, he was involved in AIA
ministerial meetings, and was disappointed at the refusal of British
Government to agree to three-judge
Diplock courts. But he said the whole
process of the agreement had made the
British authorities more sensitive in
their dealings with the Nationalist
community. In 1987 he questioned
whether the Fianna Fáil Government
was showing enough commitment to
the AIA. In 1981, as TD for Kildare, he
was appointed Agriculture Minister on
his first day in the Dáil, and Finance
Minister, 1982–6. Economist.
Personal adviser in Brussels to EC
Commissioner Richard Burke, 1977–
80. Governor, European Investment
Bank and IMF, 1982–6.

DUNGANNON
The S. Tyrone town, with a population
almost evenly comprised of Protestants
and Catholics, which has figured
heavily in events since 1968. The first
civil rights march was from Coalisland
(a nearby predominantly Catholic
village) to Dungannon on 24 August
1968. One of the points of community
tension in 1968 was the complaint of

Catholics that they were denied their fair share of houses by the Unionist-controlled local council. In August 1969 riots flared in the town in the wake of events in Londonderry. The town has suffered greatly from PIRA bombing campaign, and there have been many attacks on RUC stations in the area, and killings of members of security forces, as well as sectarian murders. In 1988–9 council chairmanship was shared between members from both communities as a gesture of reconciliation.

DUNLEATH, LORD
Active member of the House of Lords and effectively the voice of the Alliance Party at Westminster. b. London, 23 June 1933, son of Baron and Lady Dunleath. Represented N. Down in 1973 and 1982 Assemblies and in the Constitutional Convention, 1975–6. Ards Borough Council, 1977–85. In 1977 successfully sponsored legislation in the House of Lords to provide for shared schools (for Protestant and Catholic pupils), wherever there is sufficient demand from parents. He also brought forward a Bill to bring divorce law in NI broadly into line with that in GB, which led to the Government having similar legislation passed in 1978. Has extensive business interests and is president of the Royal Ulster Agricultural Society. BBC National Governor for NI, 1967–73. Resigned from Alliance Party for a period in 1979–80 to make an unsuccessful bid for NI ITV franchise.

DUNLOP, DOROTHY
OUP Assembly member for E. Belfast, 1982–6. Chairman, Health and Social Services Committee; member, Education and Security committees. BA (QUB). Formerly on staff of BBC talks department in Belfast, and later taught in several Belfast schools and in the prison education service. Belfast City Council, 1975–. Deputy Lord Mayor, 1978–9. In 1987 she was one of five Belfast OUP councillors who lost the party Whip for failing to support the anti-AIA adjournment policy, and later that year she lost her position as chairwoman of E. Belfast Unionist Association. Granddaughter of Sir Robert Woods, one-time Unionist MP at Westminster for TCD.

DUNLOP, JOHN
MP for Mid-Ulster, February 1974–83. Originally Vanguard–UUUC; UUUP, 1977–83. b. 20 May 1910. Has catering business in Moneymore, Co. Londonderry, and sat in Assembly for Vanguard, 1973–4. Joined Rev. Ian Paisley in support of Unionist Action Council strike in May 1977, and split from OUP MPs with the break-up of United Ulster Unionist Coalition in 1977. In the 1979 general election, OUP decided not to oppose him in Mid-Ulster. Unsuccessful candidate in 1982 Assembly election.

DUNLOP, STEWART
DUP Convention member for S. Antrim, 1975–6. b. 1946. Founder member of Protestant Unionist Party and DUP. Antrim District Council, 1973–.

DUNN, JAMES ALEXANDER
Parliamentary Under-Secretary, NIO, 1976–9. b. 30 January 1926. Labour MP, Kirkdale (Liverpool), 1964–81; SDP, 1981–3. A prominent figure in the Merseyside Catholic community and especially active in education and soccer circles. At NIO he had special responsibility for Agriculture, Finance, and overseeing of public bodies. Absent from NIO through illness for most of his last year in office. Commons spokesman for SDP during passage of the 1982 devolution measure, to which he gave general support

DUTCH-NORTHERN IRISH ADVISORY COMMITTEE

This committee, comprising educationists, Churchmen and others in both countries, has sponsored trips to Holland to show how the Netherlands has tackled the problems of religious and other divisions. Delegations of NI politicians to Holland have included an inter-party group in 1973, a further party in 1975, including members of the SDLP, Alliance, NILP and UPNI and a twenty-strong OUP deputation, headed by party leader Harry West. Members of paramilitary groups have attended some of the conferences sponsored by the committee.

E

ECONOMY

Economic activity in NI has traditionally been at a lower level than GB and marked by higher unemployment and lower earnings. Gross Domestic Product in NI lags well behind the UK average but not so seriously in recent years as was at first thought. In 1986 GDP was initially estimated at £6,100 million, or £3,389 per head as against £6,676 in south-east England. NI GDP was thus estimated at 69 per cent of the UK average in 1986, or 10 per cent lower than in 1982. However, the Department of Economic Development later issued corrected figures because of a computer underestimate of 10 to 15 per cent for the period 1983–6. The new 1986 figure may place GDP at 79 to 80 per cent. The decline of manufacturing industry has meant that in 1986 it accounted for only 19 per cent of GDP. Agriculture at 4 per cent was twice the UK average. The public services accounted for 35 per cent of GDP compared with 23 per cent in the

UK. In 1979 the unemployment figure of 12 per cent was exactly twice the national average; in October 1987 it was 20.3 per cent compared with the UK average of 11.1 per cent. In 1987 NI also had the highest number of unemployed out of work for a year or more – 59 per cent compared with the UK average of 47 per cent. NI also had the highest dependence on social security payments which represented 20 per cent of household income. The official publication *Regional Trends* (CSO), showed that average weekly earnings for NI men were £199.40 (GB average £224) in 1987; for women in full-time work the figure was £137.30 (GB average £148). The trade-union movement has questioned the relevance of unemployment statistics because the method of calculation has changed so frequently, making comparisons with the past less reliable. The official total of jobless reached a high point in 1986 at 130,000. The total dropped in 1987 and 1988 to 108,981 (15.7 per cent) at the end of 1988. At the same time nearly 8,000 young people were in full-time Youth Training Programmes and more than 5,000 in the YTP work-scheme, which have the strong backing of the European Social Fund. Apart from the disincentive of the violence, employment has been declining over a long period in traditional industries like shipbuilding and textiles, as well as in farming. In 1977 the extensive attractions for new industry (in financial terms, the highest in the EC) were further improved, and a new independent Economic Council was established under the chairmanship of Sir Charles Carter of Lancaster University to advise the Government on ways of achieving more rapid economic growth. It included four independent members, with five from the CBI and five from the ICTU. In 1982 Secretary of State James Prior further streamlined the Government structure concerned with industry and employment. The Commerce and Manpower departments were merged into a new Department of Economic Development, with an associated Industrial Development Board. The new board was set up at a moment when NI's industrial base was contracting rapidly, after closures or serious cutbacks in several multinationals, such as Courtaulds, British Enkalon and Michelin, and the collapse of the de Lorean car project, which had once raised employment hopes in W. Belfast. In March 1983 Prior announced new measures to help industry, including up to 80 per cent refund of corporation tax and 100 per cent de-rating of industrial premises. Government efforts to attract outside investment were increased in the mid-1980s and successful local businessmen were encouraged to join deputations to the US, Europe and the Far East. Politicians from both sides of the community also helped sell NI's attractions in the US. Although manufacturing has declined, Harland and Wolff's shipyard is the largest in the UK and Shorts has carved out a distinctive place in the world aerospace scene. NI still has a significant place in the production of engineering products, tobacco, clothing, telecommunications, electronics and oilfield equipment. Of the 400 manufacturing units in NI, around 25 per cent represent outside investment, which got a boost at the end of 1988 with a Korean project, quickly followed by a sizeable French investment. During mid-1988, all NI political parties united to oppose Government plans to privatise the shipyard and aircraft industries and the generation and supply of electricity, held by another publicly owned body, the NIE. Much effort has been directed to encouraging small firms and there was considerable support for 'enterprise zones' in Belfast and Londonderry,

while Belfast International Airport gained 'freeport' status. Large confirmed deposits of lignite in Co. Antrim held the prospect of cheaper electricity to a region denied North Sea gas. The lower tax yield in NI and the principle of parity of taxation and services established since 1945 have resulted in a large transfer of funds from the Treasury to NI in recent times. The amount has increased sharply since 1972 as NI became more closely integrated into the central administrative and policy system. During 1969–70, the subvention was £74 million; 1973–4, £314 million; 1975–6, £571 million; and 1978–9, £860 million. In the early 1980s it passed the £1,000-million mark and by 1986–7 it was around £1,700 million. (The total Treasury subvention during 1969–79 was under £4,000 million.) These figures left out of account the cost of maintaining the army in NI but it has been shown that the cost of keeping troops in NI is lower than in Germany and not much more than in GB. (*See also* European Community.)

'ÉIRE NUA' *see* Provisional Irish Republican Army

ELTON, LORD
Parliamentary Under-Secretary, NIO, 1979–81. b. 2 March 1930. MA (Oxon.). Varied teaching career in comprehensive and grammar schools and as college lecturer, 1962–72. Conservative Whip in House of Lords, 1974–6. Front-bench Conservative spokesman in Lords, 1976–9. In NIO, spokesman on all subjects in Lords and responsible for the departments of Agriculture and Education. Held posts in Whitehall at Health Department, Home Office, and Environment between 1981 and 1986.

EMERGENCY PROVISIONS ACT
see Security System section, pp. 398–406

EMPEY, REGINALD
VUPP (and later UUUM) Convention member for E. Belfast, 1975–6. b. 1947. B.Sc. (QUB). He had been vice-chairman of the Young Unionist Council (OUP) before he joined VUPP, of which he became chairman in 1975. In the Convention he was secretary of the UUUC's policy committee. Deputy leader, UUUP, 1977–84. Unsuccessfully contested E. Belfast in 1982 Assembly election. In 1985 elected as OUP councillor in Belfast. Deputy Lord Mayor, 1988–.

ENGLISH, MICHAEL
Chairman of the NI standing committee of MPs at Westminster, 1976–9. b. 24 December 1930. LLB (Liverpool). Has an Ulster family background. Labour MP for Nottingham W., 1964–83.

ENNISKILLEN BOMBING
Eleven civilians – six men and five women – were killed and sixty-three people, including children, were injured when a PIRA bomb exploded close to the Enniskillen war memorial on 8 November 1987, shortly before the annual Remembrance Sunday ceremony was due to begin. The circumstances led to widespread condemnation of the attack, which the PIRA admitted only on the following day in a statement which expressed 'deep regret' and suggested that the bomb could have been triggered by a security forces scanning device – a claim rejected as a 'lie' by the RUC. Margaret Thatcher, who attended the memorial service in Enniskillen, made a strong plea in the Commons to constitutional parties to come together in the wake of the tragedy.

ERSKINE, LORD (OF RERRICK)
Governor of NI, 1964–8. b. 14 December 1893; d. 1980. Was jeered by supporters of Rev. Ian Paisley when he attended the General Assembly of the Irish Presbyterian Church in Belfast on 5 June 1966. The protest was said to be against the 'Romeward trend' of the Church. The incident drew condemnation from the then PM, Captain Terence O'Neill, who talked of trends towards Nazism and fascism.

EUROPA HOTEL
Centrally situated Belfast hotel which has been a popular rendezvous for politicians and journalists during the Troubles. Sometimes described as NI's most-bombed building, since some twenty bombs have exploded in or near the hotel. For several years it was known as the Forum Hotel but reverted to its original title with a change of ownership in 1986.

EUROPEAN COMMUNITY
NI joined the European Community in 1973 as a region of the UK. Since its accession, which was controversial (*see* Common Market Referendum), has benefited from special treatment by the European Commission due to its social, economic and political problems. It has enjoyed priority status in most of the community's funding programmes. Up to 1988, a total of almost £1,000 million had been allocated to the region in the form of grants and loans. Special measures have been adopted to help overcome the more acute problems of NI. In 1983 the Council of Ministers adopted the 'Belfast Urban Renewal Regulation', a measure aimed at helping regenerate the city, badly affected by the decline of the textile and shipbuilding industries. This measure injected about £60 million into Belfast over a three-year period. In 1981 the 'Border Areas Regulation' was implemented and covered the border counties of NI and the Republic. The measure was extended geographically in 1985 and for another period of five years to cover the whole of NI, excluding Greater

Belfast. Aimed mainly at tourism, it has enabled local authorities to build facilities like the Ardhowen Theatre in Enniskillen, Co. Fermanagh, and the Annalong Corn Mill and Marine Park in Co. Down. On a more general level, the European Regional Development Fund's involvement in NI amounted to £280 million at the end of 1987. The European Social Fund, which is intended to help combat unemployment by training or re-training the young, the long-term unemployed, women who wish to resume work, or the handicapped, had contributed £430 million up to the end of 1987. Much of this has been allocated, in large sums, to various Government manpower-training programmes (principally, YTP and ACE). But other organisations which sustain an innovative training and enterprise development programme have been awarded financial help from Europe, such as the NI Industrial Therapy Organisation. Special measures have also been implemented in the agricultural sector to assist processing and marketing of agricultural products, drainage, and the Less Favoured Areas. There has been cash help too for the modernisation of the inshore fishing fleet and the development of aquaculture. Farming has enjoyed the price-support mechanism of the Common Agricultural Policy, though some sectors, such as pig production, have declined since 1973. EC membership has meant extra help for development of the economy. Nevertheless, additionality (that is, that EC aid should be on top of planned Government spending), or the lack of it, has long been a point of contention and has attracted widespread criticism in NI. It is argued that because of the UK Government's policy of tightly controlling public expenditure, NI's priority status in the EC spending programmes is not fully exploited and even that the considerable amounts that do come are not 'additional' in that they are, to some extent at least, compensating the British Exchequer for its own planned expenditure. For example, in 1984 a Parliamentary answer revealed a net benefit of funds of £36 million since 1973. This problem, according to Commission sources, is likely to become more acute as the EC doubles the size of its structural funds, and seeks to concentrate them much more closely on its priority development regions. In 1988 the British Government attempted to have NI excluded from the list of regions. Meanwhile, the challenge of the Single European Market in 1992 has been the subject of many warnings to industry and agriculture. In 1988 a special joint conference was held in Brussels to assess the problems posed for both NI and the Republic. An assessment for the Commission in 1988, edited by John Simpson, claimed that in most years NI had a net gain from EC funds when allowance was made for the region's attributable share of contributions to Brussels. The gain was put at £84 million for the period 1985–6. Estimates have been put forward that NI will get £100 million or more extra as a result of the treating of NI as a priority region. Since 1986 the amount of assistance to projects has fallen and at the end of 1988 there was criticism of NIO tardiness in submission of projects under the new arrangements. In 1988 the EC Commission formally approved a proposal that £30 million should be contributed to the International Fund for Ireland over three years. (*See also* Economy *and* European Parliament.)

**EUROPEAN COURT/
COMMISSION OF HUMAN
RIGHTS**
Some interesting decisions affecting NI have been handed down by these inter-

linked Strasbourg-based bodies. The first of major interest was given in 1978 when, on the application of the Republic's Government, the court dealt with charges of ill-treatment of internees during 'interrogation in depth'. The court found that some internees had been subjected to 'inhuman and degrading treatment', but not to torture. Shortly before the 1981 H-Block hunger strike, the Commission (representing the first stage of the procedure) turned down a submission by four H-Block prisoners that their treatment was a breach of the European Convention, although it criticised the 'inflexibility' of the British Government. Two members of the Commission visited the Maze Prison when Bobby Sands MP was on hunger strike, but Sands refused to follow up a complaint lodged on his behalf by his sister. This was followed by an unsuccessful move by a group of widows of victims of terrorism in NI to persuade the Commission that the Republic's Government was breaching the Convention by not taking adequate anti-terrorist measures. In October 1981 the court held that the ban on male homosexuality in NI was a breach of the Convention, and in 1982 an Order was introduced to achieve parity in the law with GB. In 1984 the Commission held that the use of plastic bullets was justified in a riot situation. It said 66,000 plastic and rubber bullets had been fired since 1969, causing thirteen deaths, and the weapon was less dangerous than alleged. In May 1988 a spokesman for the Commission criticised the power to detain suspects for up to seven days under the PTA. In December 1988 court ruled against seven-day detention, but Home Secretary Douglas Hurd announced that the Government was seeking 'temporary' derogation from the Convention while it decided on its long-term response.

EUROPEAN PARLIAMENT
NI has three seats in the Parliament. This allocation derived from a discussion at a European summit meeting in 1976, when the heads of government accepted a proposal from the Irish Republic's Government that NI should have one more seat than it was entitled to under UK representation so as to ensure that both NI communities would have a voice in the Assembly. The idea was backed by James Callaghan, for the British Government. In January 1978 the British Parliament decided that the first direct election should be held on PR in a single NI constituency – a further guarantee of a Nationalist-aligned member. Unionist MPs, who urged a straight vote as in the rest of the UK, had the support of a large section of the Conservative Party. The election on 7 June 1979 resulted in the return of the Rev. Ian Paisley (DUP); John Hume (SDLP); and John Taylor (OUP), in that order. (*See* Election Results section, pp. 333–6.) NI was previously unrepresented in the Assembly, except during 1973–4, when Rafton Pounder, Unionist MP for S. Belfast, was included in the British Conservative delegation. In Strasbourg the three MEPs, despite their other differences, have co-operated in pressing the case for special measures. The most notable example was when Hume, in 1979, put forward a motion calling for a special report on action to boost the NI economy. He was supported by Paisley and Taylor, and a special survey was carried out by a French MEP Simone Martin in 1980. The Parliament backed her report, which called, among other things, for tax exemption for new industries for at least five years, special help for Belfast housing, and a common energy price structure throughout the UK. Margaret Thatcher's decision to bring electricity charges in NI broadly into line with those in GB, and financial aid for

Belfast housing could be seen as a reply. The two Unionist MEPs and the SDLP leader have been strongly at odds on whether the Parliament should concern itself with NI political issues. In the autumn of 1982 Hume sought to have special hearings organised by the Parliament's political affairs committee to find ways in which the Community could help end the political and economic crisis in NI. But both Paisley and Taylor attacked the suggestion, saying that it conflicted with a decision by the Parliament in 1981 that it should not become involved in the political and constitutional affairs of NI. In the event, the proposal gave rise to strong opposition from the British Government, with Thatcher declaring that there would be no co-operation with such an inquiry. But the Bureau of the Parliament authorised the political affairs committee to have a special report prepared by Danish MEP Neils Haagerup. This report, adopted by the Parliament in 1984, called for power-sharing, and an integrated economic plan for NI. In May 1981 the Parliament rejected a motion calling for British 'flexibility' on the H-Block dispute, put forward by two MEPs from the Republic, Neil Blaney and Paddy Lalor, on the grounds that it was not competent to intervene in NI, and regretting the more than 2,000 deaths in the current violence. But in 1982 the Parliament passed a motion calling for a ban throughout the EC on the use of plastic bullets, which were at that time a matter of intense controversy in NI. There is an all-party committee on NI in the Parliament which has visited NI to talk to local politicians. The three original MEPs were re-elected in 1984, but Taylor has announced he will not be standing in 1989. In December 1985 the Parliament voted 150 to 28 in favour of the AIA. In October 1988 Ian Paisley was ejected from the Parliament

when he interrupted an address by Pope John Paul II. (*See also* European Community.)

EWART-BIGGS, CHRISTOPHER British ambassador to Dublin, assassinated on 21 July 1976, two weeks after he took up the post. b. 1921. Ewart-Biggs and a young woman civil servant from the NIO, Judith Cook, died when the ambassador's car was blown up by a landmine, a short distance from his official residence. The assassination gave rise to the declaration of a state of emergency in the Republic, and the introduction of additional anti-terrorist measures. In September 1976 Dublin newspapers reported that a PIRA spokesman had admitted responsibility for the murders. Ewart-Biggs was a colourful personality – 'straight out of P. G. Wodehouse' was a common assessment – and had a distinctive appearance, having worn an eye-patch since he lost his right eye in World War II. A novel which he had written in his early years was still banned in the Republic when he was appointed to Dublin. His wife Jane (created life peer, 1978), declared that she had no bitterness towards the Irish people and she joined the Peace People, and also launched a memorial prize which is awarded to authors whose works have helped towards peace and reconciliation in Ireland.

EXTRADITION *see* Mayhew, Sir Patrick

F

FAIR EMPLOYMENT Complaints of anti-Catholic bias in employment were one of the features of the civil rights campaign, and in 1976 a

Fair Employment Agency was set up to identify instances of religious discrimination and to seek remedial measures, including court action if necessary. In the late 1980s two factors served to increase the pressure for even tougher legislation. There were repeated references to the fact that a Catholic male was still two and a half times as likely to be unemployed as a Protestant male, while in the US a highly vocal Irish-American lobby succeeded in persuading several states to adopt the MacBride Principles on fair employment, which were derived from the Sullivan Principles applied to South Africa. This action was directed at making US investment in NI conditional on firms accepting the MacBride code, which the British Government criticised as positive discrimination. The code, named after the late Sean MacBride, one-time Irish Foreign Minister, urged, among other things, increased Catholic representation in workforces, including managerial and administrative posts; security for Catholics at work and on the journey to and from work; and training programmes for minority employees. In 1985, when the pro-MacBride drive was at its height, US companies in NI employed 12,000 people, and thirteen of these firms had US city pension funds invested in them. In 1987 and 1988 the British Government responded with proposals to strengthen fair employment legislation, and in December 1988 published a Bill to replace the 1976 measure. A new Fair Employment Commission was suggested, with double the resources of the FEA, and also a tribunal to adjudicate on individual cases of alleged discrimination. The tribunal was empowered to impose fines on firms of up to £30,000, while a court could impose unlimited fines or even imprisonment. Erring firms could also suffer loss of public contracts and grants. Firms would also be required to monitor the religious composition of their workforces and to abide by a code of conduct. The Irish Government and the SDLP gave the proposals a guarded welcome, and many Unionists treated them with the hostility that they had earlier directed against the FEA. Some employers remained critical of the compulsory monitoring procedures. But Secretary of State Tom King had the satisfaction of having his approach endorsed by the US ambassador in London, Charles Price, although US supporters of 'MacBride' insisted they would be continuing their campaign.

FALLS ROAD

The main Catholic district of Belfast, centred on the thoroughfare which stretches westwards from the city centre to Andersonstown. It runs parallel to the predominantly Protestant Shankill Road, from which it is separated by the Peace Line, erected after riots and house-burnings in 1969. In this area of confrontation there have been many serious incidents during the Troubles, and thousands of people moved out of their homes in the summer of 1969 when Protestant militants invaded the area and burned many homes (there were counter-claims on the Protestant side that loyalist homes had been attacked). The IRA has always looked for support to the Falls area, and it was here in the aftermath of the serious violence of 1969 that the PIRA began to assert itself. It was in the Lower Falls in the summer of 1969 that protests were mounted against RUC action in the Bogside area of Londonderry, and the Scarman report criticised the RUC for 'unjustified' firing of a Browning machine gun into Divis Flats, which resulted in a young boy's death. The erection of barricades in the area in 1969 gave rise to angry controversy, and delicate negotiations between the

Falls Road-based CCDC and the Government and security forces. These involved, at one point, a deputation to London to meet Home Secretary James Callaghan. The barriers were eventually lowered, but their existence had brought repeated protests from loyalists, who sometimes erected their own barricades in the Shankill area as a protest. A major problem for the security forces has been the refusal of people in the area to fully accept the RUC, although by 1978 the police were claiming that co-operation was increasing and people in the area were more willing to give information, particularly by way of the confidential telephone. But the Scarman report showed that the policing problem was there even before 1969. It stated that after 1968, RUC foot patrols did not go into a substantial area in the Falls on foot either late at night or early in the morning. This was the area bounded by the Falls Road, Grosvenor Road, Albert Street and Cullingtree Road. The police, according to Scarman, had code-named the area 'No-go-land'. This was virtually the area chosen for the army curfew on 3–5 July 1970, which, according to Catholics, marked the end of the 'honeymoon' with the British army as protectors of the minority. During the curfew, which extended over thirty-four hours (apart from a two-hour shopping break), five civilians were killed, and sixty injured, while fifteen soldiers were injured. The army search during the curfew yielded fifty-two pistols, thirty-five rifles, six automatic weapons, fourteen shot-guns, one hundred homemade bombs, a grenade, 250 pounds of explosives, about 21,000 rounds of ammunition and eight two-way radio sets. The operation led to strong protests from NICRA and the CCDC, and two local politicians, Gerry Fitt MP and Paddy Devlin MP, flew to London to complain that the troops had abused people,

looted, and stolen during the operation – charges broadly denied by the army. Falls Road spokesmen claimed that the army were ignoring much larger supplies of weapons and ammunition in the Shankill area. During the Troubles, the Falls has been the venue of some fierce gun battles between the security forces and the PIRA, and of bitter feuds between the PIRA and the OIRA, and between the OIRA and the IRSP. Several factories in the area were burned in 1969, and over the years there have been numerous riots and demonstrations, in many of which buses have been burned and vehicles hi-jacked. Police and army posts in the area have been attacked frequently. Easter parades to the Republican plot at Milltown cemetery, where many IRA men are buried, and funerals of members of the Republican movement have been occasions of high tension between many residents and the police and army (see Andersonstown). And the introduction of internment in 1971 and the subsequent civil disobedience campaign further alienated many residents from the authorities. Up to the 1981 hunger strike, the SDLP, with its support for constitutional politics, had majority backing in the area, and in 1977 official sources attributed PIRA's decision to regroup and alter its tactics to the disenchantment of local people with violent methods. But there was undoubtedly strong support for the H-Block protest in the Falls Road area, and in wider W. Belfast. There were many pro-hunger-strike demonstrations, and the vast turn-out for the funeral of Bobby Sands MP to Milltown cemetery testified to the growth of republicanism. PSF's decision to contest W. Belfast at the 1982 Assembly election was a direct challenge to the SDLP, and strong organisational effort and a network of PSF advice centres paid off. Gerry Adams, then vice-president of PSF, headed the poll with 25.5 per cent of first preferences, with the total SDLP vote for three candidates standing at 24.5 per cent. Adams was also returned to Westminster in the 1983 general election, unseating Gerry Fitt, who had held the seat since 1966, and he retained the seat in 1987 despite a major organisational drive by the SDLP and the decision by Alliance to stand aside. PSF also outvoted SDLP in the 1985 council elections and in two 1987 council by-elections. In 1987 and 1988 much attention was focused on demands by local politicians and Churchmen for a major development plan for the area, and the issue was also pursued by the Republic's Government in the AIA conference. The British Government responded by launching a special study. The eventual demolition of the controversial Divis Flats complex was agreed in 1987. (*See also* Central Citizens' Defence Committee.)

FARREN, SEAN NIAL
SDLP Assembly member for N. Antrim, 1982–6. SDLP chairman, 1981–6. b. 1939. Unsuccessfully contested N. Antrim in 1979, 1983 and 1987 Westminster elections. Lecturer in education at University of Ulster.

FAUL, FATHER DENIS
A leading campaigner against alleged ill-treatment of persons arrested for interrogation and of detainees during internment. b. Co. Louth, 1932. A teacher at St Patrick's Academy, Dungannon, he first attracted attention in November 1969 when he declared that Catholics felt that NI's judicial system was loaded against them. The statement was attacked by Government Ministers and brought a rebuke from Cardinal Conway, the Catholic Primate. He has been strongly critical of the army and the RUC Special Branch, but he has also repeatedly condemned PIRA violence and has

called on PIRA, without success, to declare a ceasefire. In March 1977 he described the PIRA campaign of that period as 'spurious in Republican terms' and 'directly contrary to Catholic teaching on the sacredness of human life'. As a Maze Prison chaplain during the H-Block hunger strikes, 1980–1, he strongly opposed the fasts, but at the same time urged Government reforms to defuse the crisis. The meetings of relatives which he organised in the autumn of 1981 were seen as an important element in bringing the protest to an end. PSF accused him of bringing pressure on relatives to request medical intervention where hunger-strikers had lapsed into a coma. In 1984 he suggested that only 20 per cent of Catholics would vote for removal of the border in an immediate referendum and that the ending of violence was their priority. In 1988 his repeated demands for a more generous policy of releases of young prisoners seemed to be having an impact on Government practice.

FAULKNER, LORD (OF DOWNPATRICK)
Formerly Brian Faulkner, PM, 1971–2, and Chief Executive in power-sharing administration, 1974. b. 18 February 1921 and killed in a hunting accident near his Co. Down home in March 1977. His career was the most dramatic and varied of any in NI politics. He was the last PM under the 1920 Constitution, and the first head of a Unionist Government to include a Catholic in the Cabinet. In 1974 he led the brief inter-party executive which embraced Unionists as well as members of the mainly Catholic SDLP and the Alliance Party. First spotted as a potential politician by British Labour Minister Hugh Dalton, he started out as a traditional Unionist active in the Orange Order (he was a member of the Grand Orange Lodge of Ireland), and

he was elected as MP for E. Down in 1949. At twenty-eight he was the youngest MP returned to Stormont up to that time. After three years as Government Chief Whip, he became Minister of Home Affairs in 1959 and was active in countering the IRA border campaign. In March 1963 he became Minister of Commerce in the Terence O'Neill Government, and even political opponents praised his energetic and successful approach to the attraction of new industry, particularly from overseas. He caused a major surprise in January 1969 when he resigned from the O'Neill Government in protest against the setting up of the Cameron Commission to inquire into the causes of the violence. This was obviously a climax to tensions between Faulkner and O'Neill. And when O'Neill resigned as PM in April 1969, Faulkner failed by only one vote to succeed him. Major Chichester-Clark became PM and appointed him Minister of Development, with the task of carrying through local government reform and the setting up of a central housing authority. When Chichester-Clark bowed out as Premier in 1971, he finally achieved his ambition to become PM, easily beating his only challenger, William Craig. In August 1971 he introduced internment without trial, a move which infuriated the opposition, and led to an escalation of violence. And in March 1972, what he had confidently predicted would never happen occurred overnight – the Stormont Parliament was prorogued. He joined militant Unionists in demonstrating against the action of the Heath Government, and he refused to have anything to do with the Commission set up to advise the Secretary of State. Northern Ireland, he declared, would not be treated like a 'coconut colony'. His biggest test came in 1973 when he joined with the SDLP and Alliance parties in the Sunningdale

Conference and the cross-community Executive. But power-sharing and the cross-border Council of Ireland were too much for the Unionist Party. The loyalist strike brought down the Executive in May 1974. In the Convention election he tried to bring mainline unionism behind his UPNI, a breakaway group, but it fared badly in the election. In 1976 he announced that he was quitting active politics. In 1977 he became a life peer (he could have had a peerage in 1972), and he confessed that power-sharing had cost him his political life. His autobiography, *Memoirs of a Statesman*, appeared in 1978, fifteen months after his death. His widow Lady Lucy Faulkner, a BBC Governor, 1978–85, became first chairwoman of the NI Broadcasting Council, 1981–5, and in 1985 became a member of the NI Tourist Board.

FEAKLE TALKS

Secret discussions between Protestant Churchmen, mainly from NI, and PSF and PIRA representatives in Smyth's Village Hotel, Feakle, Co. Clare, on 9–11 December 1974. The talks were criticised by many Unionists, and the Churches stressed that the clergy taking part had acted only as individuals. The talks were followed by a brief PIRA ceasefire, and later by a more extended ceasefire (or truce according to the PIRA) which petered out in renewed PIRA violence after a few months. The Churchmen involved were: Dr Arthur Butler, Church of Ireland Bishop of Connor; Dr Jack Weir, then Clerk of the Presbyterian Assembly; Rev. Eric Gallagher, former president of the Methodist Church in Ireland; Rev. Ralph Baxter, secretary, and Rev. William Arlow, assistant secretary of the Irish Council of Churches; Dr Harry Morton, secretary, British Council of Churches; Right Rev. Arthur McArthur, moderator of the United Reformed Church in England;

and Stanley Worrall, former head-master of Methodist College, Belfast, and chairman of NUM. The PSF spokesmen included the president, Ruairí Ó Brádaigh; Maire Drumm, vice-president, and Seamus Loughran, Belfast organiser. The PIRA leaders included Dáithí Ó Conaill, chief of staff and at the time regarded as the most-wanted man in Ireland, Seamus Twomey and Kevin Mallon. There was a touch of drama during the meeting, since men from the Republic's Special Branch entered the hotel, apparently as a result of a tip-off. But the PIRA men had already left. The proposals exchanged between the Churchmen and the Provisionals were as follows:

The Churchmen suggested that the PIRA would consider that its require-ments prior to a permanent ceasefire were met if the British Government issued a policy statement which included the following:

1 That the Government stated it had no political or territorial interests in Ireland beyond its obligations to NI citizens.
2 That the Government's prime concern was the achievement of peace and the promotion of such under-standing between the various sections in NI as would guarantee to all its people a full participation in the life of the community, whatever be the relationship of NI to the EC, UK or Republic.
3 Contingent on the maintenance of a declared ceasefire and effective policing, the Government would relieve the army as quickly as possible of its internal duties.
4 Until agreements about the future government of NI had been freely negotiated and guaranteed, armed forces would be retained in NI.
5 The Government recognised the right of all those who had political aims

to pursue them through the democratic process.

The PIRA's point-by-point reply was sent within a few days:

1 Until the Government clearly stated that it had no claim to sovereignty in any part of Ireland the statement was meaningless. 'We accept that economic commitments must be honoured.'
2 'A noble wish with which we concur but we believe it can only be realised in the full community of the people of Ireland.'
3 No difficulty in maintaining com-munity peace if a bilateral truce was agreed between the army and the PIRA. Discussions with loyalist groups in maintaining peace would be welcomed.
4 If declaration of intent to withdraw, PIRA accepted that there should be a limited army presence during negotiations and implementation of an agreed settlement.
5 'It is meaningless to talk of democratic processes while. . . 2,000 political prisoners are in jail.'

PIRA then sent a number of counter-proposals, including an elected all-Ireland constituent assembly which would draw up a constitution which would have to be approved by a two-thirds majority. There would be a provisional parliament for Ulster (nine counties). It called for British with-drawal within twelve months of the constitution being adopted and an amnesty for all political prisoners in Britain and Ireland. It also offered a temporary ceasefire from midnight on 22 December 1974 until midnight on 2 January 1975 to enable the Govern-ment to respond 'favourably', but said this was conditional on the army stopping raids, harassment and arrests for the same period. On 18 December Secretary of State Merlyn Rees received five of the Churchmen involved in the Feakle Talks. Afterwards he issued a statement saying that if there was a genuine cessation of violence there would be 'a new situation to which the British Government would naturally respond'. Rees stated in his memoirs that he believed the 'ignominy of Birmingham' had been a major reason for the PIRA move. On 19 December Mr Arlow, described as a 'chatterbox' by Rees, had a meeting with the PIRA chief of staff, who ordered a ceasefire over the Christmas period. The Secretary of State continued to insist that there should be no deals with PIRA, although Government officials met PSF representatives to 'explain' Government policy. But special incident centres were set up to allow PSF to make quick contact with the authorities so as to safeguard the ceasefire – a move fiercely denounced by loyalists and regarded with great suspicion by the SDLP. By Easter 1975 the PIRA apparently felt they were not getting anything tangible in political terms and violence crept back steadily.

FEELY, FRANCIS (FRANK)
SDLP Assembly member for S. Down, 1982–6. Also represented same constituency in Assembly, 1973–4, and Convention, 1975–6. b. Kiltimagh, Co. Mayo, 1937. BA (UCG); Dip.H.E. (Maynooth). Publican. Active in ALJ and in Newry civil rights committee, 1968–71. Party delegate at Atkins conference, 1980. Party spokesman on energy and transport.

FENIAN
A term sometimes applied to Catholics by extreme loyalists, but strictly referring to members of the Fenian Brotherhood, active in the nineteenth century in Britain and North America in fighting British rule in Ireland.

FERGUSON, RAYMOND
OUP Assembly member for Fermanagh–S. Tyrone, 1982–6.

Served on committees on Economic Development, and Education. Comes from a family long associated with unionism in Fermanagh. Fermanagh Council, 1977–. Chairman of Council, 1981–3. Unsuccessfully contested the Westminster seat in the 1979 general election. After the closing of the 1982 Assembly, he remained a strong advocate of devolved government. Solicitor; ex-Ulster rugby player. In November 1988 he called on Unionists to have dialogue with constitutional Nationalists in NI and Republic, but his approach was rejected by OUP conference.

FERGUSON, RICHARD
Unionist MP at Stormont for S. Antrim, 1968–70. b. Belfast, 22 August 1935. BA (TCD); LLB Hons (QUB). Member NI Bar (QC), English Bar, and in March 1983 became first NI barrister called to Republic's Inner Bar. In 1984 he moved to London, where he quickly made a reputation as defence counsel in major criminal cases. On the liberal wing of the Unionist Party, and a supporter of Terence O'Neill, he resigned from the Orange Order in August 1969. In February 1970 he resigned as MP for health reasons, and in April 1970 his home in Lisburn was damaged by a bomb. He joined the Alliance Party in March 1971.

FIANNA FÁIL
One of the two major parties in the Irish Republic, it originated from the wing of old Sinn Féin opposed to the Anglo-Irish Treaty of 1921. It first came to power under Eamon de Valera in 1932, and it has been the governing party for most of the period since. It gave way to inter-party Governments headed by Fine Gael, 1948–51, 1954–7, 1973–7, July 1981–February 1982; and November 1982–March 1987. In the 1930s it took a number of steps to underline separation from Britain –

high protective tariffs, and the distinguishing of Irish nationality from British, the abolition of the post of Governor-General. Furthermore, the 1937 Constitution contained articles stating the claim to a united Ireland. These have been regarded by NI Unionists as a threat to NI, although Southern spokesmen have always insisted that they seek unity only by consent. A Fianna Fáil policy statement in 1975 called for a British declaration of intent to withdraw from NI, but party leader Jack Lynch and his colleagues stressed that it was not comparable with the 'Brits out' demands of PSF. They said that no time scale was mentioned, and that the aim was to encourage Britain to promote unity in a peaceful way. Jack Lynch, in the early 1960s, as Minister for Industry and Commerce, broke new economic ground by giving preferential tariffs to some NI goods. But he caused anger in Britain and in NI with his criticism of British security policy in NI in 1969. There were also occasional complaints from Britain that his Government was not taking a sufficiently tough line against PIRA, notably after the Mountbatten murder. When Lynch resigned in December 1979, his favoured candidate as successor, George Colley, lost out to Charles Haughey. And Haughey gave a new direction to FF's NI policy. He stressed the need for agreement with Britain on NI's future, and clearly saw his December 1980 summit meeting with Margaret Thatcher in Dublin as a useful step. But FF's relations with Britain worsened as the Thatcher Government felt Haughey had overplayed the Dublin meeting, and when he criticised the Conservative Government's approach to the H-Block hunger strike and failed to back Britain on anti-Argentina sanctions during the Falklands conflict. The 1982 FF Government was also highly critical of

Britain's 'rolling devolution' initiative. The party gave full support to the New Ireland Forum, 1983–4, but laid greater stress on the unitary thirty-two-county-state option than the others set out in the final report. It also questioned the maintenance of the constitutional guarantee for NI in the AIA in 1985. Yet the minority Government led by Haughey, which took office in 1987, worked the AIA and pressed strongly for law-and-order reforms in NI and tougher fair employment laws. But it modified the extradition arrangements with Britain, accepted by the outgoing Fine Gael–Labour Coalition, to provide for the Irish Attorney-General to check the evidence adduced in a particular case. This, in the context of legal decisions in Britain concerning the Birmingham Six case and the Stalker inquiry, produced a major test of the AIA and the relationships implicit in it.

FIANNA NA HÉIREANN

Youth wing of the PIRA, traditionally used to provide communications, to alert terrorists as to the approach of security forces, and on occasion to stage incidents which might lure troops or police into ambush positions. The security forces claimed that after the introduction of internment without trial, the youth wing was employed increasingly in carrying bombs and in moving weapons. The exact strength of the movement is difficult to determine, but it probably reached several hundred in Belfast in the 1971–2 period, and then declined as the PIRA switched its effort more to small active service units.

FINE GAEL

One of the two main political parties in the Irish Republic. Derives from the pro-Treaty wing of the old Sinn Féin movement. In the 1920s it was known as Cumann na nGaedheal, and formed the first Government of the Irish Free State. That administration was headed by William T. Cosgrave, whose son Liam Cosgrave was to become Taoiseach, 1973–7. To many people outside the Republic, particularly NI Unionists and the British public, it has been regarded as taking a softer line than the Fianna Fáil Party on NI issues and a united Ireland. But the overall records of the two parties on these matters have differed little in practice. Although de Valera and Fianna Fáil rejected the Treaty which led to the setting up of two separate administrations in Ireland, and to the partition of the country, the future Fine Gael party was supported by Republicans like Michael Collins and by the underground Irish Republican Brotherhood. Since losing power to de Valera and Fianna Fáil in 1932, it has been unable to sustain a government from its own ranks. Out of power in the 1930s, it was allied briefly to Eoin O'Duffy's Blueshirts, a fascist-type group. When one of FG's leading figures, James Dillon, urged support for the Allies in World War II, he was expelled. The inter-party Government of 1948–51, made up of Fine Gael, the Irish Labour Party and the small Republican party, Clann na Poblachta, and led by John Costello, broke the last tenuous link with the British Commonwealth. When FG came to power in combination with the Irish Labour Party in 1973, under the leadership of Liam Cosgrave, it had acquired a left-centre image. One of the disappointments of the Fine Gael leadership in that period was the failure of the Sunningdale Conference in 1973 to provide a lasting solution in NI. And when Dr Garret FitzGerald took over as party leader in 1977, after the defeat of the Coalition, one of his first moves was to launch a fresh appraisal of policy on NI and Irish unity. In 1979 the party published a scheme for an Irish

confederation, but it failed to attract any serious interest among Unionists. The party returned to power after the June 1981 election, again in Coalition with Labour, but as a minority administration dependent on the votes of a few independents. The Coalition agreed with the British Government in November 1981 the setting up of the British-Irish Intergovernmental Council, but soon afterwards it was defeated on its Budget and lost office in the February 1982 election. Fine Gael was unhappy about the British Government's 'rolling devolution' initiative on NI in 1982, but less vehement in its denunciation than the Fianna Fáil Government. It was also critical of Taoiseach Charles Haughey's all-out assault on sanctions against Argentina during the Falklands conflict; Haughey's attitude had greatly angered the Thatcher Government. When the minority Fianna Fáil Government was defeated in the November 1982 election, Fine Gael returned to power, once more in combination with Labour and promised a 'radical new approach' to NI. In 1983 its leader Garret FitzGerald launched the New Ireland Forum, and the strong international support for its report in 1984 set the scene for the AIA in 1985. But the February 1987 election saw a new alignment. Labour had opted out of coalition politics, and Fine Gael was now exchanging transfers with the recently launched Progressive Democrats. But FG was down to fifty seats and the Prog. D.'s had only fourteen, so that FF, with eighty-one seats, was able to establish a minority administration. Dr FitzGerald resigned the next month, but party officials insisted that despite the defeat, FG had greatly improved its organisation and electoral base under his leadership. Former Minister Alan Dukes succeeded FitzGerald as leader.

FISH, HAMILTON

Chairman of us *ad hoc* Congressional Committee on Irish affairs, 1988–. b. 3 June 1926. Lawyer and member of old New York Republican family. us vice-consul in Dublin, 1951–3. New York Congressman, 1969–. Member of Congressional delegation that visited NI in 1978 and urged role for US as 'honest broker' in negotiating NI settlement. He is said to be close to President Bush.

FITT, LORD

As Gerard (Gerry) Fitt, MP at Westminster for W. Belfast, 1966–83. Has been Independent Socialist since 1979, when he resigned from the SDLP, which he had led from its foundation in 1970. He broke with the SDLP because of its initial refusal to attend the Constitutional Conference organised by Secretary of State Humphrey Atkins, and his belief that the party was becoming less socialist and 'more green Nationalist'. Earlier, he was Republican Labour and, still earlier, Irish Labour. b. Belfast, 9 April 1926. He first worked as a soap boy in a barber's shop, and then served with the British merchant navy, 1941–53, and he was in many wartime convoys to the USSR. At sea, he educated himself in law and politics and when he left the navy he devoted himself to grassroots politics in his native Dock ward in Belfast, then a tough and colourful waterfront area. His energy and keen sense of humour – he often referred to his five daughters as the 'Miss Fitts' – soon established him as a personality in local politics. In 1958 he was returned as an Irish Labour member of Belfast City Council, of which he remained a member until 1981, when his anti-hunger-strike stance brought about his defeat. In 1962 he entered the NI Parliament, gaining the Dock seat from the Unionists. In 1966 he also won the W. Belfast seat from a Unionist, and his

effective use at Westminster of material provided by the Campaign for Social Justice was an important factor in developing British Labour interest in the NI situation. He organised several trips to NI by sympathetic Labour MPs, notably on the occasion of the Londonderry civil rights march on 5 October 1968 when he received a head injury. During the five-month power-sharing Executive in 1974, he was the deputy Chief Executive – that is, deputy to Brian Faulkner. He has stood out strongly against PIRA, some of whose supporters attacked his Belfast home in August 1976. On that occasion he defended himself, his wife and some members of his family with a gun. He has been a supporter, for the most part, of the Labour Party at Westminster, and his vote was often important to the Wilson and Callaghan Governments. But he abstained in the crucial confidence vote in 1979 which brought down the Labour administration. He was demonstrating, he said, his 'disillusionment' with Roy Mason as NI Secretary of State. In 1978 he secured the passage of a Private Members' Bill to bring the law in NI on the chronically sick and disabled into line with that in GB. He lost his seat to Gerry Adams, PSF, in the 1983 election, but got over 10,000 votes, many of which were believed to have come from normally Unionist and Alliance voters. He had campaigned on an anti-PIRA ticket and his appointment as a life peer in 1983 was popular at Westminster, but not with Irish Nationalists. In 1985 he was critical of the AIA, saying that London and Dublin had come up with a deal without consulting the Unionists, and a Council of Ireland was being set up in the guise of the conference. He also accused the SDLP of showing cowardice during the hunger strike, and in boycotting the Assembly. In 1987 he angered the SDLP by calling on W. Belfast voters to support the Workers' Party.

FITZGERALD, GARRET

Leader of the Fine Gael party in the
Republic, 1977–87. Taoiseach, 1981–
March 1982; December 1982–
February 1987. b. 9 February 1926. BL,
Ph.D. (UCD); Hon LLD (New York and
St Louis). Dr FitzGerald has probably
visited NI more frequently than any
other Dublin-based politician. He has
close Northern family connections for,
while his father Desmond was the first
Foreign Minister of the Irish Free State,
his mother was an Ulster Presbyterian.
His ministerial responsibility for NI
affairs as Foreign Minister in the
Cosgrave Government, 1973–7,
covered the period of Sunningdale, the
Assembly and the Convention, so that
he was regularly involved in talks with
British Ministers on security and
political issues affecting NI. He used his
influence as Foreign Minister and as EC
president to promote cross-border
economic co-operation. After the
failure of the Convention in 1976, he
tried to encourage fresh thinking on NI
devolution and had fairly regular
meetings with most of the NI political
groups, other than the DUP. While
looking to an eventual united Ireland,
he has always stressed the need for full
consent within NI and reassurance for
Northern Protestants. He disclosed in
1978 that he had told loyalist leaders in
NI in 1974 that they would be 'bloody
fools' to join the Republic under its
existing Constitution. Formerly a
lecturer in political economy at UCD, he
operated extensively as a journalist for
British and American publications
before going on to the front bench in
the Dáil. On taking over the Fine Gael
leadership in 1977, he emphasised that
he would continue to have personal
oversight of his party's policy on NI.
Following a reassessment, Fine Gael
produced in 1979 a scheme for an Irish
confederation and while Unionists
showed no enthusiasm for the idea they
conceded for the most part that it was a

sincere effort by Dr FitzGerald to meet
Northern sensibilities. In February
1980 Dr FitzGerald said most British
politicians would prefer not to have to
maintain the link with NI and should
say so publicly. When he took office as
Taoiseach after the June 1981 general
election, he quickly announced a
'crusade' to make the Republic's
Constitution more attractive to NI
Protestants. At his London meeting
with Margaret Thatcher in November
1981 the decision to set up a British-
Irish Intergovernmental Council was
announced. But that Fine Gael–Labour
administration was dependent on the
backing of a few independents, and
their refusal to support the January
1982 Budget led to a further inconclusive election in February and a
minority Fianna Fáil Government. In
the November 1982 general election he
was once more poised for power as
Fianna Fáil lost ground, and he took
office again in December as head of a
Fine Gael–Labour Coalition with an
overall majority. During that election
campaign, he urged the setting up of
all-Ireland courts and an all-Ireland
police force to counter terrorism –
ideas which brought him into sharp
collision with Fianna Fáil leader
Charles Haughey. Speaking at QUB in
January 1983, he said his Government
wanted a 'new and dynamic relationship' with both NI communities, the
British Government and their European
friends in creating a tolerant, compassionate and just society in Ireland. He
did not want EC 'interference' in NI, but
he said there was need for international
encouragement for some solution that
would end the impasse. In March 1983
he had talks with Margaret Thatcher in
a bid to restore Anglo-Irish relations. In
April 1983 he launched the New
Ireland Forum. But this bid to give Irish
nationalism a new cohesion in its
approach to NI did not quite succeed,
for it was clear that there were

differences between himself and Charles Haughey on policy and tactics when the NIF report appeared in 1984. Also, Thatcher summarily dismissed the main options in her 'out, out, out' reply at a London news conference in November 1984, after he had talked with her at a Chequers summit meeting. Dr FitzGerald was reported to have described Thatcher's remarks as 'gratuitously offensive' when he spoke to his Parliamentary party. However, he launched a major diplomatic offensive in support of the NIF report, emphasising its point that Nationalists were prepared to consider any ideas put up. President Reagan had praised the NIF report during his 1984 visit to Ireland, and a direct appeal by Dr FitzGerald to the US Congress was sympathetically received. And apart from the international pressure on the British Government, there was clearly support in London, both official and ministerial, and within the opposition, for a new initiative. After numerous negotiating sessions, the AIA was hammered out in close secrecy and signed at Hillsborough in November 1985 by FitzGerald and Thatcher. Although it met with intense hostility from Unionists and did not produce any early progress towards power-sharing government in NI, it was still regarded as the main achievement of the Coalition Government which ended in 1987. When Haughey took over again after the election of February, FitzGerald quickly stood down as Fine Gael leader. He admitted that the rejection of divorce proposals in the 1986 referendum had been a special disappointment.

FITZSIMMONS, WILLIAM K.
Minister of Health and Social Services, 1969–72. b. Belfast, 31 January 1909. As Minister of Development in 1967, he drew up a statement on reform of local government. Unionist MP for Duncairn, 1956–72.

FLANAGAN, SIR JAMIE
Chief Constable of the RUC, 1973–6. b. 1914. The first Catholic to be appointed police chief, he had been deputy Chief Constable since November 1970. He had two especially difficult periods as Chief Constable – the UWC strike in 1974 and the PIRA ceasefire in 1975. During the 1974 strike, there was an undercurrent of criticism of the RUC by supporters of the Executive that it did not act vigorously enough against the strikers. During the ceasefire, there were indications of some unrest within the RUC on the grounds that they were being required for political reasons to 'go easy' on the PIRA.

FLANNERY, MARTIN
Chairman, Labour back-bench group on NI, 1983–. MP for Hillsborough, Sheffield. b. 2 March 1918. Urged inquiry into SAS shooting of three PIRA members in Gibraltar in 1988. Later that year criticised Labour abstentions on main Commons vote on new PTA.

FOOT, MICHAEL
Leader of British Labour Party, 1980–3. b. 23 July 1913. Deputy leader, Labour Party, 1976–80. MP for Ebbw Vale, 1960–83; Blaenau Gwent, 1983–. As leader of the Commons in the Callaghan Government, he pleased Unionists and angered the SDLP when he supported the proposal for a Speaker's Conference on the NI seats, which led to the Boundary Commission recommendation of five extra MPs. When he visited NI in February 1982 to talk to politicians and trade unionists, it was his first trip there for twenty-five years, and he stressed mainly the need for more jobs rather than pushing his party's new policy of campaigning actively for a united

Ireland by consent. He has been critical of Labour MPs who had talks with PSF while it supported violence. He also urged Unionist MPs to abandon their initial policy of absention from Westminster in protest against the AIA.

FORSYTHE, CLIFFORD

OUP MP S. Antrim, 1983–. Assembly member for S. Antrim, 1982–6. b. 24 August 1929. Served on committees on Environment, Finance and Personnel, and deputy chairman, Health and Social Services. Newtownabbey Council, 1983. Mayor of Newtown-abbey, 1981–3. Former professional footballer with Linfield and Derry City. Party spokesman on local government.

FORUM FOR A NEW IRELAND *see* New Ireland Forum

FORUM HOTEL *see* Europa Hotel

FOSTER, REVEREND IVAN

DUP Assembly member for Fermanagh–S. Tyrone, 1982–6. Served on committees on Agriculture, Education, and Devolution. b. 1943. Free Presbyterian Church minister, 1967–. Prominent in loyalist street demonstrations since 1960s and active in Vanguard movement in early 1970s. Named local commander in Fermanagh of the Third Force set up by the DUP in early 1982. In 1987 he criticised the Unionist pact for hampering the anti-AIA campaign. Has served several brief prison sentences arising from protests, including one outside the Presbyterian General Assembly in 1966; a loyalist demonstration in Armagh on the occasion of a 1969 civil rights march; and taking part in a banned parade in Castlewellan, Co. Down, in June 1985 (in default of fine). Omagh Council, 1981–5; unsuccessful candidate for Fermanagh Council, 1985. Left active politics in 1989.

FREELAND, LIEUTENANT-GENERAL SIR IAN HENRY

Army GOC and Director of Operations, NI, 1969–71. b. 14 September 1912. Sir Ian, who had been deputy Chief of the General Staff, 1968–9, was the first GOC to be overall Director of Operations in NI – a situation which arose from talks between the British and NI Governments in August 1969, when troops first went on to the streets in support of the RUC. Sir Ian had to cope with a great variety of problems – the 1969 riots and the development of barricades and no-go areas, the erection of a Peace Line between Catholic and Protestant areas in W. Belfast, and the recurring civil rights marches and loyalist counter-demon-strations. In 1970 he took a tough line with 'trouble-makers' and ran into severe criticism from NICRA and local defence committees in Catholic areas. In April 1970 he warned petrol-bombers that they could be shot, and in June 1970, that anybody carrying a firearm would be shot without warning. His most controversial operation in Belfast was the Falls Road curfew from 3–5 July 1970. From Friday night until Sunday morning a large area was sealed off and houses searched intensively. A large cache of arms and ammunition was uncovered, but there was severe violence during which five civilians were killed and sixty injured, while fifteen soldiers were injured. The curfew, which was raised for only two hours on Saturday to allow for local shopping, gave rise to allegations by the NICRA and local MPs that there had been looting, theft and abusive behaviour by the troops. General Freeland denied, however, that there had been any excessive force.

FREUD, CLEMENT

British Liberal Party spokesman on NI, 1976–9. b. 1924. A grandson of Sigmund Freud, father of modern

psychology, he supported reconciliation in statements on NI, and
sought to maintain all-party approach
to NI problems. MP for Isle of Ely,
1973–87. Popular journalist and
broadcaster.

FRIEL, BRIAN
Senator in Irish Republic, 1987–.
Nominated to Senate by Taoiseach
Charles Haughey. Internationally-
known playwright. b. Derry, 9 January
1929. Hon D.Litt. (NUI).

FRIENDS OF IRELAND
An organisation formally set up in
Washington DC on 16 March 1981 by
leading Irish-Americans associated
with Senator Edward Kennedy and
Speaker 'Tip' O'Neill. The politicians
reaffirmed support for Irish unity, but
said it must have the support of the NI
majority. They said the US had a
constructive role to play in promoting a
NI settlement, and they expressed
satisfaction that support in the US for
violence in Ireland had diminished
since they had issued their first St
Patrick's Day message in 1977. In 1982
some leaders of the Church of Ireland
and the Presbyterian Church criticised
the group for not taking enough
account of the Unionist viewpoint. The
group was particularly influential in
building US support for the AIA and the
International Fund for Ireland. In 1987
it called on the EC to back the fund, and
its chairman, Congressman Brian
Donnelly, on a visit to Belfast in 1989,
urged that grants should be targeted
more on disadvantaged areas.

FRIENDS OF THE UNION
An organisation set up in June 1986 to
'increase knowledge and understanding of the need to maintain the
union of Great Britain and Northern
Ireland'. Sixteen Conservative MPs and
eight peers were listed as trustees or
patrons of the body. Most of those

involved were active in opposing the
AIA. Prominent were the late Sir John
Biggs-Davison MP, and Ian Gow MP,
who was only Minister to resign from
Government in protest at the AIA.
Other supporters included former NI
PM Lord Moyola, the Marquess of
Salisbury, and the Earl of Caledon. In a
document sent to Margaret Thatcher in
1988 the organisation suggested that
the BIIC of 1981 should be revived to
replace the AIA.

FYFFE, WILLIAM
Unionist MP for N. Tyrone at
Stormont, 1969–72. b. Strabane,
1914. A leading local journalist, he
strongly argued against the holding of
civil rights marches in Strabane, since
they tended, he argued, to worsen
community relations. Supported
Terence O'Neill in 1969 election
campaign.

G

GARDINER REPORT
The report of the committee of inquiry,
headed by former Lord Chancellor
Lord Gardiner, which reported in
January 1975 on measures to deal with
terrorism in NI in the context of civil
liberties and human rights. The
committee also included Lord
MacDermott, former Lord Chief
Justice of NI, Alistair Buchan, J. P.
Higgins, Kathleen Jones, Michael
Morland, and John Whyte. It held that
detention without trial was a short-
term necessity, and that special
category (or political) status for
convicted prisoners should be ended,
with priority being given to a halt on
admission of new prisoners to the
status. It also said that non-jury trials
for terrorist offences should be

continued for the present and that there should be a new offence of terrorism. It recommended that the prison building programme be speeded up and that an independent police complaint procedure be introduced. The committee also said that the normal conventions of majority rule would not work in NI. It said no political framework could endure unless both communities shared in the responsibility of administering, and recognition was given to the different national inheritances of the two communities. Lord MacDermott declined to subscribe to this second point, however, since he said he could not understand what it meant.

GASTON, JOSEPH ALEXANDER
OUP Assembly member for N. Antrim, 1982–6. Served on committees on Agriculture, Education, and Security. b. 1928. Ballymoney Council, 1973–. Chairman, N. Antrim Unionist Association. Was part-time member of UDR for seven years until he lost a leg from IRA booby-trap bomb in 1975.

GIBRALTAR SHOOTINGS
On Sunday 6 March 1988 the SAS shot dead in Gibraltar three unarmed PIRA terrorists who were said to be planning to bomb a changing-of-the-guard ceremony on 8 March. Those who died – all from Belfast – were: Mairead Farrell (thirty-one); Daniel McCann (thirty); and Sean Savage (twenty-four). Farrell, a student at QUB, had served ten years for bombing the Conway Hotel, near Belfast. McCann had served two years for possession of explosives. In 1982 Savage had been charged with IRA membership and conspiracy to cause explosions, but the charges were later dropped. PIRA claimed that the SAS would have known that their volunteers were unarmed, and it emerged that British and Spanish intelligence had traced the journey of the three in their car, which had been parked close to where the guard-changing ceremony was due to take place. This car did not contain explosives. Two days after the shootings a car with explosives and a timer was found in the Spanish resort of Marbella and was said to be the actual car bomb. There was considerable controversy over the shootings. Some Labour MPs suggested that the three could have been arrested. SDLP deputy leader Seamus Mallon found a 'striking similarity' with Armagh shootings in 1982. The Irish Government said it was 'gravely perturbed' at what had happened. But British Ministers defended the action and PM Margaret Thatcher thanked the Spanish Government for the co-operation of their police. At the inquest SAS men gave evidence from behind a screen, and the jury returned a nine to two verdict of 'lawful killing'. (*See also* Andersonstown.)

GIBSON, SIMPSON
DUP Assembly member for N. Down, 1982–6. Deputy chairman, Agriculture Committee. b. 1946. Ards Council 1981–. Mayor, 1987. Vice-chairman of DUP and secretary of the Unionist Forum, an umbrella group of the Unionist parties. Member, local government Staff Commission, 1985–.

GILLILAND, DAVID
Chief Information Officer, NIO, at Stormont, 1972–87. b. Londonderry, 1927. Journalist on the *Londonderry Sentinel* and *Belfast Telegraph* before joining the NI Government Information Service in 1956. Became Principal official spokesman at Stormont when he was appointed press secretary to Lord Moyola as PM in 1969, and when he retired in 1987, he had served under eight Secretaries of State. He visited the US regularly to brief officials and journalists.

GILMOUR, SIR IAN HEDWORTH JOHN LITTLE

Conservative spokesman on NI, 1974–5. b. 8 July 1926. Conservative MP for Norfolk Central, 1962–74; Chesham, 1974–83; Chesham and Amersham, 1983–. Lord Privy Seal (deputy Foreign Secretary), 1979–81. Sir Ian was closely involved with security policy in NI between 1970 and 1974, as during this period he rose from Under-Secretary in the Defence Ministry to Secretary for Defence. As opposition spokesman on NI from June 1974 until early 1975 he gave strong support to the Labour Government's Convention initiative, and he warned that if it failed the dangers could be very great. Before he was sacked from the Government by Margaret Thatcher in 1981, he was a member of the Cabinet group discussing a NI initiative.

GLASS, JOHN BASIL CALDWELL

Deputy leader of the Alliance Party, 1976–80. b. Co. Leitrim, 1926. LLB (QUB). A leading Belfast solicitor, he was the first chairman of the Alliance Party and president, 1972–4. Represented S. Belfast in both the Assembly, 1973–4, and the Convention, 1975–6, but unsuccessful candidate there in the 1982 Assembly election. Alliance Chief Whip, 1973–6, and deputy Chief Whip of NI Executive, 1974. Unsuccessfully contested S. Belfast in the Westminster elections of October 1974 and 1979. Belfast City Council, 1977–81. Party vice-chairman, 1983–5; party chairman, 1985–7. In 1987 appointed Bankruptcy and Companies Master in High Court.

GLENDINNING, WILLIAM (WILL)

Alliance Assembly member for W. Belfast, 1982–6. Deputy chairman, Environment Committee; member of Health and Social Services Committee. Belfast City Council, 1977–87. Leader of Alliance group in City Council since

1981 and party spokesman on housing. With the closure of the Assembly he became education officer of the NI Council on Alcohol. In 1987 he and his wife Pip, also a City Councillor, resigned their seats in Lower and Upper Falls respectively, and withdrew from political activity for 'personal reasons', while remaining members of the Alliance Party.

GOODHART, SIR PHILIP CARTER

Parliamentary Under-Secretary, NIO, 1979–81. b. 3 November 1925. Conservative MP for Bromley, Beckenham, 1957–. Former Fleet Street journalist. Has served on many British delegations, including UN General Assembly, NATO Assembly, and Council of Europe. Chairman of Conservative Party's Committee on NI, 1976–9. Responsible in NIO for Department of the Environment. Trustee of Friends of the Union, 1986–.

GORMLEY, THOMAS COLUMBA

MP at Stormont for Mid-Tyrone, 1962–72. (Ind. Nationalist until 1972, when he became one of first three members of Alliance Parliamentary Party.) b. Claudy, Co. Derry, 29 July 1916; d. 1984. Strabane Rural Council, 1947. Tyrone County Council, 1950–73. Strabane District Council, 1973–7.

GOULDING, CATHAL

Chief of staff of OIRA, 1969–72. b. Dublin, 1922. Comes of strong Republican family, and his record in IRA goes back to World War II, during which he was interned by the Dublin Government. He was involved in revival of IRA organisation after the war, and in 1953, while working as a house painter in England, became associated with Seán Mac Stiofáin, who was later to become chief of staff of PIRA. They, together with another man, were sentenced to eight years' imprisonment for an arms raid on Felstead School in Essex in 1953. By 1967 he had become powerful in the IRA, and in an address at that period put forward the Marxist views which were later to become associated with Official Sinn Féin and the OIRA. In 1972 he led the OIRA in declaring a ceasefire, and he was strongly critical of the PIRA bombing campaign. In an interview with *Pravda* in 1972 he said the PIRA bombings were inhuman acts in moral terms, and provocative in political terms. He made no comment when allegations were made in a Dublin magazine in 1982 that OIRA was still involved in murders and large-scale armed robberies. The Workers' Party (formerly Official Sinn Féin, the political wing of OIRA) dismissed the charges as 'muck'. In 1983, as an executive member of the WP, he attacked PIRA for sectarianism and defended the use of supergrasses against 'undemocratic elements'.

GOW, IAN

The only Minister to resign from the Thatcher Government in protest at the AIA. b. 11 February 1937. Solicitor. MP for Eastbourne, 1974–. Parliamentary Private Secretary to Margaret Thatcher, 1979–83. He was Minister of State at the Treasury when he stepped down, saying that he was 'profoundly opposed' to the agreement because, in his opinion, it would prolong and not diminish NI's agony. When he spoke to the Assembly committee in 1985, he urged Unionists not to resort to violence in opposing the AIA. Trustee of Friends of the Union, 1986–. He said in October 1988 that he believed there was a real chance of Margaret Thatcher having a change of heart on AIA.

GOWRIE, LORD

Minister of State and deputy Secretary of State, September 1981–3. b. 26

November 1939. Educated Eton and Oxford. Member of a Southern Irish Protestant family, he came to NI with James Prior, with whom he had served as Minister of State at the Employment Department. As Minister responsible for prisons, he was closely involved in the later talks on the 1981 H-Block hunger strike. He occasionally stirred controversy – for example, by urging joint British and Irish citizenship for Northern Irish people. In 1982 he commented that the Government's plans for 'rolling devolution' might take twenty or thirty years to mature. In 1983 he described PIRA leadership as 'very intelligent, very sophisticated'. After the 1983 election, he left NI to become Minister for the Arts, and although promoted to the Cabinet in 1984, he left the Government in 1985, saying he could not live on his £33,000 ministerial salary.

GRAHAM, EDGAR SAMUEL DAVID

OUP Assembly member for S. Belfast, 1982–3. b. 1954. Shot dead by PIRA at QUB, 7 December 1983. Barrister and law lecturer, QUB. Chairman, Ulster Young Unionist Council, 1981–2. Honorary Secretary, Ulster Unionist Council, 1982. He wrote two pamphlets for his party's Devolution Group, and was responsible for legal submissions to European Commission of Human Rights on behalf of widows of terrorist victims through special unit set up by Harold McCusker MP. First chairman of Assembly's Finance and Personnel Committee.

GRAHAM, GEORGE

DUP Assembly member for S. Down, 1982–6. Served on committees on Agriculture, Health and Social Services, and Finance and Personnel. b. 1947. Co-opted in 1975, he was the first DUP member of Newry and Mourne council. In 1982 the SDLP-controlled council elected him as chairman, despite his opposition to cross-border co-operation. In 1987 he continued to attend council meetings in defiance of party policy on AIA, and resigned from DUP in January 1989.

GRAHAM, BRIGADIER PETER WALKER

Commander, UDR, May 1982–6. b. 1937. He had considerable army experience in NI before joining UDR: served two years as brigade major with the 39th Infantry Brigade, and later commanded 1st Battalion, Gordon Highlanders, during a two-year stay at Holywood barracks. Has served in Kenya, Borneo and with BAOR.

GREEN, DESMOND GEORGE RENNIE

VUPP (and later UUUM) Convention member for N. Down, 1975–6. b. 1914. Bangor Borough Council, 1971–3. N. Down District Council, 1973–. Mayor, 1979–81. As chairman of the Ulster Special Constabulary Association (organisation of ex-B Specials, of which he was former district commandant), he was involved in the loyalist strike in 1974, and in later efforts to set up a new 'home guard'. In 1974 he claimed that more than 30,000 people had registered their names as possible members of such a Third Force, but the claim was never accepted by the Government. Some members of his organisation were believed to be involved in the unofficial Ulster Service Corps, which mounted patrols in some rural areas in early 1977. When VUPP split in 1976, he supported Ernest Baird and UUUP until 1980. Elected N. Down Borough Council in 1981 as UPUP member. Unsuccessful candidate in NI Assembly elections, 1982, when his leader, Jim Kilfedder, transferred only 42 per cent of his surplus to him. He rejoined OUP soon after and in 1985 topped poll in his area as OUP

candidate but in 1986 he was expelled for failure to support council adjournment policy. In January 1989 he switched to the unofficial N. Down Conservative Association.

GREY, LORD (OF NAUNTON)

The last Governor of NI. b. Wellington, New Zealand, 15 April 1910. LLB (Auckland) and Hon LLD (QUB). A barrister and solicitor in New Zealand, he entered the British Colonial Service. Deputy Governor-General, Nigeria, 1957–9. Governor, British Guiana, 1959–64. Governor, Bahamas, 1964–8. Governor, NI, 1968–73. The post of Governor was abolished under the legislation which provided for an Assembly elected by PR and the constitutional duties of Governor were absorbed by the Secretary of State. The ending of the office was strongly criticised by Unionists who regarded it as a weakening of the link with the British Crown. After leaving, he maintained his interest in NI, notably as Chancellor of NUU (later Univeristy of Ulster).

H

HAILSHAM, LORD (OF SAINT MARYLEBONE)

Formerly Quintin McGarel Hogg, concerned with NI as Shadow Home Secretary, 1966–70, and Lord Chancellor, 1970–4, and 1979–87. b. 9 October 1907. A former Conservative MP for Oxford, he has held a variety of Government posts, including leader of the House of Lords. His father's family were Lowland Scots who were settled for more than a century at Lisburn, Co. Antrim. Lord Hailsham strongly backed James Callaghan as Home Secretary in his efforts to get reforms in NI in 1969. At that time he urged a treaty of perpetual friendship, binding GB, NI and the Republic. Such a treaty, he said, should involve a recognition of the border as a fact of the situation of indefinite duration; a human rights convention placing the rights of minorities in all three territories on a judicially enforceable, and not simply political, footing. In 1971 he created controversy with a suggestion that people accused of serious bombings should be charged with treason, which would carry the death penalty. In 1974 he urged the setting up of a 'Council of the Islands' which would bring together England, Scotland, Wales, NI, the Irish Republic, the Channel Islands, and Orkney and Shetland. He said that unless all these components prospered, none could prosper, and he suggested that it was the failure to recognise this dimension that was largely at the bottom of the 1974 loyalist strike in NI. But he also argued that the extreme Protestant viewpoint in NI had not assisted those who wanted to maintain the Union. As Lord Chancellor in the Thatcher Government he was said to be the most vocal member of the Cabinet committee which considered the issue of NI devolution. In 1986 he resisted demands by the Irish Government that the Diplock courts should be reconstructed to allow for a 'mix' of British and Irish judges or, failing that, the replacement of one-judge courts by a three-judge panel.

HALL-THOMPSON, MAJOR ROBERT LLOYD
Leader of Assembly, 1973–4, and Chief Whip in Executive. b. 9 April 1920. Represented N. Belfast in Assembly, 1973–4, and in the Convention, 1975–6. First elected to Stormont in 1969 as pro-O'Neill Unionist in Clifton. Son of former Stormont Education Minister and grandson of MP for N. Belfast at

Westminster. With split in unionism, he joined Brian Faulkner in UPNI and represented the party in the Convention. Wide variety of public interests, and heavily involved in horse racing and breeding.

HARTE, PATRICK DONAL
Fine Gael spokesman on security and NI, 1977–81. b. 1932. Elected to the Dáil as a Donegal TD in 1961, and served on Dáil committee reviewing the Republic's Constitution. Minister of State, 1981–2. Throughout the Troubles he has sought to promote peace in NI, and has maintained close contacts with a wide variety of interests, including paramilitaries. In early 1982 he complained that Donegal was being used increasingly as a terrorist base by PIRA and INLA, following a number of large seizures of arms and explosives in areas of the county adjoining the border. In 1984 he urged the Republic to assert its claim to the island of Rockall in the Atlantic, which has been claimed by Britain. On the AIA he said in 1986 that it could not work unless the NI Unionist majority gave its consent. At a meeting in Bangor, Co. Down, in December 1988 he urged Protestants to change their attitude to the AIA.

HARVEY, CECIL
Chairman of the UUUP, 1977–80, but joined DUP in 1981. Down District Council, 1981–5. b. 1918; d. 1985. Ex-member of the OUP, he was elected in S. Down as a Vanguard Unionist to the Assembly, 1973–4. In the Convention, 1975–6, he was Chief Whip of the VUPP, and represented his party on the business committee. With the split in Vanguard on the issue of a voluntary coalition, he opposed the idea and became member of the UUUM, led by Ernest Baird. When the UUUM became a separate political party as the UUUP in 1977, he was appointed chairman of

the new party, and became its prospective candidate for the Westminster S. Down seat held by Enoch Powell MP, whom he backed in the October 1974 election. He did not fight the 1979 election but in 1983 he opposed Powell and lost his deposit. He was active in the Free Presbyterian Church.

HATTERSLEY, ROY SYDNEY GEORGE
Minister of Defence (Administration), 1969–70, and mainly responsible for detailed planning for setting up UDR. b. 28 December 1932. B.Sc. (Econ.) (Hull). Labour MP for Sparkbrook (Birmingham), 1964–. Visited NI for 'Operation Motorman', 1972, as Labour Defence spokesman. In 1978, as Prices Secretary, asked Prices Commission to make informal investigation of higher prices in NI. Shadow Home Secretary, 1980–3. Deputy leader of Labour Party, 1983–.

HAUGHEY, CHARLES JAMES
Taoiseach of Irish Republic, March 1987–; 1979–June 1981; and March–December 1982. Leader of opposition, July 1981–February 1982. b. Castlebar, Co. Mayo, 16 September 1925. B.Comm., BL (UCD). One of Republic's ablest, wealthiest and most colourful politicians, he has a NI background. His parents came from Swatragh, Co. Derry, and from families with a strong Republican tradition. His father, Sean, was second-in-command of the Northern division of the IRA. He joined Fianna Fáil in Dublin in 1948, and in 1951 married Maureen Lemass, daughter of former Fianna Fáil Taoiseach Sean Lemass. After two years in Dublin Corporation, he was elected to the Dáil at the third attempt in 1957 in Dublin North-East, an area which has provided him with a strong constituency base over the years. He was Minister for Justice, 1961–4, and

Minister for Agriculture, 1964–6, when he was a strong contender for the Fianna Fáil leadership, but eventually withdrew from the contest and gave his support to Jack Lynch. He was at the centre of gun-running allegations at the height of the NI Troubles in 1970. As Finance Minister he was sacked by Lynch, and later charged with conspiracy to import arms and ammunition illegally. But he and three others were acquitted. He returned to office in the Lynch Government elected in 1977, taking over the Health Ministry. In December 1979 he succeeded Lynch as Taoiseach and Fianna Fáil leader, but the Parliamentary Party vote was indicative of his inability to win general acceptance within Fianna Fáil at that time. He defeated George Colley (Lynch's deputy and his favourite for the post) by 44 votes to 38. On taking over as head of Government, he voiced his opposition to all the activities of PIRA, undertook to maintain all existing security measures, and named peaceful reunification of Ireland as his first political priority. At his party's annual conference in Dublin in 1980 he declared that the Stormont Constitutional Conference, then under way, could not provide a conclusive settlement. He envisaged the British and Irish Governments working together to find a solution. 'For over sixty years now,' he said, 'the situation in Northern Ireland has been a source of instability, real or potential, in these islands. It has been so because the very entity itself is artificial. . . In these conditions, violence and repression were inevitable.' This approach dominated his thinking on NI as Taoiseach. Unlike his Fine Gael opposite number, Garret FitzGerald, he was not prepared to modify those parts of the Constitution which were attacked by Unionists, and he saw no merit in an internal settlement in NI. Thus, he considered the Anglo-Irish talks as the key to the situation. His summit talks with Thatcher in Dublin in December 1980 were particularly gratifying, since the British PM and three Cabinet colleagues (Secretaries for Foreign Affairs, Northern Ireland, and the Chancellor of the Exchequer) agreed to a communiqué which he described as 'a historic breakthrough'. There were to be joint studies into a wide range of subjects and the 'totality of relations between the two countries', and the possibilities of new institutions. The ground was laid for the British-Irish Intergovernmental Council, which emerged in late 1981 and, it could be argued, the AIA of 1985. But in the wake of the 1980 summit, Thatcher was obviously worried about the intense anger which the Dublin package aroused among Unionists, many of whom talked of a 'sell-out' and an attempt to revive the Sunningdale plan. This led Thatcher to repeat the NI constitutional guarantee on every possible occasion, and she also rejected any idea of concessions to the H-Block hunger-strikers for which Haughey pressed. In the event it was probably the appearance of anti-H-Block candidates which led to the downfall of the Haughey administration in the June 1981 election. And when he got back to power in 1982 as the leader of a minority Government, he had a further policy clash with Britain, since he was opposed to EC sanctions against Argentina over the Falklands. In this situation there was little surprise that NI Secretary of State James Prior went ahead with his 'rolling devolution' initiative in 1982 without consulting the Dublin Government about the details. Indeed, Thatcher rubbed in the point by saying that Britain had no obligation to consult the Republic about NI affairs. So Haughey denounced the initiative as 'unworkable'. London, however, apparently found nothing to complain

about in Haughey's anti-terrorist policy. In the November 1982 election campaign he firmly opposed suggestions by FitzGerald that there should be an all-Ireland court and cross-border police force to deal with terrorism, and he sought to portray much of British political opinion and the media as interfering in an Irish election by expressing a preference for FitzGerald. The election was certainly a severe blow to Haughey, since it gave a Fine Gael–Labour Coalition a secure majority and he left office with Anglo-Irish relations extremely strained. Unionists in NI took the change calmly, with some of them saying that they preferred the certainty of Haughey's republicanism to FitzGerald's subtlety. The SDLP looked for the restoration of a strong bipartisan policy on NI in Dublin. This emerged to the extent that Haughey joined FitzGerald in supporting the New Ireland Forum. On the NIF report, published in May 1984, Haughey angered the other participants by insisting that the report meant that only the unitary state option had been accepted and that neither federation nor joint authority would bring peace in the North. When the AIA emerged in 1985, Haughey was critical of article one which provided a constitutional guarantee for NI, and he accused NI Secretary of State Tom King of 'impertinence' in attacking the articles in the Irish Constitution which claim sovereignty over NI. At the Wolfe Tone commemoration at Bodenstown in October 1986 he said his party would seek to renegotiate the AIA when it took office again. In the event, he just failed to secure an overall majority in the February 1987 election, but he was elected Taoiseach by the casting vote of the Speaker. In power, Haughey demonstrated a new pragmatism. He dropped the renegotiation demand and stressed that he accepted the AIA as an international agreement and would seek to make it work for the benefit of people in NI. But his Government did amend the extradition arrangement with the UK to ensure that the Irish Attorney-General was able to check the evidence related to each application. Thatcher protested that Britain was being treated in this matter less favourably than other European countries and coincidentally there were several clashes between Dublin and London over law-and-order issues. But behind the scenes Haughey seemed to be anxious to get Anglo-Irish relations on a better basis. At the same time he showed anxiety to build contacts with Unionists – a gesture which brought an open response in early 1988 from OUP leader James Molyneaux. He also improved his standing in the opinion polls, apparently reflecting widespread acceptance of tough financial measures. While he was ill at the end of 1988, Thatcher hit out at the year-old extradition arrangements, but Haughey's firm but low-key retorts and handling of the meeting with her at the EC summit in Rhodes strengthened his position at home.

HAUGHEY, DENIS

SDLP Assembly member for Mid-Ulster, 1982–6. Chairman of SDLP, 1973–8. b. Coalisland, Co. Tyrone, 3 October 1944. BA Hons in political science and modern history (QUB). Active in university as member of New Ireland Society, and in civil rights movement as first chairman of Tyrone Civil Rights Association. Joined SDLP on its formation, and unsuccessful in three Westminster elections – Fermanagh–S. Tyrone in February 1974 and Mid-Ulster in 1983 and in 1987, when he pushed PSF into third place. Candidate in Convention poll in N. Antrim in 1975. SDLP delegate to Socialist International and bureau of Conferation of Socialist Parties of EC. In 1980 became full-time assistant to

party leader John Hume in his work as MEP, and also International Secretary of the party. SDLP's spokesman on agriculture.

HAYES, MAURICE N.

NI Ombudsman and Commissioner of Complaints, 1987–. b. 8 July 1927. BA Hons; Hon LLD (QUB). Has had extremely diverse career in public service. As Town Clerk of Downpatrick, 1955–73, he was seconded as first chairman of Community Relations Commission, 1969–72, and director of Ombudsman's Office, 1972–3. During 1973–4, he was Assistant Secretary in office of power-sharing Executive, and after it collapsed, senior adviser to Sir Robert (later Lord) Lowry as Convention chairman, 1974–6. In 1976 he was involved in the setting up of the Fair Employment Agency, and his civil service career between that and 1987 included a period as Head of Personnel, but was mainly in the Department of Health and Social Services, where he was Permanent Secretary, 1984–7. He has been a visiting professor at the University of Ulster, and has served on a great variety of public bodies, including the Arts Council of NI, and the BBC Advisory Committee, 1967–73.

H-BLOCKS

The Maze Prison cell blocks – so called because of their shape – which were designed to accommodate terrorist-type prisoners with the ending of special category status. (See also Special Category.) The term 'H-Block' went round the world in the spring of 1978 when some 300 Republican prisoners, campaigning for political status or the restoration of special category status, decided to step up their existing campaign of wearing only a blanket. They refused to wash, or leave their cells, or use the toilet facilities, and the walls of many of the cells were covered with excreta. They also smashed up cell furniture. For the PIRA, the protest had the effect of attracting worldwide publicity, and the British Government attempted to counter it by claiming that if the prisoners would only accept the normal prison discipline they would be able to enjoy the facilities of one of the best-equipped prisons in western Europe. The Catholic archbishop of Armagh, Dr Tomás (later Cardinal) Ó Fiaich, urged the British Government in August 1978 to do something to deal with the 'inhuman conditions' at the Maze, but the then Secretary of State, Roy Mason, ruled out any change of policy. In late 1978 and early 1979, the Government stepped up its publicity drive against the H-Block protesters since they obviously feared that the Republican campaign was making some impact in the US, notably among Irish-Americans, and possibly stimulating financial aid to Republican funds. For the first time, journalists were allowed inside the Maze Prison to describe the conditions, although they were not allowed to talk to the protesters. In 1980 the Republican prison protest took a more dramatic turn, with the arrival of the mass hunger strike. On 27 October seven prisoners – six PIRA and one INLA – at the Maze began fasting in support of the demand that, among other things, they should be allowed to wear their own clothes and be excused prison work. The British Government, through Secretary of State Humphrey Atkins, insisted that there could be no concession which could be regarded as permitting political status, although he argued that the Government was prepared to talk about improvements in conditions on purely humanitarian grounds. In October 1980 the Government announced that all male convicted prisoners would be allowed to wear official-issue, civilian-type clothing, but it emerged quickly that

this would not be seen by the protesters as meeting the 'own clothing' demand and many people sympathetic to the prisoners' cause criticised the Government for stopping short of conceding on the clothing issue. This phase of the hunger strike ended in some confusion on 18 December 1980. With one PIRA prisoner, Sean McKenna, close to death, the prisoners said they had abandoned their fast because of a message from Atkins and a thirty-four-page description of prison conditions which had been shown to them. On 25 January 1981, however, Bobby Sands, twenty-six-year-old newly elected leader of the PIRA prisoners, claimed that moves for gradual co-operation between the prisoners and the administration had broken down. On 1 March 1981 – fifth anniversary of the start of phasing out of special category – Sands began fasting on his own, and thus launched a campaign which was to drag on for seven months, provoking a political crisis in both NI and the Republic, and intense controversy in many parts of the world. In the course of the protests ten hunger-strikers died – seven from PIRA and three from INLA. On 5 May Sands, who had been elected MP for Fermanagh–S. Tyrone in the April 1981 by-election, was the first hunger-striker to die, after sixty-six days without food. His funeral from Twinbrook, W. Belfast, to Milltown cemetery was an impressive display of Republican strength, with some 70,000 people attending. The others who died were:

Francis Hughes (twenty-five), PIRA, on 12 May after fifty-nine days.

Raymond McCreesh (twenty-four), PIRA, on 21 May after sixty-one days.

Patsy O'Hara (twenty-three), leader of INLA prisoners, on 21 May after sixty-one days.

Joe McDonnell (thirty), PIRA, on 8 July after sixty-one days.

Martin Hurson (twenty-seven), PIRA, on 13 July after forty-six days.

Kevin Lynch (twenty-five), INLA, on 1 August after seventy-one days.

Kieran Doherty (twenty-five), PIRA, elected TD in Cavan–Monaghan in the June general election, on 2 August after seventy-three days.

Thomas McElwee (twenty-three), PIRA, on 8 August after sixty-five days.

Michael Devine (twenty-three), INLA, on 20 August after sixty-six days.

Basically, it was a battle of wills between the prisoners and the British Government. Outside the prison, the campaign for the 'five demands' (own clothing, no prison work, freedom of association, extra recreational facilities and more visits and letters, and restoration of remission lost on protests) was spearheaded by the National H-Block/Armagh Committee, and strongly backed by PSF. (See also National H-Block/Armagh Committee.) But there was much sympathy for the hunger-strikers in the general Nationalist-Catholic sector of the community. This often fell short of support for political status and, in common with much Dublin opinion, concentrated on British 'intransigence'. Certainly Thatcher gave a strong lead against any concessions while the hunger strike continued, and during a visit to Belfast on 28 May, she remarked that the protest 'might well be the last card' of the PIRA campaign. British information services abroad stressed the rejection by the European Commission of Human Rights of a claim by four prisoners that their treatment had breached the European Convention of Human Rights. Britain also argued that prisoners were failing to take advantage of the modern prison facilities. But the recurring deaths, the tense atmosphere and a high level of violence spurred a great variety of individuals and organisations to try their hand at reconciliation. The Catholic Church was involved at many levels. In the early stages, the Papal envoy, Monsignor John Magee, Ulster-born personal Secretary to Pope John Paul II, talked with Sands in an unsuccessful bid to persuade him to abandon the protest. Cardinal Ó Fiaich and the Bishop of Derry, Dr Edward Daly, had several meetings with Government Ministers. They urged that clothing and work should be optional, and apparently were disappointed at an early stage that the Government did not concede 'own clothing', as they had been led to believe it would. When Raymond McCreesh and Patsy O'Hara died in May, the Cardinal warned that the Government would 'face the wrath of the whole Nationalist population' if it failed to modify its 'rigid stance'. The Irish Commission for Justice and Peace (a sub-committee of the Irish Bishops' Conference) had a series of lengthy talks with Michael Alison, the Minister of State in charge of prisons up to September 1981. The Commission was optimistic about an end to the protest in July, when it produced an elaborate package of reforms, but it evidently misjudged the Government's attitude. Father Denis Faul, a prison chaplain, was also closely involved, particularly in the final stages of the hunger strike, when he organised meetings of relatives of those still fasting. In Dublin both Charles Haughey and Garret FitzGerald, as successive heads of Government, tried unsuccessfully to persuade Thatcher to soften her approach, as did SDLP leader John Hume at a meeting with the PM. In July the Irish Government also failed in a bid to enlist the support of President Reagan, at least publicly. The European Commission of Human Rights, and the International Red Cross were also briefly involved. The hunger strike had widespread repercussions in terms of violence and a political spin-off both in NI and the Republic. During the protest, sixty-one people died in violent incidents in NI. Fifteen RUC men – twelve regulars and three reservists – along with eight soldiers and seven UDR members died in bombings and shootings. Five of the soldiers died on 19 May in a landmine explosion near Camlough, Co. Armagh, home village of hunger-striker Raymond McCreesh. Thirty-four civilians were killed, including seven people (two of them girls of eleven and fourteen) who died as a result of injuries inflicted by plastic bullets fired by the police or army. In the Republic the most serious violence occurred in Dublin on 18 July, when some two hundred people were injured during a riot, when Gardaí prevented an H-Block march passing the British Embassy. As for the political effects inside NI, the by-election victory of Sands and then of his election agent, Owen Carron, in Fermanagh–S. Tyrone, were a reminder that the passions of an across-the-board nationalism could still be aroused. The by-elections also served to weaken the British argument that the protest enjoyed very little public support. In the council elections of May 1981 the atmosphere also resulted in hardened attitudes, and candidates, from several parties, campaigning directly on the H-Block issue polled 51,000 votes and won thirty-six seats. The impact on Southern Irish politics was also far-reaching. The return of two Maze prisoners as TDs – hunger-striker Kieran Doherty in Cavan–Monaghan, and Paddy Agnew in Louth – and the substantial vote for H-Block nominees were seen as playing a major part in the defeat of the Fianna Fáil Government in the June 1981 general election. The nine H-Block candidates took nearly 40,000 first-preference votes. In

Britain Thatcher had broad support in Parliament for her refusal to make concessions, and a MORI poll in May suggested that 92 per cent of English and Welsh voters rejected political status. Opposition politicians such as Labour's Don Concannon and Liberal leader David Steel visited the Maze, but saw no scope for Government concessions. Only about fourteen Labour backbenchers were sympathetic to the H-Block cause. When James Prior became Secretary of State in mid-September, there were clear signs that the hunger strike had lost its impetus. Already, the relatives of four hunger-strikers had intervened to ensure that they were fed under medical supervision. None the less, Prior's first commitment outside Government offices was a three-hour visit to the Maze Prison within four days of taking over, and he saw two of the hunger-strikers, although he did not talk to them. On 29 September Lord Gowrie, Minister of State and deputy to Prior, who had now taken responsibility for prison matters, repeated that no concessions would be made to prisoners until the protest ended. The six remaining hunger-strikers now became aware that their relatives would intervene to save their lives, and this was the factor which finally brought an end to the long-drawn-out bid to secure political status. On the afternoon of Saturday 3 October, the six men still fasting agreed to take food. Three days later the Secretary of State announced that all prisoners would be allowed to wear their own clothing at all times. At the same time protesters would have 50 per cent of lost remission restored. But the Government refused to meet the demand for an end to prison work and for free association, although it hinted at some improvement on these points. Unionists protested strongly at the clothing and remission moves, and some Republicans who had backed the protest consoled themselves with the claim that the overall result of the hunger strike had been to give international recognition to the prisoners' political status. And in 1982 the demand for segregation of Republican and loyalist prisoners, which had seemed a minor element in 1980–1, suddenly began to be pressed by both sides. The Government showed itself opposed to segregation in principle and hinted at collusion between Republican and loyalist prisoners to achieve separation. The Maze H-Blocks were again in the world headlines when, on 23 September 1983, thirty-eight PIRA prisoners staged the biggest break-out in British prison history. During the operation, which involved the hijacking of a prison food lorry, a prison officer, James Ferris, forty-three, died and six other officers suffered knife and gunshot wounds. (Ferris's death was first believed to be due to stabbing, but a court in 1988 held it could have arisen from natural causes.) Fifteen of the escapees were swiftly recaptured, while another four were picked up within three days. But nineteen got away, including PIRA leader in the H-Blocks, Brendan McFarlane, who was subsequently extradited from Holland in 1986. 'The Great Escape', as PIRA dubbed it, was a serious embarrassment to NI Ministers, and security was tightened as a result of the Hennessy report on the escape. In April 1988 eighteen of the original escapees were given sentences ranging from five to eight years on firearms and other charges, but sixteen of them were found not guilty of murdering a prison officer. Gerard Kelly, who like McFarlane had been extradited from Holland, was found not guilty of attempted murder. Neither he nor McFarlane could be charged with murder because of the terms of the extradition. Both men got five years for the escape attempt and other offences.

Lord Chief Justice Lowry sharply criticised the evidence of prison officers, saying much of it had been unreliable and contradictory. At that time, ten of the escapees were still at large: three were dead, and seven were in custody in the Republic or in England, including Gerard McDonnell, sentenced for his part in the Brighton hotel bombing. In 1988 the remaining ninety-two special category prisoners moved to the H-Blocks but retained their privileges.

HEATH, EDWARD RICHARD GEORGE

Conservative PM, 1970–4, and opposition leader, 1965–70 and 1974–5. MP for Bexley Sidcup, 1974–83; Old Bexley and Sidcup, 1983–. b. 9 July 1916. There were three decisive points in Edward Heath's policy towards NI as PM and Conservative leader. Firstly, he switched the emphasis of Tory policy away from positive support of the Union. In November 1971 he said: 'Many Catholics in Northern Ireland would like to see Northern Ireland unified with the South. That is understandable. It is legitimate that they should seek to further that aim by democratic and constitutional means. If at some future date the majority of the people in Northern Ireland want unification and express that desire in the appropriate constitutional manner, I do not believe any British Government would stand in the way. But that is not what the majority want today.' Secondly, he moved swiftly to suspend Stormont in March 1972, in the wake of 'Bloody Sunday' in Londonderry, defying the advice of the NI Premier, Brian Faulkner, and risking a loyalist backlash. Thirdly, he brought all his Prime Ministerial power to bear at the Sunningdale Conference in December 1973 to get the power-sharing administration established. The previous August he made a two-day visit to NI during which he urged politicians to get on with the job of making the Assembly work. On that occasion he made one of his few gestures to unionism when he attended the Belfast memorial service for the former PM, Lord Brookeborough. Earlier visits to NI were in December 1971 (essentially a pre-Christmas visit to the army), and on 16–17 November 1972, when he was pondering the scope of the British political initiative. One of his most surprising comments was made in Dublin in September 1973 after talks with Taoiseach Liam Cosgrave and other Ministers. In a BBC interview he mentioned the possibility of NI being fully integrated with GB. After protests from Harold Wilson, the opposition leader, and many sections of NI and Dublin opinion, he claimed that he was not advocating integration as a solution. In his *Memoirs of a Statesman*, the late Brian (Lord) Faulkner quotes Heath as saying in the critical pre-direct-rule talks at Downing Street that NI should have a county-council- or Greater-London-Council-type administration. Visiting Belfast in January 1983, he described himself as 'the best friend Ulster ever had'. In 1984 he complained that the Wilson Government had not done enough in 1974 to maintain the power-sharing Executive.

HENDRON, JAMES
Alliance Convention member for S. Belfast, 1975–6. b. Belfast, 1931. Solicitor. Founder member and ex-chairman of the Alliance Party. His brother, Dr Joseph Hendron, was SDLP Convention member for W. Belfast.

HENDRON, DR JOSEPH GERARD
SDLP Assembly member for W. Belfast, 1982–6. b. Belfast, 1932. MB (QUB); MRCGP, DPH, Dip. Obst., RCOG. General medical practitioner in Falls

Road area of Belfast and party's health spokesman. NI Assembly, 1973–4. Convention member for W. Belfast, 1975–6, while his brother James was an Alliance Convention member for S. Belfast. Belfast City Council, 1981–. Chairman of the SDLP Constituency Representatives, 1980–. In the 1983 Westminster election, he was runner-up to Gerry Adams, who won the seat for PSF, but Gerry Fitt blamed him for his loss of the seat, saying Dr Hendron was unable to attract the non-Nationalist support which had gone to him (Fitt). In 1987 he again ran second to Adams despite a strong SDLP campaign and the decision of Alliance to stand aside. In 1988 he urged massive economic aid for W. Belfast, claiming that unemployed young people were being sucked into paramilitary organisations.

HENNESSY REPORT *see* H-Blocks

HERMON, SIR JOHN
Chief Constable of the RUC, January 1980–9. b. Larne, Co. Antrim, 1928. He had been in the RUC for twenty-nine years when he was appointed Chief Constable, having risen through the ranks. In 1963, when he became a head constable, he was also the first RUC officer to go to Bramshill police training college in England. In 1966 he was district inspector in charge of the Cookstown area, and in the following year deputy Commandant of the RUC training centre at Enniskillen. He was promoted to Chief Superintendent in 1970, Assistant Chief Constable, 1974, and in 1975 was awarded the OBE. By 1976 he was deputy Chief Constable (operations) and when he went on attachment to Scotland Yard in 1979, he was widely tipped for the top post. As Chief Constable, he faced a wide variety of challenges. In the early years he had to cope with the revival of street violence during the 1981 hunger strike.

In 1982 the Armagh 'shoot to kill' controversy surfaced and was still producing a spin-off in 1988. He has clashed with the local police federation on policy and internal matters, and the EOC over the sacking of women officers. When the Rev. Ian Paisley launched his Third Force at the end of 1981, Sir John gave a strong warning that no private army would be allowed to usurp the authority of the police or army. At private conferences he has proved a highly articulate defender of the RUC, and has been a strict disciplinarian, apparently unworried by his detractors. There have been periodic 'hiccups' in his relations with the Garda chiefs, but these have not affected the developing cross-border security co-operation, notably since the signing of the AIA, and he has attended most of the official conferences held under the agreement. In 1986 he succeeded in dispelling doubts in Dublin that he would be able to handle effectively the loyalist protests against the AIA and new public order legislation. While acknowledging the 'deep-seated' Unionist opposition to the agreement, he insisted that the RUC had acted impartially throughout, and he has claimed increasing acceptability of the police in the Nationalist community. Following the decision not to bring prosecutions against RUC men over an alleged cover-up of evidence related to the 1982 Armagh shootings, the Police Authority in 1988 voted by a majority of one not to pursue disciplinary inquiries against Sir John and two of his senior colleagues. Sir John's subsequent decision to bring disciplinary charges against twenty junior members of the force drew wide criticism. He has indicated his intention to retire during May 1989.

HERRON, THOMAS (TOMMY)
Vice-chairman and leading spokesman of the UDA, who was found shot dead at Drumbo, near Lisburn, in September 1973. b. 1937. An open verdict was returned at the inquest. UDA leaders dismissed the idea of a serious political motive, ruling out both PIRA and Protestant paramilitary involvement. They suggested that 'cranks', bitterly opposed to Herron, had been responsible. He stood unsuccessfully as a Vanguard Unionist candidate in the Assembly election in 1973.

HESLIP, HERBERT
OUP member for S. Down in the Assembly, 1973–4, and Convention, 1975–6. b. Ballinaskeagh, Co. Down, 1913. Farmer. For many years a leading figure in unionism and local government in S. Down. Member of Down County Council, 1968–73. Banbridge District Council, 1973–85. Vice-president, Down Orange Welfare. Deputy Speaker of NI Assembly, 1973–4.

HILLERY, DR PATRICK JOHN
President of Irish Republic, 1976–. b. 2 May 1923. B.Sc., MB, B.Ch., BAO (UCD). Dr Hillery made his most dramatic intervention in NI affairs on 6 July 1970, as the Republic's Minister for Foreign Affairs. He drove secretly to Belfast and appeared on the Falls Road. He had not consulted the British Government, and there was an angry protest from Britain's Foreign Secretary Sir Alec Douglas-Home, who said it was a 'serious diplomatic discourtesy' and would add to the difficulties of those working for peace. Taoiseach Jack Lynch defended the visit, saying that there was fear on the Falls and it was vitally important that it should not be exploited by subversive elements. Dr Hillery was Foreign Minister, 1969–73, and earlier ministerial posts were: Education, 1959–65; Industry and Commerce, 1965–6; and Labour, 1966–9. He was EC Commissioner for Social Affairs,

1973–6, and one of his earliest
announcements in that office was the
setting up of an EC Commission office
in Belfast.

HOLDEN, SIR DAVID CHARLES BERESFORD

Head of the NI civil service and
Permanent Secretary, Department of
Finance, 1973–6. b. 26 July 1915.
Educated at King's College, Cambridge.
Joined the NI civil service in 1937, and
after retirement in 1976, served for a
year as Director of the Ulster Office in
London.

HOLLYWOOD, SEAN

SDLP candidate who lost by 3,567 votes
to Enoch Powell (OUP, UUUC) in S.
Down in the Westminster election,
October 1974. b. 1945. BA (QUB).
Teacher. Caught attention as main
opponent to Enoch Powell in heavily
publicised campaign. His strong
showing in a constituency where the
Unionist majority had often reached
10,000 to 20,000 clearly owed much to
his ability to pull over some votes of
Unionists unhappy at Powell's can-
didature. Newry and Mourne District
Council, 1973–7. Unsuccessful SDLP
Convention candidate in N. Down,
1975. In 1978 he was at variance with
the party on the power-sharing issue.
Left politics to pursue interest in stage
and drama.

HOUSE, LIEUTENANT-GENERAL SIR DAVID

Army GOC, NI, 1975–7. b. 8 August
1922. General House took over in NI
when the PIRA ceasefire was petering
out. One of his major tasks was to deal
with the outbreak of violence in S.
Armagh, including the killing of ten
Protestant workers in a minibus in
January 1976. This led to the
introduction of the undercover Special
Air Service into S. Armagh, and soon
afterwards it was permitted to operate
anywhere in NI, mainly to counter
sectarian assassinations. In 1977 he left
the army to become Black Rod in the
House of Lords.

HOWE, SIR GEOFFREY

Foreign and Commonwealth Secretary,
1983–. b. 20 December 1926. QC. As
Chancellor of the Exchequer in
December 1980, he was one of Cabinet
team who had talks in Dublin with
Charles Haughey's Government,
which led to the declaration that the
Thatcher and Haughey Governments
would consider the 'totality of relationships' between the two countries. Sir
Geoffrey has backed the radical
external approach to NI affairs which
led to the AIA, and which was at odds
with Thatcher's initial insistence that
the Irish Government had no right to be
consulted on NI matters. In 1988, when
relations between London and Dublin
were strained, mainly over security
issues, he argued that this was exactly
the situation the AIA was designed to
deal with. And although Haughey, on a
US visit in 1988, was critical of British
policy, Sir Geoffrey described the
Taoiseach as 'an outstanding patriot'
and said he did not underestimate the
'hurt' felt by the Irish recently. In
November 1988 he visited Dublin for
talks with the Government, which was
urging greater use of extra-territorial
legislation as an alternative, but Sir
Geoffrey declared that the use of such
legislation was no substitute for
extradition.

HOWELL, DAVID

Parliamentary Under-Secretary, NIO,
1972–3. b. 18 January 1936. Energy
Minister, 1979–81; Transport
Minister, 1981–3. Conservative MP for
Guildford, 1966–. After a short period
in the economic section of the
Treasury, he was leader writer and
special correspondent of the London
Daily Telegraph, 1960–4. As director

of the Conservative Political Centre, he had a hand in drafting the party's 1964 election manifesto. At the NIO he had charge of the departments of Finance, Commerce and Agriculture.

HULL, WILLIAM (BILLY)

Chairman of LAW, 1969–73. b. Belfast, 1912. Member NILP, 1948–73. He became well known as a voice of Protestant workers at the height of the violence. He left the NILP in protest against Harold Wilson's attitude to NI. He had helped organise the Workers' Committee for the Defence of the Constitution, which preceded LAW, and as convenor of shop stewards at the Belfast shipyard engine works, was one of a small group which organised LAW throughout NI to the point when it claimed about 100,000 members. After the murder of three Scottish soldiers in Belfast in early 1971, he led a march of 9,000 engineering workers to Unionist headquarters – a protest which was regarded as one of the main factors which led to the resignation soon afterwards of James Chichester-Clark from the Premiership. He was also involved in planning the forty-eight-hour loyalist strike when direct rule was introduced in 1972. Most of LAW's supporters linked up with the UWC in early 1973, when Hull differed with some of the other leaders on tactics.

HUME, JOHN

SDLP MEP for NI, 1979–. Leader, SDLP, November 1979–. MP for Foyle, 1983–. Assembly member for Londonderry, 1973–4 and 1982–6; Convention member, 1975–6. Head of Commerce Department in power-sharing NI Executive, 1974, and deputy leader, SDLP, 1973–9. b. Londonderry, 18 January 1937. MA (Maynooth). An ex-teacher, he first came to political prominence in the civil rights movement in Londonderry in 1968, and was vice-chairman of the Derry Citizens'

Action Committee, 1968–9. In the Stormont general election of February 1969, he was returned as MP for Foyle, unseating the Nationalist leader, Eddie McAteer. During the election campaign, he urged the establishment of a social democratic party. He was a founder member of the SDLP in 1970, and soon emerged as the party's chief policy-maker. He was elected to the Assembly, 1973–4, from Londonderry and was heavily engaged in the negotiations with Secretary of State William Whitelaw, and in the Sunningdale Conference, which led to the setting up of the Executive. As head of the Commerce Department, he was deeply involved with the economic problems thrown up by the loyalist strike in 1974. He fought the London-derry seat unsuccessfully in the West-minster election of October 1974. He was returned to the Convention for Londonderry, and after the failure of the Convention joined his then party colleague, Paddy Devlin, in private but unsuccessful talks with Austin Ardill and the Rev. Martin Smyth, Official Unionists, on a possible political settlement. He then became active in liaising with politicians in Europe and the US, and in 1977 he became part-time adviser on consumer affairs to the EC Commissioner, Richard Burke. This entailed considerable travel within the Common Market area. In 1978 the main political parties in the Republic took up in principle his plea that they should seek to spell out in detail their intentions on eventual Irish unity. He suggested at the same time that more thought should be given to a federal solution. In 1978 he was unanimously selected as the SDLP candidate for one of the three NI seats in the 1979 European direct elections. He fought a vigorous campaign, essentially on EC issues, but claimed that the new Parliament would lead to co-operation between MEPs from NI and the

Republic, and would form a 'healing process' in Irish affairs. On the first count, he secured 140,622 votes, or 24.5 per cent – that is, just short of the quota. He had more votes than the combined total of the two Official Unionists, and the poll was a record one for the SDLP. He was elected on the third count, with 146,072 and became a member of the socialist group in the European Assembly, and a member of the Assembly's regional committee. He succeeded Gerry Fitt MP as party leader. Fitt had resigned because of the initial refusal of the SDLP to attend the 1980 Constitutional Conference promoted by Secretary of State Humphrey Atkins, and also because he argued that the SDLP had abandoned a socialist approach and become simply a Nationalist party – a contention hotly denied by Hume. Hume later claimed that at the Atkins conference the SDLP had proposed that power-sharing government should be limited to ten years, and he said it was clear that Unionists were totally opposed to partnership government. He again cited Unionist opposition to power-sharing as one of the reasons for rejecting the 'rolling devolution' scheme put forward by Secretary of State James Prior in 1982. Dubbing the plan 'unworkable', he also complained that the Irish dimension was far too limited. During the passage of the legislation, Hume urged that a Parliamentary tier of the British-Irish Inter-governmental Council should have responsibility for security, civil rights and 'identity'. In the event, he led the SDLP into the October 1982 Assembly elections, with a boycott of the Assembly itself and called for a 'Council for a New Ireland', which would bring together politicians from the Republic and NI to draw up a realistic Irish unity blueprint. The proposal led to the New Ireland Forum. After the polls, he said the

Assembly was 'dead as a dodo'. In the European Parliament in 1980 he spearheaded a new economic initiative for NI, which was supported by the other two local MEPs, and which led to a special European Parliament report on ways of strengthening the local economy. He has made frequent visits to the US, making political contacts at many levels and receiving honorary degrees from several universities. In March 1982 he was one of President Reagan's guests at a St Patrick's Day lunch in the White House, at which the Republic's Taoiseach, Charles Haughey, was guest of honour. Hume used the occasion to exlain SDLP policy to Congressional leaders. In 1983 he pressed in European Parliament for an inquiry by its political affairs committee into NI's economy and political situation. The idea was adopted, despite opposition from the British Government and Unionists. In the 1983 Westminster election, he won easily the new Foyle constituency – the first time a non-Unionist had got a Westminster seat in the Londonderry area since the establishment of NI. In 1984 he saw the NIF report as a pointer to a new era of negotiations aimed at resolving the NI situation, and he had an insider's view of the testing exchanges between London and Dublin which led finally to the AIA in 1985. He sought to blunt the Unionist assault on the AIA by arguing that it was not an end in itself but the beginning of a process in which the two traditions could reach an accommodation. He insisted that devolution had to be judged on whether it was likely to contribute to such a solution, but it was 1988 before he led his party into serious talks with Secretary of State Tom King on the issue of a local administration. By that time he had also become involved in controversial discussions with PSF president Gerry Adams, aimed, he said, at bringing not a ceasefire but a permanent end to violence. Hume had annoyed the Garret FitzGerald Government with his brief but unsuccessful meeting with PIRA in February 1985, and these exchanges with PSF in 1988 also raised some doubts in Dublin, as well as outright hostility from Unionists, who said they would not have talks with the SDLP while the contacts continued. The SDLP leader apparently saw the talks with PSF as an opportunity to press his claim that the AIA effectively meant that Britain had disclaimed any long-term interest in having a presence in Ireland, and that the 'armed struggle' was, therefore, irrelevant. The talks with PSF ended in September 1988. He also dismissed scepticism within NI about the possibility of a political breakthrough. But his appeal to Unionists at the 1988 SDLP annual conference to enter into dialogue outside, but parallel to, the AIA was rejected. In his address he accused PIRA of 'showing the hallmarks of undiluted fascism'.

HUNGER STRIKE *see* H-Blocks

HUNT REPORT
The report produced by the committee headed by Lord Hunt which led to far-reaching reforms in the NI security forces in 1969. The report recommended an unarmed RUC and replacement of the controversial USC by a new part-time force under the army GOC (it emerged as the UDR), as well as the setting up of a Police Reserve. The proposal for ending the USC was deeply resented by many Unionists, and led to serious rioting in Protestant areas of Belfast. It was welcomed by those who had supported the civil rights campaign.

HURD, DOUGLAS RICHARD
NI Secretary of State, September 1984–September 1985. Previously

Minister of State at the Home Office, 1983–4, and at the Foreign and Commonwealth Office, 1979–83. MP for Mid Oxon., February 1974–83; MP for Witney, 1983–. b. 8 March 1930. Although he had made political contacts in NI as an opposition spokesman in the 1970s, his appointment was a surprise. In the event his brief stay at Stormont turned out to be a crucial period, since it marked the decisive stage of negotiations preceding the signing of the AIA. But there were ups and downs in London–Dublin relations during his tenure at the NIO. Thatcher had angered the Irish Government and the SDLP with her comment after the November 1984 London summit meeting with Garret FitzGerald that it was 'out, out, out' to the three options of the New Ireland Forum. This had temporarily heartened Unionists, but soon they were using the Assembly as a platform for repeated allegations that the British Government was planning a 'back-doors' deal with Dublin. By March 1985, when Hurd asked junior Minister Chris Patten to mediate between the NI parties, he had already received two reports from the Assembly Devolution Committee. The appointment of a mediator was a signal of Hurd's discontent with their efforts. The feeling seems to have been mutual, for in their one meeting with Hurd the committee found him cold and aloof and their minutes referred to 'a somewhat cavalier attitude to the committee and the Assembly'. The mediation attempt failed as Unionists were in no mood for compromise and the SDLP were still looking for major Irish Government involvement in NI affairs. Hurd was believed to have been influential in bringing about a change of attitude by Thatcher, and he may have been helped in this by her strong interest in cross-border security. This could only have been heightened by the PIRA assault on

Newry police station in February 1985, in which nine RUC officers died. Oddly enough, Hurd's sudden departure from the NIO in 1985 to succeed Leon Brittan as Home Secretary owed something to what was widely seen as Brittan's mishandling of the controversy over the BBC *Real Lives* film featuring local politicians: Gregory Campbell (DUP) and Martin McGuinness (PSF). As a thriller writer, Hurd produced in 1975 a novel, *Vote to Kill*, dealing with an IRA plot to kill the PM and which was dedicated to Edward Heath, to whom he had been Political Secretary, 1970–4. His refusal as Secretary of State to have meetings with PSF elected representatives led to references to a meeting which he held privately in 1978 with Gerry Adams and Danny Morrison of PSF in preparation for a BBC programme. In 1987, as Home Secretary, he allowed the six men convicted for the Birmingham pub bombings of 1974 to go to the Court of Appeal, but the appeal failed there and in the Lords. In 1988 Hurd was active in promoting new anti-terrorist measures, and his ban on broadcasts by supporters of terrorism and new official secrets legislation drew particular criticism from the media.

HUTCHINSON, DOUGLAS
DUP Assembly, 1973–4, and Convention, 1975–6, member for Armagh. b. Richhill, Co. Armagh, 1918. One of the Rev. Ian Paisley's most active supporters, he was on Armagh Rural Council, 1953–73, and Armagh District Council, 1973–. Former member, USC. In Convention election he said he would share power in government only with those who supported the link with GB. Sentenced to one month's imprisonment after incidents in November 1968 in Armagh, following the civil rights march and loyalist counter-demonstrations there. Expelled from

Orange Order for criticism of leadership. Unsuccessfully contested 1982 Assembly election in Armagh.

HUTTON, SIR JAMES BRIAN EDWARD
Lord Chief Justice, NI, 1988–. b. 29 June 1931. Called to NI Bar, 1954. QC (NI), 1970. Called to English Bar, 1972. Senior Crown Counsel, NI, 1973–9. High Court judge, NI, 1979–88. Appointed Lord Chief Justice at a time when the Irish Government was pressing for major changes in court system in NI in the context of the AIA. In 1978 was member of British defence team in European Court of Human Rights when Britain was found guilty of ill-treating internees in 1971.

HUTTON, NORMAN
General secretary of the OUP, 1974–83. b. 1943. A former businessman, he was responsible for planning the party's election campaigns, and was heavily involved in carrying through constituency reorganisation to deal with the five extra Westminster seats.

I

ILLEGAL ORGANISATIONS *see* Security System section, p. 400, for list of bodies proscribed under the Emergency Provisions Act

INDEPENDENT ORANGE ORDER
A relatively small organisation which was originally a breakaway from the main Orange Order. It was founded in 1903 after a row following a Belfast by-election in which the official Unionist candidate was defeated by a shipyard worker, T. H. Sloan. When Sloan was expelled from the Orange

Order he and his friends set up the Independent Orange Order. It called on its members to 'hold out the right hand of fellowship to those who, while worshipping at other shrines, are yet our countrymen'. It holds its own 12 July demonstrations, some of which have been addressed by the Rev. Ian Paisley, who broke with the main Order in 1962. In 1982 the Rev. Martin Smyth MP, as head of the main Order, said he hoped that the official and independent Orange Orders would eventually reunite. In 1985 the Independent Order criticised Orangemen in Canada for taking part in a 'reconciliation seminar' with Catholics.

INDEPENDENT UNIONIST GROUP *see* Progressive Unionist Party

INTEGRATION

The idea of complete absorption of NI into the UK without any regional self-government. It has been ruled out by the main parties in GB and was not backed by any group in the Constitutional Convention, 1975–6. After the collapse of the Convention, however, a section of the OUP seemed to be attracted to the possibility, provided that NI was given parity with the rest of the UK in representation at Westminster, and in local government. This presumably inspired the party's suggestions of administrative devolution in the 1982 Assembly. The decision of the Callaghan Government in 1978 to introduce five extra Westminster seats was interpreted by the SDLP as a lurch towards integration. However, British Governments, both Conservative and Labour, have continued to look for devolved government, and have maintained a separate statute book for local legislation during direct rule, and devolution was envisaged in the AIA. Opinion polls have shown around 80

per cent of Protestants in NI prepared to accept integration but, predictably, little support among Nationalists. An Integration Group was set up in NI in 1984 to promote the idea, and the Campaign for Equal Citizenship has also drawn integrationists to its ranks.

INTERNATIONAL FUND FOR IRELAND

Set up in 1986 to back the AIA with economic measures in NI and, to a lesser extent, in border areas of the Republic. Fund developed from anxiety in US to encourage reconciliation in the wake of the AIA. Washington contributed $120 million over three years up to 1988, and there have been suggestions that the aid will be extended. In 1987 Canada pledged $10 million over ten years, and New Zealand $1 million over the same period. In 1988 the EC Commission proposed £9.75 million per year for three years. The fund is administered by a board headed by Belfast solicitor Charles Brett, former Housing Executive chairman, who has stressed the independence of the board from political control. Its second report, at the end of 1988, stated that grants to 858 projects totalled £26,579,000, and represented 4,500 permanent jobs. The SDLP has been supportive of the initiative, while quarrelling with some of its grants policies. Several Irish-American groups have been critical of the administration of the fund, but the US Senate Appropriations Committee has praised its approach. Unionists have condemned the fund as an attempt to bribe them to accept the AIA. Before leaving office, President Reagan promised a further contribution in 1989.

IRELAND FUNDS

Funds established in the US, Canada, Australia and GB 'to promote peace, culture and charity in all of Ireland', with priority being given to projects that are innovative, featuring self-help and a high degree of community involvement. The funds derive from the Ireland Fund set up in US in 1976 and which in 1987 merged with the Irish American Foundation, and up to 1987 total contributions in US were over $8 million. The Canadian fund was set up in 1978; the Australian, in 1987; and the British in 1988. All now operate together under the chairmanship of Dr Tony O'Reilly, who headed the US fund from the outset. The funds have had the endorsement of both the British and Irish Governments, and that of President Reagan and the Prime Ministers of Canada and Australia. Fifty per cent of grant aid goes to NI projects.

IRISH-AMERICAN UNITY CONFERENCE
Irish-American group which has been critical of British policy in Ireland. In January 1988 its chairman Jim Delaney was also opposed to the Republic's Government's changed attitude to extradition and 'heavy tactics' by its security forces in searching for arms. About the same time, its publicity director Gerry Coleman, on a visit to Belfast, said the group would make an in-depth study of the operation of the International Fund for Ireland because he did not find it helping people in deprived Nationalist areas. The organisation has helped to raise money for some job-creation projects in NI which have been refused Government assistance.

IRISH ASSOCIATION FOR CULTURAL, ECONOMIC AND SOCIAL RELATIONS
Founded on an all-Ireland basis in 1938 to bring together people of differing religious and political views. Idea originated with Maj.-Gen. Hugh Montgomery, of Fivemiletown, Co.

Tyrone, and its first president was the liberal-minded Lord Charlemont, a former NI Education Minister. The association was largely inactive during World War II. Since then it has organised regular addresses by leading politicians, academics and Churchmen.

IRISH DIMENSION
A term which came into popular usage in 1973, when the Conservative Government published its Green Paper on NI. It was used to denote the desire of the bulk of the Catholic minority for an eventual united Ireland. It was a counter-balance to the British Dimension, the term used to describe the Unionist attachment to Britain. It was reflected in the plan for a Council of Ireland, which emerged in the Sunningdale Agreement, and which attracted the fierce opposition of loyalists. The scheme foundered with the collapse of the power-sharing Executive in 1974, but found strong expression in the AIA in 1985.

IRISH INDEPENDENCE PARTY
Party launched in 1977 which sought a British withdrawal from NI to prepare the way for negotiation of NI's future status in Ireland. Its main initial tactic was to seek agreed anti-Unionist candidates in Westminster elections. The leading figures in the new group were former Unity MP for Fermanagh–S. Tyrone, Frank McManus, and Fergus McAteer, the Derry Nationalist and son of former Nationalist leader, Eddie McAteer, who had also expressed support for some move towards independence. Its main support was drawn from W. Ulster, N. Antrim, and S. Down, and it attracted the interest of several Independent and Nationalist councillors. In the Westminster election in May 1979 it ran four candidates, and secured 3.3 per cent of the total vote, with the best showing by Pat Fahy in Mid-Ulster with a vote of

12,055. Soon afterwards, Fahy was appointed party leader, with McManus, deputy leader, and McAteer, chairman. The party improved its share of the vote to 3.9 per cent in the 1981 council elections, but opted out of the 1982 Assembly elections because of its intense opposition to the 'rolling devolution' scheme. Its showing was seriously affected by the electoral participation of PSF since 1982, and in the 1985 council elections it took only 1.1 per cent of the votes and four seats.

IRISH NATIONAL CAUCUS

The American umbrella group for the majority of Irish-American organisations. It embraces the Gaelic Athletic Association and the AOH, Irish county associations, and scores of local bodies in New York, Boston, Philadelphia, and other US cities with strong Irish-American links. In 1978 it sent a three-man inquiry team to NI, headed by its national co-ordinator, Father Sean McManus (brother of ex-MP Frank McManus), which urged a 'peace forum' on NI in Washington and reported to this effect to the *ad hoc* Congressional Committee on Irish affairs. The visiting team had talks with the IRA, UDA, UVF and some other loyalist organisations, and said that paramilitary organisations must be included in any search for a solution. In 1978 Jack Lynch, as Taoiseach of the Republic, attacked the Caucus for giving support to the PIRA, but spokesmen of the Caucus have insisted that it has no connection with any organisation outside the US, and that it has been cleared of any suspicion of support of violence by FBI and other inquiries. In the 1980 presidential election, it claimed as a victory the call for Irish unity in the Democratic platform. But it failed to get any commitment from the Republicans, and was clearly disappointed by the

election of Ronald Reagan. In 1985 the INC mounted an extensive campaign against a new US–UK extradition treaty which could affect the position of terrorist suspects in America because it removed the 'political' defence hitherto available. But the treaty, which had the support of President Reagan, was cleared by the Senate in 1986. The INC then turned its attention to requiring US firms operating in NI to adopt stringent new rules known as the 'MacBride Principles' to force the companies to employ more Catholics. In 1987 and 1988 it had several successes in securing legislative backing for the policy in several states, against British lobbying in other states. In the run-up to the 1988 presidential election, however, the Caucus was able to point to Democratic contender Michael Dukakis, Governor of Massachusetts, as the first Governor to sign 'MacBride' into State law. At the end of 1988 it criticised the new Fair Employment Bill for not having goals or timetables, and described it as 'too little too late'.

IRISH NATIONAL LIBERATION ARMY

An illegal Republican paramilitary group set up in 1975 as the military wing of the IRSP and which rapidly gained a reputation for ruthlessness. Its initial strength derived mainly from ex-OIRA members angry at the OIRA ceasefire in 1972, and it is believed to have gained recruits from PIRA during its ceasefire in 1975, when its members were active in the feud between the OIRA and the IRSP. One of its first acts was to kill OIRA commander Billy McMillen in Belfast in April 1975. Its main support has come from the Lower Falls and Markets areas in Belfast, and from parts of Co. Derry, notably S. Derry. Many of its attacks have been on members of the security forces, but it first attracted world attention when it claimed to have placed the car bomb which killed Conservative NI spokesman Airey Neave at Westminster in March 1979. In a statement issued through a Belfast office of IRSP it said that he had been specifically selected for assassination because of his 'rabid militarist calls for more repression against the Irish people'. INLA also said that its primary aim was to secure a British military, political and economic withdrawal from Ireland, and it denied that it was a cover group for PIRA. In fact, PIRA members tended to talk of INLA as 'wild men'. It was declared illegal throughout the UK in July 1979, when NI Secretary of State Humphrey Atkins told Parliament that it was engaged in violence and contacts with terrorist groups abroad. Government security experts claimed that it was getting arms, including the Russian AK-47 rifle, from the Middle East. In the succeeding years INLA stepped up its activities. It was said to be responsible for nearly thirty deaths in NI in 1982. Seventeen of these were caused by the bombing on 6 December of the Droppin' Well pub disco in Ballykelly, Co. Londonderry. Eleven of the victims were off-duty soldiers stationed nearby and most of the others local people. It was the second-highest death toll in any incident during the Troubles, being exceeded only by the Warrenpoint bombing in 1979. In the 1981 H-Block hunger strike, three INLA prisoners died. In the later stages of the protest, Belfast IRSP councillor Sean Flynn said they could not replace hunger-strikers at the same rate as previously, since INLA had only 28 prisoners against PIRA's 380 (see H-Blocks). A period of internal disagreement coincided with the hunger strike, and the injuring of Harry Flynn, press officer of the IRSP, in a machine-gun attack in Dublin was believed to be associated with the feud. The differences were apparently patched up as the operation of

informers gave rise to mass arrests of INLA members in 1982. In July 1982 the IRSP publication, *Starry Plough*, denied that there was any split between IRSP and INLA and it also said that the INLA structure had been reformed with a new chief of staff from NI. In September 1982 it brought strong criticism from residents in the Divis Flats in the Lower Falls Road area of Belfast, when it set off a bomb which killed two local boys of eleven and fourteen and a soldier. The flats were regarded as one of INLA's main strongholds. In a statement in September 1982 it said certain Unionist politicians were on a 'hit list' because they had been responsible for inciting the murders of 700 innocent Catholics over the previous ten years. In January 1982 it claimed to have shot dead E. Belfast loyalist John McKeague. In March 1981 it shot and seriously wounded Belfast UDA councillor Sammy Millar at his Shankill Road home. In October 1981 it killed a senior Belfast UDA man, Billy McCullough, in retaliation, it said, for recent loyalist murders of Catholics. In May 1981 it placed a powerful blast incendiary bomb at the Lisburn home of DUP Assembly member Rev. William Beattie but it was detected before it went off. Soon afterwards, it shot and seriously wounded Belfast DUP councillor Billy Dickson (an Assembly candidate) at his home. In January 1983 the Republic's Government proscribed the organisation, which meant that conviction for membership could result in up to seven years' imprisonment. The organisation was said to have committed 'particularly vicious outrages' both north and south of the border and in London. In the Republic INLA was suspected of the murder of a Garda in Co. Dublin in early 1982. In September that year it blew up the radar station at Schull, Co. Cork, and it was also thought to have carried out a series of armed robberies in the Republic during 1982. On 25 November 1981 an INLA bomb exploded at a British army camp at Herford, West Germany, but caused no injuries. A similar bomb failed to explode at the British Consulate in Hamburg the day before. INLA recruited dissident PIRA members from time to time, and one of these was Dominic McGlinchey, who is reputed to have taken over the leadership of the organisation at the point of a gun, and who was to make legal history when he was extradited from the Republic in 1982. (He was later re-extradited when a murder charge failed.) The supergrass system dealt a body blow to INLA – twenty-seven alleged members were convicted on the evidence of supergrass Harry Kirkpatrick. Although all but two had their convictions quashed on appeal in 1986, the authorities acquired a great deal of intelligence in the process. The releases also sparked off new problems since there were sharp differences among the former accused, which were to result in a bloody internal feud. Between December 1986 and March 1987, twelve people died and several were injured as a breakaway group styling itself the Irish People's Liberation Organisation (and also the INLA Army Council) sought to force the dissolution of the organisation. The succession of murders caused such horror in the Nationalist community that two W. Belfast priests, Father Gerry Reynolds and Father Arthur Reid, became involved in March 1987 as mediators, and eventually secured a truce. IPLO leader Gerard Steenson was among those shot dead by INLA GHQ gunmen. One of the victims of the IPLO was Thomas Power, whose prison writings were claimed to provide a missing political element for INLA. Mary McGlinchey, wife of Dominic, was shot dead during the feud, but

apparently for reasons unconnected with it. By late 1987 a reorganised INLA was said to have some fifty activists, and in August 1988 one of its members was shot dead by the security forces in an attack on a border post at Clady, Co. Tyrone. 'Border Fox' Dessie O'Hare, jailed in the Republic on a kidnapping charge, had been prominent in INLA before his expulsion in September 1987. He and another man died as a result of a Garda shootout in Co. Kilkenny in November 1987. (See also Irish People's Liberation Organisation and Irish Republican Socialist Party.)

IRISH NORTHERN AID COMMITTEE

The US-based committee, popularly known as NORAID, established in 1969 for the declared purpose of providing funds for the relief of families deprived of wage-earners because of the struggle against Britain. The body has been at the centre of angry controversy since its inception. The money raised – probably around $5 million by 1987 – has been handled in Ireland by people associated with PSF, and there have been frequent allegations that some of the money is siphoned off, either in Dublin or in the US, for the purchase of arms for PIRA. NORAID spokesmen have denied this, and PSF has retorted that PIRA has its own means of raising money. British and Irish Government Ministers, on visits to the US, have warned people not to help NORAID. The organisation has about a hundred local groups in centres with substantial Irish-American populations, such as New York, Boston, Philadelphia and Chicago, and it makes no secret of its anti-British stance. In 1977 the organisation was required, as a result of a case brought by the Justice Department, to register as an agent of PIRA under the Foreign Agents' Act. Although this meant that it had to give more detailed information about its activities, it was not a serious obstacle to its operations. NORAID claims that the money it raises is distributed through PSF in Dublin and the Green Cross in Belfast. The organisation got a big fillip from the H-Block hunger strike in 1981, when its income was around $400,000. In 1987 it declared its transfers to Ireland at $200,000. In November 1982 the chairman and founder of NORAID, Michael Flannery, then aged eighty, was one of five men acquitted in New York of conspiracy to supply arms to PIRA. The accused pleaded successfully before a jury that the CIA were aware of the activities of their supplier, and were involved in monitoring the supply of arms to PIRA. Flannery, an IRA man in the 1920s, said that while he had not been personally involved in gun-running to PIRA, such activity would have his blessing. He also denied that NORAID money had been used for buying arms. He was at the centre of controversy when he was chosen to head the New York St Patrick's day parade in 1983. But the veteran Republican left the organisation in 1988 in protest at the PSF decision to take Dáil seats if elected. At the same time the organisation has had to cope with the situation created by the AIA, which has proved attractive to many Irish-Americans and added to NORAID's fund-raising problems. In recent years publicity director Martin Galvin has become the best-known NORAID figure, particularly because of his repeated defiance of a Government order banning him from NI. He first defied the ban in 1984, when the RUC made an unsuccessful bid to arrest him at a W. Belfast rally, during which Sean Downes was killed by a plastic baton round fired by an RUC officer at close range. In 1985 he was at the funeral in Derry of a PIRA man, and in 1987 he visited the relatives of eight PIRA men shot dead by the security forces at

Loughall, Co. Armagh. He is on record as condemning the killing of civilians in incidents such as the Harrods bombing in London in 1983, but he has defended PIRA attacks on security forces.

IRISH PEOPLE'S LIBERATION ORGANISATION

The INLA faction which tried in 1986–7 to force the disbandment of IRSP–INLA – a move which led to a bitter feud and to the killings of twelve people over a three-month period. When a truce was finally arranged in March 1987, through the mediation of two Belfast priests, IPLO had failed in its aim, and it then continued as a separate organisation and held a convention in Galway in May 1987. In the same year, using the cover-name of Catholic Reaction Force, it claimed the fatal shooting of Belfast loyalist George Seawright. In August 1988 it admitted several explosions in Belfast, and the sending of letter-bombs to Rev. William McCrea MP and Ken Maginnis MP which were defused. In October 1988 the organisation was accused by PIRA of unprovoked attacks on people in W. Belfast and warned that PIRA might intervene. (*See also* Irish National Liberation Army *and* Irish Republican Socialist Party.)

IRISH REPUBLICAN SOCIALIST PARTY

Formed December 1974 and essentially a breakaway group from Official Sinn Féin plus dissidents from PIRA unhappy at their freshly declared ceasefire. By March 1975 they were claiming some 700 members in Belfast. Their best-known personality at that time was former Mid-Ulster MP Bernadette McAliskey, who with other leaders insisted that it did not have a military wing. Its founder was Seamus Costello, who was shot dead in Dublin in 1977. At first it seemed that the group would fight elections, with

Bernadette McAliskey a possible candidate for the Convention, but they decided to boycott the election. In early 1975 there was a bitter feud between the OIRA and the IRSP, with claims of assassinations on both sides. When Cathal Goulding, chief of staff of the OIRA, spoke at the funeral of Sean Fox of the OIRA in Belfast's Milltown cemetery in February 1975, he supported the OIRA claim that Fox had been shot by the IRSP. And he described the IRSP as 'a few misguided and confused malcontents'. The feud was a particularly vicious one, and involved shootings both north and south of the border. A leading Official Republican in Belfast, Billy McMillen, shot dead in Belfast in April 1975, was said to be one of the victims. At one point, the IRSP temporarily disbanded its Belfast organisation and Dublin Senator Michael Mullen acted as intermediary in a bid to stop the inter-factional shootings. When it was registered as a political party in the Republic in May 1975, it claimed nearly 400 members in NI. In September 1975 it denied any link with the South Armagh Republican Action Force, which had claimed killings at an Orange Hall in Newtownhamilton. But in 1976, 1977 and 1978 the security authorities alleged that the IRSP's military wing, the Irish National Liberation Army, had been responsible for several murders and attempted murders. In December 1977 there were clear indications that the IRSP was moving closer to PSF, many of whose members attended Seamus Costello's funeral in October. INLA claimed in 1982 that Costello had been shot by a member of OIRA. Certainly, the 1981 hunger strike brought closer co-operation with PSF, although the IRSP has always regarded itself as being to the left of the Provisionals. In the 1981 council elections, it took two seats in Belfast but, unlike PSF, it opted out of the 1982 Assembly

election. There was further convulsion in the IRSP–INLA network between 1983 and 1987 when senior figures were implicated by supergrasses. When twenty-five of those accused on the word of INLA informer Harry Kirkpatrick were freed at the end of 1986, a struggle for power within INLA led to the feud in which twelve people died. A faction calling itself the Irish People's Liberation Organisation tried to force the disbandment of IRSP–INLA but failed in the end and went its own way. In 1987 the reformed IRSP–INLA reportedly began to concentrate on developing a political philosophy with a Marxist-Leninist slant, while building links with revolutionary groups like the French Action Directe. At an IRSP rally in Derry in October 1988 party spokesman Kevin McQuillan said that draconian laws would not demoralise people: 'We would contend that the opposite will be the case.' (*See also* Irish National Liberation Army *and* Irish People's Liberation Organisation.)

J

JELLICOE REPORT *see* Security System section, p. 399

JOHN, BRYNMOR THOMAS British Labour Party spokesman on NI, June 1979–80. b. 18 April 1934; d. 1988. LLB (London). Solicitor. Labour MP for Pontypridd, 1970–88. Parliamentary Under-Secretary, Defence, 1974–6; Minister of State, Home Affairs, 1976–9. Defence spokesman, 1980.

K

KANE, ALAN JAMES
DUP Assembly member for Mid-Ulster, 1982–6. Youngest member of Assembly; served on Education and Finance and Personnel scrutiny committees. b. 1958. Barrister. Cookstown Council, 1981–; chairman, 1985–. General Secretary of DUP. In 1987 he urged withdrawal of support from RUC once new public-order laws became effective, declaring that NI was 'beginning to look like a police state'.

KELLY, LORD JUSTICE SIR (JOHN WILLIAM) BASIL
Judge of NI High Court, 1973–, and NI Attorney-General, 1968–72. b. 10 May 1920. LLB Hons (TCD). QC, 1958. Unionist MP for Mid-Down at Stormont, 1964–72, and senior Crown Counsel in Tyrone, Fermanagh and Armagh before becoming Attorney-General. He had a key role as law officer of the NI Government in the civil rights period and in the months preceding the imposition of direct rule. In a debate in the NI Commons in 1969, he stated that Westminster had the power to interfere with the powers of the NI Parliament, but that it would be against convention to do so. But he stressed that law was stronger than convention. In May 1971 he was accused by opposition MPs of showing political bias in ordering court prosecutions. But an opposition motion to this effect was rejected by twenty-five votes to nine. In 1983 he presided at a trial of thirty-eight people implicated in PIRA terrorism by supergrass Christopher Black and passed sentences totalling 4,000 years. In 1986 the Court of Appeal quashed the convictions of eighteen of those convicted.

KENNEDY, DENNIS
Head of NI office of the EC Commission, 1985–. b. Lisburn, 3 August 1936. BA (QUB); Ph.D. (TCD). Previous career mainly journalistic in Ireland, US, and Ethiopia. Chief leader writer, *Belfast Telegraph*, 1964–6. *Irish Times* diplomatic correspondent, 1969, and deputy editor, 1983–5. Wrote mainly on diplomatic, European and Third World affairs, 'with occasional commentaries on NI problem in marked contrast to traditional sentimental nationalism of *Irish Times*'. Author, *The Widening Gulf: Northern attitudes to the independent Irish state 1919–49*.

KENNEDY, EDWARD
One of group of Irish-Americans who have been keenly interested in NI situation. b. 22 February 1932. Brother of late President John F. Kennedy. Senator (Teddy) Kennedy's attitude to NI has altered with the growth of PIRA violence. In October 1971 he spoke in Congress in support of a motion calling for the immediate withdrawal of British troops and the calling of a conference of all parties for the purpose of establishing a united Ireland. He argued that this was the only realistic way to bring peace, but his remarks were strongly criticised within NI, especially by Unionists and the Alliance Party. US official spokesmen stressed that Senator Kennedy was not reflecting US Government policy. But he repeated his plea for withdrawal of troops in 1972, saying that they had become a symbol of Protestant supremacy, and he vigorously attacked internment without trial, which he regarded as discriminating against Catholics. When the power-sharing Executive fell in 1974, he described it as a tragedy for the cause of peace in NI, and said Britain could not yield to the tactics of extremists. He has repeatedly advised Irish-Americans not to give moral or

financial support to terrorists. In 1977 he joined with other Irish-American leaders to sponsor a call for peace in NI, and he was among those who urged President Carter to promise US economic aid for NI in the event of a political settlement. The President did this in August 1977. Kennedy took a strong united Ireland line during his unsuccessful campaign for the Democratic presidential nomination in 1980. He was one of the founders in 1981 of the Friends of Ireland group made up of leading Irish-American politicians and in 1983 was one of the sponsors of a Senate motion calling for a united Ireland. He has used his influence to secure support for both the NIF report and the AIA, and has maintained close contacts with Irish Governments. On a visit to Dublin in November 1988 he said the general impression among Irish-Americans was that the AIA had been slow to achieve progress in the areas of fair employment and the administration of justice in NI.

KENNEDY, JOHN ANDREW DUNN

Clerk to the NI Assembly, 1982–6. b. Londonderry. Barrister. Served on NI Parliamentary staffs, 1962–72, Assembly, 1973–4, and Convention, 1975–6. Head of Office of Law Reform, Stormont, 1976–82. Although the Assembly ceased to function in 1986, he retained the office of Clerk.

KENNEDY, JOSEPH

US Congressman for Massachusetts, son of late Senator Robert Kennedy. b. 24 September 1952. BA (University of Massachusetts). During visit to NI in April 1988 his criticisms of British policy brought unfavourable comments from British press. He accused Britain of not doing enough to counter anti-Catholic discrimination in

jobs. He also spoke of the need to encourage non-violent change, but commented that those individuals who had chosen violence as a means to political change 'do so as a direct result of the prejudice and seeming intractability of the British position'.

KENNEDY, PATRICK

Republican Labour MP for Belfast Central, 1969–72. b. 1943. Became leader of Republican Labour Party when Gerry Fitt MP left in 1970 to head the newly formed SDLP. He had been prominent in opposition protests against the Unionist Government in 1969, and in support of the civil rights campaign. In June 1969 he declared that if extreme Unionists were going to police their side of Belfast, 'we must do something to police our end of the city'. In September 1969 he flew to London in CCDC deputation for a meeting with Home Secretary James Callaghan to discuss the tension over demands for removal of barricades in W. Belfast. In 1970 he refused to join the SDLP, and in July 1971 he withdrew from Stormont, and soon afterwards introduced Joe Cahill as leader of the PIRA at a Belfast news conference. He failed to secure election to the Assembly in 1973 as a candidate in W. Belfast.

KEOGH, MICHAEL

Nationalist MP for S. Down, 1967–72. When editor of the former Newry weekly newspaper, *Frontier Sentinel*, he retained the seat for the Nationalist Party in a by-election in 1967, with a majority of 5,627 over a Unionist candidate. In the 1969 general election, when no Unionist stood, his majority over a PD candidate was 220. In 1972 he took a strong line against PIRA bombing in Newry, which he said was hitting severely at community relations in the town.

KERNOHAN, (THOMAS) HUGH
Ombudsman and Commissioner of
Complaints, NI, 1980–7. b. 11 May
1932. Official (latterly Secretary) of NI
Employers' Association, 1953–80. In
August 1982 a Westminster select
committee praised Kernohan's work
and said he seemed to be 'trusted
equally by all sectors of the
population'.

KIDD, SIR ROBERT HILL
Head of the NI civil service, 1976–9.
b. 3 February 1918. BA, B. Litt. (TCD).
Served in army in World War II. Joined
NI civil service in 1947; second
Secretary in Department of Finance,
1969–76, with rank of Permanent
Secretary. In 1980 he carried out a
review of NI's industrial incentives.
Active in Co-operation North
movement.

KILFEDDER, JAMES ALEXANDER
MP for N. Down, 1970–. (OUP,
1970–9; UPUP, 1979–.) Speaker, NI
Assembly, 1982–6. b. Kinlough, Co.
Leitrim, 16 July 1928. BA (TCD). Gave
up his London barrister's practice
when he entered Parliament. He was
MP for W. Belfast, 1964–6, and during
that time he was for a period Secretary
of the Unionist MPs, and of a number of
Conservative committees, including
that on NI. He has always pursued a
highly individualistic course, and in
1977 he parted from the other Official
Unionist MPs at Westminster, com-
plaining that Enoch Powell was
dictating policy. In early 1979 he
finally broke with the OUP after an
exchange of letters with party leader
Harry West. In the 1979 election he
was opposed by Clifford Smyth for the
OUP, but held the seat easily. Apparently, his devotion to constituency
work has been the key to his success,
since he was able to beat off an earlier
challenge in the February 1974 election
when Roy Bradford stood against him

as a Pro-Assembly Unionist. He topped
the poll in N. Down in the Assembly
contests of 1973 and 1982, and also in
the Convention election. His first-
preference vote in 1973 of 20,684 was
the largest of the whole election. In the
1979 European election, which he
fought as 'Ulster Unionist', he got over
38,000 first-preference votes, and on
the sixth count he was runner-up to
John Taylor (OUP), last of the three
successful candidates. (In the 1984
European election he lost his deposit.)
In 1979 he founded the Ulster Progressive Unionist Party, but the party
name was changed to Ulster Popular
Unionist Party in 1980 because of
confusion with the PUP. Although he
was critical of the 'rolling devolution'
scheme, he accepted nomination as
Speaker of the 1982 Assembly. He was
elected by DUP and Alliance votes, with
the OUP opposing, and his Speaker's
salary of £18,000, together with his
Westminster salary, made him the UK's
best-paid politician. In the 1983
Westminster election he held off,
without the use of posters, a strong
challenge from OUP and Alliance in the
reduced N. Down constituency. In the
1986 by-election he had a 22,000
majority over Alliance, but this
dropped to 3,953 in the 1987 general
election, when Robert McCartney QC,
standing as a 'Real Unionist', was
runner-up, with Alliance in third place.

KINAHAN, CHARLES
Alliance Convention member for S.
Antrim, 1975–6. b. Belfast, 1915.
Brother of Sir Robin Kinahan, Unionist
MP for Clifton at Stormont, 1958–9.
Unsuccessfully contested S. Antrim
Westminster seat in February and
October 1974. Vice-chairman,
Alliance Party, 1978. Antrim Borough
Council, 1973–85.

KING, GENERAL SIR FRANK DOUGLAS

Army GOC, NI, February 1973–August 1975. b. 9 March 1919. He arrived in NI at a time when sectarian assass-inations were running at a high rate. But his most testing time came in 1974, when the loyalist strike, which led to the downfall of the power-sharing Executive, posed new problems for the army. Some Executive Ministers and many opponents of the stoppage accused the army of not moving swiftly in the first few days of the strike to dismantle UDA and other loyalist barricades. There were also complaints that the army was reluctant to take on oil distribution when petrol supplies were halted by the strikers, and disappointment that the army did not have the expertise to run the power stations. There was a widespread belief that General King was not anxious that troops should become involved in strike-breaking activities. After he left NI, he said in an interview that 'if you get a large section of the population which is bent on a particular course, then it is a difficult thing to stop them taking that course'. General King also provoked controversy in April 1975, when he said in a speech in Nottingham that the phased release of internees could help the PIRA. Since the statement came at a moment when the PIRA ceasefire was showing signs of petering out, and politicians were preparing for the Convention elections, the comment was highly unwelcome to the Govern-ment. It pleased loyalists, dismayed the SDLP, and brought the remark from PSF that the army wanted to show the British Government who was boss. General King claimed that his words had been taken out of context, since what he meant was that 'in a ceasefire situation it is obviously necessary to take steps to bring about a situation of normality without lowering our guard'.

KING, THOMAS JEREMY (TOM)

NI Secretary of State, September 1985–. Successively held three Cabinet offices (Environment, Transport and Employment) before moving to NI. MP for Bridgewater, 1970–. b. 13 June 1933. He had some familiarity with NI as a businessman and shadow Energy Secretary before his Cabinet appoint-ments and arrival at Stormont in 1985. He inherited the negotiations over the AIA at an advanced stage, and in less than two months he had to face the wrath of Unionists when it was signed at Hillsborough on 15 November 1985, and a few days after the signing, he was physically attacked by loyalists outside Belfast City Hall. In an apparent attempt to sell the accord to Unionists, he stressed his own Unionist convictions, and disclosed that he had urged the Irish Government to drop the claim to NI in the Irish Constitution. On 4 December 1985, on a visit to Brussels, he embarrassed Margaret Thatcher when he said that Dr FitzGerald, by signing the AIA, 'has in fact accepted that for all practical purposes and into perpetuity there will never be a united Ireland'. Dr FitzGerald attacked the comment as 'inaccurate', and King apologised in the Commons. Thus, there were some doubts in Nationalist circles about King's level of enthusiasm for the AIA. But his general approach was to defend it strongly and to point to the 473–47 vote by which the agreement was endorsed at Westminster, and to challenge Unionists, whose attitude he described as 'misconceived and negative', to enter into dialogue with him. He shrugged off massive demon-strations against the agreement, as well as the fifteen protest by-elections in January 1986, showing an increase in the overall Unionist vote. Indeed, King took encouragement from the 10.8 per cent swing in the Nationalist vote against PSF since 1983. Unionist 'withdrawal of consent' from the Government and boycott of Ministers, together with a virtual halt to business in loyalist-controlled councils and abstention of most Unionist MPs from Westminster, did not greatly hamper his administrative task. When the 3 March 1986 Unionist 'day of action' against the AIA produced violence and intimidation, King accused Unionist MPs of making common cause with paramilitaries, despite the clear condemnation of the violence by Unionist leaders. But while steadily denying to Unionists any suspension of the AIA as a basis for renewed talks, he also faced pressure from the Irish Government for action to meet Nationalist grievances. In particular, Dublin was concerned about delay in reshaping Diplock non-jury courts by having three judges instead of one, but Irish Ministers gradually accepted that the RUC was showing impartiality in the handling of loyalist parades. The Stormont Assembly, launched by James Prior, was wound up in June 1986 by King, who obviously resented the fact that it had become a platform for Unionist attacks on Government policy. In February 1987 the return to office in the Republic of Fianna Fáil, led by Charles Haughey, created a new situation for King. Indeed, Haughey, as opposition leader, had cited King's Brussels speech as vindicating his own criticism of the AIA, and there was uncertainty as to how far the new Irish Government would work the agreement. In the event, Haughey, who led a minority Government, said he would adhere to an international agreement, but he was clearly looking for tangible results from it. King's attitude reflected the desire of Margaret Thatcher that there should be effective extradition of terrorist suspects from the Republic, but Fianna Fáil questioned the quality of justice in Britain and particularly in NI, and when it supported a Dáil vote

on extradition it was with the proviso that the Irish Attorney-General should have a flavour of the evidence in advance. Late 1987 and early 1988 produced a variety of other security-related issues which saw King at variance with Irish Ministers in the Ministerial Conference. These included the refusal to prosecute RUC officers allegedly involved in 'shoot to kill' incidents in Co. Armagh in 1982, the rejection of the appeal of the Birmingham Six, and the continuing argument about the courts in NI. But King had the satisfaction of getting strong backing from the Republic for action to prevent arms landed from Libya being used by PIRA. Meanwhile, in 1987 the Unionist leaders had begun tentative 'talks about talks' with King aimed, they said, at finding out whether the British Government was prepared to consider a replacement for the AIA as a preliminary to serious political talks. King was unable to satisfy Unionist wishes, and in mid-1988 opened talks with the SDLP. In July 1988 he retained his post in a Cabinet reshuffle when his length of service would have indicated a move. In the autumn of 1988, although he concentrated very heavily on tightening security measures in response to PIRA attacks – a favourite demand of Unionists – the two Unionist leaders continued to resist any idea of contributing to the review of the working of the AIA Conference and Secretariat. In this situation he sought a response from the wider community, setting the end of 1988 as the deadline for submissions. At the same time his situation was not made easier by the London–Dublin row on extradition centred on the Republic's refusal to extradite Father Patrick Ryan. In October 1988 two men and a woman from the Republic were convicted of conspiracy to murder him, when they were tried at Winchester Crown Court.

Two of them had been arrested close to his Wiltshire home. In early 1989 he made a fresh attempt to promote inter-party talks.

KINGSMILLS MASSACRE
Ten Protestant workmen were shot dead in a van at Kingsmills in S. Armagh on 5 January 1976, when they were travelling home from work at Glenanne spinning mill. The shooting was claimed by the S. Armagh Repub-lican Action Force, regarded as a cover name for PIRA. The shootings occurred during a series of tit-for-tat murders, with five Catholic men being killed in two incidents (near Lurgan and at Whitecross) on 4 January.

KINNOCK, NEIL GORDON
Leader of British Labour Party, 1983–. MP for Bedwelty, 1970–83; Islwyn, 1983–. b. 28 March 1942. Kinnock has pursued a generally low-key line on NI, leaving it to his frontbench spokes-men to make most of the running. But on a visit to NI in December 1984 he described Margaret Thatcher's initial 'out, out, out' reference to the New Ireland Forum report as unhelpful, and said Labour's approach would be 'in, in, in' as a basis for discussion. He said at the same time that Dublin would have to play a part in any solution, although documents produced by the Unionist community would also have to be taken into account. He has given steady backing to the AIA but at a private meeting in December 1986 he was ready to listen to Unionist leaders express their opposition to the AIA and their worries about the security situation. The meeting took place at a time when Unionists were refusing to meet the Secretary of State, but they rejected any suggestion that they were trying to build pre-election bridges with Labour. Within the party, he has opposed left-wing moves to remove from party policy the need for consent

of Unionists to a united Ireland. On a visit to NI in January 1987 he defended the action of his party spokesman in meeting PSF councillors, while also saying that he ruled out meetings between himself and PSF as not being 'productive'.

KIRK, HERBERT VICTOR
Minister of Finance, 1966–72. b. Belfast, 5 June 1912. A chartered accountant, he was earlier Minister of Labour and Minister of Education and an influential figure in unionism for many years. Was a member of Brian Faulkner's team at the Darlington and Sunningdale conferences, but he did not seek re-election after the Stormont Parliament was suspended.

KIRKPATRICK, THOMAS JAMES (JIM)
OUP Assembly member for S. Belfast, 1982–6. Served on Economic Develop-ment Committee. b. 1937. Manu-facturer (engineering). Ex-UDR officer. Belfast City Council, 1985–. Resigned as secretary of the OUP group on the council when he was barred from a meeting with Unionist leaders because of his opposition to the adjournment policy against the AIA.

KOCH, EDWARD (ED)
Mayor (Democrat) of New York, 1978–. b. 12 December 1924. Lawyer. Congressman, 1969–77. As a long-time critic of British policy in NI, he caused surprise when he rejected the idea of Britain as an 'occupying force', after a peace pilgrimage to NI in July 1988 with Cardinal O'Connor of New York. He also suggested that Britain was playing a constructive role in NI. His remarks on his return to New York were praised by Margaret Thatcher, but infuriated some Irish-Americans who called for a retraction. Koch, with an election approaching, responded by admitting to 'an unfortunate use of

language', and called on Britain to fix a date for withdrawal from NI. Conservative MPs accused him of cowardice.

L

LABOUR COMMITTEE ON IRELAND
A left-wing pressure group seeking to persuade the British Labour movement to adopt a policy of British withdrawal from NI, and an end to emergency powers, including the abolition of non-jury courts and use of plastic bullets. Most of its supporters have voiced opposition to the AIA. It has organised fringe meetings at Labour Party conferences, and one of its speakers at a 1986 conference was Armagh PSF councillor Tommy Carroll. In the 1987 general election, the LCI sent a questionnaire to all 633 Labour candidates but only 55 made any reply, and of those who did 40 backed British withdrawal 'within the lifetime of the next Government'.

LABOUR '87
Founded in March 1987, the party brought together the long-standing but declining ULP and NILP, the two-year-old LPNI, and Newtownabbey Labour Party. The party was said to be trade-union based, and its first vice-chairman, Paddy Devlin, said it would have fraternal relations with Labour parties in GB and the Republic, but no direct connection, and its position was that it was impractical in existing circumstances to change NI's constitutional status. A resolution at its initial meeting said that while the AIA had not brought about a significant decrease in violence or sectarian tensions, it had not brought about the

'catastrophic' confrontation many had forecast. In 1989 the party proposed a two-chamber assembly – the lower, more powerful chamber elected by PR, and the second representing a variety of interests.

LABOUR PARTY, BRITISH
For much of its life, the British Labour movement has been inclined to sympathise with Irish nationalism and to regard NI unionism with some hostility. But it was not until 1981 that the party committed itself to campaign actively for a united Ireland by consent. Its Nationalist stance has been partly due to the influence of people of Irish background in the Labour and trade-union movement in GB, and partly a reaction to the long association between British Conservatism and NI unionism, which was effectively ruptured when a Conservative Government suspended the Stormont Parliament in 1972. The NI civil rights campaign also attracted considerable support from Labour MPs, notably through the Campaign for Democracy in Ulster. On the left wing of the party there has been some backing for the 'troops out' movement and general disengagement from NI. At the same time many British Labour activists regarded themselves as having more in common with the SDLP than with the former NILP, despite the latter's loose association with the British Labour Party. Labour Ministers, however, notably since James Callaghan's visit to NI as Home Secretary in 1969, have sought to strike a fairly even balance between the NI parties, in keeping with the broad consensus policy between the major British parties. The Callaghan Government, none the less, was accused by the SDLP and by some of its own supporters of adopting an un-characteristic attitude when it backed extra MPs for NI in 1978 and 1979, since this was a long-standing demand

of Unionists. Many critics of the Government saw it as yielding to pressure and seeking to neutralise Unionist votes in the lobbies in the light of the Government's minority position. Both the Government and the Unionists denied any deal as such, but it became clear just before the fall of the Labour Government in April 1979 that it had been prepared to trade a major inquiry into NI fuel costs for Unionist support. Labour Ministers insisted that they could not oppose extra MPs for NI while retaining Scottish and Welsh representation in their devolution proposals. At its 1979 conference the party rejected a motion passed originally in 1921 calling for withdrawal from Ireland. In 1982 Labour opposition gave general support to the new NI Assembly plan, while pressing for changes to enlarge the Irish dimension. At its 1982 annual conference the party called for a ban on the use of plastic bullets throughout the UK, despite a warning from its NI spokesman Don Concannon that he could not have his hands tied on the issue. The 1983 election manifesto repeated the commitment to Irish unity by consent, and also called for repeal of the Prevention of Terrorism Act and reform of non-jury courts. Under Neil Kinnock's leadership the party welcomed the NIF report and deplored Margaret Thatcher's 'out, out, out' to the document in 1984, and gave firm backing to the AIA. But he and his friends have resisted moves within the party to remove the Unionist veto on constitutional change, and he met the two Unionist leaders at the end of 1986 at a time when they were refusing to meet Ministers. On a visit to NI in January 1987 he defended meetings between his party spokesman and PSF councillors but insisted that it would not be productive if he himself were to hold such meetings. In October 1986 front-bench spokesman Stuart Bell said

the party saw the AIA as a move towards a united Ireland, but they would not be 'bounced' into a 'troops out' policy or setting a date for British withdrawal. The 1986 party conference heavily rejected a call for removal of troops and voted ten to one in a block vote against the termination of British sovereignty in NI. In 1988 a party document warned against precipitate withdrawal from NI, but urged harmonisation of economic policies, North and South, and a suggestion of interim financial arrangements associated with Irish unity was welcomed by Charles Haughey. On a visit to NI in December 1988 Kinnock said there must be no concession to terrorism by withdrawing army families threatened by PIRA. But the party's criticisms of some of the security measures introduced at that time were strongly articulated by party spokesman Kevin McNamara. Two front-bench spokespersons resigned because of the leadership's decision not to vote against the new Prevention of Terrorism Bill in the main Commons division, although it did put forward specific criticisms.

LABOUR PARTY, IRISH
For many years the Republic's third largest party, but in the February 1987 general election it dropped to fourth place, behind the recently formed Progressive Democrats. It won twelve seats to the Prog. D.'s fourteen, and its 6.4 per cent vote was its worst performance since 1933. In the early 1960s it was linked to the NILP for a time through a Council of Labour. In 1972 it backed the SDLP policy statement, 'Towards a New Ireland'. While it was in Coalition Government with Fine Gael, 1973–7, there were some differences of emphasis on NI within the party. One of its Ministers, Dr Conor Cruise O'Brien, was highly critical of the articles in the

Constitution claiming all-Ireland jurisdiction. At the 1978 party conference,
Frank Cluskey, who succeeded
Brendan Corish as leader in 1977,
criticised Jack Lynch's comments on NI
as likely to help the 'godfathers' of the
IRA. Michael O'Leary, Cluskey's
successor (who joined Fine Gael in
1982), maintained close contact with
the NI parties. The party decided,
however, not to invite the SDLP to send
representatives to its 1982 conference.
It was partner with Fine Gael in the
1982–7 Coalition, with its leader Dick
Spring as deputy to Taoiseach Garret
FitzGerald. The party participated
fully in the New Ireland Forum, and
Spring was active in the negotiations
which led to the AIA. But in January
1987 the party pulled out of the
Coalition to pursue its own budgetary
policy, and FitzGerald advised his
supporters to give their transfers not to
Labour but to the Progressive
Democrats. In 1988 Spring accused
Britain of 'arrogance' in its approach to
Anglo-Irish relations, but warned
against suspension of the AIA.

LAIRD, JOHN

OUP member for W. Belfast in
Assembly, 1973–4, and Convention,
1975–6. b. 1944. Succeeded his father,
Dr Norman Laird, as Stormont MP for
St Anne's, Belfast, in a by-election in
1970. At twenty-six, he was then the
youngest MP at Stormont. Chairman,
Young Unionist Council, 1970.
Topped the poll in W. Belfast in both
the Assembly and Convention elections.
In the Assembly he opposed power-
sharing and led an unsuccessful
demand for renegotiation of the
Sunningdale Agreement. Joint
Honorary Secretary of the Ulster
Unionist Council, 1976–8. Established
his own public relations agency when
Convention ended.

LARKIN, AIDAN JOSEPH

SDLP Assembly member for Mid-
Ulster, 1973–4. b. Cookstown, 1946.
MA (QUB). Barrister; formerly teacher.
Magherafelt District Council, 1973–7.

LENIHAN, BRIAN JOSEPH

Tánaiste (deputy Taoiseach) and
Foreign Minister, Irish Republic,
March 1987–. b. Dundalk, 1930. A
prominent Fianna Fáil politician, first
elected to the Dáil in 1961, he has had
considerable contact with NI affairs.
He was Foreign Minister in 1974
during the period of the NI power-
sharing Executive, and again in 1979–
81, when there were problems in
Anglo-Irish relations. When Fianna
Fáil took power in March 1987, he
immediately became involved as co-
chairman of the Anglo-Irish Ministerial
Conference and set the tone for
relations between the new Dublin
administration and NI Secretary of
State Tom King. He had previously
held a variety of Cabinet posts and
served, 1973–7, as leader of the Fianna
Fáil Party in the Senate and the party
delegation in the European Assembly.
Deputy leader, Fianna Fáil, 1983–.
In November 1988 he assured
Unionists that the AIA was not a vehicle
designed to destroy them. At the same
time, he said, the achievements of the
AIA had so far failed to fulfil the hopes
and expectations of many Nationalists.
In late 1988, while Lenihan was ill,
Energy and Communications Minister
Ray Burke deputised for him at AIA
meetings.

LENNON, GERALD (GERRY)

Opposition (Nationalist) leader in NI
Senate, 1965–71. b. 1907; d. 1976. He
was the longest-serving Nationalist
Senator, having entered the House in
1944. In 1962 and 1963 he had several
meetings with the grand master of the
Orange Order in Ireland, Sir George
Clark, in an effort to remove what he

termed 'the stigma of religious discrimination in NI'. The Orange–Green talks did not produce any significant result. He was national president of the AOH for the last year of his life.

LIBERAL PARTY, BRITISH

With its backing, historically, for Irish Home Rule, the party tended to support the civil rights campaign. Jeremy Thorpe, as party leader, was highly critical of successive Unionist Governments in speeches to the Liberal conference and to Ulster Liberal Party gatherings. In 1971 he suggested dual British-Irish nationality as an approach to NI problem. On that occasion the Liberal assembly first voted for the replacement of British troops by a UN force, but reversed that decision after a NI delegate protested that this would be capitulation to gunmen on both sides. At the start of the Troubles the party urged that there should be PR in Stormont elections and the setting up of a Council of Ireland. It also came out against internment without trial. In 1979 it suggested that NI should have a small advisory committee, elected by PR, as a first step towards the restoration of devolved government. In 1982 it gave general support to the 'rolling devolution' initiative. However, in 1985, against the wishes of party leader David Steel, the party's annual conference voted for a commitment to a united Ireland and the withdrawal of British troops. But that was effectively set aside in 1985 when the Liberal–SDP Alliance accepted the principle of consent along with power-sharing government and a British-Irish Security Commission – a switch in policy which angered some Dublin politicians. The NI Alliance Party, under the leadership of John Cushnahan, developed close links with the party, and these were strengthened when the Liberals and the SDP agreed

to merge as the Social and Liberal Democrats in March 1988. The new party leader, Paddy Ashdown, visited NI in 1988 and renewed contact with the Alliance Party.

LIDDLE, LIEUTENANT-COLONEL GEORGE

Imperial grand master of the Orange Order, 1982–5. b. 1901; d. 1988. Colonel Liddle was associated in his youth with the formation of the Ulster Special Constabulary (B Specials) in Co. Fermanagh. He was later in charge of the force in that county, where he was prominent in both unionism and orangeism. He succeeded the Rev. Martin Smyth MP as Imperial grand master. At the time of his appointment he was grand master of the Order in Fermanagh. He served for many years on the Ulster Unionist Council.

LINDSAY, KENNEDY

VUPP Assembly, 1973–4, and Convention, 1975–6, member for S. Antrim. b. Saskatchewan, Canada, 1924. BA, Ph. D. (TCD, Edinburgh, London). Held university appointments in Canada, US, UK, West Indies and Nigeria, and during an Assembly debate he donned a Nigerian ceremonial robe to make a point. In the Convention he launched the British Ulster Dominion Party, and stood unsuccessfully in District Council elections in Newtownabbey in 1977. In the 1982 Assembly election, he was an unsuccessful UUUP candidate in S. Antrim. Author, *British Intelligence Services in Action*.

LOGUE, HUGH

SDLP Assembly member for Londonderry, 1982–6. Also represented the constituency in the 1973–4 Assembly and the 1975–6 Convention. b. Londonderry, 1949.

SDLP executive, 1970–3, and chairman, SDLP policy committee, 1971. NICRA executive, 1971–3. Economic affairs spokesman of SDLP, 1975–. In 1974 he called for disbandment of the UDR because, he said, many of its members had supported the loyalist strike. After the collapse of the Executive in August 1974, he said that a statement of British disengagement would end the uncertainty and desperate political vacuum. After the winding up of the Convention, he was active in political journalism. Unsuccessfully contested Londonderry in February 1974 and 1979 Westminster elections. Member of the Irish Commission for Justice and Peace which had important role in the H-Block hunger-strike controversy in 1981. In 1987 he was appointed to the EC Commission's Science Research and Development Directorate in Brussels.

LONDONDERRY/DERRY
The city where the civil rights demonstration in Duke Street on 5 October 1968 put the movement on the TV screens and newspaper front pages throughout the world. The dual name of the city epitomises its eventful history. The name Derry is based on the original Irish, Doire, and tends to be favoured more by Nationalists, who sought in the City Council in 1978 and 1983 to have Derry adopted as the official name of the city. The suggestion was bitterly attacked by Unionists, but in 1984 the Government agreed that henceforth the City Council would be known as Derry although the official name of the city would continue to be Londonderry. This NIO concession to Nationalists led local Unionists to call, without success, for a separate council for the Waterside area of the city and to impose a ban on attending council meetings. The city's official title denotes the British connection and the role of the City of London companies in the development of the city. It has been symbolic for loyalists since Protestants defied James II in the siege of 1689. Local conditions were a key issue in the civil rights controversy. One of the reforms demanded was the abolition of the corporation, dominated by Unionists because ward boundaries had been drawn in a manner which meant that a Unionist minority was able to secure a majority in the City Council. One of the earliest reforms granted by the O'Neill Government was the replacement of the council by a nine-man Development Commission. This reform was announced only a month or so after the Duke Street demonstration. The march route had been heavily restricted by the Government, but some 200 people, including opposition MPs from Stormont, a few British Labour MPs, civil rights leaders and local civil rights groups, defied the ban. TV film of the event showed the attempts of the RUC to prevent the march and the ensuing confused confrontation in which police batons and placard poles were intermingled with bleeding faces. The publicity spin-off for the civil rights movement was astonishing. It was highly damaging to the NI Government and an embarrassment to the British Labour administration, headed by Harold Wilson, whose sympathies were largely with the marchers. There is no doubt that the event caused Britain to put heavy pressure on Stormont for reforms. But it was not until 1969, and after even larger civil rights demonstrations in the city, that Derry came to play a decisive role in reducing the power and authority of the NI Government. The riots which blew up on the edge of the Catholic Bogside in the wake of the Protestant Apprentice Boys' 12 August march led to British troops being introduced in the streets. The barricades went up in the Bogside

and the adjoining Catholic area, Creggan, and behind them the PIRA planned bombing and other missions which caused substantial damage to the city. The existence of 'Free Derry', as extreme Republicans termed it, raised tensions in loyalist areas, and there were many sectarian killings in the city and county. The refusal by the authorities to agree to an impartial inquiry into the shooting dead by the army of two Derry men – Seamus Cusack and Desmond Beattie – on 8 July 1971 led to the withdrawal of the SDLP from Stormont. The SDLP contested the official explanation that Cusack was shot when he was seen to raise a rifle against troops, and Beattie when he was about to throw a nail bomb. The 'Bloody Sunday' affair, in which thirteen civilians were shot dead by paratroopers on the edge of the Bogside on 30 January 1972, was one of the incidents which precipitated direct rule from Westminster. At the end of July 1972 the security forces mounted 'Operation Motorman' to end the no-go areas and moved in strength into the Bogside and Creggan, with little more than token resistance from PIRA. With the reform of local government in 1973, the Development Commission was replaced by an enlarged District Council, in which PR gave Nationalists a majority of two. In 1978, as a result of a special Derry–Donegal survey, EC money became available to help finance a second bridge across the River Foyle and to improve the harbour, and road and telephone links with Donegal. There was still sporadic violence but by 1978 there was some easing of traffic checks at the approaches to the old walled city. However, tension rose sharply during the 1981 hunger strike, and in that and the following year there were many deaths arising from PIRA and INLA activity. There was also intense controversy over deaths caused by the

operations of the security forces, notably through the use of plastic bullets. But 6 December 1982 brought the heaviest death toll in any incident in County Derry during the Troubles. Seventeen people died in the bombing of the Droppin' Well pub disco at Ballykelly. Eleven were soldiers stationed nearby, and most of the civilian victims were from Ballykelly itself. INLA claimed the attack, and mentioned that warnings had been given to pubs serving members of the security forces. The SDLP took control of the City Council after the 1981 council elections, but PSF got a boost in the 1982 Assembly election, when its best-known Derry-city figure, Martin McGuinness, was returned. With some 9,000 unemployed in the city, the Government announced in 1982 an 'enterprise zone', with special inducements for investment. Throughout the 1980s considerable effort has been put into improving facilities for sport and shopping, and rehousing has changed out of all recognition the city of the early civil rights demonstrations. Cross-community campaigns have been launched in a bid to attract US investment, notably through a link-up with Boston. There have also been moves to reduce the sectarian element in the three-hundredth anniversary of the siege in the 1989 celebrations. None the less, local politics remain lively. In 1983 the area got its first non-Unionist MP at Westminster since NI was established, when SDLP leader and MEP John Hume took the new Foyle seat. In the City Council the arrival of PSF members in 1985 and the Unionist boycott imposed in the wake of the AIA heightened tension, but divisions in unionism led to an independent Unionist, Jim Guy, being installed as Mayor in 1987–8 with the support of the SDLP. (*See also* Derry Citizens' Action Committee *and* Derry Citizens' Defence Association)

LONG, CAPTAIN WILLIAM JOSEPH

Minister of Home Affairs, December 1968–March 1969, a period which included the eventful PD march from Belfast to Londonderry. b. Stockton-on-Tees, 23 April 1922. Stormont MP, 1962–72, and held a number of junior posts before becoming Minister of Education in 1969. Minister of Development, 1969.

LONG KESH see H-Blocks and Security System section, p. 403

LOUGHGALL SHOOTINGS

On 8 May 1987 an eight-man PIRA unit was wiped out by the SAS when it attacked Loughgall (Co. Armagh) RUC station. A passing motorist also died in the shooting. The PIRA gang included some of its most experienced gunmen and bombers, apparently drawn from the E. Tyrone–Monaghan ASUs which had been active in attacks on border RUC stations and in the killings of UDR men and Protestant farmers on the Fermanagh border. PIRA sources denied that the ambush had been due to a tip-off from within PIRA; they suggested that police and SAS had been standing by at RUC stations likely to be attacked. The RUC claimed that weapons recovered from the bodies had been used in seven murders and nine attempted murders in the previous two years.

LOWRY, LORD

As Sir Robert Lowry he was chairman of the Constitutional Convention, 1975–6. b. 30 January 1919. QC, 1956. Lord Chief Justice of NI, 1971–88. Sir Robert presided over the Convention's public sittings, and behind the scenes, with the assistance of advisers, he tried to reconcile the conflicting views of the political parties on the type of admin-istration which would prove viable. Notably, he had a scheme prepared for

voluntary coalition, as distinct from imposed power-sharing. The circum-stances which had given rise to the document proved a major point of controversy, and on the United Unionist side only William Craig and a few of his supporters were attracted to the idea. Despite the failure of the exercise, Sir Robert's efforts were praised on all sides of the Convention. Raised to peerage in 1979. PIRA made an unsuccessful bid to assassinate him at Queen's University, Belfast, in March 1982. Four shots were fired, and one injured a QUB professor. After the signing of the AIA in 1985, he was said by Whitehall sources to be against the idea of three-judge Diplock courts – a proposal pressed by the Irish Gov-ernment and also opposed by the then Lord Chancellor, Lord Hailsham.

LOYAL CITIZENS OF ULSTER

A small militant group which first appeared in Londonderry in October 1968. Its leader, Major Ronald Bunting, threatened that it would hold a meeting on the city walls to coincide with a sit-down in Guildhall Square below by supporters of the Derry Citizens' Action Committee. But the counter-demonstration was banned by William Craig, as Minister of Home Affairs. In January 1969 it announced a counter-demonstration to a PD march in Newry, but it did not proceed with its plan. The LCU appeared at a variety of loyalist demonstrations in 1968 and 1969.

LYELL, LORD

Parliamentary Under-Secretary, NIO, April 1984–. b. 27 March 1939. He is 3rd Baron (Charles Lyell) and member of Queen's Bodyguard for Scotland. Chartered accountant. At Stormont has had responsibility for Agriculture, and NIO spokesman in Lords, where he was a Government Whip, 1979–84. Has given strong warnings to local farmers of the challenge they face in 1992 when the Single European Market takes effect.

LYNCH, JOHN (JACK)

Fianna Fáil Taoiseach of Irish Republic, 1966–73 and 1977–9. b. Cork, 15 August 1917. Hon LLD (TCD and NUI); Hon DCL (University College, N. Carolina). Began as civil servant in Department of Justice, 1936, and called to Bar, 1945. TD for Cork Constituencies, 1948–81. Junior Minister, 1951–4. Minister for Lands, 1951; Minister for Gaeltacht, 1957; Minister for Education, 1957–9; Minister for Industry and Commerce, 1959–65; Minister for Finance, 1965–6, when he succeeded Sean Lemass as Taoiseach. As Minister for Industry and Commerce he developed improved economic relations with NI, and had talks with Brian Faulkner, NI Commerce Minister, at the same period as Sean Lemass's historic trip to Stormont in 1965. He brought in special preferential tariffs for some NI goods. As Taoiseach, he had talks at Stormont with PM Terence O'Neill in 1967, and his car was snowballed at Stormont by supporters of the Rev. Ian Paisley. During the early years of the Troubles, his words and actions became a matter of intense controversy in NI. Many Catholics looked to him for moral and sometimes material support. Unionists blamed him for what they termed 'interference in the internal affairs of the United Kingdom'. During the violent clashes in the Bogside area of Derry, he said in a broadcast on 13 August 1969 that it was evident that the Stormont Government was no longer in control of the situation: 'Indeed, the present situation is the inevitable outcome of the policies pursued for decades by successive Stormont Governments. It is clear also that the Irish Government can no longer stand by and see innocent people injured and perhaps worse.' He called for a UN peace-keeping force and said he had asked the British Government to see that 'police attacks on the people of Derry should cease immediately'. Lynch also announced that army field hospitals would be set up at points along the border to treat people who did not wish to go to hospitals in NI. The Scarman report on the Troubles said of Lynch's statement: 'There is no doubt that this broadcast strengthened the will of the Bogsiders to obstruct any attempt by the police to enter their area, and to harass them by missile and petrol bomb attacks, whenever they appeared on the perimeter.' The NI Premier, Major Chichester-Clark, reacted angrily. He said he had heard the broadcast with indignation, and he would hold Lynch personally responsible for any worsening of feeling which his 'inflammatory and ill-considered remarks' might cause. In 1970, during what became known as the 'arms trial crisis', Lynch sacked two Ministers, Charles Haughey and Neil Blaney, who were later acquitted of charges of being involved in arms deals. Lynch also rejected suggestions that Fianna Fáil had been involved in the setting up of the PIRA. He rejected, too, a claim by Blaney that twenty-five Senators and TDs in Dublin had given their guns for use in NI. In 1973 he lost the general election, which he said he had called partly because of the NI situation. In 1975 Fianna Fáil's policy statement, calling on the British Government to declare its commitment to an ordered withdrawal from NI, brought angry protests from many quarters. In Britain and in NI, and to some extent in the Republic, he was accused of adopting PIRA policy. This Lynch hotly denied, and in 1977 he scored a surprise election triumph over the Fine Gael–Labour coalition, led by Liam Cosgrave. He got an unprecedented twenty-seat majority in the Dáil. Some tension developed in relations between London and Dublin. British Ministers thought he could do more to tighten cross-border security and they argued that the Lynch Government was discouraging a political settlement by stressing Irish unity too strongly. At the 1978 annual conference of Fianna Fáil in Dublin he announced a special party group to study North–South relations. At the end of 1978 he tried unsuccessfully to persuade the British Government to join the new European Monetary System so as to avoid problems in cross-border currency. In September 1979, in the wake of the murder of Lord Mountbatten, he had talks in London with Margaret Thatcher on ways of strengthening cross-border security. Improvements were agreed, but Lynch ruled out in advance two moves sought by the British security forces: the right of the British army to 'hot pursuit' of suspected terrorists across the border, and permission for RUC detectives to interrogate persons held in the Republic. Towards the end of 1979, pressure built up against Lynch in his own party, and in December he gave way to Charles Haughey as party leader and Taoiseach, and in 1981 also gave up his Dáil seat.

LYNCH, SEAMUS

Regional chairman and national vice-president of the Workers' Party (formerly Official Sinn Féin nationally and Republican Clubs in NI), 1978–. b. 1945. Belfast City Council, 1977–81 and 1985–. Unsuccessfully contested N. Belfast in 1979, 1983 and 1987 general elections, and in 1986 by-election, and also in 1982 Assembly election. He has consistently called for dialogue among the constitutional parties aimed at securing devolved government. Helped change WP attitude to AIA in Republic to a more sceptical approach.

M

MCALISKEY, JOSEPHINE BERNADETTE

Unity MP for Mid-Ulster, 1969; Independent, 1970–4. b. Cookstown, Co. Tyrone, 23 April 1947. Final-year psychology student at QUB, 1969. As Bernadette Devlin, she first came to prominence in the civil rights campaign as a member of the PD movement. She took part in the student demonstrations in Belfast in the summer of 1968, and in all the major NICRA marches that year in Dungannon, Armagh, and in Duke Street, Derry, on 5 October. She was also in the Belfast–Londonderry PD march in January 1969, when it was attacked by militant loyalists at Burntollet. She lost her first election when she stood against Major Chichester-Clark (who was soon to become PM) in S. Londonderry in March 1969. But the next month she won a by-election in Mid-Ulster for Westminster, defeating the Unionist candidate (widow of the former MP) by 4,211 votes in a poll of 92 per cent. She became the youngest woman ever to be elected to Westminster, and the youngest MP for fifty years. She took her seat on her twenty-second birthday. It was, she said, 'the arrival of a peasant in the halls of the great'. Her sponsors were Gerry Fitt MP, and Labour MP Paul Rose, chairman of the Campaign for Democracy in Ulster. Ignoring tradition, she made her maiden speech an hour after taking her seat. In it she attacked the Unionist Government of Captain O'Neill and said an extreme, but possible, solution would be the abolition of Stormont.

The Home Secretary, James Callaghan, spoke of her 'brilliance' and said he looked to the day when she might be standing at the Government despatch box. Conservative MP, Norman St John Stevas, said that not since the days of F.E. Smith had the House listened to such an electrifying maiden speech. Newspapers hailed her triumph, not only as the voice of NICRA, but of the student generation. The maiden speech was sandwiched between lunch with the Government Chief Whip and dinner with Lord Longford. But soon Bernadette Devlin was to make very different headlines. In the 'battle of the Bogside' in Londonderry in August 1969, she became the focus of world attention. The slight, five-foot tall MP was to be seen encouraging the Bogsiders to raise their barricades against the police. The report of the Scarman Tribunal had described how she was involved in 'inconclusive' telephone conversations from the Bogside to Major Chichester-Clark (then PM) and Lord Stonham (Minister of State, Home Office) at the height of the violence on 13 August 1969. Of that same day, Scarman also noted: 'She was seen in the afternoon to be actively defending the Rossville Street barricades, taking missiles up to its defenders, and shouting encouragement to them. In the morning she led a flag party to the high flats where she unfurled at one end of the roof the 'Starry Plough' flag of the Connolly Association.' Bernadette Devlin now became to her admirers 'an Irish Joan of Arc', and to at least one Unionist MP (Stratton Mills) a 'mini-skirted Castro'. In August 1969, on a trip to the US, she raised £50,000 for relief in NI. In December 1969 she was sentenced to six months' imprisonment at Derry Magistrates' Court for incitement to riot and obstruction and disorderly behaviour, arising from the Bogside incidents. She went to Armagh Prison

in June 1970, after she had increased her Mid-Ulster majority to nearly 6,000 in the general election. When she was jailed, there were protest marches and demonstrations in many parts of NI and a protest march in London. In July 1971 she announced that she was going to have a baby. Newspaper opinion was divided. Some papers praised her courage and her insistence that her private life was her own; one critical paper said she seemed to have become a lost leader. In January 1972 she punched the Home Secretary, Reginald Maudling, in the Commons. She accused him of lying about the events of 'Bloody Sunday' in Derry, in which thirteen people had died. The scene was unprecedented in recent history, and she said later that the reaction to it showed a lot about the English. It had created more popular outrage than the Derry shootings. In April 1973 she married Michael McAliskey, a schoolmaster, at a quiet, early morning ceremony. Once again, it was an event on her birthday – her twenty-sixth – and the wedding was at a Catholic church near her home town of Cookstown. In the February 1974 general election she lost her Mid-Ulster seat. The intervention of the SDLP split the anti-Unionist vote, and a Vanguard Unionist, John Dunlop, was returned. The old unity of the civil rights movement had vanished and she helped found the IRSP at the end of 1974. When the 1975 feud developed between the OIRA and the IRSP, she strongly denied that the IRSP had a military wing. On a lecture tour in the US in 1976 she attacked the Peace People as dishonest and said she was not going to tell the PIRA to stop fighting. They were fighting British imperialism in the only way they knew how, she said. In the 1979 European election she championed the Republican prisoners engaged in protests at the Maze Prison to secure political status, but PSF made it clear that it was not supporting her, and it urged voters to boycott the election. She was eliminated on the third count, although she managed to save her deposit. On 16 February 1981 she and her husband were seriously injured when they were shot in their home at Derrylaughan, near Coalisland, Co. Tyrone, by loyalist gunmen. An army patrol arrived quickly and she later acknowledged the value of emergency treatment given by the soldiers. In 1980 and 1981 she was the main spokes-woman of the National H-Block/Armagh Committee. In September 1981 she was expelled from Spain when she arrived to speak at an H-Block meeting in the Basque country. But she managed to slip into Spain again from France, and addressed a meeting without being apprehended. In 1982 she stood unsuccessfully in both the Republic's general elections as PD candidate. She contested Dublin North Central – Charles Haughey's constituency. In 1987 and 1988 she campaigned strongly against extradition from the Republic.

MCALLISTER, JAMES

PSF Assembly member for Armagh, 1982–6. b. Crossmaglen, Co. Armagh, 1944. Both his parents' families were deeply involved in Republicanism, and his own activity in the movement dates from the early 1960s. After a period in England, he resumed his interest in 1974, and was PRO of the S. Armagh Hunger Strike Action Committee in 1981, and then became chairman of PSF in S. Armagh. Newry and Mourne Council, 1985–. Stood unsuccessfully in Newry and Armagh in 1983 and 1987 elections, and in 1986 by-election.

MCATEER, EDWARD (EDDIE)

Leader of the Nationalist Party at Stormont, 1964–9. b. Coatbridge, Glasgow, 1914; d. 1986. A civil servant from 1930 until 1944, when he started his own accountancy business. He was returned unopposed as Nationalist MP for Mid-Derry in 1945, and again in 1949. He represented Foyle from 1953 until 1969, when he lost to John Hume. He was on Derry Corporation from 1952 until 1958. Early in his career he published a blueprint for civil disobedience entitled 'Irish Action', but in the civil rights campaign he frequently urged moderation. He accepted the role of official opposition leader at Stormont in 1965, and he argued that much trouble might have been avoided if Unionists had offered concessions at that period, and he brought his own brand of wit and sarcasm to parliamentary proceedings. His brother, Hugh McAteer, was at one time chief of staff of the IRA, and staged an escape from Crumlin Road Prison in Belfast. In 1977 Eddie McAteer gave support to the newly established IIP.

MACBRIDE, SEAN

The Nobel Peace Prize winner of 1974 and international jurist and diplomat, who was involved in peace talks in 1977 aimed at securing a paramilitary ceasefire in NI. b. 27 January 1904; d. 1988. MacBride was among the most prominent IRA leaders in the 1920s and 1930s. He was reputedly chief of staff for a time, and was imprisoned three times between 1918 and 1930. He urged a concentration on constitutional action during the 1940s and became leader of the Republican party, Clann na Poblachta, and a member of the Dáil, 1947–58. He was Minister for External Affairs in the inter-party Government, 1948–51. He was Assistant UN Secretary-General and UN Commissioner in Namibia, 1973–4, and returned to Dublin when he left this post. In 1977 he was awarded the Lenin Peace Prize. In that year he tried, without success, to get agreement between loyalist and IRA paramilitaries in NI. These talks also involved Desmond Boal, the NI lawyer and former Unionist MP and first chairman of the DUP. The contacts were made in great secrecy and did not involve face-to-face talks between the two sides. Churchmen were used to some extent as intermediaries. Despite his early involvement with the IRA, he has stressed his opposition to the PIRA campaign. He summed up his view by saying that there were injustices in NI, but they were not unbearable and there were probably other ways of remedying the situation. It was disclosed in British Cabinet papers released in January 1980 that MacBride had a meeting at Stormont in 1949 with the then PM Lord Brookeborough. But MacBride said there had been no negotiations as such. Opposed divorce in Republic's 1986 referendum. In 1985 he was associated with the MacBride Principles, which proposed tighter rules against discrimination in jobs than the existing legislation in NI.

MACBRIDE PRINCIPLES see Fair Employment *and* MacBride, Sean

MCCANN, EAMONN
Civil rights activist, b. 10 March 1943. Expelled from QUB, 1965, when reading psychology. President of university 'Literific' Society and vice-president of Labour Club. One of the organisers of civil rights march in Londonderry, 5 October 1968. As chairman of Derry Labour Party, unsuccessfully contested Foyle in Stormont 1969 general election and Londonderry in 1970 Westminster election. Active in 'battle of the Bogside' in Derry and author of *War in an Irish Town*. His Foyle campaign included a demand for take-over of all vacant property suitable for housing accommodation. Later, he took up journalism and became well known as a broadcaster.

MCCARTNEY, ROBERT
OUP Assembly member for N. Down, 1982–6. Served on committees on Economic Development, and Finance and Personnel. b. 1936. A native of the Shankill area of Belfast, he was a QC and one of NI's most successful barristers when he caught the political limelight in 1981 with a sharp attack on the Rev. Ian Paisley, whom he called a 'fascist'. In October 1981 he led a delegation of NI lawyers and business-men in talks with Taoiseach Dr Garret FitzGerald, on his 'constitutional crusade'. In August 1982, as chairman of the OUP's newly formed Union Group, he visited the US, and in a speech to the Irish Forum in San Francisco described as 'simplistic and dangerous nonsense' the idea that Ireland's problems would be solved if only the British left. When the Assembly collapsed in 1986, he launched an intensive drive as leader of the Campaign for Equal Citizenship, urging national parties to organise in NI. In 1987 he was expelled from the OUP when he stood unsuccessfully against Jim Kilfedder in N. Down in the general election, because there was an agreement among Unionist parties, in their anti-AIA campaign, that sitting Unionists should not be opposed. Standing as a 'Real Unionist', he got within 4,000 votes of Kilfedder. Soon afterwards he stood down as CEC president, but returned to the post in 1988 amid suggestions that he might contest the 1989 European election.

MCCLOSKEY, VINCENT
SDLP Assembly, 1973–4, and Convention, 1975–6, member for S. Antrim. b. Belfast, 1920. Formerly, National Democratic Party. Lisburn Rural District Council, 1968–73.

MCCLURE, WILLIAM JAMES
DUP Assembly member for Londonderry, 1982–6. Deputy

chairman, Health and Social Services Committee. Was Convention member for the same constituency, 1975–6. b. 1927. Founder member of DUP; chairman, 1974, of the party's Londonderry association. Party chairman, 1978–. Prominent in anti-AIA campaign, and in 1987 he became a member of two District Councils – Coleraine and Ballymoney. He had been on the Coleraine Council since 1977, and was then co-opted on to the Ballymoney Council to avoid a by-election arising from the resignation of a DUP member in protest at the AIA. Past grand master of Independent Orange Order.

MCCONNELL, ROBERT DODD (BERTIE)

All. Assembly, 1973–4, and Convention, 1975–6, member for N. Down. b. Bangor, Co. Down, 1921. Blinded in World War II, during army service, he served on Bangor Borough Council, 1958–73, and N. Down Council, 1973–81. MP for Bangor in NI Parliament, 1969–72; elected as pro-O'Neill Unionist and joined Alliance Party in 1972 as one of first members of Alliance Parliamentary Party. President, Alliance Party, 1976.

MCCREA, RAYMOND STUART

DUP Assembly member for S. Belfast, 1982–6. Served on committees on Environment, and Health and Social Services. b. 1945. Belfast City Council, 1977–85. Leader, DUP group on City Council, 1981. Unsuccessfully contested S. Belfast in 1983 Westminster election.

MCCREA, REVEREND ROBERT THOMAS WILLIAM

DUP MP for Mid-Ulster, 1983–. Assembly member for Mid-Ulster, 1982–6. Served on committees on Agriculture, Education, Health and Social Services. b. 6 February 1948. A

Free Presbyterian Minister prominent in loyalist politics since 1971, when he was sentenced to six months' imprisonment for riotous behaviour in Dungiven, Co. Londonderry. Widely known as a Gospel singer. Chairman, United Loyalist Front, 1972. Magherafelt Council, 1973–. Chairman, DUP, 1976. Housing Executive Board, 1979–80. Unsuccessfully contested S. Belfast by-election, 1982. His 1983 election majority of 78 in Mid-Ulster was the smallest of the election in NI. But he raised it to over 9,000 in the 1986 by-election and 1987 general election.

MCCULLOUGH, RAYMOND

OUP Assembly member for S. Down, 1982–5. Deputy chairman, Agriculture Committee; member, Environment Committee. Banbridge Council, 1973–85; served as chairman and vice-chairman. b. 1919; d. 1985. On executive of Official Unionist Party; Honorary Secretary, S. Down Unionist Association; and on committee, Grand Orange Lodge of Ireland.

MCCUSKER, JAMES HAROLD

OUP MP for Upper Bann, 1983–. MP for Armagh, 1974–83. Assembly member for Armagh, 1982–6. Deputy leader, Official Unionist Party, 1982–. b. 7 February 1940. A teacher and later production manager, he was Secretary and Whip of the Unionist Coalition MPs, 1975–6. Active in pressing for tougher security measures in S. Armagh. Voted with the Labour Government in crucial confidence vote which led to the defeat of the Callaghan Government and the 1979 general election. He held off a challenge from the DUP in that election, and in the 1982 Assembly election topped the poll in Armagh. In 1981 he was responsible for setting up a unit based at OUP headquarters which sought to persuade the European Commission on Human Rights that border security was inadequate, and that widows of innocent victims of the violence should be regarded as suffering a deprivation of human rights. In criticism of the AIA in 1986 he said independence might become a viable option, since Unionists were being ignored by Westminster. He said he was not advocating independence, but the Union should be on terms which were mutually acceptable, 'and not those acceptable to Margaret Thatcher and the Tory party'. In 1987 he served a short sentence in Belfast Prison for withholding car tax in protest at the AIA. He was a member of the OUP–DUP task force which reported to Unionist leaders on strategy in opposing the AIA in the summer of 1987.

MCDONALD, JAMES
SDLP Assembly member for S. Antrim, 1982–6. b. 1930. Craigavon Council, 1973–85. First SDLP deputy Mayor of Craigavon, 1979. Unsuccessfully contested Convention election in S. Antrim, 1975.

MCFAUL, KENNETH
Founder member of DUP and former member of Protestant Unionist Party. b. 1948. Left DUP in 1984 after the selection of Jim Allister as candidate for the E. Antrim constituency in the 1983 general election. Carrickfergus Borough Council, 1973–85; Mayor, 1981–3. Convention member for N. Antrim, 1975–6. Unsuccessful candidate in N. Antrim in Assembly election, 1982.

MAC GIOLLA, TOMÁS
President of the Workers' Party and its predecessor, Official Sinn Féin, January 1970–88, and earlier president of Sinn Féin, 1962–70. He presided at the Dublin meeting in December 1969 at which the walk-out of the future

Provisional members occurred. b. 1924. BA, B.Comm. (UCD). TD, 1982–. Has frequently visited NI, particularly to speak in elections. In 1972 he was cleared of a charge of membership of the OIRA. In that year he was twice deported from Britain, but in 1976 Home Secretary Roy Jenkins resisted Conservative demands that he should be expelled. On that occasion he addressed a private meeting of MPs at the House of Commons, which had been arranged by Labour MP Joan Maynard. Unsuccessfully contested the 1979 European election in Dublin. In early 1987 he strongly denied reports that WP was associated with OIRA and that violence and robberies had been carried out in NI, the Republic and GB by people linked with the party.

MCGLONE, PATRICK (PATSY)
General Secretary of SDLP, 1986–. b. 8 July 1959. BA Hons (UU). A former civil servant (Environment), he joined SDLP in 1983, and after holding party posts in Co. Derry, including secretaryship of S. Derry executive, he was elected to executive in 1985, when he also became chairman of University of Ulster branch. Unsuccessful candidate, Magherafelt District Council, 1985. Member, GAA.

MCGONAGLE, STEPHEN
Parliamentary Commissioner for Administration (Ombudsman) and Commissioner for Complaints, 1974–9. Irish Senator, 1983–7. b. Londonderry, 1914. Leading local trade unionist before appointment as Ombudsman; district secretary of the ITGWU and president of the NI Committee of ICTU, 1972. He became vice-chairman of Londonderry Development Commission in 1969, but resigned in August 1971, as a protest against the introduction of internment without trial. Chairman of Police Complaints Board set up in 1977

to independently investigate complaints against the RUC, but resigned from this post in 1983, after Unionist protests that it was inconsistent with membership of Irish Senate. In 1982 presided at initial, short-lived inquiry into homosexual scandal at Kincora boys' home in E. Belfast. Irish Labour Party delegate to New Ireland Forum, 1983–4.

MCGRADY, EDWARD KEVIN (EDDIE)

SDLP MP for S. Down, 1987–. SDLP Assembly member for S. Down, 1982–6. Also elected for S. Down to Assembly, 1973–4, and Convention, 1975–6. b. 3 June 1935. First chairman SDLP, 1971–3. Head of Department of Executive Planning and Co-ordination in NI Executive, 1974. Downpatrick Urban Council, 1961–73 (chairman, 1964–73); Down District Council, 1973– (chairman, 1974–5). McGrady was particularly critical of Secretary of State Merlyn Rees after the fall of the Executive. He said that a remark by Rees that he had not expected the Executive to endure showed the 'duplicity and dishonesty' of British policy. Chief Whip, SDLP, 1979–. Unsuccessfully stood against Enoch Powell in S. Down in 1979 and 1983 general elections, and 1986 by-election, and finally won the seat in 1987, when the rise in the Nationalist electorate defeated a strong Powell campaign. Has been prominent in highlighting health dangers from Sellafield nuclear plant, and opposing effect of expenditure cuts on local hospitals. Unenthusiastic about talks between SDLP and PSF in 1988. Party spokesman on local government.

MCGUINNESS, (JAMES) MARTIN

PSF Assembly member for Londonderry, 1982–6. Vice-president, PSF, 1983–. b. Bogside area of Derry, 1950. An active Republican since 1969, he

was a member of the top-level PIRA delegation which met NI Secretary of State William Whitelaw in London, July 1972. The previous year he had become leader of PIRA in Derry, and he has been imprisoned on several occasions both in NI and the Republic. In 1981 he gave the oration at funeral of PIRA hunger-striker Francis Hughes in Bellaghy, Co. Derry, and has been prominent at many PIRA funerals. With PSF's entry into the NI electoral scene, he became a major figure in the movement. In 1984 he indicated that PIRA would be dropping punishment shootings, but the practice continued. In 1985 he denied that he was PIRA chief of staff, and claimed that the allegation was part of a British plan to have him assassinated. This was during the angry controversy which erupted over the BBC *Real Lives* TV programme in which he was featured, and which was eventually transmitted with minor changes despite opposition from the Government. Stood unsuccessfully in Foyle against John Hume in the 1983 and 1987 Westminster elections.

MCGURRAN, MALACHY

Chairman of the six-county executive of Republican Clubs and vice-president of Official Sinn Féin from 1970 until his death from bone cancer in July 1978. b. Lurgan, 1938. Active in the 1956 IRA campaign and interned for a time. Candidate for Armagh in October 1974 general election and 1975 Convention election. Craigavon District Council, 1977–8.

MCIVOR, (WILLIAM) BASIL

Education Minister in Executive, 1974. b. 17 June 1928. LLB (QUB). Barrister, 1950. Unionist MP for Larkfield, 1969–72. Minister of Community Relations, 1971. After direct rule, he dissociated himself from Unionist attacks on Secretary of State William Whitelaw. One of the Unionist team at the Sunningdale Conference, December 1973. As head of the Education Department in the power-sharing Executive, he announced the scheme for shared schools for Protestant and Catholic pupils, but the scheme was never implemented owing to the short life of the Executive. In 1981 he became first chairman of Lagan College – NI's first integrated school. Resident Magistrate, 1976–. In 1987 four Unionist MPs tabled a Commons' motion calling for his removal from the Bench on the grounds that he had shown bias against Unionists and Orangemen in a case at Ballymoney.

MCKAY, JOHN ALEXANDER
OUP member of Convention, 1975–6, for Fermanagh–S. Tyrone. b. 1945.

MCKEAGUE, JOHN DUNLOP
A leading Belfast loyalist who was shot dead by an INLA gunman in his E. Belfast shop in January 1982. b. 1930. First came to prominence as chairman of the Shankill Defence Association, 1969–70. He stood unsuccessfully as Protestant Unionist candidate for Belfast Corporation by-election in Victoria in 1969, and as an Independent in N. Belfast at the 1970 Westminster election. He was often described as a founder of the loyalist paramilitary group, the Red Hand Commandos, but always denied that he was involved with the organisation. He was cleared in 1969 of charges of conspiracy to cause explosions. In October 1969 he was sentenced to three months' imprisonment for unlawful assembly. In 1971 his elderly mother was burned to death when his shop and flat in E. Belfast were set on fire by petrol bombs. *Loyalist News*, the paper run by McKeague, said she had been 'murdered by the enemies of Ulster'. In the same year he and two others were the first persons to be accused under the Incitement to Hatred

Act, after they published a *Loyalist Song Book*. The jury disagreed at the first trial and they were acquitted at the retrial. In 1976, as a member of the ULCCC, he was prominent in advocating independence for NI.

MCKEE, JOHN (JACK)
DUP Assembly member for N. Antrim, 1982–6. Served on committees on Environment, and Health and Social Services. b. 1944. Larne Council, 1973–. Leader of DUP on Larne Council, 1981–; Mayor, 1984–.

MCKEOWN, CIARAN
One of the three founders of the Peace People in 1976. b. Londonderry, 24 December 1943. Graduated in philosophy at QUB, 1966, and in that year president of the Students' Union. President of Union of Students of Ireland, 1967. On Belfast staff of *Irish Press* (Dublin), before joining Peace People full time in 1976. In 1977 awarded scholarship worth £4,000 a year by Norwegian Government to help with peace work and the writing of articles for the Norwegian Institute for Peace Research. Director and editor of *Fortnight*, NI current affairs magazine, for a period during 1977. Editor, Peace People newspaper, 1978–9. Stood down as chairman of Peace People executive in 1978 and resigned in 1980. In 1988 he resigned as Secretary of the Lyric Theatre, Belfast, with which he had been associated for eleven years.

MCLACHLAN, PETER
UPNI Assembly member for S. Antrim, 1973–4. b. 1937. In 1977 he became a full-time official of the Peace People and was elected chairman when the original leaders stood down from the executive in 1978. He resigned from this post in February 1980, and became Secretary of the Belfast Voluntary Welfare Society. Worked in a great

variety of posts – teacher, civil servant at Stormont and Westminster, secretary to the Youth Orchestra of Great Britain, personal assistant to Fleet Street newspaper chief Cecil King – before taking charge of NI desk at Conservative Central Office in 1970. Parliamentary lobbyist at Westminster, 1972–3. In the Assembly he was one of Brian Faulkner's closest advisers, particularly during the Sunningdale Conference. But he declined a post in the Executive, arguing that he would be better employed as a backbencher and in building up UPNI. Stood unsuccessfully in Westminster election in E. Belfast in 1974 and in Convention election in S. Antrim in 1975. Specially interested in penal reform and community groups and chairman of NI Federation of Housing Associations, 1977. Active in Campaign for a Devolved Parliament group launched in 1988.

MCMANUS, FRANCIS JOSEPH (FRANK)

Unity MP for Fermanagh–S. Tyrone, 1970–4. b. Enniskillen, 16 August 1942. BA, Dip.Ed. (QUB). Chairman of Fermanagh Civil Rights Association, 1968–71, and leading speaker at civil rights demonstrations throughout NI. Chairman, Northern Resistance Movement, 1972. Chairman, Comhairle Uladh (Republican-oriented, nine-county forum), 1972. Leading figure in Unity Movement which contested a variety of elections, and in 1977 one of founders of IIP of which he became deputy leader in 1981. In 1971 he was sentenced to six months' imprisonment for defying a parade ban in Enniskillen. In same year he was cleared of charge relating to PIRA documents. Injured by one of four shots fired at him in September 1973. Irish representative of US-based Irish National Caucus, 1976–.

MCMASTER, STANLEY EDWARD

Unionist MP for E. Belfast, 1959–74. b. 23 September 1926. Barrister in practice in London. Lecturer in company law, Regent Street Polytechnic.

MCNAMARA, (JOSEPH) KEVIN

Labour front-bench spokesman on NI, 1987–. Chairman of party's NI committee, 1974–9. b. 5 September 1934. Labour MP for Kingston-upon-Hull North/Central since 1966. Lecturer in law. Co. Down family background. Has maintained interest in NI since he was prominent in Campaign for Democracy in Ulster. In 1987 he said Neil Kinnock had appointed him front-bench spokesman not in spite of, but because of, his record of campaigning for Irish unity. He claimed that bipartisanship with the Conservatives on NI had ended in 1981 when Labour became committed to a united Ireland by consent. Reviewing the AIA in 1988, he voiced disappointment that it had not achieved more in internal reforms in NI, but said there were signs of flexibility among Unionists which was essential to any resolution of the conflict. Expressed hope in 1988 that he would become last NI Secretary of State.

MCQUADE, JOHN

DUP MP for N. Belfast, 1979–83. b. 1912; d. 1984. Ex-docker, ex-soldier, ex-boxer, he was one of the best-known personalities on the Protestant Shankill Road in Belfast. Unionist MP for Woodvale at Stormont, 1965–72, he broke with the Unionist Parliamentary Party in 1971, and resigned as MP when Stormont was suspended in 1972. He then joined the DUP, and was returned as a DUP Assembly member for N. Belfast, 1973–4. When the Assembly was prorogued in May 1974, he refused to take his salary and donated it to a holiday fund for old

people. In February 1974 he unsuccessfully contested W. Belfast as UUUC
candidate. He then broke with the DUP
but rejoined in 1979, and with a split in
the Unionist vote, gained N. Belfast
from the Official Unionists by a
majority of 995 in a seven-candidate
contest in which he obtained 27.6 per
cent of the vote.

MACRORY, SIR PATRICK
Chairman of the review body which
produced the plan for local government reform in NI, 1970. b. 21 March
1911. A barrister, Sir Patrick was a
director of a variety of top companies
and a member of the NI Development
Council, 1956–64. The Macrory
proposals produced a great deal of
controversy. They were strongly
attacked by existing councillors, and
supported by the NICRA. They were
accepted by the Chichester-Clark
Government, and the twenty-six
District Councils which replaced the
former complex structure were first
elected in 1973. Apart from the
councils, the scheme provided for area
boards for education, library and
health services, which were strongly
attacked by Unionists on the grounds
that the majority of members of the
boards were nominated by the
Government rather than elected
representatives. The disappearance of
the Assembly removed what was
intended to be the top tier of local
government, and this has been dubbed
the 'Macrory gap'. Its absence has been
frequently criticised by Sir Patrick. In
1984 Sir Patrick was chairman of a
'think tank' under the auspices of the
Institute for European Defence and
Strategic Studies which urged the
setting up of a joint British-Irish
Security Commission to fight
terrorism.

MCSORLEY, MARY KATHERINE
SDLP Assembly member for Mid-

Ulster, 1982–6. Magherafelt Council,
1978–. Party spokeswoman on
tourism. Member, local government
Staff Commission, 1985–. In 1989
became first SDLP-elected representative to accept a royal honour (MBE); the
party, angered at her action, said she
could not run as SDLP candidate in May
1989 District Council elections.

MAC STIOFÁIN, SEÁN
Chief of staff of PIRA, 1970–2. b.
Leytonstone, London, 17 February
1928. John Edward Drayton
Stephenson's adoption of an Irish
background and dedication to IRA aims
were apparently due to the influence of
his mother, who claimed to be a native
of Belfast. After National Service with
the RAF (he became a corporal), he
joined some London-Irish associations
and, presumably, the IRA. In 1953 he
and two other men – one of them
Cathal Goulding, who was later to
become chief of staff of the OIRA – were
sentenced to eight years' imprisonment
for stealing one hundred and eight
rifles and eight Bren guns from the
cadet armoury of Felstead School in
Essex. After his release in 1959, he
travelled to Dublin (the first time he
had been in Ireland) and became
salesman for an Irish language
organisation. By this time he was a
fluent Irish speaker. He soon became
immersed in IRA intelligence work, and
he devoted his organisational skill to
the building up of PIRA after the split in
the Republican movement. At the
height of the PIRA campaign he made
many secret trips to NI, but he was
believed to be interested in moving over
eventually to the political side of the
PIRA. In 1972 he said he was interested
in peace, but not peace at any price, and
the British must first agree to the basic
PIRA aims. In November 1972 he was
arrested in Co. Dublin soon after he
had recorded a controversial interview
with RTE journalist, Kevin O'Kelly.

Jailed for six months for PIRA membership. PIRA made an unsuccessful bid to free him when he was taken to a Dublin hospital on hunger strike. In January 1973 he ended the fifty-seven-day hunger strike after PIRA leadership stated that it was 'serving no useful purpose'. He then ceased to be PIRA chief of staff. At end of 1981 he resigned from PSF after its Ard Fheis had shown a majority opposed to the 'Éire Nua' federal policy. In March 1983 he appealed for a PIRA ceasefire. A *Sunday Times* report in 1985 that he had been a Garda informer for twenty years was dismissed by PSF as 'British propaganda'.

MAGINNIS, JOHN EDWARD

Unionist MP for Armagh, 1959–February 1974. b. Tandragee, Co. Armagh, 7 March 1919. Served in RUC, 1939–45. Group Secretary, Ulster Farmers' Union, 1956–9. Stood unsuccessfully as UPNI candidate in Armagh at the Convention election, 1975.

MAGINNIS, KENNETH (KEN)

OUP MP for Fermanagh–S. Tyrone, 1983–. Assembly member for same constituency, 1982–6. b. 1938. Teacher. Formerly served in Ulster Special Constabulary (B Specials), and was later part-time Major and Company Commander, UDR, for eleven years. Official Unionist security spokesman, 1982–. Chairman of Assembly's security committee, 1983–6. Deputy chairman, Finance and Personnel Committee. Dungannon Council, 1981–. Unsuccessfully contested Fermanagh–S. Tyrone by-election, August 1981, but had 7,000-plus majority in 1983 election when SDLP competed for Nationalist vote and raised majority to over 12,000 in 1986 by-election and 1987 general election. As OUP security spokesman he has repeatedly called for stronger

action against PIRA in border areas (there are more than 190 unsolved murders in his constituency), and in 1988 he was urging selective internment. Has supported power-sharing in government, which he has termed 'responsibility sharing'. In 1987 he served a brief prison sentence for refusal to pay car tax in protest at the AIA. In 1988 he was named 'Parliamentarian of the Year' by the *Spectator* magazine.

MAGUIRE, FRANCIS (FRANK)

Independent MP for Fermanagh–S. Tyrone, October 1974–81. b. 1929; d. 5 March 1981. A publican, he was active in the Republican movement and was interned for nearly two years in the late 1950s. As an MP he took a special interest in the welfare of Irish prisoners in English jails. He came close to practising the abstentionist policy so often favoured by Republicans, and rarely attended at Westminster and still had not made a maiden speech at the time of his death. But he did support the Callaghan Government in some key divisions, and his absence from the final vote of confidence contributed to its defeat. In the 1979 election he increased his majority and his death gave rise to the by-election in which hunger-striker Bobby Sands was elected.

MAGUIRE, PAUL

All. Assembly member for N. Belfast, 1982–6, Health and Social Services Committee. Barrister and lecturer in law, QUB, and party spokesman on legal affairs. Party adviser at Stormont Constitutional Conference, 1980.

MALLON, SEAMUS

SDLP MP for Newry and Armagh, 1986–. Deputy leader of SDLP, 1979–. b. Markethill, Co. Armagh, 1936. Elected Assembly member for Armagh in 1982, but disqualified on grounds that he was a member of the Republic's Senate. Former Co. Armagh Gaelic footballer and head teacher. Prominent in civil rights campaign and chairman, Mid-Armagh Anti-Discrimination Committee, 1963–8. Armagh Council, 1973–. Represented Armagh in both the 1973–4 Assembly and the 1975–6 Convention. Unsuccessfully contested Armagh in Westminster elections, October 1974, 1979 and the new constituency of Newry and Armagh in 1983. But in the January 1986 by-election forced by Unionists in protest at the AIA, his persistence was rewarded, and he unseated Jim Nicholson of the OUP by some 2,500 votes, and doubled that majority in 1987. Before becoming deputy leader to John Hume, he had been chairman of the SDLP in the 1973 Assembly and chairman of constituency representatives, 1977–9. His appointment to the Republic's Senate by Taoiseach Charles Haughey in May 1982 was a major surprise. When it led to his exclusion from the Assembly, Mallon protested that the situation highlighted the 'incongruity' of British political involvement in Irish affairs. Despite the SDLP decision not to attend the Assembly, he was unseated in an Election Court on a petition brought by Armagh MP Harold McCusker. From 1979 to 1982 he was party spokesman on relations with Westminster, and in 1982 took over as law-and-order spokesman. In that capacity he was particularly critical of the NIO's handling of controversial RUC shootings in Armagh in 1982, and in the wake of the AIA urged a speed-up in reform of the judiciary. In 1988 he called for a rethink of the Republic's neutrality policy. He was critical of several of the anti-terrorist measures introduced in late 1988, including intensive house searches in Nationalist areas.

MANSFIELD AND MANSFIELD, LORD

Minister of State, NIO, 1983–4. b. 7 July 1930. (Heir, Viscount Stormont.) Minister of State, Scottish Office, 1979–83. Member of British delegation to European Parliament, 1973–5. Opposition spokesman in House of Lords, 1975–9. Apart from being departmental spokesman in the Lords, he took responsibility for Agriculture in NIO. Resigned for health reasons.

MARKETS

A district close to the centre of Belfast, where there were many bombing and shooting incidents in 1969–70. At the start of the Troubles, OIRA had a strong presence in the area, and after 1972 it was largely displaced by INLA, which continued to be active in the area in the early 1980s. The area has been transformed by new housing developments.

MARSHALL, JAMES

Labour front-bench spokesman on NI, 1987–. MP for Leicester South, October 1974–83; 1987–. b. 13 March 1941. Assistant Government Whip, 1977–9. Strongly against privatisation of Short Brothers plc in 1988.

MARTIN, THOMAS GEOFFREY

Head of EC office in Belfast, 1979–85. b. 26 July 1940. B.Sc. Hons (QUB). President of the National Union of Students, 1966–8. Diplomatic staff, Commonwealth Secretariat, 1974–9. After the Dublin summit of December 1980, he suggested that the EC could provide 'a useful institutional relationship' in the future strategy of Anglo-Irish relations, and that the European dimension could have a growing importance in NI affairs. Moved to EC post in Bangkok.

MASON, LORD (OF BARNSLEY)

As Roy Mason, NI Secretary of State, September 1976–May 1979. b. 18 April 1924. As a boy of fourteen he went down the mines in his native Barnsley, Yorkshire, and remained in the coal industry until 1953, when he became Labour MP for Barnsley. Labour Party spokesman on Defence, Home Affairs and Post Office, 1960–4. Minister of State, Board of Trade, 1964–7. Minister of Defence, Equipment, 1967–8. Minister of Power, 1968–9. President of the Board of Trade, 1969–70. Secretary for Defence, 1974–6. His appointment to Stormont was unexpected, and regarded by many non-Unionists as indicating a tougher direct-rule regime than that of his predecessor, Merlyn Rees. Some SDLP members suggested that he was concerned only with a military solution. He was also handicapped in some quarters by a statement which he had made as Defence Secretary in April 1974: 'Pressure is mounting on the mainland to pull out the troops. Equally, demands are being made to set a date for withdrawal, thereby forcing the warring factions to get together and hammer out a solution.' The comment caused alarm in the three-party NI Executive, and deputy Chief Executive Gerry Fitt flew to London to seek clarification from the PM Harold Wilson. In a statement after a Cabinet meeting, the PM said the troops would stay in the front line against terrorism, and a statement from the Defence Ministry said Mason did not intend to suggest any change of policy. At the same time, he was responsible for a military initiative in NI: the introduction of units of the controversial SAS in S. Armagh in 1976. As Defence Secretary, he called an early morning meeting of his top advisers and presented the plan to Wilson, who accepted it immediately as an answer to some horrific murders in the area. At

Stormont Mason was helped by three factors: his experience of the army role during his previous two years at the Defence Ministry; a more friendly attitude towards him by the Conservative opposition than Rees had enjoyed; and the tendency for violence to decline, notably from the loyalist side. In his early months in NI he ran into criticism from the media because of an attempt to introduce voluntary censorship of news of 'sensitive terrorist incidents'. He wanted to bring in the equivalent of the Whitehall 'D' notice system which is designed to discourage the dissemination of information likely to be damaging to national security. He was also opposed to the BBC and ITV broadcasting interviews in support of allegations of ill-treatment directed against the RUC. This was clearly part of a psychological approach. At his initial news conference in September 1976 he spoke of the IRA 'reeling'; at the end of the year the 'net was tightening on the terrorist'; and by the end of 1977 the 'corner is being turned in the war against the terrorists'. Certainly, the security forces achieved major successes in terms of arrests during 1977, and there was a distinct drop in the level of killings and bombings. But at the end of 1977, with a fireman's strike, the PIRA mounted a new incendiary bomb campaign, which caused heavy damage. And the PIRA said Mason was being a 'fool' to predict their defeat. One of the important changes which he made in security policy during 1977 was to increase the covert tactics of the army, and the SAS was allowed to operate throughout NI. Other features of his security approach were to enlarge the role of the RUC and UDR (more 'Ulsterisation' of security is the local phrase). At the start of 1978 he also aimed to switch a larger section of the army locally from men on four-month

188

tours to units which would remain on a long-stay basis, that is, for two years. In 1977 he had a substantial political success in defeating the efforts of the UUAC to repeat the triumph of the 1974 UWC strike. During that year, he also made two attempts to get some movement towards a political settlement. After talks with the various parties in February and March, he reported to Parliament that there was little sign of bridging the divide. Towards the end of the year he had more talks on the possibility of 'interim devolution', but these rapidly petered out. Mason also put emphasis on bringing forward controversial legislation during direct rule – a regime which he claimed was 'positive, compassionate and caring'. Legislation was brought forward to bring the laws on divorce and homosexuality into line with those in GB and the Government committed itself to comprehensive education. The courts' system in NI was substantially reformed. As Secretary of State, he forcefully projected his dominant personality on the local scene. In 1987 Lord Mason claimed that PIRA 'high command' had admitted, after he left NI, that if his policies had continued for another six months, they would have been defeated.

MATES, MICHAEL JOHN
Conservative MP for Petersfield, 1974–, and chairman of the Anglo-Irish all-party committee at Westminster, 1979–. b. 9 June 1934. Served with army in NI as Lieutenant Colonel. Secretary of Conservative back-bench committee on NI, 1974–9; vice-chairman, 1979–81. Differed strongly from right-wing MPs on Conservative NI Committee who were critical of the James Prior 'rolling devolution' initiative. Regular media commentator on NI affairs and defence issues, and is chairman of the Commons Select Committee on Defence. His inde-

pendent stance was illustrated by his spearheading in 1988 of the Conservative back-bench revolt on the poll tax. Supporter of the AIA and has been active in pressing for a parliamentary tier of MPs and TDs.

MAUDLING, REGINALD
As Home Secretary, responsible for NI affairs at Westminster, 1970–2. b. 7 March 1917; d. February 1979. Conservative MP for Barnet, 1950–79. When he took over from James Callaghan when the Conservatives returned to power in 1970, he made it clear that he would continue to support reform moves in NI. But with the PM, Edward Heath, concerning himself closely with NI matters, Maudling's influence was secondary. His relaxed approach also brought criticism within NI when he stated in March 1971 that London and Stormont Governments were in agreement on security, and shortly afterwards NI Premier James Chichester-Clark resigned, leaving little doubt that he was dissatisfied with Westminster's approach to law and order. Best remembered in NI for having coined the phrase 'acceptable level of violence'. The remark drew a strong protest from the NI Government despite his denial that he was in any way complacent. In January 1972, when he made his statement on 'Bloody Sunday' in the Commons, he was struck by the Mid-Ulster MP, Bernadette Devlin (later McAliskey). He is believed to have only reluctantly backed the decision of the Faulkner Government to introduce internment without trial in 1971.

MAWHINNEY, BRIAN STANLEY
Under-Secretary, NIO, 1986–. b. 26 July 1940. B.Sc. (QUB); M.Sc. (University of Michigan); Ph.D. (London). He was the first Ulster-born MP appointed a NI Minister since direct rule. He took responsibility for the

Education Department five months after being appointed Parliamentary Private Secretary to Secretary of State Tom King. His appointment brought a mixed response from local politicians. Some welcomed the idea of local knowledge being available in the ministerial sphere, but some Unionists saw it as an attempt to damp down loyalist protests against the AIA. In some speeches he sought to counter the Unionist claim that the AIA was a threat to the Union. As Conservative MP for Peterborough, 1979–, he was active in the party's NI Committee, and in 1980 suggested a NI Assembly which has been widely regarded as the inspiration for the 'rolling devolution' plan of James Prior. In 1988 his proposed educational reforms followed those in GB, but the exclusion of Irish from the list of core subjects and the commitment of resources to the promotion of integrated schools caused controversy. In the summer of 1988, in his role as Minister for Information, he visited the US to present the Government's case on fair employment and other issues. In February 1989 he was asked by Secretary of State Tom King to sound out the political parties on the possibility of dialogue. Author of *Conflict and Christianity in Northern Ireland*.

MAWHINNEY, GORDON

All. Assembly member for S. Antrim, 1982–6. Served on committees on Economic Development, Environment, and Security. Deputy leader, Alliance Party, 1987–; Chief Whip, 1984–6. Candidate, Newtownabbey Borough Council, 1981. b. 1943. Specialist in valuation and rating. Participant in Duisburg Talks, October 1988.

MAYHEW, SIR PATRICK

Attorney-General, 1987–. b. 11 September 1929. QC, 1972. Minister of State, Home Office, 1981–3. Solicitor-

General, 1983–7. MP for Tunbridge Wells, February 1974–. Sir Patrick was frequently in the news in 1987 and 1988, when his office was affected by new Irish legislation on extradition from the Republic that required him to provide an outline of evidence in each case. He shared PM Margaret Thatcher's objections to the procedure and was particularly angered by the refusal of his Irish opposite number, John Murray, to authorise the extradition of Father Patrick Ryan on terrorist charges at the end of 1988. Sir Patrick has been mentioned as a possible future NI Secretary of State.

MAZE PRISON *see* H-Blocks *and* Security System section, p. 403

MELCHETT, LORD

Minister of State and House of Lords spokesman, NIO, 1976–9. b. 24 February 1948. BA (Cantab.); MA (Keele). Government Whip, 1974–5, Parliamentary Under-Secretary, Trade, 1975–6. Chairman, Government working party on pop festivals, 1975–6, and has described himself as a punk rock fan. Responsibilities at NIO: departments of Education, and Health and Social Services; also probation, court services; youth matters. His strong support of comprehensive education proved controversial in NI.

MI5 *see* Security System section, pp. 406–7

MI6 *see* Security System section, pp. 407–9

MILES, OLIVER

Joint head of AIA Secretariat at Maryfield, 1988–. b. 1936. A former Ambassador to Libya, who was pulled out of Tripoli after the Libyan People's Bureau siege in London, he was said to have been chosen for the NI post because of the importance attached by the Government to countering the flow of arms from Libya to PIRA.

MILLAR, FRANCIS (FRANK)
Ind. U. Assembly member for N. Belfast, 1982–6. Served on committees on Economic Development and Environment. Was Ind. Loyalist member of the 1973–4 Assembly and UUUC member of the Convention, 1975–6. b. Belfast, 1925. Founder member, Belfast Protestant Action, 1956–64. Belfast City Council, 1972–. As a former shipyard worker and shop steward he was active in 1988 in opposing privatisation of Harland and Wolff plc.

MILLAR, FRANCIS (FRANK)
Elected unopposed to Assembly for S. Belfast at by-election, March 1984. General Secretary, OUP, 1983–7. b. Belfast, 1954; son of Ind. U. councillor Frank Millar. Press officer, Young Unionist Council, 1972–3. Research officer for OUP MPs at Westminster, 1977–81. Press officer at party HQ, 1981–3, before becoming youngest-ever general secretary of the party. One of three members of Unionist inter-party task force set up by Unionist leaders to advise on tactics in opposing the AIA. His resignation as general secretary in September 1987, to become a TV researcher in London, was believed to be due to disappointment that the task-force report had not been more fully implemented. In the 1987 general election he was the party's candidate in W. Belfast, polling some 7,000 votes. He rejected suggestions that the OUP should have stood aside to maximise vote against sitting PSF MP Gerry Adams. He said that for the party to have called for support for the SDLP would have incurred the contempt of Unionists across NI.

MILLS, SIR PETER
Parliamentary Under-Secretary, NIO,

1972–4, with special responsibility for Agriculture. Previously, Parliamentary Secretary, MAFF. b. 1921. Conservative MP for Torrington, 1964–70; Devon West, 1974–9; Devon West and Torridge, 1983–7. Retired in 1987.

MILLS, WILLIAM STRATTON
MP for N. Belfast, 1959–74. b. 1 July 1922. One of a group of Unionist MPs – styled a 'truth squad' by the party – who visited the US and Canada in August 1969 to counter statements by Bernadette Devlin MP. He had served on several Conservative Party committees, including the executive of the 1922 (backbenchers') Committee, and as vice-chairman of the NI Committee. But in February 1971 he voted against the Heath Government as a protest against its 'inadequate security policy' in NI. After the introduction of direct rule, he expressed the view that any future Stormont Assembly should not be dominated by one party and should not have control of security. This was unwelcome to many Unionists, and when he failed to persuade the party's Standing Committee in 1972 that members of Vanguard should be expelled, he resigned from the party. He continued to sit at Westminster, initially as an Ind. Unionist and then as an Alliance MP from 1973 until the February 1974 general election.

MINFORD, NATHANIEL (NAT)
Speaker of the NI Assembly, 1973–4. b. 1913; d. 1975. Unionist MP for Antrim, 1960–72. Leader of the Commons, 1971–2. Elected to Assembly for S. Antrim, 1973.

MITCHELL, SIR DAVID BOWER
Parliamentary Under-Secretary, NIO, January 1981–3. b. 20 June 1928. Conservative MP for Basingstoke, 1964–83; Hampshire North West, 1983–. He took charge of the

Environment Department at Stormont – the department which has the most wide-ranging responsibilities, taking in much of local government, housing and planning, the 'enterprise zones' in Belfast and Londonderry and the Belfast integrated operation, for which EC aid was provided. Under-Secretary of State at Transport, 1983–6; Minister of State, 1986–8. Left Government, 1988.

MITCHELL, CAPTAIN ROBERT
Unionist MP for N. Armagh, 1969–72. b. 1912. Lurgan Borough Council, 1957–73; Coleraine Council, 1977–. Captain Mitchell, as secretary of the Unionist Backbenchers' Committee, 1971–2, was often critical of the Government's law-and-order policies. He questioned the value of the Unionist anti-AIA council boycott campaign.

MOLYNEAUX, JAMES HENRY
Leader of the Official Unionist Party, 1979–. MP for S. Antrim, 1970–83; MP for Lagan Valley, 1983–. Assembly member for S. Antrim, 1982–6. Privy Councillor, 1983. b. 27 August 1920. He was Whip and Secretary of the Unionist Coalition MPs from March to October 1974. He had been defeated by Harry West in a contest for the party leadership in January 1974, but he succeeded West as leader of the coalition MPs when West lost his seat in October 1974. Molyneaux held this post until the break-up of the coalition in 1977, and he continued as leader of the Official Unionist MPs. Vice-president of the Ulster Unionist Council, deputy grand master of the Orange Order, and Sovereign Commonwealth grand master of the Royal Black Institution. His early period of leadership was marked by the adoption of a neutral stance at Westminster, in contrast to the party's former close association with the Conservative Party. He had a leading role in persuading the Callaghan Government to give NI more MPs. In early 1977 he advocated some form of interim devolution, but his critics within unionism accused him of seeking integration rather than full devolution. When he took over the party leadership in 1979, the party was somewhat demoralised by the triumph of the Rev. Ian Paisley in the European election. But he vigorously defended the OUP decision to stand aside from the Atkins Constitutional Conference at Stormont in 1980, and seemed to be determined to build a more broadly based leadership and to tighten party organisation at the grass roots. At the same time, he tried to project himself to a greater extent through the media. Despite this, the DUP achieved a small lead in votes over the OUP in the 1981 council elections, and this was followed by some rumblings against his leadership. In the run-up to the 1982 Assembly elections, he was active in Parliament and outside, warning that the Prior plan was a serious threat to unionism. He pressed one argument repeatedly – that the 'rolling devolution' Assembly could not produce majority-rule government since it basically sought to re-establish the Sunningdale formula, both in terms of power-sharing government and a new cross-border institution. At the end of 1981 he announced the setting up of a Council for the Union 'to defeat the drift towards a united Ireland, as indicated by the Anglo-Irish talks'. In his speech at the Royal Black Preceptory demonstration at Scarva, Co. Armagh, in 1982 he commented that 'certain not-so-loyal Crown servants' had not been surprised by the murder of the Rev. Robert Bradford. James Prior described it as an 'appalling charge' and referred it to the Chief Constable. In the 1982 Assembly election he led his party to a modest victory – the OUP took five more seats

than the DUP, and achieved a 3 per cent swing in votes from the DUP as compared with the 1981 council elections. His own first-preference vote of 19,978 in S. Antrim was the largest of the whole election. In the 1983 Westminster election he tried to establish an electoral pact with DUP in marginal seats, but largely failed. His majority in the 1983 Westminster election in the new seat, Lagan Valley, was more than 17,000 and the OUP achievement in taking eleven NI seats in that election, putting it ahead of the SDP in Parliament, strengthened his position as leader. Margaret Thatcher appointed him a Privy Councillor in 1983, but his efforts, in partnership with Rev. Ian Paisley, to persuade the PM to drop plans to give the Republic a direct say in NI affairs failed. The AIA was clearly a major blow to the OUP leader, who had taken comfort from Thatcher's rejection in 1984 of the main options of the NIF report. An immediate consequence of the Hillsborough Agreement was a cementing of the Molyneaux–Paisley joint leadership of unionism, which had been evident earlier in action against PSF membership of councils. They led the 'Ulster Says No' campaign with considerable vigour, and Molyneaux's majority in Lagan Valley in the 1986 protest by-election rose to nearly 30,000. With his attachment to Westminster, the Unionist ploy of staying away from Parliament cannot have been easy for him, and he had the painful experience of seeing OUP representation reduced in the by-elections with the defeat of Jim Nicholson in Newry and Armagh, and again in the 1987 general election with Enoch Powell unseated in S. Down. The drop in the overall Unionist vote in 1987 was apparently taken by Molyneaux as a signal that a more sophisticated campaign was called for, and one result was the start in 1987 of

'talks about talks' with Secretary of State Tom King. No great optimism surrounded the discussions, however, for while Unionists were prepared to offer a role in Government to the SDLP, it was nothing like full-blooded power-sharing, which, indeed, the OUP leader described as a 'dead duck' in July 1988. And direct talks with Dublin were envisaged by Unionists only after a devolved administration had been established in NI. In the spring of 1988, with Irish Premier Charles Haughey offering talks to Unionist leaders without conditions, Molyneaux made several intriguing comments about the possibility of North–South contacts short of a summit. One upshot was nervousness in the DUP, but by late 1988 the Molyneaux–Paisley axis remained intact. The Molyneaux affability was shown to have concealed some unexpected toughness, for the anti-AIA campaign called for the expulsion of the N. Down association of the party in the run-up to the 1987 election. It also entailed the expulsion of some councillors opposed to the boycott of local government. He made his own personal protest at the AIA by resigning as a JP in 1987.

MONDAY CLUB
The Ulster Monday Club was established in 1975 and is linked to the National Monday Club, which has frequently featured Unionists at its Conservative conference gatherings. National Monday Club chairman David Storey told the local club at its tenth anniversary luncheon in 1985 that if terrorism in NI were to triumph, Ireland could become Britain's Cuba.

MORGAN, WILLIAM JAMES
OUP Assembly, 1973–4, and Convention, 1975–6, member for N. Belfast. b. 1914. MP for Oldpark (Belfast) at Stormont, 1949–58. MP for Clifton (Belfast) at Stormont,

1959–69. Minister of Health and Local Government, 1961–4. Minister of Labour, 1964–5; Minister of Health and Social Services, 1965–9; NI Senate, 1970–2. Took strong line against the Council of Ireland proposal during Assembly debate on Sunningdale proposals, and on this issue transferred support from Brian Faulkner to Harry West in May 1974.

MORRELL, LESLIE JAMES
Head of the Department of Agriculture in NI Executive, 1974. b. Enniskillen, 1931. B.Agr. (QUB). Farms near Coleraine and active in Royal Ulster Agricultural Society. Assembly member for Londonderry, 1973–4, but failed there in Convention election, 1975. Deputy Leader of UPNI, 1974–81. Londonderry County Council, 1969–73. Coleraine District Council, 1973–7.

MORRISON, DANIEL GERARD (DANNY)
PSF Assembly member for Mid-Ulster, 1982–6. b. 1953. A former internee; a charge of PIRA membership was dropped in 1979. Became well known through TV appearances during the 1981 Maze Prison hunger strike, because he was nominated by Bobby Sands MP as external spokesman for the fasting prisoners. PSF director of publicity, 1981–. (Also editor for a time of *An Phoblacht/Republican News*.) His remark at the PSF Ard Fheis in 1981 about Republicans 'with an Armalite in one hand and a ballot paper in the other, we will take power in Ireland', has become a familiar phrase to illustrate the stance of the movement. In January 1982 he was arrested when trying to enter the US from Canada with Owen Carron MP. In December 1982 he was banned from entering GB when invited by GLC leader Ken Livingstone to speak to Labour MPs and councillors in London. In the

1983 general election he was only 78 votes behind the DUP winner in Mid-Ulster, but in the 1986 by-election the DUP margin had increased to nearly 10,000, and he was just a little ahead of SDLP. In 1987 he did not contest the seat. In the 1984 European election he secured 13.3 per cent of the first-preference votes (91,476) to emerge as runner-up. Has had key role in projecting the PSF case, and has acknowledged the problems posed for the political wing by PIRA blunders and bombings involving civilians. He has had much to do with achieving the dominance of the Northern element in PSF.

MORRISON, GEORGE
VUPP (and later UUUM) Convention member for S. Antrim, 1975–6. b. 1924. A founder member of the Vanguard Unionist Party, he is a former chairman of the Lisburn branch. In the row over William Craig's plan in the Convention for a voluntary coalition between Unionists and the SDLP he opposed Craig and became a member of UUUM, later the UUUP, led by Ernest Baird. Lisburn Borough Council, 1973–85. Joined OUP, 1983. Grand master, Co. Antrim, in Orange Order, 1985–.

MORROW, ADAM JAMES (ADDIE)
All. Assembly member for E. Belfast, 1982–6. Served on Agriculture and Education scrutiny committees. All. deputy leader, 1984–7. Castlereagh Council, 1973– (deputy Mayor, 1981). b. 1929. He was a founder member of Alliance Party, and as he had a large dairy farm in Castlereagh, was a natural for party spokesman on agriculture. Unsuccessfully contested Strangford in 1983 and 1987 general elections. Founder member of Corrymeela Community.

MOWLAM, MARJORIE

Labour Party junior front-bench spokeswoman on NI, 1988–. b. 18 September 1949. MA, Ph.D. (University of Iowa). MP for Redcar, 1987–. In 1988 she was critical of new education proposals in NI on the grounds that they did not do enough to encourage integrated education or promote the Irish language, and they did not make religious education a core subject.

MOYLE, ROLAND DUNSTAN

Minister of State, NIO, 1974–6. Labour MP for Lewisham North, 1966–74; Lewisham East, 1974–83. Defeated 1983. b. 12 March 1928. Son of late Baron Moyle, a Labour peer. MA, LLB (Cantab.). Barrister. In the NIO he took charge of the departments of Education and Environment after the collapse of the NI Executive.

MOYNIHAN, DANIEL PATRICK

US Senator (New York State), 1977–. b. 16 March 1927. Associated with Senator Edward Kennedy and other Irish-American Democratic politicians in urging peace in NI and in setting up the Friends of Ireland Group in 1981. In June 1979 he said he hoped to see Ireland united, and that American interest in NI was consistent. 'I hope it will not be supposed that we will be everlastingly patient,' he said. He also attacked the PIRA as a 'band of sadistic murderers'. Strong advocate in Senate of International Fund for Ireland.

MOYOLA, LORD

Formerly Major James Chichester-Clark, PM of NI, May 1969–March 1971. b. 12 February 1923. Returned unopposed as Unionist MP for S. Derry in 1960; again unopposed in 1965, but had to fight off a challenge from Bernadette Devlin (PD) in 1969. Unionist Chief Whip in 1963, leader of the Commons, 1966, and succeeded Harry West as Minister of Agriculture

in 1967. On 23 April 1969 he resigned from the O'Neill Government, following speculation that he might become Premier if Captain O'Neill resigned. He gave as his reason for resignation the timing of the 'one man, one vote' reform, although he said he was not against the principle of the reform. Five days later O'Neill stood down, and on 1 May 1969 Chichester-Clark was elected PM by seventeen votes to sixteen over Brian Faulkner. One of his first acts was to order an amnesty for those convicted of, or charged with, political offences since the previous October. The Rev. Ian Paisley was among those released from prison. But neither this gesture, nor an appeal to opposition MPs to join in a declaration that NI was at peace and would remain so, brought any response. The demands for reform were intensified and the violence grew to a climax in August 1969 when the serious rioting in the Bogside area of Londonderry and in Belfast forced the Chichester-Clark Government to ask for troops to be sent to help maintain order. The situation led to angry exchanges between Chichester-Clark and the Republic's Taoiseach Jack Lynch. Lynch had called for UN intervention, moved army field hospitals to the border, and arranged special camps in the Republic to accommodate people who had fled their homes in NI. Chichester-Clark attacked Lynch for 'inflammatory and ill-considered' comments. The entry of British troops subtly changed the position of Chichester-Clark and his Government. At Downing Street talks with PM Harold Wilson the NI Premier agreed that the army GOC should be director of security operations. At Downing Street, Wilson gave a TV interview in which he indicated that the USC (B Specials) would be phased out. This was denied by Chichester-Clark and his Ministers, but by October the USC was on the way out, the RUC was being disarmed, and the Inspector-General of the RUC, Anthony Peacocke, had been succeeded by Sir Arthur Young. It was all extremely embarrassing for Chichester-Clark, who argued, however, that the new UDR would essentially fill the role of the USC. The Home Secretary James Callaghan, who had ministerial responsibility for NI, had, in the meantime, twice visited the region to encourage reforms such as anti-discrimination measures, action to ensure fair housing allocations, and to improve community relations. The NI Premier now had to face a double threat – a loyalist backlash, reflected in widespread violence, including shooting and the erection of barricades in loyalist areas, and on the other side, the obvious growth of the IRA, with rioting in Republican areas, which produced a threat from the GOC, General Freeland, that troops might shoot to kill. Besides, he had to face the loss of two Stormont seats to the Rev. Ian Paisley and his deputy, the Rev. William Beattie, and in June 1970 the election which brought the Conservatives back to power also returned Paisley to Westminster. Early July brought a fierce gun battle in the Falls Road area between the army and IRA snipers after soldiers had begun to search houses in the area. A three-day curfew was clamped on the Falls area, and more than 100 firearms and some 20,000 rounds of ammunition were found by soldiers. But the continued existence of Republican no-go areas made many Unionists furious with Chichester-Clark. Groups of para-militaries mushroomed in loyalist areas of Belfast. At the same time the PIRA emerged, and the murder of three young Scottish soldiers in Belfast in March 1971 was the signal for a new loyalist campaign demanding Chichester-Clark's resignation. On 18 March the Premier flew to London for

talks with Heath and other Ministers. He pressed for some dramatic security initiative, but Heath would only authorise an extra 1,300 troops, and many Unionists regarded this as derisory. Chichester-Clark was believed to have pressed for, among other things, saturation by the security forces of areas which he considered were dominated by the PIRA. Some of his colleagues wanted internment without trial. Two days later he resigned from the Premiership, after the Defence Secretary, Lord Carrington, had flown to Belfast for special talks with the NI Cabinet. In a statement he repeated his view that some further security initiative was needed. He also said: 'I have decided to resign because I see no other way of bringing home to all concerned the realities of the present constitutional, political and security situation.' In 1985 he was critical of lack of consultation with Unionists over AIA. Trustee, Friends of the Union Group, 1986–.

MURNAGHAN, SHEELAGH MARY
Only Liberal MP to sit in NI Parliament. b. Dublin, 26 May 1924. LLB (QUB). Irish hockey international. A barrister, she was MP for QUB, 1961–9, and prominent in pressing for reforms, notably the introduction of PR voting in NI. Member of NI Advisory Commission and Community Relations Commission, 1972–3. Served as chairwoman of Industrial and National Insurance Tribunals. Associated with a great variety of bodies, including United Nations Association, Protestant and Catholic Encounter, and a committee devoted to finding sites for the settlement of itinerants.

MURRAY, HAROLD (HARRY)
Chairman of the Ulster Workers' Council during the loyalist strike in

May 1974. b. 1921. A Belfast shipyard shop steward, he announced the decision of the UWC to mount the stoppage which brought about the collapse of the power-sharing Executive. He was a leading spokesman of the strikers throughout the stoppage. But after the fall of the Executive, he split with the loyalist paramilitaries. At an Oxford conference on NI in July 1974 he ran into criticism from loyalists when he said that he would talk to the PIRA on condition that they put down their guns and bombs. He said his own methods had proved the best in the end since he had brought a country to a standstill in five days while PIRA had not been able to do it in five years. In July 1974 he resigned from the UWC and said that both communities would have to be brought together, and he proposed to devote himself to promoting peace. In 1975 he stood unsuccessfully as an Alliance candidate in a N. Down Borough Council by-election in Bangor, but he said later that he had not actually joined the Alliance Party. In 1982 he was involved in an effort to re-form the UWC as an organisation campaigning for jobs and worker unity, and free of paramilitary links.

N

NAPIER, SIR OLIVER

All. Assembly member for E. Belfast, 1982–6. Served on committees on Economic Development, and Finance and Personnel. Leader of Alliance, 1972–84, of which he was one of the founders, and earlier prominent in the NUM. b. 11 July 1935. LLB (QUB). Belfast solicitor. Elected in E. Belfast to both the Assembly, 1973–4, and Convention, 1975–6. Took a prominent role in the Sunningdale

Conference in 1973, and became Head of the Office of Law Reform in the power-sharing Executive. Belfast City Council, 1977–. In the 1979 Westminster election, he stood unsuccessfully in E. Belfast, where the Alliance Party had high hopes of gaining the seat. But although he polled strongly, the seat went to DUP and he was in third place. He had another disappointment in the 1979 European election, in which he secured 39,026 (6.8 per cent) first-preference votes. He headed his party delegation in the Atkins conference at Stormont in 1980, pressing the case for partnership government, and gave strong support to the 1982 Assembly. In the 1983 Westminster election in E. Belfast he again ran third despite party hopes that he might capture the seat and his vote further declined in the 1986 by-election. When he stepped down from the party leadership in 1984, Secretary of State Douglas Hurd said that all who had sought a political solution in NI owed him a deep debt of gratitude. Knighted in 1985. In 1988 became chairman of the Standing Advisory Commission on Human Rights.

NATIONAL COUNCIL FOR CIVIL LIBERTIES

The London-based civil rights body which has targeted many NI issues over the years. In 1967 it was represented at the launching of NICRA, which was modelled on the London organisation. It has frequently argued that many NI emergency powers have been counter-productive in tackling violence. In particular, it has opposed the seven-day detention power and exclusion orders, introduced under the PTA. It was critical of the supergrass system, and in 1988 was opposed to the ending of the 'right to silence' and the restrictions imposed on broadcasting. In January 1989 it adopted 'Liberty' as its short title.

NATIONAL DEMOCRATIC PARTY

A political party formed in 1965 which operated mainly in the Greater Belfast area until 1970. It developed from the National Unity movement established in 1959 to press for reform of the Nationalist Party. National Unity organised a conference in April 1964, which gave rise to a 'National Political Front'. This included Nationalist MPs and 'new frontier Nationalists' who sought a more democratically organised party. But the NPF collapsed after only five months, since there was disagreement about party organisation, and the provisional council of the NDP complained that the Nationalist MPs had not consulted them before deciding not to contest the Fermanagh–S. Tyrone seat. The 'new frontier' Nationalists then set up the NDP which had a high proportion of teachers in its ranks. It produced a variety of discussion papers but had little electoral success. When it was wound up, its members had a strong influence within the newly established SDLP.

NATIONAL H-BLOCK/ARMAGH COMMITTEE

The committee which publicised throughout the world the case for political status for Republican prisoners in the Maze and Armagh prisons during the 1980–1 hunger strikes. The committee, which covered a wide spectrum of nationalism, operated with such skill that it created serious problems for the British information services in the US, Canada, Europe, and many other areas. Its chairman was Father Piaras Ó Duill, and its main spokeswoman, Bernadette McAliskey. The committee supplanted the Relatives Action Committee which operated in the initial phase of the campaign. (*See also* H-Blocks.)

NATIONALIST PARTY

Deriving from the old Irish Parliamentary Party, it was the main vehicle of anti-partition politics until the civil rights campaign developed in 1968–9. For much of its existence it was very locally based, and there was a good deal of clerical influence within it. In the 1960s, under the leadership of Eddie McAteer, there was an attempt to give it a more radical image and a constituency-based organisation, but the more dynamic approach of the civil rights movement proved to have greater popular appeal. Much of its support went over to the SDLP, and one of its MPs, Austin Currie, was a founder of the SDLP.

NEAVE, AIREY MIDDLETON SHEFFIELD

Conservative MP for Abingdon, 1953–79; spokesman on NI, 1975–9. b. 23 January 1916; killed by car bomb as he drove out of House of Commons car park, 30 March 1979, an event which cast a shadow over the start of general election campaign. BA Hons (Oxon.). Barrister. Notable army record in World War II. Wounded and taken prisoner by Germans in France, 1940, and first British officer to escape from Colditz POW camp, 1942. Attached after the war to British War Crimes Executive and served indictments on Göring and other leading war criminals tried at Nuremberg. Masterminded campaign for election of Margaret Thatcher as Conservative leader, and headed her private office from 1975 until his death. Between 1975 and September 1976 he was extremely critical of Government security policy in NI and also critical of RUC interrogation techniques, but took a more friendly attitude when Roy Mason succeeded Merlyn Rees as Secretary of State in 1976. He claimed that increased army covert operations and other measures to tighten security were due to Conservative prompting. Often critical of British media which, he argued, over-publicised the PIRA and magnified faults of security forces. In early 1978 his speeches and notably his reference to power-sharing as being 'no longer practical politics' caused Unionists to look on him with a more friendly eye, and the SDLP to see his policy as a retreat from that of Edward Heath and William Whitelaw. In particular, he urged the setting up of regional councils in NI. Responsibility for his murder was claimed by the INLA, and it led to strict new rules restricting the movements of visitors to Westminster. In 1986 Enoch Powell claimed he had been killed not by the INLA but by 'high contracting parties' for political purposes.

NEEDHAM, RICHARD FRANCIS

Under-Secretary, NIO, September 1985–. b. 29 January 1942. Conservative MP for Chippenham, 1979–83; Wiltshire N., 1983–. Since he is 6th Earl of Kilmorey – an Irish title which he does not use – he has close family associations with S. Down, and as Parliamentary Private Secretary to James Prior when he was NI Secretary of State, he had the advantage of considerable familiarity with local problems when he took over responsibility for the departments of Environment and Health and Social Services. In several areas he had to take emergency action to overcome the difficulties posed by the disruptive tactics employed by DUP and OUP councillors in protest at the AIA. In 1986 he encountered controversy over his plans for Sunday opening of pubs and on economy measures in the health services. In 1987 he launched the Lagan Bank and Castle Court schemes for Belfast. In 1988 he was active in pushing plans to deal with deprivation in W. and N. Belfast, and also for improving Derry city's environment.

Has written a book, *Honourable Member*, on the work of an MP.

NEESON, SEAN

All. Assembly member for N. Antrim, 1982–6; served on Economic Development and Education committees. b. 1946. Chairman, Alliance Party, 1982–3. Carrickfergus Council, 1977–88. Neeson, who was deputy Speaker in the Assembly and economic spokesman of his party, stood down from active politics in 1988 because, he said, of the need to find a job to support his family.

NEILL, MAJOR SIR IVAN

Last Speaker of NI House of Commons, 1969–72. b. Belfast, 1 July 1906. B.Sc. (Econ.) (QUB). MP for Ballynafeigh (Belfast), 1949–72. Minister of Labour and National Insurance, 1950–61; additionally, Minister of Home Affairs, August–October 1952. Minister of Education, 1962. Minister of Finance and leader of Commons, 1964–5. (Resigned from Government, 1965.) Minister of Development, 1968. Alderman and councillor, Belfast City Council, 1964–70.

NEWE, GERARD BENEDICT

Minister of State in PM's office, NI Government, 1971–2. b. Cushendall, Co. Antrim, 5 February 1907; d. November 1982. MA (QUB), D.Litt. (NUU). Newe was the only Catholic to serve in a NI Government during the fifty-one years' operation of the Government of Ireland Act, 1920. He was invited by PM Brian Faulkner to join the Government to help promote better community relations, and his acceptance of the appointment caused misgivings among some of his co-religionists. He made it clear that he was not, and never had been, a member of the Unionist Party. He believed that people must have the right to work peacefully for a united Ireland, if they wished, but he recognised the social and economic benefits for NI of the link with Britain. He was regional organiser and secretary to the NI Council of Social Service, 1948–72. Founder member of Protestant and Catholic Encounter.

NEW IRELAND FORUM

The conference of the four main Nationalist parties – Fianna Fáil, Fine Gael, Irish Labour Party and SDLP – which had its initial meeting in Dublin in May 1983, with the aim of working out an agreed approach to a NI settlement. The body owed its existence primarily to SDLP leader John Hume, who had pressed strongly for an agreed Nationalist strategy. The NIF produced its report on 3 May 1984, which comprised a detailed historical analysis from the Nationalist standpoint, together with options for a new all-Ireland constitution. The parties made it clear that their first preference was for a unitary thirty-two-county state, but they also put forward the options of a federal arrangement and joint authority in NI exercised by the London and Dublin Governments equally. The report also stated: 'The parties in the Forum also remain open to discuss other views which may contribute to political development.' It was clear, however, that Fianna Fáil was laying much greater stress on the unitary-state idea than Fine Gael or Labour, and the Coalition Government led by Garret FitzGerald put strong emphasis on the offer to discuss other views 'with all others involved in the problem of NI who oppose the use of violence'. Secretary of State James Prior said the British Government could not accept the 'Nationalist interpretation' of past events or the dismissal of the strenuous efforts of successive UK Governments to deal with 'the intractable problems of NI'. Although the Government welcomed 'positive elements' in the report, it found the Forum's account of the British position to be 'one-sided and unacceptable'. The UK Government, said Prior, stood by its undertaking that NI should not cease to be part of the UK without the consent of a majority of its people 'and remains willing to give effect to any majority wish which might be expressed in favour of unity' – a clear pointer to the constitutional formula of the AIA. The Secretary of State said Unionist opposition to Irish unity was to the principle rather than the form, and there was no reason to expect consent to change in sovereignty in NI in any of the three forms suggested. But he said it remained necessary to face the problems of division and violence in NI 'including the feelings of alienation among the Nationalist community'. In NI only the SDLP wholeheartedly backed the report. To Unionists it was another example of outside interference. To PSF it was 'a major dilution of national aspirations'. But British Labour spokesman Peter Archer described it as 'a unique initiative in recent Irish history'. The report attracted considerable international interest and support and although Thatcher dismayed the Irish Government with a comment in November 1984 that it was 'out, out, out' to the three options of the NIF report, diplomatic pressure, notably from the US and Europe, was seen as a key element in the British-Irish negotiating process which led eventually to the AIA in November 1985.

NEW IRELAND GROUP/
MOVEMENT see Robb, John

NEW LODGE ROAD

District adjoining Antrim Road in N. Belfast, which has been regarded as a stronghold of PIRA. Centre of demonstrations and hi-jacking when PIRA is active.

NEWMAN, SIR KENNETH LESLIE
Chief Constable of the RUC, 1976–9.
b. 1926. Served with Palestine Police,
1946–8, and with London Metropolitan Police, 1948–73. Became
Commander at New Scotland Yard,
1972, in charge of the community
relations branch. Senior deputy Chief
Constable, RUC, 1973–6. As Chief
Constable of the RUC, he was
responsible for setting up regional
crime squads to deal with terrorism
and for closer intelligence liaison with
the army. His period as Chief
Constable was also marked by the
introduction of the policy known as
'primacy of the police' which gave the
RUC a more dominant role in security
relative to the army. But there was also
continuing criticism of RUC interrogation practices, criticism which Sir
Kenneth attacked as 'less than fair'. But
a number of reforms were made in
interrogation procedures (*see* Bennett
Report). On leaving the RUC, he
became Commandant of the Police
Staff College at Bramshill and was
Metropolitan Police Commissioner,
1982–7. Professor of law at Bristol
University, 1987.

NEWRY
The border town in S. Down with a
mainly Catholic population, which
demonstrated strong support for the
civil rights movement in 1968 and
1969. There was a riot in the town on
11 January 1969 when some police
vehicles were set on fire and others
pushed into the canal. Ten members of
the RUC and twenty-eight civilians were
injured and there was much damage to
shops. Spokesmen for NICRA and PD
deplored the violence and said it would
not help the civil rights movement. In
August 1969 there was prolonged
rioting and severe damage to public

buildings and private property. The
Scarman tribunal found that an action
committee had planned the takeover of
the town, but that it had been foiled by
skilled police work and lack of public
support. The introduction of internment in 1971 brought further violent
scenes. In October 1971 the shooting
dead by the army of three youths who
had failed to halt was followed by
burning and looting on a large scale.
The town suffered several bomb
attacks, notably during 1971. The
biggest protest march was held on 6
February 1972, after 'Bloody Sunday'.
In August 1972 the Newry branch of
NICRA made a strong appeal to PIRA to
call off its bombing campaign. But PIRA
remained active in the area, and there
was some evidence that local units of
OIRA were slow to observe the ceasefire
called by their leaders in 1972. There
have been considerable efforts in the
1980s to counter the heavy local
unemployment and to encourage
tourism, but PIRA has been active in the
town and adjoining border areas. In the
autumn of 1984 there were ten bomb
attacks in eight weeks in the town
centre, and on 28 February 1985 nine
RUC officers, including two women
constables, died in a mortar attack on
the RUC station. It was the highest RUC
death toll in a single incident since the
force was formed. Three RUC men also
died in a PIRA attack in the summer of
1986. But violent incidents failed to
deter shoppers from the South crossing
in large numbers to take advantage of
lower prices – a traffic only damped
down by new border rules introduced
by the Haughey Government in 1987
and at variance with EC law. Some
intriguing situations have developed in
local council politics. In 1981 the SDLP-
controlled council appointed a DUP
chairman, but in the wake of the AIA,
Unionists voted with PSF to keep SDLP
out of the chair and to sustain an IIP
chairman.

NEWS, HUGH
SDLP Assembly member for Armagh, 1982–6. Also represented the constituency in the 1973–4 Assembly and the 1975–6 Convention. b. Lurgan, 1931. Publican and pharmaceutical chemist. Lurgan Borough Council (Independent Citizens' Association member), 1964–7. Craigavon District Council, 1973–. National vice-president, AOH, 1974.

NEW ULSTER MOVEMENT
A movement which developed in early 1969 to urge moderation and non-sectarianism in politics and to press for reforms. It was among the first groups to call for a Community Relations Commission, a Central Housing Executive and the abolition of the USC. In a pamphlet in 1971, *The Reform of Stormont*, it put forward proposals for power-sharing in government and later that year urged the suspension of the Stormont Parliament. Many of its early members (it claimed a membership of 7,000 in 1969) became active in the Alliance Party. Its first chairman, Brian W. Walker, became director of Oxfam in 1974, and he was succeeded by Dr Stanley Worrall, former headmaster of Methodist College Belfast.

NEW ULSTER POLITICAL RESEARCH GROUP *see* Ulster Defence Association

NICHOLSON, JAMES (JIM)
OUP MP for Newry and Armagh, 1983–6. Assembly member for Armagh, 1982–6; served on Agriculture Committee. b. 1945. Armagh Council, 1975–. Secretary–organiser, Mid/S. Armagh Unionist Association, 1973–83. He took the new seat of Newry and Armagh in 1983 against the odds, when the overall Nationalist majority was split between SDLP and PSF, and the DUP backed him. But he lost to SDLP deputy leader Seamus

Mallon in the 1986 by-election, called in protest at the AIA, and so could be said to be the main casualty from the Unionist tactic. He made an unsuccessful bid to regain the seat in 1987, and was adopted as prospective OUP candidate for the 1989 European election.

NO-GO AREAS
The term coined for the districts behind the barricades between the summer of 1969 and July 1972, where paramilitary groups, rather than the forces of law and order, tended to hold sway. The most notable were the Bogside in Londonderry – Free Derry – and parts of W. Belfast, although similar enclaves existed in other places. The term persisted for some time after the barriers had come down, and even after 'Operation Motorman', undertaken by the security forces on 31 July 1972, which sought to re-establish official control in such areas. Although most of the no-go areas were PIRA dominated, loyalists on occasions set up their own no-go areas, particularly in the Shankill–Woodvale district of Belfast, through the agency of the UDA. Some of these moves were designed to pressurise the Government to act against the Republican no-go areas. Some loyalists continued to see a no-go element in the refusal of the Government to allow the deployment of the UDR in some Republican districts.

NORAID *see* Irish Northern Aid Committee

NORTHERN CONSENSUS GROUP
A group of professional people, Protestant and Catholic, who have been calling since 1982 for a political solution within NI, involving both traditions in government. It gave evidence to NIF and to the Assembly committee on the AIA, and has had talks with British and Irish Ministers. Leading members include Professor

Desmond Rea, Professor Robert W. Stout, John G. Neill, and Terence Donaghy, a Belfast solicitor.

NORTHERN IRELAND CIVIL RIGHTS ASSOCIATION

The body established in January 1967, which spearheaded the civil rights campaign. Its constitution was similar to that of the London-based National Council for Civil Liberties, whose secretary, Tony Smythe, attended the inaugural meeting in Belfast. Its initial committee comprised Noel Harris (chairman), of the Draughtsmen and Allied Trades' Association; Dr Con McCluskey (vice-chairman), of the Campaign for Social Justice; Fred Heatley (treasurer), of the Wolfe Tone Society; Jack Bennett (information officer), of the Wolfe Tone Society; Michael Dolley (QUB); Ken Banks (trade union); Kevin Agnew (Republican); Betty Sinclair (Belfast Trades' Council); Joe Sherry (Republican Labour Party); John Quinn (Ulster Liberal Party); Paddy Devlin (NILP); Terence O'Brien (unattached); and Robin Cole (chairman of Young Unionist Group at QUB), co-opted. The basic aims of NICRA were: one man, one vote in council elections; ending of 'gerrymandered' electoral boundaries; machinery to prevent discrimination by public authorities and to deal with complaints; fair allocation of public housing; repeal of Special Powers Act; and disbanding of B Specials. NICRA's initial impact was in organising protest marches. The first was held at Dungannon, Co. Tyrone, on 24 August 1968, on the suggestion of Nationalist MP Austin Currie, who had already staged a sit-in at a house in nearby Caledon over a housing allocation. Some 4,000 people singing 'We shall overcome' marked this first NICRA event, but it was the next march in Londonderry, on 5 October 1968,

which put the civil rights campaign in the world headlines and on TV. Several leading opposition figures, including Gerry Fitt MP and Nationalist leader Eddie McAteer MP, were injured in a clash with the RUC. Lord Cameron, in his report, found that they had been batoned without justification or excuse, although Fitt's conduct was described as 'reckless and wholly irresponsible'. The Duke Street affair, in which eleven policemen and seventy-seven civilians were hurt, made a big impression internationally and par-ticularly on Labour opinion in Britain. It brought strong pressure from the Wilson Government on Stormont to introduce reforms. The NICRA campaign was attacked by Unionists as a front for the IRA. The Cameron Commission held that while there had been evidence that IRA members were active in the association, there was no sign that they were dominant or in a position to control or direct the policy of NICRA. With the arrival of intern-ment, it was engaged in promoting a civil disobedience campaign, which led to widespread withholding of rent and rates. The setting up of the power-sharing Executive led to some alien-ation from the SDLP. During the Convention, it was active in pressing for a Bill of Rights. It also became a point of contact for outside bodies interested in civil rights. Old con-troversies within the movement were revived in 1988, when events were organised to mark the twentieth anniversary of the initial demonstration.

NORTHERN IRELAND LABOUR PARTY

A socialist party drawing its support mainly from Greater Belfast, founded in 1924. The party, which had only limited electoral success, was essentially neutral on the border issue until 1949. In that year its annual conference supported the link with Britain, and this gained it more Protestant support but added to its difficulties in attracting Catholic votes. The peak of its success was from 1958 to 1965, when it had four MPs at Stormont, all from Belfast constituencies. Indeed, in 1962 it was only 8,000 votes short of the Unionist total in the city. One of its weaknesses was its failure to secure full trade-union backing, and the British Labour Party was only fitfully interested in its fate, occasionally providing money for Westminster elections and the endorsement of candidates by the national leader. It never won a Westminster seat, despite amassing nearly 100,000 votes in the 1970 election but it often polled strongly in E. Belfast. Its main personalities in its heyday were secretary Sam Napier, Billy (now Lord) Blease, Charles Brett (chairman for a time), and Stormont MPs Tom Boyd, Billy Boyd, Vivian Simpson, David Bleakley and Paddy Devlin. Devlin, MP for Falls, was one of the founders of the SDLP, and the creation of that party made the task of the NILP even more uphill. In the 1973-4 Assembly and 1975-6 Convention it held only one seat (David Bleakley), and in the 1977 and 1981 council elections took only one seat (in Ards). In the 1973 Assembly election it supported power-sharing, but when the Executive collapsed it came out against both a Council of Ireland and formal power-sharing. When all three Belfast candidates lost their deposits in the 1979 Westminster election, and the party opted out of the 1982 Assembly contest, few people saw any future for it, and it was absorbed in Labour '87, set up in 1987.

Ó BRÁDAIGH, RUAIRÍ

President of PSF, 1970–83. b. 1932. An ex-technical school teacher, he was a TD for a period in the 1950s, being elected for Sinn Féin on an abstentionist ticket in Longford–Westmeath. He is also believed to have been chief of staff of the IRA for two periods before the organisation split at the end of 1969. In 1973 he was sentenced in Dublin to six months' imprisonment for PIRA membership. He was the first person to be prosecuted under the provision of the Republic's Offences Against the State Act, which allows a court to convict on the evidence of a senior Garda officer that a person is a member of a proscribed organisation. He took part in the Feakle talks with Protestant Churchmen in 1974. He brought a certain organisational flair to the central direction of PSF, and energetically promoted the federal 'Éire Nua' policy. He opposed the dropping of this policy in 1981, telling the Ard Fheis: 'Don't swop a policy for a slogan.' He was active in building up contacts with revolutionary groups abroad, and in opposing the EC. In 1983 he was succeeded as president of PSF by Gerry Adams, and at the 1986 Ard Fheis also lost out to Adams on the issue of the ending of the traditional policy of abstention from the Dáil. Ó Brádaigh led the resistance to change, but Adams and his supporters won the day easily. Ó Brádaigh was among a group which then set up Republican Sinn Féin.

O'BRIEN, CONOR CRUISE

Irish politician and journalist. b. 3 November 1917. BA, Ph.D. (TCD). In his many-sided career, he has often spoken out on NI, and took a strongly individualist viewpoint as Irish Labour Party spokesman when he was elected to the Dáil in 1969, and later as Minister for Posts and Telegraphs in the Coalition Government of 1973–7. He was defeated in the Dáil general election in 1977, but was then elected to the Senate from TCD. He resigned from the Senate in 1979. In his earlier career he had been in the Irish diplomatic service and in 1961 represented the UN Secretary-General in Katanga. He was vice-chancellor of the University of Ghana, 1962–5, and Professor of Humanities at New York University, 1965–9. His general theme on NI has been that repeated calls from the Republic for a united Ireland are counter-productive, and may even encourage violence. In opposition after the defeat of the Coalition Government in 1977, he resigned from the Irish Labour Parliamentary Party so that he could be free to speak on NI. At a conference on NI at Oxford University in September 1977 he argued forcibly that opinion surveys showed that there was not a majority in the whole of Ireland in favour of Irish unity – a claim which was hotly contested inside the Republic. As Minister for Posts and Telegraphs, he banned broadcasts by illegal paramilitary organisations and PSF. In his book, *States of Ireland* (1972), he suggested that the NI civil rights campaign had failed to make use of its victories and allowed itself to be used as a spring-board for the re-emergence of the IRA. From 1978 to 1980 he was editor-in-chief, the *Observer*, London. He was critical of the AIA and in 1988 he suggested that the AIA would fade away gradually; he hoped it would be followed by talks, not about moving towards a united Ireland, but about how to live and work together, while agreeing to differ on political allegiance.

Ó CONAILL, DÁITHÍ
A leading strategist of the Provisional Republican movement, 1972–86.

b. Cork, 1937. He is believed to have joined the IRA at the age of eighteen, and he was wounded in the 1956 IRA campaign. In 1958 he escaped from the Curragh camp in the Republic, where he had been interned. He worked for a time as a teacher of building and woodwork at Ballyshannon, Co. Donegal, vocational school. In 1960 he was sentenced to eight years' imprisonment for carrying a gun and ammunition with intent to endanger life, but he served only three years. In 1971 he narrowly avoided capture when Interpol set up a big search operation after a consignment of Czechoslovakian arms had been found at Amsterdam airport. He had been travelling with a companion, Maria McGuire, who later fled to England and described her IRA experiences in a book: *To Take Arms*. He was said to have invented the car bomb, and by April 1973, when he slipped through a police-and-army security net to give an oration in Milltown cemetery, Belfast, he was believed to have become chief of staff of the PIRA. In a TV interview in 1974 he stated – as he did on many other occasions – that there would be no end to the PIRA campaign until the British made a declaration of intent to withdraw from NI. By 1974 he was a vice-president of PSF, and he was among the PIRA leaders who talked to Protestant Churchmen at the secret meeting in Feakle, Co. Clare – the meeting which led to the 1975 PIRA ceasefire. His arrest in Dublin during the ceasefire was presented by the PIRA as a bid by Dublin to end what the PIRA called a 'truce'. He was sentenced to twelve months' imprisonment for PIRA membership, and was again arrested in July 1976, coincidentally on the same day as the British ambassador in Dublin, Christopher Ewart-Biggs, was killed in a landmine explosion. After his release in 1977, he appeared to be absorbed by political work, but there were strong Unionist protests when he slipped into Derry at Easter 1978 to address a Republican ceremony, just as he had done four years earlier. In the 1981 general election in the Republic he was active in supporting the H-Block candidates, and in the February 1982 election he was PSF's director of elections. In one respect, though, his influence waned in the 1980s. He had encouraged some contacts with Protestant paramilitaries, and had seen the 'Éire Nua' federal policy as a concession of sorts to loyalists. But his arguments were swept aside by NI delegates at the 1981 Ard Fheis who brought about the defeat of the federal idea. Soon after the PIRA bombings in London in July 1982, he threatened more bombs in Britain when he spoke at a rally in Monaghan. But in 1986 he walked out of the PSF Ard Fheis, when it voted to end abstention from the Dáil, and became one of the founders of Republican Sinn Féin.

O'DONOGHUE, PATRICK

SDLP Assembly member for S. Down, 1982–6. Also represented S. Down in the 1973–4 Assembly and the 1975–6 Convention. b. Castlewellan, Co. Down, 1930. Deputy Speaker in the 1973 Assembly. SDLP spokesman on Education. Down District Council, 1973–85. Active in ALJ and GAA. In a speech in Galway in 1974 he suggested that the British had recognised that they could not solve the Irish problem and that 'the long, complex and dangerous business' of British disengagement had already begun.

OFFICIAL IRISH REPUBLICAN ARMY

The term 'Official IRA' dates from the beginning of 1970, when the split in the Republican movement meant that there were now two branches, the Officials and the Provisionals, each comprising an IRA, or military, wing, and a political counterpart, Sinn Féin.

In NI the 'Officials' are often dubbed the 'Stickies', because of their practice of sticking on coat lapels their Easter lilies during the annual commemorations of the 1916 Easter Rising in Dublin. OIRA appears to have been largely inactive since the summer of 1972 when it declared a ceasefire. It represented those militant Republicans who remained loyal to Cathal Goulding as chief of staff, when the movement divided on the issue of parliamentary action during the December 1969–January 1970 period. There was majority support in the IRA at the end of 1969 for switching to political action – that is, seeking to have candidates elected to the Parliaments in Dublin, Belfast and London on a leftist, broadly Marxist policy. Clearly, Goulding and many of his associates felt that the lack of public support for the IRA border campaign in 1956–62 suggested that Republicans generally wanted more emphasis on strictly political action. But those who sought this new approach failed to secure a two-thirds majority at the Dublin Ard Fheis of Sinn Féin in January 1970. At that point the Provisionals walked out of the meeting and because they went off to hold a meeting in Kevin Street, Dublin, and established their HQ there, they were initially known as Kevin Street Sinn Féin to distinguish them from the Officials, who for similar reasons were frequently described as Gardiner Place Sinn Féin. Each side claimed to be the true inheritor of 1916, and the OIRA said later that it had been able to hold 70 per cent of the total of IRA volunteers when the PIRA broke away. In NI the IRA strength in 1970 was probably about 600, and mainly in Belfast. All the indications, however, were that PIRA rapidly outstripped the Officials in number. Notably in the Belfast Republican areas, the Provisionals built on the strength of local defence committees and were widely accepted as the defenders of the people against loyalist attacks. The OIRA also had to face the taunts of the new 'Provos' that it was totally unprepared in the Belfast violence of 1969. The OIRA insisted that the split in the movement had been engineered by Fianna Fáil agents so that a separate IRA would develop in the North and outside the Republic. Certainly, the tension between Officials and Provisionals was intense in 1970–1, and in March 1971 there was a fierce gun battle between the two groups in the Lower Falls area of Belfast. One man was shot dead and several wounded, with the British army standing carefully aside. A ceasefire was quickly negotiated in this inter-IRA struggle, but there were to be many more clashes between the two groups. In Belfast and many other centres the annual Easter parades to cemeteries where Republicans are buried were split into separate Official and Provisional efforts. The OIRA was still involved in violence in early 1971. It bombed a Shankill Road public house in Belfast in April. But Cathal Goulding's warning that PIRA tactics were likely to bring internment without trial in NI proved to be justified. And although OIRA, like PIRA, had been keeping many of its members away from their usual haunts, a good many key OIRA members were rounded up in the dawn swoop on 9 August 1971. PIRA claimed that only thirty of its members had been arrested, but this was probably a serious under-estimation. OIRA suffered, though, from the handicap that many of its activists were people who had a record in the IRA earlier and thus figured in Special Branch lists. Internment, however, created extra problems for OIRA because it stirred up hostility towards the British authorities and the NI Government on a massive scale. It was an emotion more geared to PIRA strategy than to the politically

oriented approach of Cathal Goulding and his friends. Violence became much more the order of the day for OIRA. In December 1971 it killed Unionist Senator Jack Barnhill in Strabane, and burned the Rostrevor home of the Stormont Speaker, Ivan Neill. In February 1972 – that is, immediately after 'Bloody Sunday' in Londonderry – it claimed responsibility for an explosion at the Aldershot (Hampshire) HQ of the Parachute Regiment. Seven people were killed, including five women canteen workers. Also in February it mounted an assassination attempt on Unionist Government Minister John Taylor in Armagh. He was hit by six bullets and had his jaw shattered. In March 1972 Cathal Goulding and three other men were charged in Dublin with membership of an illegal organisation, but they were freed after the prosecution had applied for the charges to be struck out. When direct rule of NI from Westminster was announced at the end of March, OIRA announced that it would continue the struggle. In April 1972 OIRA was responsible for a spate of violence in Belfast, including many attacks on RUC stations. These were in response to the shooting dead by soldiers of Joe McCann, one of OIRA's most revered leaders. Even members of the Provisionals turned out in a separate parade among the 5,000 people at McCann's funeral. In May 1972 OIRA admitted that it had shot dead Ranger William Best, of the Royal Irish Rangers, home on leave in Derry. They said it was a reprisal for crimes by the British army, but it brought angry protests from many Bogside women and calls for OIRA to leave the Bogside and Creggan areas. On Monday 29 May 1972 OIRA announced a ceasefire. It said it was doing so in accordance with the wishes of the people it represented in NI, although it reserved the right to act in self-defence and to defend areas attacked by British troops or 'sectarian forces'. This ceasefire followed an anxious meeting of the OIRA leadership from all thirty-two counties of Ireland, including some women who were said to be local OIRA commanders. It was stated that the decision had been taken by an overwhelming majority. Goulding seems to have argued that the PIRA bombing campaign could only increase sectarianism. He also claimed the PIRA would soon be forced to call a ceasefire as well, but this prediction was only partially borne out, for the PIRA ceasefire, which came soon afterwards, was short-lived. The Goulding policy was to seek to develop class politics, and to secure more joint action with Protestants on issues such as housing. This concentration by OIRA on community politics meant that it tended to coalesce completely in most areas with the Republican Clubs – that is, the NI equivalent of Sinn Féin (the Workers' Party) in the Republic. In 1973 there was trouble between PIRA and OIRA prisoners in Crumlin Road Prison in Belfast, and in 1974, after clashes at the Maze Prison, twenty-one OIRA men there were moved to Crumlin Road Prison for ten days. But PIRA and OIRA made common cause on occasional anti-internment protests and worked together to some extent in the Catholic areas of Belfast to reduce hardship during the loyalist strike in 1974. OIRA guns were brought out again in the spring of 1975, when it was involved in a bitter struggle with the newly formed IRSP. There were deaths and injuries on both sides in Belfast, and a suspicion among the security forces that the IRSP had drawn some recruits from PIRA members who were doubtful about their ceasefire. In April 1982 the Dublin magazine *Magill* claimed that OIRA was still active, well-armed and engaged in recent years in murders, robberies and intimidation. It

also alleged that Seamus Costello, leader of IRSP, had been killed by a senior member of OIRA in 1977. The magazine added that £2 million had been taken in armed robberies since 1972, and that one major bank robbery had been carried out in NI immediately before the Republic's general election in June 1981. It also asserted that almost all the hundred or so members of OIRA, including several of its leaders, were members of the Workers' Party. A spokesman for the WP dismissed the allegations as 'muck' and the WP president, Tomás Mac Giolla (elected a TD in the November 1982 election), said he had no knowledge of the continued existence of OIRA, and certainly they had no association with any military organisation. In July 1982 INLA claimed that OIRA had provided information for 'loyalist death squads' which had resulted in the deaths of three Republican activists in Belfast – Miriam Daly, Ronnie Bunting and Noel Little. INLA also said it had murdered Jim Flynn in Dublin after they had been informed by former OIRA members that he had murdered Seamus Costello. In May 1983 the Republic's Justice Minister, Michael Noonan, said he could confirm that OIRA was still in existence. Its continued activity in NI was also reported by the RUC at that time. In December 1985 the WP denied allegations by the Republic's Labour Minister, Ruairí Quinn, that OIRA still existed and had links with the WP. The party described it as a 'smear tactic'.

OFFICIAL SINN FÉIN *see* Workers' Party, The

OFFICIAL UNIONIST PARTY *see* Ulster Unionist Party

O'HANLON, PATRICK MICHAEL SDLP Assembly member for Armagh, 1973–4. b. Drogheda, 8 May 1944. B. Comm. (UCD). Independent MP for S.

Armagh, 1969–72. Active in civil rights campaign. Founder member of SDLP. Party Chief Whip in the Assembly, 1974. Member of several party delegations in talks with Republic's Government, 1973–4. Unsuccessful candidate in Convention election, 1975, and Assembly election, 1982. Called to the NI Bar in 1986.

O'HARE, PASCHAL JOSEPH
SDLP Assembly member for N. Belfast, 1982–6. b. 1932. Belfast City Council, 1973–85. Solicitor. A founder member and former executive member of the SDLP, he stood unsuccessfully in the 1975 Convention election for W. Belfast and the 1979 Westminster election in N. Belfast. Resigned from SDLP in 1985 because of the party's involvement in the AIA, which he regarded as an acceptance by the Republic's Government of 'a settlement in a six-county context'. In 1986 he called for talks with men of violence, both Republican and loyalist.

O'KENNEDY, MICHAEL
Minister of Agriculture in Republic, 1987–. Foreign Minister, 1977–9. EC Commissioner, 1981–2. b. 21 February 1936. MA (NUI). Barrister and classical scholar. Fianna Fáil Senator, 1965–9; TD, 1969–81. Minister of Transport and Power, 1973; Minister of Finance, 1979–81. As Foreign Minister, he was the member of Lynch's Government most closely involved with NI affairs, and he was an early advocate of the idea of an all-Ireland court to deal with terrorism. As Foreign Minister, he was closely involved with the EC-backed Derry–Donegal schemes. In August 1979, while president of the EC Council of Ministers, he urged early efforts to break the NI 'political log-jam' through informal talks between the British and Irish Governments and the NI parties. In October 1979 he reached agreement in London with NI Secretary of State Humphrey Atkins on secret anti-terrorist measures. In 1985 he came out strongly against any internal settlement in NI.

OLDFIELD, SIR MAURICE
Chief Security Co-ordinator, NI, from 1979 until his death in 1980. b. 16 November 1915. Sir Maurice, who retired from the Foreign Office in 1977, held a great variety of diplomatic posts, including counsellor in Washington, but his real fame rested on his post as head of the Secret Intelligence Service (MI6) between 1965 and 1977. The NI appointment was said to be aimed at increasing pressure on terrorists and bringing them to justice. It followed reports that the army was anxious to see more co-ordination of the security effort and that there were differences between the intelligence services, army and RUC. Sir Maurice (dubbed 'Maurice the Mole' by PIRA) kept a very low profile in NI, and in 1986 Thatcher told the Commons that he had been a homosexual and had admitted such activities although there was no reason to suggest that security had ever been compromised. But several of his former associates in MI6 rejected this suggestion of homosexuality. In 1975 PIRA planted a bomb outside his London flat.

OLIVER, JOHN ANDREW
Chief adviser to chairman of Constitutional Convention, 1975–6. b. Belfast, 1913. BA, Ph.D. (QUB). Entered NI civil service in 1936 and rose to be Permanent Secretary in Development Ministry in 1970, and Housing Department, 1974. Retired from civil service in 1976, and books include an analysis of NI's constitutional options, *Ulster Today and Tomorrow* (1978).

O'MALLEY, DESMOND

Leader (and founder) of the Republic's Progressive Democrats, 1985–. He was Parliamentary Secretary to Taoiseach Jack Lynch, Minister for Defence, and Government Chief Whip at the start of the NI Troubles in 1969, and held various Cabinet posts in Fianna Fáil Governments until 1982. In 1984 he was expelled from Fianna Fáil for challenging the line of the then Taoiseach, Charles Haughey, that the unitary state was the only acceptable form of Irish unity. The following year he launched Prog. D. with the object of 'breaking the mould of Irish politics'. In the 1987 election he emerged at the head of a fourteen-strong Dáil party and has been a strong advocate of devolution in NI and of co-operation with the Alliance Party.

OMBUDSMAN

Popular title for Parliamentary Commissioner for Administration, who deals with complaints of maladministration against Stormont departments. The office was established in 1969, and later linked with that of Commissioner of Complaints.

O'NEILL, LORD (OF THE MAINE)

PM of NI, 1963–9. b. 10 September 1914. Captain Terence O'Neill has an Anglo-Irish background – among his ancestors were the ancient Ulster O'Neill family, and the English Chichesters. When, in 1963, Lord Brookeborough resigned after twenty years as PM, O'Neill had been Finance Minister for seven years and seemed the natural successor. He quickly made it clear that he was set on a reformist course: firstly, in terms of stronger cross-border economic links; and secondly, in trying to accommodate the political ambitions of an increasingly educated Catholic community. In January 1965 he sprang a surprise with

an unannounced visit to Stormont of the Republic's Taoiseach Sean Lemass. Even the majority of his Cabinet colleagues were not told of the meeting in advance, and the trip angered right-wing Unionists, always suspicious of Southern motives. The Rev. Ian Paisley attacked the visit in what can be seen as the start of his 'O'Neill must go' campaign. The extremist UVF emerged on the loyalist side, and the civil rights campaign built up to the torrent of protest reached in 1968. The violent scenes at the civil rights march on 5 October 1968 went round the world on TV and made a tremendous impression on the PM. He saw that reforms must be pressed forward, and in this he clashed with those who shared the view of Home Affairs Minister William Craig that the civil rights agitation was an expression of republicanism, encour-aged by the IRA. In December 1968 O'Neill sacked Craig, and made it evident that he regarded him as an advocate of UDI. He warned against the growth of a 'Protestant Sinn Féin' and appealed to the protest marchers to get off the streets. At the end of 1968 he announced a five-point programme of reforms – a points system for housing allocations, an Ombudsman, the ending of the company vote in council elections, a review of the Special Powers Act, and the setting up of the Londonderry Development Commission. In London the British PM, Harold Wilson, spoke of Captain O'Neill being 'blackmailed by thugs' and he warned that there would be a reappraisal of NI's position if he was overthrown. In the event, Captain O'Neill decided to challenge his Unionist critics in a general election in February 1969. But this 'cross-roads election', as he termed it, was extremely confused. He took the gamble of endorsing pro-O'Neill candidates who, in many cases, were opposing the official nominees of the local Unionist associations. Although his leadership was confirmed by the Unionist Parliamentary Party after the election, with twenty-three MPs voting for, Brian Faulkner against, and William Craig abstaining, the election left a legacy of bitterness throughout unionism. Also, the pressure for change from the civil rights movement was intensified. On 28 April 1969 O'Neill resigned as PM and was succeeded by James Chichester-Clark, who had resigned from the O'Neill Government five days before. In the House of Lords O'Neill has spoken frequently on NI issues. In comments on the 1968–9 period, he has said that the Troubles in NI had to happen, and that West-minster only acted when there was trouble. But for trouble, he said in a 1978 radio interview, Britain would probably still be in India. He supported the 1974 power-sharing project, but he insisted that there had been two mistakes – an over-elaborate cross-border Council of Ireland, and the withdrawal from Stormont of Secretary of State William Whitelaw before the new administration got under way.

O'NEILL, PHELIM *see* Rathcavan, Lord

O'NEILL, THOMAS P. ('TIP')
Speaker of the US House of Representatives, 1974–86. b. 1912. One of a group of Irish-American politicians, including Senator Edward Kennedy, who have maintained interest in Washington DC in NI issues and warned Americans against giving aid to funds which could help finance violence in Ireland. These politicians set up the Friends of Ireland Group in 1981. President Carter praised his efforts to promote reconciliation in Ireland, and Jack Lynch, former Taoiseach of the Republic, called him 'a true friend of Ireland'. In April 1979

he paid a brief visit to NI with other Congressmen and urged the new Conservative Government to launch a political initiative in NI. In a speech in Dublin he complained that NI had been made a 'political football' at West-minster – a comment criticised by Thatcher and Labour spokesmen. O'Neill's influence was crucial in getting Congressional and White House opinion behind the NIF report after Thatcher had curtly dismissed its options towards the end of 1984. He was also insistent on economic aid for NI to back the AIA. In 1989, for personal reasons, he declined President Bush's offer of the post of ambassador to Ireland.

'OPERATION MOTORMAN'
Code name of the security forces operation in the early hours of 31 July 1972 to clear barricades in no-go areas in Londonderry and Belfast. Some 21,000 troops, together with 9,000 mobilised UDR men and 6,000 members of the RUC, were involved. In Derry, 1,500 troops with armoured cars and other vehicles swept into the Bogside and Creggan areas. The operation had clearly been signalled in advance and resistance was confined to minor sniping and two people were killed by the army. There had been talk previously of at least 100 deaths if the areas were reoccupied. There was little resistance in Belfast Republican areas, and loyalists helped to dismantle their own barricades which they claimed were simply a response to the existence of Republican no-go areas. The Secretary of State William Whitelaw told a news conference that the operation had been designed to 'remove the capacity of the IRA to create violence and terror'. Shortly before he spoke, six people were killed in the Derry village of Claudy when three car bombs exploded. It was immediately assumed to be an IRA reply

to 'Motorman', although the IRA denied responsibility.

ORANGE ORDER

The largest Protestant organisation in NI, where it probably has between 80,000 and 100,000 active members, with between 4,000 and 5,000 members in the Republic. The Loyal Orange Institution owes its character to the victories of King William III (William of Orange) in the religious wars of the late seventeenth century. Its annual twelfth of July demonstrations at more than twenty centres in NI celebrate King William's victory over King James at the Battle of the Boyne. It was formed in September 1795, in Co. Armagh, after a clash between Protestants and Catholics at the 'Battle of the Diamond'. Its lodges were based on those of the Masonic Order. Although one of its main objectives is the defence of the Protestant succession to the British throne, its relations with London have often been strained. The Order fiercely resented the ban on Orange processions in the 1860s, and it was widely defied. The Order took on a distinctly Unionist flavour when Home Rule threatened. The effective beginning of the Unionist Party was a meeting of seven Orangemen, elected as MPs at Westminster in January 1886. The Unionist-Conservative link was forged in the opposition to Liberal plans for Irish Home Rule. A leading Conservative, Lord Randolph Churchill, 'played the Orange card' when he told an anti-Home Rule rally in Belfast's Ulster Hall: 'Ulster will fight and Ulster will be right.' Orangemen did not want the devolution accorded to NI in 1921, but once the state had been established, they defended it energetically and attacked any idea of a link-up with the South. Most Ministers in Unionist governments were Orangemen, and the controversial B Specials, the auxiliary police force which many Unionists regarded as Ulster's army, were almost exclusively Orangemen. While the defence of civil and religious liberty is a prime Orange aim, it attacked the civil rights movement as Republican- or Communist-inspired. The imposition of direct rule and the scheme for power-sharing between Protestants and Catholics in government got little support from Orangemen. The Order remains close to the OUP, although the ties have been loosened a little by the fragmentation of unionism. And throughout the violence the Order has been calling for tougher security policies, particularly against the IRA, and its leaders have claimed that it has exercised a restraining influence on loyalists. When the Order's World Council met in Belfast in 1976, there were representatives present from ten countries – NI, the Republic, England, Scotland, US, Canada, New Zealand, Australia, Ghana and Togoland. There were also said to be plans to set up lodges in South Africa and Sweden. There is a lodge at the House of Commons founded originally by James Craig, NI's first PM, and in the past military lodges existed in places like Hong Kong, Singapore and Egypt. It was reported in 1982 that there had been a 48 per cent increase in membership in Africa in the previous three years. One lodge established in Ghana in 1985 was said to comprise 300 men and women, all former Catholics. The World Council met in Belfast in 1985 to make plans for celebrations in 1990 of the three-hundredth anniversary of the Battle of the Boyne. It also appointed an Australian, John Gowans, as Imperial grand master. S. Belfast OUP MP, Rev. Martin Smyth, who was formerly Imperial grand master, has been grand master in Ireland since 1972. In 1986 Belfast grand master John McCrea became grand secretary of the Order in

Ireland in succession to Walter Williams, who had held office for thirty years. But the secretaryship was then made an honorary post, and George Patton was named full-time executive officer. The Order has been active in opposition to the AIA, and was also highly critical of new public order laws introduced in 1987. In 1988 Orangemen had their own celebrations of the tercentenary of King William's arrival in England, but they had no part in the official celebrations (confined to GB) of the 'glorious revolution'. They were refused permission to hold a special service in Exeter cathedral. (In 1986 Queen Beatrix of the Netherlands said the Dutch deplored the fact that the name 'Orange', which to them had become symbolic of tolerance, should in a different setting be associated with intolerance.) The senior branch of the Order is known as the Royal Black Institution – it is headed by OUP leader James Molyneaux MP – and it is also closely associated with the Apprentice Boys of Derry, with membership often overlapping. There are also women's and junior branches.

ORANGE VOLUNTEERS

A loyalist paramilitary group started in 1972 with about 500 members and closely linked with the Vanguard movement. Its membership was restricted to Orangemen and ex-servicemen, and it frequently provided stewards at rallies addressed by William Craig. In 1974, when it was thought to have grown to about 3,000 members, it was involved in setting up road blocks and in communications during the loyalist strike. It also supported the more limited loyalist strike in May 1977.

O'REILLY, JAMES

Nationalist MP for Mourne, 1958–72. He was Whip for his party in the later days of the Stormont Parliament, and frequently spoke on farming issues. In 1964 he unsuccessfully promoted a bill to establish an Ombudsman in NI. In the 1971 census he refused to complete his return, and went to prison rather than pay a fine. He said he was protesting against the 'biased administration of justice'.

ORME, STANLEY

Minister of State, NIO, 1974–6. b. 5 April 1923. Soon after he was elected Labour MP for Salford W. in 1964, Orme visited NI at the invitation of Gerry Fitt, the W. Belfast MP, to study the local situation in company with several other Labour MPS. Soon afterwards, when the Campaign for Democracy in Ulster was formed at Westminster, Orme became associated with it, and was a strong critic of Unionist administrations. He opposed internment without trial, and in 1973 told an audience in Dublin that he believed in the eventual reunification of Ireland. He was at that time a frontbench Labour spokesman, and prominently associated with the left-wing *Tribune* group of MPS. When he was appointed to the NIO in 1974, the move was immediately criticised by Unionists. The OUP, in a statement, questioned whether he could deal with NI matters impartially in view of the 'somewhat partisan' opinions which he had aired previously. Friction with the Unionists was increased when he took up a highly critical attitude towards the UWC strike in May 1974. As the Minister responsible for Economic Affairs, he had charge of the departments of Commerce and Manpower Services, and made several overseas trips in a bid to find new industrial investment. He was Minister of Social Security, 1976–9. Since 1983, MP for Salford E. Chairman, Parliamentary Labour Party, 1987–.

ORR, CAPTAIN LAWRENCE PERCY STORY (WILLIE)

Leader of the Unionist MPs at Westminster, 1954–74, and MP for S. Down, 1950–74. b. Belfast, 16 September 1918. Son of a former Dean of Dromore, he was Unionist organiser in S. Down before becoming the first MP for the newly created constituency. Former Imperial grand master of the Orange Order, he revived the Orange Lodge (LOL 1688) in House of Commons in 1955. He was an officer of many Conservative committees during his long career in Parliament. In August 1974 he announced he would not be standing again, and supported Enoch Powell as his successor.

OVEREND, ROBERT

Initially VUPP and later UUUM Convention member for Mid-Ulster, 1975–6. b. 1931. Magherafelt District Council, 1977–85. A farmer and pedigree-livestock dealer, prominent in the Orange Order and Apprentice Boys of Derry. Unsuccessful UUUP candidate in Mid-Ulster in 1982 Assembly election.

OWEN, DAVID

Leader of SDP, 1983–. b. 2 July 1938. MP for Plymouth Devonport (Labour, 1966–81 and SDP, 1981–). After holding a number of junior posts in Labour Government, he was Foreign Secretary, 1976–7. In 1981 he was one of 'gang of four' who founded SDP and he was joint leader of SDP–Liberal Alliance. But after the 1987 general election, he opposed the merger between the two parties which produced the SLD. He has visited NI several times, and said in Belfast in October 1988 that if there was a build-up of members, it could open the door to SDP candidates standing in NI. In 1988 he also supported Margaret Thatcher in her criticisms of the Republic over extradition, and urged

that Gerry Adams should lose his MP status because of abstention from Parliament.

P

PAISLEY, EILEEN

Wife of the Rev. Ian Paisley. DUP Assembly, 1973–4, and Convention, 1975–6, member for E. Belfast. b. Belfast. Belfast City Council, 1967–75. In 1982 she was a member of a joint OUP–DUP publicity team visiting the US. She stood in for her husband, who had been refused a US visa.

PAISLEY, REVEREND IAN RICHARD KYLE

Democratic Unionist MEP for NI, June 1979–. MP for N. Antrim, 1970–. Assembly member for N. Antrim, 1982–6. Chairman of Agriculture Committee; member, Security Committee. Leader of DUP, 1971–. b. 6 April 1926. Son of a Baptist minister, he is reputed to have started preaching at the age of sixteen. In 1951 he started a Free Presbyterian Church in the Ravenhill Road area of Belfast, where he later erected his large Martyrs' Memorial Church. But it was in 1963 that his interest in political action developed. He organised a march to protest against the lowering of the Union flag on Belfast City Hall to mark the death of Pope John XXIII. And when it was the first loyalist march to be banned under the Special Powers Act, he persisted with his plan. He was fined £10, and said he would go to prison rather than pay the fine. But the fine was paid anonymously, and Paisley alleged that it had been paid by the Government. In 1964, during the Westminster general election campaign in W. Belfast, he made a big issue of the display of a tricolour flag in the window of the Republican HQ in Divis Street, adjoining the Catholic Falls Road. The RUC broke into the premises and removed the flag. The flag was later replaced, and when the police returned, serious rioting broke out. These incidents established a pattern of protest which he was to employ in many different circumstances. The visit of the Republic's Taoiseach, Sean Lemass, to Stormont in January 1965 gave him a new and potent campaign issue. He insisted, with his booming oratory, that the threat of a united Ireland had been opened up by the 'treachery' of PM Captain O'Neill. The 'O'Neill must go' drive was pursued at rallies and meetings. In June 1966 he infuriated O'Neill by having a march to the General Assembly of the Presbyterian Church in Belfast to protest against its 'Romeward trend'. The Governor, Lord Erskine, and Church dignitaries had abuse shouted at them outside the hall, and in Parliament the PM deplored what he called 'tendencies towards nazism and fascism'. O'Neill also accused Paisley of having associations with the UVF, something which Paisley firmly denied. But Paisley had now set up two organisations – the Ulster Constitution Defence Committee and Ulster Protestant Volunteers – which were to figure frequently in counter-demonstrations during the civil rights campaign. One of the largest demonstrations which Paisley and his supporters mounted against a civil rights march was in Armagh on 30 November 1968. He and Major Ronald Bunting arrived in Armagh early in the morning and, with their supporters, blocked the town centre, forcing the civil rights demonstrators to cut short their parade. Paisley and Bunting had to serve six weeks' imprisonment for unlawful assembly. The resignation of O'Neill in April

1969 brought the comment from Paisley that he had 'brought down a Captain and could bring down a Major as well'. The Major, of course, was Major Chichester-Clark, who succeeded O'Neill. Paisley's chance to challenge the new Government came in April 1970, when by-elections were held in two Co. Antrim seats – Bannside (former seat of Captain O'Neill) and S. Antrim. Paisley won the Bannside constituency and his colleague, the Rev. William Beattie, the S. Antrim seat. It was a double blow to the Government and two months later Paisley achieved another parliamentary success – he gained the N. Antrim seat in the Westminster election. In 1971 he set up the Democratic Unionist Party to replace the Protestant Unionist Party. Towards the end of 1971 he angered many Unionists by predicting direct rule from Westminster, despite denials from London and by NI PM Brian Faulkner. At that period he seemed to be keen on integration of NI with GB, with a Greater Ulster Council at Stormont. And his concentration on attacks on the 'theocratic' nature of the Republic's Constitution gave rise to suggestions that Paisley was softening a little in his attitude towards the South – an impression which he moved quickly to dispel. The Sunningdale Conference, aimed at setting up the power-sharing Executive, was his next major target. He claimed that by excluding his party from full participation in Sunningdale the Government had gone back on its White Paper promise. And he and his supporters now adopted a wrecking approach towards the Assembly. On 22 January 1974 he and several of his loyalist colleagues were removed bodily from the Chamber after they had refused to give up the front-bench seats to the new Executive members and had mounted a noisy protest. Paisley himself was carried out by eight uniformed policemen. In February 1974 he increased his N. Antrim majority in the general election from under 3,000 in 1970 to some 27,000. Although he was abroad when the loyalist strike started in May 1974, he soon became deeply involved with the message, 'This is one we can't afford to lose.' He, together with Harry West and William Craig, represented the UUUC leadership in the strike committee, and his oratory was employed frequently at the anti-Executive rallies at Stormont and elsewhere. With the fall of the Executive, he was active in calling for new elections. These were granted in terms of the Constitutional Convention, and in the Convention, Paisley served on UUUC deputations which met the Alliance Party. There were conflicting assessments of his position in the Convention. Some Official Unionists said he had been more conciliatory in private than in public towards some form of partnership government. His public stance was certainly one of full support for the majority Convention report. After the Convention was wound up, it was clear however that his relations with many Official Unionists were strained. Paisley and Ernest Baird backed a United Unionist Action Council, designed to take a more militant line towards direct rule and in favour of tougher security. But the Official Unionists opted out, and refused to back a loyalist strike called in May 1977, with the support of the loyalist paramilitaries. The strike was only a shadow of the 1974 affair, and Paisley's prestige undoubtedly suffered, not least because of an unredeemed pledge to quit politics if it failed. It also meant a break with the OUP MPs. The Scarman report has dealt with the suggestion that Paisley had been largely responsible for the disturbances of 1969. It said: 'Those who live in a free country must accept as legitimate the powerful expression of views opposed to their own, even if, as often happens, it is accompanied by exaggeration, scurrility and abuse. Dr Paisley's spoken words were always powerful and must have frequently appeared to some as provocative: his newspaper [*Protestant Telegraph*] was such that its style and substance were likely to rouse the enthusiasm of his supporters and the fury of his opponents. We are satisfied that Dr Paisley's role in the events under review was fundamentally similiar to that of the political leaders on the other side of the sectarian divide. While his speeches and writings must have been one of the many factors increasing tension in 1969, he neither plotted nor organised the disorders under review and there is no evidence that he was a party to any of the acts of violence investigated by us.' The European election in June 1979 was seized by Paisley as an opportunity to demonstrate that he had more popular support than the Official Unionists. And since his party had gained two seats from the OUP in the May general election, he was well placed to stage a successful campaign. He travelled throughout NI, attacking the EC as both disastrous in economic terms and as a threat to Protestantism. In the event, he headed the poll easily, with more than 170,000 votes, or just under 30 per cent of first preferences, and 8 per cent ahead of the total OUP vote for two candidates. He claimed that the election gave him a mandate to speak for the NI majority in any political negotiations, and to answer criticisms at Strasbourg by MEPs from the Republic. At the first session in Strasbourg in July 1979 he intervened twice. On the opening day he was the first MEP to speak, apart from the acting president, when he protested that the Union flag was flying the wrong way up outside the Parliament Buildings. Later, he interrupted Jack

216

Lynch (president in office of the European Council), saying that he was protesting against the Republic's refusal to sign the European Convention on Terrorism. In the European Parliament he was appointed member of the Energy Committee and later of the Political Affairs Committee. In July 1979 he strongly attacked any suggestion that Pope John Paul II should enter NI during the Irish Papal visit in September. Paisley's campaigning in the early 1980s was directed at some familiar targets. In 1980 he castigated the OUP for failing to take part in the Atkins conference, in which the DUP stood out against power-sharing. His other main assaults were on Anglo-Irish contacts and Government security policy. The Thatcher–Haughey meeting in Dublin in December 1980, with its launch of joint studies by the British and Irish Governments was presented by him as a threat comparable to that faced by Edward Carson and Ulster loyalists in 1912. He accused Thatcher, when he met her privately, of 'undermining' NI's constitutional guarantee, a contention which she angrily repudiated. In February 1981 he organised a demonstration involving 500 men who paraded late at night on a Co. Antrim hillside, brandishing gun licences. This dramatic gesture was followed by a new 'Ulster declaration' on the lines of the original Covenant, to be signed by loyalists as a protest against the Thatcher–Haughey 'conspiracy'. It was linked to eleven 'Carson trail' rallies, culminating in a march to Stormont on 28 March, attended by some 30,000 people. Meantime, he was suspended from the Commons for five days for calling Secretary of State Humphrey Atkins a 'liar' when MPs discussed the murder of Sir Norman Stronge and his son. In the May 1981 council elections, the DUP put itself marginally ahead of the OUP in total

votes. After the assassination of S. Belfast MP, the Rev. Robert Bradford, in November 1981, he was involved in another Parliamentary scene. He and his two party colleagues, Peter Robinson and John McQuade, were ordered out of the Commons by the Speaker when they noisily interrupted Secretary of State James Prior as he was giving the Government's reaction to the killing. At that point Paisley was promoting a Third Force to protect loyalists, and it was claimed that 5,000 members of the force paraded at a rally in Newtownards on 23 November which he addressed. That was the day designated by Unionists as a 'Day of Action' to demand a tougher security policy. Many Protestants stopped work and OUP and DUP leaders spoke at separate rallies. In early December 1981 he claimed that the Third Force had 15,000–20,000 members, and was organised on a county basis. Soon afterwards, some Irish-American Congressmen, headed by Senator Edward Kennedy, urged the State Department to withdraw his US visa in the light of his recent activities. Just before Christmas the visa was withdrawn, on the grounds of the 'divisiveness' of his recent statements and actions so that he was unable to visit the US in January 1982, on a joint DUP–OUP publicity operation. He made the best of it, however, since he travelled to Canada, and got on to the US national TV networks from Toronto, while his wife read his speeches in the US. James Prior's 'rolling devolution' initiative in 1982 was a further occasion for friction between the DUP and OUP. Paisley shared with the OUP a dislike of the 'cross-community support' condition attached to devolved government. But he argued that it was the last chance in his lifetime to secure devolved government at Stormont, and that the initial scrutiny powers could be a powerful check on direct rule. He was disappointed, however, by the election results, since the OUP took twenty-six Assembly seats to the DUP's twenty-one. He took over the chairmanship of the Assembly's Agriculture committee, and to those who marvelled at his spread of commitments, taking in Strasbourg and Westminster, he explained that he would give up his Westminster seat if devolved government was achieved. He also found time to protest on the ground during Pope John Paul II's visit to Britain. In 1983 his N. Antrim seat was cut in half by redistribution, but he held it by a 13,000-plus majority. The 1984 European election was a further personal triumph, when he took more than one-third of all the votes (230,251 first preferences). But when the AIA was signed, he threw in his lot with OUP leader James Molyneaux to mount the 'Ulster Says No' campaign with a massive rally in Belfast and a variety of other protest actions – virtual withdrawal from Parliament, the forcing of by-elections in all Unionist-held seats, a boycott of Ministers, adjournment of Unionist-controlled councils, and protests against new public order laws in 1987, which were presented as deriving from Dublin pressure. When the fifteen protest by-elections were held in January 1986, the device of a 'dummy candidate' had to be resorted to in N. Antrim to enable Paisley to chalk up a 33,000-plus majority. Given the long-standing rivalry with the OUP, he braved some opposition from within the DUP to keep in harness with the Glengall Street HQ. In particular, he stamped on plans to oppose the OUP in E. Antrim in the 1987 election. But in that election he sensed the need for something more imaginative than the anti-AIA campaign to date. The commitment of no talks until the AIA was at least suspended was interpreted as allowing the two Unionist leaders to engage in probing 'talks about talks'

with NI Secretary of State Tom King which, surprisingly, reached into the summer of 1988. Publicly, the exchanges were aimed at securing a British Government assurance that it would consider an alternative to the AIA more acceptable to Unionists, with the hint of generosity towards the SDLP in new arrangements for internal government if the AIA could be set aside. In early 1988 it seemed that a rift might be developing between Paisley and Molyneaux, when the latter seemed to be responding with some warmth to the public statements of Taoiseach Charles Haughey. But at mid-1988 both were saying that there could be no talks with the Dublin Government before an agreed internal NI settlement, and both were rejecting power-sharing. The upsurge in PIRA violence in July–August 1988 found Paisley demanding capital punishment and detention of Republican terrorist suspects. In October 1988 Paisley was ejected from the European Parliament when he interrupted an address by Pope John Paul II. His daughter Rhonda, who wrote a book on her father in 1988, was Lady Mayoress of Belfast, 1986–7, when party press officer Sammy Wilson was first DUP Lord Mayor. At the same time Paisley's son Ian became chairman of the Young Democrats at QUB.

PARKER COMMITTEE
The committee, headed by Lord Parker, which reported in 1972 on the methods used in interrogating detainees in NI. The committee was particularly concerned with the 'five techniques' which were held by the European Court of Human Rights in January 1978 to amount to inhuman and degrading treatment, but not to torture. Lord Parker and John Boyd-Carpenter held that the methods could be justified in exceptional circumstances, subject to certain further

safeguards. But the third member, Lord Gardiner, said he did not believe such measures were morally justifiable, whether in peacetime or even in war against a ruthless enemy. The PM, Edward Heath, told MPs that the five techniques – hooding, wall-standing, subjection to noise and deprivation of food and sleep – would not be used again.

PASCOE, LIEUTENANT-GENERAL SIR ROBERT
Army GOC, NI, 1985–8. b. 1932. Was army Commander at a time when the Government was pressing for greater cross-border security co-operation in face of a PIRA build-up, and when the Irish Government through the AIA was calling for more sensitivity towards the Catholic minority in day-to-day operations. Had previously served in NI with Royal Greenjackets between 1971 and 1974, and at HQ in Lisburn in 1980. ADC to the Queen, 1989–.

PASSMORE, THOMAS
OUP Assembly member for W. Belfast, 1982–6. Served on committees on Education, Health and Social Services, and Security. b. 1931; d. 1989. A prominent Orangeman, he was grand master in Belfast, 1974–84, and Irish deputy grand master for twenty years prior to his death. He stood unsuccessfully in W. Belfast in the 1979 and 1983 elections, and was chairman for some years of Woodvale Unionist Association. In the Assembly he was frequently critical of Government security policy. When his father was shot dead by PIRA at their W. Belfast home in 1976, he said that he thought he himself had been the intended target.

PATTEN, CHRISTOPHER FRANCIS
Parliamentary Under-Secretary, NIO, 1983–5. b. 12 May 1944. Balliol College, Oxford. Director, Conservative Research Department, 1974–9. MP for Bath, 1979–. During his period in NI, he was regarded as one of the most able junior Ministers under direct rule. But he was somewhat more popular with the SDLP than with Unionists, who were intensely angry at his decision as Environment Minister in 1984 to adopt Derry City Council as the official title, thus dropping the name 'Londonderry'. He was called 'Lundy' by some Unionists in the Assembly, and there were references to his Catholicism. In 1985 Secretary of State James Prior got him to investigate the chances of breaking the political deadlock, but the inquiry was short-lived, and in September 1985 he returned to Whitehall as Minister of State at Education, 1985–6. Minister for Overseas Development, 1986–.

PATTEN, JOHN HAGGIT CHARLES
Parliamentary Under-Secretary, NIO, 1981–3. b. 17 July 1945. Cambridge University. Fellow of Hertford College, Oxford, 1972–. Conservative MP for Oxford, 1979–83; Oxford W. and Abingdon, 1983–. Oxford City Council, 1973–6. Took charge of Department of Health and Social Services at Stormont, and spokesman in Commons for those matters for which Lord Gowrie had responsibility, such as finance and police and prison administration. Parliamentary Under-Secretary, Department of Health in London, 1983–5; Minister of State, Home Office, 1987–.

PEACE LINE
The barrier put up by British troops between the Catholic Falls area and the Protestant Shankill area in Belfast in September 1969. Sometimes known as the Orange–Green line, it was erected because of the violent disturbances in the summer of 1969. Since 1982 it has

been converted into a brick wall and similar barriers have been erected in some other confrontation areas of the city.

PEACE PEOPLE
The peace movement established in August 1976, and inspired by the deaths of the three Maguire children, who had been struck by a gunman's getaway car in the Andersonstown area of Belfast. It was founded by Betty Williams, Mairead Corrigan, and Ciaran McKeown. Betty Williams and Mairead Corrigan were awarded the 1976 Nobel Peace Prize. The movement was initially marked by large rallies in Belfast and other centres in NI, and rallies of supporters in London, Dublin, and various places abroad. The movement has had strong financial support from Norway, and substantial aid from Germany, the US and several other countries. It has defined its aim as a 'non-violent movement towards a just and peaceful society'. In 1977 it began to switch its effort from large meetings to small groups, particularly in areas of confrontation, and to encourage increased community effort, better recreational facilities and, in some cases, the establishment of local industry. It created a good deal of controversy because its leaders were critical of established politicians. It set up its own forum for discussion – the Peace Assembly – which brought together annually delegates from groups throughout NI to debate current social and political issues. In February 1980 there was serious internal dissension, although not apparently on policy. Betty Williams resigned for family reasons, and she settled in the US in 1982. Peter McLachlan, who had become chairman of the movement in 1978, also left in 1980. Ciaran McKeown initially resumed his journalistic career but later turned to typesetting. He was associated for

several years with Belfast's Lyric Theatre until he resigned from the secretaryship in 1988. Mairead Corrigan was chairwoman, 1980–1, when she married Jackie Maguire, whose wife Anne (Mairead's sister) had committed suicide the previous year. She was said to have been heartbroken at the loss of her children and the continuing violence. Mairead Corrigan-Maguire has continued with the organisation, working on the ground and raising money for it in the US. In 1986 she claimed that the split in the movement had arisen because the German organisation wanted to provide money on condition that the PP avoided controversy, and they could not do that. In the 1980s the movement has been media-shy, but in 1988 it was still getting financial backing from several countries, including Norway where it organises regular camps for young people. It also had an active 'Youth for Peace' group, and was promoting a five-a-side football league to bring Protestants and Catholics together, and organising religiously mixed group holidays in GB and Europe. Much effort was also going into welfare for families of paramilitary prisoners and it was running buses to the prisons for relatives.

PEACOCKE, JOSEPH ANTHONY
The last head of the RUC to hold the title of Inspector-General. He was criticised by the Scarman tribunal for his handling of the situation in the riots of August 1969. b. 1908; d. November 1975. He joined the RUC as a cadet in 1932, and became Inspector-General in February 1969. But he held the post only until October 1969, when he was succeeded by Sir Arthur Young with the rank of Chief Constable. The direction of the RUC had been one of the controversial aspects of 1969, and he was widely blamed for not having

called for army assistance before 14 August. The Scarman report said Peacocke had acted in August as though RUC strength were sufficient to maintain the public peace. 'It was not until he was confronted with the physical exhaustion of the police in Londonderry on the 14th and in Belfast on the 15th that he was brought to the decision to call in the aid of the army. Had he correctly appreciated the situation before the outbreak of the mid-August disturbances, it is likely that the Apprentice Boys' parade [in Derry] would not have taken place, and the police would have been sufficiently reinforced to prevent disorder arising in the city. Had he correctly apprec-iated the threat to Belfast that emerged on 13 August he would have saved the city the tragedy of the 15th. We have no doubt that he was well aware of the existence of political pressures against calling in the army, but their existence constituted no excuse, as he himself recognised when in evidence he stoutly and honourably asserted that they did not influence his decision.' This reference to 'political pressure' related to the point that entry of the army to the streets would involve the British Government in a reappraisal of the whole position of the Stormont administration.

PENDRY, THOMAS (TOM)
Parliamentary Under-Secretary, NIO, October 1978–May 1979. b. 10 June 1934. Labour MP for Stalybridge and Hyde, 1970–. Opposition Whip, 1971–4. Government Whip, 1974–7. Appointed to NIO to look after Finance and Agriculture owing to illness of James Dunn MP. Chairman, All-Party Football Committee.

PENTLAND, JOHN WESLEY
DUP Assembly member for N. Down, 1982–6. Served on committees on Economic Development, Health and

Social Services, Finance and Personnel. Member of former Lurgan Borough Council and deputy Mayor in early 1960s. Institute of Travel and Tourism; British Travel Association.

PEOPLE'S DEMOCRACY
A radical leftist group, which had its beginnings at QUB on 9 October 1968. After a student march to Belfast city centre to demand an impartial inquiry into police brutality in Londonderry and the repeal of the Special Powers Act and the Public Order Act, among other things, a committee of ten was established at the inaugural meeting. Apart from the repeal of what it regarded as repressive legislation, it also urged one man, one vote, with the redrawing of electoral boundaries, and action to outlaw discrimination in jobs and housing allocations. Its best-known original members were Bernadette Devlin, Kevin Boyle and Michael Farrell. Its most dramatic move was a four-day march from Belfast to Londonderry, starting on 1 January 1969, with between forty and seventy people taking part. The project was attacked as provocative by loyalists, and it was harassed by extreme elements at various points. The most serious incident was near Burntollet Bridge in Co. Derry, when the marchers were ambushed by some 200 loyalists. Stones and sticks were used in the assault and thirteen marchers had to have hospital treatment. The affair gave rise to angry recriminations, and criticism of the RUC by civil rights spokesmen. In the February 1969 Stormont general election, PD tried its appeal at the polls. None of its eight candidates was successful, but it got a total of 23,645 votes and the PD nominee was only 220 behind the Nationalist in S. Down. In 1972 it put out a detailed policy statement, pro-posing a secular, all-Ireland republic, with the dissolution of both the existing

states. It said there was no point in submerging the North in the 'gombeen state' in the South. It also called for the disbanding of the RUC and UDR. PD has frequently campaigned in close association with PIRA but in 1974 the PIRA called PD 'weak and pseudo-revolutionary'. PD secured two council seats in Belfast in the 1981 local government contests. It expressed total opposition to the 1982 'rolling devolution' initiative, but put up its two councillors – Fergus O'Hare and John McAnulty – in W. and N. Belfast in the Assembly election. They got fewer than 500 votes between them. Bernadette McAliskey (née Devlin) stood unsuccessfully as PD candidate in the 1982 general elections in the Republic.

PLASTIC BULLET *see* Security System section, pp. 395–6

POOTS, CHARLES BOUCHER
DUP Assembly, 1973–4, and Convention, 1974–5, member for N. Down. b. 1929. Member, Lisburn District Council, 1973–. Unsuccessful candidate for Stormont Iveagh seat, 1969. Treasurer, Hillsborough Free Presbyterian Church. In the Assembly in January 1974 he was suspended for a day for calling Chief Executive Brian Faulkner 'a lying tramp'. Stood unsuccessfully in 1982 Assembly election.

POPULATION
NI's population in 1986 was estimated at around 1,567,000 or nearly 2 per cent above the 1981 census return of 1,488,077. In 1981 calculations were made more difficult by the efforts of Republican supporters to disrupt the count as part of their Maze Prison protest. The 1981 total did not take account of non-returns estimated at about 19,000. The 1971 census total was 1,536,065. In 1981 the Registrar-General reckoned that NI was losing

10,000 people a year through emigration. A notable switch in population was that the city of Belfast had 100,000 fewer people than in 1971, but there were 50,000 more in Greater Belfast and adjoining towns, reflecting the tendency to move from the inner city to developing suburbs. In 1986 NI was recorded as the most sparsely populated part of the UK, with 111 persons per square kilometre, but it was forecast that by the year 2001 the population would rise by 7.3 per cent. In 1986 NI had the youngest population of any region of UK, with 8.7 per cent of population under five years of age, and with those over retirement age making up only 14.4 per cent of population against the UK average of 18.1 per cent.

PORTER, SIR ROBERT WILSON
Minister of Home Affairs, 1969–70. b. Londonderry, 23 December 1923. LLB (QUB). QC, 1965. Unionist MP for QUB, 1966–9; Lagan Valley, 1969–72. Minister of Health and Social Services, 1969. One of the strongest supporters of Terence O'Neill as PM. In the Chichester-Clark Government he took part in the crucial Downing Street talks in August 1969. He often argued that unionism could no longer operate on the 'no surrender' approach, or 'stand still while the rest of the world is changing'. In June 1972 he resigned from the Unionist Party because Faulkner, as PM, had associated himself with the Vanguard movement in attacking direct rule. He joined the Alliance Party soon afterwards and resumed his Bar practice, occasionally acting as deputy Recorder of Belfast and frequently as a prosecuting counsel in terrorist cases. County Court judge, 1978–.

POUNDER, RAFTON JOHN
Unionist MP for S. Belfast, 1963–74. b. Belfast, 13 May 1933. Chartered

222

accountant; internal auditor, QUB, 1962–3. Parliamentary Private Secretary to Conservative Industry Minister, 1970–1. Member, UK delegation, European Parliament, 1973–4. Staff of EC Commission, 1974–6, working on scheme for Court of Auditors to check Common Market spending and counter abuses. Defeated by UUUC candidate in S. Belfast, February 1974. Secretary, NI Bankers' Association, 1977–.

POWELL, JOHN ENOCH

Unionist MP for S. Down, October 1974–87. b. 16 June 1912. MA (Cantab.). Enoch Powell had been Conservative MP for Wolverhampton S.W., 1950–74. Minister of Health, 1960–3, and an internationally known personality before he became interested in NI affairs. He displayed his Unionist sympathies intermittently for some years, notably by addressing party meetings in NI before his break with the Conservatives left him without a seat in Parliament. So his entry into active NI politics in 1974 was seen as being of mutual benefit to the Unionists and to Powell. He had been out of the Commons for some six months when he was selected as Unionist candidate in S. Down, and the Unionists saw him as a controversialist with the ability to project their case in GB. The were disappointed, however, to find that his majority in October 1974 over the SDLP candidate in S. Down was only 3,500 in a seat which normally yielded Unionist majorities of 10,000 or more. But in the circumstances of direct rule, his mastery of parliamentary and Whitehall procedure was a real asset to the UUUC, particularly since several of their MPs were new to Westminster and lacked even Stormont experience. Powell's support for Labour in the election was an embarrassment to many Unionists, who believed that

despite Edward Heath's suspension of Stormont, every effort should be made to restore the former Conservative-Unionist partnership – a belief which was strengthened when Margaret Thatcher took over as Conservative leader. Powell's tactics were, however, to extract as much advantage as possible from the narrowly balanced Parliament, and he pointed to the Labour Government's acceptance of the case for more NI seats at Westminster as one of the key gains. He was also regarded on all sides in NI as basically an integrationist who had little time for the revival of a strong devolved government at Stormont, but he answered this point by saying that he always stuck to the letter of his election manifesto. On the Common Market issue, his unwavering opposition reflected the majority view in unionism. As S. Down MP, he displayed little friendliness towards the Republic, which he has always described as a foreign state. He questioned, among other things, the right of the Republic's citizens to enjoy equal voting rights in Britain. By having a house in S. Down and by intensive canvassing, he sought to dispel the 'carpetbagger' image, and when he came to fight his second election in S. Down in 1979, he substantially increased his majority. He was also helped by the fact that the Bill to give NI five extra MPs had been put on the statute book, and it was accepted that he had played a major part in the campaign to achieve increased representation. In 1982 he mounted a major attack on the Prior 'rolling devolution' initiative. He saw it as closely tied up with the Anglo-Irish talks, which he regarded as an 'Anglo-American plot' to secure a united Ireland within NATO. Undeterred by Government denials, he spoke vigorously against the devolution Bill both inside and outside Parliament, and reinforced the efforts of Conservative right-wing critics during the committee stage of the measure by some skilful filibustering. But Powell proved to be one of the most forceful Parliamentary supporters of Thatcher during the Falklands operation. He was among leading politicians to whom she accorded a personal briefing on the crisis, and there were Conservative MPs who thought he should be back in Government. In 1982, at age seventy, he was reselected as candidate by S. Down Unionists. In the 1983 election he survived in S. Down despite the handicaps of boundary changes favouring the SDLP, and opposition from the DUP. A PSF vote of more than 4,000 blunted the SDLP challenge and gave him a majority of 548. In 1985 he regarded the signing of the AIA as treachery by the Thatcher Government, and as confirming his warnings of US pressure on Britain. He joined, some thought hesitantly, his Unionist colleagues in forcing protest by-elections, and his majority in S. Down, with the DUP giving support, rose to 1,842. But he stood aside from many Unionist demonstrations against the AIA; he did not boycott Parliament, join illegal parades, or stop paying rates. The rise in the Nationalist vote in S. Down, together with a weakening of support for PSF, however, proved too much for him in the 1987 general election. He lost by some 700 votes to his long-time opponent Eddie McGrady (SDLP). But he remained on the OUP executive, and although he did not go to the Lords in the dissolution honours, many MPs felt that he might be elevated eventually.

PREVENTION OF TERRORISM ACT *see* Security System section, pp. 398–406

PRIOR, LORD
As James Prior, NI Secretary of State,

September 1981–September 1984. b. 11 October 1927. Educated Charterhouse and Pembroke College, Cambridge. Conservative MP for Lowestoft, 1959–83. MP for Waveney, 1983–7. Employment Secretary, 1979–81. His appointment to NI came after repeated rumours that he was favourite to succeed Humphrey Atkins but that he had told Margaret Thatcher he would prefer to resign rather than leave Employment. At the time he was known to have qualms about Government economic policy, and to be high on the PM's list of Cabinet 'Wets'. He was also reckoned to be a possible future challenger for the Conservative leadership. In the end, he deferred to the PM's wishes. It was his duty, he said, to put the nation first, and he seems to have been concerned with the 'international dimension' of the NI job. Thatcher also allowed him to remain on the influential Cabinet Economic Committee, and to take three of his close political friends to NI with him – Lord Gowrie, Nicholas Scott and John Patten. In his first Stormont statement, he said he was prepared to lay his political reputation 'on the line' in a bid to secure a political settlement. His immediate challenge was the H-Block hunger strike, which had already led to the deaths of ten Republican prisoners. It was however, petering out as next-of-kin of those close to death sought medical intervention, and within a month PIRA and INLA bowed to the inevitable. Prior announced only one substantial concession when the protest ended – the right of all prisoners to wear their own clothes at all times. But the easing of tension was followed by a new upsurge of violence and the murder of the Rev. Robert Bradford, MP for S. Belfast. He was now brought face to face with loyalist wrath – notably at Bradford's funeral – and calls from Official and Democratic Unionists for a tougher security policy.

The DUP-sponsored Third Force appeared at several rallies, and Rev. Ian Paisley mounted night-time demonstrations on lonely hillsides to dramatise his campaign. But Prior continued to pursue the possibilities of political advance, despite the obvious lack of agreement on how devolution could be achieved. His first thoughts were directed to the setting up of a local administration to which he would appoint Ministers – rather like a US President. But he abandoned this quickly for what became known as 'rolling devolution' (see Systems of Government section, p. 367). He got little encouragement for his gradualist approach. Both main Unionist parties were obsessed by fears of new pressure for power-sharing and the shadow of the new British-Irish Intergovernmental Council. The DUP, though, were more enthusiastic than the OUP about the Assembly's scrutiny powers. The SDLP were sharply critical of what they saw as the absence of any firm assurances on power-sharing and an Irish dimension. The major Dublin parties were equally unfriendly to the proposals, and Prior had to face strong criticism from the Conservative far-right during the passage of the legislation in the spring of 1982. At the same time, Charles Haughey's refusal to back sanctions against Argentina during the Falklands crisis brought Anglo-Irish relations to a new low. But despite this unhappy context, Prior pressed on with the initiative, and the 20 October 1982 poll found the SDLP fighting the election, but committed to boycotting the Assembly. This was clearly disappointing for Prior, who was also unable to take any comfort from the achievement of PSF in getting five seats and 10 per cent of the vote in contesting a Stormont election for the first time. He saw the Assembly start with fifty-nine members present: twenty-six OUP; twenty-one DUP; ten

All.; one UPUP; and one Indepedent Unionist. The fourteen SDLP and five PSF members stayed away. He sought to boost the Assembly's prestige by addressing it on security policy within three weeks of its first meeting, but it was evident that a host of questions hung over this latest British initiative. Prior had the satisfaction, however, of having the Assembly plan supported in the 1983 Conservative manifesto. There had been some doubts as to whether he would return to NI after the 1983 election, but Thatcher acceded to his request for a further period as Secretary of State. By the time he left NI in 1984, it was clear that the Assembly would not produce a political solution. Shortly before his departure to become chairman of GEC, he ran into criticism for saying that mistakes had been made in banning Martin Galvin of NORAID from the UK. In 1985 he referred to his differences with Thatcher and admitted that they sometimes shouted at each other. 'It is hell being a rebel if you are a Tory,' he said. In 1987 he left the Commons and was appointed a life peer.

PRIVY COUNCIL
The Privy Council in NI has been suspended since direct rule. In the old Stormont Parliament all Cabinet Ministers were appointed to the Privy Council for life. Some senior judges were also admitted to the Council, which met at the Governor's residence at Hillsborough. Ex-Cabinet Ministers have been permitted to retain the title. Ministers in the power-sharing Executive of 1974 had no Privy Council membership. After the signing of the AIA, some NI Privy Councillors met to consider whether they could make any useful move, but no action resulted.

PRO-ASSEMBLY UNIONISTS
The name given to Unionists who

supported the approach to partnership government in the Government's 1973 White Paper. When the NI Executive collapsed in 1974, many of them moved to UPNI or the Alliance Party.

PROGRESSIVE DEMOCRATS

The Republic's newest party, which replaced Irish Labour as the third party in the State at the 1987 election. It took fourteen seats to Labour's twelve. Founded by Desmond O'Malley (formerly Fianna Fáil), it has put forward radical proposals for a new constitution for the Republic. These include the dropping of the existing territorial claim to NI and its replacement by an aspiration, seen by the party as more in the spirit of the AIA, and a clear separation of Church and State. The proposals were adopted at conference in September 1988. In 1988 the party seemed set to agree with Alliance in NI and SLD in GB a common platform for the 1989 European election. Its NI spokeswoman, Geraldine Kennedy, also became Chief Whip in 1988.

PROGRESSIVE UNIONIST PARTY

Started in the Shankill Road area of Belfast in 1978 as the Independent Unionist Group, becoming PUP in 1979. Alderman Hugh Smyth, an Ind. Unionist member of the Convention, 1975–6, was among the founders; he stood unsuccessfully in W. Belfast in the 1982 Assembly election. It urged in a statement in June 1978 that there should be a devolved administration based on a 153-seat parliament, with departments run by committees elected by the parliament, which would have power to co-opt non-voting members from outside. The party tried unsuc-cessfully to take part in the Stormont Constitutional Conference in 1980.

PROTESTANT ACTION FORCE *see* Ulster Volunteer Force

PROTESTANT ACTION GROUP *see* Ulster Protestant Action Group

PROTESTANT AND CATHOLIC ENCOUNTER

An organisation established in 1968 to bring together people of differing religious and political affiliations so as to promote harmony and goodwill. It aims at the creation of a 'social order based upon justice and charity, and enlivened by mutual respect and understanding'. It is run by a central council, bringing together Churchmen, academics, and others, and has groups in many towns and villages. It works through conferences, social events, and a magazine.

PROTESTANT TASK FORCE

Believed to be a small group involved in assassinations of people it claimed were associated with the PIRA. In press interview in November 1974, an unofficial spokesman of the organ-isation in mid-Ulster stated that they had murdered twenty-eight people in two months. He also said that the PTF had no scruples in dealing with Republicans, was restricted to ex-servicemen, and unconnected with any leading loyalist paramilitary group.

PROTESTANT UNIONIST PARTY

The party led by the Rev. Ian Paisley which gave way to the DUP in 1971. The term 'Protestant Unionist' was used by four candidates in the Belfast Corporation elections in 1964. Prot. U. nominees stood unsuccessfully in the 1969 Stormont election, and its first successes were achieved in April 1970, when Paisley and the Rev. William Beattie won the Bannside and S. Antrim by-elections. In June 1970 Paisley won N. Antrim in the Westminster election as a Protestant Unionist.

PROVISIONAL IRISH REPUBLICAN ARMY

The PIRA, the dominant element in the NI violence, dates effectively from December 1969. In that month the IRA army council voted by three to one to give at least token recognition to the three Parliaments – Westminster, Dublin and Stormont. This switch in policy ran directly against the traditional abstentionism and physical-force policy of the IRA. It was too much for the more militant members, who split off to create the PIRA. The break was mirrored in Sinn Féin, the political counterpart of the IRA. When the Sinn Féin Ard Fheis (annual convention) met in Dublin in January 1970, there was a majority for a change in policy, but not the necessary two-thirds majority. So the new Provisionals walked out of the meeting in the Intercontinental Hotel to set up their organisation in Kevin Street, Dublin. There were now two IRAS – Provisional and Official – and the same applied to Sinn Féin. Events in NI, and particularly in Belfast, meant that PIRA was better placed than the Officials to attract public support in the Northern ghettoes. For the IRA, so far as it existed in Belfast in the violent summer of 1969, had little credibility. Falls Road Catholics complained that it was unable to prevent the burning of Catholic homes. 'IRA – I Ran Away' was scrawled on some walls in W. Belfast. The Scarman Tribunal, which investigated the early Troubles, said that the main difference between the Derry Citizens' Defence Association, which had some IRA members, and the IRA in Belfast was that the DCDA was ready while the IRA in Belfast was not. Scarman also found that while there was IRA influence in the 1969 riots in Belfast, Derry and Newry, the IRA did not start or plan the riots, and that the evidence was that they were taken by surprise and did less than many of their

supporters felt they should have done. But Stormont was convinced that there was a strong IRA influence in the civil rights campaign. The point was made many times by William Craig, as Minister of Home Affairs. Scarman published a letter from the head of the RUC Special Branch to the Minister of Home Affairs, dated 18 August 1969. This claimed that at the end of May 1969 members of Republican Clubs controlled two-thirds of the executives of all local civil rights associations in NI, while six of the fourteen members of the NICRA executive were from the Republican movement. The head of the Special Branch also stated that the citizens' defence committees which had developed in Belfast, Derry, Newry, Lurgan, and other towns were all IRA-dominated, and that IRA units in these areas had been making hundreds of petrol bombs and some grenades. They were also instructing people in the use of petrol bombs through the citizens' defence committees. Thus, the situation in NI was highly favourable to the Provisionals, who attracted not only many young recruits but a high proportion of veterans of former IRA campaigns, and one survivor of the 1916 Easter Rising in Dublin – the late Joe Clarke. The Provisionals were short of both arms and ammunition at the start of 1970, but friendly sources in Dublin provided some, others were shipped in secretly from Britain and the Continent. The guns which they got from the Republic were, of course, sometimes intended for the local defence committees. And the charging in the Republic in 1970 of two Cabinet Ministers (Charles Haughey and Neil Blaney) with illegal dealing in arms was seen by PIRA chiefs as having a valuable publicity spin-off, even if both Ministers were later cleared. The Provisionals duplicated the military organisation of the former IRA. In Belfast, for example, there was a commander and brigade staff, and three battalions. By mid-1970 PIRA strength overall was believed to be around 1,500, including 800 in NI, divided roughly as follows: Belfast, 600; Derry, 100; other areas, 100. The growing Provisional strength was reflected in the big increase in violence in 1970 compared with 1969. Twenty-three civilians and two RUC men died during the year. There were 153 explosions compared with 8 in 1969. Street violence also remained at a high level in 1970, and the security forces held that much of it could be traced to inspiration by PIRA. PIRA further stepped up attacks in 1971. It was held responsible for most of the 304 explosions between January and July. In February 1971 General Farrar-Hockley, Commander of Land Forces, named five men as leaders of the PIRA in Belfast, and blamed them for recent rioting. They were Francis Card, William McKee, Liam Hannaway and his son, Kevin, and Patrick Leo Martin. About the same time, the army blamed the Provisionals for organising attacks by children, and claimed that the PIRA were using petrol bombs, grenades and rifles against the troops. In the early part of 1971 a bitter feud went on between the PIRA and OIRA and there was much of what the authorities termed inter-factional shooting. The murder in Belfast of three young Scottish soldiers in March 1971 brought strident loyalist demands for the use of internment without trial against PIRA. The army and police began to lean heavily on PIRA suspects. Billy McKee, the Belfast commander, was arrested in March. His successor, Joe Cahill, held a news conference in Belfast in the summer of 1971, much to the discomfiture of the Government and security chiefs. At that period the leading figures in the top PIRA leadership were Seán Mac Stiofáin, English-born chief of staff, and Dáithí

Ó Conaill. In July 1971 there was a big round-up of people believed to be connected with both wings of the IRA. It was designed to secure information for the coming internment operation. Government intelligence was satisfied that most of the thirty people killed up to 9 August 1971 – the date of the start of internment – had been victims of PIRA. They comprised eleven soldiers, two policemen and seventeen civilians. The European Court of Human Rights report on the ill-treatment of some of the IRA suspects interned in August 1971 stated: 'Prior to August 1971, the intelligence obtained by the police had failed to provide anything but a very general picture of the IRA organisation.' The internment move was designed to sweep up activists and sympathisers of the IRA. Of the 454 originally taken into custody, 350 were interned, and it was evidently the Government's belief that the operation would deprive the Provisionals of their more experienced people and damp down the violence. But the reality was otherwise: the use of internment alienated a huge section of the Catholic population, increased support for PIRA, and violence was intensified. From the date of intern-ment (9 August) to the end of 1971, the count of violence was: 143 people killed (including 46 members of security forces); 729 explosions; 1,437 shooting incidents. Security forces put the great bulk down to PIRA, and loyalists were accused of only one killing. At this point, PIRA had assembled a great diversity of weapons, despite the uncovering of a Czech-oslovakian arms deal in Amsterdam in October 1971. Apart from the old stand-by of the IRA, the Thompson sub-machine-gun (the 'Chicago piano'), it had also some US-made M1 carbines and Garard rifles, and a variety of .303 rifles and German and American pistols. It was using the car bomb, the nail bomb (usually a beer can containing nails wrapped in explosive), and the hold-all bag bomb, often left outside business premises. It had also displayed ingenuity in producing small incendiary devices which could easily be hidden in shops. Two popular types were the cigarette- packet incendiary, and the device in which a contraceptive acted as a fuse, with the detonation achieved by acid burning through the rubber. The existence of internment made it easier for the Provisionals to get funds from abroad, particularly from Irish-Americans. The Provisionals were also helped by the non-accept-ability of the RUC in many Catholic areas, and they got a new boost at the start of 1972, when thirteen people were shot dead by the army in Derry on what became known as 'Bloody Sunday'. In March 1972 Provisional Sinn Féin launched its 'Éire Nua' policy – a scheme for four provincial parliaments in Ireland – which was also linked with demands for the abolition of Stormont, a declaration of intent of British withdrawal, and a full amnesty for all political prisoners. PIRA ordered a three-day ceasefire in association with this policy, but they called it off because they had not got a British response, and arrests had been continued by the security forces. In fact, there were 900 internees at the end of March 1972, when direct rule was imposed from London, and they were all held because of alleged IRA involvement. But the closing down of the Stormont Parliament was not enough to induce PIRA to drop its campaign. Its determination to fight on was announced after a Dublin meeting in April which was said to have been attended by representatives of every active service unit. On 29 May 1972 the OIRA declared a ceasefire, which soon took on permanence. Exactly four weeks later, PIRA began a truce of its own, but it lasted only thirteen days.

The collapse occurred after a row about housing in Belfast. Two days before the ceasefire ended, a party of PIRA leaders were flown secretly to London for talks with Secretary of State William Whitelaw. The Govern-ment was believed to have received intelligence suggesting that PIRA was ready to make major concessions, but the talks proved unproductive. The restart of the PIRA campaign produced a massive upsurge in violence. For July 1972 alone there was an unpre-cedented tally of violence: 74 civilians and 21 members of the security forces killed, nearly 200 explosions and 2,800 shooting incidents. Throughout 1972 there had also been a mounting toll of sectarian assassinations carried out, for the most part, by loyalists. Faced with this two-pronged campaign, the Government decided to move against the no-go areas. But few PIRA men remained in the W. Belfast Republican areas or in the Bogside area of Londonderry, since the Government's intentions had been signalled well in advance. The second half of 1972 was a period of strong pressure on the Provisionals both in NI and in the Republic, and there were sporadic incidents involving members of PIRA and OIRA. A leading Belfast PIRA man, Martin Meehan, was recaptured in Belfast in August – he had escaped from Belfast Prison at the end of 1971. Documents seized by the security forces in Belfast were claimed to reveal a good deal about the PIRA structure in the city and especially its measures to prevent 'leaks'. It was also stated about the same time in *An Phoblacht*, the Provisional newspaper, that of the forty-four PIRA members killed since 1969, eighteen had been executed for mistakes or for giving information to the security forces. In November 1972 the PIRA chief of staff, Seán Mac Stiofáin, was arrested after he had given an interview to RTE. He was charged with IRA membership and then went on hunger strike, and an unsuccessful attempt was made to rescue him from a Dublin hospital. With Ruairí Ó Brádaigh, president of PSF, held in December 1972 for alleged IRA membership, there were rumours that Mac Stíofáin was seeking a larger political role. The British Government was claiming that it was getting truce 'feelers' from PIRA, despite denials by the organisation. There was a leadership crisis in PIRA when Mac Stíofáin abandoned his hunger strike. He was thought to have been succeeded by a three-man council made up of Dáithí Ó Conaill, Joe Cahill, and Gerry Adams, a Belfast Provisional who was one of the deputation flown secretly to London in July 1972 to meet Whitelaw. At the end of 1972 Whitelaw said in London that 1,000 IRA men had been arrested and convicted during 1972 and the organisation's command structure greatly weakened. There were also signs that PIRA was finding difficulty in getting conventional explosives because of the clamp-down in the South. The weed-killer chemical sodium chlorate was figuring increasingly in PIRA weapons. At this period, PIRA continued its attacks alongside loyalist violence on a substantial scale. Official estimates suggested that between 1 April 1972 and 31 January 1973, PIRA was responsible for about 300 deaths, including some 120 members of the security forces. In the case of 'factional' or 'sectarian' assassinations, PIRA was blamed for thirty-four and the loyalists for seventy. Throughout 1973, when the total of deaths was 250 – 171 civilians and 79 security forces – the pattern of PIRA bombing and shooting of soldiers and policemen was continued, while the loyalists concentrated on the shooting of Catholics. In February PIRA warned the UDA that it

would take 'ruthless action' against it to halt sectarian killings. PIRA called for the rejection of the British Government White Paper which led to the Assembly system, and it also called for a boycott of the 1973 council elections. In May 1973 Joe Cahill was sentenced to five years' imprisonment arising from gun-running charges associated with the vessel *Claudia*, seized off Waterford with a cargo of arms and ammunition from Libya – a precursor of future supplies along the same route. In May 1973 the Government published figures of IRA casualties going back to 1969. It claimed that 123 IRA men had been killed. PIRA admitted that it had lost ninety-nine men, and said the British claim was 'outlandish'. In 1974 there was some falling off in PIRA violence. In part, this was believed to be due to a desire to encourage the loyalists to make the running against the Government in their opposition to the Sunningdale Agreement and power-sharing. But PIRA had its own troubles at this time. A coup for the authorities was the uncovering in the select Malone Road area of Belfast of the brigade HQ of PIRA. In a flat, and posing as a businessman, was Brendan Hughes, the brigade commander, and one of his aides. About the same time several other key figures in PIRA in the city were also picked up. In the Commons, PM Harold Wilson referred to documents seized at the Provisionals' HQ which, he said, were a 'specific and calculated' plan to take over certain areas of Belfast by creating inter-sectarian hatred, chaos, violence and hardship. The areas to be taken over were said to include loyalist districts like Woodvale and Sandy Row, together with key buildings, such as Telephone House, the gas works, BBC and UTV. PIRA admitted that the plans had been drawn up some time before as a doomsday contingency. The end of 1974 was a period of mixed fortunes for the Provisionals. On the one hand, they came under greater pressure after the passing at Westminster of new and tougher anti-terrorist legislation in the wake of the Birmingham bombings. On the other, their leaders became involved in secret talks with Protestant Churchmen in Feakle, Co. Clare. PIRA immediately came under suspicion for the bombings which resulted in the deaths in November of nineteen people in two Birmingham pubs. The Provisionals denied that they had been responsible but there were later PIRA statements promising an inquiry into the bombings, although no result of such an investigation was ever issued. Meantime, six men had been jailed for life for the Birmingham bombings. (There were many claims that the men were innocent, but in 1988 their appeals were rejected by the Court of Appeal and the Lords.) The immediate effect of the Birmingham tragedy was to unite Parliament in support of the Prevention of Terrorism Act, which declared the IRA illegal in GB, allowed suspects to be held without charge for up to seven days, and permitted the expulsion of people to either NI or the Republic. The upshot of the Feakle Talks with Churchmen was that there was a flurry of talks in mid-December. The Secretary of State Merlyn Rees met some of the Churchmen to hear the Provisionals' demands, which included a call for a declaration of intent of British withdrawal. (Six months later, one of the Churchmen, the Rev. William Arlow, claimed that the Government had told the Provisionals that the army would be withdrawn if the Convention broke down – a claim denied by Rees.) There was also a lengthy secret meeting of the PIRA army council, and its then chief of staff, Dáithí Ó Conaill, met Arlow in Dublin. The only public response from the British Government was a comment by

Rees that they would naturally respond to any genuine cessation of violence. PIRA then announced a ceasefire from 22 December to 2 January 1975, to give the Government time, they said, to consider their proposals. In an atmosphere in which many politicians, and particularly the loyalists, were highly suspicious of what was going on, the Government insisted that there was no question of negotiations with PIRA. But there were meetings between Government officials and members of PSF. So the ceasefire was extended first to 16 January and then to 10 February when an open-ended ceasefire was announced. It emerged that a plan to monitor the ceasefire involved the setting up of 'incident centres' manned by PSF in Catholic areas of Belfast and Londonderry and other major towns. These would be in instant contact with Government officials with the object of avoiding a breakdown of the ceasefire through misunderstanding about individual incidents. There was a great deal of scepticism about the operation. Loyalists feared 'Provo policing', the SDLP were worried that the Provisionals were being given new credibility through ready access to Government; and Official Republicans saw signs of co-operation with the RUC through 'Royal Ulster Provisionals', a charge which PIRA were quick to deny. Not all the PIRA activists put away their guns; some joined the IRSP which was engaged in a feud with OIRA. In March 1975 the Belfast sisters, Dolours and Marion Price, sentenced for the London car bombings, were moved from Durham Jail to Armagh Women's Prison – a decision which was seen as a definite gesture by the Government towards the PIRA ceasefire. The ceasefire became more fragile, and more controversial, as time went on. At the beginning of July four soldiers were killed in an ambush in S. Armagh, and the Secretary of State told Parliament that one of the key questions was whether the Provisionals could control their followers. By mid-August the number of soldiers killed still stood at four during the ceasefire period, compared with nineteen in the same period of 1974. But the total of civilian deaths had risen by 26 to 119, and since the increase was entirely accounted for by a rise in the number of Protestants murdered (57), the security forces suspected that some of the PIRA effort had been switched to revenge killings of loyalists in view of the continued assassinations of Catholics. There were also murmurings from loyalist politicians at what they saw as a deliberate policy by the security forces of turning a blind eye to Provisionals who had returned to their old haunts in W. Belfast. Notably, there was confusion as to whether Seamus Twomey, a former PIRA commander in the city, was still on the wanted list. The implication seemed to be that, with the suspension of the detention process at the start of the ceasefire in February, Provisionals were only being arrested where specific charges could be brought against them. One of the imponderables of the situation was the extent to which PIRA had been preparing during the ceasefire for a new onslaught. Certainly, it had gone to the length of establishing a new 4th battalion in Belfast. In September six men were killed during a raid on an Orange Hall at Tullyvallen in S. Armagh. Although the raid was claimed by the 'South Armagh Republican Action Force', this was treated by the authorities as a cover for PIRA. Indeed, S. Armagh, which Secretary of State Merlyn Rees had described as 'bandit country', was never effectively covered by the ceasefire. How far this was due to lack of control by the PIRA army council was never very clear. In November 1976 it was claimed that PIRA had carried out

twenty-one killings in the area during the nine months of the ceasefire. In that month three soldiers were killed in a S. Armagh border dug-out by PIRA and two soldiers were killed by an explosion. Outside S. Armagh, September had brought eighteen PIRA explosions in one day throughout NI. In November the Government closed the incident centres, but PSF claimed that contacts continued with the Government and that there was still a 'truce situation'. On 5 December the Secretary of State ordered the release of the last seventy-five detainees, among them fifty-seven members of the PIRA. The 1975 security figures reflected the ceasefire in several respects. The 30 deaths of members of the security forces compared with 50 in 1974; the number of shooting incidents was down from 3,206 to 1,803; and the total of explosions from 685 to 399. Then, 1976 opened with the shooting dead by PIRA of ten Protestant workers, when their bus was ambushed in S. Armagh. The incident on 5 January on the Whitecross−Newry road was not claimed by PIRA, but British security forces insisted that it had been carried out by a PIRA unit based in the Republic. The killings were, apparently, a reprisal for the murder of five Catholics in two separate incidents in Co. Armagh the previous day. With many Catholics in S. Armagh voicing their fears of loyalist vengeance, the British Government announced that men of the Special Air Service (SAS) would be sent into the area. Although there had been many reports of SAS units operating earlier, these had always been denied by the British authorities. In February the ceasefire finally came to an end, with the death in prison in England of IRA hunger-striker Frank Stagg. His death provoked widespread violence in NI. In April the arrival of James Callaghan as PM was the signal for more PIRA attacks on troops. During the month, five part-time UDR men died. In May there was a further round of bombing, which was repeated in August at the time of the internment anniversary. Two events then occurred which created problems for PIRA chiefs. The Peace People movement got off the ground in Belfast, and probably accounted in part for an increased flow of information to the security forces. And in September Roy Mason, who had been Defence Secretary, succeeded Merlyn Rees as NI Secretary of State. He had a reputation for toughness, and while his immediate claim that PIRA were 'reeling' caused problems for him, he was obviously intent on stepping up army undercover activity. He also permitted the SAS to operate anywhere in NI. By late autumn he claimed in Parliament that 690 members of PIRA had been charged since the start of the year, that is, more than twice the total (320) in 1975. The weight of police and army intelligence was directed to cataloguing the movements of suspected terrorists and their life-style, contacts, 'safe houses', and general tactics. But the Mason approach did not prevent a sharp rise in the level of violence in 1976, mostly by PIRA. The number killed was 297, an increase of 50. Twenty-nine soldiers died, as against nineteen in 1975; and twenty-three RUC members against eleven in 1975. The total of 766 explosions was roughly double the 1975 figure. In 1977 there were signs that the pressure by the security forces on PIRA was beginning to tell. It was also apparently short of explosives, and the car bomb had all but vanished. In February, however, PIRA activated an earlier threat when it killed three businessmen and injured four others. At Easter the feud between PIRA and OIRA also flared up again. The response of PIRA to growing undercover police and army activity was to mount a large-scale reorganisation. The effect of this was to substitute very small active service units – possibly with only two or three members – for its larger companies. It is also likely that the new tactics were based on the 'need to know' principle – that is, probably only one member of a bombing unit would be informed in advance of the actual target. The organisation had also come to rely largely on the small incendiary device, with only a very limited explosive content. Increased 'knee-cappings' – shooting through the knees as a punishment – reflected a growing effort by PIRA to punish members who were careless and to increase 'policing' in Republican areas by dealing with those whom they termed 'petty criminals'. The end of 1977 brought a serious loss for PIRA – the recapture in Dublin of Seamus Twomey, its chief of staff. The total of soldiers killed by PIRA in 1977 was 29 – the same figure as in 1976 – but violence generally had dropped sharply, and the total death toll was down to 112. PIRA began 1978 with an atrocity which horrified even its own sympathisers, and which it rapidly acknowledged to have been a mistake. On 17 February fire bombs were used to attack the La Mon House Hotel, near Comber, Co. Down, while it was crowded with about five hundred people attending two social functions. Twelve people died instantly in the blaze, and twenty-three were badly burned. Following the attack, the security forces clamped down heavily on PSF and mounted a big effort to prove that it was working closely with PIRA. Meantime, PIRA prisoners in the Maze Prison staged a protest against the withdrawal of special category status. They refused to leave their cells to wash or go to the toilet. In August 1978 PIRA was blamed by the security forces for a series of bomb attacks on British army barracks in West Germany. On 21 September PIRA bomb attacks destroyed the terminal building at Eglinton airfield, and caused other extensive damage. In November the organisation murdered the deputy governor of Belfast Prison, Albert Miles, and bombed the centres of many towns and villages; on 30 November explosives and fire bombs were set off in fourteen centres. At the same time PIRA warned that it was 'preparing for a long war'. In November the Intelligence Staff of the Defence Ministry concluded that PIRA was still a force to be reckoned with. The Ministry's report, which was regarded as top secret, apparently fell into PIRA hands in May 1979. The leak of the report was obviously an embarrassment to Ministers. It predicted that PIRA would have the manpower to sustain violence during the next five years and that it would show 'more precise targeting and greater expertise'. And it said that the calibre of members of ASUs did not support the view that they were merely 'mindless hooligans'. It suggested that the Provisional leadership was committed to a long campaign of attrition, and events in the first half of 1979 indicated that it had settled on striking at a variety of targets – shops, offices, hotels, security installations – and keeping up its assault on members of the security forces and prison officers at about the same level as in 1978. PIRA's activities in the early 1980s became more diffuse, since some members were diverted to promoting the hunger-strike campaign and the efforts of H-Block and PSF candidates in Dáil elections in 1981 and 1982, and the 1982 NI Assembly election. This increased political involvement seems to have had full PIRA backing, and its muscle was obviously an element in strengthening anti-H-Block demon-strations, particularly the closing of business premises in Republican areas. The organisation had also to cope with the appearance of informers on a large

scale, so that 1982 became known as 'the year of the supergrass'. PIRA let it be known in early 1982 that there would be an amnesty for informers who made themselves and the extent of their disclosures known. This contrasted with the established PIRA practice of killing informers. But there were signs that the 1981 hunger strike brought extra recruits and resources and an increase in Republican solidarity. Army intelligence sources had reported in 1980 that PIRA strength could be 'measured in tens' but later the same year ex-GOC Sir Timothy Creasey talked of 500 hard-core terrorists overall in NI. But the deaths of ten hunger-strikers, seven of them PIRA and including Bobby Sands MP, undoubtedly spurred support from US Irish Republican sympathisers and others in Europe and elsewhere. And PIRA chiefs were obviously impressed by the arguments of people like Gerry Adams (later to become PSF president and MP for W. Belfast), that the Republican movement must have an increasing political content, with no prospect of 'Brits out' being achieved in the foreseeable future. Two PIRA prisoners in the Maze won Dáil seats in the June 1981 election. They were hunger-striker Kieran Doherty (Cavan–Monaghan), who later died from his fast, and Paddy Agnew (Louth) (see H-Blocks). In the early 1980s PIRA's NI campaign became extremely varied. Russian RPG rockets (handled with varying confidence), the M-60 machine gun, car and beer-keg bombs and landmines with plastic, gelignite and other inferior explosives, homemade mortars, and more sophisticated incendiaries incor-porating silicon chips – all these figured in assaults. Much of PIRA's effort in this period was directed against the security forces, but there were also attacks on property and two coal boats, the *Nellie M* and *St Bedan*, were sunk in Lough

Foyle. Some forty-two deaths were believed to have resulted from PIRA attacks in 1982. But the assassination which attracted most attention at this period was that of the S. Belfast Official Unionist MP, the Rev. Robert Bradford, shot in November 1981 at a community centre in Finaghy. He was the first Westminster MP for a NI seat to be killed in the Troubles. PIRA accused him of being 'one of the key people responsible for winding up the loyalist paramilitary sectarian machine'. In March 1982 it made an unsuccessful bid to assassinate Lord Chief Justice Lord Lowry at QUB. Immediately before that there was a lull in PIRA activity, and a PIRA spokesman admitted in March 1982 that they had supply and other problems. These no doubt included difficulties in getting explosives across the border, with the stepped-up operations of anti-terrorist units in the Republic. In mid-November 1982 three PIRA members were shot dead by the RUC near Lurgan when they were alleged to have driven through a check-point. The incident provoked much controversy and allegations that the RUC was operating a new 'shoot to kill' policy. This was denied by the authorities, although they admitted to the existence of specialised RUC anti-terrorist units. Controversy over the shootings had still not run its course by early 1989, when the House of Lords was due to consider whether RUC officers involved should be compelled to give evidence at the inquest. The Lurgan shootings came two weeks after three RUC men had been killed by a PIRA landmine in the area. The extent to which PIRA should mount attacks in GB has always been a matter of debate within the organisation. The result has been intermittent action there which has probably added greatly to the detection problems of the anti-terrorist squads. But PIRA chiefs are obviously attracted

by the greater publicity attached to such incidents. In October 1981 it placed a bomb in the car of Maj.-Gen. Sir Stuart Pringle, Commandant General of the Royal Marines, at his London home, as a result of which he lost a leg. The next month and on the eve of its assassination of Robert Bradford, it seriously damaged with a bomb the London home of Sir Michael Havers, the Attorney-General, although no one was injured. On 10 October 1981 it set off a nail bomb outside Chelsea barracks in London which killed a woman and injured twenty-three soldiers and seventeen civilians. But PIRA bombings in London on 20 July 1982 were much more spectacular, and clearly intended to dispel suggestions by the security forces that they were a waning force. Attacks by nail bombs on the Household Cavalry at Hyde Park and an army band at Regent's Park left ten soldiers dead and some fifty people injured, both soldiers and civilians, while seven army horses also died in the Hyde Park bombing. Margaret Thatcher denounced the attacks as 'callous and cowardly'. In the mid-1980s, in the course of the supergrass trials, some of the mystique of PIRA was dispelled by detailed disclosures on the life-style and *modus operandi* of ASUs. Scores of alleged PIRA members found themselves charged on the word of informers like Christopher Black, Robert Quigley, Kevin McGrady and Raymond Gilmour. The supergrass system was bitterly criticised by Nationalists and by the Irish Government, as well as a section of loyalism. Cardinal Ó Fiaich described it as 'internment under another name'. It eventually collapsed as many convictions were overturned on appeal, and some informers retracted their stories. But the widespread arrests disrupted many PIRA units, and in face of the challenge of the 'converted terrorist' – the RUC term – the PIRA army council set about reorganisation and the diversifying of tactics. One dramatic move was the mass break-out of thirty-eight prisoners from the Maze Prison in September 1983, with nineteen getting away. In early 1984 PIRA also shot dead the assistant governor of the prison because, according to prison officers, he threatened the PIRA command structure at the Maze. With PIRA apparently gearing up for fresh attacks in mainland Britain, British, Irish and US intelligence units had a major success in September 1984, when the trawler *Marita Ann* was intercepted off the Kerry coast with a huge cargo of arms and ammunition which it had transported across the Atlantic for PIRA. Thatcher remained a prime target of PIRA and in October 1984 it came close to killing her with its bombing of the Grand Hotel in Brighton. Among the aims of PIRA chiefs were the countering of Government attempts to promote an image of normality within NI, and to 'sicken' mainland opinion. (Interestingly, a 1984 MORI poll in GB showed 50 per cent of people believing that any attempt to solve the NI problem must have the co-operation of PIRA.) The Brighton bombing led to a major increase in anti-terrorist measures in GB, and killed PIRA's 1985 plan to bomb major seaside resorts. It was not until the summer of 1988 that PIRA struck again in London, with a bomb at the Inglis army barracks at Mill Hill, in which one soldier died. In the interim, its grand plan seemed to be to switch targets in a random way. In 1985, however, it mounted a sustained assault on RUC stations, mainly in border areas, to which it linked murder threats against contractors and their employees who became involved in repair of the stations. In the course of this campaign it killed nine RUC officers in a mortar attack on Newry station.

But at the same time, PIRA was quietly building up substantial supplies of new weapons and explosives from Libya. Two such shipments are believed to have reached Ireland in 1985 and two more in 1986. But this reinforcement of the PIRA effort seems not to have been suspected until the Irish-crewed vessel *Eksund* was intercepted by French customs in October 1987, with a massive cargo of weaponry and explosives, including ground-to-air missiles, heavy machine guns and plastic explosive. Libya denied involvement but French intelligence was satisfied that the *Eksund* had been loaded at Tripoli, and was intended to be shared between PIRA and a European terrorist group, possibly the Basque ETA which has always had strong links with PIRA. Libya's Colonel Gaddafi has repeatedly expressed sympathy with Irish republicanism, and his anger at British support for US air raids on Libya gave him an extra reason for wanting to hit British interests. As the extent of Libyan arms in PIRA hands became apparent, there was alarm in both British and Irish security establishments. They were forced to conclude that the PIRA arsenal was larger than ever before, and there were extensive searches on both sides of the border. Part of the Libyan haul was uncovered on a beach near Malin Head in Co. Donegal and there was a variety of smaller seizures. Many new PIRA bunkers were revealed on farms and in remote areas, ready to receive arms and to provide a choice of 'hides'. The AIA was a new spur to North–South security co-operation, and put severe pressure on PIRA lines of communication, where occasional carelessness proved costly to the organisation in terms of arms seizures. None the less, the widespread perception of PIRA as almost a spent force after the Enniskillen Remembrance Sunday atrocity in 1987, when it felt obliged to express 'deep regret' for the bombing in which eleven civilians died, was soon dispelled. Following Enniskillen, there was a series of similar blunders by PIRA which led to deaths of innocent civilians, but PIRA shrugged off such embarrassments, even if some PSF members found 'contradictions' arising from the armed struggle where PSF was seeking to maximise its vote. PIRA also has its own political role. No major Republican departure in policy (for example, the 1986 decision to end abstention from the Dáil) is taken without PIRA endorsement. PIRA has also hit at British Ministers' description of it as 'Marxist' and has also apparently ruled out any idea of a further ceasefire. But in the late 1980s it does seem to have suffered from lack of experienced terrorists to match the new sophistication of its weaponry. Some of its losses were obvious, including fourteen members shot dead by the SAS: eight as they attacked Loughgall RUC station (May 1987); three in Gibraltar (March 1988); and three more in Tyrone (August 1988). Indeed, PIRA suffered twenty-two casualties within NI between 1 January 1987 and 31 August 1988. But it also inflicted appreciable losses on the security forces during the same period: the twenty-four regular soldiers killed included eight in a landmine attack on their bus near Ballygawley (August 1988); six bombed in Lisburn after taking part in a 'fun run' (June 1988); and two shot dead after being attacked by mourners at a PIRA funeral in Belfast (March 1988). During the same twenty months, nineteen RUC members and eighteen UDR soldiers died. PIRA also mounted attacks on members of the security forces in Europe, forcing a change of car number plates by BAOR. In 1988 three off-duty RAF men died in Holland, and a soldier in Belgium. The inclusion of the Czechoslovakian

explosive Semtex in Libyan supplies also gave its campaign a new edge. Smaller and more powerful bombs resulted, and were evident in landmines in rural areas and a renewal of the assault on Belfast city centre in the summer of 1988. It used one of its new heavy machine guns to bring down an army helicopter in S. Armagh in 1988, and kept the security forces guessing as to how it might deploy ground-to-air missiles. In 1987 it killed Lord Justice Gibson and his wife Cecily and also UDA leader John McMichael, and in 1988 threatened civil servants and bombed the home of Stormont civil service chief Sir Kenneth Bloomfield, who escaped injury. At the end of 1988 PIRA attacked several housing estates occupied by army families. As the twentieth anniversary approached of the entry of the army in August 1969, it also mentioned politicians and members of the royal family as likely targets. It came under pressure from PSF to avoid the civilian casualties which were a strong feature of PIRA violence in 1987–8, and in response it was announced that a Donegal-based unit active on the Fermanagh border had been disbanded in January 1989.

PROVISIONAL SINN FÉIN
The political counterpart of PIRA, which dates from January 1970, when the split occurred in the Republican movement. At the Ard Fheis (annual conference) in Dublin, the dispute centred on whether Sinn Féin should drop its long-standing policy of non-recognition of the Parliaments in Belfast and Dublin. Those against recognition called themselves the Provisionals – an echo of the 'Provisional Government' of 1916 – and they walked out to set up their own organisation with HQ in Kevin Street, Dublin. There was another important point of difference between the two groups. Those who remained in what

became known as Official Sinn Féin (eventually the Worker's Party) inclined to a Marxist approach. PSF policy was rooted in the demand for British withdrawal from NI, usually expressed in the slogan 'Brits out'. Originally, it favoured a phased withdrawal and Ruairí Ó Brádaigh, who became its president in 1970, defended this approach on the grounds that they did not want a sudden British pull-out which could create a Congo situation. But its 1980 Ard Fheis committed the party to calling for immediate British withdrawal. At the 1981 Ard Fheis it effectively abandoned its initial policy of a federal Ireland, with parliaments for each of the four provinces, which it called 'Éire Nua'. This issue produced bitter debate, with the change spearheaded by the NI leaders, headed by the then vice-president Gerry Adams, while leading Southern figures such as Ó Brádaigh, and Dáithí Ó Conaill argued for the status quo. The federal idea was seen by its supporters as a gesture to NI loyalists, but the new NI leaders of PSF were in no mood for compromise and the change was sealed at the 1982 Ard Fheis. In 1981 PSF also decided to take up any seats won in council elections in NI. This removed an anomaly because the party was already contesting local elections in the Republic and it held thirty-six seats on twenty-six councils in fourteen counties. (During the 1956 IRA campaign, the former Sinn Féin took four Dáil seats on an abstentionist basis, one being held by Ó Brádaigh.) Increasingly, there was pressure from within PSF to seek elected status since one of the party's obvious aims was to supplant the SDLP as the main voice of NI Nationalists. In the early 1980s PSF's total membership is believed to have been around 5,000 with 400 branches (or *cumainn*) throughout Ireland. Although a registered political party in the Republic, its spokesmen have been denied access to TV and radio there. This ban was first imposed by the Coalition Government of 1973–7, and the then Minister for Posts and Telegraphs, Dr Conor Cruise O'Brien, defended it on the grounds that PSF was essentially a front for PIRA. This ban was continued by successive governments, including those of Fianna Fáil, and it survived a PSF challenge to its constitutionality in the Courts in 1982. In NI a long-standing ban on Sinn Féin was raised by the British Government in 1974 in the hope that it would contest the 1975 Convention elections. But it decided to ignore these contests, although Albert Price, father of the Price sisters (who had been convicted of the London bombings in 1973), supported PSF policies when he stood unsuccessfully as an Independent in W. Belfast in the February 1974 Westminster election. At this period Maire Drumm was the leading PSF personality in Belfast, as a vice-president. She was murdered by loyalists in the city's Mater Hospital in 1976. Senior Belfast members of PSF were involved in talks with British officials in 1975, and party members manned the seven incident centres set up to monitor the PIRA ceasefire and maintain contact with the NIO. Although the British Government insisted that the officials were doing no more than explaining British policy and were not engaged in negotiations, the exercise brought sharp criticism from Unionist and other politicians in NI, who claimed that it tended to give credibility to PSF. There is no bar to dual membership of PSF and PIRA, and most leading people in Sinn Féin have had a background associated with PIRA or the earlier IRA. Normally, at least one member of the PSF executive, or ard comhairle, is on PIRA's army council. In Belfast PIRA statements are put out through the PSF office via telex to the media. Far from retreating from support for the campaign of violence,

PSF spokesmen have increasingly insisted that political action cannot succeed in itself in the NI situation in advancing its aims. At the 1982 Ard Fheis it was decided that all future PSF candidates must give their 'unambivalent' support to the 'armed struggle'. At the 1981 Ard Fheis PSF's director of publicity, Danny Morrison, articulated the policy in these words: 'Who here really believes that we can win the war through the ballot-box? But will anyone here object if, with a ballot paper in this hand and an Armalite in this hand, we take power in Ireland?' Morrison was speaking at a point where two PIRA prisoners in the Maze had secured election in the Republic's general election of June 1981 – hunger-striker Kieran Doherty (who fasted to death) in Cavan–Monaghan; and Paddy Agnew in Louth. PSF joined other anti-H-Block elements in that campaign, but PSF alone was unable to repeat these successes in the February 1982 election and it had under 2 per cent of the vote in the 1987 Dáil election. In NI the hunger strike brought Sinn Féin more substantial benefits. In Fermanagh–S. Tyrone it had backed PIRA hunger-striker Bobby Sands in his successful campaign in the April 1981 by-election for Westminster. And a rank-and-file member of PSF, Owen Carron, was elected as an abstentionist to fill the vacancy created by Sands's death. The October 1982 Assembly election found PSF urging initially a boycott of the new institution and the election, but it also committed itself to fighting the election on an abstentionist ticket if a general Nationalist boycott could not be achieved. In the event SDLP's decision to run candidates, but not to attend the Assembly, seems to have benefited PSF, which ran twelve candidates. Many Nationalists apparently saw PSF as representing a more dynamic boycott policy at a time when there was intense polarisation in the community. The outcome for PSF was highly gratifying in terms of its overall 10 per cent vote, but it might have expected to get more than the five seats which it actually won, since Alliance, with fewer votes, had got ten seats. None the less, it was a breakthrough, and encouraged PSF to talk of fighting as many as possible of the seventeen new Westminster seats. The first major controversy sparked off by the election came in December 1982 when two of the successful PSF Assembly candidates, Gerry Adams (W. Belfast) and Danny Morrison (Mid-Ulster), were invited to London by GLC leader Ken Livingstone to explain their policies. Both were banned from GB by Home Secretary William Whitelaw under the Prevention of Terrorism Act. The ban also applied to Derry Assembly member, Martin McGuinness. Thatcher claimed that the ban had been imposed for security and not political reasons. The 1983 Westminster election was broadly successful for PSF. It did not make a net advance in terms of seats, since it gained only W. Belfast and lost Fermanagh–S. Tyrone, but it achieved its target of 100,000 votes and had a percentage poll of 13.4 – 3 per cent more than in the 1982 Assembly election. It also failed by only 78 votes to win Mid-Ulster. Gerry Adams's victory in W. Belfast attracted attention for two reasons – it led to the unseating of colourful MP Gerry Fitt, who had held the seat for seventeen years, and it was secured in face of strong warnings from the Catholic Church against supporting a group committed to backing PIRA violence. Adams's triumph also reinforced his growing authority in PSF, and it was no surprise that he was elected president later that year. The balance of power in PSF had now shifted decisively to the North. The 1984 European election saw Danny Morrison (PSF publicity director) virtually maintain the PSF 1983 vote in percentage terms, although he was 10 per cent behind John Hume. In 1984 the organisation developed its advice-centre network and strongly pushed community issues in readiness for its foray into council politics in NI in 1985. Unionists, outraged at Gerry Adams's description of the 1984 Brighton bombing as 'an inevitable result of Britain's inter-ference in Irish affairs' and 'a democratic act', made repeated calls for proscription of PSF. In the event, PSF was well satisfied with the outcome of the 1985 elections – it ended up with fifty-nine council seats and 11.8 per cent of the votes. Indeed, the PSF showing set alarm bells ringing in London and Dublin and undoubtedly helped along the Anglo-Irish process, which was to produce the AIA later that year. British and Irish Ministers looked to the AIA to strengthen the appeal of the SDLP, and Thatcher also looked for easier extradition from the South and stronger cross-border security co-operation – both prospects unwelcome to the Provisionals. Certainly, PSF found the going hard in the January 1986 by-elections forced by the Unionists in protest at the AIA. In four constituencies where there was a PSF–SDLP clash, there was a 6 per cent swing from PSF to SDLP as compared with 1983, a trend which helped SDLP to gain Newry and Armagh. PSF in the council chambers infuriated Unionists, and Ministers refused to talk to PSF councillors, although they recognised the few PSF council chairmen. In 1986 Adams and his supporters forced another major change on the party – a decision to occupy any Dáil seats won in elections. The question gave rise to angry debate, and Southern tradition-alists like Ó Brádaigh and Ó Conaill walked out of PSF to establish Republican Sinn Féin. But the general loss in membership to RSF was

minimal. In the 1987 Westminster election PSF also felt the effects of the AIA. The PSF vote dropped 2 per cent compared with 1983, while the SDLP put on 3 per cent. The party took comfort, however, from its retention of W. Belfast, where SDLP mounted a determined challenge and got Alliance votes. Shortly before the 1987 election, PSF put out a policy document, 'Scenario for Peace', which suggested an all-Ireland convention to work out a new Irish constitution, British financial support for a time towards a united Ireland, and written guarantees for loyalists. In 1988 the party seemed to be in a mood of reassessment and to be looking for a pan-Nationalist front. And in the first nine months of 1988 it had talks with the SDLP. These apparently left both parties as far apart as ever, although the PSF argued that they had helped morale in the Nationalist community. The PSF analysis of the situation was firmly rejected by John Hume, who failed to persuade Gerry Adams that the AIA had made simple 'Brits out' politics redundant. For PSF, the test of the 1989 council elections loomed ahead, with the party allowing its nominees to sign a statutory anti-violence declaration, despite the possibility of civil actions in the courts when it was breached. Its leaders were also active in seeking ways round the broadcasting ban imposed in late 1988 on supporters outside election periods. There were moves to build a nationalist grouping wider than PSF to fight the 1989 European election. In January 1989 the Ard Fheis featured a strong appeal to PIRA to try to avoid accidental civilian deaths likely to frighten off electoral support.

PYM, LORD
As Francis Pym, NI Secretary of State, November 1973–February 1974. b. 13 February 1922. MP for Cambridgeshire S.E., 1983–7. Defence Secretary,

1979–82. Foreign Secretary, 1982–3. On taking office as Secretary of State, he was immediately plunged into the Sunningdale Conference, but in the event, the PM, Edward Heath, and his predecessor as NI Secretary, William Whitelaw, were more directly involved in the negotiations which led to the setting up of the three-party power-sharing Executive on 1 January 1974. He was, however, involved in the Stormont ceremony of the swearing-in of the new Executive members. Shortly afterwards, there was a PIRA threat to kill him because he had interned a Derry man. He had no real opportunity to make his presence felt in NI since the Conservatives were defeated in the February 1974 general election, and he was succeeded by Labour's Merlyn Rees.

R

RATHCAVAN, LORD

As Phelim O'Neill, first leader of the Alliance Parliamentary Party, 1972–3. b. 2 November 1909. One of NI's most individualistic politicians, he switched from the Unionist Party to the Alliance Party shortly before direct rule was declared in 1972, and with two other MPs formed the first Alliance group at Stormont. A cousin of Terence O'Neill (PM, 1963–9) and son of first Lord Rathcavan (first Speaker at Stormont and for many years MP for N. Antrim at Westminster), Phelim O'Neill rarely toed the party line, and often treated Ministers scornfully in the former Stormont House of Commons. He described his politics as 'left-wing Conservative'. He was Unionist MP for N. Antrim at Westminster from 1952 to 1959, and Stormont MP for N. Antrim, 1969–72. He was Minister of Education in NI Government in 1969 and Minister of Agriculture, 1969–71. He led the Alliance delegation at the Darlington conference in 1972. He was expelled from the Orange Order in 1958 after attending a Catholic service during a community week in Bally-money. When he switched to Alliance he said that whether they liked it or not, both the Unionists and the SDLP were sectarian parties. He succeeded to the title in 1982, when his father died aged ninety-nine.

REAGAN, RONALD

US President, 1981–9. b. 6 February 1911. One of the many US Presidents who can claim Irish ancestry. His great-grandfather, Michael O'Regan, left Ballyporeen, on the Tipperary–Cork border, during the Irish potato famine in the 1840s. The family went first to the Peckham area of London, and later to Illinois. Although his parents were married in a Catholic Church in Fulton, Illinois, his Protestant mother brought him up in her faith. In the early period of his presidency, he avoided any deep entanglement with the Irish issue. Although Taoiseach Charles Haughey was among St Patrick's Day guests at the White House in 1981, the President did not endorse Haughey's bid to make Irish unity a stated objective of US foreign policy. In his 1981 St Patrick's Day statement he 'took note' of the violence and suffering in NI and the importance to the US of a 'peaceful, just and swift solution'. He also urged Americans on this and other occasions not to give money which might be used for violence. While welcoming the Anglo-Irish initiative, the President made it clear in a letter to Taoiseach Garret FitzGerald in December 1981 that his administration had no position on the question of Irish unity. He said it was not for the US to chart a course which others must follow, and that if solutions in NI were to endure, they must come from the people who lived there. He also appears not to have responded to a plea by the Irish Government in 1981 to intervene with Britain over the Maze hunger strike. But the following year, the President did see the Republic having some role in a settlement, while Thatcher was insisting that Britain had no obligation to consult the Republic on NI affairs. Certainly, Reagan praised the New Ireland Forum initiative on his visit to the Republic in 1984. It seems likely that Speaker 'Tip' O'Neill was a strong influence on the President in securing a positive White House approach to a strong Anglo-Irish initiative, and the idea of US financial aid to back it. It appears that within a month of her 'out, out, out' comments on the Forum options, Thatcher was being told by the President in Washington (December 1984) of his deep interest in progress on NI at a meeting arranged to discuss the Star Wars project. When the AIA was signed, he stressed strong US support for it. The President has clearly enjoyed his St Patrick's Day parties in Washington. At a 1987 gathering he recalled that St Patrick had died in AD 461, adding: 'Leave it to the Irish to be carrying on a wake for 1,500 years.'

RED HAND COMMANDOS

A loyalist paramilitary group launched in 1972, and declared illegal in 1973 at the same time as the UFF. It was believed to be involved in sectarian assassinations. In 1974 the RHC in Fermanagh and S. Tyrone wrote to a local newspaper threatening to shoot five Catholics for every Protestant killed in border areas. When Secretary of State Merlyn Rees met loyalist paramilitaries on 7 August 1974, it was claimed that the UVF delegate also spoke for the RHC. It announced a ceasefire a few days later, but said it reserved the right to defend loyalist

lives and property. In 1978 there was further evidence of its association with the UVF – a statement from a prisoners' council representing both organisations in the Maze Prison. There was a claim that it had murdered E. Belfast loyalist John McKeague in 1982, but the INLA claim was generally accepted. McKeague always denied reports that he had been one of the founders of RHC. In 1985 it claimed to have placed a bomb in Castlewellan after the banning of an Orange parade in the town, but nothing was found. In 1987 it claimed a blast bomb in Short Strand in Belfast.

REES, MERLYN

Secretary of State for NI, March 1974–September 1976. b. 18 December 1920. When he arrived at Stormont, Merlyn Rees had been Labour Party spokesman on NI for two years. He had been at the Home Office with James Callaghan in 1969, and as a teacher he was familiar with Irish history. He was immediately faced with a crisis. The general election which had brought Labour to office and Rees to Stormont had also given the UUUC eleven of the twelve NI seats at Westminster. And the loyalists were not slow to claim the result as a landslide against the whole existence of the power-sharing Executive at Stormont which had taken office on 1 January. The UUUC was pledged to fight the Sunningdale Agreement, on which the Executive was based. Its main slogan was 'Dublin is just a Sunningdale away', indicating its opposition not only to Unionists joining the SDLP in government, but to any cross-border Council of Ireland. With nearly 60 per cent of all votes secured by anti-White Paper candidates, 51 per cent by loyalists alone, the UUUC presented the outcome as a vote of no confidence in the Executive and demanded fresh Assembly elections. At the same time, PIRA stepped up its bombing campaign, and made it more difficult for Rees to accelerate the phasing out of internment. Then, on 13 May 1974, he faced his biggest test. Loyalists, led by the Ulster Workers' Council, which brought together politicians and paramilitary leaders, as well as some key shop stewards, mounted what they called a 'constitutional stoppage': With loyalist paramilitary groups backing the strike, together with power workers, much of industry came to a standstill. And with many accusations of intimidation directed against the strikers, Rees was under intense pressure to use troops to keep power stations going and to maintain essential supplies. The Executive, whose morale was already shaken by the election result, was urging Rees to adopt a much tougher line against the strikers. But while he refused to negotiate with the strike organisers, Rees and the British Government were obviously cautious about using the army directly to help break the strike. And this attitude clearly reflected the senior army view that 'the game isn't worth the candle'. Rees also appears to have been doubtful about the capacity of the Executive to survive in any event. With vital services threatened, particularly sewerage, the Unionist members resigned on the fifteenth day of the strike, and the Secretary of State decided to end the Executive and resume direct rule. Rees told MPs that NI now needed a breathing space. He also called the loyalists 'Ulster Protestant Nationalists'. On 4 July 1974 Rees announced a new initiative – an elected Constitutional Convention to work out a political settlement. And during that summer he resisted strong pressure from Unionists for a new Home Guard or Third Force to supplement the efforts of the RUC and UDR. In mid-September he had talks with the Dublin Government aimed at improving cross-border security

co-operation. But the SDLP was clearly unhappy with Rees: the party's then deputy leader, John Hume, said in October that he had lost all credibility. In November 1974 came the horrific Birmingham bombings and Rees was immediately involved in bringing in the new Prevention of Terrorism legislation so far as it affected NI. The effect was to allow people to be deported from Britain to both the Republic and NI, and after protests that this would turn NI into a 'Devil's Island', Rees took power to expel people from NI to the Republic. Oddly enough, the tightening of security laws coincided with a meeting in early December 1974 between Churchmen and Provisionals (both IRA and Sinn Féin) at Feakle, Co. Clare – a meeting which was kept secret until it had ended and which was widely criticised by loyalists. But it offered Rees a pause in PIRA violence. After a brief stop over Christmas, the Provisionals declared a ceasefire on 10 February 1975. The Feakle Talks had produced a document which the Churchmen involved conveyed to Rees. But he insisted that the PIRA demands (including a call for a declaration of intent of British withdrawal) would not be considered by the Government, although 'a genuine and sustained cessation of violence over a period would create a new situation'. None the less, the ceasefire got a degree of official co-operation. Rees authorised the setting up of seven 'incident centres' manned by Provisionals so that they could make contact easily with Government officials. The purpose was to prevent a small incident developing into a threat to the ceasefire. But the exercise was regarded with great suspicion by loyalists, and the army, apparently, were also unhappy about it. The Secretary of State was evidently activated by the hope that the Provisionals might become 'politicised' as a result of the facility, which he had also granted them, of direct talks, if not negotiations, with Government officials. But the Provisionals showed no interest in the Convention elections in 1975, and more importantly, these elections gave the UUUC a decisive overall majority. This ruled out any prospect of a repeat of the power-sharing experiment. By the summer of 1975, the PIRA ceasefire was no more than a technicality. The overall total of deaths in 1975 was 247. This included an estimated 144 deaths arising from inter-factional or sectarian assas-sinations, many of them carried out by loyalists. However, at the end of 1975 Rees set free the last of those detained without trial. And in 1976 he witnessed the final collapse of the Constitutional Convention, and the death toll increased yet again. In September Rees moved to the post of Home Secretary, and was succeeded by the Defence Secretary, Roy Mason. As Shadow Home Secretary in August 1979, he declared that PIRA could not be defeated militarily, and that any attempt to reintroduce internment would be 'a grave error of judgement'. In his memoirs, published in 1985, he said: 'The hope of finding a successful solution lies with the Northern Irish people, not with outsiders in Dublin and London talking by proxy.' In November 1987 he urged a top-level reassessment of the AIA and revealed in the Commons that he was 'extremely worried' about allegations of army undercover activities in NI during his period of office.

REFORMS
The changes which have taken place outside the security field include: the closing down of the Stormont Parlia-ment in March 1972, and the intro-duction of direct rule from Westminster (interrupted only by the five-month tenure of the NI Executive in 1974); the

acceptance of the principle of one man, one vote and the use of PR for all elections except those for Westminster; the dismantling of the system of local government and its replacement by area boards to cover health, education, libraries and so on, with twenty-six District Councils with very limited powers; the setting up of a central Housing Executive to look after all public housing; the establishment of a Community Relations Department and Community Relations Commission (both subsequently dropped); the appointment of a Standing Advisory Commission on Human Rights, and the creation of an Ombudsman and Commissioner of Complaints to inquire into charges of maladmin-istration by Government departments and other public bodies (the posts have been merged); the setting up of a Fair Employment Agency and an Equal Opportunities Commission to guard against discrimination in employment on grounds of religion or sex respectively. In 1980 divorce laws were brought into line with those in GB, and in 1982 the laws on homosexuality were treated similarly after they had been condemned by the European Court of Human Rights. In 1988 laws against sex discrimination in employment were strengthened and at the end of the year a new Fair Employment Bill was presented to Parliament.

REID, RICHARD
DUP Convention member for Mid-Ulster, 1975–6. b. 1922. Cookstown District Council, 1973–81. Refused to stand again after a party disagreement. Founder member of the DUP.

RELIGION
The Churches may still exercise vast influence in NI, which has about fifty sects in addition to the main denom-inations, but the 1981 census showed

nearly one person in five refusing to state their religion. This was about twice the non-return level of the previous census in 1971. The main Churches had the following declared members in 1981: Catholic, 414,532; Presbyterian, 339,818; Church of Ireland, 281,472; Methodist, 58,731; Baptist, 16,375; Brethren, 12,158; Free Presbyterians (led by Rev. Ian Paisley), 9,621; Congregationalist, 8,265. More than 10,000 gave an indefinite answer, while 14,318 used the term, 'Protestant', and 8,695 described themselves simply as 'Christian'. There were 517 Jews and 26 members of the highly localised 'Cooneyites'. But there were also 1,171 agnostics and 730 atheists, while 274,584 did not give any answer. Expert calculations since the 1981 census suggest that the Catholic share of the NI population was 39 per cent in 1987, as compared with the estimate current for many years of 35 per cent. There are doubts as to whether the religious question will be included in the 1991 census. In 1981 the then Health Minister, John Patten, commented that the information obtained on religion was of very little value in the light of public response.

REPUBLICAN CLUBS *see* Workers' Party, The

REPUBLICAN LABOUR PARTY
Founded in Belfast in 1960, when two MPs for Stormont seats of Dock and Falls, Gerry Fitt (Dock Labour Party) and Harry Diamond (Socialist Republican), decided to unite under one label. It supported a non-violent republicanism, linked to socialist objectives, and when Fitt was elected to Westminster for W. Belfast in 1966, he supported the British Labour Party in the lobbies. Harry Diamond, who had represented the Falls constituency under various labels, including Éire

Labour and Socialist Republican, lost the seat in 1969 general election to Paddy Devlin of the NILP. But Paddy Kennedy gained the Belfast Central seat. In the 1969 election, Rep. Lab. ran five candidates, and got 2.4 per cent of the total vote. The party was active in the civil rights campaign, but it split in 1970 when Fitt assumed the leadership of the newly formed SDLP. When Kennedy withdrew from Stormont in 1971, the party also withdrew its six councillors from Belfast Corporation, and it was heavily engaged in the civil disobedience campaign directed against internment without trial. Kennedy's failure to win a seat in the 1973 Assembly election marked the disappearance of Rep. Lab. as an electoral force.

REPUBLICAN SINN FÉIN
The breakaway group which emerged after the PSF Ard Fheis in 1986 voted to end abstention from the Dáil. It opposed the change, and included the two main PSF figures in the Republic – Ruairí Ó Brádaigh, former president, and Dáithí Ó Conaill, ex-PIRA chief of staff. Ó Brádaigh became first president and Ó Conaill first vice-president. According to a spokesman, RSF would remain in support of the armed struggle and Republican prisoners. At its 1988 Ard Fheis it reaffirmed support for 'an armed struggle to re-establish the democratic socialist republic'.

RICHARDS, SIR BROOKS
Security Co-ordinator, NIO, 1980–1. b. 18 July 1918. Succeeded late Sir Maurice Oldfield in Stormont post after a long career in the diplomatic service and a period at the Cabinet Office as Intelligence Co-ordinator.

RICHARDSON, SIR ROBERT FRANCIS
Army GOC, NI, 1982–5. b. 2 March

1929. Commanded 39th Infantry Brigade in NI, 1974–5. Army's director of manning, 1980–1. In March 1983 he said it was important to reduce the role of the army to the point where it was seen by everyone as supporting the civil power, and not the visible embodiment of that power.

RITCHIE, BRIGADIER CHARLES
Commander, UDR, 1988–. b. 1942. After Sandhurst, commissioned in Royal Scots Regiment, 1961; served two brief tours in NI, 1971–2, with another Scottish regiment. He returned to Sandhurst as an instructor until 1978 when he became a staff officer with the British Commanders in Chief (Soviet Mission) in West Germany. After attending the National Defence College in 1981, he returned to NI to command 3rd (Co. Down) Battalion UDR until 1983. His two most recent appointments were at the Joint Staff Defence College at Greenwich until 1985 and Assistant Director Military Assistance Overseas (Army). In the 1960s he served a year in Libya and from 1965 to 1967 he was ADC to the Governor of Victoria in Australia.

ROBB, JOHN
Founder of the New Ireland Group in 1982, and earlier the New Ireland Movement. Irish Senator, 1982–. b. 1932. As a Protestant Ulsterman, and a surgeon at the Royal Victoria Hospital in Belfast in the early 1970s, he was so moved by the results of the bombing that he began campaigning for a new approach to local problems. His proposals have included the idea of Britain and the Republic foregoing all claims to sovereignty over NI so that they could jointly sponsor a new constitutional convention in NI and jointly guarantee its outcome. He says he was greatly influenced by the philosophy of Gandhi during a visit to India and by seeing Mother Theresa of

Calcutta visiting a Belfast woman blinded by the violence and who was the mother of eight children. His appointment by Charles Haughey to the Irish Senate in 1982 caused some surprise, and one of his first acts there was to call for cross-border extradition arrangements. Member of RTE Authority, 1973–7.

ROBINSON, PETER DAVID
Deputy leader of the DUP; MP for E. Belfast, 1979–. Assembly member for E. Belfast, 1982–6. b. 1948. His career has epitomised the rise of the DUP. In 1975 he became full-time general secretary, and was an unsuccessful candidate that year in the Convention election in E. Belfast. But two years later he was on Castlereagh Council, and in 1979 gained a surprise victory in E. Belfast, when he unseated William Craig, OUP, by sixty-four votes in a five-way contest. As deputy leader of the DUP, he has been at Rev. Ian Paisley's side in the various DUP campaigns, notably in opposition to the Anglo-Irish talks in early 1981 and the AIA since 1985. In 1981 he was associated with the Third Force and demands for tougher security, and with the 'Ulster Resistance' organisation which developed in the early days of the anti-AIA campaign. With his two party colleagues, he was suspended from the Commons in 1981 in the row arising from the assassination of the Rev. Robert Bradford MP. In the 1982 Assembly elections he headed the poll in E. Belfast, and was chairman of the Assembly's Environment Committee and deputy chairman of the Devolution Committee. In August 1986 he accompanied some hundreds of loyalists on a late-night incursion into the Co. Monaghan village of Clontibret to prove, he claimed, that there was a 'gaping hole' in border security. Two members of the Garda Síochána were injured by loyalists and

this led to Secretary of State Tom King expressing his regret to Dublin for the incident. Robinson was eventually fined IR£15,000 for unlawful assembly. In 1987 he was active in protests against the new public order laws, and was a member of a three-man task force set up by the two Unionist leaders to consider anti-AIA strategy. In October 1987 he resigned as DUP deputy leader, apparently because he disagreed with tactics in the anti-AIA campaign, but took up the post again three months later without making any detailed explanation. He served several brief prison sentences for refusal to pay fines arising from protests against the AIA and the public order laws. At one point in 1988 both he and his wife, Iris, were in prison at the same time. Mayor of Castlereagh, 1986. Participant in Duisburg Talks, October 1988.

RODGERS, BRID
General Secretary of SDLP, 1981–3. Irish Senator, 1983–7. Party chairwoman, 1978–80. Advisory Commission on Human Rights, 1977–80. Craigavon Council, 1985–. Formerly on Southern Education and Library Board.

ROLLING DEVOLUTION see
Systems of Government section, p. 367

ROSE, PAUL
Labour MP for Blackley, Manchester, 1964–79, and chairman of the Campaign for Democracy in Ulster, 1965–73. b. 26 December 1935. LLB Hons (Manchester). He led many deputations of MPs to see Ministers in the early days of the civil rights campaign, and frequently visited NI on fact-finding trips. Resigned as chairman in 1973 on the publication of the White Paper on the future government of NI and from Parliament in 1979 in frustration at the role of backbenchers.

ROSS, LORD (OF NEWPORT)
As Stephen Ross, Liberal Party spokesman on NI, June 1979–83. b. 1926. Liberal MP for Isle of Wight, February 1974–87. LLB, MA (Edinburgh).

ROSS, WILLIAM
OUP MP for E. Londonderry, 1983–. MP for Londonderry, 1974–83. b. 4 February 1936. Farms at Dungiven, Co. Londonderry, and agricultural spokesman of the OUP Parliamentary Party, 1974–. Secretary of the local Unionist Association before entering Parliament. In April 1982 he resigned from the National Union of Conservative and Unionist Associations and three of its committees as a protest against James Prior's 'rolling devolution' initiative. In 1987 he urged a return to the Airey Neave formula of 1979 for local government. Member of the Monday Club. In 1988 he opposed power-sharing because it would have an in-built Nationalist veto.

ROSSI, SIR HUGH
Minister of State, NIO, 1979–81. b. 21 June 1927. LLB (London). Solicitor. Knight of Holy Sepulchre, 1966. Conservative MP for Hornsey, 1966–83; Hornsey and Woodgreen, 1983–. Government Whip, 1970–2. Council of Europe Whip, 1971–3. Lord Commissioner of Treasury, 1972–4. Parliamentary Under-Secretary, Department of Environment, 1974. Deputy leader, UK delegation to Council of Europe, 1972–3. Responsible at NIO for Finance and Manpower Services. On leaving NIO, he became Social Security Minister. He was dropped from the Government after the 1983 election but given knighthood.

ROWNTREE TRUST
The Joseph Rowntree Social Service Trust has contributed substantially to

help political parties and pressure groups in NI. Its total grants in 1974 amounted to £70,000. Some £11,000 of this went to the SDLP, including a contribution to the party's election expenses in October 1974. The Alliance Party, NILP and the New Ulster Movement have also been helped, and the Trust assisted the loyalist paramilitaries to finance a conference in Belfast in 1975, and contributed to the expenses of para-military delegates attending an Oxford conference on NI in 1974.

ROYAL BLACK INSTITUTION

Effectively the senior branch of the Orange Order. Its full title is the Imperial Grand Black Chapter of the British Commonwealth. Like the Orange Order, it has a substantial membership outside NI, including lodges in GB, US, Canada, Australia, New Zealand and various African countries. Its HQ is at Lurgan, Co. Armagh, and its sovereign grand master is OUP leader James Molyneaux MP. Its main demonstrations are staged on the last Saturday of August each year, when some 30,000 members parade with bands and banners. The 'Blackmen', as they are commonly termed, also sponsor an event on 13 July each year – the 'sham fight' at Scarva, Co. Armagh – when a colourful mock battle is staged between 'King William' and 'King James'. Although there are few political speeches at its demonstrations, it is just as committed as the Orange Order generally to unionism and defence of Protestantism.

ROYAL ULSTER CONSTABULARY
see Security System section, pp. 385–9

RUBBER BULLET see Security
System section, p. 395

S

SANDELSON, NEVILLE DEVONSHIRE
SDP spokesman on NI, 1981–3. b. 27 November 1923. MP for Hayes and Harlington, 1971–83. (Labour, 1971–81; SDP, 1981–3.)

SANDS, ROBERT (BOBBY)
Anti-H-Block MP for Fermanagh–S. Tyrone, April–May 1981. b. Rathcoole, Belfast, 1954; d. 5 May 1981 on hunger strike in Maze Prison, on sixty-sixth day of his fast in support of the demand for political status or the 'five demands' (see H-Blocks). He was the first of ten Republican prisoners to die during the protest. In 1972 Sands's family moved from Rathcoole to Twinbrook, on the fringe of W. Belfast, and are said to have been forced by loyalists to move home. He was sentenced in 1973 to five years' imprisonment on an arms charge, and had special category status in the Maze Prison until his release in April 1976. Soon afterwards, he and three others were found in a car with weapons. In 1977 he was sentenced to fourteen years' imprisonment, and alleged that he had been subjected to ill-treatment while being interrogated at Castle-reagh. He immediately joined PIRA prisoners protesting against the denial of special category status, and during the 1980 hunger strike became leader of the PIRA prisoners in the H-Blocks. On 1 March 1981 he began his fast 'unto death' in support of political status, and the readiness of some 30,000 voters in Fermanagh–S. Tyrone to give him a majority in the April by-election (see Election Results section, p. 338) gave a new spur to repub-licanism. Many politicians and Churchmen sought to persuade him to end his fast, among them Monsignor

John Magee, Newry-born emissary of Pope John Paul II, who gave Sands a crucifix sent by the Pope. Westminster moved quickly to prevent another hunger-striker being nominated for the by-election following his death. Teheran named one of its thorough-fares Bobby Sands Street.

SANDY ROW

Ultra-loyalist area close to central Belfast, usually linked with the Shankill Road as denoting militant Protest-antism. During the 1969 violence, local people put up barricades at the Boyne Bridge to prevent, they said, Repub-licans entering from the nearby Grosvenor Road area. Some bomb damage was caused to pubs and other premises in the main thoroughfare. Housing in the area has been radically improved.

SAOR ÉIRE

This name appeared originally in Dublin in 1931 as the title of a strongly left-wing Republican group, which was declared illegal for a time in Southern Ireland. It had some support from the IRA at the time. The name emerged again in the early 1960s as the Saor Éire Action Group, and it was blamed for many bank raids in the Republic in 1966 and 1967. In 1971 a Marxist journal, *Red Mole,* carried what purported to be a statement from Saor Éire strongly criticising the Official Republican movement. In 1973 there were claims of a threat by its Derry unit to avenge sectarian murders by loyalists. In the same year there were reports of misappropriation of funds by some of its leaders. In 1975 it was credited with a threat to take action against either the IRSP or the OIRA if those two groups did not cease their feud in Belfast. The group has been regarded by the security forces in NI as a minor element in the violence, and little credence is attached to a claim that it was responsible for

killing some members of the security forces in 1972.

SCARMAN TRIBUNAL

The inquiry body which investigated the riots and shootings in the summer of 1969. Mr Justice (now Lord) Scarman presided, and he was assisted by two NI businessmen – William Marshall, Protestant, and George Lavery, Catholic. It heard 400 witnesses at 170 sittings. It reported in April 1972 that there was no plot to overthrow the NI Government or to mount an armed insurrection. The riots were described as communal distur-bances arising from a complex political, social and economic situation. It also said that while there was no conspiracy, it would be the height of naïveté to deny that the teenage hooligans, who almost invariably threw the first stones, were manipulated and encouraged by those seeking to discredit the Government. The tribunal found that the RUC was seriously at fault on six occasions. It said there was lack of firm direction in handling the disturbances in Derry during the early evening of 12 August; in the decision to put the USC (B Specials) on riot control in Dungannon and Armagh without disarming them; and in the use of Browning machine guns in Belfast on 14 and 15 August. It described as 'wholly unjustifiable' the firing of a Browning gun into Divis Flats on the Falls Road, where Patrick Rooney, aged nine, had been shot dead. The RUC were also blamed for failing to prevent Protestant mobs from burning the homes of Catholics in Belfast, and for failure to take any effective action to disperse crowds or protect lives and property in the riot areas on 15 August before the army came in. The tribunal said the RUC did, however, struggle manfully to do their duty in a situation they could not control, and their courage had been beyond praise.

The report added: 'Once large-scale communal disturbances occur, they are not susceptible to control by police. Either they must be suppressed by over-whelming force which, save in the last resort, is not acceptable in our society – and it was not within the control of the NI Government – or a political solution must be devised.' The tribunal cleared the RUC of the charge that it was a partisan force co-operating with Protestant mobs to attack Catholics. But it added that the incidents in W. Belfast on 14 August had resulted in a complete loss of confidence by the Catholic community in the police force as it was then constituted. The USC was said to have neither the training nor the equipment for riot duty, and outside Belfast it had shown on several occasions a lack of discipline with firearms. The tribunal found that politicians opposed to the Government, and specifically the Rev. Ian Paisley, had not been implicated in the violence, although their speeches had helped to build up tension. It found that the Protestant and Catholic communities had exhibited the same fears, the same sort of self-help, and the same distrust of lawful authority. (*See also* Security System section, p. 384.)

SCOTT, NICHOLAS PAUL

Deputy Secretary of State, NIO, 1986–7; Under-Secretary, NIO, 1981–6. b. 1933. Conservative MP for Chelsea, 1974–, and Paddington S., 1966–74. Under-Secretary, Employment, 1974. He faced a great variety of problems during a Stormont career longer than that of any Minister under direct rule. As Under-Secretary, he dealt with education and, later, security, and rode out the storm over the mass escape from the Maze Prison in 1983. In education he encountered criticism over school closures and the future of the Catholic training colleges, and merged the New University of

Ulster and the Ulster Polytechnic to create the University of Ulster. He campaigned for greater co-operation between Catholic and State schools. But it was his role as a strong defender of the AIA which attracted most attention. This earned him esteem in Dublin Government and SDLP circles, but Unionists showed him only hostility, and some of them dubbed him 'Minister of Discord', and welcomed his departure in the June 1987 reshuffle. Despite his left-of-centre stance in the Conservative Party, his work was clearly valued by Margaret Thatcher, who apparently saw the need to keep him at Stormont in 1985, when she was forced to move Secretary of State Douglas Hurd to the Home Office. His safe Chelsea seat was probably another factor. His vigorous response to loyalist protests over the AIA in 1986 earned him promotion to Minister of State and deputy Secretary of State and he emerged as a strong personality in the Joint Ministerial Conference of the AIA, where he pushed security reforms and maintained close contacts with Dublin. Social Security Minister, 1987–.

SCOTTISH UNIONIST PARTY

Set up in April 1986 to support the Unionist campaign against the AIA. Backed by Orange Order in Scotland. Initially, its chairman, Bill McMurdo, said they would be fighting nine seats in the 1987 general election, including that of Scottish Secretary Malcolm Rifkind, but later the party decided simply to work actively against the Conservatives, and its efforts contributed to the poor showing of Government candidates.

SEAWRIGHT, GEORGE

Militant loyalist politician, fatally wounded in IPLO shooting in November 1987, and who died the following month. Born in Glasgow, his power base was in the Shankill area of Belfast, and he was elected to Belfast City Council in 1981, and to the Assembly in 1982 on the slogan 'A Protestant candidate for a Protestant people'. In the Assembly he served on committees on Health and Social Services, Finance and Personnel, and Security. He was expelled from the DUP for failing to clarify a comment at a Belfast Education and Library Board meeting in 1984 that Catholics and their priests should be burned, following objections by Catholic parents to the playing of the British national anthem at joint school concerts. The incident also led to a three-month suspended sentence and £100 fine. In 1986 he was active in protests directed at Secretary of State Tom King over the AIA; the first led to a three-month suspended sentence and the second to a nine-month sentence. His other activities included support for loyalist prisoners' campaigns and denunciation of rerouting of Orange parades. But he bowed out of politics when he failed to take N. Belfast in the 1987 election. A massive funeral on the Shankill was attended by represent-atives of all the main sections of unionism. His wife, Elizabeth, won his council seat.

SHANKILL DEFENCE ASSOCIATION

A loyalist vigilante group formed in the Shankill Road area of Belfast in the violent summer of 1969. It was under the chairmanship of John McKeague, and soon claimed a membership of 1,000. Its members, armed on occasion, were involved in clashes in areas adjoining the Falls Road, and according to the Scarman report, it was 'active in assisting Protestant families to move out of Hooker Street, and there is evidence, which we accept, that it encouraged Catholic families to move out of Protestant streets south of

the Ardoyne'. On 2 August 1969 it was claimed by the security forces that SDA members had set up a cordon round the Unity Flats complex, occupied by Catholics, and had tried to force their way into the flats after reports that Junior Orangemen had been attacked in the area. Petrol bombs were used in the rioting which followed, and the SDA was particularly critical of the use by the RUC of water cannon. They gave a warning that the people of the Shankill would not have any further confidence in the RUC. The UCDC, headed by the Rev. Ian Paisley, denied that either the UCDC or the UPV had any connection with the SDA. Many members of the SDA were believed to be members of the USC. When the Hunt report in 1969 recommended the replacement of the USC by a new part-time force under the army GOC, the SDA called for the resignation of the Chichester-Clark Government, and said the time was fast approaching when responsible leaders of the SDA would not be able to restrain the 'backlash of outraged loyalist opinion'. In October 1969 there was serious rioting on the Shankill Road, and the RUC suffered its first casualty when Constable Victor Arbuckle was shot dead. In November 1969 SDA chairman John McKeague was cleared of a charge of conspiracy to cause explosions.

SHANKILL ROAD

The Belfast area which is a major loyalist stronghold. Organisations like the UVF and the UDA have drawn much of their support from the Shankill. In 1969 there were serious riots in the area, and the Peace Line was erected between the Shankill Road and the adjoining (Catholic) Falls Road to prevent confrontations between hostile crowds. By a strange irony, the first RUC man to be shot dead (Constable Victor Arbuckle) was killed during a riot on the Shankill Road in October

1969. The character of the area has been greatly affected by large-scale demolition and slow redevelopment. In 1978 the UVF was threatening to prevent further demolition. In 1988 the Shankill Community Council was calling for revitalisation of the area if it was not to sink into deprivation. The district was expected to benefit from Government measures announced later that year to help run-down areas of the city.

SHAW, SIR GILES
As Giles Shaw, Parliamentary Under-Secretary, NIO, 1979–81. b. 1931. MA (Cantab.) and president of the Union, 1954. Marketing director, Rowntree Mackintosh Limited, 1970–4. Conservative MP for Pudsey, February 1974–. Responsible at NIO for the departments of Commerce and Agriculture. After serving in several departments, including Minister of State at Home Office, and Trade and Industry, he left Government in 1987.

SHILLINGTON, SIR GRAHAM
Chief Constable of the RUC, 1970–3. b. Portadown, Co. Armagh, 1911. When he took charge of the RUC, he had been deputy Chief Constable for nearly two years, and had been concerned with the reorganisation of the force as a consequence of the Hunt report. Earlier, he had been RUC City Commissioner in Belfast. His appointment as Chief Constable was welcomed by Unionists, but questioned by civil rights supporters. His tenure of office as Chief Constable covered the introduction of internment and the violence which followed direct rule. He also had to cope with a high level of sectarian assassinations.

SHORT STRAND
A mainly Catholic enclave in predominantly Protestant E. Belfast. In the early days of the Troubles, notably in

1972, there were clashes between Protestants and Catholics, and occasionally serious riots on the fringes of the district.

SILENT TOO LONG
An organisation established in 1981 of relatives of innocent Catholic victims of violence. It claimed at that time that the deaths of 600 such victims had been virtually ignored by the authorities. In 1986 a publicity trip to the US by representatives of the organisation was sponsored by NORAID.

SIMPSON, FREDERICK VIVIAN
NILP MP for Oldpark, 1958–72. b. Dublin, 23 August 1903; d. 1977. Draper and footwear merchant in Carrickfergus, where he served in local council, 1947–58. Methodist lay preacher.

SIMPSON, MARY
OUP Assembly member for Armagh, 1982–6. Served on committees on Education and Environment. Craigavon Council, 1977–. Mayor of Craigavon, 1981–2. Honorary Secretary, Central Armagh Unionist Association, 1974–.

SIMPSON, DR ROBERT
First Minister of Community Relations, 1969–71, the appointment being part of the reform package arising from the visit of James Callaghan as Home Secretary. On taking office, Dr Simpson resigned from the Masonic and Orange Orders. b. Ballymena, 3 July 1923. MB (QUB). Unionist MP for Mid-Antrim, 1952–72.

SIX COUNTIES
A term sometimes used to designate NI, particularly in Nationalist circles.

SMITH, SIR HOWARD
Last UK Government representative, NI, 1971–2. b. 15 October 1919. He was the last holder of an office which

extended from 1969 until the introduction of direct rule in March 1972. His main activity was in the crucial period leading up to direct rule, including 'Bloody Sunday' in Londonderry. He became ambassador to Moscow in 1976 and later that year was appointed by Home Secretary Merlyn Rees as head of MI5.

SMYTH, CLIFFORD A.

DUP Assembly, 1973–4, Convention, 1975–6, member for N. Antrim. b. Londonderry, 1944. BA (QUB). Chairman, QUB Conservative and Unionist Association, 1971. He was elected to the Assembly in June 1974, after it had already been prorogued, heading the poll in the by-election. In the Convention, he was secretary of the UUUC. In 1977 he returned to the OUP (as a student he had been secretary of the Young Unionist Council) and unsuccessfully contested N. Down in 1979 Westminster election. In 1986–7 he was chairman of the CEC, but stood down after disagreeing about the movement's direction, while claiming that he still supported the concept of equal citizenship.

SMYTH, HUGH

Independent Unionist Assembly, 1973–4, and Convention, 1975–6, member for W. Belfast. b. Shankill, Belfast, 1941. Belfast City Council, 1972–. Deputy Lord Mayor, 1983. Heavily involved in political and welfare work in the Shankill area, he was one of the founders of the Loyalist Front, which was active in 1974, and which had the support of the UVF. After the 1974 loyalist strike, he claimed that loyalist leaders had only shown their hand when they were sure that the strike was going to succeed, and that in future the decisions must be taken by the workers. He helped to found the short-lived Volunteer Political Party – political arm of the UVF – and in 1978

he was appointed leader of the Belfast-based Independent Unionist Group which became Progressive Unionist Party in 1979. Unsuccessful candidate in W. Belfast for 1982 Assembly.

SMYTH, REVEREND (WILLIAM) MARTIN

OUP MP for S. Belfast, 1982–. Grand master of the Orange Order in Ireland, 1972–. b. Belfast, 1931. Originally joined junior Orange lodge in Sandy Row area of Belfast, and for ten years (1972–82) combined his career as a Presbyterian Minister (Alexandra Church in N. Belfast) with leadership of the Orange Order and the post of vice-president of the council of the OUP. During that period, he was Imperial grand master of the Orange Order as well as head of the Order in Ireland. On his election as MP for S. Belfast in the February 1982 by-election (created by the assassination of the Rev. Robert Bradford), he resigned his church ministry and the post of Imperial grand master of the Orange Order. He also suggested that he should give up the post of Irish grand master, but was persuaded by Orange colleagues to remain. He made his first election bid in the Convention election of 1975, and headed the poll in S. Belfast. When the Convention broke up, he incurred some criticism from Unionists for taking part in secret, but unsuccessful, talks with the SDLP, represented by John Hume and Paddy Devlin, in an attempt to break the political deadlock. His win in the 1982 by-election in S. Belfast was psychologically important for his party since it seemed to mark a halt to the loss of electoral ground to the DUP. He has been strongly critical of the AIA, but in 1987 urged the development of a federal system of government covering the whole UK, with a provincial parliament in Belfast, and a place for the return of the Republic to the UK. NI, he said, had not been the success it should have been because British Governments had not the will to make it work. Chairman of the 1982 Assembly's Health and Social Services, and Finance and Personnel committees. Member of Devolution Committee. ·

SOCIAL AND LIBERAL DEMOCRATS

The party launched in March 1987 with the merger of the Liberal Party and the bulk of the SDP. Known nationally as the Democrats, the party has established close links with the NI Alliance Party, and both parties are expected to join with the Progressive Democrats in the Republic on a single manifesto for the 1989 European elections. Alliance leader Dr John Alderdice said in 1988 that the SLD and Alliance were working very closely together and he did not rule out a future merger. Paddy Ashdown, elected first leader of the new party in July 1988, also took the post of party spokesman on NI.

SOCIAL DEMOCRATIC PARTY

In 1982 the SDP claimed to be the only major national party recruiting members in NI. This may have been partly due to the influence of one of its founders, Shirley Williams, who had taken a special interest in NI affairs as a member of Labour's NEC and as a Home Office Minister at the start of the Troubles. In the 1987 general election the SDP, then in partnership with the Liberals, co-operated closely with the Alliance Party in NI, and there was much common ground in their manifestos. SDP leader Dr David Owen was a little less enthusiastic about the AIA than most Westminster politicians. He did not think enough had been done to grapple with the problems of the community within NI. He hoped profoundly that it would work, 'but I am a bit dubious,' he said. In 1988,

when the bulk of the SDP had teamed up with the Liberals in the SLD, the NI branch of SDP was pressing party chiefs to run candidates in NI at the next election.

SOCIAL DEMOCRATIC AND LABOUR PARTY

The party which speaks for most Catholics in NI. Founded on 21 August 1970, it absorbed most supporters of the old Nationalist Party, National Democratic Party and Republican Labour Party. It joined the Confederation of Socialist Parties of the European Community. The party was launched by seven Stormont politicians: Gerry Fitt MP, then Republican Labour, who became party leader; three Independent MPs, who had been prominent in the civil rights campaign – John Hume, Ivan Cooper and Paddy O'Hanlon; Austin Currie, a Nationalist MP; Paddy Devlin, NILP MP; and Paddy Wilson, Republican Labour Senator, who was to become a murder victim. It presented itself as a radical, left-of-centre party, which would seek civil rights for all and just distribution of wealth. It would work to promote friendship and understanding between North and South, with a view to the eventual unity of Ireland, through the consent of the majority of the people, North and South. The SDLP's first major move was to withdraw from Stormont in July 1971. It stated that it was withdrawing its consent from the institutions of government. With the introduction of internment without trial in August 1971, it sponsored a civil disobedience campaign, involving the withholding of rents and rates. In the autumn of 1971 it was involved in the Assembly of the Northern Irish People – the unofficial 'Dungiven Parliament'. With the imposition of direct rule in 1972, it proposed a form of condominium, with Britain and the Republic exercising joint sovereignty over NI. There would be an Assembly elected by PR, but legislation would have to be approved by commissioners appointed by the British and Irish Governments. The Executive would be elected by the Assembly, also by PR. The party also called for a declaration by Britain in favour of Irish unity, and the setting up of a 'National Senate' by the Assembly and the Dáil to plan progress towards Irish unity. The SDLP opted out of the Darlington conference, organised in September 1972 by Secretary of State William Whitelaw, despite an appeal by Edward Heath. But it took comfort from the Government's Green Paper, which urged power-sharing between the communities and an Irish dimension, and it supported the White Paper which followed. Its Assembly election manifesto stressed partnership government and a cross-border Council of Ireland. In the election the SDLP got nineteen of the seventy-eight seats, and 22.1 per cent of first-preference votes. It had four seats in the 1974 power-sharing Executive, including that of deputy Chief Executive, held by Gerry Fitt. The collapse of the Executive as a result of the loyalist strike was a serious blow to the party. It angrily blamed the British Government for failing to tackle the paramilitary groups backing the stoppage. In its Convention manifesto, *Speak with Strength*, it stuck to the main points of its policy, with perhaps a shade less emphasis on the Irish dimension. It secured 23.7 per cent of first-preference votes but got only seventeen seats, two fewer than in the Assembly. The loyalist majority in the Convention showed no disposition to accept power-sharing other than in the framework of departmental committees. And since the UUUC rejected William Craig's plan for an emergency voluntary coalition, the SDLP was never called upon to declare its attitude to a

scheme which fell short of full power-sharing and excluded a Council of Ireland. After the Convention was wound up, the party's deputy leader, John Hume, and Paddy Devlin had private exploratory talks with the Rev. Martin Smyth and Austin Ardill of the Official Unionists, but the exchanges were unproductive. With renewed direct rule, the SDLP became unhappy at what it saw as lack of effort by the British Government to deal with 'loyalist intransigence'. It also saw evidence of a trend towards integration, with Westminster support for five extra NI MPs. In a policy statement, *Facing Reality*, endorsed at its 1977 conference, it urged an 'agreed Ireland – the essential unity of whose people would have evolved in agreement over the years, whose institutions of government would reflect both its unity and diversity, and whose people would live in a harmonious relationship with Britain'. Many Unionists regarded the statement as more angled towards a united Ireland than previous statements, but this was denied by party spokesmen. They also rejected the claim of Paddy Devlin that there was a move away from socialism, and Devlin was expelled in the autumn of 1977. In 1978 the three major Dublin parties indicated that they would respond to a plea by John Hume that they should spell out precisely their ideas for Irish unity. In local government elections the party has established a firm base. In the 1977 District Council elections, it won 113 seats (20.6 per cent of first-preference votes) as compared with 83 seats in 1973. At its 1978 conference the party renewed its call for the British and Irish Governments and both sides of the NI community to get together to work out a settlement, but its motion also referred to eventual British withdrawal as 'desirable and inevitable' and this point was seized on by Unionist critics.

In the 1979 Westminster election the party retained W. Belfast, but did not come close to winning any other seat. Its Chief Whip, Austin Currie, resigned to fight, unsuccessfully, Fermanagh–S. Tyrone as Independent SDLP. In the 1979 European election the party's deputy leader, John Hume, achieved a record vote for the party – nearly 25 per cent – in taking one of the three NI seats in the European Parliament. The announcement of a Constitutional Conference by Secretary of State Humphrey Atkins in November 1979 created a crisis for the party. The SDLP regarded the agenda as far too limited to produce a political settlement. Gerry Fitt immediately denounced its attitude and resigned from the party, claiming that it was losing it socialism and becoming 'green Nationalist'. John Hume rejected the charge and succeeded Fitt as party leader. In the end the SDLP did join the Stormont conference, after persuading the Secretary of State to set up a parallel meeting in which cross-border relations, security and the economy could be discussed. In the main conference the party proposed a power-sharing administration in which places would be allocated in proportion to party strength. In the parallel conference it attacked Government policy, and when the main conference failed to produce agreement, it turned down a further Government idea of a fifty-member advisory council. During the H-Block hunger strike, it called for concessions short of political status, but its proposals were rejected by the Government. Throughout the hunger strike it suffered some internal strains as a result of its decision to stay out of the Fermanagh–S. Tyrone by-elections, and the Maze protest also hit its expectations in the 1981 council elections. Although it lost only a few council seats, its share of the poll dropped 3 per cent to 17.5 per cent. In

1982 the party came out strongly against the 'rolling devolution' plan, which it attacked as 'unworkable', and it was firmly supported in this view by the Republic's Taoiseach, Charles Haughey, while the Fine Gael leader, Dr Garret FitzGerald, also expressed reservations. The SDLP went into the election urging a 'Council for a New Ireland' to enable politicians from NI and the Republic to get together to discuss the implications of Irish unity. It also decided not to attend the Assembly. It had to face widespread competition from PSF candidates in strongly Nationalist areas, and in consequence its total of fourteen Assembly seats was down on both the 1973 Assembly and the 1975 Convention. With just under 19 per cent of first preferences, its share of the vote was also down on previous Stormont elections, although an improvement on the 1981 council contests. It also lost one of its Assembly seats in Armagh when its deputy leader, Seamus Mallon, was unseated because of his membership of the Republic's Senate. At its 1983 conference, the party reaffirmed its opposition to the Assembly, and backed Hume's call for it to meet the PSF challenge 'head on' and contest all seventeen seats at the Westminster election. It did so and fought on the platform of support for the New Ireland Forum. It maintained its vote numerically, but because of the larger poll and PSF competition, its share of the poll dropped to 18 per cent and it secured only the Foyle seat, taken by John Hume. For the party, 1984 was a period of great uncertainty. Margaret Thatcher was thought to be planning some new Anglo-Irish initiative in the light of the Assembly's failure to produce an acceptable scheme for devolution. But the party was unprepared for the PM's sharp rebuff to the main Forum options in November

1984. Her 'out, out, out' remarks
seemed to preclude any major move by
London. But the SDLP, like the Irish
Government, built on the international
diplomatic support for the Forum. The
US Congress had unanimously backed
the NIF report in May 1984, and it also
had a favourable response in Europe,
while the British Labour Party was
inclined to say 'in, in, in'. The SDLP
benefited, strangely enough, from PSF's
strong showing in its first council
elections contest in 1985. A total of
fifty-nine PSF councillors left the SDLP
position virtually unchanged, but it
was a new spur to London and Dublin
to seek some way of strengthening
constitutional politics. The outcome
was the AIA of 1985, but SDLP hopes
that it might lead to inter-party talks
were swiftly disappointed. John Hume,
who pressed the AIA as the beginning of
a process of reconciliation, made no
headway in face of the fierce opposition of Unionists, who presented the
AIA as the brainchild of the SDLP and
Dublin, accepted by Thatcher against
her better judgement. But immediate
SDLP disappointments were out-
weighed by its electoral gains. First,
Seamus Mallon took Newry and
Armagh in the 1986 by-elections, and
then Eddie McGrady unseated veteran
MP Enoch Powell in S. Down in the
1987 election. The decline in the PSF
vote was a factor in both victories. By
1988 public opinion polls in NI were
showing Catholics not greatly
impressed by the fruits of the AIA.
There were many rumours, but few
tangible signs of a political breakthrough. John Hume (joined later by
some of his colleagues) had talks over
nine months with PSF president Gerry
Adams, aimed, apparently, at persuading PSF that the AIA had shown the
British Government to be essentially
neutral in its attitude to a British
presence in Ireland and that violence
was unnecessary. The talks, unsur-

prisingly, did not lead to agreement.

SOLEY, CLIVE
Labour front-bench spokesman on NI,
1981–5. b. 7 May 1939. BA Hons
(Strathclyde); DASS (Southampton). MP
for Hammersmith W., 1979–83;
Hammersmith, 1983–. In January
1983 he suggested an all-Ireland
economic council and an all-Ireland
court and police force to strengthen
cross-border security.

SOUTH ARMAGH REPUBLICAN ACTION FORCE
An organisation which claimed many
murders in S. Armagh, particularly in
1975. Regarded by the security forces
as a 'flag of convenience' for some local
PIRA units.

SPEAKER'S CONFERENCE
Conference headed by Speaker of the
Commons, George Thomas MP, which
reported in February 1978 that NI
should have seventeen MPs at Westminster instead of twelve. It also
suggested that the NI Boundary
Commission should be free to vary this
figure by one either way to facilitate
drawing of boundaries and the
Commission settled on seventeen seats,
which took effect in 1983. The
conference represented all the parties,
and included three NI MPs – Enoch
Powell, James Molyneaux (both OUP),
and Gerry Fitt (SDLP), who was alone
in standing out against any increased
representation.

SPECIAL AIR SERVICE *see* Security
System section, pp. 392 *and* 408

SPECIAL CATEGORY
The special status accorded to
prisoners who were members of
paramilitary organisations, as a result
of a decision by William Whitelaw,
Secretary of State, in June 1972, after a
prolonged hunger strike by prisoners in

Belfast Prison. The privileges applied to prisoners sentenced to more than nine months' imprisonment for offences related to the civil disturbances. Because of the lack of cell accommodation they were housed in compounds. They were not required to work, could wear their own clothes, and were allowed extra visits and food parcels. By 31 December 1974, the number of prisoners enjoying special category, or political, status had risen to 1,116, including 51 women. At that time there were 545 male special category prisoners at the Maze Prison; 502 at Magilligan, Co. Derry, and 18 in Belfast. The women were in Armagh Prison. The prisoners were from both wings of the IRA and the various loyalist paramilitary groups, and the paramilitary organisations ran a prisoner-of-war-type regime in the compounds, some of which had ninety prisoners each. The Gardiner committee, in 1975, came out against special category status. It said it meant virtually the loss of disciplinary control by the prison authorities. Merlyn Rees, as Secretary of State, announced the phasing out of special category as from 1 March 1976. This meant that no one convicted of an offence committed after that date was admitted to special category status and in 1980, Secretary of State Humphrey Atkins stopped all new admissions to special category. At the end of 1976 the total of special category prisoners was more than 1,500; by mid-1978 it had dropped to about 800. Prisoners who would normally have been placed in compounds were now put in cells, and 8 new blocks, each with 100 cells, were built at the Maze Prison. They became known as H-Blocks because of the layout, and were linked to recreational facilities, as well as special workshops and vocational training accommodation. But Republican prisoners immediately made it clear they would

refuse to co-operate with the removal of special status. They refused to wear prison clothing, and simply covered themselves with a blanket; hence the description of the protest as 'on the blanket'. With the British Government refusing to make any concessions to the protesters, the prisoners involved – they now numbered more than 300 – began to intensify their protest in March 1978. They refused to wash or use the toilets, and smashed up the furniture in their cells. This 'dirty protest' continued, with one interruption, until March 1981, when it was dropped so as to focus attention on Bobby Sands's hunger strike. At the beginning of 1983 230 prisoners at the Maze were still enjoying special category, and living in compounds. There were 105 in the PIRA–INLA compound, 12 OIRA, 67 UVF, and 46 UDA. But by 1988, when the remaining occupants of the compounds moved into H-Block cells, without giving up their privileges, they totalled about ninety. (*See also* H-Blocks.)

SPECIAL POWERS ACT *see* Security System section, pp. 398–406

SPEERS, JAMES ALEXANDER (JIM)
OUP Assembly member for Armagh, April 1983–6. Served on committees on Agriculture, Environment, and deputy chairman Health and Social Services. b. 1946. Local official of Ulster Farmers' Union. Armagh Council, 1977–. Secretary, Mid- and S. Armagh Unionist Association, 1970–. Stood unsuccessfully in 1982 Assembly election in Armagh, but returned in April 1983 by-election following disqualification of Seamus Mallon (SDLP).

SPENCE, AUGUSTUS (GUSTY)
Best-known figure in the revived UVF, the illegal loyalist paramilitary group.

b. Belfast, 1933. Like many UVF men, he had served in the army – with the Royal Ulster Rifles in West Germany and later in Cyprus during the EOKA campaign. He was sentenced to twenty years' imprisonment in 1966 for shooting a young Catholic barman at a public house in Malvern Street in the Shankill Road area of Belfast. Soon afterwards, the UVF was proscribed. He and his friends always insisted that he was innocent of the crime. On several occasions he went on hunger strike to support his claim, and in 1972, when he was given parole to attend his daughter's wedding, UVF members 'kidnapped' him to draw attention to his case. Four months later, he was recaptured, but his friends said he had given himself up because of his heart condition. Among militant loyalists on the Shankill Road, he remained a local hero. Tea towels were produced with his portrait, and facsimile five-pound notes were printed on which the Queen's head was replaced by Spence's. 'His only crime was loyalty' was the slogan used by those who campaigned for his release. In 1977, as UVF commander inside the Maze Prison, he issued a message supporting reconciliation and attacking violence, which, he said, could now be counter-productive. He believed that the loyalists had achieved their aim of self-determination. He was also reported to be learning Irish, and his general attitude was not welcomed by all UVF prisoners. In March 1978 he resigned as UVF commander in the prison. Spence was finally released in December 1984, when he was said to be in very poor health. In an interview for the *Shankill Bulletin* in June 1985 he said his future would be in some sort of community politics. He criticised the two main Unionist parties for failing to outflank PSF by talking to the SDLP.

STALKER AFFAIR

The shooting dead by the RUC in Co. Armagh in 1982 of six unarmed Catholic men, five of them with alleged terrorist links, has proved a traumatic affair for the force. The RUC has consistently denied suggestions of an official shoot-to-kill policy but Dublin politicians and the SDLP have complained that there was an official cover-up of some aspects of the killings. The deaths were investigated initially by Manchester's former deputy Chief Constable John Stalker, who claimed that he had been hampered in his inquiries. He was taken off the case when he faced disciplinary charges, which were later dropped, and the investigation was continued by W. Yorkshire Chief Constable Colin Sampson. Reports of the inquiries were not published, but in 1988 Attorney-General Sir Patrick Mayhew said that while there was evidence of attempts to pervert the course of justice, there would be no prosecution of police officers, on the grounds of national security. The NI Police Authority also decided, by one vote, that there would be no disciplinary charges against the three top officers of the RUC. But a report to the RUC Chief Constable Sir John Hermon by Staffordshire Chief Constable Charles Kelly led to disciplinary charges against twenty junior officers, due to be dealt with in early 1989.

STALLARD, LORD

Chairman of the Labour Party's back-bench NI committee at Westminster, 1979–83. b. 1921. MP for St Pancras N., 1970–4; MP for Camden, St Pancras N., 1974–83. Minister of State (Housing), 1974–6. Government Whip, 1976–9.

STANDING ADVISORY COMMISSION ON HUMAN RIGHTS

An official body set up under the Constitution Act of 1973 to monitor the effectiveness of laws against discrimination on the grounds of religion or politics. The Commission has taken a highly independent line. In May 1979 it recommended to the Secretary of State the dropping of the power to intern without trial. It has prompted widespread discussion on a possible Bill of Rights, and while it basically favours such a measure for the whole UK, it said in its 1980–1 report that there might be circumstances which would justify a Bill for NI alone. Earlier, it urged that the laws on divorce and homosexuality should be brought into line with those in GB. The divorce reform took effect in 1980 but the homosexuality laws were only changed in 1982 after a ruling by the European Court of Human Rights. In 1981 the Commission was strongly critical of the change in electoral law passed in the wake of the election of hunger-striker Bobby Sands as an MP, which prevented a convicted prisoner being nominated. The Commission said it was an infringement of the citizen's right to choose. In the wake of the AIA it supported the case for three-judge courts to deal with terrorist-type offences. In 1988 it also urged the ending of PTA exclusion orders banning UK citizens from GB or NI, and an easement of port-control procedures. It called for review of the law on the use of reasonable force by the security forces, which it said was 'vague and unsatisfactory'. It suggested 'clear and comprehensive' measures on fair employment, and questioned whether the new police complaints procedure was sufficiently impartial. In January 1989 the Commission accused the Government of failing to consult more widely before introducing anti-terrorist measures. It considered that the anti-violence declaration for councillors would be counter-productive; that a new broadcasting restriction affecting supporters of violence was too wide; and described as disappointing the Government's decision to derogate from the European Convention to maintain the seven-day detention power. It also protested that ending of the 'right to silence' had been rushed. The chairman, appointed in 1988, is Sir Oliver Napier.

STANLEY, SIR JOHN PAUL

NI Minister of State and deputy Secretary of State, 15 June 1987–26 July 1988. Conservative MP for Tonbridge and Malling, 1983–. b. 19 January 1942. Parliamentary Private Secretary to Margaret Thatcher, 1976–9; Housing Minister, 1979–83; Minister for Armed Forces, 1983–7. His Defence Ministry job had given him some familiarity with local security problems, and with his close contacts with the PM, his move to Stormont was variously interpreted as heralding a tougher security policy, a gesture to Unionists still furious at the AIA, and as providing an 'eyes and ears' for Thatcher in the Stormont scene. In the event, he stayed only thirteen months. In the July 1988 reshuffle he resigned for 'personal reasons' and returned to the back benches. Secretary of State Tom King praised his work and the PM awarded him a knighthood. At Stormont he inherited his predecessor's portfolios – law and order and finance – but not Nicholas Scott's flair for public relations. He was involved in several critical meetings of the AIA conference, and in 1988 had to face an upsurge of PIRA violence, but he made few public comments and his previous unpopularity among officials in Whitehall apparently pursued him to Belfast.

STEWART, IAN
Minister of State and deputy to Secretary of State, NI, 26 July 1988–. Conservative MP for Hitchin, October 1974–83; Hertfordshire N., 1983–. b. 10 August 1935. MA, D.Litt. (Cantab.). Merchant banker before entering Government in January 1983 as Under-Secretary at Defence (Procurement); Economic Secretary to Treasury, November 1983. Promoted Minister of State at Treasury, 1984. Became Minister for Armed Forces, 15 June 1987, in succession to John Stanley and again succeeded him in the NIO. His first engagement was a meeting of the Anglo-Irish conference on 27 July at which, apparently, cross-border security was put on a better basis after a period of increased PIRA activity. Soon after his arrival at Stormont he annoyed the Irish Government by revealing an agreement on over-flying of the border for bomb disposal.

'STICKIES' *see* Official Irish Republican Army

STORMONT
The seat of Government in NI, on a commanding site about eight kilometres from Belfast city centre. Comprises Parliament Buildings, Stormont Castle (Secretary of State's office), and Stormont House (residence of Speaker of NI Commons, but has provided accommodation for British Ministers under direct rule). Parliament Buildings was a gift to the people of NI and was designed by Sir Arnold Thornley in Greek classical style, and with exterior faced in Portland stone above a plinth of unpolished granite from the Mountains of Mourne. The building is 110 metres long, 49 metres wide, and rises to 28 metres.

STOWE, SIR KENNETH RONALD
Permanent Secretary, NIO, October 1979–81. b. 17 July 1927. MA (Oxon.). Principal private secretary to the Prime Minister, 1973–9. During his earlier civil service career, he was seconded to the UN Secretariat in 1958.

STRABANE
The Co. Tyrone border town often cited as an example of under-development in W. Ulster. Its rate of unemployment has nearly always exceeded 25 per cent and in 1988 it was around 30 per cent. Male unemployment has sometimes approached 80 per cent. The town has suffered heavily from violence, and throughout the Troubles there have been frequent allegations that PIRA has been able to operate from adjoining areas of Co. Donegal in the Republic. In the early 1980s there were suggestions that INLA also had bases in Donegal where in late 1982 there were many seizures of arms and explosives by Gardaí. In February 1985 three PIRA members were shot dead, apparently by the SAS, close to the town. The shooting dead of Unionist Senator Jack Barnhill by OIRA there in 1971 was one of the earliest political assassinations. In the early days of the civil rights campaign there were many rallies in the town. At one of these meetings in June 1969 the differing approaches of political speakers underlined the difficulty of keeping the movement together as the reforms developed. The election of Ivan Barr (PSF) as council chairman in 1988 led to lively exchanges in the council chamber.

STRONGE, JAMES
OUP MP for Mid-Armagh in Stormont Parliament, 1969–72. b. 1933. Shot dead along with his father, Sir Norman Stronge, aged eighty-six, ex-Speaker of the Stormont Commons, by PIRA in January 1981. They were killed at their

home, Tynan Abbey, close to the border, and the house was destroyed by explosives which set it on fire. The PIRA admission described them as 'symbols of hated unionism' and said the killings were a reprisal for loyalist assassinations of Nationalist people. In the 1969 general election, James Stronge succeeded his father in the seat which Sir Norman had held for thirty-one years, and where he had been opposed only once (1965). Stronge was firmly against the Sunningdale Agreement, which he described as 'a great act of political appeasement'.

SUNNINGDALE CONFERENCE

The conference between the British and Irish Governments and the three parties involved in the NI Executive held at the Sunningdale (Berkshire) Civil Service College, 6–9 December 1973. Agreement to set up the power-sharing Executive made up of the Unionists led by Brian Faulkner, the SDLP and the Alliance Party, and the distribution of offices had been reached at talks at Stormont on 21 November 1973. The Sunningdale Conference was intended to establish the 'Irish dimension' and the political framework in which the new government would operate. But the proposed formal conference to sign the declaration on the status of NI was never held and in May 1974 the Executive collapsed in face of the UWC loyalist strike. Main points of the Sunningdale Agreement:

1 The Government of the Republic and the SDLP upheld their aspiration for a united Ireland, but only by consent. The Unionist and Alliance parties voiced the desire of the majority in NI to remain part of the UK.
2 The Irish Government fully accepted and solemnly declared that there could be no change in the status of NI until a majority of the people of NI desired a change in that status.

3 The British Government solemnly declared that it was, and would remain, its policy to support the wishes of the majority of the people of NI. The present status of NI is that it is part of the UK. If in the future the majority of the people of NI should indicate a wish to become part of a united Ireland, the British Government would support that wish.
4 Declarations to this effect by both Governments would be registered at the UN.
5 A Council of Ireland would be set up, limited to representatives from both parts of Ireland, but with 'appropriate safeguards' for the British Government's financial and other interests. The Council of Ministers, which must make decisions by unanimous vote, would have seven Ministers from either side, and there would also be a Consultative Assembly with an advisory role. The Assembly would have sixty members – thirty from the Dáil and thirty from the NI Assembly. They would be elected by the members of each Parliament on PR.
6 The Council was to have a wide range of functions, including the study of the impact of EC membership, development of resources, co-operative ventures in trade and industry, electricity generation, tourism, roads and transport, public health advisory services, sport, culture and the arts.
7 It was agreed that persons committing crimes of violence, however motivated, in any part of Ireland should be brought to trial, irrespective of the part of Ireland in which they were located. The conference discussed various approaches, including extradition, the creation of a common law enforcement area in which an all-Ireland court would have jurisdiction, and the extension of the jurisdiction of domestic courts so as to enable them to try offences committed outside the jurisdiction. Because of the

legal complexity of these problems, it was agreed that the British and Irish Governments should set up a Joint Law Commission to examine the various proposals. (In the event, this was the only point in the Sunningdale Agreement which was jointly implemented. The Commission's report led to reciprocal legislation, which permitted a person accused of a terrorist offence to be brought to trial on whichever side of the border he is arrested.)

8 In the field of human rights the Council of Ireland would consider what further legislation was needed.

9 On law and order and policing, it was accepted that the two parts of Ireland were to a considerable extent inter-dependent, and that the problems of political violence and identification with the police service could not be solved without taking account of that fact.

10 Accordingly, the British Government stated that, as soon as the security problems were resolved and the new institutions were seen to be working effectively, they would wish to discuss the devolution of responsibility for normal policing, and how this might be achieved, with the NI Executive and the police. The Irish Government agreed to set up a police authority (it did not do so) and together with the NI police authority would consult with the Council of Ministers on appointments. The Secretary of State undertook to set up an all-party Assembly committee to examine how best to introduce effective policing.

11 The conference took note of the reaffirmation by the British Government of its intention to bring detention without trial to an end as soon as the security situation permitted.

The PM, Edward Heath, presided at the conference, travelling back and forth by helicopter to Chequers, his country home. The Council of Ireland and policing were the crunch issues, and there is much evidence that Brian Faulkner's team were divided on the Council, and that strong pressure was brought to bear by Heath to get quick agreement. The NI Secretary of State, Francis Pym, also attended, but since he had only recently taken over at Stormont, his role was inevitably limited. The Irish team was headed by Taoiseach Liam Cosgrave, the SDLP delegates were led by Gerry Fitt and the Alliance Party members by Oliver Napier. The loyalists opposed to the Sunningdale exercise – that is, the Unionists led by Harry West, the Rev. Ian Paisley and William Craig – were not invited to the talks. After Paisley and Craig had protested at this, they were invited to one session, but rejected this as inadequate. When the communiqué appeared they sharply attacked it, and in early January 1974, Faulkner lost his battle to 'sell' Sunningdale to the Unionist Council and the power-sharing Executive lasted only five months (January–May 1974).

SUPERGRASS SYSTEM

Between 1981 and 1986 the supergrass system proved to be one of the most controversial features of the administration of justice in NI. The British Government and the RUC strongly defended the use of accomplice evidence as being well-established in English law. RUC Chief Constable Sir John Hermon saw the use of 'converted terrorists' as a fully justified means of bringing paramilitary gunmen and bombers to book. But the charging of large numbers of defendants on the word of a supergrass emerging from the ranks of a terrorist group was a practice with little support in the Nationalist community, and it was also widely attacked by Irish Governments and British Labour politicians. It also attracted considerable criticism among lawyers, particularly when the prosecution used the novel device of a Bill of Indictment, which avoided witnesses having to give evidence at a preliminary hearing as well as at the trial. Critics accused the RUC of using blackmail, intimidation and the offers of large sums of money to produce informers willing to speak in court against alleged fellow terrorists. Some supergrasses were given immunity from prosecution, police protection, and the means to start a new life outside NI. The informers came from PIRA (including Christopher Black and Raymond Gilmour), INLA (Harry Kirkpatrick and Jackie Grimley, among others), and the UVF (William 'Budgie' Allen and Joseph Bennett were the best-known). In the period 1981 to 1983 evidence from nearly thirty supergrasses led to charges against some three hundred people, but thirteen of these retracted their evidence before the trials began. In his report on emergency legislation in 1984 Sir George Baker agreed with the use of supergrasses, but recommended that there should be no more than twenty defendants in any trial and that fewer charges should be brought. In the event, the proportion of convictions dropped, and many appeals were successful. In 1986, when the Court of Appeal quashed the convictions of eighteen men jailed on the word of PIRA supergrass Christopher Black, Labour spokesman Peter Archer said it was the 'last nail in the coffin' of a discredited system. Irish Ministers claimed that it had been ended as a result of the AIA – something which GB denied. The RUC consoled itself with the thought that evidence presented in the various trials had cast a revealing light on the *modus operandi* of paramilitaries.

TARA
A secret loyalist organisation which began as an anti-Catholic, anti-Communist pressure group in the mid-1960s, but which took on a paramilitary character with the outbreak of violence in 1969. It described itself as 'the hard core of Protestant resistance', and in a statement issued in August 1971, it urged loyalists to organise themselves into platoons of twenty under the command of someone capable of acting as a sergeant. It said that every effort must be made to arm these platoons with 'whatever weapons are available'. Its membership was drawn mainly from Orange ranks, and it disclaimed any connection with any other political or paramilitary group. It also said that the Catholic Church should be declared illegal, and all its schools closed. In September 1986 the group said the Republic was a haven for PIRA and it threatened attacks on Dublin and towns in the South, and action against those involved in cross-border trade.

TARTAN GANGS
Gangs of Protestant youths who often wore tartan scarves in memory of the three young soldiers of the Royal Highland Fusiliers who were shot dead in Belfast on 10 March 1971. (Both the OIRA and PIRA denied responsibility for the murders.) The tartan gangs were largely based in Protestant estates in the Belfast area. The slogan 'Tartan Rule OK' became common in 1971 and 1972, and they were active during the loyalist strike in 1974, when they were frequently accused of intimidation of shopkeepers and workers who wanted to stay at work.

TAYLOR, JOHN DAVID
OUP MEP for NI, June 1979–89. MP for

Strangford, 1983–. Assembly member for N. Down, 1982–6. Served on the Agriculture Committee. Minister of State, Home Affairs, 1970–2. b. Armagh, 24 December 1937. B.Sc. (QUB). Joined Young Unionist movement at QUB and was youngest Stormont Unionist MP when returned for S. Tyrone in 1965. He was Parliamentary Secretary at Home Affairs, 1969–70. He was one of twelve Unionist MPs who, in February 1969, signed a statement saying that only a change of leadership from Terence O'Neill could unite the party. At Home Affairs he was sometimes critical of the British Government's approach to security and he was boycotted for a period by the SDLP when he was appointed to the Cabinet in August 1970. In 1972 OIRA tried to assassinate him in Armagh city. In a hail of machine-gun bullets his jawbone was shattered and he had to have extensive plastic surgery. As Assembly member for Fermanagh–S. Tyrone, 1973–4, he was a strong opponent of the Sunningdale Agreement. At the meeting of the Ulster Unionist Council in January 1974 he moved the motion criticising the deal. The motion was carried and Brian Faulkner resigned as Unionist Party leader. On several occasions between 1972 and 1974 he mentioned the possibility of negotiated independence for NI, stressing that this was very different from UDI. In April 1974 he said that, apart from integration, this might be the only option open to loyalists. A prominent Orangeman, he told the 12 July demonstration in Belfast in 1974 that a new Home Guard should be set up 'with or without London Government legislation'. He was returned to the Convention in 1975 from N. Down, and after its collapse in 1976, he became OUP spokesman on the EC. In the European election in 1979 he was

returned as one of the three MEPs from NI, but he had to wait until the sixth count, when he benefited from the lower preferences of OUP leader Harry West, who had been eliminated. He campaigned on the line that local issues should not be pursued in the European Assembly, and that there must be extensive renegotiation of the EC to help areas like NI. In the European Parliament he joined British Conservatives in the European Democratic Group, and as a member of the Parliament's regional committee urged greater EC aid for NI. He also opposed discussion in the Parliament of constitutional and security issues affecting NI. In 1981 he urged his party to be 'more positive' about devolution, and when the OUP boycotted economic talks with Secretary of State James Prior, he insisted on attending. In January 1982 he took part in 'Operation USA', a joint OUP–DUP mission to the US to present the Unionist viewpoint. When the 1982 Stormont Assembly held its initial sitting, he was described as 'father of the House', since he was the longest-serving member of Stormont institutions actually attending. He was elected to represent the new parliamentary constituency of Strangford in June 1983. His re-election to the European Parliament in 1984 meant that he joined Rev. Ian Paisley and John Hume in having a 'dual mandate' – a position he argued against in 1979. In his opposition to the AIA he was critical of the boycott of councils, and in 1987 he also urged the return of MPs to Westminster to put the Unionist case. He also wanted a bigger anti-AIA effort in mainland constituencies and more support for the newly founded Scottish Unionist Party. In 1987 he broke with the European Democratic Group (which includes British Tory MEPs) because of the EDG's support for the AIA, and joined the European Right

Group. He rejected suggestions that the ERG was 'fascist' in character, and he was elected to the Parliament's Agriculture Committee on the nomination of the ERG. In 1988 he ruled out power-sharing with John Hume in view of the latter's talks with PSF, and confirmed that he would not be standing in the 1989 European election.

THATCHER, MARGARET HILDA British PM, 1979–. Leader of the Conservative Party, 1975–. MP for Finchley, 1959–. b. 13 October 1925. As Conservative leader, she seemed initially to be anxious to rebuild the links between the Conservative Party and the Official Unionists, shattered by the Heath Government's abolition of the NI Parliament in 1972. On her third visit to NI as opposition leader in June 1978, she voiced strong support for the UK link. She said it was fashionable to talk of a federal Ireland, but it was a fashion her party did not intend to follow. She also expressed support for the restoration of a top tier of local government – one of the demands of Official Unionists. Her attitude was criticised by the SDLP and the Liberals. The promise of a regional council or councils was contained in the Conservative manifesto in 1979, but it was conditional on a failure to achieve devolved government. Thatcher acknowledged in her first Commons speech as PM that political progress in NI would not be easy, and she indicated a tough security policy in NI and ruled out any amnesty for convicted terrorists. The OUP MPs, or the majority of them, helped Thatcher bring down the Labour Government but they made it clear during the election that they would maintain their neutral stance. After the killing of eighteen soldiers and the murder of Lord Mountbatten in August 1979, she made a one-day trip to NI to see the security situation

for herself. On a seven-hour visit she became the first PM to visit S. Armagh and Crossmaglen during a rapid border tour. Soon afterwards, she met Taoiseach Jack Lynch in London to urge closer cross-border security co-operation. In Anglo-Irish relations, her December 1980 meeting in Dublin with Charles Haughey, the Fianna Fáil Taoiseach, was regarded as a land-mark, since it promised a review 'of the totality of relations between the two countries'. It was also the most powerful British Government dele-gation ever to have visited Dublin, for she was accompanied by Foreign Secretary Lord Carrington, Chancellor of the Exchequer Sir Geoffrey Howe, and NI Secretary of State Humphrey Atkins. Predictably, it drew fierce opposition from Unionists and heartened Nationalists, despite her claim that the summit held no con-stitutional threat to NI. At a private meeting at Westminster the Rev. Ian Paisley accused her of 'undermining the NI constitutional guarantee', but she denied that she was doing anything of the sort and said she was 'dismayed' by the accusation. She rejected sug-gestions from Unionists that the setting up in 1981 of the British-Irish Inter-governmental Council was in any sense a 'sell-out', and stressed the importance of friendship with the Republic, as well as security and economic co-operation. She agreed with Taoiseach Dr Garret FitzGerald in November 1981 that the two Governments should pursue the idea of an Advisory Council and Parliamentary tier of the BIIC. She had a deteriorating relationship, however, with Haughey, and was particularly angered by his opposition during the Falklands crisis to anti-Argentina sanctions. And she included Enoch Powell MP in Privy Council briefings on the Falklands, although he had several times alleged that the Foreign Office was intriguing against NI's position.

She also kept lines open to OUP leader James Molyneaux (appointed PC, 1983). Her basic unionism was underlined by her declaration in July 1982 that 'no commitment exists for HM Government to consult the Irish Government on matters affecting Northern Ireland'. She said that had always been her Government's position, but in Dublin the Fianna Fáil Government said it was difficult to find any justification for Thatcher's claim. In the H-Block hunger strike she stood out against any major concessions, and was accused by those sympathetic to the protest of being the real obstacle to a settlement. She certainly reflected Unionist attitudes during the crisis and angered the SDLP, whose leader, John Hume, had a tense meeting with her at the height of the dispute. Her relationship with NI Secretary of State James Prior was uneasy at the time of his appointment in September 1981. He was among the Cabinet 'Wets' in his doubts about Government economic policy, and she insisted on moving him from Employment to the NIO – a move which it had seemed initially he might oppose to the point of resignation. When Prior brought forward his 'rolling devolution' initiative, Whitehall sources suggested that she was distancing herself a little from the plan. The PIRA attack on the Conservative conference in Brighton in October 1984 (see Brighton Hotel Bombing) probably swung her thoughts away from Irish political to mainly security issues. Thus, in November 1984 Garret FitzGerald's initial efforts to sell her the approach of the NIF report clearly failed. She publicly dismissed the main Forum options with the words 'out, out, out', to the delight of Unionists and the dismay of Dublin and the SDLP. But the communiqué issued after that London summit committed London and Dublin to reflecting the identities of both

communities 'in the structures and process of Northern Ireland'. The patient diplomacy of FitzGerald concentrated on this point and also the Forum's readiness to accept other ideas outside the main options. Pressure for a new departure in British-Irish relations was also evident in the Cabinet Office and Foreign Office, as well as in Europe and in the US. By February Thatcher in Washington was speaking of her 'excellent relations' with FitzGerald and she told Congress that they would 'continue to consult together in the quest for peace'. (The Irish Government's move in pushing through a special Bill to seize £1.7 million held in an Irish bank, allegedly for PIRA, particularly appealed to the PM.) That quest led to the AIA in November 1985, and the Republic's strong consultative role in NI. She was clearly disappointed by the fierce resistance of Unionists to the agreement, but while repeatedly voicing her own support for the Union, she made no move to appease them. She was also apparently unimpressed by the Republic's anti-terrorist efforts in the wake of the agreement. In particular, she was angered by the Fianna Fáil Government's decision to attach to the new extradition arrangements the proviso that the Irish Attorney-General must have a preview of the evidence supporting each application. Her close relationship with US President Reagan was partly reflected in their common anxiety to defeat terrorism, and both saw PIRA in an international context especially after Libya's role in directly supplying arms to PIRA had been disclosed. There was little surprise that Thatcher went personally to the memorial service for the victims of the Enniskillen bombing in 1987, or that she chose to make her next visit to NI in September 1988, after PIRA had stepped up its assaults, notably against the army. For she was preparing a major security initiative:

she returned to Brighton for the Conservative conference four years after the PIRA attempt there on her life to tell the party that 'this Government will never surrender to the IRA – never'. By then, there had been four Secretaries of State at Stormont during her Premiership and she must have felt that she alone provided continuity in terms of Government experience of NI affairs.

THIRD FORCE

A DUP-sponsored vigilante organisation set up towards the end of 1981. It made an appearance at several rallies addressed by the Rev. Ian Paisley, and it was claimed that its existence had reduced the number of murders of Protestants in border areas. It was organised on a county basis, and a strength of 15,000 to 20,000 was mentioned. It occasionally set up road checks, but around March 1982 adopted a lower profile, although it was claimed that it was still active in offering protection to loyalists living in isolated areas. The launching of the organisation was accompanied by warnings from the authorities that private armies would not be tolerated, and sharp criticism from Nationalists.

THOMPSON, FRANCIS HENRY ESMOND

OUP Convention member for Mid-Ulster, 1975–6. b. Maghera, Co. Derry, 1929. OUP executive, 1971–. Ex-Royal Navy, ex-UDR.

THOMPSON, ROY

DUP Assembly member for S. Antrim, 1982–6. Served on committees on Agriculture, Economic Development, and Security. Dairy farmer. b. 1946. Founder member, DUP, and serves on party executive. Antrim Council, 1981–. In 1987 he was potential candidate in S. Antrim when the DUP decided not to oppose the sitting OUP member.

THOMPSON, WILLIAM JOHN

OUP Assembly member for Mid-Ulster, 1982–6. Chairman, Finance and Personnel Committee; served on committees on Education, Health and Social Services, and Security. Also represented the constituency in 1973–4 Assembly and 1975–6 Convention. b. 1939. Returned in 1973 as anti-White Paper Unionist. Member of OUP committee which drew up party's Convention manifesto. Resigned in January 1983 from OUP's Assembly party as a protest against its refusal to join Assembly committees, but remained party member. Omagh District Council, 1981–. Secretary, Mid- and W. Tyrone Unionist Association, 1972–. Methodist lay preacher.

TIGER BAY

A militant Protestant area adjoining North Queen Street in N. Belfast which has tended to erupt violently when Unionist interests are thought to be threatened.

TIME TO GO

A group launched in July 1988 to promote debate on the withdrawal of troops from NI. Diverse supporters included historian A.J.P. Taylor, *Mirror* group political editor Joe Haines (he was Press Secretary to Harold Wilson in Downing Street), actress Julie Christie, and Labour MP Clare Short, whose parents came from Crossmaglen, Co. Armagh.

TRIMBLE, WILLIAM DAVID

VUPP Convention member for S. Belfast, 1975–6. b. 1944. Unsuccessfully contested N. Down in Assembly election, 1973. He was assistant dean of the Faculty of Law at QUB when he was elected to the Convention, and in the early stages of the Convention took a key role in drafting UUUC proposals. In the split in the Vanguard Party over the plan put forward by William Craig for a voluntary coalition including the SDLP, he supported Craig and then became deputy leader of VUPP. When the VUPP abandoned its party political role in 1978, he joined the OUP and continued to press the case for devolved government. In 1981 he was an unsuccessful candidate for Lisburn Borough Council. He was associated for a time with Ulster Clubs movement before becoming an OUP executive member. In 1988 he was unsuccessful contender for his party's nomination in 1989 European election. Chairman, Lagan Valley Unionist Association.

TROOPS OUT MOVEMENT

A group which operates from a London office and campaigns for the immediate withdrawal of British troops from NI. It has been active since the end of 1969. It organises conferences on the issue, and occasionally sends deputations to NI, which include leading leftist figures in trade unions and trade councils. It has had the support of a small number of Labour MPs, and has been particularly critical of strong anti-terrorist measures. In 1988, when it claimed to be drawing increased support in GB, it condemned the move to ban TV and radio interviews with PSF.

TURNLY, JOHN

IIP councillor, who was shot dead by the UFF in June 1980. He had been SDLP Convention member for N. Antrim, 1975–6, and joined the newly established IIP in 1977, after a policy disagreement with SDLP. b. Ballycastle, Co. Antrim, 1935. A company director who had spent some years in Japan, and a Protestant, he was sitting in his car with his Japanese wife and their two children, when he was killed. One of three men convicted of the murder claimed that he had been working for the SAS. Larne Council, 1973–80. Unsuccessfully contested N. Antrim in

1974 Assembly by-election and 1979 Westminster election.

TUZO, GENERAL SIR HARRY CRAUFURD

Army GOC, NI, 1971–3. b. 1917. Oxford-educated, with a flair for diplomacy, he had a larger political role than any other GOC during the period of violence. He arrived in February 1971, and immediately became involved in the arguments between Stormont and Whitehall which preceded the resignation of Major Chichester-Clark as PM. In a BBC TV interview in June 1971, he said he did not think a permanent solution could be achieved by military means. He thought that about half the Catholic population in NI had Republican aspirations, and of these 25 per cent were prepared to lend passive or active support to the IRA or similar organisations. He was reputed to have agreed to internment without trial only with great reluctance. He once described it as 'distasteful'. But he said the alternatives were to kill IRA men or to bring them before courts where juries could be fixed or witnesses intimidated. He had to cope with the upsurge of violence after the intro- duction of internment, and following direct rule. With the escalating PIRA bombing campaign, he developed undercover army activity against the paramilitaries. These included the Military Reconnaissance Force, which went to the length of setting up a fake laundry service, which was eventually uncovered by the PIRA. He was also responsible for the direction of 'Operation Motorman', mounted in the summer of 1972 for the reoccupation of no-go areas.

TWOMEY, SEAMUS

Became a leading figure in PIRA in 1971, when he succeeded Joe Cahill as head of the organisation in Belfast.

b. Belfast, 1919. Believed to have joined the IRA originally in the 1940s, but was not active in the 1956 campaign. In August 1969 he rejoined the IRA and was one of the leaders of Republican auxiliaries active during loyalist attacks in the Falls Road area. At that time he was manager of a Falls Road bookmaker's. In 1972, as brigade commander in Belfast, he negotiated a brief truce with the British army. Soon afterwards, he was flown to London for the secret talks with Secretary of State William Whitelaw. Became chief of staff of PIRA in March 1973, but after three months as leader he was arrested in the Republic and sentenced to three years' imprisonment for PIRA membership. But in October 1973 he made a dramatic helicopter escape from Dublin's Mountjoy Prison, together with two other leading Republicans, Kevin Mallon and Joe O'Hagan. In 1974 he acted again as chief of staff when Dáithí Ó Conaill was arrested, and he attended the Feakle meeting with Protestant Churchmen in December 1974. During the ceasefire in 1975, at an Easter ceremony at Milltown cemetery in Belfast, he warned that the PIRA would go back to war if its demands were not met in full. In an interview published in the autumn of 1977 Twomey described himself as chief of staff. In December 1977 he was recaptured by the Gardaí in Dublin. He was released in January 1982, and was active in the PSF election campaign in the Republic in February 1982. In 1988 some Conservative MPS protested that the US authorities were continuing to permit Twomey to address NORAID meetings.

TYRIE, ANDREW (ANDY)
Commander of the UDA, 1973–88. b. Belfast, 1940. He was in the UVF before becoming a UDA officer on the Shankill Road in Belfast, and then head of the paramilitary organisation. He was

prominently associated with the loyalist strike in 1974, and the unsuccessful loyalist stoppage in 1977. A tough man of few words, he was credited initially with taking action to 'clean up' the organisation and restrain its violent fringes, and he said on several occasions that the UDA must not get into confrontation with the Catholic community. In July 1974 he led a UDA deputation in talks with the SDLP – a discussion which showed agreement only on opposition to internment. In 1976 he took the UDA out of the ULCCC after claiming that some ULCCC members had been talking to Republicans about independence. But in 1979 the UDA, under his leadership, sponsored the New Ulster Political Research Group, which produced a plan for negotiated independence for NI, and he visited the US with UDA deputation for talks with politicians to promote the policy. Independence was also a central point of policy for the political party, the ULDP, which the UDA launched in 1981. All the indications are that Tyrie has faced a serious problem in reconciling conflicting views within the UDA on what its role should be. In early 1981 he said the UDA might have to cross the border to 'terrorise terrorists', a threat which precipitated fresh demands for the proscription of the organisation. In 1984 terrorist charges against him were dropped, and in 1986 a charge of possessing documents likely to be of use to terrorists was dismissed. Coincidentally, there was growing emphasis on military action within the organisation which was reflected in increased activity by the UFF (violent wing of the organisation). The UDA, while giving muscle to the anti-AIA protest, was critical of its direction and leadership and put forward a new 'Common Sense' plan for devolved power-sharing. But while this political initiative was attracting praise in unexpected quarters, there was also publicity on protection rackets associated with the UDA. The leadership of the UDA had indeed become a hot seat, and Tyrie faced particular hostility from sections of the organisation in late 1987 and early 1988, and was finally ousted in March 1988 shortly after a mystery booby-trap bomb had been found attached to his car. Earlier, he had rejected suggestions that the killing by PIRA in December 1987 of his deputy, John McMichael, had any links with the investigation of racketeering. In 1984 he was co-author of a play, *This is It!*, with the theme of an Ulster identity. (*See also* Ulster Defence Association.)

U

ULSTER
A term frequently applied to NI. It is strictly the name of one of the four ancient provinces in Ireland. Historically nine counties, it varied in size and when NI was formed, three counties – Cavan, Monaghan and Donegal – were separated from the other six and placed in what is now the Republic of Ireland.

ULSTER ARMY COUNCIL
A grouping of loyalist paramilitary organisations which had a vital role in building support for the 1974 loyalist strike. The body was formed in December 1973 and included the UDA, UVF, Ulster Special Constabulary Association, Loyalist Defence Volunteers, Orange Volunteers, and Red Hand Commandos. It said it would work closely with the newly formed UUUC. When the UUUC politicians held a conference in Portrush, Co. Antrim, in April 1974, it joined the UUUC in urging the politicians

to call for an end to the power-sharing Executive, a return to direct rule without any power of veto for the Secretary of State, new elections on PR in smaller constituencies, and an end even to discussion of a Council of Ireland. The UAC warned on the eve of the 1974 loyalist strike that 'if Westminster is not prepared to restore democracy, that is, the will of the people made clear in an election, then the only way it can be restored is by a *coup d'état*'. After the strike, it was replaced by the Ulster Loyalist Central Co-ordinating Committee in 1974.

ULSTER CITIZEN ARMY
The name cropped up several times in 1974, apparently being the title of a group of dissidents from the UDA and UVF. In February 1974 it put out a statement saying that it would assassinate business executives and army officers if the Government succeeded in throwing NI into 'vicious sectarian warfare'. Then in October 1974 it was issuing handbills which alleged that 'power-crazed animals have taken over control of the loyalist paramilitary organisations and have embarked on a programme of wanton slaughter, intimidation, robbery and extortion'. It said that during the previous month a dozen people had been butchered by psychopaths, acting on the orders of loyalist leaders. It promised to supply the addresses of those involved to the security forces. The UCA was also believed to have operated under the name 'The Covenanters'.

ULSTER CLUBS
The organisation was formed in the autumn of 1985 to oppose the rerouting of traditional loyalist parades. After November 1985, it pledged to destroy the AIA. It regarded itself as an umbrella organisation to which all Unionists could belong but

denied that it was a paramilitary body. By January 1986 it claimed to have 8,000 members in 48 branches. It had four main aims: to assert the right to self-determination of the Northern Irish people; to maintain the Union so long as it is in NI's interest; to combat the encroachment of Irish nationalism; and to unify the talents, abilities and resources of Unionists. In short, the aim was to defend NI and the Protestant faith. It professed to stick by the constitutional process but was sceptical about its value and the attitude was to 'hope for the best but to prepare for the worst'. The leader of the Ulster Clubs, Alan Wright, said that he had no faith in the political system after Nationalists had got every concession going for sixteen years through violence. After the January 1986 by-elections, Ulster Clubs said it was instigating a campaign of withdrawal of consent and civil disobedience and awaited a call to action by Unionist political leaders. Alan Wright had lost his father, a policeman, killed by INLA. In 1988 a number of its members were fined for breaches of the new public order legislation. In October 1988 Alan Wright was jailed for failure to pay fines for car tax offences as a protest at the AIA and non-payment of fines for taking part in parades illegal under the public order laws. In October 1988 the membership of Ulster Clubs was said to be about 12,000. Wright stood down as leader in February 1989, because he was considering entering Bible College.

ULSTER CONSTITUTION DEFENCE COMMITTEE

Set up in 1966 under the chairmanship of Rev. Ian Paisley, and active initially in mounting counter-demonstrations to Republican Easter parades and later to coincide with civil rights marches. Closely linked with UPV. In June 1966 Paisley said in a speech in Holywood,

Co. Down, that the UCDC had absolutely no connection with the UVF, which had just been proscribed. The UCDC was prominent in Paisley's 'O'Neill must go' campaign.

ULSTER DEFENCE ASSOCIATION

The largest Protestant paramilitary organisation. Started in September 1971 as a co-ordinating body for loyalist vigilante groups, many of them calling themselves 'Defence Associations', which had grown up in Protestant areas of Belfast and in estates in adjoining areas, such as Newtownabbey, Dundonald and Lisburn. It adopted the motto 'Law before Violence', and took on a distinctly working-class image, excluding MPs and clergymen from membership. It is organised on military lines and at its peak in 1972 it probably had about 40,000 members. By 1978 this had dropped to between 10,000 and 12,000 – a reduction brought about, according to its spokesmen, not by lack of support, but because of a deliberate policy of limiting membership to a readily controllable size. In the 1980s that total is thought to have dropped further, although the organisation has mounted occasional recruiting campaigns. In 1986 one of its recruiting posters showed a member holding an automatic weapon. Indeed, its varied history has been marked by violence (frequently through its now overt military arm, the illegal Ulster Freedom Fighters), by strong-arm tactics in support of loyalist protests, by forays into political thinking (in recent years via the NUPRG and ULDP), and even some acceptance of Gaelic culture as an element in the Ulster identity. This confused image dates from its earliest days. Its first leader, Charles Harding Smith, was acquitted, together with five other men, of being concerned in dealing in £350,000-worth of arms, including a large number of rifles, in early 1972. Smith claimed that meetings set up in London at the time, and which came to the attention of the Special Branch, were really intended to trap PIRA arms dealers. He also said that he had assisted the security forces in NI, and at the trial a letter was read from the Assistant Chief Constable of the RUC, stating that on many occasions Smith had been a pacifier in quarrels between Protestants and Catholics in Belfast. According to police evidence, an official document listing names and ranks of junior PIRA officers, and mentioning Seamus Twomey, Belfast commander of the PIRA, had been found at Smith's Belfast home. In the anti-direct-rule protests of 1972 the UDA was closely involved with the Vanguard movement and LAW, and intermittently with the more violent UVF. Its largest demonstrations took the form of massive parades in Belfast in the summer of 1972. Thousands of UDA men, sometimes masked and wearing combat jackets with military style caps or bush hats, marched through the city centre. In July and August 1972 local units set up their own no-go areas in some loyalist districts of Belfast as a protest against the existence of no-go areas in the Bogside and Creggan areas of Derry. The erection of barricades often entailed the use of concrete mixers, cement blocks and metal spikes. One dispute, on 3 July 1972, over a plan for loyalist barricades between the Springfield (Catholic) and Shankill (Protestant) areas led to about 8,000 uniformed UDA men, many of them carrying iron bars, confronting some 250 troops for an hour and a half while anxious negotiations went on between UDA chiefs and senior officials and army officers. The situation, the ugliest involving Protestants and the security forces since the Shankill Road riots of 1969, was regarded by the UDA as an

impressive demonstration of the speed with which they could rally a large force of their supporters. But this incident, and the massive parades, were regarded by Catholic interests as evidence that the security forces were adopting too soft a line towards loyalist militants. Privately, however, the army was talking toughly to the UDA. In the no-go row the UDA held its hand over the 12 July period of 1972 and then its thirteen-man council had talks with Secretary of State William Whitelaw. They got the impression that Government action was pending against the Derry barricades, and in the event the Bogside and Creggan were opened up in 'Operation Motorman' at the end of July. But in the autumn of 1972, when the UDA mounted street protests against the Government's security policy, they were involved in disputes with the army about the circumstances in which some Protestants had been killed. In mid-October, after a meeting between UDA leaders and the army, there was a statement that both sides would try to take the heat out of the situation, and an assurance that all complaints against the army would be investigated by the RUC. In September 1973 Tommy Herron, who had been the UDA's deputy leader until he unsuccessfully fought the Assembly election in E. Belfast, was murdered in mysterious circumstances. His body was found near Lisburn and he had been shot in the head. There were many rumours that he had been killed by loyalist extremists but this was rejected by the UDA, who said they were satisfied that no Protestant organisation had been involved. The biggest operation of the UDA was in the loyalist strike of May 1974, which led to the break-up of the power-sharing administration. The UDA was first involved in the 'Ulster Army Council', a small grouping of Protestant paramilitaries, and then in the larger Ulster Workers' Council, which organised the strike effort. The UDA commander, Andy Tyrie, was on the UWC Co-ordinating Committee, and the organisation provided much of the muscle in mounting road blocks. Critics of the strike alleged that the UDA had been heavily engaged in intimidation of people who wanted to stay at work. In June, after the fall of the Executive, the UDA said that while it ruled out talks with PIRA, it was prepared to meet elected representatives, including PSF. In the same month the UDA issued a statement on behalf of the UFF, saying that it wanted an end to violence. It now became clear that the UFF was indeed the violent wing of the UDA. When it first became active in mid-1973, it was thought to be a breakaway group from the UDA. PIRA made contradictory allegations about its make-up, saying in January 1974 that it was a British army killer squad, and then six months later that it was composed of 'criminals from the Catholic and Protestant communities'. From 1974 on there were numerous UFF telephone claims of murders of Catholics (often alleging that their victims had PIRA associations), and bomb attacks on Catholic churches, schools and public houses. The phone calls were often said to be from 'Captain White' or 'Captain Black'. Among such claims were the murder of Fine Gael Senator Billy Fox in Co. Monaghan in March 1974, and of SDLP Senator Paddy Wilson in Belfast in June 1973. The claim in respect of Senator Fox was not, however, taken seriously in the Republic. The UDA's June 1974 statement, saying that the UFF had seen enough of violence, added that it would be happy if, after the Assembly elections, it was discovered that all shades of opinion could work together. But the UFF reserved the 'right' to retaliate if attacks were made on loyalist areas. In July 1977 the UFF in Londonderry claimed to have bombed a Catholic church at Greysteel, Co. Derry, in reprisal, they said, for the burning of Bellaghy Orange Hall. In June 1979 eleven Scottish UDA men were given heavy prison sentences for furthering the aims of the organisation by unlawfully acquiring arms and ammunition. One group of seven were given 164 years between them, and the supreme commander of the UDA in Scotland, James Hamilton, aged forty-four, was sentenced to 15 years – the heaviest sentence. Four others were sentenced to between seven and twelve years for furthering the aims of the UDA in Paisley and the west of Scotland. The judge, Lord Wylie, spoke of a 'reign of terror' by the UDA commander in Paisley, William Currie, who was sentenced to twelve years' imprisonment. (The Scottish connection was stressed again in February 1981, when a Scottish member claimed on TV that there were 2,000 UDA members in Scotland. He also said there were Scottish stockpiles of arms and 'safe houses' for loyalist fugitives, and that arms and ammunition had been smuggled to NI through Larne.) A clandestine news conference in Belfast in 1979, following the PIRA murder of Lord Mountbatten, was told that it had been reorganised and re-equipped and was now the most powerful loyalist paramilitary organisation. It also claimed to have drawn up a 'death list' of known Republicans in NI, GB and the Republic. Almost immediately afterwards, it claimed the murder of a twenty-seven-year-old married man in N. Belfast. Two men jailed for the murder of IIP councillor John Turnly in Carnlough, Co. Antrim, in June 1980 were said by the prosecution to be members of the UFF. It was active during the H-Block hunger strike, and is believed to have carried out at least

274

five sectarian murders during 1981. In September 1981 it referred to another 'death list', this time related to alleged PIRA and INLA informers. In 1981 INLA shot dead a leading UDA man, Billy McCullough, on the Shankill Road in Belfast, in retaliation, it said, for loyalist murders of Catholics. In the same year it shot and seriously injured UDA councillor Sammy Millar at his home in the Shankill area. In the early 1980s the UDA seemed to be beset by uncertainties, with an internal clash between those who argued for more political action and those who regarded it as essentially a Protestant counter-terror organisation. It refused to back the Rev. Ian Paisley's 'Day of Action' and Third Force in 1981, and seemed to ridicule the idea of protest marches. But in April and May 1981 it mounted some local shows of strength, putting some 2,500 men on the Shankill Road, in what was termed 'purely defensive mobilisation' and several hundred men on parade in the Fountain area of Londonderry. In February 1981 Tyrie threatened that UDA men might cross the border to 'terrorise the terrorists'. This statement revived demands from Nationalists for the outlawing of the organisation, but proscription was once more rejected by the NIO. But the security forces kept up pressure on the UDA, and in April 1982 terrorist charges were brought against several leading members but were later dropped. The court was told during a preliminary hearing that files on judges, police and IRA suspects had been found during the police raids. In the mid- and late 1980s the UFF was frequently involved in sectarian murders, and the seizures in 1988 of large quantities of weapons and ammunition intended for the UDA raised fears of major confrontations between loyalists and PIRA. In early January 1988 the UDA's Belfast HQ was raided by the RUC, who took away

documents. The UDA seemed to be intent on avenging the murder, in December 1987, by PIRA of the UDA's deputy leader, John McMichael, who died when a bomb went off under his car outside his Lisburn home. In October 1988 the UFF claimed the murder of prominent UDA man James Craig, who was shot dead in a bar in E. Belfast. They accused him of 'treason' and linked his actions to the killing of McMichael. When McMichael died, there were suggestions that he might have been set up for PIRA by people within the UDA who resented his investigation of UDA racketeering, although Andy Tyrie rejected the idea of any such connection. The killing of Craig came shortly after another leading UDA man, Billy Quee, was shot dead in N. Belfast by IPLO. In 1985 charges against both Craig and Quee of extorting money from building contractors had failed. (In 1988 security sources were suggesting that the UDA might be raising as much as £3 million a year from a variety of protection rackets.) But alongside strictly paramilitary activities, the UDA has always sought to project a political dimension, something which its Nationalist critics have tended to regard as a smokescreen for violence. In August 1974, after the UDA had resigned from the UWC and the ULCCC, it had a meeting with SDLP representatives. The SDLP spokesmen were Gerry Fitt, John Hume, Paddy Devlin, Ivan Cooper and Hugh Logue. The UDA was represented by Andy Tyrie, Bill Snoddy, Tommy Lyttle, and Ronnie Reid. But while there was united opposition to internment, there was no agreement about the political future. The UDA said the SDLP had been hypocritical, and insisted that it should drop its united Ireland aspiration. Fitt felt that the meeting had shown an intense power struggle within the UDA. In November 1974 a UDA delegation visited Libya, headed by its political adviser, Glen Barr, a Vanguard Assembly member. The meeting created controversy, since a PSF deputation was in Libya at the same time. Both sides denied that there had been any negotiations between them, and a Dublin banker who had arranged the UDA visit said it had been concerned with the development of offshore oil and other resources. But in a personal comment Barr admitted that the deputation had been seeking possible economic aid for an independent NI. During the Constitutional Convention, Barr's support for Vanguard leader William Craig's idea of a voluntary coalition, including the SDLP, seems to have influenced UDA thinking. Andy Tyrie expressed support for Craig's scheme, and blamed the Rev. Ian Paisley and Harry West for the failure of the Convention, and suggested that they would be responsible for further deaths. But whatever their reservations about loyalist politicians, the UDA supported the United Unionist Action Council when it mounted a strike in May 1977 as a protest against Government security policy and continued direct rule. The Rev. Ian Paisley and Ernest Baird were the two main politicians involved in the UUAC, and the strike turned out to be a half-hearted affair. In early 1978 the UDA warned against retaliation by Protestants when twelve people were burned to death in the La Mon House Hotel which had been fire-bombed by PIRA. It also warned in July 1978 that it would 'no longer be the willing tool of any aspiring or ready-made politician'. In February 1979 a deputation visited the US for talks with leading politicians. In March 1979 a plan for an independent NI was proposed by the New Ulster Political Research Group, which the UDA had set up in January 1978, after discussions between Andy Tyrie and Glen Barr. They claimed that nego-

tiated independence was the only settlement acceptable to both sides of the community. The proposal envisaged that an Assembly would be elected for four years, but Ministers would be appointed – as in the US – and neither they, nor the PM, would sit in the Assembly. The Ministers would be chosen by the elected president, his deputy, and the PM, although they would have to be endorsed by the Assembly, which would deal with legislation. In the May 1981 council elections, one NUPRG candidate out of three was returned in Belfast (Sammy Millar, who had been seriously injured in an assassination attempt). Soon afterwards, and coincidental with the withdrawal of NUPRG chairman Glen Barr from active politics, the Ulster Loyalist Democratic Party was launched in June 1981 to replace it. Its line seemed to be independence within the Commonwealth and the EC, which its first chairman, John McMichael, suggested would be acceptable to many Catholics. The party seemed to take a good deal of encouragement from the support for independence from the *Sunday Times* and ex-PM James Callaghan. But it found the electoral going hard. It failed in its first bid – a Belfast council by-election in E. Belfast in August 1981, where the candidate received 3.2 per cent of the vote. John McMichael got fewer than 600 votes in the S. Belfast by-election in February 1982. Its two candidates in the 1982 Assembly election (both in N. Belfast) polled only 1,086 votes (0.2 per cent). The party did not contest the 1983 general election or the 1984 election for the European Parliament. It contested the 1985 District Council elections with only two candidates, but neither succeeded and they gained only 782 votes (0.1 per cent). In the protest actions against the AIA the UDA voiced its opposition but seemed content that mainstream Unionist political leaders took the lead. In particular, it ruled out any repetition of the 1974 stoppage but favoured civil disobedience, and its members were active in protests against the AIA and in the March 1986 'Day of Action'. ULDP did not contest the January 1986 by-elections and in February John McMichael caused some surprise by urging that PSF be included in any constitutional conference. What the conference should discuss emerged at the end of January 1987 when the UDA published 'Common Sense'. The document showed sensitivity to the Ulster-identity issue and to minorities; it envisaged an Assembly and Executive, elected by PR and resulting in an all-party coalition, a Bill of Rights and a written Constitution. The proposals received a very favourable response in Britain and in Ireland, and SDLP leader John Hume termed it 'constructive' and said his party was prepared to treat it as a basis for discussion despite its 'surprising source'. The NIO broadly welcomed it. But the UDA supported the Unionist demand that the AIA must be set aside, at least temporarily, for negotiations to go ahead, and with the continuing political impasse, UDA activity tended to switch towards the military. Its involvement in the importation in 1988 of large quantities of sophisticated weaponry, and growing fragmentation at the top, together with UFF sectarian murders, created a dangerous mixture. The murder by PIRA of McMichael in December 1987 was followed three months later by the ousting of Tyrie as leader, soon after a bomb was found under his car. Tyrie's leadership was replaced by collective control by the six members of the inner council. They claimed that, together with the UFF, they would direct a military campaign against PIRA, and build on the political front created by their devolution document. No 'innocent Catholic' had

anything to fear from them, they said. But in March 1988 three men – two of them ex-UDR – were sentenced for their part in an armed raid of a massive haul of weapons for the UDA from a UDR camp in Coleraine. In October 1988 four members of a UDA killer squad from N. Belfast were jailed for life, with Mr Justice Nicholson commenting that the UDA was 'comparable in many ways' to PIRA and INLA. In November 1988 Judge Nicholson urged the Protestant community to stop the UDA 'living off them', when he sentenced Davy Payne, a one-time prominent UDA man, to nineteen years' imprisonment for possession of the biggest haul of loyalist arms uncovered during the Troubles at Portadown in January 1987; two accomplices were sentenced to fourteen years. The following month four UDA men were sentenced to a total of thirty years on blackmail charges after two of the accused had been filmed by TV investigator Roger Cook, who posed as an English financier planning a major development in Co. Armagh. The two principals were sentenced to ten years each and two others to seven and three years respectively. Both the UDA and UFF were named in the broadcasting ban applied to paramilitary organisations in November 1988. Towards the end of 1988 the ULDP in Londonderry said that it would contest the 1989 District Council election and Gary McMichael, son of the murdered UDA leader, said that he would seek the nomination for the European election. At that time the ULDP was claiming to be wholly independent of the UDA. (*See also* Tyrie, Andrew.)

ULSTER DEFENCE REGIMENT *see* Security System section, pp. 397–8

ULSTER DOMINION GROUP *see* British Ulster Dominion Party

ULSTER FREEDOM FIGHTERS
Illegal military wing of the UDA (*see* Ulster Defence Association).

ULSTER INDEPENDENCE ASSOCIATION
A group campaigning for an independent, sovereign NI. Urges an assembly of up to 100 members elected by PR list system, with a consensus government and non-political president. The transfer of responsibility from Westminster would be achieved by negotiation, particularly on interim financial arrangements. It would seek a declaration from the Republic that it respects the sovereignty of an independent, peaceful NI. Claims some Catholic support. The association was active in 1979 in seeking to arrange a Washington peace forum, and it handled invitations on behalf of Congressman Mario Biaggi, chairman of the *ad hoc* Congressional Committee on Irish affairs in Washington. Its chairman, George Allport, a businessman, visited the US in 1977 and 1979 for talks with politicians. One of its deputy leaders was E. Belfast loyalist John McKeague, shot dead in 1982 by INLA.

ULSTER INDEPENDENCE COMMITTEE
The committee was formed early in 1988 under the leadership of the Rev. Hugh Ross, a Presbyterian minister from Newmills, Dungannon, Co. Tyrone. It seeks an end to sectarian politics through unity on a common Ulster identity. It advocates a written Constitution, a Bill of Rights and the existence of a sovereign, independent NI as an alternative to the 'tyrannical and arbitrary rule of the London/Dublin coalition' leading to a united Ireland. After a series of summer rallies and speaking engagements, Mr Ross said that eleven branches had been formed.

ULSTER INDEPENDENCE PARTY
Launched on a small scale in October 1977 with the object of securing 'by democratic means, a sovereign, free and independent Ulster'. Government would be based on proportional power-sharing at all levels, and the party said Protestants and Catholics should join hands in a spirit of friendship. An initial statement said that in May 1976 the Ulster Independence movement had issued an economic survey and feasibility study. This had been published in the US in July 1976 by the Ulster Heritage Society, under the title *Towards an Independent Ulster*. These documents had shown that NI, with an export performance much superior to that of either GB or the Republic, could be economically feasible on its own. In January 1978 the UIP said it could not accept the idea of 'interim independence' mentioned as a possibility by the Catholic Primate, Cardinal Ó Fiaich, since this would be a contradiction in terms.

ULSTER LIBERAL PARTY
The party, linked with the British Liberal Party, has been at a low ebb in recent years, and the presumption is that many of its supporters moved to the Alliance Party. Sheelagh Murnaghan sat in the former Stormont Parliament for QUB. She and the former chairperson, Rev. Albert McElroy, were prominent in the demand for reforms. Two candidates who stood in the Assembly elections in 1973 forfeited their deposits and the party was not represented in the Convention election in 1975. In 1977 and 1978 it organised 'fringe' meetings on NI at the British Liberal assemblies. The party put up a candidate, Jim Murray, a teacher, in the 1979 European election, but he received only 932 first-preference votes (0.1 per cent). In the next few years its activities seemed to

be minimal, although it did sponsor a candidate in S. Belfast in the 1982 Assembly election, who secured sixty-five votes. In 1985 the party had one candidate, Michael Colin J. McGuigan, for Ards Borough Council, and he polled only thirty-five votes. It has not fought any subsequent election up to 1988.

ULSTER LOYALIST ASSOCIATION

A body prominent between 1969 and 1972 in opposing any interference with the NI Constitution, and urging stronger security policies, notably against the PIRA. Its leading figures were William Craig, the Rev. Martin Smyth and Captain Austin Ardill, and many of its members were also Orangemen. The ULA organised a series of rallies throughout NI, and Captain Ardill, speaking as chairman in 1971, called for the severing of diplomatic relations with the Republic and the sealing of the border.

ULSTER LOYALIST CENTRAL CO-ORDINATING COMMITTEE

The organisation set up after the 1974 loyalist strike to act as a forum for loyalist paramilitary organisations. It replaced the Ulster Army Council set up in 1973. The ULCCC originally included the UDA, UVF, RHC, LAW, VSC, Orange Volunteers, and Down Orange Welfare. In 1976 the UDA and Down Orange Welfare withdrew after suggestions that some members of the ULCCC were meeting members of the PIRA and talking to a wide range of Catholics about the possibility of an independent NI. Its co-chairman, loyalist John McKeague, was shot dead in his E. Belfast shop in January 1982. A claim by INLA that it was responsible was generally accepted, although there had been a telephone claim of responsibility, allegedly from the RHC.

ULSTER LOYALIST DEMOCRATIC PARTY

The UDA-sponsored political party set up in June 1981 (see Ulster Defence Association).

ULSTER POPULAR UNIONIST PARTY

Founded by James Kilfedder MP in January 1980 as the Ulster Progressive Unionist Party but the name was changed in March to Popular Unionist to avoid confusion with the Progressive Unionist Party of Hugh Smyth. Kilfedder's break with OUP resulted from disagreements on party policy and leadership after 1976 when the leader at Westminster was James Molyneaux. The formal break came when Kilfedder took offence at a personal letter written to him by party leader Harry West. Encouraged by a 23,625 majority over OUP opposition in the 1979 general election, and runner-up in the election to the European Parliament in May 1979, the UPUP was launched in 1980. Its first electoral test was the District Council elections of 1981 when twenty candidates (including seven women), were promoted, and a temporary electoral pact concluded with nine UPNI candidates. Five UPUP candidates were elected, two in Ards and three in N. Down. The appearance of being more than a personality party took a knock in the Assembly election of 1982 when two candidates polled 2.5 quotas but only Kilfedder was elected as his surplus transferred more to other parties than to his running mate George Green. In 1983 Kilfedder was the sole flag-bearer for his party in the new constituency of N. Down, which he held against OUP, Alliance Party and SDLP competition, with 22,861 votes, and a majority of 13,846. He also contested the 1984 election for the European Parliament, receiving 20,092 votes (2.9 per cent), but he did not stand under his party label but as Speaker of the NI Assembly. By the time of the 1985 District Council elections some of his members had drifted back to the main parties and the five UPUP candidates polled 3,139 votes (0.5 per cent), and three were elected, two in N. Down and Kilfedder's sister Gladys McIntyre in Ards. In the aftermath of the AIA in 1985, by which he felt strongly betrayed by the Conservatives, he resigned his seat with the other Unionist MPs and fought the January by-elections without opposition from OUP or DUP. At the general election of June 1987 he remained unopposed by OUP and DUP but his majority was reduced to 3,953 by Robert McCartney QC, an expelled OUP member standing as a 'Real Unionist' candidate. At the end of 1988 the party remained largely a 'personality party' with a few members in district councils.

ULSTER PROTESTANT ACTION GROUP

A paramilitary group active mainly in 1974 which was responsible for the assassination of many Catholics. The security forces believed that it was comprised of dissident members of the UDA. In a statement in October 1974 it said that the assassinations would continue 'until the Provisional IRA are exterminated'. The group apparently adopted the name of an organisation active before the Troubles in encouraging the employment of Protestants in industry. The name 'Protestant Action' reappeared in 1981 when there were claims at a clandestine news conference that it would kill 'active Republicans'. In 1982 it claimed the murders of several people, including a PSF election worker in Armagh. At that time there were suggestions that it had some link with the illegal RHC.

ULSTER PROTESTANT VOLUNTEERS

A loyalist paramilitary group associated with the UCDC. It was involved in many counter-demonstrations to civil rights meetings in the period 1968–7. Organised in local divisions, it styled itself 'a united Society of Protestant patriots, pledged by all lawful methods to uphold and maintain the constitution of NI as an integral part of the UK so long as the UK maintains a Protestant monarchy and the terms of the revolution settlement'. The UPV accompanied most of the Rev. Ian Paisley's parades during the early civil rights period.

ULSTER RESISTANCE

The organisation was launched at an invitation-only rally in the Ulster Hall, Belfast, in November 1986. It was attended by the Rev. Ian Paisley MP, Peter Robinson MP, and the Rev. Ivan Foster. Rallies were then held in other towns such as Portadown, Kilkeel, Larne and Londonderry and the organisation became identified with a red beret. At one time it was said to have comprised nine battalions. Since the summer of 1987 very little was heard of the organisation. It was rumoured that relations with the DUP and politicians began to cool when the politicians opted for talks rather than a more hostile campaign against the AIA and the British Government. However, a major arms find in Co. Armagh in November 1988 – with weapons similar to those seized earlier from the UDA at Portadown and the UVF in Belfast – the discovery of five red berets and the arrest of a former DUP District Council candidate brought Ulster Resistance and the links with DUP under close scrutiny. A statement by DUP said that they had been informed that the organisation was being put on ice in the summer of 1987, and party association and contacts were ended, though individuals may have continued membership. Experts accepted that the arms had been dumped and had not been used for terrorist acts and Ulster Resistance had no record of paramilitary involvement.

ULSTER SERVICE CORPS

A loyalist vigilante group established in 1977, with the support of the United Unionist Action Council. In the spring of 1977 it mounted road blocks from time to time in parts of S. Derry, Armagh and Tyrone, and claimed to have some liaison with members of the RUC and UDR, although this was denied by the authorities. Its activities included observation of alleged PIRA 'safe houses'. It claimed to have a membership of about 500 throughout NI. Some of its members were summoned for obstruction, and a spokesman for the Government accused it of wasting the time of the security forces who had to be diverted to deal with it. The SDLP protested strongly that there was evidence of collusion with the UDR to the extent that joint patrols were operated in some areas of mid-Ulster. Most of its original members are believed to have served with the former Ulster Special Constabulary (B Specials).

ULSTER SPECIAL
CONSTABULARY *see* Security System section, pp. 383–5

ULSTER SPECIAL
CONSTABULARY ASSOCIATION

An association bringing together ex-B Specials, who were disbanded officially in 1970, following the adoption by the Government of the Hunt report. The USCA has operated as a pressure group, calling for tougher anti-IRA measures and more local control of security. It has been associated with loyalist paramilitary groups, notably in support of the loyalist strike in 1974.

Exact strength uncertain, but probably had backing of 10,000 ex-B Specials in 1970.

ULSTER UNIONIST PARTY

Popularly styled the Official Unionist Party in recent years, it is the largest political entity in NI. It is substantially the party which provided the Government of NI at Stormont from 1921 to March 1972, when direct rule from London was imposed. Up to the late 1960s, when pro- and anti-Premier O'Neill factions became sharply differentiated, the party was essentially a coalition embracing a left-to-right spectrum of opinion committed to the maintenance of the link with Britain and the defence of the NI Parliament. In the face of demands for reform from the civil rights movement, and tensions caused by the violence, it was weakened by a series of breakaway movements: supporters of O'Neill who moved to the Alliance Party or out of active politics; anti-O'Neill people who moved to Vanguard or the DUP; pro-Faulkner members who moved to UPNI. In most of the Parliaments from 1921 until 1972, the Unionists held around forty of the fifty-two seats in the NI House of Commons, and they usually held at least ten of the twelve Westminster seats. It was unquestionably a party of government, and some Unionist MPs had never had to fight an election. So the closing down of the old Stormont Parliament in 1972 was a severe shock, and one which eventually forced the hard core of the party into combination with smaller Unionist parties. Under the pressure of events, the working-class element in the party became more powerful, and the influence of the 'county families' was visibly reduced. Key meetings of the party ceased to be held midweek when few average workers were able to attend. An enlarged executive took charge of policy, instead of the former

1,000-strong Unionist Council and 300-member Standing Committee which had held frequent meetings during the O'Neill crisis. And although the party was a branch of the British Conservative Party, entitled to send full voting representatives to party conferences, the action of the Heath Government in suspending Stormont strained to breaking point an inter-party link which had existed from the days of the earliest Home Rule controversy in the late nineteenth century. In the 1973 election to the new Assembly, the party was split between those who followed Faulkner's lead and backed the power-sharing policy of Westminster and those who opposed the British Government's White Paper. The election resulted in the return of twenty-three candidates supporting the White Paper, and ten who were against. A major crisis for the party developed in January 1974, after Faulkner and his colleagues had joined a power-sharing Executive which included the SDLP and the Alliance Party. The Ulster Unionist Council rejected by 427 to 374 the Sunningdale Agreement, which provided the basis for the Executive. This brought about the resignation of Faulkner as party leader, and he was succeeded by Harry West. Soon afterwards, the February 1974 Westminster election gave the anti-Sunningdale Unionists the opportunity to test their support. They chose to join with the DUP and Vanguard in the UUUC. The Unionist Coalition secured eleven out of the twelve seats, and West was returned in Fermanagh–S. Tyrone. He led the Coalition at Westminster into a neutral stance at a time when their votes, if they had been sought, could have kept the Heath Government in office. The fact that the Unionist Coalition had got more than 50 per cent of the votes in NI was a severe blow to the three-party Executive. But the new Labour Government was just as committed to power-sharing as the Conservatives, and by rejecting the demand for fresh Assembly elections, the Executive survived until the loyalist strike, organised by the UWC and backed by the Official Unionists and its partners, effectively brought life to a standstill in May 1974. The Coalition continued into the elections for the Constitutional Convention in 1975, but the fragmentation of unionism had its effects. The Official Unionists now obtained 25.8 per cent of the votes, and nineteen seats; they were no longer the predominant party, and if they were still against any partnership with the SDLP, they had to face the fact that they must co-operate with some other parties to achieve anything. The Official Unionists together with the DUP and Vanguard backed the majority Convention report which provided for majority Cabinet rule, and argued that opposition influence should be achieved through a system of committees linked to the various Stormont departments. But it did not meet Westminster's criteria for devolved government. In the later stage of the Convention the Official Unionists stood out against the move by William Craig to try to get agreement for a voluntary coalition which would include the SDLP for the period of the emergency. And it now formed part of the UUUC which included the DUP and those members (the majority) of Vanguard who disagreed with Craig, and who now made up the UUUM under Ernest Baird, who had been Craig's deputy in Vanguard. After the break-up of the Convention in 1976, two Official Unionists (the Rev. Martin Smyth and Captain Austin Ardill) became involved in private, but unsuccessful, talks with John Hume and Paddy Devlin of the SDLP. The secrecy surrounding these talks gave rise to friction between the party and the Rev.

Ian Paisley and Ernest Baird. This gap was widened in 1977 when the Official Unionists stood aside from the Action Council which organised the loyalist strike – a largely abortive stoppage – in May 1977 against direct rule and in support of a tougher security policy. The Official Unionists also refused to support a parallel operation – an unofficial vigilante group known as the Ulster Service Corps, which appeared briefly in some areas during 1977. Again, Official Unionists declined to have any UUUC endorsement of their candidates in the May 1977 District Council elections. In that election Official Unionists had 29.6 per cent of the first-preference votes and 33.8 per cent of the seats (178). In June 1977 the Official Unionists accepted 'the *de facto* collapse of the UUUC'. The party was now set upon a more independent course, and the Parliamentary Unionist Coalition at Westminster also ended. Six Official Unionist MPs, under the leadership of James Molyneaux, became a separate group, and William Craig joined them in 1978. Since October 1974, Enoch Powell in S. Down had been an OUP MP, and his aversion to the Conservatives, plus tactical awareness were obviously factors in securing from a Labour Government, lacking an overall majority after April 1976, support for a Speaker's conference to examine the long-standing demand of Unionists for extra seats for NI at Westminster. This all-party conference reported in 1978 in favour of five extra NI seats, with discretion to the Boundary Commission to have one more or one less. But the Conservatives, also with an eye to Unionist votes at Westminster, strongly backed the OUP call for the introduction of regional councils in NI as a way of filling the administrative gap created by the absence of any Stormont Assembly. In 1978 the Official Unionists turned down a plea

by the DUP for some sort of agreement on the allocation of candidates in the coming Westminster elections. Party leader Harry West pointed out to the Rev. Ian Paisley that the party's constitution prevented it giving any directions to local associations on the choice of candidates. Although the OUP retains its long-standing association with the Orange Order, its importance has declined in recent years with the divisions in unionism. In the 1979 European election, one of its two candidates, John Taylor, was successful on the sixth count, but party leader Harry West was eliminated. The party's overall performance was not impressive. The combined total of first preferences for the party was 21.8 per cent compared with 29.8 per cent for DUP leader, the Rev. Ian Paisley, and 24.5 per cent for SDLP candidate John Hume. West conceded that perhaps 100,000 party supporters had refused to back the party line of calling for extensive renegotiation of the EC as distinct from the outright opposition of Paisley. The result led directly to the resignation of Harry West as party leader in July 1979. The Parliamentary leader, James Molyneaux, succeeded him. But the hopes of the OUP that the Thatcher Government would prove helpful to their aims were soon disappointed. The party's annual report regretted that the PM 'has followed, not her own instincts, but those of Lord Carrington and the Foreign Office'. There was some surprise, however, that the OUP decided to boycott the Stormont Constitutional Conference announced by Secretary of State Humphrey Atkins in November 1979. Molyneaux called it 'a time-wasting exercise and window-dressing'. But although the party stayed away from the discussions, it sent proposals for majority government to the PM. When the failure of the Constitutional Conference

283

was followed by a plan for a fifty-member Advisory Council, this too was turned down by the party. The OUP was also highly suspicious of the London–Dublin contacts, and especially the December 1980 summit in Dublin at which Margaret Thatcher and Charles Haughey initiated a review of 'the totality of relations between the two countries'. Although the PM repeated on every possible occasion the constitutional pledge on NI, many OUP people, and notably Enoch Powell, saw a Foreign Office conspiratorial approach in every Anglo-Irish gesture. OUP–DUP rivalry was renewed in the 1981 council elections, and again the OUP fell behind the DUP, if only marginally, in terms of votes, although it maintained its superiority in seats. The OUP also became quickly antagonistic towards Atkins's successor, James Prior. After the murder of the party's S. Belfast MP, the Rev. Robert Bradford, in November 1981, its anger was directed at the Government's security policy. It joined in the loyalist 'Day of Action' on 23 November, when rallies and meetings were sponsored by both the OUP and DUP to demand a more aggressive approach to security by the authorities. It also co-operated for a time with the DUP in the adjournment of loyalist-controlled councils as part of the security protest. The OUP tended, however, to distance itself from the DUP, and rejected the DUP suggestion that a united Unionist candidate should be run in the S. Belfast by-election in February 1982, and it had the satisfaction of seeing its candidate, the Rev. Martin Smyth, win easily, with the DUP in third place. Prior's 'rolling devolution' initiative in 1982 found the OUP slightly divided, but most opinion went along with the leadership in regarding the Assembly as a revival of power-sharing and Sunningdale and as an institution which could fit in with

Government plans for a Parliamentary tier of the British-Irish Intergovernmental Council. Since the DUP was welcoming the scrutiny powers of the proposed Assembly, many OUP members saw the possibility of outflanking the Rev. Ian Paisley in the Assembly elections. OUP MPs, for the most part, were active in opposing the legislation for the Assembly and they co-operated, to some extent, with right-wing Conservatives who mounted a filibuster on the committee stage. They also propagated the view that Thatcher was by no means wholeheartedly behind the Prior plan. When the Falklands crisis broke, the OUP MPs threw themselves enthusiastically behind the PM's strong response, and even drew parallels with the Irish Republic's claims over NI. They were aided in this by the Republic's opposition to sanctions against Argentina, and Thatcher pointedly included Enoch Powell in her Privy Council briefings on the situation. Prior warned against making comparisons between the Falklands and the NI situation. In the end the OUP had to face the fact that Prior had got his Assembly measure through virtually unscathed, but they did recover their lead in the popular vote in the Assembly elections, with 29.7 per cent to 23 per cent, and got twenty-six seats to the DUP's twenty-one. In the 1983 Westminster election the party went a small way with the Rev. Ian Paisley's bid to secure an electoral pact. It reached an arrangement on three seats whereas the DUP leader wanted to cover six. The 1983 Westminster election represented the party's best showing since before direct rule. It took 34 per cent of the vote and eleven of the seventeen seats. It thus pulled 14 per cent ahead of DUP which got three seats and 20 per cent of the vote. There was, however, a 'limited understanding' between the two parties. This meant that DUP did not contest Newry and Armagh, and Fermanagh–S. Tyrone while OUP stood down in Foyle. However, in the personality contest of the second election to the European Parliament in 1984 the Rev. Ian Paisley and DUP pulled ahead with 33.6 per cent to 20 per cent for John Taylor (OUP). The results of the 1985 District Council elections showed that OUP had reversed the 1981 position and confirmed their position ahead of DUP in 1982 and 1983. OUP polled 29.5 per cent of the votes compared to 24.3 per cent for DUP and won 180 seats to 142. The signing of the AIA six months later forced the two party leaders to co-operate over their tactics of constitutional opposition. The by-election tactic, when fifteen Unionist MPs resigned their seats and forced by-elections as a test of opinion on the AIA, saw them poll 418,230 votes in what was the fourth-best poll since 1920. But they lost one seat, Newry and Armagh, to Seamus Mallon (SDLP), and by restricted competition as in 1983, there was no guide as to whether public opinion was behind the more radical young bloods of the DUP or the more restrained OUP. After the March 'Day of Action' and some minor violence, the differences became more apparent. Despite the clear frustration of some DUP members the two parties contested the 1987 general election in the same constituencies as in 1983. While another seat was lost, S. Down, and the vote fell to below 400,000, OUP was seen to be clearly ahead with 37.8 per cent to 11.7 per cent. The vote fell because of limited competition in the hope of electing a block of fourteen MPs; but it also fell because of Alliance Party criticism of the Unionist negative stance and boycott of Parliament, and because of competition from Campaign for Equal Citizenship arguments by Robert McCartney QC in N. Down. The return of the Conservative

Government with a majority of 101 and committed to the AIA forced a rethink of Unionist strategy. MPs returned to Westminster, Unionist leaders began a series of 'talks about talks' on whether the Government was willing to consider an alternative to the AIA. Early in 1988 the nature of the talks changed and a set of proposals was submitted. The boycott of District Council business gradually petered out. When no reply was received to the outline proposals after eight months, they were sent to the PM and her reply commented that they were 'interesting and progressive'. Within OUP, criticism of the links with DUP have become muted as the association has become a restraint on DUP. Further, despite some pressure, especially from Fermanagh Unionists, Ken Maginnis and Raymond Ferguson, and the Charter Group, for progress on devolution, the position of the leadership was secure at the November 1988 conference. With devolution available only under the AIA and much opinion in favour of integration, the conference acclaimed Molyneaux's assertion that 'this is no time for turning' and his appeal to 'stand fast'.

ULSTER VANGUARD
A pressure group within unionism, led by William Craig, and launched at the beginning of 1972, when the possibility of direct rule from Westminster began to be discussed seriously. Its purpose was to provide an umbrella organisation for loyalists in a bid to overcome the weaknesses of their party divisions. It had strong support from loyalist paramilitary groups. The deputy leaders, at the start, were the Rev. Martin Smyth and Captain Austin Ardill. Vanguard organised rallies, to which Craig travelled frequently in an open car with a motor cycle escort provided by the Vanguard Service Corps, a paramilitary group directly

linked with the organisation. A rally in Ormeau Park, Belfast, in March 1972 attracted about 60,000 people, and it mounted a forty-eight-hour strike by its supporters against direct rule. William Craig's remark at the Ormeau Park rally that 'if the politicians fail, it will be our duty to liquidate the enemy', brought angry protests from his critics that Vanguard was a fascist movement. Craig denied that it was neo-Nazi. He said that any para-military appearance was due simply to the symbolic gesture of men of different political affiliations standing together shoulder to shoulder. Vanguard turned out in strength for a demonstration at Parliament Buildings on 28 March 1972 to protest against the introduction of direct rule. It was the last sitting day of the old Stormont Parliament, and Craig appeared on the balcony of Parliament Buildings and was joined by PM Brian Faulkner and several Cabinet Ministers. But the unity was more apparent than real on that occasion, and Faulkner made it clear later that he was embarrassed by the link-up with Vanguard. In May 1972 Vanguard shed some support among Official Unionists with a policy statement entitled 'Ulster – a Nation'. It said that NI might, if reluctantly, have to go it alone. More immediately, it called for renegotiation of the relationship with Westminster to ensure local control of security in view of the unilateral application of direct rule. In 1973 the setting up of the Vanguard Unionist Progressive Party meant the disappearance of Vanguard as an umbrella group. But Ulster Vanguard re-emerged in February 1978, when VUPP was wound up as a political party. Craig, who had now rejoined the OUP, remained at its head, and David Trimble, the deputy leader of VUPP, was appointed his deputy. (*See also* Vanguard Unionist Progressive Party.)

ULSTER VOLUNTEER FORCE

Illegal Protestant paramilitary force, sometimes described as the 'secret Protestant army'. Also uses the cover name Protestant Action Force. In 1966 it revived the title applied to the Unionist-Protestant force established in 1912 to fight Irish Home Rule. Known sometimes as 'Carson's Army', after Lord Carson, the original UVF organised the training of volunteers as well as gun-running to Ulster. When war broke out in 1914, and Home Rule was set aside for the moment, its members very largely became the 36th (Ulster) Division in the British army, which suffered severe losses at the Battle of the Somme in July 1916. The new UVF of the 1960s was completely opposed to the liberal Unionist regime of Terence O'Neill. It first attracted attention in May 1966, when a statement over the name 'Capt. Wm. Johnston' threatened war against the IRA, and said that it was the UVF's intention to kill IRA men mercilessly. Six days later, a man named John Scullion was fatally stabbed on the Falls Road in Belfast. On 26 June an eighteen-year-old Catholic barman, Peter Ward, was shot dead as he left a bar in the Protestant Shankill Road area of the city. Augustus (Gusty) Spence, the best-known UVF leader, was sentenced to life imprisonment for this murder. PM O'Neill announced in Parliament that the UVF was to be declared illegal. He said that 'this evil thing in our midst' had misappropriated the name UVF and would now take its proper place alongside the IRA in the schedule of illegal bodies. He also branded it as 'a dangerous conspiracy'. The PM claimed that the Rev. Ian Paisley had links with the UVF and that he had voiced support for it in speeches, but Paisley and his newspaper angrily denied that he had been associated with the organisation or had advocated violence. The UVF, now organising underground on military lines, and apparently attracting mainly ex-soldiers, is thought to have attained a strength of about 1,500 by 1972. In that year – the year in which direct rule from Westminster was imposed – it was heavily involved in the assassination of Catholics. It also claimed to be well armed with a variety of weapons, including Browning, Bren, Sterling and Thompson guns. In October 1972 it admitted to a raid on a military arsenal in Lurgan, Co. Armagh.

Its main centres of strength at that time were the Shankill area of Belfast, E. Antrim and Co. Armagh. In July 1972 Gusty Spence, then described as second-in-command, vanished while on two days' parole from Belfast Prison. He was said to have been held by his UVF comrades in a bid to force a new trial for Spence, but a few months later he was recaptured and went to the Maze Prison to preside over the compound where UVF prisoners who had special category status were held. In April 1974 Secretary of State Merlyn Rees removed the proscription on the UVF to encourage it to turn to political activity and in the October 1974 election the Volunteer Political Party chairman, Ken Gibson, was a candidate in W. Belfast. (*See also* Volunteer Political Party.) But on 3 October 1975 the UVF admitted that it had been responsible for most of the violence of the previous day in which twelve people died and about forty were injured, most of them Catholics. In declaring the organisation illegal again, Rees said that the UVF had shown that it was still wedded to violence, including the murder of innocent citizens. In reply, the UVF threatened further 'anti-IRA action' and expressed its 'utter disgust' at what it said was the failure of the military and civil authorities to act effectively against the PIRA. Shortly before it was banned, leading members of the UVF

met Government officials and put a series of demands to the Government. These were, apparently, that the IRSP should be declared illegal and that the incident centres set up to monitor the PIRA ceasefire should be closed. However, these talks were unproductive. In fact, the security forces were already poised to swoop on the homes of UVF suspects in Belfast and E. Antrim. On 5 October 1,000 troops and police were involved in the operation, which had been planned since a day in the previous August when a twenty-seven-year-old UVF officer ran to a police station in Carrickfergus to report that a UVF court-martial was under way in the Royal British Legion Hall in the town. He feared that he was going to be tried and shot by the UVF, and his information on the organisation proved to be the link the security forces needed to break up a strong UVF unit in that area. In March 1977 after a £2 million trial, the most costly in NI's criminal history, twenty-six UVF men were given a total of 700 years' imprisonment, including eight life sentences. There were fifty-five charges against the men, including four murders. One was the murder of a UVF man, and two others were the murders of UDA men Hugh McVeigh and David Douglas, whose bodies were found in a shallow grave in Co. Antrim five months after they disappeared. About the same time, ten men from the Ballyclare, Co. Antrim, unit were sentenced for a variety of terrorist offences, and it is known that units in Bangor, Co. Down, and Coleraine, Co. Londonderry, also found difficulty in surviving arrests in early 1977. The UVF probably maintains a small but ruthless organisation in Belfast, and it has a welfare section which looks after assistance for prisoners and their families. In June 1977 there were confused reports about a ceasefire, which seemed to confirm the belief that the UVF was somewhat divided in its leadership. In June 1979 nine Scottish UVF members were sentenced to between twelve and eighteen years' imprisonment for plotting to further the aims of the UVF. Four of the men were also convicted of bombing two Glasgow pubs and the judge, Lord Ross, described the gang as 'wicked, brutal and senseless'. He also urged that the organisation should be declared illegal in Scotland. The convictions were believed to have broken up a sixty-strong UVF unit in Glasgow which had been engaged in supplying explosives to the UVF in NI. In the early 1980s the UVF suffered from informers both in Belfast and in Co. Armagh. Eighteen of twenty men arrested in Co. Armagh in 1982, on the evidence of ex-UVF informer Clifford McKeown, pleaded guilty to a variety of terrorist offences, some of which indicated that the organisation was then involved in sectarian murder attempts. In the Shankill area in the same year, police raids broke up a UVF group and uncovered firearms, including a homemade machine gun, and ammunition, and seven UVF men from Larne got a total of eighty-nine years' imprisonment on charges such as armed robbery and having guns and bombs. There were reports about the same time of internal differences in the organisation, notably in Belfast. In 1982 the UVF reacted angrily to a comment by the Chief Constable that weapons favoured by PIRA had been found in the possession of loyalists. In a statement the UVF asked: 'Is he not aware that the black market on which these weapons are purchased is not interested in the politics of Northern Ireland, but only in the cash and business which our conflict brings?' The same statement described the UVF as 'political soldiers with the spirit of 1912'. The organisation suffered a severe blow in April 1983, when one of

its battalion commanders, Joseph Bennett, turned supergrass and gave evidence which resulted in the conviction of fourteen leading members, two of whom were sentenced to life imprisonment. Those convicted included John Graham, described as 'brigadier-general'. Bennett was given immunity in respect of two murders and other offences. In the summer of 1983 there were more arrests arising from the activities of informers. In fact, the evidence since then was of more and more UVF members being made amenable for crimes. In June 1985 six UVF men were sentenced for eighty crimes, including four murders; another received seventeen years for the attempted murder of *Sunday World* journalist, Jim Campbell. The only 'good news' for the organisation in 1985 was the collapse of the trial of supergrass William 'Budgie' Allen when Judge Higgins said his evidence was 'seriously flawed and unworthy of belief'. As a result twenty persons named by him were released, but five others, who had confessed, were sentenced. There was some evidence in 1987 and 1988 of PIRA and INLA using those named in such trials as targets for assassination. In addition to the loss of personnel due to court cases and assassinations, sources of arms for the organisation were also drying up. In 1988 a plot to smuggle arms from Toronto to NI via Liverpool was broken up. A Canadian citizen and a man from Liverpool were jailed for four years each for their involvement, and another Canadian was jailed in Canada. A fourth man was fighting efforts to return him for trial in GB. Early in 1988 the UVF share of a consignment of arms was discovered at Ligoniel in Belfast. In January 1988 a court was told of drugs stolen from the Royal Victoria Hospital being supplied to the UVF.

ULSTER WORKERS' COUNCIL

The body which organised and ran the loyalist strike in May 1974, which led to the collapse of the power-sharing administration. By the cutting of power supplies and extensive backing from Protestant paramilitary groups, it halted industrial and other activity, and the chaotic situation which had developed after fourteen days caused Unionist members to resign from the Executive and so render it ineffective. The UWC operated through a co-ordinating committee, headed by Vanguard Assembly member Glen Barr. It included three leading politicians – Harry West (OUP); Rev. Ian Paisley (DUP); and William Craig (Vanguard). Among the paramilitary representatives were Andy Tyrie (UDA), Colonel Brush (Down Orange Welfare), Ken Gibson and Bill Hannigan (UVF political spokesmen), George Green (USC Association) and Bob Marno (Orange Volunteers). Its best-known spokesmen during the stoppage were Jim Smyth and Harry Murray, and other members were Billy Kelly (power workers), Hugh Petrie and Tom Beattie. The UWC was again active in the 1977 loyalist strike – a more limited affair – which had been backed by the United Unionist Action Council. But failure to halt electricity supplies in 1977 reduced its effectiveness. And in 1977 the OUP and Vanguard were opposed to the strike, although it was supported by the Rev. Ian Paisley and Ernest Baird, then leading the UUUP. In February 1981 its former chairman Harry Murray announced that the UWC was being re-formed to campaign for jobs and to promote the unity of workers. He said it would not have paramilitary links.

UNIONIST COALITION see United Ulster Unionist Council

UNIONIST PARTY OF NORTHERN IRELAND

Formed by those ex-members of the OUP who continued to support Brian Faulkner after the Sunningdale proposals had been rejected by the OUP, and Faulkner had resigned as party leader. Initially those who had rallied round Faulkner simply adopted the description 'Unionist Pro-Assembly', and six candidates employing this label unsuccessfully contested the February 1974 Westminster election. UPNI was formally launched in September 1974, four months after the collapse of the Executive, and Faulkner boldly expressed the view that it could become the 'mainstream' Unionist Party. But two of its nominees failed to get elected in the October 1974 Westminster election. In the Constitutional Convention, UPNI continued its support for power-sharing, and stressed the need for a strong regional government, with a maintenance of the UK link. But it dropped the idea of a Council of Ireland, which it held to be counter-productive in developing social and economic co-operation between NI and the Irish Republic. Its total of first-preference votes in the election was 50,891 (7.7 per cent of the total) and it got five seats out of the seventy-eight. In 1976, after the failure of the Convention, Faulkner (later Lord Faulkner) withdrew from the leadership of the party, and from active politics, and he died in a hunting accident in 1977. He was succeeded by Anne Dickson. In the 1977 District Council elections, the party fought on a narrow front, with only twenty-four candidates, and secured 13,691 first-preference votes (2.4 per cent of the total) and took 6 seats out of the 526. The party's viewpoint was represented in the House of Lords by Lord Brookeborough and Lord Moyola, and it continued to enjoy the support of several other former members of Unionist governments, including Sir John Andrews. In 1978 there were some rumours of a possible link-up with the OUP, but the party continued to differ with the OUP on the power-sharing issue, and seemed to be determined to maintain its independent stance. In the 1979 Westminster election it ran three candidates in Belfast, but its total vote was only 8,021 (1.2 per cent of the total vote) and all three candidates lost their deposits. In the 1979 European election it fared no better. Its candidate, consultant engineer Eddie Cummings, had 0.6 per cent of first-preference votes and lost his deposit. Because of its poor showing in the 1981 council elections, when it shared seven seats and 1.9 per cent of the votes in a temporary coalition with UPUP, the party decided to wind up its organisation.

UNITED LABOUR PARTY

A party launched in 1978, with the declared aim of trying to establish a government in NI based on democratic socialism. Paddy Devlin, formerly of the SDLP, was one of the founders. Its draft constitution urged co-operation with other Labour movements throughout the British Isles. It also stated that the constitutional position of NI should only be changed if that would further political accommodation and have majority support from the electors. Devlin got just over 6,000 first-preference votes when he ran unsuccessfully as ULP candidate in the 1979 European election, and its nominee in the S. Belfast by-election for Westminster in 1982 secured 303 votes. It was absorbed in Labour '87, set up in 1987.

UNITED ULSTER UNIONIST COUNCIL

Sometimes called the Unionist Coalition, it was set up in January 1974 to fight the Sunningdale Agreement which it saw as a step to a united Ireland. It followed on the split in the Unionist Party, which elected Harry West as leader in succession to Brian Faulkner, who had become Chief Minister in the power-sharing Executive. The UUUC comprised the OUP, headed by West, the DUP, led by the Rev. Ian Paisley, and the Vanguard Unionists, headed by William Craig. The group won eleven of the twelve NI seats in the February 1974 Westminster election. After the election a UUUC conference in April 1974 at Portrush, Co. Antrim, set out its immediate programme. It included the ending of the power-sharing Executive, fresh elections using PR but in smaller constituencies, the removal of the Secretary of State's veto power and an end to the Council of Ireland or even discussion of it. In Parliament these MPs formed a Unionist Parliamentary Coalition led by West, and later James Molyneaux MP succeeded West when the latter lost his Fermanagh–S. Tyrone seat in October 1974. The support of the UUUC for the UWC strike in May 1974 was an important element in the success of the stoppage. It continued to operate in the Convention election in 1975, and in the Convention it carried through the majority report which failed, however, to get backing from other parties. Craig's support for the idea of a voluntary coalition, embracing the SDLP for an emergency period, led to a split in Vanguard, the majority of whose Convention members remained loyal to the UUUC when Craig was expelled from the Unionist Coalition. In early 1977 the UUUC, now made up of the OUP, DUP and the UUUM, headed by Ernest Baird (the UUUM included the majority section of Vanguard which had refused to follow Craig), began to show signs of serious internal strain. This was aggravated by the formation by the UUUC steering committee of United Unionist Action Council, which eventually took in paramilitary groups and mounted the abortive 'loyalist strike' in May 1977. The OUP condemned this venture, and the UUUC effectively collapsed. The Parliamentary Coalition at Westminster also broke up at the time of the May stoppage, since two of its MPs, the Rev. Ian Paisley and John Dunlop, supported the stoppage. But the UUUC experiment at Westminster had important political implications. It marked the real break between the Conservative Party and Ulster Unionists in Parliament, and the end of Labour's overall majority in the Commons in 1976 gave the Unionist MPs the influence in 1977 to secure Labour Government support for a Speaker's conference to consider extra NI seats at Westminster – a long-standing demand of all shades of unionism and a move hitherto opposed by Labour – and the NI Boundary Commission recommended seventeen seats. The change took effect in the 1983 election and immediately benefited the OUP and SDLP.

UNITED ULSTER UNIONIST MOVEMENT *see* United Ulster Unionist Party *and* Vanguard Unionist Progressive Party

UNITED ULSTER UNIONIST PARTY
The party led by Ernest Baird which emerged to fight the District Council elections in May 1977. It was based on the UUUM – the breakaway movement from the Vanguard Party during the Constitutional Convention. UUUM was made up of the former Vanguard Convention members who were opposed to William Craig's idea of a voluntary coalition. Initially, UUUM campaigned for the creation of a single,

united Unionist party. When this appeared unattainable, Baird announced that the UUUM would become a political party as UUUP. In the 1977 council elections, it got 3.2 per cent of first-preference votes and twelve seats. In the 1979 Westminster election it retained Mid-Ulster, where the sitting MP, John Dunlop, was not opposed by the OUP. Ernest Baird was unsuccessful in Fermanagh–S. Tyrone. The party share of the vote in the election was 5.6 per cent (two seats contested). The party contested only seven District Councils in 1981 and won five seats with 4,653 votes (0.7 per cent). Although it was evident that the DUP had now captured the more fundamentalist Unionist vote, UUUP made a final effort in the 1982 Assembly election. It ran twelve candidates, but none was returned, and its share of the total vote was 1.8 per cent. The candidates included party leader Ernest Baird, deputy leader Reg Empey, and John Dunlop MP. The party did not contest the 1983 Westminster election or any subsequent election and ceased to exist.

UNITED UNIONIST ACTION COUNCIL
The body which organised vigilante patrols, known as the Ulster Service Corps, in the spring of 1977. It also promoted the loyalist strike in May 1977 against direct rule and in favour of tougher security measures – a stoppage which drew much less support than the UWC strike of 1974. The UUAC included the Rev. Ian Paisley and Ernest Baird, and its chairman was former Unionist MP Joseph Burns. It included representatives of the UWC, UDA, Orange Volunteers and Down Orange Welfare. The UUAC was technically a sub-committee of the steering committee of the UUUC. It was not, however, supported by the OUP or the VUPP and, unlike the organisers of

the 1974 stoppage, failed to get the backing of the power workers.

UNITY MOVEMENT
An anti-Unionist group launched in April 1973. Its main personality was Frank McManus, then MP for Fermanagh–S. Tyrone. In May 1973 it issued a manifesto calling for an amnesty for all political prisoners, disbandment of the RUC, the setting up of a new police force, and repeal of all 'offensive and repressive' legislation. In the February 1974 Westminster election, McManus lost his seat and another Unity candidate in Armagh polled very few votes. In 1977 McManus was one of the founders of the Irish Independence Party.

V

VANGUARD SERVICE CORPS
The paramilitary organisation linked with Ulster Vanguard in its early years. When Ulster Vanguard became the Vanguard Unionist Progressive Party in 1973, the VSC took the title 'Ulster Volunteer Service Corps'. Its main purpose was to provide an escort for Vanguard speakers.

VANGUARD UNIONIST PROGRESSIVE PARTY
A political party which developed out of the Vanguard movement, led by William Craig. It was established as a party in March 1973, and mainly comprised ex-members of the Unionist Party disenchanted with the policies of recent leaders – Terence O'Neill, James Chichester-Clark and Brian Faulkner. In the Assembly election of 1973 it secured seven seats and 10.5 per cent of the total vote, and in the Convention election of 1975 (as part of the UUUC) it doubled its representation to fourteen

seats, although its share of the total vote had increased only to 12.7 per cent. This indicated the shrewdness with which the UUUC had distributed its candidates. VUPP reflected the strong opposition to direct rule of the Vanguard movement from which it sprang. It also opposed the British Government's White Paper on which the Assembly was based, and it pressed for tough measures against the PIRA. In the Convention, it was seriously split over Craig's support for the idea of voluntary coalition with the SDLP. Apart from Craig himself and two other members, David Trimble and Glen Barr, the rest of the party broke away under the leadership of Ernest Baird, deputy leader, to form the UUUM, which in 1977 became the UUUP. The VUPP did not contest the 1977 District Council elections as an entity and in February 1978 it ceased to be a political party and reverted to its former status of the Vanguard movement. Craig, then MP for E. Belfast, moved to the OUP. The VUPP's other MP elected in 1977, John Dunlop in Mid-Ulster, had already joined the UUUP. In 1982 Craig, clearly disillusioned with the OUP, stood as Vanguard Unionist in the Assembly election in E. Belfast, but got only 2,000 first-preference votes. (*See also* Ulster Vanguard.)

VAN STRAUBENZEE, SIR WILLIAM RADCLIFFE
Minister of State, NIO, 1972–4. b. 27 January 1924. Conservative MP for Wokingham, 1959–87. Church (of England) Commissioner, 1967–. Known as 'the Bishop' in Westminster circles, he presided as NI Minister of State over a committee which drew up proposals to counter religious and political discrimination in jobs, and which led eventually to the setting up of the Fair Employment Agency.

VIGGERS, PETER

Parliamentary Under-Secretary, NIO, 1986–. b. 13 March 1938. Conservative MP for Gosport since February 1974. Parliamentary Private Secretary to Solicitor-General, 1979–83; Parliamentary Private Secretary to first Secretary at Treasury, 1983–6. His appointment to Stormont as Industry Minister was his first Government job, but he had some previous business contacts with NI. He arrived at a difficult moment, with Unionist hostility to Ministers at its height in the wake of the AIA. Also, his predecessor at the Department of Economic Affairs, Dr Rhodes Boyson, had run into criticism for suggesting that there should be a Government-supported system of emigration and that he would be raising the matter with US and Canadian immigration officials. Viggers did not pursue this idea, and although he was active in pushing small-firm developments locally and seeking to find outside industrial investment, he was able to record only modest gains in jobs, and trade unionists argued that changes in the official statistics tended to understate real unemployment. In 1988 he found all the local political parties united against him when he proposed privatisation of the Belfast shipyard, Harland and Wolff plc, Short Brothers' aerospace factories, and the NIE. Even the IDB's successful attraction of substantial investment from Korea and France in the latter part of 1988 did not dispel concern at the principle and handling of the privatisation issue.

VITTY, DENNY

DUP Assembly member for E. Belfast, 1982–6. Served on committee on Economic Development. b. 1950. Castlereagh Council, 1977–. Mayor, 1987–8. Chairman, DUP's E. Belfast Association.

VOLUNTEER POLITICAL PARTY

Political wing of Protestant para-military organisation, the UVF, it emerged briefly in September 1974. Its chairman, Ken Gibson, contested the October 1974 Westminster election in W. Belfast. He had some support from the UDA in the area but polled only 2,690 votes. The VPP supported the link with Britain, and said either a united Ireland or UDI would mean higher taxes and a cut in social security benefits. (*See also* Ulster Volunteer Force.)

W

WALKER, (ALFRED) CECIL

OUP MP for N. Belfast, 1983–. b. 17 December 1924. Manager of timber firm before entering Parliament. He has repeatedly expressed concern about the high level of sectarian killings in his constituency. In 1988 became first MP to go to prison for refusing to pay a fine for contravening new public order laws, which, he claimed, were 'shackling traditional freedoms'. With the SDLP standing aside and a united Unionist vote, he had a majority of some 16,000 in the 1986 by-election held to protest against the AIA, but his winning margin was halved to some 8,000 in 1987 when he was opposed by George Seawright, standing as a Protestant Unionist.

WARRENPOINT

South Co. Down port and seaside resort, near which eighteen soldiers died on 27 August 1979 in two PIRA explosions. It was the largest death toll in any incident up to that date. The ambush came only a few hours after Lord Mountbatten had been killed when his boat was blown up by PIRA off the Co. Sligo coast in the Republic.

WATERS, LIEUTENANT-GENERAL SIR JOHN

Army GOC, NI, June 1988–. b. 2 September 1935. Sandhurst. Commissioned Gloucestershire Regiment, 1955. Served in NI early in the Troubles; after a second tour, promoted to command regiment in 1975. Commanded 3rd Infantry Brigade (based at Portadown), 1979–81. Deputy Commander Land Forces in Falklands campaign, 1982. Commander, 4th Armoured Division, BAOR, 1983–5. Commandant, Staff College, Camberley, 1986–8. His experience of service in other trouble spots – Aden, Persian Gulf, Cyprus, Belize – has resulted in the description 'one of the most experienced anti-terrorist experts in the army'. His arrival in NI as GOC in June 1988 coincided with an upsurge in PIRA attacks on regular soldiers, the establishment of a new brigade based at Armagh, and enhanced cross-border security co-operation.

WELLS, JAMES HENRY

DUP Assembly member for S. Down, 1982–6. Served on committees on Environment, and Health and Social Services. b. 1957. BA Hons, Diploma in Town and Country Planning (QUB). Lisburn Borough Council, 1981–5; Banbridge District Council, 1985–8. Announced decision to leave active politics 26 September 1988 because of his inability to gain full-time employment while involved in politics.

WEST, HENRY WILLIAM (HARRY)

Leader of the OUP, 1974–9. b. Enniskillen, 27 March 1917. Large-scale farmer in Co. Fermanagh, High Sheriff, Fermanagh, 1954. President, Ulster Farmers' Union, 1955–6. Unionist MP for Enniskillen, 1954–72. Parliamentary Secretary, Ministry of Agriculture, 1958. Minister of Agriculture, 1960–6 and 1971–2. MP for Fermanagh–S. Tyrone, 1974, and leader of United Unionist Parliamentary Coalition at Westminster, 1974. Elected from Fermanagh–S. Tyrone to Assembly, 1973–4, and Constitutional Convention, 1975–6. During the 1968–71 period, he led the West Ulster Unionist Council and strongly criticised reforms which he saw as weakening unionism and the position of the NI Government. In particular, he opposed local government changes and the setting up of a central housing authority. He also resisted the idea of an unarmed police force, and the abolition of the USC. But he resigned from the West Ulster Unionist Council in June 1971, and accepted Brian Faulkner's invitation to return as Minister of Agriculture. He was not, however, prepared to follow Faulkner on the issue of power-sharing government and the Sunningdale Agreement, and in January 1974 he was elected to succeed Faulkner as OUP leader, when the Ulster Unionist Council rejected the Sunningdale package. He aligned the OUP with the DUP and Vanguard in the UUUC and he gained the Fermanagh–S. Tyrone seat as official UUUC candidate in the February 1974 election. He lost it again in October 1974 when anti-Unionists combined to support Frank Maguire, Independent. In the Assembly he led his party in opposition to the three-party Executive, although he dissociated his supporters from rowdy scenes in and around the Assembly chamber. He backed the UWC strike in May 1974 which led to the fall of the Executive. In the Constitutional Convention, he continued to resist the idea of power-sharing at Cabinet level, although he always insisted that his attitude was not anti-Catholic, but only directed to refusing co-operation in government with those who sought a united Ireland. In early 1977 he gradually drifted apart from the Rev. Ian Paisley and Ernest Baird, the other two leaders of the UUUC. The differences centred on a Unionist Action Council which mounted a strike in May 1977 against direct rule and in favour of a much tougher security policy. West and his party refused to back the strike, which got only limited support from loyalists, and the result was to confirm the break-up of the UUUC. Between 1977 and 1979 he was engaged in many discussions with Secretary of State Roy Mason on the possibility of some form of interim devolution, but the talks were unproductive. In the European Parliament election in June 1979, he secured just under 57,000 first-preference votes, which inevitably led to comparisons with the Rev. Ian Paisley's 170,000, and he was eliminated on the fourth count. He claimed that some 100,000 OUP voters had refused to turn out because of their doubts about the Common Market. But he immediately tendered his resignation as party leader, and on 2 July – within four weeks of the election – he confirmed this and was succeeded by James Molyneaux MP. He lost to hunger-striker Bobby Sands, with a united anti-Unionist vote behind him, in the April 1981 Westminster by-election in Fermanagh–S. Tyrone. In 1987–8 he was the leading figure in the Charter Group, which challenged OUP leadership and called for devolution.

WEST ULSTER UNIONIST COUNCIL

A large pressure group within the OUP, active between 1969 and 1971 in defending traditional unionism. It opposed reforms such as the reduction of the powers of local authorities and the setting up of a central housing authority. It also demanded tougher security policies. It was spearheaded by Fermanagh Unionist Association, and although the bulk of its membership was made up of Unionist associations in W. Ulster, it also had the support of several constituency associations in Belfast and E. Ulster. It was frequently attacked by liberal Unionists as a divisive force, but Harry West MP, who led it for most of the time, insisted that it spoke for the majority of grass-roots Unionists. He resigned from the council in 1971, when he became Minister of Agriculture in the Faulkner Government.

WHITELAW, LORD

As William Whitelaw, first Secretary of State of NI, March 1972–November 1973. b. 28 June 1918. Golfing blue, Cambridge University, 1936–9. Took up farming on Cumberland estate after resigning army commission, 1947. Conservative MP for Penrith and the Border, 1955–83. Chief Conservative Whip, 1964–70. Lord President of the Council and leader of the Commons, 1970–2. Employment Secretary, 1973–4. Chairman, Conservative Party, 1974–5. Deputy leader of Conservative party, 1975–9 and spokesman on Home Affairs, 1975–9. Deputy PM, 1979–88 (also Home Secretary, 1979–83, Lord President of the Council and leader of Lords, 1983–88). On taking over at Stormont in 1972, the genial Whitelaw had to face a double threat – the wrath of loyalists deprived of a local Parliament and Government and a big effort by the PIRA, so that the overall result was a year with 467 violent deaths. In a bid to keep a brief PIRA ceasefire going, he tried a controversial initiative in early July 1972. He met PIRA leaders secretly in London, but the Provisionals' terms were too sweeping to be acceptable to the British Government. The Secretary of State reported to MPs that the PIRA wanted:

1 A public declaration that the Irish people as a whole should decide the future of Ireland.

2 The withdrawal of all British troops from Irish soil by 1 January 1975.
3 Pending the withdrawal, all troops should be withdrawn immediately from 'sensitive areas'.
4 A general amnesty for all political prisoners, internees and persons on the wanted list.

Whitelaw also said the Provisionals had expressed regret that internment had not been halted in response to their ceasefire, which had been ended after a fortnight, following a single dispute about housing in W. Belfast which, Whitelaw claimed, could easily have been resolved peacefully. The thinking behind the meeting with PIRA, according to the Minister of State at the time, David Howell (*The Times*, 10 February 1975) was that the Government wanted to show that everything had been tried, including truce and meeting, so that PIRA would be seen to be concerned only with violence. But it is also thought that the Government had intelligence that PIRA planned concessions which never materialised. About the same time, Whitelaw made what he later admitted to Parliament was a mistake – he agreed to special privileges for convicted terrorists who belonged to the political paramilitary groups. This 'special category' system began, following a hunger strike in Belfast Prison during which PIRA leader Billy McKee was close to death. But after 'Bloody Friday' in Belfast – 21 July 1972 – when ten civilians and three soldiers died in the city, Whitelaw ordered the takeover of the no-go areas. These were the areas, mainly in W. Belfast and in Londonderry's Bogside, where there was little control by the security forces. On 31 July 1972 the army moved into the areas in strength in 'Operation Motorman', and while two people were killed by troops in Derry, there was little resistance generally. But despite the continuance of violence, both from PIRA and loyalist groups, he tried to move the emphasis to political progress, and organised a conference of local political parties at Darlington in September 1972. Too few parties accepted to make the exercise worth while. None the less, at the end of October 1972 he produced a discussion paper (a 'green paper' in British Parliamentary terms, but the phrase was officially avoided) which pointed to the need to recognise both the British and Irish dimensions in the NI situation. In March 1973 this was translated into a White Paper which set out the Government's plans for new-style devolved government. It proposed a seventy-eight member Assembly elected by PR, and power-sharing between the parties as an alternative to majority government. Unionists were sharply divided on the document, but SDLP and Alliance gave it a general welcome. Whitelaw began the most severe test of his diplomacy on 5 October 1973 (that is, precisely five years after the violent scenes in Derry's Duke Street) when he met the delegations from three parties at Stormont Castle. The Unionists were led by Brian Faulkner, the SDLP by Gerry Fitt, and Alliance by Oliver Napier. The talks were patiently piloted by Whitelaw over seven weeks, and often they came close to breakdown. But finally, on 21 November 1973, a formula was agreed for a three-party Executive (in effect, a coalition). But the final seal on strategy and details of the Council of Ireland had to be left to a conference at Sunningdale in Berkshire, in early December, attended by PM Edward Heath and by Irish Ministers, headed by the Taoiseach Liam Cosgrave. Immediately before the conference Whitelaw moved to the Department of Employment, and he was succeeded by Francis Pym as NI Secretary of State. As Conservative deputy leader, he resisted pressures from within the party to depart from the broadly bipartisan approach to NI which had been established in 1969. As Home Secretary and deputy Premier in the Thatcher Government, he was a member of the Cabinet committee considering efforts to restore devolution to NI. He caused some surprise when he hinted at the 1982 Conservative conference that citizens of the Irish Republic living in GB might lose their voting rights. In December 1982 he banned two PSF Assembly members, Gerry Adams and Danny Morrison, from entering GB because of their alleged links with terrorism. One of his last acts as Home Secretary in June 1983 was to remove the ban on Adams, once he had been elected in W. Belfast. Although on Cabinet committee which planned the AIA, he declared in 1987 that the political log jam could only be broken by NI politicians themselves. He suggested that if they were to sink their differences and work together, they would have a very strong hand to play with any British Government. On loyalist protests against the AIA, he said the Government would not bow to any kind of undemocratic pressure. When he retired from the Government for health reasons in 1988, he said the collapse of power-sharing in 1974 had been 'one of the great sadnesses of my life'. Memoirs expected in 1989.

WHITTEN, HERBERT

OUP member of NI Assembly, 1973–4, and Convention, 1975–6, elected from Armagh. b. Portadown, Co. Armagh, 1909; d. December 1981. He was one of three OUP members of the Assembly who voted against a vote of confidence in the power-sharing Executive in February 1974. Prominent in Orange Order in Co. Armagh. Stormont MP for Central Armagh, 1969–72. Portadown Borough Council, 1968–72, Mayor,

1968–9; Craigavon District Council, 1973–81.

WIDGERY REPORT *see* 'Bloody Sunday'

WILLIAMS, BETTY

One of the three founders of the Peace People in 1976. She was joint recipient, with Mairead Corrigan, of the Nobel Peace Prize, 1976. b. Belfast, 1943. A housewife from Andersonstown, one of Belfast's Republican strongholds, she witnessed the tragedy (that is, the accident in which the three Maguire children were killed) which inspired her, together with Mairead Corrigan and Ciaran McKeown, to launch the Peace People movement. She travelled abroad extensively to talk about the movement. In 1980 she stepped down from the PP executive, although continuing to campaign for it. Before leaving NI to live in the US in 1982, she said she had had 200 job refusals in eighteen months. In December 1982 she married an American businessman, Jim Perkins, in Florida. In 1986, when she returned for a TV programme to mark the tenth anniversary of PP, her two co-founders declined to meet her. She said her crime had been to accept the £38,000 Nobel Prize. 'I took it; I needed the money; I am guilty as charged,' she said.

WILSON, LORD (OF RIEVAULX)

As Harold Wilson, Labour PM, 1964–70 and 1974–6. b. 11 March 1916. Harold Wilson's career touched NI at many points. As a young civil servant, he toyed with the idea of seeking the post of economic adviser to the NI Government. As Labour Party leader (1963–76), he was highly conscious of the importance of the Irish vote in Britain. He often remarked that he had reminded successive Irish leaders that he had more Irish people in his Huyton (Liverpool) constituency than they had in theirs. As PM at the start of the civil rights campaign in 1968, he and Home Secretary James Callaghan had to deal with the crisis produced by the demands for reform and later in 1969, with the serious violence in Belfast, Londonderry and other towns. Harold Wilson had, apparently, already made up his mind to send troops to NI when the appeal for them came from Stormont in August 1969. And he personally handled the critical talks with NI Ministers which set the stage for reforms – social, political and in the reorganisation of the RUC and disbandment of the B Specials. His most comprehensive statement of his personal views was in a speech as opposition leader in the Commons in November 1971. He urged more attention to the aspiration of a united Ireland, while stressing that it could come only with the agreement of people in NI. But he said the dream must be there. 'If men of moderation have nothing to hope for, men of violence will have something to shoot for.' So he suggested talks between the Westminster, Dublin and Stormont Parliaments which could lead to a Constitutional Commission which would work out arrangements for a united Ireland, which could become effective fifteen years after agreement had been reached, provided that political violence had ceased. He also urged the participation of Catholics at all levels of Government, and the removal of all security powers from Stormont and their transfer to London. His approach was condemned by Unionists and by some members of the NILP, but given a cautious welcome by Catholic politicians. Wilson had never been enthusiastic about direct rule, but he backed the decision of the Heath Government to impose it in 1972. In 1974 he returned to power to face the challenge of the loyalist strike, and was attacked both by loyalists and by the

SDLP. The Unionists resented fiercely his speech on 25 May 1974, in which he condemned the strike organisers as people 'purporting to act as though they were an elected government, spending their lives sponging on Westminster'. The SDLP said he had failed to act toughly enough to smash the strike. In 1975 he travelled to Stormont to announce the Convention election, and he saw the Convention fail before he left office in 1976. Life peer, 1983.

WILSON, GERARD PATRICK (PADDY)
SDLP Senator who was stabbed to death at a lonely quarry on the Upper Hightown Road in N. Belfast on 26 June 1973. b. 1933. A woman friend, to whom he had given a lift in his car, was murdered at the same time. The murders were claimed by the UFF as part of a campaign to secure the release of their members from detention. He had been elected to Senate in 1968 as Rep. Lab. but left that party in 1970 when he was one of the founders of the SDLP. He was also a Belfast City Councillor. At the time of his death he had been acting as election agent to Gerry Fitt MP for the Assembly elections.

WILSON, HUGH
Alliance Assembly, 1973–4, and Convention, 1975–6, member for N. Antrim. b. Ballyclare, Co. Antrim, 1905. MB, B.Ch., BAO (QUB). Consultant surgeon (FRCS). Narrowly defeated in Larne by William Craig in the 1969 Stormont election. Unsuccessfully contested N. Antrim seat (held by the Rev. Ian Paisley) in Westminster election, October 1974. Member of Larne Borough Council, 1977–85.

WILSON, JAMES (JIM)
Secretary and chief executive, Ulster

Unionist Party, November 1987–. b. 15 December 1941. Chairman, Ballyclare Unionist Association, 1982–. Newtownabbey Council, 1975–. North Eastern Education and Library Board, 1981–5. Prominent in Orange and Black institutions. In 1987 general election he was seconded by party to help Jim Kilfedder (UPUP) in his N. Down campaign.

WILSON, SAMUEL (SAMMY)
First DUP Lord Mayor of Belfast, 1986–7. Press Officer, DUP, 1982–. b. 4 April 1953. Belfast City Council, 1981–. Teacher of economics. Was Lord Mayor at height of Unionist local government campaign against AIA, and refused to meet Dublin's Lord Mayor because of it. Strong supporter of devolution, with 'left-of-centre approach in national politics'.

WINDLESHAM, LORD
Minister of State, NIO, 1972–3. b. 28 January 1932. Lord Windlesham, a Catholic, was deputy to William Whitelaw when he took over as Secretary of State, NI, in March 1972. Has strong Irish links – his ancestor, Richard Hennessy (1720–1800), b. Co. Cork, went to Cognac, France, in 1765, and founded the firm of Hennessy. At the NIO Lord Windlesham was spokesman in the House of Lords, and his responsibilities included community relations, Home Affairs and Development. In 1973 he became Government leader in the Lords, and Conservative leader there when Labour came to power in 1974.

WOMEN TOGETHER
A peace movement launched in November 1970, which has brought together women from Protestant and Catholic areas to campaign against violence. The group was strongly criticised by PSF, some of whose supporters disrupted WT meetings.

Monica Patterson, who was chair-woman of the movement from 1970 to 1973, says that it quickly achieved the position where it was listened to by the army chiefs, the Secretary of State and even PM Harold Wilson. She said that if it vouched for the innocence of youths who had been 'lifted', they were released. 'We were out on the streets,' she wrote in 1978, 'stopping rowdyism between gangs of youths. . . stopping armed youths engaged in vandalism of property, sweeping the streets and having burned-out vehicles removed. . . supporting the victims of intimidation.'

WOOD, ANDREW
Director, NI Information Service, February 1987–. b. 1943. Head of Information in NIO (London), 1983–7; Chief Press Officer, Home Office, 1980–3; and Press Officer, Downing Street, 1976–80. Before joining civil service, worked for newspapers on Teeside, BBC radio news, BBC TV features, and *Visnews*.

WOODFIELD, SIR PHILIP JOHN
Permanent Secretary, NIO, 1981–3. b. 30 August 1923. His arrival as head of the official side of the NIO almost coincided with James Prior's appointment as Secretary of State, and he brought to the post very diverse political experience, including a spell in the early 1970s as deputy Secretary at Stormont. He joined the Home Office in 1950 and served there for three different periods, and from 1961 to 1965 he was at 10 Downing Street, as private secretary to three PMs – Macmillan, Douglas-Home, and Wilson. He was also with the Federal Government of Nigeria from 1955 to 1957, and in 1966 was secretary to Lord Mountbatten's committee of inquiry into prison conditions. In 1987 he was named as first Ombudsman for the security services, MI5 and MI6.

WORKERS' PARTY, THE

A Republican party with a strong socialist content operating in both NI and the Republic. Up to 1982 it was known as Official Sinn Féin in the Republic and Republican Clubs in NI. In 1982 its three Dáil TDs supported Charles Haughey as Taoiseach and enabled him to form a minority government. Its change of name was clearly designed to dissociate itself from paramilitarism, since with the split in the Republican movement in 1970, Official Sinn Féin and the Republican Clubs were the political counterpart of the OIRA. As Republican Clubs, the organisation was declared illegal in NI in March 1967 by William Craig as Minister of Home Affairs. In April 1973 – that is, a year after the OIRA had begun its ceasefire – the proscription was removed. It was a move by the British Government to try to bring more militant elements into the political process. By that time the Republican Clubs had become more Marxist, in line with the general trend in Official Sinn Féin. In the Assembly election in 1973 they opposed the Government's White Paper and urged an all-Ireland socialist republic. They put up ten candidates, but emphasised that, if elected, they would only take their seats when internment ended, and emergency powers were dropped. But none of their nominees was returned, and the party's total first-preference vote was 13,064 (1.8 per cent of the total). They adopted a very similar approach in the Convention elections, but again failed to secure a seat with 2.2 per cent of the vote. In the District Council elections in May 1977 they got six seats out of the 526, with 14,277 first-preference votes (2.6 per cent of the total). But in the 1981 council elections they lost three of their six seats, and had only 1.8 per cent of first-preferences, while in the 1985 council contests, their vote dropped slightly to 1.6 per cent but they gained one seat. In the 1982 Assembly election the party improved its showing in terms of the overall vote, with 2.7 per cent of first-preferences, but failed to secure any representation. Its vote in the European election in 1984 was 1.3 per cent. It also contests Westminster elections, but has not so far achieved a significant vote. The WP refused to take part in the NIF, and its attitude to the AIA was 'reluctantly in favour', although its TDs backed the agreement in the Dáil. Subsequently, the party in NI convinced the WP to take a more critical stance. In NI the party stressed its demand for devolution worked out by local parties, and argued that the AIA must deliver peace in the first instance. Seamus Lynch, Northern chairman, dismissed as 'laughable' press allegations in 1987 that the party was linked with the OIRA and serious crime.

WRIGHT, JAMES CLAUDE

Speaker, US House of Representatives, 1987–. b. 22 December 1922. Congressman, 1954–. Majority leader (Democrat) in House, 1976–87. His family forebears were from Castlecaulfield, Co. Tyrone, and he has shown the same close interest in Irish affairs as his predecessor, 'Tip' O'Neill. Former Presbyterian lay minister.

WRIGHT, SIR JOHN OLIVER

First UK Government representative in NI, August 1969–March 1970. b. 6 March 1921. A senior diplomat, he was sent to NI in a 'watch-dog' role for PM Harold Wilson. He was engaged in the delicate negotiations about the removal of barricades in Belfast's Falls Road in 1969, and in monitoring the NI Government's reform programme. On leaving, he said that Britain had tended to neglect NI in the past, and NI had tended willingly to run its own affairs, and this had been wrong for both sides of the equation. British ambassador to

West Germany, 1975–81. With increased Irish-American activity and with US opinion playing an increasing role in Anglo-Irish exchanges, his appointment as ambassador to Washington DC in 1982 was seen by NIO as timely. He stayed there until 1986. Co-chairman, Anglo-Irish Encounter, 1986–.

Y

YOUNG, SIR ARTHUR EDWIN
Chief Constable, RUC, 1969–70. b. 1908; d. January 1979. Sir Arthur interrupted his career as City of London Police Commissioner to take over control of the RUC during the crucial period of reorganisation of the RUC arising from the Hunt report. He did so at the personal request of PM Harold Wilson, who saw Sir Arthur's experience of terrorism in Malaya and elsewhere as valuable in restoring the morale of the force, which had been shaken by the violence of the summer of 1969. In reorganising the RUC he angered many Unionists, some of whom dubbed him 'Mr Softly, Softly'.

YOUNG CITIZENS VOLUNTEER FORCE
A Protestant extremist youth group active mainly in 1974 and 1975. An RUC detective told a court in February 1975 that it had been formed for the sole purpose of killing Catholics. In the summer of 1974 there were reports that it was involved in petrol-bombing of Catholic homes.

YOUNG MILITANTS
A loyalist paramilitary group first mentioned in 1972, when it was assumed to be a breakaway from the UDA. But this was denied by the UDA. It claimed several explosions in NI and the Republic.

ELECTION RESULTS
1968–88

1968 STORMONT BY-ELECTIONS

Lisnaskea, 22 March 1968

Elec. 10,600	% Poll 83.0
Brooke, J. (U.)	4,428
Patterson, F. (Ind. U.)	3,270
Wynne, J. (U. Lib.)	1,102
U. maj.	1,158
No change	

Londonderry City, 16 May 1968

Elec. 19,688	% Poll 68.8
Anderson, A.W. (U.)	9,122
Wilcox, Mrs J. (NILP)	3,944
U. maj.	5,178
No change	

South Antrim, 6 November 1968

Elec. 38,672	% Poll 49.6
Ferguson, R. (U.)	16,288
Coulthard, J. (NILP)	2,848
U. maj.	13,440
No change	

1969 STORMONT GENERAL ELECTION

The Stormont general election on 24 February 1969 was dubbed by PM Captain Terence O'Neill the 'cross-roads election'. He insisted that it was the last chance for Northern Irish people to vote for sensible, reformist policies that would enable NI to have the respect of Westminster, and that would assure its continued membership of the UK. At the same time civil rights supporters were suspicious of the will, or the ability, of the Premier to deliver reforms. And within unionism he was assailed by many, who suggested he was selling out to those who wanted a united Ireland. So the election battle took on a wholly new character – there were Unofficial Unionists who supported O'Neill against Official Unionists who opposed him. There were Independents who represented the broad civil rights platform, and People's Democracy candidates who spoke for the more revolutionary wing. The PM had been strongly criticised for attacking Official Unionists who did not share his view. But the Premier replied that he could not support those who equivocated or hedged, and who did not back vital parts of the Unionist manifesto. He was under fire from the former PM Lord Brookeborough, and from his ex-ministerial colleague, Brian Faulkner, who had resigned from the Government the previous month. The overall result of the election posed no problem for Unionists, who improved their position slightly. Of the thirty-nine Unionist MPs, twenty-four were Official (pro-O'Neill) and three Unofficial (pro-O'Neill), while ten were Official (anti-O'Neill) and two were Official but unclear in their attitude to the Premier. The NILP retained two seats, and while Rep. Lab.

lost Falls, it won Central and held Dock. But the Nationalist Party lost three of its nine seats to Independents identified with the civil rights movement and, most notably, the Foyle seat of party leader Eddie McAteer to John Hume. But the divisions at the grass roots of unionism were serious, and tensions were steadily building up with civil rights marches and loyalist counter-demonstrations. And although Captain O'Neill declared after the election that he would stay on and fight, he resigned two months later. The turnout was 71.9 per cent.

Overall figures, 1969 Stormont general election

Party	Votes	% Valid poll
Off. U. (pro-O'Neill)	173,805	31.1
Off. U. (anti-O'Neill)	95,696	17.1
Unoff. U. (pro-O'Neill)	72,120	12.9
Ind. U.	13,932	2.5
Prot. U.	20,991	3.8
NILP	45,113	8.1
Rep. Lab.	13,155	2.4
Nat.	42,315	7.6
Nat. Dem.	26,009	4.6
PD	23,645	4.2
PPP	2,992	0.5
U. Lib.	7,337	1.3
Independents	21,977	3.9
Total valid votes	559,087	100.0
Spoiled votes	4,783	
Total votes polled	563,870	

Belfast – Ballynafeigh

Elec. 14,572	% Poll 64.0
*Neill, I. (U.)	6,523
Holmes, E. (NILP)	2,675
U. maj.	3,848
No change	

Belfast – Bloomfield

Elec. 21,142	% Poll 70.4
*Scott, W. (U.)	9,084
Spence, W. (Prot. U.)	3,568
Caldwell, W. (NILP)	2,196
U. maj.	5,516
No change	

Belfast – Central

Elec. 6,384	% Poll 58.3
Kennedy, P. (Rep. Lab.)	2,032
*Brennan, J. (Nat. Dem.)	1,538
Rep. Lab. maj.	494
Rep. Lab. gain	

Belfast – Clifton

Elec. 16,196	% Poll 74.5

Hall-Thompson, L. (Unoff. U.)	6,066
*Morgan, W. (U.)	3,215
Thompson, N. (NILP)	1,681
McKeown, M. (Nat. Dem.)	1,079

| Unoff. U. maj. | 2,851 |
| Unoff. U. gain | |

Belfast – Cromac

Elec. 13,541	% Poll 61.5

*Kennedy, W. (U.)	6,320
Barkley, J. (NILP)	1,134
Wiegleb, E. (PD)	752

| U. maj. | 5,186 |
| No change | |

Belfast – Dock

Elec. 7,212	% Poll 73.0

| *Fitt, G. (Rep. Lab.) | 3,274 |
| Smith, H. (U.) | 1,936 |

| Rep. Lab. maj. | 1,338 |
| No change | |

Belfast – Duncairn

Elec. 18,415	% Poll 66.0

| *Fitzsimmons, W. (U.) | 7,435 |
| Porter, N. (Unoff. U.) | 4,321 |

| U. maj. | 3,114 |
| No change | |

Belfast – Falls

Elec. 19,802	% Poll 60.5

| Devlin, P. (NILP) | 6,275 |
| *Diamond, H. (Rep. Lab.) | 5,549 |

| NILP maj. | 726 |
| NILP gain | |

Belfast – Oldpark

Elec. 17,817	% Poll 69.0

| *Simpson, V. (NILP) | 6,779 |
| Cairns, J. (U.) | 5,224 |

| NILP maj. | 1,555 |
| No change | |

Belfast – Pottinger

Elec. 8,328	% Poll 68.5

| Cardwell, J. (U.) | 2,902 |
| McBirney, M. (NILP) | 2,744 |

| U. maj. | 158 |
| U. gain | |

Belfast – St Anne's

Elec. 19,041	% Poll 71.0

*Laird, Dr N. (U.)	7,126
McKee, Sir C. (Unoff. U.)	4,183
Murphy, J. (Nat. Dem.)	2,136

| U. maj. | 2,943 |
| No change | |

Belfast – Shankill

Elec. 18,186	% Poll 72.0

*Boal, D. (U.)	6,384
Walsh. H. (Unoff. U.)	4,545
Overend, D. (NILP)	1,997

| U. maj. | 1,839 |
| No change | |

Belfast – Victoria

Elec. 19,504	% Poll 76.0

*Bradford, R. (U.)	9,249
Coulthard, J. (NILP)	2,972
Bunting, R. (Prot. U.)	2,489

| U. maj. | 6,277 |
| No change | |

Belfast – Willowfield

Elec. 12,427	% Poll 68.9

*Caldwell, T. (Unoff. U.)	4,613
Hinds, W. (U.)	2,134
Boyd, B. (NILP)	1,747

| Unoff. U. maj. | 2,479 |
| Unoff. U. gain | |

Belfast – Windsor

*Kirk, H. V. (U.)	unopposed

Belfast – Woodvale

Elec. 19,984	% Poll 72.2

*McQuade, J. (U.)	7,209
Boyd, W. R. (NILP)	3,878
Bell, L. (Unoff. U.)	3,231

| U. maj. | 3,331 |
| No change | |

Bannside

Elec. 20,635	% Poll 78.7

*O'Neill, Capt. T. (U.)	7,745
Paisley, Rev. I. (Prot. U.)	6,331
Farrell, M. (PD)	2,310

| U. maj. | 1,414 |
| No change | |

Carrick

Elec. 22,905	% Poll 64.3

| Dickson, Mrs A. (U.) | 9,529 |
| Craig, J. (Unoff. U.) | 5,246 |

| U. maj. | 4,283 |
| No change | |

Larkfield

Elec. 20,774	% Poll 68.3

McIvor, B. (U.)	8,501
Sherry, T. (Nat. Dem.)	2,386
Magee, T. (NILP)	1,714
O'Hare, G. (Rep. Lab.)	1,591

| U. maj. | 6,115 |
| New seat | |

Larne

Elec. 20,728	% Poll 79.5
*Craig, W. (U.)	8,550
Wilson, H. (Unoff. U.)	7,897
U. maj.	653
No change	

Antrim

*Minford, N. (U.)	unopposed

Mid-Antrim

Elec. 21,992	% Poll 58.8
*Simpson, Dr R. (U.)	10,249
Galbraith, R.H. (NILP)	2,124
U. maj.	8,125
No change	

Newtownabbey

Elec. 22,151	% Poll 59.9
Bailie, R. (U.)	9,852
McDowell, J.W. (NILP)	3,410
U. maj.	6,442
New seat	

North Antrim

Elec. 19,611	% Poll 63.0
*O'Neill, P. (U.)	9,142
Wylie, Rev. J.W. (Prot. U.)	3,241
U. maj.	5,901
No change	

South Antrim

Elec. 24,693	% Poll 64.7
*Ferguson, R. (U.)	10,761
Beattie, Rev. W. (Prot. U.)	5,362
U. maj.	5,399
No change	

Ards

*Long, Capt. W. (U.)	unopposed

Bangor

Elec. 20,886	% Poll 61.8
McConnell, R.D. (Unoff. U.)	7,714
Campbell, R. (U.)	5,190
Unoff. U. maj.	2,524
New seat	

East Down

Elec. 18,230	% Poll 86.0
*Faulkner, B. (U.)	8,136
McGrady, E. (Nat. Dem.)	6,427
Rowan-Hamilton, Lt.-Col. D. (Unoff. U.)	1,248
U. maj.	1,709
No change	

Iveagh

Elec. 16,172	% Poll 70.0
*McGowan, S. (U.)	6,869
Poots, C. (Prot. U.)	4,365
U. maj.	2,504
No change	

Lagan Valley

*Porter, R., QC (U.)	unopposed

Mid-Down

Kelly, B., QC (U.)	unopposed

Mourne

Elec. 16,272	% Poll 81.0
*O'Reilly, J. (Nat.)	7,335
Newell, C. (U.)	5,960
Nat. maj.	1,375
No change	

North Down

Elec. 18,408	% Poll 57.0
*Babington, R. (U.)	9,013
Murnaghan, Miss S. (U. Lib.)	1,567
U. maj.	7,446
No change	

South Down

Elec. 17,486	% Poll 56.0
*Keogh, M. (Nat.)	4,830
Woods, P. (PD)	4,610
Nat. maj.	220
No change	

West Down

Elec. 16,584	% Poll 77.7
*Dobson, J. (U.)	7,608
Buller, A.W. (Unoff. U.)	5,219
U. maj.	2,389
No change	

Central Armagh

*Whitten, H. (U.)	unopposed

Mid-Armagh

Elec. 15,901	% Poll 80.8
Stronge, J. (U.)	6,932
Toman, C. (PD)	3,551
Magowan, I. (Unoff. U.)	2,321
U. maj.	3,381
No change	

North Armagh

Elec. 20,652	% Poll 72.0
Mitchell, R.J. (U.)	9,087
Kennedy, A. (Nat. Dem.)	5,847
U. maj.	3,240
No change	

South Armagh

Elec. 18,140	% Poll 71.0

O'Hanlon, P. (Ind.)	6,442
*Richardson, E. (Nat.)	4,332
Byrne, P. (NILP)	1,794

| Ind. maj. | 2,110 |
| Ind. gain | |

Londonderry City

Elec. 19,344	% Poll 81.5

*Anderson, A. (U.)	6,480
Wilton, C. (U. Lib.)	5,770
Campbell, P. (Unoff. U.)	4,181

| U. maj. | 710 |
| No change | |

Foyle

Elec. 19,875	% Poll 84.0

Hume, J. (Ind.)	8,920
*McAteer, E. (Nat.)	5,267
McCann, E. (NILP)	1,993

| Ind. maj. | 3,653 |
| Ind. gain | |

Mid-Londonderry

Elec. 16,411	% Poll 82.0

Cooper, I. (Ind.)	6,056
Shields, R. (U.)	4,438
*Gormley, P. (Nat.)	2,229
O'Kane, J. (Rep. Lab.)	709

| Ind. maj. | 1,618 |
| Ind. gain | |

North Londonderry

Elec. 24,457	% Poll 76.6

| *Burns, J. (U.) | 9,364 |
| Barr, J. (Unoff. U.) | 9,249 |

| U. maj. | 115 |
| No change | |

South Londonderry

Elec. 18,393	% Poll 83.5

| *Chichester-Clark, Maj. J. (U.) | 9,195 |
| Devlin, Miss B. (PD) | 5,812 |

| U. maj. | 3,383 |
| No change | |

East Tyrone

Elec. 17,358	% Poll 89.9

| *Currie, A. (Nat.) | 9,065 |
| Curran, E. (U.) | 6,501 |

| Nat. maj. | 2,564 |
| No change | |

Mid-Tyrone

Elec. 11,779	% Poll 69.4

| *Gormley, T. (Nat.) | 5,149 |
| McDonald, P. (PPP) | 2,992 |

| Nat. maj. | 2,157 |
| No change | |

North Tyrone

Elec. 18,024	% Poll 85.5
Fyffe, W. (U.)	8,290
McLaughlin, D. (Nat. Dem.)	6,596
O'Kane, L. (Ind.)	559
U. maj.	1,694
No change	

South Tyrone

Elec. 17,132	% Poll 83.6
*Taylor, J. (U.)	7,683
Eakins, Rev. G. (Unoff. U.)	6,533
U. maj.	1,150
No change	

West Tyrone

*O'Connor, R. (Nat.)	unopposed

Enniskillen

Elec. 11,695	% Poll 87.0
*West, H. (U.)	4,891
Bowes-Egan, M. (PD)	2,784
Archdale, D. (Unoff. U.)	2,418
U. maj.	2,107
No change	

Lisnaskea

Elec. 10,506	% Poll 88.0
*Brooke, Capt. J. (U.)	4,794
Henderson, Maj. J. (Unoff. U.)	2,702
Carey, M. (PD)	1,726
U. maj.	2,092
No change	

South Fermanagh

Elec. 8,322	% Poll 74.9
*Carron, J. (Nat.)	4,108
Cosgrove, P. (PD)	2,100
Nat. maj.	2,008
No change	

1969 WESTMINSTER BY-ELECTION

In the by-election caused by the death of George Forrest, the Unionist MP for Mid-Ulster, his wife, Anna, the Unionist candidate, was defeated by Bernadette Devlin, Unity, in a hard-fought contest.

Mid-Ulster, 17 April 1969

Elec. 68,973	% Poll 91.5
Devlin, Miss B. (Unity)	33,648
Forrest, Mrs A. (U.)	29,437
Unity maj.	4,211
Unity gain	

1970 STORMONT BY-ELECTIONS

The two by-elections which took place in 1970 were probably the most vital in the history of the Stormont House of Commons. They were at Bannside, vacated by the former PM, Captain Terence O'Neill, and at S. Antrim, left vacant by the resignation of one of his leading supporters, Richard Ferguson, a young barrister. First, the by-elections were a test of Unionist feeling on the reforms carried through by the Chichester-Clark Government. Second, they were a measure of the support for the Rev. Ian Paisley, since he was standing in Bannside and the deputy leader of his Protestant Unionist Party, the Rev. William Beattie, in S. Antrim. In the event, the Government suffered a shattering defeat, losing both seats.

Bannside, 16 April 1970

Elec. 22,954	% Poll 79.6
Paisley, Rev. I. (Prot. U.)	7,981
Minford, Dr B. (U.)	6,778
McHugh, P. (NILP)	3,514
Prot. U. maj.	1,203
Prot. U. gain	

South Antrim, 16 April 1970

Elec. 28,633	% Poll 70.9
Beattie, Rev. W. (Prot. U.)	7,137
Morgan, W. (U.)	6,179
Corkey, D. (Ind.)	5,212
Whitby, A. (NILP)	1,773
Prot. U. maj.	958
Prot. U. gain	

1970 WESTMINSTER GENERAL ELECTION

The main local feature of the 18 June 1970 Westminster general election was that, for the first time, official Unionists secured only eight of the twelve seats. The Rev. Ian Paisley gained N. Antrim and Frank McManus, Unity, Fermanagh–S. Tyrone, while Gerry Fitt held W. Belfast, and Bernadette Devlin held Mid-Ulster. In UK terms, the big change was that James Callaghan was no longer master-minding the reforms from London, since the Conservatives had returned to power and Reginald Maudling had replaced Callaghan at the Home Office. The turnout was 76.8 per cent.

Overall figures, 1970 Westminster general election

Party	Votes	% Valid poll
Unionists	422,041	54.3
NILP	98,194	12.6
Unity	76,185	9.8
Independent (B. Devlin)	37,739	4.8
Prot. U.	35,303	4.5
Rep. Lab.	30,649	3.9
Nat.	27,006	3.5
U. Lib.	12,005	1.5
Nat. Dem.	10,349	1.3
Others	29,642	3.8
Total valid votes	779,113	100.0
Spoiled votes	2,176	
Total votes polled	781,289	

East Belfast

Elec. 59,524	% Poll 75.7
*McMaster, S.R. (U.)	26,778
Bleakley, D.W. (NILP)	18,259
U. maj.	8,519
No change	

North Belfast

Elec. 75,740	% Poll 78.1
*Mills, S. (U.)	28,668
Sharkey, J. (NILP)	18,894
Beattie, Rev. W. (Prot. U.)	11,173
McKeague, J.D. (Ind.)	441
U. maj.	9,774
No change	

South Belfast

Elec. 57,112	% Poll 68.4
*Pounder, R. (U.)	27,523
Coulthard, J. (NILP)	11,567
U. maj.	15,956
No change	

West Belfast

Elec. 68,665	% Poll 84.6
*Fitt, G. (Rep. Lab.)	30,649
McRoberts, B. (U.)	27,451
Rep. Lab. maj.	3,198
No change	

North Antrim

Elec. 79,930	% Poll 73.4
Paisley, Rev. I. (Prot. U.)	24,130
*Clark, H.M. (U.)	21,451
McHugh, P. (NILP)	6,476
McDonnell, A. (Nat. Dem.)	4,312
Moore, G. (U. Lib.)	2,269
Prot. U. maj.	2,679
Prot. U. gain	

South Antrim

Elec. 143,274	% Poll 68.0
Molyneaux, J. (U.)	59,589
Johnston, R. (NILP)	19,971
Caldwell, H. (Ind. U.)	10,938
MacAllister, J. (Nat. Dem.)	6,037
Smith, A.M. (U. Lib.)	913
U. maj.	39,618
No change	

Armagh

Elec. 86,847	% Poll 78.5
*Maginnis, J. (U.)	37,667
Lewis, H. (Unity)	21,696
Holmes, E. (NILP)	8,781
U. maj.	15,971
No change	

North Down

Elec. 121,196	% Poll 66.6
Kilfedder, J. (U.)	55,679
Young, K. (NILP)	14,246
Nixon, R. (Ind. U.)	6,408
McGladdery, J.R. (Ind.)	3,321
Simonds-Gooding, H. (U. Lib.)	1,076
U. maj. (largest in UK)	41,433
No change	

South Down

Elec. 87,079	% Poll 73.9
*Orr, L.P.S. (U.)	34,894
Golding, H. (Unity)	21,676
Quinn, J.G. (U. Lib.)	7,747
U. maj.	13,218
No change	

Fermanagh–South Tyrone

Elec. 70,381	% Poll 91.2
McManus, F. (Unity)	32,813
*Hamilton, Lord (U.)	31,390
Unity maj.	1,423
Unity gain	

Londonderry

Elec. 90,302	% Poll 81.6
*Chichester-Clark, R. (U.)	39,141
McAteer, E. (Nat.)	27,006
McCann, E. (Ind. Lab.)	7,565
U. maj.	12,135
No change	

Mid-Ulster

Elec. 77,143	% Poll 91.4
*Devlin, Miss B. (Ind.)	37,739
Thornton, W.N.J. (U.)	31,810
Cunningham, M. (Ind. Unity)	771
O'Neill, P. (Nat. Soc.)	198
Ind. maj.	5,929
Ind. gain	

313

1973 DISTRICT COUNCIL ELECTIONS

In the first election for the twenty-six new district councils, held on 30 May 1973, PR (STV) was used in NI for the first time since the 1920s. Parties tended to regard the contest as a trial run for the coming Assembly election. Unionist and loyalist candidates secured more than 300 of the 526 seats. Official Unionists and Unionists, adopted almost exclusively by OUP associations, got control of twelve councils, with 233 seats, and Loyalist Coalition candidates controlled Larne. The DUP won twenty-one seats, and a variety of other loyalists had about sixty in all. The SDLP took eighty-three seats, and were the largest party in three councils, while Alliance took sixty-three seats and Republican Clubs seven. The turnout was 68.1 per cent.

Party composition of councils, 1973

Council	DUP	VULC	Loy. Coal.	Off. U.	Ind. U.	All.	NILP	SDLP	Rep. C.	Nat./ Unity	Others
Antrim	1	1	0	9	0	2	0	0	0	0	2
Ards	0	1	0	11	0	2	1	1	0	0	1
Armagh	2	0	0	11	0	1	0	5	0	0	1
Ballymena	5	1	0	9	0	1	0	0	0	0	5
Ballymoney	1	0	0	9	0	1	0	2	0	0	3
Banbridge	0	0	0	11	0	0	0	1	0	0	3
Belfast	2	1	2	25	2	8	2	7	2	0	0
Carrickfergus	0	0	6	6	0	3	0	0	0	0	0
Castlereagh	0	0	3	10	0	5	0	0	0	0	1
Coleraine	0	0	0	13	1	3	0	1	0	0	2
Cookstown	0	0	1	8	0	0	0	3	1	0	2
Craigavon	3	2	3	10	0	4	0	2	0	0	1
Down	0	1	0	8	0	2	0	8	0	0	1
Dungannon	0	0	0	11	0	0	0	5	0	4	0
Fermanagh	0	0	0	9	1	0	0	4	0	4	2
Larne	0	0	8	1	0	3	0	0	0	0	3
Limavady	0	0	0	8	0	2	0	4	0	0	1
Lisburn	4	1	0	14	0	3	0	1	0	0	0
Londonderry	0	0	9	0	0	4	0	10	1	3	0
Magherafelt	0	1	1	5	0	0	0	6	1	0	1
Moyle	0	0	0	7	0	0	0	2	0	0	7
Newry and Mourne	0	0	0	3	0	4	0	13	2	0	8
Newtownabbey	3	0	2	12	0	3	1	0	0	0	0
North Down	0	0	4	9	0	7	0	0	0	0	0
Omagh	0	0	0	8	0	3	0	4	0	2	3
Strabane	0	0	1	6	0	2	0	4	0	0	2
Total	21	9	40	233	4	63	4	83	7	13	49

**Overall figures,
1973 district council elections**

Party	1st-preference votes	% votes
DUP	29,610	4.3
VULC	14,467	2.1
Loy. Coal.	52,875	7.7
Off. U.	286,112	41.4
Ind. U.	7,818	1.1
All.	94,474	13.7
NILP	17,422	2.5
SDLP	92,600	13.4
Rep. C.	20,680	3.0
Rep. Lab.	2,594	0.4
Nat./Unity	16,737	2.4
Ind./Non Party	51,197	7.4
Others	4,393	0.6
Total	690,979	100.0

1973 NI ASSEMBLY ELECTION
The Assembly of seventy-eight members was elected by PR (STV) on 28 June 1973, contested by 219 candidates. Because of the divisions in unionism, the party labels were not always an accurate guide to the attitude of candidates to the British Government's White Paper, which envisaged a partnership government. For example, several Official Unionists were against the scheme and the policy of the party leader, Brian Faulkner. So the anti-White Paper Unionists were split between ten Official candidates, here described as 'Unionists', the Vanguard Unionist Loyalist Coalition (led by William Craig), the Democratic Unionist Loyalist Coalition (led by Rev. Ian Paisley) and three members of the West Belfast Loyalist Coalition. The Alliance Party and Northern Ireland Labour Party did less well than they expected, and for the first time in the history of NI no Nationalist was elected. The SDLP, with nineteen seats, established itself as the second party. The electorate stood at 1,022,820 and the turnout was 72.3 per cent.

Seats and votes, 1973 NI Assembly election

Party	Seats	1st-preference votes	% Valid poll
Official Unionists	24	211,362	29.3
Unionists	8	61,183	8.5
DULC	8	78,228	10.8
VULC	7	75,759	10.5
WBLC	3	16,869	2.3
Other Loyalist	0	3,734	0.5
SDLP	19	159,773	22.1
Alliance	8	66,541	9.2
NILP	1	18,675	2.6
Rep. C.	0	13,064	1.8
Nat.	0	8,270	1.2
Rep. Lab.	0	1,750	0.2
U. Lib.	0	811	0.1
Communist	0	123	0.0
Independents	0	6,099	0.9
Total	78	722,241	100.0

East Belfast	Elec. 80,421	% Poll 71.7
6 elected	Quota 8,113	1st-preference votes
Count 1	Bradford, R.H. (Off. U.)	13,187
Count 13	Cardwell, J. (Off. U.)	5,001
Count 16	Paisley, Mrs E. (DULC)	5,518
Count 18	Napier, O.J. (All.)	4,941
Count 18	Bleakley, D.W. (NILP)	4,425
Count 18	Agnew, N. (Off. U.)	3,615

North Belfast	Elec. 75,768	% Poll 68.7
6 elected	Quota 7,255	1st-preference votes
Count 1	Fitt, G. (SDLP)	8,264
Count 11	McQuade, J. (DULC)	5,148
Count 14	Hall-Thompson, L. (Off. U.)	5,694
Count 15	Morgan, W.J. (Off. U.)	5,190
Count 15	Millar, F. (U.)	4,187
Count 15	Ferguson, J. (All.)	1,958

South Belfast	Elec. 75,990	% Poll 70.6
6 elected	Quota 7,532	1st-preference votes
Count 11	McIvor, W.B. (Off. U.)	6,930
Count 12	Glass, J.B.C. (All.)	5,148
Count 14	Burns, T.E. (DULC)	4,640
Count 15	Elder, N. (Off. U.)	4,807
Count 15	Kirk, H.V. (Off. U.)	5,426
Count 16	Magee, R.A.E. (Off. U.)	3,656

West Belfast	Elec. 70,791	% Poll 62.5
6 elected	Quota 5,911	1st-preference votes
Count 1	Laird, J.D. (U.)	11,479
Count 1	Devlin, P.J. (SDLP)	7,743
Count 3	Smyth, H. (Ind. U.)	3,625
Count 9	Coulter, R.J. (U.)	1,765
Count 12	Cooper, R.G. (All.)	3,160
Count 12	Gillespie, D.E. (SDLP)	1,940

North Antrim	Elec. 99,635	% Poll 72.5
7 elected	Quota 8,907	1st-preference votes
Count 1	Paisley, Rev. I.R.K. (DULC)	14,533
Count 1	Baxter, J.L. (Off. U.)	9,009
Count 2	Craig, W. (VULC)	8,538
Count 12	O'Hagan, J.J. (SDLP)	6,204
Count 15	McCarthy, D. (Off. U.)	5,125
Count 15	Wilson, J. (All.)	2,876
Count 15	Craig, J. (DULC)	3,871

South Antrim	Elec. 114,240	% Poll 66.9
8 elected	Quota 8,338	1st-preference votes
Count 1	Beattie, Rev. W.J. (DULC)	10,126
Count 1	Dickson, Mrs A.L. (Off. U.)	9,033
Count 9	McCloskey, E.V. (SDLP)	7,899
Count 13	Crothers, D.S.F. (All.)	5,975
Count 17	Minford, N.O. (Off. U.)	5,289
Count 18	Ardill, R.A. (Off. U.)	5,234
Count 18	Lindsay, K. (VULC)	3,055
Count 18	McLachlan, P. (Off. U.)	3,983

Armagh	Elec. 89,056	% Poll 71.1
7 elected	Quota 7,676	1st-preference votes
Count 1	O'Hanlon, P.M. (SDLP)	8,219
Count 1	Mallon, S.F. (SDLP)	7,995
Count 7	Whitten, H. (Off. U.)	6,891
Count 8	Carson, T.D. (VULC)	6,866
Count 10	Stronge, J.M. (Off. U.)	4,355
Count 12	News, H. (SDLP)	4,731
Count 12	Hutchinson, D. (DULC)	4,552

North Down	Elec. 89,682	% Poll 69.4
7 elected	Quota 7,682	1st-preference votes
Count 1	Kilfedder, J.A. (Off. U.)	20,684
Count 2	Brooke, J. (Off. U.)	6,160
Count 12	Poots, C.B. (DULC)	4,364
Count 13	Dunleath, Lord (All.)	4,482
Count 13	Campbell, R.W. (Off. U.)	3,760
Count 13	Brownlow, W.S. (Off. U.)	2,620
Count 13	McConnell, R.D. (All.)	3,271

South Down	Elec. 89,324	% Poll 73.2
7 elected	Quota 8,005	1st-preference votes
Count 1	Faulkner, A.B.D. (Off. U.)	16,287
Count 7	McGrady, E.R. (SDLP)	7,870
Count 12	Broadhurst, R.J.C. (Off. U.)	1,515
Count 14	Feely, F. (SDLP)	6,857
Count 15	O'Donoghue, P. (SDLP)	4,322
Count 17	Harvey, C. (VULC)	5,006
Count 17	Heslip, J. (U.)	3,838

Fermanagh–South Tyrone	Elec. 68,733	% Poll 84.6
5 elected	Quota 9,488	1st-preference votes
Count 1	Currie, J.A. (SDLP)	11,016
Count 4	Baird, E.A. (VULC)	8,456
Count 7	Taylor, J.D. (U.)	8,410
Count 7	Daly, T.A. (SDLP)	7,511
Count 7	West, H.W. (U.)	8,198

Londonderry	Elec. 89,849	% Poll 75.9
7 elected	Quota 8,308	1st-preference votes
Count 1	Hume, J. (SDLP)	12,596
Count 1	Morrell, L.J. (U.)	9,685
Count 2	Logue, H.A. (SDLP)	7,230
Count 3	Douglas, W.A.B. (U.)	8,245
Count 9	Barr, G. (VULC)	6,511
Count 11	Canavan, M.W.E. (SDLP)	3,647
Count 11	Conn, Mrs S.E. (U.)	6,550

Mid-Ulster	Elec. 79,331	% Poll 82.4
6 elected	Quota 9,145	1st-preference votes
Count 1	Cooper, I.A. (SDLP)	12,614
Count 1	Pollock, T.D. (Off. U.)	9,557
Count 10	Duffy, P.A. (SDLP)	4,437
Count 11	Dunlop, J. (VULC)	7,082
Count 11	Thompson, W.J. (U.)	5,352
Count 13	Larkin, A.J. (SDLP)	4,045

FEBRUARY 1974 WESTMINSTER GENERAL ELECTION

This election, held on 28 February, proved to have enormous political repercussions. It was fought in constituencies revised by the Boundary Commission. Changes were made in seven constituencies – E. Belfast, N. Belfast, S. Belfast, W. Belfast, N. Antrim, S. Antrim and N. Down. The NI powersharing Executive had been in office only since the start of the year and the UUUC campaign was directed both against the principle of partnership with the SDLP and the idea of a Council of Ireland as envisaged in the Sunningdale Agreement. The three Executive parties – Brian Faulkner's Unionists, the SDLP and the Alliance Party – were seriously embarrassed at having to defend a system that had barely got off the ground while competing against one another in the elections. To maximise its effort, the UUUC had a single candidate in each constituency, and it adopted what proved to be a telling slogan, 'Dublin is just a Sunningdale away.' The UUUC got eleven of the twelve seats, with Gerry Fitt, deputy Chief Executive, retaining his W. Belfast seat for the SDLP. The UUUC, having secured more than half the total votes cast, claimed that the result was a vote of no confidence in the new administration. The turnout was 70.4 per cent.

319

**Overall figures,
February 1974
Westminster general election**

Party	Votes	% Valid poll
UUUC:		
OUP	232,103	32.3
VUPP	75,944	10.6
DUP	58,656	8.2
U. Pro-A.	94,301	13.1
All.	22,660	3.2
NILP	17,284	2.4
SDLP	160,437	22.4
Rep. C.	15,152	2.1
Unity	17,593	2.4
Independents	23,496	3.3
Total valid votes	717,626	100.0
Spoiled votes	4,676	
Total votes polled	722,302	

*INDICATES OUTGOING MP

East Belfast

Elec. 78,821	% Poll 73.1
Craig, W. (VUPP-UUUC)	27,817
*McMaster, S.R. (U. Pro-A.)	20,077
Bleakley, D.W. (NILP)	8,122
Gillespie, D.E. (SDLP)	1,502
UUUC maj.	7,740

North Belfast

Elec. 71,081	% Poll 69.9
Carson, J. (OUP-UUUC)	21,531
Smyth, D.W. (U. Pro-A.)	12,755
Donnelly, T. (SDLP)	12,003
Scott, A. (NILP)	2,917
UUUC maj.	8,776

South Belfast

Elec. 74,534	% Poll 69.8
Bradford, Rev. R.J. (VUPP-UUUC)	22,083
*Pounder, R.J. (U. Pro-A.)	18,085
Cook, D.S. (All.)	5,118
Caraher, J.B. (SDLP)	4,149
Holmes, J.E. (NILP)	2,455
UUUC maj.	3,998

West Belfast

Elec. 65,651	% Poll 73.0
*Fitt, G. (SDLP)	19,554
McQuade, J. (DUP-UUUC)	17,374
Price, A. (Ind.)	5,662
Brady, J. (Rep. C.)	3,088
Boyd, W.R. (NILP)	1,989
SDLP maj.	2,180

North Antrim

Elec. 102,983	% Poll 63.4
*Paisley, Rev. I.R.K.	
(DUP-UUUC)	41,282
Utley, T.E. (U. Pro-A.)	13,651
McAlister, Miss M.	
(SDLP)	10,056
UUUC maj.	27,631

South Antrim

Elec. 116,710	% Poll 61.5
*Molyneaux, J.H.	
(OUP-UUUC)	48,203
Kinahan, C.H.G. (All.)	12,559
Rowan, P.J. (SDLP)	8,769
Kidd, R.J. (Ind.)	1,801
UUUC maj.	35,644

Armagh

Elec. 90,262	% Poll 67.7
McCusker, J.H.	
(OUP-UUUC)	33,194
O'Hanlon, P.M. (SDLP)	18,090
Glendinning, R.J. (All.)	4,983
Moore, T.O. (Rep. C.)	4,129
Lewis, H. (Unity)	1,364
UUUC maj.	15,104
No change	

North Down

Elec. 92,800	% Poll 67.6
*Kilfedder, J.A.	
(OUP-UUUC)	38,169
Bradford, R.H.	
(U. Pro-A.)	21,943
Curran, D. (SDLP)	2,376
UUUC maj.	16,226

South Down

Elec. 90,613	% Poll 66.6
*Orr, L.P.S.	
(OUP-UUUC)	31,088
Hollywood, S. (SDLP)	25,486
Golding, H. (Rep. C.)	3,046
UUUC maj.	5,602
No change	

Fermanagh–South Tyrone

Elec. 70,615	% Poll 87.6
West, H W.	
(OUP-UUUC)	26,858
*McManus, F.J. (Unity)	16,229
Haughey, P.D. (SDLP)	15,410
Brown, H.I. (U. Pro-A.)	3,157
UUUC maj.	10,629
UUUC gain	

Londonderry

Elec. 92,192	% Poll 68.1
Ross, W. (OUP-UUUC)	33,060
Logue, H.A. (SDLP)	23,670
Montgomery, M.J. (Rep. C.)	4,889
Foster, R.J. (Lab. and TU)	1,162
UUUC maj.	9,390
No change	

Mid-Ulster

Elec. 80,982	% Poll 82.7
Dunlop, J. (VUPP-UUUC)	26,044
Cooper, I.A. (SDLP)	19,372
*McAliskey, Mrs B. (Ind. Soc.)	16,672
Thornton, W.N.J. (U. Pro-A.)	4,633
UUUC maj.	6,672
UUUC gain	

1974 NI ASSEMBLY BY-ELECTION

The by-election was caused by the death of David McCarthy (Pro-Faulkner Unionist) in a car accident on 15 July 1973. The UWC strike in May 1974 forced the postponement of polling for four weeks until 20 June. By that time the whole political landscape had changed: the Executive had fallen on 28 May and the NI Assembly Prorogation Order had prorogued the Assembly for four months from 29 May. Hence, while the Assembly remained in existence it could not perform any of its functions. Despite this, 46.7 per cent of the electorate voted on 20 June and Clifford Smyth was elected on the first count, with the prospect of performing only constituency duties.

North Antrim, 20 June 1974

Elec. 104,168 Quota 24,069	% Poll 46.7
Party candidates	1st-preference votes
Smyth, A.C. (DUP-UUUC)	29,739
Turnly, J. (SDLP)	10,421
Agnew, Dr Iris (U. Pro-A.)	5,546
Fawcett, J. (All.)	2,430

Smyth elected on the first count.

OCTOBER 1974 WESTMINSTER GENERAL ELECTION

The Westminster election of 10 October brought only one change of party strength. The OUP leader, Harry West, lost his Fermanagh–South Tyrone seat to Independent Frank Maguire, who had stood as an agreed anti-Unionist nominee. In a sense, the contest was a test of the standing of the UUUC after its successful campaign against the power-sharing Executive, and also of the more independent line adopted by Unionists at Westminster. After the election, West was succeeded as UUUC Parliamentary leader by James Molyneaux, and Enoch Powell's election in South Down provided valuable Parliamentary expertise for the UUUC. Gerry Fitt, for the SDLP, stressed partnership in government, and Brian Faulkner's newly established UPNI made its first election bid, and one which proved disappointing for it. Alliance ran five candidates, but found that its call for an end to violence as the first priority did not make sufficient impact. The turnout was 68.5 per cent.

Overall figures, October 1974 Westminster general election

Party	Votes	% Valid poll
UUUC:		
OUP	256,065	36.5
VUPP	92,262	13.1
DUP	59,451	8.5
UPNI	20,454	2.9
Ind. U.	7,942	1.1
All.	44,644	6.3
NILP	11,539	1.6
SDLP	154,193	22.0
Rep. C.	21,633	3.1
Ind. N.	32,795	4.7
Others	1,386	0.2
Total valid votes	702,364	100.0
Spoiled votes	7,805	
Total votes polled	710,169	

*INDICATES OUTGOING MP

East Belfast

Elec. 79,629	% Poll 67.4
*Craig, W. (VUPP-UUUC)	31,594
McLachlan, P. (UPNI)	14,417
Bleakley, D. (NILP)	7,415
UUUC maj. No change	17,177

North Belfast

Elec. 71,774	% Poll 66.6
*Carson, J. (OUP-UUUC)	29,622
Donnelly, T. (SDLP)	11,400
Ferguson, J. (All.)	3,807
Boyd, W. (NILP)	2,481
UUUC maj. No change	18,222

323

South Belfast

Elec. 75,147	% Poll 67.9,
*Bradford, Rev. R.J.	
(VUPP-UUUC)	30,116
Glass, B. (All.)	11,715
McMaster, S. (Ind. U.)	4,982
Caraher, B. (SDLP)	2,390
Holmes, E. (NILP)	1,643
UUUC maj.	18,401
No change	

West Belfast

Elec. 66,278	% Poll 67.2
*Fitt, G. (SDLP)	21,821
McQuade, J.	
(DUP-UUUC)	16,265
O'Kane, Mrs K.	
(Rep. C.)	3,547
Gibson, S. McK. (VPP)	2,690
Kerins, P. (CPI)	203
SDLP maj.	5,556
No change	

North Antrim

Elec. 103,763	% Poll 57.7
*Paisley, Rev. I.R.K.	
(DUP-UUUC)	43,186
Wilson, H. (All.)	8,689
McAlister, Miss M.	
(SDLP)	7,616
UUUC maj.	34,497
No change	

South Antrim

Elec. 118,483	% Poll 58.0
*Molyneaux, J.	
(OUP-UUUC)	48,892
Kinahan, C. (All.)	10,460
Rowan, P. (SDLP)	9,061
UUUC maj.	38,432
No change	

Armagh

Elec. 91,085	% Poll 69.5
*McCusker, H.	
(OUP-UUUC)	37,518
Mallon, S. (SDLP)	19,855
McGurran, M. (Rep. C.)	5,138
UUUC maj.	17,663
No change	

North Down

Elec. 93,641	% Poll 61.2
*Kilfedder, J.A.	
(OUP-UUUC)	40,996
Jones, K. (All.)	9,973
Brownlow, W. (UPNI)	6,037
UUUC maj.	31,023
No change	

South Down

Elec. 91,792	% Poll 70.0
Powell, E. (OUP-UUUC)	33,614
Hollywood, S. (SDLP)	30,047
O'Hanlon, G. (Rep. C.)	2,327
Vipond, D. (CPI)	152
UUUC maj.	3,567
No change	

Fermanagh–South Tyrone

Elec. 71,343	% Poll 88.7
Maguire, F. (Ind.)	32,795
*West, H.W. (OUP-UUUC)	30,285
Evans, A.J. (CPI)	185
Ind. maj.	2,510
Ind. gain	

Londonderry

Elec. 93,207	% Poll 71.3
*Ross, W. (OUP-UUUC)	35,138
Hume, J. (SDLP)	26,118
Montgomery, M.J. (Rep. C.)	2,530
Foster, R. (Lab. and TU)	846
UUUC maj.	9,020
No change	

Mid-Ulster

Elec. 82,718	% Poll 79.2
*Dunlop, J. (VUPP-UUUC)	30,552
Cooper, I. (SDLP)	25,885
Donnelly, F. (Rep. C.)	8,091
UUUC maj.	4,667
No change	

1975 CONVENTION ELECTION

The election for the Constitutional Convention, like the Assembly contest, was conducted on PR (STV) for seventy-eight seats based on the twelve Westminster constituencies. It was held on 1 May 1975. Because it was not a Parliamentary election, but simply the return of delegates to an elected conference, the clash was purely on the basis of what type of constitution would have the widest acceptance in the NI community and would be approved by Westminster. The UUUC, embracing the OUP, DUP and VUPP, were firmly committed to having 'British Parliamentary standards' – that is, majority rule on the Westminster model – whereas the parties representing the former power-sharing Executive – that is, SDLP, Alliance and UPNI – urged partnership government of the type which they felt had not had a fair trial in the Assembly. The UUUC, with a special steering committee, worked with great skill to deploy their candidates in order to secure the maximum advantage from PR. In the event a total of 165 candidates contested the 78 seats – 54 fewer than in the Assembly election. The electorate stood at 1,026,987 and the total turnout was 65.8 per cent as compared with 72.3 per cent in the Assembly election, indicating perhaps a little election weariness, since this was the seventh poll in NI in little more than two years.

Seats and votes, 1975 Convention election

Party	Seats	1st-preference votes	% Valid poll
UUUC:			
OUP	19	169,797	25.8
DUP	12	97,073	14.8
VUPP	14	83,507	12.7
Ind. U.	1	5,687	0.9
Other Loyalists	1	4,453	0.6
SDLP	17	156,049	23.7
All.	8	64,657	9.8
UPNI	5	50,891	7.7
Rep. C.	0	14,515	2.2
NILP	1	9,102	1.4
Communist	0	378	0.1
Independents	0	2,052	0.3
Total	78	658,161	100.0

East Belfast	Elec. 78,340	% Poll 65.3
6 elected	Quota 7,166	1st-preference votes
Count 1	Craig, W. (VUPP-UUUC)	11,958
Count 6	Napier, O. (All.)	6,341
Count 8	Empey, R. (VUPP-UUUC)	4,657
Count 11	Cardwell, J. (UPNI)	3,039
Count 11	Paisley, Mrs E. (DUP-UUUC)	3,606
Count 11	Bleakley, D. (NILP)	3,998

North Belfast	Elec. 70,673	% Poll 63.3
6 elected	Quota 6,230	1st-preference votes
Count 1	Fitt, G. (SDLP)	6,454
Count 1	Bell, W. (OUP-UUUC)	6,268
Count 7	Millar, F. (Ind. U.-UUUC)	5,687
Count 8	Morgan, W. (OUP-UUUC)	5,558
Count 10	Hall-Thompson, L. (UPNI)	3,577
Count 10	Annon, W.T. (DUP-UUUC)	4,132

South Belfast	Elec. 73,324	% Poll 66.3
6 elected	Quota 6,831	1st-preference votes
Count 1	Smyth, Rev. M. (OUP-UUUC)	15,061
Count 1	Glass, B. (All.)	7,961
Count 2	Burchill, J. (OUP-UUUC)	4,230
Count 8	Hendron, J. (All.)	2,499
Count 9	Trimble, D. (VUPP-UUUC)	2,429
Count 11	Burns, T. (DUP-UUUC)	2,529

West Belfast	Elec. 63,869	% Poll 58.7
6 elected	Quota 5,103	1st-preference votes
Count 1	Laird, J. (OUP-UUUC)	8,433
Count 1	Devlin, P. (SDLP)	6,267
Count 6	Coulter, Miss J. (OUP-UUUC)	2,325
Count 8	Cooper, R. (All.)	3,293
Count 8	Hendron, Dr J.G. (SDLP)	2,840
Count 8	Smyth, H. (Ind. Loy.)	2,644

North Antrim	Elec. 103,469	% Poll 61.0
7 elected	Quota 7,778	1st-preference votes
Count 1	Paisley, Rev. I. (DUP-UUUC)	19,335
Count 2	McFaul, K. (DUP-UUUC)	7,658
Count 2	Smyth, C. (DUP-UUUC)	5,806
Count 9	Wilson, H. (All.)	4,601
Count 10	Turnly, J. (SDLP)	4,888
Count 12	Wright, W. (VUPP-UUUC)	2,761
Count 12	Allen, D. (VUPP-UUUC)	2,268

South Antrim	Elec. 119,723	% Poll 58.6
8 elected	Quota 7,646	1st-preference votes
Count 1	Beattie, Rev. W. (DUP-UUUC)	11,834
Count 1	Ardill, A. (OUP-UUUC)	10,895
Count 4	McCloskey, V. (SDLP)	6,756
Count 8	Kinahan, C. (All.)	5,294
Count 9	Dickson, Mrs A. (UPNI)	5,723
Count 11	Dunlop, S. (DUP-UUUC)	2,461
Count 11	Lindsay, K. (VUPP-UUUC)	4,529
Count 12	Morrison, G. (VUPP-UUUC)	2,943

Armagh	Elec. 90,640	% Poll 67.7
7 elected	Quota 7,424	1st-preference votes
Count 1	Mallon, S. (SDLP)	8,999
Count 1	Armstrong, M. (OUP-UUUC)	8,802
Count 1	Hutchinson, D. (DUP-UUUC)	7,746
Count 9	Whitten, H. (OUP-UUUC)	4,843
Count 9	Carson, T.D. (VUPP-UUUC)	5,974
Count 9	Black, A. (VUPP-UUUC)	5,435
Count 9	News, H. (SDLP)	3,303

North Down	Elec. 93,884	% Poll 62.6
7 elected	Quota 7,223	1st-preference votes
Count 1	Kilfedder, J. (OUP-UUUC)	21,693
Count 1	Taylor, J. (OUP-UUUC)	7,238
Count 3	Green, G. (VUPP-UUUC)	4,408
Count 6	Poots, C. (DUP-UUUC)	2,962
Count 7	Dunleath, Lord (All.)	4,616
Count 8	McConnell, R. (All.)	3,099
Count 8	Brookeborough, Lord (UPNI)	3,555

South Down	Elec. 89,912	% Poll 68.9
7 elected	Quota 7,594	1st-preference votes
Count 1	Feely, F. (SDLP)	9,730
Count 1	Harvey, C. (VUPP-UUUC)	8,843
Count 2	McGrady, E. (SDLP)	7,257
Count 4	O'Donoghue, P. (SDLP)	6,657
Count 9	Faulkner, B. (UPNI)	6,035
Count 9	Brush, E. (OUP-UUUC)	6,293
Count 9	Heslip, H. (OUP-UUUC)	6,380

Fermanagh–South Tyrone	Elec. 70,344	% Poll 78.4
5 elected	Quota 8,843	1st-preference votes
Count 1	West, H. (OUP-UUUC)	12,922
Count 1	Currie, A. (SDLP)	9,984
Count 3	Baird, E. (VUPP-UUUC)	8,067
Count 7	Daly, T. (SDLP)	7,145
Count 9	McKay, J. (OUP-UUUC)	3,194

Londonderry	Elec. 92,003	% Poll 69.8
7 elected	Quota 7,801	1st-preference votes
Count 1	Hume, J. (SDLP)	11,941
Count 1	Conn, Mrs S. (OUP-UUUC)	8,789
Count 1	Barr, G. (VUPP-UUUC)	7,883
Count 4	Logue, H. (SDLP)	6,661
Count 5	Douglas, W. (OUP-UUUC)	4,939
Count 6	Canavan, M. (SDLP)	4,600
Count 12	McClure, J. (DUP-UUUC)	3,436

Mid-Ulster	Elec. 80,806	% Poll 72.5
6 elected	Quota 8,068	1st-preference votes
Count 1	Thompson, W. (OUP-UUUC)	9,342
Count 1	Cooper, I. (SDLP)	9,073
Count 1	Reid, R. (DUP-UUUC)	8,250
Count 10	Duffy, P. (SDLP)	4,130
Count 11	Thompson, E. (OUP-UUUC)	4,292
Count 11	Overend, R. (VUPP-UUUC)	5,573

1977 DISTRICT COUNCIL ELECTIONS

The second election for the twenty-six district councils was held on 18 May 1977, in the immediate aftermath of the abortive UUAC strike against the security policy pursued by the direct rule regime. The refusal of OUP to join with Paisley (DUP) and Baird (UUUP) in the strike produced a terminal rift in the UUUC and, for the first time since 1974, candidates from the main Unionist parties stood without the endorsement of the UUUC. Two main features emerged from the elections: first, despite a party system which was still fragmenting, political support concentrated on four main parties – OUP, SDLP, Alliance and DUP – who together won 77.3 per cent of the vote and 82.7 per cent of the seats; second,

Overall figures, 1977 district council elections

Party	1st-preference votes	% votes
DUP	70,850	12.7
UUUP	17,901	3.2
Loy.	13,218	2.4
OUP	164,900	29.6
VUPP	8,135	1.5
UPNI	13,691	2.4
All.	80,011	14.4
NILP	4,732	0.8
SDLP	114,776	20.6
Rep. C.	14,277	2.6
Nat./Unity	8,161	1.5
Others	46,055	8.3
Total	556,707	100.0

there was a radical change away from council control by a single party with an absolute majority of seats. Only three councils – Antrim and Banbridge (OUP) and Ballymena (DUP) – were controlled by a single party, in contrast to 1973 when twelve were dominated by OUP and one by loyalists. In 1977 OUP was the largest party on ten

councils and SDLP on six, but both depended on support from other parties to win control. These features and the break-up of the UUUC opened the way to bargaining for position on some councils. The turnout was 57.9 per cent, 10.2 per cent lower than 1973.

Party composition of councils, 1977

Council	DUP	UUUP	Loy.	VUPP	OUP	UPNI	All.	SDLP	Rep. C.	Nat./ Unity	Others
Antrim	3	0	0	0	8	0	2	0	0	0	2
Ards	3	0	0	0	6	0	5	1	0	0	2
Armagh	2	1	0	0	9	0	0	7	0	0	1
Ballymena	11	0	2	0	4	0	1	0	0	0	3
Ballymoney	3	0	1	0	5	0	1	3	0	0	3
Banbridge	3	0	1	0	8	0	0	2	0	0	1
Belfast	7	0	2	0	15	2	13	8	3	0	1
Carrickfergus	3	0	1	0	5	1	5	0	0	0	0
Castlereagh	4	0	0	0	7	0	7	0	0	0	1
Coleraine	2	0	1	0	10	0	2	2	0	0	3
Cookstown	1	3	0	0	4	0	0	5	0	0	2
Craigavon	4	1	0	0	10	0	3	6	1	0	0
Down	0	0	0	0	7	0	3	10	0	0	0
Dungannon	2	0	0	0	8	0	0	6	0	0	4
Fermanagh	0	3	0	0	6	0	0	7	0	2	2
Larne	3	0	1	3	1	0	4	1	0	0	2
Limavady	2	0	0	0	6	0	0	6	0	0	1
Lisburn	6	2	0	0	9	1	3	2	0	0	0
Londonderry	2	0	0	0	6	0	2	13	0	4	0
Magherafelt	3	1	0	0	4	0	0	5	1	0	1
Moyle	2	0	0	0	5	0	0	3	0	0	6
Newry and Mourne	1	0	0	0	7	0	3	15	0	0	4
Newtownabbey	4	0	1	0	8	1	6	0	0	0	1
North Down	1	1	1	2	7	1	7	0	0	0	0
Omagh	0	0	0	0	8	0	3	6	1	0	2
Strabane	2	0	0	0	5	0	0	5	0	0	3
Total	74	12	11	5	178	6	70	113	6	6	45

1979 WESTMINSTER GENERAL ELECTION

The 3 May 1979 Westminster general election found Unionists, anti-Unionists and centre parties all split, and three seats, E. Belfast, N. Belfast and N. Down changed hands. The first two were gained from OUP by DUP, each by a narrow majority. In N. Down, although there was no change of MP, James Kilfedder's victory in face of opposition from the OUP, from which he had just resigned, was in effect an Ind. Unionist gain. The turnout was 68.4 per cent.

Overall figures, 1979 Westminster general election

Party	Votes	% Valid poll
OUP	254,578	36.6
SDLP	126,325	18.3
All.	82,892	11.8
DUP	70,975	10.2
UUUP	39,856	5.7
Ind. U.	36,989	5.3
IIP	23,086	3.3
Ind. N.	22,398	3.2
Rep. C.	12,098	1.7
Ind. SDLP	10,785	1.6
UPNI	8,021	1.2
NILP	4,411	0.6
Others	3,573	2.1

Total valid votes	695,987	100.0

Spoiled votes	7,512	

Total votes polled	703,499	

*INDICATES OUTGOING MP

East Belfast

Elec. 75,496	% Poll 67.6
Robinson, P. (DUP)	15,994
*Craig, W. (OUP)	15,930
Napier, O. (All.)	15,066
Agnew, N. (UPNI)	2,017
Chambers, G. (NILP)	1,982

DUP maj.   64
DUP gain

North Belfast

Elec. 65,099	% Poll 66.0
McQuade, J. (DUP)	11,690
Walker, C. (OUP)	10,695
O'Hare, P. (SDLP)	7,823
Dickson, Mrs A. (UPNI)	4,220
Cushnahan, J. (All.)	4,120
Lynch, S. (Rep. C.)	1,907
Carr, A. (NILP)	1,889

DUP maj.   995
DUP gain

South Belfast

Elec. 68,946	% Poll 68.0
*Bradford, Rev. R. (OUP)	28,875
Glass, B. (All.)	11,745
McDonnell, A. (SDLP)	3,694
Brennan, V. (UPNI)	1,784
Dudgeon, J. (Lab. Integrationist)	692

OUP maj.   17,130
No change

West Belfast

Elec. 58,915	% Poll 60.4
*Fitt, G. (SDLP)	16,480
Passmore, T. (OUP)	8,245
Dickson, W. (DUP)	3,716
Brennan, B. (Rep. C.)	2,282
Cousins, J. (All.)	2,024
Peters, D. (NILP)	540
SDLP maj.	8,235
No change	

North Antrim

Elec. 102,224	% Poll 62.6
*Paisley, Rev. I. (DUP)	33,941
Burchill, J. (OUP)	15,398
Wilson, H. (All.)	7,797
Farren, S. (SDLP)	4,867
Turnly, J. (IIP)	3,689
DUP maj.	18,543
No change	

South Antrim

Elec. 126,493	% Poll 58.8
*Molyneaux, J. (OUP)	50,782
Kinahan, C. (All.)	11,914
Rowan, P. (SDLP)	7,432
Kidd, R. (ULP)	1,895
Smyth, K. (Rep. C.)	1,615
OUP maj.	38,868
No change	

Armagh

Elec. 93,097	% Poll 70.9
*McCusker, H. (OUP)	31,668
Mallon, S. (SDLP)	23,545
Calvert, D. (DUP)	5,634
Moore, T. (Rep. C.)	2,310
Ramsay, W. (All.)	2,074
OUP maj.	8,123
No change	

North Down

Elec. 99,889	% Poll 62.4
*Kilfedder, J. (Ind. U.)	36,989
Jones, K. (All.)	13,364
Smyth, C. (OUP)	11,728
Ind. U. maj.	23,625
Ind. U. gain	

South Down

Elec. 89,597	% Poll 72.0
*Powell, E. (OUP)	32,254
McGrady, E. (SDLP)	24,033
Forde, P. (All.)	4,407
Markey, J. (IIP)	1,853
O'Hagan, D. (Rep. C.)	1,682
Rice, S. (Ind.)	216
Courtney, P. (Reform)	31
OUP maj.	8,221
No change	

Fermanagh–South Tyrone

Elec. 71,541	% Poll 88.9
*Maguire, F. (Ind.)	22,398
Ferguson, R. (OUP)	17,411
Currie, A. (Ind. SDLP)	10,785
Baird, E. (UUUP)	10,607
Acheson, P. (All.)	1,070
Ind. maj.	4,987
No change	

Londonderry

Elec. 94,800	% Poll 67.6
*Ross, W. (OUP)	31,592
Logue, H. (SDLP)	19,185
Barr, A. (All.)	5,830
McAteer, F. (IIP)	5,489
Melaugh, E. (Rep. C.)	888
Webster, B. (Derry Lab.)	639
OUP maj.	12,407
No change	

Mid-Ulster

Elec. 81,499	% Poll 80.9
*Dunlop, J. (UUUP)	29,249
Duffy, P. (SDLP)	19,266
Fahy, P. (IIP)	12,055
Lagan, A. (All.)	3,481
Donnelly, F. (Rep. C.)	1,414
UUUP maj.	9,983
No change	

1979 EUROPEAN PARLIAMENT ELECTION

The election for the European Parliament on 7 June 1979 resulted in the three NI seats being filled by: the Rev. Ian Paisley MP, leader of the DUP, John Hume, deputy leader of the SDLP, and John Taylor, OUP EC spokesman. Paisley's easy victory on the first count, and Hume's record SDLP poll, with the two OUPs – party leader Harry West and John Taylor – well behind in first preferences, was regarded as something of a watershed in local politics. The Alliance Party also lost ground seriously by comparison with the 1979 Westminster election. The DUP campaign was characterised by Paisley's condemnation of the EC, and his repeated declarations that he would seek to counter Catholic influence at Strasbourg. And he insisted that his vote meant that he must be regarded as speaking for the NI majority. The OUP, while accepting the UK's commitment to EC membership, called for major changes to meet NI conditions. They claimed that the result showed that many of their supporters, being opposed to the Common Market, had deserted to Paisley. Both the SDLP and Alliance took a strong pro-European line, but urged more effort to meet regional needs. Hume, as a candidate of the European Socialist group, accepted the Socialist manifesto, with its commitment to deal energetically with unemployment. He also argued that the new European Parliament would have a healing effect locally, because MEPs from both NI and the Republic would be likely to find themselves on the same side in European politics. The election took place in the single NI constituency, with voting by PR (STV) and the outcome was in accordance with the intention of the European summit meeting which had allocated a third seat to NI in the hope that this would ensure representation of both communities. The turnout of nearly 57 per cent reflected a higher level of interest than in GB.

Note The method of determining the number of votes transferred from one candidate to another under this PR system can vary, according to usage in different countries. In NI the method employed in this election allowed for the calculation of transfers to be determined to two decimal places. This differs from the system which obtains in the Republic, where only whole numbers of votes are transferred.

1979 European Parliament election

Details of the count

3 seats

Electorate 1,029,490	Percentage poll 56.92
Valid votes 572,239	Quota 143,060
Spoiled votes 13,774	Votes unaccounted for 47

First count

Party candidates	1st-preference votes	% valid poll
Paisley, Rev. I. (DUP)	170,688	29.8
Hume, J. (SDLP)	140,622	24.6
Taylor, J. (OUP)	68,185	11.9
West, H. (OUP)	56,984	10.0
Napier, O. (All.)	39,026	6.8
Kilfedder, J. (Ulster Unionist)	38,198	6.7
McAliskey, Mrs B. (Ind.)	33,969	5.9
Bleakley, D. (Utd. Community)	9,383	1.6
Devlin, P. (ULP)	6,122	1.1
Cummings, E. (UPNI)	3,712	0.6
Brennan, B. (Rep. C.)	3,258	0.6
Donnelly, F. (Rep. C.)	1,160	0.2
Murray, J. (U. Lib.)	932	0.2

Paisley elected; his surplus votes were distributed.

Second count

Party candidates	Distribution of surplus votes	Total votes
Hume	+54.56	140,676.56
Taylor	+9,043.68	77,228.68
West	+4,179.04	61,163.04
Kilfedder	+12,424.32	50,622.32
Napier	+378.08	39,404.08
McAliskey	+6.72	33,975.72
Bleakley	+217.76	9,600.76
Devlin	+24.80	6,146.80
Cummings	+124.96	3,836.96
Brennan	+5.44	3,263.44
Donnelly	+4.00	1,164.00
Murray	+16.00	948.00

Non-transferable votes, 1,148.64. Bleakley, Brennan, Cummings, Devlin, Donnelly and Murray eliminated, all with lost deposits. Their votes were distributed.

Third count

Party candidates	Distribution of votes	Total votes
Hume	+5,396.00	146,072.56
Taylor	+2,979.28	80,207.96
West	+789.12	61,952.16
Kilfedder	+3,363.84	53,986.16
Napier	+6,298.88	45,702.96
McAliskey	+2,129.72	36,105.44

Accumulative non-transferable votes, 5,151.76. Hume elected. McAliskey eliminated; her votes were distributed.

Fourth count

Party candidates	Distribution of votes	Total votes
Taylor	+197.96	80,405.92
West	+187.96	62,140.12
Kilfedder	+637.72	54,623.88
Napier	+5,560.80	51,263.76

Accumulative non-transferable votes, 34,672.76. Napier eliminated; his votes were distributed.

Fifth count

Party candidates	Distribution of votes	Total votes
Taylor	+16,001.44	96,407.36
Kilfedder	+14,760.08	69,383.96
West	+3,775.52	65,915.64

Accumulative non-transferable votes, 51,399.48. West eliminated; his votes were distributed.

Sixth count

Party candidates	Distribution of votes	Total votes
Taylor	+57,059.00	153,466.36
Kilfedder	+3,174.00	72,557.96

Accumulative non-transferable votes, 57,082.12. Taylor elected.

1981 DISTRICT COUNCIL ELECTIONS

The district council elections on 20 May 1981 were marked by a highly polarised atmosphere, largely due to the H-Block hunger strike, and the results showed a decline in support for centre parties. The DUP took most satisfaction from the outcome, because it succeeded in replacing OUP as the party with the largest popular vote, but its lead was so slender (0.1 per cent) that it left the OUP the strongest party in terms of seats. But the DUP more than doubled its share of the first-preference votes as compared with 1977 – 26.6 per cent against 12.7 per cent – and its total of seats increased by 68 to 142. The OUP, however, got 152 seats compared with 178 in the 1977 election; that is, it lost 5 per cent of the total seats although its share of the vote dropped by only 3 per cent. The OUP first-preference votes reached 26.5 per cent against 29.6 per cent four years earlier. The Alliance Party fared worst – its vote dropped from 14.4 per cent to

Overall figures, 1981 district council elections

Party	1st-preference votes	% votes
DUP	176,816	26.6
Loy.	21,699	3.3
OUP	176,342	26.5
UPUP/UPNI	12,491	1.9
All.	59,219	8.9
Lab.	9,854	1.5
WPRC	12,237	1.8
SDLP	116,487	17.5
IIP	25,859	3.9
Nat.	9,487	1.4
Others	45,011	6.7
Total	665,502	100.0

8.9 per cent, and it now held thirty-eight seats instead of seventy. The SDLP also lost ground, although much less dramatically. Its percentage poll was 17.5 as compared with 20.6 in 1977, although, because of the larger turnout, it dropped fewer than 2,000 votes overall. Its tally of seats fell from 113 to 103 in face of increased competition from a variety of Republicans and Nationalists, but most notably from the Irish

Independence Party. The IIP, which came into being soon after the 1977 elections, took 3.9 per cent of the votes and picked up twenty-one seats. The smaller parties found the going hard. A combination of UPUP and UPNI got seven seats and 1.9 per cent of votes. WPRC halved its representation with three seats and 1.8 per cent of votes; IRSP and PD got two seats each, and the NILP held its single seat. The turnout was 66.2 per cent.

Party composition of councils, 1981

Council	DUP	Loy.	OUP	UPUP/ UPNI	All.	Lab.	WPRC	SDLP	IIP	Nat.	Others
Antrim	4	0	7	0	1	0	0	2	1	0	0
Ards	7	0	3	2	3	1	0	1	0	0	0
Armagh	3	1	8	0	0	0	0	7	0	0	1
Ballymena	13	0	5	0	0	0	0	0	0	0	3
Ballymoney	7	0	3	0	1	0	0	2	0	0	3
Banbridge	4	0	8	0	0	0	0	2	0	0	1
Belfast	15	3	13	1	7	1	0	6	0	4	1
Carrickfergus	7	2	3	0	3	0	0	0	0	0	0
Castlereagh	9	0	5	0	4	0	0	0	0	0	1
Coleraine	6	0	8	0	1	0	0	2	0	0	3
Cookstown	3	1	4	0	0	0	0	5	0	0	2
Craigavon	7	1	9	0	1	0	2	5	0	0	0
Down	3	0	6	0	1	1	1	8	0	0	0
Dungannon	3	0	8	0	0	0	0	3	1	0	5
Fermanagh	2	0	8	0	0	0	0	4	4	0	2
Larne	6	1	4	0	3	0	0	0	0	0	1
Limavady	2	0	6	0	0	0	0	5	1	0	1
Lisburn	10	1	8	0	2	0	0	2	0	0	0
Londonderry	5	0	4	0	0	0	0	14	4	0	0
Magherafelt	4	1	2	0	0	0	0	5	1	0	2
Moyle	2	1	4	0	0	0	0	5	0	0	4
Newry and Mourne	2	0	6	0	0	0	0	16	4	0	2
Newtownabbey	5	2	9	0	3	1	0	0	0	0	1
North Down	5	1	4	4	6	0	0	0	0	0	0
Omagh	4	0	4	0	2	0	0	5	5	0	0
Strabane	4	0	3	0	0	0	0	4	0	0	4
Total	142	15	152	7	38	4	3	103	21	4	37

APRIL 1981 WESTMINSTER BY-ELECTION

The by-election, created by the death of Frank Maguire, Ind. MP for Fermanagh–S. Tyrone, aroused world-wide interest, because it resolved itself into a straight fight between Bobby Sands, leader of the H-Block hunger-strikers, and Harry West (OUP), who had held the seat briefly in 1974. Sands had been on hunger strike since 1 March and was said to have lost about 13 kilograms in weight by polling day. His campaign from his Maze Prison cell stimulated widespread media attention, and in the end provoked an astonishing unity among all shades of Nationalists. Failure to fight the seat created angry dissension within the SDLP. The British authorities made it clear that Sands's narrow victory would not weaken their opposition to H-Block demands, but the result was a powerful boost to the hunger-strike campaign.

Fermanagh–South Tyrone, 9 April 1981

Elec. 72,283	% Poll 86.9
Sands, R.G. (Anti-H-Block/Armagh Political Prisoner)	30,492
West, H.W. (OUP)	29,046
Anti-H-Block/Armagh Political Prisoner maj.	1,446
Spoiled votes	3,280

AUGUST 1981 WESTMINSTER BY-ELECTION

In this second by-election in Fermanagh–S. Tyrone in five months, to fill the vacancy created by the death of hunger-striker Bobby Sands, his election agent, Owen Carron, was successful in a six-cornered contest. With the hunger strike still going on, and the previous by-election result having failed to move the British Government, there was some surprise that Carron, an ordinary member of PSF, got 786 votes more than Sands, despite the split in the anti-Unionist vote. The OUP vote, with a new candidate in Ken Maginnis, a Dungannon councillor, was virtually the same as in the April contest.

Fermanagh–South Tyrone, 20 August 1981

Elec. 72,834	% Poll 88.6
Carron, O. (Anti-H-Block Proxy Political Prisoner	31,278
Maginnis, K. (OUP)	29,048
Close, S. (All.)	1,930
Moore, T. (WPRC)	1,132
Green, M. (General Amnesty)	249
Hall-Raleigh, S. (Peace)	90
Anti-H-Block Proxy Political Prisoner maj.	2,230
Spoiled votes	804

1982 WESTMINSTER BY-ELECTION

The by-election on 4 March 1982, to fill the vacancy arising from the murder of the Rev. Robert Bradford, OUP MP for S. Belfast, developed into a bitter struggle between the OUP and the DUP, who were particularly angry at the refusal of the 'Officials' to consider the idea of a United Unionist candidate. The DUP selected a strong contender in the Rev. William McCrea, of Magherafelt, a well-known gospel singer. But in an eight-cornered contest, the OUP nominee, the Rev. Martin Smyth, head of the Orange Order, had a 5,397 majority over Alliance candidate David Cook, and the DUP candidate was in third place.

South Belfast, 4 March 1982

Elec. 66,219	% Poll 66.2
Smyth, Rev. M. (OUP)	17,123
Cook, D. (All.)	11,726
McCrea, Rev. W. (DUP)	9,818
McDonnell, Dr A. (SDLP)	3,839
McMichael, J. (ULDP)	576
Caul, B. (ULP)	303
Narain, J. (One Human Family)	137
Hall-Raleigh, S. (Peace State)	12
OUP maj.	5,397
No change	

1982 NI ASSEMBLY ELECTION

The 'rolling devolution' election on 20 October 1982 was notable for two things – the achievement of PSF, in its first Stormont election, of taking five of the seventy-eight seats with more than 10 per cent of the first-preference votes, and the re-emergence of the OUP as the largest group, with twenty-six seats. The PSF showed an advance of 2.4 per cent over the aggregate pro-H-Block vote in the 1981 district council elections, and it contested only seven of the twelve constituencies. It was unlucky in that it might have expected to get two more seats on the basis of its voting strength. The PSF gains led to SDLP losses, and the total of SDLP seats, at fourteen, was five down on the 1973 Assembly and three down on the 1975 Convention, although it made a small recovery in terms of first-preference votes as against the 1981 district council elections. Both SDLP and PSF fought on an abstentionist policy. PSF simply called for British withdrawal,

and the SDLP argued that the Assembly was 'unworkable' since Unionists continued to reject power-sharing and the Government had failed to promise a strong enough Irish dimension. On the Unionist side, the DUP had hoped to repeat its 1981 district council performance of a slight lead in votes over the OUP, but in the event OUP had a 7 per cent margin over the DUP in first-preference votes. Both the OUP and the DUP pledged themselves to seek to persuade the Government to concede majority rule, but the DUP was more enthusiastic than the OUP about the interim scrutiny powers given to the Assembly. With almost the same percentage of first-preference votes as in the 1973 Assembly election, Alliance profited from late transfers to give it ten seats – two more than it held in 1973 and in the 1975 Convention. For the most part, the smaller parties and Independents fared badly. The electorate stood at 1,048,807 and the turnout was 63.5 per cent.

Seats and votes, 1982 NI Assembly election

Party	Seats	1st-preference votes	% Valid poll
OUP	26	188,277	29.7
DUP	21	145,528	23.0
SDLP	14	118,891	18.8
PSF	5	64,191	10.1
Alliance	10	58,851	9.3
WP	0	17,216	2.7
UPUP	1	14,916	2.3
UUUP	0	11,550	1.8
Other Unionists	1	9,502	1.6
Others	0	4,198	0.7
Total	78	633,120	100.0

East Belfast	Elec. 74,273		% Poll 54.8
6 elected	Quota 5,632		1st-preference votes
Count 1	Robinson, P. (DUP)		15,319
Count 1	Burchill, J. (OUP)		7,345
Count 1	Napier, O. (All.)		6,037
Count 2	Vitty, D. (DUP)		235
Count 10	Dunlop, Mrs D. (OUP)		1,696
Count 10	Morrow, A. (All.)		2,966

North Belfast	Elec. 62,391		% Poll 59.2
5 elected	Quota 5,957		1st-preference votes
Count 1	Carson, J. (OUP)		7,798
Count 11	Seawright, G. (DUP)		4,929
Count 13	Millar, F. (Ind. U.)		2,047
Count 14	O'Hare, P. (SDLP)		3,190
Count 14	Maguire, P. (All.)		2,527

South Belfast	Elec. 66,683		% Poll 58.1
5 elected	Quota 6,245		1st-preference votes
Count 1	Smyth, Rev. M. (OUP)		13,337
Count 1	Cook, D. (All.)		6,514
Count 4	McCrea, S. (DUP)		4,091
Count 6	Graham, E. (OUP)		2,875
Count 6	Kirkpatrick, J. (OUP)		1,126

West Belfast	Elec. 57,726	% Poll 62.5
4 elected	Quota 6,852	1st-preference votes
Count 1	Adams, G. (PSF)	9,740
Count 5	Hendron, Dr J. (SDLP)	5,207
Count 8	Passmore, T. (OUP)	4,505
Count 8	Glendinning, W. (All.)	2,733

North Antrim	Elec. 104,683	% Poll 57.5
8 elected	Quota 6,512	1st-preference votes
Count 1	Paisley, Rev. I. (DUP)	9,231
Count 2	Allister, J. (DUP)	5,835
Count 6	Gaston, J. (OUP)	5,856
Count 8	Farren, S. (SDLP)	5,006
Count 9	Neeson, S. (All.)	3,258
Count 10	McKee, J. (DUP)	4,515
Count 10	Beggs, R. (OUP)	4,885
Count 11	Cousley, C. (DUP)	4,133

South Antrim	Elec. 131,734	% Poll 52.0
10 elected	Quota 6,041	1st-preference votes
Count 1	Molyneaux, J. (OUP)	19,978
Count 1	Beattie, Rev. W. (DUP)	7,489
Count 2	Agnew, F. (OUP)	3,302
Count 2	Davis, I. (DUP)	5,394
Count 18	Forsythe, C. (OUP)	1,612
Count 19	Thompson, R. (DUP)	2,646
Count 22	McDonald, J. (SDLP)	2,071
Count 23	Close, S. (All.)	2,916
Count 23	Mawhinney, G. (All.)	2,660
Count 23	Bell, W. (OUP)	979

This count, involving twenty-six candidates, is believed to have established a record for the UK and the Republic. It extended over more than thirty hours.

Armagh	Elec. 95,610	% Poll 66.9
7 elected	Quota 7,739	1st-preference votes
Count 1	McCusker, H. (OUP)	19,547
Count 1	Mallon, S. (SDLP)	8,528
Count 7	Nicholson, J. (OUP)	2,590
Count 9	McAllister, J. (PSF)	5,182
Count 11	Simpson, Mrs M. (OUP)	721
Count 13	Calvert, D. (DUP)	2,661
Count 14	News, H. (SDLP)	2,871

North Down	Elec. 103,619	% Poll 53.8
8 elected	Quota 6,069	1st-preference votes
Count 1	Kilfedder, J. (UPUP)	13,958
Count 2	Taylor, J. (OUP)	5,852
Count 6	Gibson, S. (DUP)	4,500
Count 8	Cushnahan, J. (All.)	4,416
Count 9	Dunleath, Lord (All.)	3,841
Count 10	Pentland, W. (DUP)	3,340
Count 11	McCartney, R. (OUP)	3,782
Count 13	Bleakes, W. (OUP)	2,692

South Down	Elec. 93,261	% Poll 65.6
7 elected	Quota 7,382	1st-preference votes
Count 1	Feely, F. (SDLP)	7,391
Count 2	McGrady, E. (SDLP)	7,313
Count 6	Brown, W. (OUP)	5,220
Count 7	O'Donoghue, P. (SDLP)	5,916
Count 10	McCullough, R. (OUP)	5,802
Count 11	Graham, G. (DUP)	4,075
Count 11	Wells, J. (DUP)	3,779

Fermanagh–South Tyrone	Elec. 73,930	% Poll 82.9
5 elected	Quota 9,864	1st-preference votes
Count 1	Carron, O. (PSF)	14,025
Count 1	Maginnis, K. (OUP)	10,117
Count 8	Ferguson, R. (OUP)	5,877
Count 9	Currie, A. (SDLP)	6,800
Count 10	Foster, Rev. I. (DUP)	4,324

Londonderry	Elec. 100,198	% Poll 66.0
7 elected	Quota 8,058	1st-preference votes
Count 1	Hume, J. (SDLP)	12,282
Count 1	McGuinness, M. (PSF)	8,207
Count 10	McClure, J. (DUP)	6,857
Count 10	Allen, J. (OUP)	6,107
Count 11	Douglas, W. (OUP)	5,031
Count 13	Logue, H. (SDLP)	4,828
Count 13	Campbell, G. (DUP)	5,305

Mid-Ulster	Elec. 84,699	% Poll 75.5
6 elected	Quota 8,853	1st-preference votes
Count 1	McCrea, Rev. W. (DUP)	10,445
Count 6	Haughey, D. (SDLP)	8,413
Count 10	Thompson, W. (OUP)	5,546
Count 11	Kane, A. (DUP)	3,981
Count 12	McSorley, Mrs M. (SDLP)	4,169
Count 12	Morrison, D. (PSF)	6,927

1983 NI ASSEMBLY BY-ELECTION

The by-election on 20 April 1983 was created by the unseating, by an Election Court, of Seamus Mallon (SDLP, Armagh) on the grounds that he was disqualified from Assembly membership because he was also an Irish Senator at the time of the Assembly election in October 1982. The SDLP called on voters to ignore the by-election. There were 571 spoiled votes.

Armagh, 20 April 1983

Elec. 95,100	% Poll 34.07
Quota 15,914	

Party candidates	1st-preference votes
Speers, J. (OUP)	26,907
French, T. (WP)	4,920

Speers elected on the first count.

1983 WESTMINSTER GENERAL ELECTION

The 9 June 1983 Westminster election was fought on seventeen seats – five extra as compared with the 1979 election. The Boundary Commission gave additional representation to five of the previous constituencies: Londonderry – Foyle; Armagh – Newry and Armagh; N. Antrim – E. Antrim; S. Antrim – Lagan Valley; and N. Down – Strangford. The other constituencies were adjusted accordingly and renamed as necessary. The main feature of the results was the dominance of the OUP, which took eleven seats and 34 per cent of the poll and went strongly ahead of the DUP, with three seats and a 20 per cent vote. UPUP had one seat. Thus, Unionists had fifteen of the seats, with the other two going to PSF (W. Belfast) and SDLP (Foyle). The campaign had been marked by a bitter struggle on both sides of the community, although a very limited accommodation between OUP and DUP meant that there was only one Unionist in three constituencies – Foyle, Newry and Armagh, and Fermanagh–S. Tyrone. SDLP rejected any idea of a pact with PSF, and fought all seventeen seats – the only party to do so. None the less, SDLP's share of the vote was down slightly as compared with the 1982 Assembly election – to 17.9 per cent – while PSF passed its target vote of 100,000 and achieved a 13.4 per cent poll, about 3 per cent up on the Assembly election. Main interest was centred in W. Belfast where Gerry Adams of PSF repeated his 1982 Assembly election success and unseated veteran MP Gerry Fitt. Owen Carron of PSF, who won the August 1981 by-election in Fermanagh–S. Tyrone, was defeated by Ken Maginnis (OUP). There was a high turnout of 73.3 per cent of the 1,048,766 electors.

Overall figures,
1983 Westminster general election

Party	Votes	% Valid poll
OUP	259,952	34.0
DUP	152,749	20.0
SDLP	137,012	17.9
PSF	102,701	13.4
All.	61,275	8.0
UPUP	22,861	3.0
WP	14,650	1.9
Ind.	10,326	1.3
Others	3,399	0.3
Total valid votes	764,925	100.0
Spoiled votes	4,353	
Total votes polled	769,278	

*INDICATES OUTGOING MP

East Belfast

Elec. 55,581	% Poll 70.0
*Robinson, P. (DUP)	17,631
Burchill, J. (OUP)	9,642
Napier, O. (All.)	9,373
Donaldson, D. (PSF)	682
Tang, Mrs M. (Lab. and TU)	584
Prendiville, P. (SDLP)	519
Cullen, F. (WP)	421
Boyd, H. (Anti-Noise)	59
DUP maj.	7,989

North Belfast

Elec. 61,128	% Poll 69.4
Walker, A.C. (OUP)	15,339
Seawright, G. (DUP)	8,260
Feeny, B. (SDLP)	5,944
Austin, J. (PSF)	5,451
Maguire, P. (All.)	3,879
Lynch, S. (WP)	2,412
Gault, W. (Ind. DUP)	1,134
OUP maj.	7,079

South Belfast

Elec. 53,694	% Poll 69.6
*Smyth, Rev. M. (OUP)	18,669
Cook, D. (All.)	8,945
McCrea, R.S. (DUP)	4,565
McDonnell, A. (SDLP)	3,216
McKnight, S. (PSF)	1,107
Carr, G. (WP)	856
OUP maj.	9,724

West Belfast

Elec. 59,750	% Poll 74.3
Adams, G. (PSF)	16,379
Hendron, Dr J. (SDLP)	10,934
*Fitt, G. (Ind.)	10,326
Passmore, T. (OUP)	2,435
Haffey, G.A. (DUP)	2,399
McMahon, Ms M. (WP)	1,893
PSF maj.	5,445

North Antrim

Elec. 63,254	% Poll 69.9
*Paisley, Rev. I. (DUP)	23,922
Coulter, Rev. R. (OUP)	10,749
Farren, S. (SDLP)	6,193
McMahon, P. (PSF)	2,860
Samuel, M.H. (Ecol.)	451
DUP maj.	13,173

South Antrim

Elec. 59,300	% Poll 65.5
Forsythe, C. (OUP)	17,727
Thompson, R. (DUP)	10,935
Mawhinney, G. (All.)	4,612
Maginness, A. (SDLP)	3,377
Laverty, S. (PSF)	1,629
Smyth, K. (WP)	549
OUP maj.	6,792

East Antrim

Elec. 58,780	% Poll 65.0
Beggs, R. (OUP)	14,293
Allister, J. (DUP)	13,926
Neeson, S. (All.)	7,620
O'Cleary, M. (SDLP)	1,047
Cunning, W. (Ind.)	741
Kelly, A. (WP)	581
OUP maj.	367

North Down

Elec. 61,574	% Poll 66.2
*Kilfedder, J. (UPUP)	22,861
Cushnahan, J. (All.)	9,015
McCartney, R. (OUP)	8,261
Ó Baoill, C. (SDLP)	645
UPUP maj.	13,846

South Down

Elec. 66,987	% Poll 76.6
*Powell, E. (OUP)	20,693
McGrady, E. (SDLP)	20,145
Fitzsimmons, P. (PSF)	4,074
Harvey, C. (DUP)	3,743
Forde, P.M.D. (All.)	1,823
Magee, Ms M. (WP)	851
OUP maj.	548

Strangford

Elec. 60,232	% Poll 64.9
Taylor, J. (OUP)	19,086
Gibson, S. (DUP)	11,716
Morrow, A. (All.)	6,171
Curry, J. (SDLP)	1,713
Heath, R. (Ind. Lab.)	430
OUP maj.	7,370

Lagan Valley

Elec. 60,099	% Poll 67.5
*Molyneaux, J. (OUP)	24,017
Beattie, Rev. W. (DUP)	6,801
Close, S. (All.)	4,593
Boomer, C. (SDLP)	2,603
McAuley, R. (PSF)	1,751
Loughlin, G. (WP)	809
OUP maj.	17,216

Upper Bann

Elec. 60,797	% Poll 72.0
*McCusker, H. (OUP)	24,888
McDonald, J. (SDLP)	7,807
Wells, J. (DUP)	4,547
Curran, B. (PSF)	4,110
French, T. (WP)	2,392
OUP maj.	17,081

Newry and Armagh

Elec. 62,387	% Poll 76.0°
Nicholson, J. (OUP)	18,988
Mallon, S. (SDLP)	17,434
McAllister, J. (PSF)	9,928
Moore, T. (WP)	1,070
OUP maj.	1,554

Fermanagh–South Tyrone

Elec. 67,880	% Poll 88.6
Maginnis, K. (OUP)	28,630
*Carron, O. (PSF)	20,954
Flanagan, Mrs R. (SDLP)	9,923
Kettyles, D. (WP)	649
OUP maj.	7,676

Mid-Ulster

Elec. 63,899	% Poll 84.3
McCrea, Rev. W. (DUP)	16,174
Morrison, D.G. (PSF)	16,096
Haughey, P.D. (SDLP)	12,044
Thompson, W.J. (OUP)	7,066
Lagan, Dr J.A. (All.)	1,735
Owens, T.A. (WP)	766
DUP maj.	78

East Londonderry

Elec. 67,365	% Poll 76.3
*Ross, W. (OUP)	19,469
McClure, J. (DUP)	12,207
Doherty, A. (SDLP)	9,397
Davey, J. (PSF)	7,073
McGrath, Mrs M. (All.)	2,401
Donnelly, F. (WP)	819
OUP maj.	7,262

Foyle

Elec. 67,431	% Poll 77.6
Hume, J. (SDLP)	24,071
Campbell, G. (DUP)	15,923
McGuinness, M. (PSF)	10,607
O'Grady, G. (All.)	1,108
Melaugh, E. (WP)	582
SDLP maj.	8,148

1984 NI ASSEMBLY BY-ELECTION

In the 1 March 1984 by-election, caused by the murder of Edgar Graham (OUP, S. Belfast) by PIRA in December 1983, Frank Millar (OUP) was returned unopposed.

South Belfast, 1 March 1984

Millar, Frank (OUP)	unopposed

1984 EUROPEAN PARLIAMENT ELECTION

NI representation at Strasbourg was unchanged as a result of the election on 14 June 1984, with the three seats being taken by the Rev. Ian Paisley (DUP), John Hume (SDLP) and John Taylor (OUP). But there were some notable polling features. The overall vote showed an increase of 7.4 per cent (about 120,000 votes) and Paisley demonstrated even more convincingly than in 1979 his dominance as a Unionist standard-bearer. He took almost exactly one-third of all the votes cast – a rise of about 4 per cent. For the OUP John Taylor maintained his party's 1979 share of the vote at 21.4 per cent. The OUP had run two candidates in 1979, but on this occasion Taylor was his party's sole representative. John Hume put on about 11,000 extra votes as compared with 1979, but his share of the poll dropped by 1.7 per cent, no doubt due partly to the substantial PSF challenge mounted by Danny Morrison, who took over 13 per cent of first-preference votes. Alliance lost some ground. As in 1979, the contest was essentially a counting of party heads rather than any real test of EC policies.

1984 European Parliament election

Details of the count		
3 seats		

Electorate 1,065,363	Percentage poll 65.4	
Valid votes 685,317	Quota 171,330	
Spoiled votes 11,654	Votes unaccounted for 23	

First count

Party candidates	1st-preference votes	% valid poll
Paisley, Rev. I. (DUP)	230,251	33.6
Hume, J. (SDLP)	151,399	22.1
Taylor, J. (OUP)	147,169	21.5
Morrison, D. (PSF)	91,476	13.3
Cook, D. (All.)	34,046	5.0
Kilfedder, J. (UPUP)	20,092	2.9
Lynch, S. (WP)	8,712	1.3
McGuigan, C. (Ecol.)	2,172	0.3

Paisley elected; his surplus votes were distributed.

Second count

Party candidates	Distribution of surplus votes	Total votes
Taylor	+38,545.52	185,714.52
Hume	+265.20	151,664.20
Morrison	+49.40	91,525.40
Kilfedder	+18,201.82	38,293.82
Cook	+846.04	34,892.04
Lynch	+101.14	8,813.14
McGuigan	+64.74	2,236.74

Non-transferable votes, 847.14. Taylor elected. Lynch and McGuigan eliminated, with lost deposits; their votes were distributed.

Third count

Party candidates	Distribution of votes	Total votes
Hume	+4,646.12	156,310.32
Morrison	+1,119.12	92,644.52
Kilfedder	+561.78	38,854.60
Cook	+2,509.24	37,401.28

Accumulative non-transferable votes, 3,061.76. Cook and Kilfedder eliminated, with lost deposits; their votes were distributed.

Fourth count

Party candidates	Distribution of votes	Total votes
Hume	+26,946.00	183,256.32
Morrison	+435.00	93,079.52

Accumulative non-transferable votes, 51,936.64. Hume elected.

1985 DISTRICT COUNCIL ELECTIONS

Before these elections the boundaries of the twenty-six district councils and the 526 wards were reviewed by an independent Boundary Commission. The result was no significant change in council boundaries but an increase in the number of wards to 566. The OUP and PSF had most reason to be happy with the outcome of the 15 May 1985 district council elections. The OUP recovered well from its marginal defeat by the DUP in the 1981 elections in terms of first-preference votes. With 29.5 per cent of first-preference votes, it was a full 5 per cent ahead of the DUP's 24.3 per cent and took 190 seats against the DUP's 142. This underlined the DUP's problem of matching, in elections, the massive personal vote achieved by the Rev. Ian Paisley in the European elections. PSF was fighting district council elections for the first time, and with 11.8 per cent of the vote and fifty-nine seats, it improved on its own understated predictions by more than twenty seats. SDLP was not much affected by the PSF intervention – its 17.8 per cent showing was slightly up on 1981 (17.5 per cent), although its total of seats dropped by 2 to 101. Alliance recorded 7.1 per cent of the vote, which was a drop on its poll of 8.9 per cent in 1981 when its support was squeezed in a highly polarised contest. The Alliance total of thirty-four seats was four down on 1981. WP gained one seat as compared with 1981 (a total of four), but its poll of 1.6 per cent was very slightly down on 1981 (1.8 per cent). IIP evidently suffered most from the PSF challenge – it took only four seats against twenty-one in 1981 and saw its poll decline from 3.9 per cent to 1.1 per cent. A feature of the elections was that single-party control was achieved in only two councils – Banbridge (OUP) and Ballymena (DUP). The overall valid poll was 60.1 per cent (4 per cent down on 1981) but it varied from 83 per cent in Cookstown and Fermanagh to 45.7 per cent in N. Down.

Overall figures, 1985 district council elections

Party	1st-preference votes	% votes
DUP	155,297	24.3
Loy.	19,712	3.1
OUP	188,497	29.5
All.	45,394	7.1
Lab.	3,692	0.6
WP	10,276	1.6
SDLP	113,967	17.8
PSF	75,686	11.8
IIP	7,459	1.1
Nat.	8,191	1.3
Others	11,451	1.8
Total	639,622	100.0

Party composition of councils, 1985

Council	DUP	Loy.	OUP	All.	Lab.	WP	SDLP	PSF	IIP	Nat.	Others
Antrim	5	0	9	1	0	0	3	1	0	0	0
Ards	8	1	6	3	1	0	0	0	0	0	1
Armagh	3	0	11	0	0	0	7	1	0	0	0
Ballymena	15	0	6	0	0	0	1	0	0	0	1
Ballymoney	6	0	6	0	0	0	2	1	0	0	1
Banbridge	3	0	8	0	0	0	3	0	0	0	1
Belfast	11	4	14	8	0	1	6	7	0	0	0
Carrickfergus	3	1	7	3	0	0	0	0	0	0	1
Castlereagh	10	0	8	3	0	0	0	0	0	0	0
Coleraine	6	0	10	2	0	0	2	0	0	0	1
Cookstown	5	1	3	0	0	0	3	4	0	0	0
Craigavon	6	0	11	0	0	2	5	2	0	0	0
Derry	5	0	5	0	0	0	14	5	1	0	0
Down	3	0	7	0	0	1	10	2	0	0	0
Dungannon	3	0	8	0	0	0	5	4	0	2	0
Fermanagh	2	0	8	0	0	0	4	8	1	0	0
Larne	6	0	6	2	0	0	0	0	0	1	0
Limavady	2	0	7	0	0	0	4	2	0	0	0
Lisburn	8	0	13	3	0	0	2	2	0	0	0
Magherafelt	4	0	3	0	0	0	4	4	0	0	0
Moyle	3	2	2	0	0	0	4	2	0	0	2
Newry and Mourne	2	0	7	0	0	0	14	5	1	1	0
Newtownabbey	9	2	10	2	1	0	0	0	0	0	1
North Down	6	3	8	7	0	0	0	0	0	0	0
Omagh	4	0	4	0	0	0	5	6	1	0	1
Strabane	4	0	3	0	0	0	3	3	0	2	0
Total	142	14	190	34	2	4	101	59	4	6	10

1985 NI ASSEMBLY BY-ELECTION

The by-election in S. Down on 17 October 1985 was caused by the death of Raymond McCullough (OUP) in June 1985. The turnout of 21.3 per cent was one of the lowest ever recorded in an election in NI. Elected on the first count, the successful candidate, Jeffrey Donaldson (OUP), was twenty-two years old and became the youngest member of the NI Assembly.

South Down, 17 October 1985

| Elec. 98,126 | % Poll 21.3 |
| Quota 10,184 | |

Party candidates	1st-preference votes
Donaldson, J. (OUP)	17,528
Smyth, Mrs E. (Utd. Ulster Loyalist)	2,838

Donaldson elected on the first count.

1986 WESTMINSTER BY-ELECTIONS

Fifteen by-elections on 23 January 1986 were forced by all the sitting Unionist MPs – eleven OUP, three DUP and one UPUP – to allow Unionists to express their opposition to the AIA. When the British Government rejected a call for a local referendum on the issue, the MPs resigned simultaneously on the understanding that they would be the sole Unionist nominees in their seats. The SDLP members, as supporters of the AIA, were not anxious to help the Unionist manoeuvre, and therefore limited their interest to the four seats which they regarded as marginal – Mid-Ulster, Fermanagh–S. Tyrone, S. Down, and Newry and Armagh. Unionists were forced to run a 'token' candidate, using the name of Irish Foreign Minister 'Peter Barry', in four other constituencies to avoid any 'unopposed' return. (Unionist supporter Wesley Robert Williamson changed his name by deed poll to 'Peter Barry' in order to provide 'opposition' in constituencies where other pro-AIA parties refused to contest.) Although Unionists failed to reach a reputed half-million-vote target, they recorded 418,230 votes against the AIA, but at the expense of losing Newry and Armagh to the SDLP's deputy leader, Seamus Mallon. The Unionist vote represented 71.5 per cent of the total valid poll, which compared with 62.3 per cent in the 1983 election. This was just under 44 per cent of the total electorate. The SDLP also had the satisfaction of seeing the PSF vote drop by 5.4 per cent in the four 'marginals', and their own vote rise by 6 per cent, which was seized on by the British and Irish Governments as one of the fruits of the AIA. Alliance and WP benefited in votes, particularly in seats where they were the sole opponents of Unionists but still suffered defeat by large majorities. Overall turnout was 62.2 per cent compared with 72.4 per cent in the same seats in 1983.

Overall figures, 1986 Westminster by-elections

Party	Votes	% Valid poll
OUP	302,198	51.7
DUP	85,239	14.6
SDLP	70,917	12.1
PSF	38,821	6.6
All.	32,095	5.5
UPUP	30,793	5.2
WP	18,148	3.1
'P. Barry'	6,777	1.2
Total valid votes	584,988	100.0
Spoiled votes	7,888	
Total votes polled	592,876	

* INDICATES OUTGOING MP

East Belfast

Elec. 55,319	% Poll 61.9
*Robinson, P. (DUP)	27,607
Napier, Sir O. (All.)	5,917
Cullen, F. (WP)	578
DUP maj.	21,690
No change	

North Belfast

Elec. 59,820	% Poll 51.5
*Walker, A.C. (OUP)	21,649
Maguire, P. (All.)	5,072
Lynch, S. (WP)	3,563
OUP maj.	16,577
No change	

South Belfast

Elec. 53,971	% Poll 56.9
*Smyth, Rev. M. (OUP)	21,771
Cook, D. (All.)	7,635
Carr, G. (WP)	1,109
OUP maj.	14,136
No change	

North Antrim

Elec. 65,334	% Poll 54.7
*Paisley, Rev. I. (DUP)	33,937
'Barry, P.' (AIA)	913
DUP maj.	33,024
No change	

South Antrim

Elec. 61,296	% Poll 53.5
*Forsythe, C. (OUP)	30,087
'Barry, P.' (AIA)	1,870
OUP maj.	28,217
No change	

East Antrim

Elec. 60,851	% Poll 59.1
*Beggs, R. (OUP)	30,386
Neeson, S. (All.)	5,405
OUP maj.	24,981
No change	

North Down

Elec. 64,278	% Poll 60.6
*Kilfedder, J. (UPUP)	30,793
Cushnahan, J. (All.)	8,066
UPUP maj.	22,727
No change	

South Down

Elec. 70,108	% Poll 74.0
*Powell, E. (OUP)	24,963
McGrady, E. (SDLP)	23,121
McDowell, H.F. (PSF)	2,936
Magee, S.D. (WP)	522
OUP maj.	1,842
No change	

Strangford

Elec. 62,896	% Poll 56.1
*Taylor, J.D. (OUP)	32,627
'Barry, P.' (AIA)	1,993
OUP maj.	30,634
No change	

Lagan Valley

Elec. 63,369	% Poll 57.8
*Molyneaux, J.H. (OUP)	32,514
Lowry, J.T. (WP)	3,328
OUP maj.	29,186
No change	

Upper Bann

Elec. 63,663	% Poll 57.9
*McCusker, H. (OUP)	29,311
French, T. (WP)	6,978
OUP maj.	22,333
No change	

Newry and Armagh

Elec. 65,482	% Poll 76.9
Mallon, S. (SDLP)	22,694
*Nicholson, J. (OUP)	20,111
McAllister, J. (PSF)	6,609
McCusker, P. (WP)	515
SDLP maj.	2,583
SDLP gain	

Fermanagh–South Tyrone

Elec. 69,919	% Poll 80.9
*Maginnis, K. (OUP)	27,857
Carron, O. (PSF)	15,278
Currie, J.A. (SDLP)	12,081
Kettyles, D. (WP)	864
OUP maj.	12,579
No change	

Mid-Ulster

Elec. 66,830	% Poll 77.6
*McCrea, Rev. W. (DUP)	23,695
Morrison, D.G. (PSF)	13,998
Colton, A. (SDLP)	13,021
Owens, T.A. (WP)	691
DUP maj.	9,697
No change	

East Londonderry

Elec. 70,375	% Poll 48.4
*Ross, W. (OUP)	30,922
'Barry, P.' (AIA)	2,001
OUP maj.	28,921
No change	

1987 WESTMINSTER GENERAL ELECTION

The 11 June 1987 general election showed an unexpected drop in the total Unionist poll, including independents, as compared with the 1983 general election, given the continuing strong campaign by Unionists against the AIA. Indeed, hostility to the agreement was the main feature of the common manifesto on which the OUP, DUP, and Jim Kilfedder (UPUP) fought the election. The drop of 2.3 per cent to 54.8 per cent in their share of the poll, as against 1983, seemed to reflect misgivings by some Unionist voters about the virtue of the boycott of Parliamentary proceedings by their MPs as part of the anti-AIA protest. Unionist representation also dropped to thirteen when the OUP suffered a severe loss in the defeat of veteran parliamentarian Enoch Powell in S. Down, where an increase in his personal vote was not enough to hold off the challenge of Eddie McGrady (SDLP). Although disappointed by its failure to dislodge PSF president Gerry Adams in W. Belfast, the SDLP apparently profited in most seats from the existence of the AIA. Its share of the poll was up by 3.2 per cent as compared with 1983. This was largely at the expense of PSF, which dropped by 2 per cent but remained at 35 per cent of the Nationalist vote. Alliance was 2 per cent up on 1983 at 10 per cent and the WP also did better than in the last election. The turnout fell by 5.9 per cent to 67.4 per cent, as compared with 1983.

Overall figures, 1987 Westminster general election

Party	Votes	% Valid poll
OUP	276,230	37.8
SDLP	154,087	21.1
DUP	85,642	11.7
PSF	83,389	11.4
All.	72,671	10.0
WP	19,294	2.6
UPUP	18,420	2.5
RU	14,467	2.0
PUP	5,671	0.9
Ecol.	281	0.0
Total valid votes	730,152	100.0
Spoiled votes	4,851	
Total votes polled	735,003	

East Belfast

Elec. 54,666	% Poll 60.6
*Robinson, P. (DUP)	20,372
Alderdice, Dr J. (All.)	10,574
Cullen, F. (WP)	1,314
O'Donnell, J. (PSF)	649
DUP maj.	9,798
No change	

North Belfast

Elec. 59,159	% Poll 62.7
*Walker, A.C. (OUP)	14,355
Maginness, A. (SDLP)	5,795
Seawright, G. (Prot. U.)	5,671
McManus, P. (PSF)	5,062
Lynch, S. (WP)	3,062
Campbell, T. (All.)	2,871
OUP maj.	8,560
No change	

South Belfast

Elec. 54,284	% Poll 60.6
*Smyth, Rev. M. (OUP)	18,917
Cook, D. (All.)	6,963
McDonnell, Dr A. (SDLP)	4,268
Carr, G. (WP)	1,528
McKnight, S. (PSF)	1,030
OUP maj.	11,954
No change	

West Belfast

Elec. 59,400	% Poll 69.6
*Adams, G. (PSF)	16,862
Hendron, Dr J. (SDLP)	14,641
Millar, F. (OUP)	7,646
McMahon, Ms M. (WP)	1,819
PSF maj.	2,221
No change	

North Antrim

Elec. 65,774	% Poll 63.3
*Paisley, Rev. I. (DUP)	28,383
Farren, S. (SDLP)	5,149
Williams, G. (All.)	5,140
Regan, S. (PSF)	2,633
DUP maj.	23,234
No change	

South Antrim

Elec. 61,706	% Poll 59.4
*Forsythe, C. (OUP)	25,395
Mawhinney, G. (All.)	5,808
McClelland, D. (SDLP)	3,611
Cushinan, H. (PSF)	1,592
OUP maj.	19,587
No change	

East Antrim

Elec. 60,600	% Poll 55.5
*Beggs, R. (OUP)	23,942
Neeson, S. (All.)	8,582
Kelly, A. (WP)	936
OUP maj.	15,360
No change	

North Down

Elec. 65,044	% Poll 63.0
*Kilfedder, J. (UPUP)	18,420
McCartney, R. (RU)	14,467
Cushnahan, J. (All.)	7,932
UPUP maj.	3,953
No change	

South Down

Elec. 71,443	% Poll 79.6
McGrady, E. (SDLP)	26,579
*Powell, E. (OUP)	25,848
Ritchie, Ms G. (PSF)	2,363
Laird, Miss S.E. (All.)	1,069
O'Hagan, D. (WP)	675
SDLP maj.	731
SDLP gain	

Strangford

Elec. 64,475	% Poll 57.9
*Taylor, J. (OUP)	28,199
Morrow, A. (All.)	7,553
Hynds, Miss I. (WP)	1,385
OUP maj.	20,646
No change	

Lagan Valley

Elec. 64,937	% Poll 64.4
*Molyneaux, J. (OUP)	29,101
Close, S. (All.)	5,728
McDonnell, B. (SDLP)	2,888
Rice, P.J. (PSF)	2,656
Lowry, J.T. (WP)	1,215
OUP maj.	23,373
No change	

Upper Bann

Elec. 64,596	% Poll 66.0
*McCusker, H. (OUP)	26,037
Rodgers, Mrs B. (SDLP)	8,676
Curran, B. (PSF)	3,126
Cook, Mrs F. (All.)	2,487
French, T. (WP)	2,004
OUP maj.	17,361
No change	

Newry and Armagh

Elec. 66,151	% Poll 79.4
*Mallon, S. (SDLP)	25,137
Nicholson, J. (OUP)	19,812
McAllister, J. (PSF)	6,173
Jeffrey, W.H. (All.)	664
O'Hanlon, G. (WP)	482

SDLP maj.	5,325
No change	

Fermanagh–South Tyrone

Elec. 69,131	% Poll 80.8
*Maginnis, K. (OUP)	27,446
Corrigan, P. (PSF)	14,623
Flanagan, Mrs R. (SDLP)	10,581
Kettyles, D. (WP)	1,784
Haslett, J. (All.)	941

OUP maj.	12,823
No change	

Mid-Ulster

Elec. 67,343	% Poll 77.9
*McCrea, Rev. W. (DUP)	23,004
Haughey, P.D. (SDLP)	13,644
Begley, S. (PSF)	12,449
Bogan, P. (All.)	1,846
McClean, P.J. (WP)	1,133

DUP maj.	9,360
No change	

East Londonderry

Elec. 71,097	% Poll 69.1
*Ross, W. (OUP)	29,532
Doherty, A. (SDLP)	9,375
Davey, J. (PSF)	5,464
McGowan, J. (All.)	3,237
Donnelly, F. (WP)	935
Samuel, M.H. (Ecol.)	281

OUP maj.	20,157
No change	

Foyle

Elec. 70,583	% Poll 69.5
*Hume, J. (SDLP)	23,743
Campbell, G. (DUP)	13,883
McGuinness, M. (PSF)	8,707
Zammitt, Mrs E. (All.)	1,276
Melaugh, E. (WP)	1,022

SDLP maj.	9,860
No change	

SYSTEMS OF GOVERNMENT
1968–88

Government: Two Systems Fall

There can be few parts of the world where two totally different systems of government have collapsed in the space of little more than two years. But this was the experience of NI between 1972 and 1974.

From June 1921 to March 1972 NI had its own Parliament and Government within the UK. The system derived from the Government of Ireland Act, 1920, which was designed to set up Parliaments in both parts of Ireland, with a Council of Ireland to look after matters of mutual concern, and possibly lead eventually to a united Ireland. Like later political approaches by Westminster, it was aimed at reconciling the conflicting desires of Ulster Unionists and Irish Nationalists. It was more Home Rule than Unionists wanted, and less ambitious than that desired by Nationalists. In fact, Southern Ireland opted for independence, and the 1920 Act became operative only in NI. Unionists, who had shown no enthusiasm for devolution, quickly came to see the advantages of a limited self-government. Ulster Nationalists refused to co-operate in promoting the new Northern state. Events tended to give permanence to partition. The Southern Irish state adopted a more separatist Constitution in 1937, and became a full Republic in 1949. At that point the NI Parliament was given the right to veto any attempt to move NI out of the UK. The pre-1972 Stormont Parliament was closely modelled on Westminster. The fifty-two-seat Commons, elected by straight vote in single-member constituencies, followed the procedure and ceremonial of its Westminster opposite number, and the twenty-six-member Senate (with two ex-officio, the Lord Mayor of Belfast and the Mayor of Derry, and twenty-four members elected on PR by the Commons) had delaying powers very like those of the House of Lords. But in practice the upper house, with its Unionist majority, rarely opposed anything of substance originating in the Commons. Usually, two out of three MPs were Unionists, and this majority was reflected in the

Senate. All the administrations set up between 1921 and 1972 were Unionist controlled. NI continued to send MPs to Westminster – at least twelve, and thirteen when QUB had a seat – although NI matters received little attention in the British Parliament.

Some British Ministers have regarded the old Stormont system as nearer to dominion status than to simple devolution. Under a convention established in 1922, it was not possible for an MP at Westminster to raise any issue within the direct responsibility of a Stormont Minister. Thus, while the 1920 Act declared that the power of Westminster in NI was not diminished in any way by local self-government, the reality was somewhat different. Westminster Ministers considered their responsibilities in relation to NI to be limited to issues such as foreign trade, defence, major taxation, customs and excise and the High Court. The Home Secretary had Cabinet responsibility for NI affairs, and he had a few officials engaged part time in dealing with them, but until the civil rights movement developed, few Home Secretaries got beyond rare and brief token trips to NI. So it required considerable ingenuity for a NI MP to find a topic on which he could put a question to a Minister. The NI Government, normally comprising the PM and seven or eight full Cabinet Ministers and a few junior Ministers, controlled most domestic affairs and internal law and order.

Up to the late 1960s, relations between London and Belfast were generally amicable. After 1945, Whitehall allowed NI to give more generous financial inducements to new industry than applied in GB and finances generally were adjusted to NI's advantage. Some local taxes, such as motor duty, entertainment tax and death duties, often differed from those in GB. And although NI had been required by the 1920 Act to make an annual 'imperial contribution' to meet items of national expenditure, such as defence, foreign representation and the national debt, it was accepted in London that this must be a declining liability in face of the high costs of social services. NI had contributed about £460 million by way of 'imperial contribution' when it was finally abolished under direct rule. The principle of equality of basic social services throughout the UK implied that there could be no variation in major taxes, and NI never exercised a limited power to reduce income tax (*see* Economy). The general pattern of the Stormont Budget was settled in discussions between the Finance Minister and Treasury officials in London, and there was a Joint

Exchequer Board to consider any disputed matters. In matters such as social legislation, including divorce, NI very often went its own way.

But the continuing split in the NI community was underlined by the impact of the civil rights movement. The long-entrenched Stormont system came under severe pressure, both from anti-Unionists and from Westminster, and increasing violence soon made it a world issue as well. The NI Government did make changes to meet some of the criticism (*see* Cameron Commission *and* Reforms), but the serious violence in the summer of 1969 and the increasing alienation of the Parliamentary opposition put large question marks over the very existence of Stormont. The need for army support for the police brought a real change in the relationship between Stormont and Whitehall. An army commander took charge of anti-terrorist operations (*see* Security System section, p. 390), and a new post of British Government representative was established so that the British Government would have its own watch-dog official at Stormont. The failure of internment without trial to halt the PIRA campaign, and the shooting dead by the army of thirteen civilians in Londonderry (*see* 'Bloody Sunday') persuaded the Heath Government that all security and law-and-order powers should be transferred to Westminster. Three NI Premiers – O'Neill, Chichester-Clark, and Faulkner – had tried to restore stability, but in March 1972 the Conservative Government suspended the NI Parliament. It was an act which pleased anti-Unionists, but horrified even the most moderate of Unionists.

For the first time in fifty-one years, NI was now ruled wholly from London (*see* Direct Rule, pp. 371–3). It got its own Secretary of State, similar to Scotland and Wales, and the first holder of the new office was William Whitelaw, a senior Conservative politician, who was assisted by a small team of junior Ministers. NI was governed under a Temporary Provisions Act, and NI legislation was brought forward by way of Orders in Council, which could not be amended on the floor of the Commons. In a bid to make direct rule more palatable, Whitelaw set up a locally recruited Advisory Commission, but Unionists boycotted it. Brian Faulkner (later Lord Faulkner), NI's last PM, who with his colleagues had resigned rather than accept the loss of law-and-order powers, said he was against NI being treated 'like a coconut colony'. The other members of the last Stormont

Cabinet under the 1920 Act were: Home Affairs, Brian Faulkner and John Taylor (Minister of State); Finance, Herbert Kirk; Health and Social Services, William Fitzsimmons; Development, Roy Bradford; Education, William Long; Agriculture, Harry West; Commerce, Robin Bailie; leader of Commons, Nat Minford; leader of Senate, John Andrews; Community Relations, David Bleakley (March–September 1971) and Basil McIvor (September 1971–March 1972). Outside the Cabinet were John Brooke (later Lord Brookeborough), Minister of State in Finance, and Gerard B. Newe, Minister of State in the PM's department.

In 1973 the Heath Government tried a new political initiative. A periodic referendum to test opinion on NI's constitutional status in relation to the UK and the Republic was introduced to take the border issue out of day-to-day politics (*see* Border Poll). NI was given a seventy-eight-member Assembly, elected by PR, with the object of giving minorities a bigger chance of representation and therefore participation in Government. The scheme was embodied in the NI Constitution Act of 1973, which also abolished the office of Governor. Towards the end of 1973, talks involving the Secretary of State, Unionists, led by Brian Faulkner, the SDLP and Alliance parties, brought agreement on the setting up of an Executive involving these parties. The new administration's approach was worked out at a conference in December which was attended by the Executive parties and by British Ministers headed by Heath, and Ministers from the Republic, led by Liam Cosgrave (*see* Sunningdale Conference).

The new Coalition took office on 1 January 1974 after being sworn in by the new Secretary of State, Francis Pym. Its members were: Chief Executive, Brian Faulkner (Unionist); deputy Chief Executive, Gerry Fitt (SDLP); Legal Minister and head of Office of Law Reform, Oliver Napier (Alliance); Minister of Information, John L. Baxter (Unionist); Minister of Environment, Roy Bradford (Unionist); Minister of Housing, Local Government and Planning, Austin Currie (SDLP); Minister of Health and Social Services, Paddy Devlin (SDLP); Minister of Commerce, John Hume (SDLP); Minister of Finance, Herbert Kirk (Unionist); Minister of Education, Basil McIvor (Unionist); Minister of Agriculture, Leslie Morrell (Unionist). Ministers outside the Executive were: Community Relations, Ivan Cooper (SDLP); Manpower Services, Robert Cooper (Alliance); Planning and Co-ordination, Eddie McGrady (SDLP); Chief Whip,

Robert Lloyd Hall-Thompson (Unionist).

The new administration rapidly ran into trouble. While it had a majority in the Assembly, it faced violent opposition from loyalists opposed to power-sharing, and at one sitting demonstrating loyalists were ejected from the Chamber by the police. At the same time Brian Faulkner was defeated in the Unionist Council, the one-thousand-strong main governing body of his party, when he tried to get endorsement of the Sunningdale Agreement. Then in February 1974 a Westminster general election showed a majority for candidates of the three anti-power-sharing Unionist groups united within the UUUC, which won eleven of the twelve seats at Westminster. Finally, a loyalist strike, aimed against power-sharing and a Council of Ireland, led to the resignation in May of the Unionist members of the Executive, and the collapse of the administration. Direct rule was then resumed under the Labour Government, with Merlyn Rees as Secretary of State, and the Assembly was prorogued. Legal authority for continuing direct rule was provided by the Northern Ireland Act of 1974, which made temporary provision for the Government of NI by the Secretary of State and his ministerial team, subject to annual renewal.

The Labour Government moved quickly to try to break the political deadlock and to replace the now defunct Assembly. In July 1974 it announced that local political parties were to be given the opportunity to produce a viable constitution. For this purpose a seventy-eight-member Constitutional Convention was elected in 1975, but the project finally failed in 1976. In the aftermath of the Convention, the Government sought to widen consultation outside and inside Parliament on NI legislation. A new NI Committee of MPs was set up to allow for general debates on local policy, for example on the economy, housing, agriculture and so on. And copies of Orders were shown in advance to local parties to enable them to put forward their views. The Labour Government (after James Callaghan became PM) accepted that there was a case for more than twelve NI MPs at Westminster – a long-standing claim of Unionists. The idea of extra representation was endorsed by the Speaker's conference in 1978.

After the failure of the Convention, the British Government did not rush into any new initiative. But in November 1977 Roy Mason, as Secretary of State, put forward a tentative plan for discussion by the parties. The plan was discussed by the Secretary of State and representatives of the parties at the end of 1977 and beginning of 1978, but the initial exchanges did not suggest any agreement. At the same time the Conservative opposition was urging that the first priority should be given to local-government reform – a course frequently urged by many Unionists. But the SDLP made it clear that they feared that a reform of councils would lead to Unionist domination, and remarks in Parliament by the Secretary of State indicated that he supported this view.

With the resumption of direct rule after the collapse of the Convention, the aim was to harmonise NI policy and legislation with the UK, and some of the departments established for the convenience of the Executive were dropped and others merged. The work of the Department of Community Relations was taken over by the Department of Education, and the departments of Environment, and Housing, Planning and Local Government were merged into a single Environment Department. By 1976 the following departments were in existence – Agriculture, Commerce, Environment, Education, Finance, Health and Social Services, Manpower Services, and Civil Service.

With the election of the Conservative Government in May 1979, it appeared at first as if its manifesto commitment to a regional council or councils for NI would be introduced. However, after the death of Airey Neave (with whom the policy was identified) at the hands of an INLA bomb attached to his car in the House of Commons car park, the policy changed. A twin-track policy was developed amid increasing external pressure from the US. First, the new Secretary of State, Humphrey Atkins, sought to establish whether a basis existed for devolution. After the publication of a White Paper, *Proposals for Further Discussion,* he called the parties to a Constitutional Conference. But by November 1980 there was still no agreement on the formation of an executive. Although in July 1981 Atkins proposed to create an advisory council of MPs, MEPs and other elected representatives, the proposal was lost in the communal tension of the H-Block hunger strike. The second track had begun in December 1980 with a unique, high-level meeting of British and Irish Ministers in Dublin. In a serious effort to improve UK–Republic relations a series of joint studies was instigated in January 1981 on security, mutual understanding, citizens' rights, economic co-operation and possible new institutional structures.

In 1981 a British-Irish Intergovernmental Council was created as a forum for discussion, and provision was made for a Parliamentary tier at some stage. While relations did deteriorate during the Falklands crisis, the institution for mutual contact had been established.

Despite the experience of his predecessor, James Prior, the new Secretary of State and the most senior politician to hold this post since William Whitelaw, was willing to put his reputation on the line 'to get political progress'. At first Prior investigated the possibilities of an Assembly together with local Ministers nominated by himself, with a separation of administrative and legislative responsibility on the US model. It was a concept which had surfaced vaguely from time to time, but in the end he settled on the idea of 'rolling devolution', a system where an Assembly would start off with only a consultative and scrutiny role. This could later be extended to embrace the devolution of one or more local departments, but this devolution would depend on the achievement in the Assembly of 'cross-community support'. The Secretary of State and his colleagues saw it as an infinitely flexible pattern, adding some local democracy to direct rule to start with, and allowing for an input from elected politicians. It was also seen, by the small group of Cabinet Ministers who settled NI policy, as a means of getting more political support for security policy and giving a semblance of stability which might help in the attraction of outside industrial investment at a time when unemployment was running at around 20 per cent.

The scheme which eventually emerged in early 1982 was based, as in 1973, on a seventy-eight-seat Assembly elected by PR in the twelve Westminster constituencies. (If the plan for seventeen NI seats had been approved by Parliament at that time, the Assembly would probably have had eighty-five seats – five in each constituency.) The Devolution Bill provided that the Assembly could apply to Westminster for devolved powers if 70 per cent, or fifty-five members, backed the proposal. This weighted majority was intended to guard against Unionists only being in a position to apply. The Bill also provided that the Assembly could discuss local legislation and set up scrutiny committees for each of the six Stormont departments, and an amendment allowed for a non-statutory security committee. Assembly members would get a salary of £8,700, and committee chairmen an extra £2,900. Members of the Assembly could join a Parliamentary tier of the BIIC as individuals.

Predictably, the reaction of the parties was mixed. Both the OUP and DUP rejected the weighted majority and 'cross-community support' provisions as a revival of the 1973 'power-sharing', although the DUP was attracted more so than the OUP to the initial scrutiny powers. To Alliance it was a last chance for NI to solve its own problems. The SDLP regarded the scheme as 'unworkable' and an 'expensive charade' (views echoed by the Haughey Government in the Republic). PSF, contesting a Stormont election for the first time, sought to displace the SDLP as the main voice of Nationalists and win political support for its 'Brits out' approach. The Secretary of State had to face a filibuster in Parliament from about twenty right-wing Conservative MPs, some of whom were opposed to him for other political reasons and argued that the Conservative 1979 manifesto should be implemented since there was no prospect of agreement on devolution (*see* Conservative Party, British), and some of whom were frankly integrationist. But the measure was put through without difficulty after a 'guillotine' motion (unusual for a constitutional Bill) had been implemented, and with general support from the opposition parties. Labour's attempt to make the scheme more acceptable to the SDLP led to an amendment to provide that both Lords and Commons would be able to pronounce on 'cross-community support'. The change did not, however, persuade the SDLP that there was any real Irish dimension.

Thus, the stage was set for the election on 20 October 1982. With both the SDLP and PSF fighting on an abstentionist platform, although differing on the issue of violence, the Government's hopes for the Assembly were distinctly limited. With the SDLP getting fourteen seats (three down on the Convention and five fewer than in the 1973 Assembly), and PSF a surprising five seats, a total of fifty-nine members attended the opening session of the Assembly. OUP had twenty-six, the DUP twenty-one, and Alliance ten, with two other Unionists, one of whom, James Kilfedder MP, was elected Speaker. The Secretary of State accepted an early invitation to address the Assembly and junior Ministers appeared at committees. But they were not responsible to the Assembly and their appearances took on the form of a public relations exercise. The absence of SDLP members obviously made it impossible to achieve the cross-community support necessary for devolution. Ministers continued to grant SDLP access despite their abstention; even PSF had access but on a narrower, 'constituency interests' basis only. Indeed, when the SDLP were engaged in their alternative New Ireland Forum strategy, it was clearly demonstrated that neither they nor surrogates would engage the Assembly in discussions. The main work of the Assembly was, therefore, the scrutiny of Government departments and to provide advice on draft legislation. It did not have power, which remained with the Secretary of State and his Ministers, but influence, which was more difficult to evaluate.

The work of the Assembly fell into three periods. First, from November 1982 to May 1984, when the absence of SDLP and the boycott by OUP over the allocation of chairmanships (until February 1983) and over security policy after the Darkley massacre in November 1983 (until May 1984) gave the Assembly an uncertain future. In their absence, the most committed parties, DUP and Alliance, worked the system as best they could.

The second phase, and its most fruitful, extended from May 1984 to November 1985 and the signing of the AIA. It was marked by the full operation of the committee system and the issue of three reports from the Devolution Committee. But in 1985, especially under the new Secretary of State, Douglas Hurd, it was clear that expectations from the Assembly were low and, instead, a UK–Republic deal was pursued, based on the 'fourth option' of the New Ireland Forum report in 1984.

The third phase was from 15 November 1985 until dissolution on 23 June 1986, and was one of protest against the AIA (*see* Anglo-Irish Agreement). The response outside NI to what was represented as the settlement of a historic difference between the UK and the Republic in the AIA was a general, if not effusive, welcome. Inside NI Nationalists gave it an immediate welcome which grew in strength as they witnessed Unionist discomfiture at the hands of a former political friend in the Conservative Party. Unionist rage at the role given to the Republic in the internal affairs of part of the UK crossed all classes and shades of political opinion. It was directed into protests at Belfast City Hall and at Maryfield, into fifteen simultaneous by-elections when Unionist MPs resigned their seats, into the boycott of District Council business, and other forms of showing the withdrawal of the Unionist consent from the new form of government which was portrayed as 'joint rule'. The existence of the NI Assembly as a representative body resulted in its conversion into a platform for protest. The scrutiny function of the six committees was suspended, the Devolution Committee was wound up and a new committee on the government of NI was set up to examine the effects of the AIA on the Northern Ireland Constitution Act, 1973, and the Northern Ireland Assembly Act, 1982. As a result the Alliance members withdrew, leaving forty-nine members attending, the NIO withdrew committee staff and cut off access to persons and papers in the departments. The Committee on the Government of Northern Ireland still issued three reports but the fate of the Assembly had been sealed. Around the time when arrangements for fresh elections would normally have been announced, it was dissolved by the British Government on 23 June 1986, and some of its protesting members were carried from the building in the early hours of the next morning by the police.

It is difficult to evaluate the earlier constructive phases of the Assembly. It did enable members to exercise a representative function which had been absent since the end of the first Assembly in 1974. The Assembly held 221 plenary sessions – about 70 per year; the various lobbies showed an awareness that it could influence decisions, and 426 witnesses gave evidence to the committees. The scrutiny committees prepared 118 reports, containing 998 recommendations of which 2 in 3 were accepted. They also had an input into draft legislation for NI. Its passing may have been welcomed by some, and to an extent it was inevitable, but its absence did not diminish the need to subject the direct-rule regime to a system of political and administrative accountability.

Despite the commitment of the signatories of the AIA to devolution in NI (article four), no new proposal has been made and it has not been a subject of a conference meeting. The expectation by Government that, once the overarching framework of relations between the UK and the Republic was established, devolution would follow naturally, proved facile. Unionists, with two electoral mandates behind them in 1986 and 1987, could not accept devolution under the AIA framework. After the June 1987 election Paisley and Molyneaux engaged in 'talks about talks' with the Secretary of State on the principle of suspending the conference to enable inter-party talks to begin. Early in 1988 outline proposals were submitted which had not produced a detailed reply by the end of the year. The Secretary of State also held talks with other parties, including SDLP, but without any indication that the 'widespread acceptance' criteria for devolution had been established. Further, soon after the Unionist proposals to the Secretary of State, SDLP began a series of private meetings with PSF which set back any possibility of direct talks with Unionists. SDLP also stated that they were not committed in principle to devolution but only in so far as it would contribute to a solution of the problem as they identified it; and that they opposed any suspension of the AIA, suggesting instead that inter-party talks run parallel with the conference and the Maryfield secretariat. Finally, in November 1988 the AIA had been in existence for three years and a review of the working of the conference (under article eleven) began.

Since the first meeting of the conference in December 1985 it had met twenty-five times: eleven meetings were held in Belfast, nine in London and five in Dublin. There had been ten meetings in the first year, four in the second, ten in the third year, and a further two meetings in the review period. After each meeting of the conference, a brief communiqué was issued outlining the main areas discussed but the sketchy details have been criticised. The Diplock courts, the administration of justice, the relationship of the security forces and the police with the Nationalist minority, flags and emblems, parades, the Irish language, fair employment and housing conditions have been among the subjects discussed. However, in the third year many of the events causing greatest concern were British-Irish issues, such as the Birmingham Six and Guildford bomb cases, the Gibraltar SAS killings, and extradition cases. At the end of the year it was clear that despite the AIA and the conference machinery, 'megaphone diplomacy' between the two countries was all too evident. In the event, the review of the working of the conference, which was expected to be brief, was extended to March 1989.

A Parliamentary tier, with twenty-five members drawn from Lords and Commons and twenty-five from Dáil and Senate, was expected to hold its first meeting in June 1989. Two seats were being allocated to Unionist MPs and one to SDLP, but Unionists refused to take part since they regarded the body as inseparable from the AIA process.

Direct Rule

Since the introduction of direct rule in 1972 there have been eight

Secretaries of State for NI. William Whitelaw (Cons.), March 1972–November 1973; Francis Pym (Cons.), November 1973–February 1974; Merlyn Rees (Lab.), March 1974–September 1976; Roy Mason (Lab.), September 1976–May 1979; Humphrey Atkins (Cons.), May 1979–September 1981; James Prior (Cons.), September 1981–September 1984; Douglas Hurd (Cons.), September 1984–September 1985; Tom King (Cons.), September 1985–.

The Secretary of State keeps key responsibilities in his own hands and delegates individual departments to his junior Ministers. Tom King, Secretary of State since September 1985, retained responsibility for political and constitutional matters, security policy and operations, and broad economic and other policies. His Minister of State and deputy, Ian Stewart, appointed in July 1988, is responsible for law and order and for the Department of Finance and Personnel. There are four Under-Secretaries of State: Richard Needham, responsible for a wide range of services in the departments of Health and Social Services and for the Environment; Lord Lyell, responsible for the Department of Agriculture and for NI issues in the House of Lords; Peter Viggers, responsible for the Department of Economic Development and the Commons spokesman on Agriculture; Brian Mawhinney, responsible for the Department of Education and for political affairs and the information section of the NIO.

By 1988, in almost seventeen years of direct rule, forty-one Ministers – thirty-one Conservative and ten Labour – have held office in NI. The average length of service has been two years, two months, but as always, the average hides many differences. The longest-serving Minister was Nicholas Scott (Cons.) with five years, nine months, from September 1981 to June 1987; a Labour predecessor, Don Concannon, remains second-longest with four years, eleven months, from June 1974 to May 1979, but Lord Lyell will complete five years in April 1989. Those Ministers with the shortest service were Francis Pym (Cons.) with three months, Tom Pendry (Lab.) six months, Paul Channon (Cons.) seven months and Lord Belstead (Cons.) nine months. The circumstances in which James Prior (Cons.) was appointed Secretary of State in 1981 have tended to result in a NI posting being described as 'internal exile'. But it is clear from an examination of Ministers' previous experience and their subsequent appointments that the NIO is regarded as a revealer of potential ministerial talent, just like any other posting. Indeed, it could be argued that because NI has something of the hothouse atmosphere given its news profile, and with two local TV and radio stations and local newspapers, the postings provide Ministers with a higher public profile than comparable-level jobs elsewhere. A NIO appointment, however, does require additional air travel but the job is not especially demanding and does not necessarily require additional time away from home. A recent Parliamentary question revealed that in the period 1 June to 31 October 1988 Ministers spent on average 36.5 nights in NI out of a possible 153: Richard Needham remained 51 nights, Lord Lyell 47 and Tom King 34. Further, for most who had served in NI the appointment was a stepping stone to a further promotion.

In earlier times direct rule was accepted because it provided stable institutions pending devolution. But with the prospect of devolution now even more remote and available only in the context of the AIA, direct rule, always lacking in legitimacy, has become even less acceptable given the strong consultative role for the Government of the Republic. With the rise in violence in each of the three years since the signing of the AIA in 1985 and the new flow of weapons to paramilitary groups, the community was united only in horror at the latest atrocity. Public opinion in the Unionist community has moved away from devolution and direct rule in favour of complete integration with Britain; Nationalists still prefer devolution with power-sharing, especially since the Anglo-Irish Conference is still in place. The result has been a more unstable form of direct rule. Hence, while considerable effort has been made to integrate NI into UK policies and legislation, it remains a place apart as far as the political parties are concerned and the conditional membership of the UK, underlined in article one of the AIA, continues to distinguish NI from other parts of the UK.

NI Government Departments

In 1982 the number of Stormont departments was reduced to six – Agriculture, Economic Development, Education, Environment, Finance and Personnel, and Health and Social Services. Civil Service affairs were absorbed into the Finance and Personnel Department in April, and Commerce and Manpower were merged into a Department of Economic Development in September. With the setting up of the DED, a new Industrial Development Board, linked with the department, took responsibility for attracting outside industrial investment. Since then the departments and their responsibilities have been as follows:

Agriculture Development and improvement of agriculture, forestry and fishing industries; animal health, drainage schemes, the recreational use of water and forest. Extensive advisory services, agricultural research, education and training. Agricultural census and farm income data. Agent for MAFF in economic support for agriculture and implementation of EC Common Agricultural Policy.

Economic Development Industrial development, employment and training of labour, and relations with commerce and industry generally. The IDB is responsible for the development of industry, for attracting new projects, for the care and maintenance of existing industry, including trade promotion, marketing, and assistance to research and development projects. It provides funds for, and liaises with, the Local Enterprise Development Unit on the promotion of small businesses; responsible for energy supply, aircraft and ship-building; development of tourism and harbours (other than fishing harbours); mineral development; consumer protection; registration of companies, societies, credit unions and trade unions; supervision of industrial assurance and unit trusts, industrial science and technology promotion. It is also responsible for the administration of Government policy in relation to the employment and training of labour.

Education Development of primary, secondary and further education, community and adult education, and special education; oversight of the five area education and library boards; teacher training; teachers' salaries and superannuation; examinations; the arts and libraries; youth services; sport and recreation and community services and facilities; and the improvement of community relations. These services are administered for the department by the five education and library boards.

Environment Planning and development; housing and landscaping; water and sewerage; construction and maintenance of roads and bridges; ordnance survey and land registry; transport and traffic, including safety and licensing; fire protection; pollution control; amenity lands and parks; Government records; regional rate collection; the Development Officer service.

Finance and Personnel   Control of spending of NI departments; liaison with Treasury and NIO on financial matters; economic and social planning and research; *Digest of Statistics*; Ulster Savings; borrowing; loan advances; charities; valuation. Formulation and co-ordination of policy for personnel management; pay and conditions in civil service; central management services and computer services. Staffs the Civil Service Commission.

Health and Social Services   Social Security (all cash social services); personal and public health services, including hospitals, general practitioners, dentists and so on, and personal social services (child care and adoption). These services are administered for the department by four health and social services boards and a Central Service Agency. Since April 1982 the Central Service Agency is also responsible for registration of births, marriages and deaths; miscellaneous licensing, and the census of population.

The head of the NI Civil Service is responsible for the co-ordination of the work of the six NI departments and is supported by a central secretariat. The post carries the rank of Permanent Secretary with responsibilities as chief adviser to the Secretary of State on all transferred matters.

The NI departments are, therefore, separate from the NIO, but under the Northern Ireland Act, 1974, and in the absence of devolution, they are subject to the direction and control of the Secretary of State and his Ministers, who are responsible for the excepted, reserved and transferred matters described in the Northern Ireland Constitution Act, 1973. The London divisions of the NIO provide liaison between the Treasury and other Whitehall departments and NI departments. The Belfast divisions of the NIO are mainly concerned with the administration of reserved and excepted matters, especially law and order. The NIO is also headed by a Permanent Secretary, and both the Belfast and London divisions deal with political and constitutional affairs and security. In addition the NIO has some specific functions, dealing with electoral matters, international matters, criminal law, including special powers, prevention and detection of crime, police, traffic wardens, treatment of offenders, firearms and explosives, compensation of victims of crime, and civil emergency planning.

Since the creation of the NIO as a separate department of State in 1972, NI has benefited from increased public expenditure under direct rule. From 1972 to 1979 NI per capita public expenditure rose by 17 per cent compared to a rise of 2 per cent in Wales and a reduction of 8 per cent in Scotland. Despite the Conservative Government's commitment to cut public expenditure, the NI programme continued to expand by 2 per cent until 1985. Standardising on England as 100, the per capita public expenditure figures for the parts of the UK in 1987 to 1988 were: England 100, Scotland 129, Wales 115, NI 150. For the period 1989–90 planned public expenditure for NI was £5,468 million. Expenditure by NI departments has been fitted into the UK Public Expenditure Survey Cycle (PESC) since 1968 and PESC control procedures since 1972. The NI programme is in two sections: first, the NI departments administering matters transferred in the Northern Ireland Constitution Act, 1973; and second, the expenditure by UK departments, namely, NIO, M.o.D. and the Foreign Office, on excepted and reserved matters. The Secretary of State has overall responsibility for both sections of the programme. In this way NI public expenditure is integrated into the UK pattern and system of control. But the procedure for handling NI legislation has attracted sharp criticism. While legislation in the excepted category is the form of a Bill and subject to full scrutiny, legislation on transferred or reserved matters is by Order in Council and can be debated, usually late at night, but not amended. In effect, once laid before Parliament, the legislation becomes law in forty days or law immediately, subject only to a 'prayer' by the House within forty days. The procedure also suffers by contrast with Scottish and Welsh legislation, where the normal Bill procedure and the second reading stage are taken by a Scottish or Welsh Grand Committee and the committee stage by the Scottish or Welsh Standing Committee, guaranteeing local influence. The existence of the NI Assembly, 1982–6, did provide additional local input on proposed laws with advice on some forty-three pieces of proposed legislation.

OFFICE HOLDERS IN
NORTHERN IRELAND
1968–88

KEY

————— Termination of regime (e.g., Stormont, NI Executive)
or of department

– – – – – Change of administration or of Minister

NOTE

*During the life of the NI Executive, 1 January–28 May 1974,
the British Ministers assisted the Secretary of State with his
functions.

	Home Secretary/Secretary of State	N I Prime Minister/Chief Executive	Home Affairs	Finance	Development	Health & Social Services	Commerce	Agriculture	Education	New Departments
1968	CALLAGHAN	T. O'NEILL	CRAIG	KIRK	FITZ-SIMMONS	MORGAN	FAULKNER	CHICHESTER-CLARK	LONG	
1969	_June_	_May_ CHICHESTER-CLARK	_December_ LONG _March_	KIRK	NEILL / LONG	_January_ PORTER	FAULKNER	CHICHESTER-CLARK	FITZ-SIMMONS / P. O'NEILL	Community Relations _October_ SIMPSON
1970		CHICHESTER-CLARK	PORTER _August_ CHICHESTER-CLARK & TAYLOR	KIRK	FAULKNER	FITZ-SIMMONS	BRADFORD	P. O'NEILL	LONG	SIMPSON
1971	MAUDLING	_March_ FAULKNER	FAULKNER & TAYLOR	KIRK	BRADFORD	FITZ-SIMMONS	BAILIE	WEST	LONG	BLEAKLEY _September_ McIVOR
Direct Rule 1972	_March_ Secretary of State WHITELAW	Secretary of State WHITELAW	LORD WINDLESHAM _June_	HOWELL	LORD WINDLESHAM	CHANNON _November_	HOWELL	HOWELL	CHANNON	LORD WINDLESHAM
1973	WHITELAW			_January_ HOWELL	HOWELL	VAN STRAUBENZEE		MILLS	VAN STRAUBENZEE / LORD BELSTEAD	VAN STRAUBENZEE
1974	_December_									

278

	Prime Minister	Chief Executive FAULKNER / Deputy FITT	Finance	Housing, Planning & Local Govt.	Environment	Health & Social Services	Manpower Services	Commerce	Agriculture	Education	Community Relations	Planning & Co-Ordination	Legal & Law Reform
*January 1974 Executive	PYM	FAULKNER / FITT	KIRK	CURRIE	BRADFORD	DEVLIN	R.COOPER	HUME	MORRELL	McIVOR	I. COOPER	McGRADY	NAPIER
— March —													
May 1974 Direct Rule Resumed	REES		CONCANNON	CONCANNON	MOYLE	LORD DONALDSON	ORME	ORME	LORD DONALDSON	MOYLE	MOYLE		
1975													
— April REES (Finance) —													
1976 — September —	MASON		DUNN	CONCANNON (Environment)	CONCANNON	CONCANNON	MOYLE	MOYLE	DUNN	LORD DONALDSON (Education); CARTER			
1977				CARTER	CARTER	LORD MELCHETT	CONCANNON	CONCANNON	PENDRY	LORD MELCHETT			
1978			PENDRY										
1979 — May —	ATKINS		ROSSI	GOODHART	GOODHART	ALISON	ROSSI	SHAW	SHAW	LORD ELTON			
1980													
1981 — September —	PRIOR		LORD GOWRIE	MITCHELL	MITCHELL	J. PATTEN	BUTLER	BUTLER	BUTLER	SCOTT			

379

	Secretary of State	Finance & Personnel	Environment	Health & Social Services	Economic Development	Agriculture	Education
1982	PRIOR	LORD GOWRIE	MITCHELL	J.PATTEN	BUTLER	BUTLER	SCOTT
1983	_September_	_June_ BUTLER			_September_	LORD MANSFIELD _April_	
1984	HURD	BOYSON	C.PATTEN	C.PATTEN	BOYSON	LORD LYELL	_January_
1985	_September_	_September_					
1986	KING	SCOTT	NEEDHAM	NEEDHAM	_September_		MAWHINNEY
1987		_June_ STANLEY			VIGGERS		
1988		_July_ STEWART					

THE SECURITY SYSTEM

THE EBB AND FLOW OF VIOLENCE

Sharp controversy over the proliferation of anti-terrorist measures in recent times is the latest indicator of the core position of law-and-order issues in the NI crisis. They featured strongly in the civil rights campaign; they were crucial in the Westminster calculations when direct rule was imposed in 1972, and they were perhaps the key consideration for the British Government in signing the AIA in 1985.

The civil rights movement had a variety of targets in the law-and-order sphere. It was critical of the Special Powers Act, with its far-reaching provisions relating to searches and internment without trial. In policing, it questioned the attitude of the RUC in its dealings with the Catholic minority, and argued that its organisation made it the tool of the NI Government rather than an independent police force. The USC, usually dubbed the 'B Specials', was attacked as a loyalist army because it had no Catholic membership. To a lesser extent there was criticism of the administration of justice, with the suggestion that too many ex-Unionist politicians were appointed to the bench. NI Ministers defended the Special Powers Act as vital in dealing with the IRA threat, and they pointed to the Offences Against the State Act in the Republic to counter subversion. The Special Powers Act continued to be used by the British Government to enforce internment up to the autumn of 1972. But the critics of the USC had an easy victory. It was swept away in the context of reform of the RUC.

The USC had been set up in 1920 to counter the IRA, and it was undoubtedly a potent symbol of local law-and-order for most Unionists. And Unionist leaders were apt to answer critics by pointing out that the force had been established originally by the British Government. However, Lord Brookeborough, former NI PM, very much regarded himself as the 'father' of the B Specials. Tim Pat Coogan, in his book *The IRA*, described the USC as 'the rock on which any mass movement by the IRA in the North has always foundered'. Wallace Clark, historian of the USC, said: 'Historians of the future, if there is any fairness in the world, will give the Ulster Special Constabulary the credit for having one of the most dedicated and effective part-time forces ever raised within the British Commonwealth.' He conceded, however, that some of its leaders had been at fault in not eradicating 'a few extremists or bad characters'. But the Scarman tribunal had no doubts about the non-acceptability of the USC to the minority community. It was 'totally distrusted by the Catholics', who saw it as 'the strong arm of the Protestant ascendancy'. Scarman added that the B Specials could not show themselves in a Catholic area without heightening tension, and they were neither trained nor equipped for riot-control duty.

Scarman has recorded the somewhat confused role of the USC in the summer of 1969. In July the Minister of Home Affairs, Robert Porter QC, authorised its use in riot control, with batons but without firearms. After protests from the USC, however, he allowed officers and NCOs to carry arms. On 13 August NI PM James Chichester-Clark indicated in a broadcast that the USC would not be used for riot control, but next day an instruction was issued stating that they should be so used, but equipped, 'where possible', with batons. It was not until 15 August that the USC was expressly ordered to report with their firearms. This was after the call-out which seems to have been mandatory before the army could go on the streets in support of the RUC. In 1969 there were about 10,000 members on the USC's books. A few hundred of these were full time, and another three hundred were mobilised for full-time duty with the RUC in 1969. Scarman found that the force was not effective when used in communal disturbances in Belfast, and that it had shown lack of proper discipline, particularly in the use of firearms, when employed outside Belfast. But the tribunal praised the USC for protecting Catholic-owned pubs in Belfast from Protestant mobs.

During discussions in Downing Street in August 1969 between the British and NI Governments, the PM, Harold Wilson, indicated in a TV interview that the USC would be phased out. But after the discussions, NI PM James Chichester-Clark and his colleagues rejected the idea of abolition of the 'Specials'. The issue produced acrimonious debate within unionism, with right-wing critics of the NI Government claiming that the public was not being told the whole truth. In the end the abolition of the USC was recommended in the Hunt report, published in the autumn of 1969, and the force was eventually stood down on 30 April 1970. With the disappearance of

the USC, security became the responsibility of three main elements –
the RUC, the regular army and the UDR, a mainly part-time force
which was designed to undertake much of the work of the former B
Specials.

THE ROYAL ULSTER CONSTABULARY

In the wake of serious riots in the summer of 1969 it was clear that
the British Government was intent on securing a new-look police
force. Thus the Home Secretary, James Callaghan, inspired the
mounting of a special committee of inquiry (*see* Hunt Report). The
Cameron Commission, in its initial look at the underlying causes of
the crisis, had complained of RUC mistakes, and the Scarman
tribunal, in its investigation of the bitter disturbances of 1969, had
recognised the 'fateful split between the Catholic community and the
police'. Scarman said the RUC had been ready to do its duty as much
in face of Protestant as of Catholic mobs, 'But it is painfully clear
from the evidence adduced before us that by July [1969] the Catholic
minority no longer believed that the RUC was impartial and that
Catholic and civil rights activists were publicly asserting this lack of
confidence.' Thus, while accepting that the RUC had made mistakes,
Scarman rejected 'the general case of a partisan force co-operating
with Protestant mobs to attack Catholic people'. Scarman held,
however, that there had been six occasions during the 1969 troubles
when the RUC had been 'seriously at fault':

12 AUGUST	Incursion by members of the RUC Reserve Force into Rossville Street, Londonderry.
13 AUGUST	Decision to put armed members of the USC on riot duty in Dungannon, Co. Tyrone, without an experienced police officer to take command.
14 AUGUST	A similar decision in Armagh city.
14–15 AUGUST	The use of Browning machine guns in Belfast.
14–16 AUGUST	Failure to prevent Protestant mobs burning down Catholic houses in Conway Street and Brookfield Street in Belfast.
15 AUGUST	Failure to take effective action to restrain or disperse mobs or to protect lives and property in riot areas during daylight and before the arrival of the army.

The burden of the Scarman criticism of the RUC was that its senior officers acted as though the strength of the force was sufficient to maintain the public peace. This meant that the army had not been called in until the Inspector-General of the RUC was confronted with the physical exhaustion of police in Londonderry on 14 August 1969 and in Belfast the following day. It found that the force had struggled manfully to do its duty in a situation which it could not control, and that its courage, as long hours of stress and strain took their toll, was beyond praise.

James Callaghan, who as Home Secretary was responsible for police matters in GB, took an exceptional interest in changing the RUC image. His first move was to arrange for Sir Arthur Young of the City of London Police to take over as the head of the force. In consequence of the Hunt recommendations the RUC lost much of its paramilitary character which it had inherited from the old Royal Irish Constabulary in 1922. Instead, it was remodelled on police forces in GB, and the term 'police service' became official jargon. Under Stormont Governments, the Ministry of Home Affairs handled broad police matters, but under the Police Act of 1970, a Police Authority, representative of the main sections of the community, was set up. It was given the responsibility to maintain an adequate and efficient police force. Operational control of the RUC was vested in the Chief Constable, and the title 'Inspector-General' was dropped. The general rank structure was also altered to conform with practice in GB.

The size of the RUC, limited to 3,500 men and women up to 31 March 1970, had to be quickly reassessed in the light of the security demands. The establishment was increased to 4,940 in 1970, to 6,500 in 1974, to 7,500 in 1979, to 8,000 in 1982, and to 8,250 in 1984. At the end of 1987 the total strength of the regular force was 8,236 with a 2,987 full-time Reserve (establishment 2,750, but raised to 3,000 in 1988); and 1,659 part-time Reserve (establishment 2,150). The RUC also has a substantial civilian backup, which stood at 336 when it was first announced by Secretary of State James Prior in 1982.

It has been Government policy since the mid-1970s to achieve the 'primacy of the police', that is, a situation in which the RUC is in charge of the peace-keeping effort everywhere in NI. This 'Ulsterisation' approach meant that by the mid-1980s the RUC was paramount, with the UDR providing the backup in 80 per cent of NI, and the army giving support elsewhere, mainly in W. Belfast and the border area, including Derry city. Earlier there had been some examples of police–army friction, and this was one of the reasons for the appointment of the late Sir Maurice Oldfield (ex-head of MI6) as Security Co-ordinator in 1979 – a post finally dropped in early 1982. In practice close consultation developed between the army and the police. Although, technically, 'tasking' is carried out by the RUC, it does not have any direct control of army personnel. The RUC's role has also changed considerably over the years with the development of anti-terrorist units, including covert operations, and the extension of computer-based intelligence.

The AIA has meant that the Chief Constable is drawn into regular discussions with British and Irish Ministers; he has had more contact than previously with the Garda Commissioner and there is a permanent 'hot line' between the two forces. But there have been strong hints that the AIA has been less productive in cross-border security than the UK Government had hoped. In September 1986 Secretary of State Tom King told the British Irish Association of his impatience for faster progress in this area, and by late 1988 extradition from the Republic was still a matter of angry criticism by Margaret Thatcher. She described the refusal of the Irish Government to extradite Father Patrick Ryan to the UK on terrorist charges as 'an insult to the British people'. The Dublin authorities had pointed to comments in Parliament and the British media coverage as reasons for their decision.

Legacy of Complaints

A long legacy of complaints by the Nationalist community about RUC methods has prevented all-round acceptability of the force in Catholic areas, despite major efforts to improve its image. Repeated stress on the need to attract more Catholic recruits led to only an approximate 10 per cent minority element in 1988. The negative factors in relations with the minority have included: allegations of maltreatment of suspects at the Castlereagh interrogation centre in the late 1970s, which led to TV monitoring (*see* Bennett Report); the tensions surrounding the 1981 H-Block hunger strike; controversial shootings, including the killing of PIRA and INLA men in Co. Armagh in 1982, which were the subject of the Stalker/Sampson reports; the bitter debate over the supergrass era (1981–6), when Chief Constable Sir John Hermon strenuously defended the use of 'converted terrorists' as a powerful weapon against the paramilitaries; and RUC support in the late 1980s for even tougher anti-terrorist measures at a time when the Irish Government was still seeking court reforms in the context of the AIA. The NIO, Police Authority and RUC have been active in seeking to allay Nationalist worries. In 1987 a code of professional ethics was introduced, requiring RUC officers to act impartially and without regard to religion, political beliefs or aspirations. And a new independent Police Complaints Commission (chairman, James Grew) became effective in 1988.

The hostility of Unionists to the AIA raised difficulties for the RUC. Some street protests against the agreement led to clashes between police and demonstrators, who resented attempts to re-route parades away from Catholic areas, notably in Portadown, where there was some serious rioting. In 1986 loyalists were involved in some 500 incidents of intimidation of RUC families, 120 of whom were forced to move home. But Unionist opposition to the new Public Order legislation (effective 2 April 1987), which required seven days' notice for all parades, including traditional parades, was much less strident than had been threatened. There were 96 illegal parades in 1987 out of a total of 2,112, but only 18 led to disorder.

In the late 1980s there have been frequent rows over the policing of PIRA funerals. In 1987 alone there were twenty-three such funerals, and RUC efforts to prevent paramilitary displays produced much controversy and some violent confrontations. But in 1988 there were five deaths at two funerals in W. Belfast which were not closely policed (*see* Andersonstown).

The RUC has become heavily involved in countering paramilitary racketeering (both by Republicans and loyalists), and has begun penetrating an area of funding – the apparently legitimate business associated with paramilitary organisations – a penetration that will be made easier by new powers proposed in late 1988.

The continuing PIRA campaign has offered by far the biggest challenge. In 1985 there was the ironic situation that overall terrorist activity was at its lowest for fifteen years, but the number of police officers killed (twenty-three) was the highest since 1976. This was due largely to the PIRA campaign against RUC stations, mainly in border areas. Thirteen stations were bombed or mortared, and eleven officers killed, nine in a single attack on Newry station in 1985. A further twenty-eight RUC members died in 1986 and 1987, but there was a falling off in police casualties in 1988, when PIRA switched its attack to the army. PIRA and INLA murders were running at about seventy per year during the early 1980s, which included the H-Block hunger-strike period, then dropped to about forty annually until 1986. But in 1987 they rose to sixty-nine out of an overall total of ninety-three deaths. This made 1987 the worst year for terrorist killings since 1981, when 101 people died. But thirty-one of those killed in 1987 were counted as known terrorists. (Loyalist groups were also active in 1986 and 1987, killing twenty-five people during the two-year period, many of them sectarian murders.) PIRA activity became intense in the summer of 1988, when twenty-six people died in August alone. At the same time PIRA stepped up its bombing campaign, even hitting Belfast city centre. For the RUC there was some comfort in large seizures of PIRA arms in Belfast and border districts, but the Chief Constable gave constant reminders of the large hauls of Czechoslovakian Semtex explosive and sophisticated weapons, including ground-to-air weapons from Libyan shipments, which were still believed to be hidden on both sides of the border.

It was also symptomatic of the tense security situation that new appointments to the Police Authority in 1988 were not publicly announced. At the end of 1988 the authority was seeking a new Chief Constable to succeed Sir John Hermon, who had announced that he would retire in May 1989. No RUC officer was short-listed for the post, and the authority selected Dublin-born Metropolitan Police Assistant Commissioner Hugh Annesley. His wide experience and recent involvement in handling anti-terrorist operations in GB – entailing co-operation with both RUC and Gardaí – were apparently conclusive for the authority. He was also described by authority chairman Tom Rainey as 'a man of sensitivity'.

THE ARMY

In pre-1969 days NI, with its 2,000-strong garrison, was a popular posting with the army, so it was a major surprise when, in the summer of 1969, the army found itself on the streets of NI in a peace-keeping role. For the NI Government, it was a hard decision to call for troops, since it was all too aware that once the army was involved, there could not fail to be a basic change in Stormont–Westminster relations. Ministers took their decision on 14 August 1969, after RUC officers accepted that their men were too exhausted to maintain their efforts to deal with violence on the edge of Derry's Bogside and in Belfast.

Home Secretary James Callaghan, for the British Government,

endorsed the request and at 5 p.m. on 14 August a company of the Prince of Wales Own Regiment went on duty in the centre of Derry. Next day 600 men of the 3rd Battalion, Light Infantry, entered W. Belfast with fixed bayonets to provide a buffer between Protestant and Catholic crowds on what later became known as the 'Peace Line'.

In many Catholic areas of Belfast the soldiers got a warm welcome because they were treated as an insurance against loyalist incursions. This situation did not persist, though, since the rise of PIRA led most Republicans to renew their natural resentment towards British forces. The Falls Road curfew in July 1970 also tended to harden Catholic attitudes against the army. The army also displayed some extra toughness in face of attacks. Army GOC and Director of Operations General Freeland warned in April 1970 that anyone throwing a petrol bomb after a warning risked being shot.

Stormont could not have any control of the army constitutionally, and it had been agreed to put the RUC under the army commander in relation to anti-terrorist operations. The army in such a situation found itself caught up in local politics. Unionists in 1969 resented what they regarded as toleration by the army of no-go areas in W. Belfast and in the Bogside and Creggan areas of Derry. But incidents involving the army had on occasion far-reaching political consequences. It was the shooting by the army in Derry of two men in July 1971 which led to the withdrawal of the SDLP from Stormont. The SDLP was acting in pursuance of an ultimatum that it would leave Parliament if a public inquiry into the shooting was refused. The shooting dead by the army of thirteen men in Derry in January 1972 was crucial in persuading the British Government to suspend Stormont (*see* 'Bloody Sunday'). The Heath Government wanted the NI Government to surrender to Westminster all law-and-order powers, and when Brian Faulkner and his colleagues refused to do so, they were left with only the option of resignation. Heath was able to act firmly because he was aware of full support from the opposition leader, Harold Wilson, who had been doubtful since 1969 about allowing Stormont any real security powers. On this point, Lord O'Neill of the Maine, former NI PM, claimed in 1978 that Stormont had been deprived of any power of decision in security matters after the entry of the army in support of the civil power.

Undoubtedly, the NI campaign proved more costly in terms of manpower than the Government originally expected. There were seven major units (around 7,000 troops) involved in 1970. In 1971 this had risen to nine units (and this was a smaller commitment than the NI Government was demanding); while at the time of 'Operation Motorman' in 1972, there were some nineteen units, or 21,000 troops, in NI. By 1975 there were fifteen units, in 1979 thirteen, and in 1982 nine. Since unit strengths vary, the numbers of troops are a more accurate guide. By 1980 the figure was 11,500; in November 1981, 10,763; and at the end of 1982, 10,500. In addition, one spearhead unit stationed in GB has been available at all times to be moved swiftly to NI. Originally most army units came from West Germany on four-month tours of duty. Up to 1978 nine major units had completed six tours, and six major units had seven tours. But in 1977 Secretary of State Roy Mason announced that there would be more long-stay units, starting with one extra in the autumn of 1978. By 1982 all but 2,000 troops (or three units) were on two-year tours of duty.

The army in NI has been temporarily reinforced to deal with two loyalist strikes – in 1974 and 1977 – and during the 1981 hunger strike. In 1974 the attitude of the army chiefs to the loyalist bid to bring down the power-sharing Executive stirred controversy. The power-sharing parties were deeply disappointed that the army could not provide the expertise to run the power stations and they believed more should have been done by troops to counter the erection of barricades and road blocks by supporters of the stoppage. The army, though, was obviously reluctant to put itself in a position of all-out confrontation with the loyalists once it was clear that the strike had considerable Protestant support. This approach was summed up by one senior army officer in the words, 'The game isn't worth the candle.' So, inevitably, the collapse of the Executive gave rise to some angry recriminations, some of them directed against the army. In 1977 the UUAC strike in May led to the deployment of an extra three infantry battalions, but the limited nature of the stoppage did not put any serious strain on army resources.

The PIRA ceasefire in 1975 raised very different problems for the army. The British Government had gone to the extent of co-operating with PSF in setting up a system for monitoring the ceasefire, and it was obviously gambling on PIRA deciding at last to abandon its shooting war. So Ministers were keen to avoid a situation in which the army gave PIRA an excuse to resume its campaign. The army itself described its stance as 'lowering its profile, but not lowering its guard'. But to some Conservative MPs and to most Unionists it seemed that the army was going very easy on the PIRA and that their men on the wanted list were being allowed to move freely. The authorities denied, however, that people wanted for specific crimes were being ignored, and in the event the ceasefire petered out rapidly, with PIRA resuming its activities seriously in the second half of 1975.

The feature of 1976 was the introduction of the undercover SAS to fight the PIRA in S. Armagh, after serious violence there. Probably fewer than one hundred SAS men were involved initially, but the move achieved a real reduction in PIRA assaults in this key border area. Later, the SAS (and undercover men from other units) were permitted to operate anywhere in NI, largely due to the growth of sectarian assassinations in the 'murder triangle', embracing parts of counties Tyrone and Armagh and in areas like N. Belfast. The SAS has continued to be employed in difficult surveillance operations, and its most dramatic operation was the shooting dead of eight PIRA members attacking Loughgall RUC station in May 1987 (see Lough-gall Shootings).

The year 1977 brought the implementation of the policy of 'primacy of the police', which meant that the army no longer controlled security but operated in support of the RUC. The 'primacy' policy does not mean, however, that the army comes under RUC command, but that soldiers support the police where necessary in anti-terrorist operations. There is very close liaison between the army GOC and the RUC Chief Constable, and similar contacts down the chain of command in both forces. The army still retains an important role in areas where the terrorist threat is still regarded as significant – that is, along the border and in W. Belfast and in the Bogside area of Derry. In the hunger-strike situation in 1981 the army proved 'indispensable', according to the RUC Chief Constable. But as the 1980s progressed, the fall in the overall level of violence was reflected in the decline of army strength. By 1985 it was down to 9,000 – 4,000 below the 1978 level. In the wake of the AIA, however, the wave of PIRA attacks on border police stations and army posts led to an extra two battalions being moved in during early 1986. This raised army strength to ten battalions (10,000 troops) instead of eight, and this strength was still maintained at the end of 1988. The stepping up of the PIRA campaign in 1987 and 1988, with the aid of arms from Libya, led to the revival of 3rd Brigade (which had earlier operated in S. Armagh), based at Drumadd barracks in Co. Armagh, to operate as a border force from Carlingford Lough to Strabane. It became operational on 1 July 1988, with two battalions, plus SAS, and meshed in with UDR border units to increase patrolling and covert operations along the frontier with the Republic. The aim was two-fold – to disrupt PIRA operations and to prevent movements of arms across the border. During the period 1987 to 1988, tall army observation posts, complete with living accommodation, had been erected at high points in S. Armagh to make surveillance easier, often to the annoyance of local residents. The establishment of the border brigade still left Belfast and most of the eastern part of NI under 39th Brigade at Lisburn, and most of the western part under the brigade at Derry.

In 1988 the locally based Royal Irish Rangers were used for the first time during the Troubles, when the 1st Battalion was stationed at Lisnaskea, Co. Fermanagh. Army sources said they were pleased with the initial reaction, and it seemed likely that the 2nd Battalion would also have an early tour of duty. There had been nervousness about the idea in Whitehall for some years, and the SDLP had warned against using the regiment in NI. It still remains speculative whether the Gurkhas will be used eventually. Also in 1988 six battalions were on extended tours of duty (two years), accompanied by their families, while four battalions were on short-term or *roulement* tours (four and a half months). At the end of 1988 estates occupied by army families became targets of PIRA, apparently in retaliation for intensive army house searches in Republican areas.

Eye in the Sky

For the army in NI adaptation has been the name of the game. Initially, it was faced largely by community conflict situations, allied to street disturbances in what the Ministry of Defence expected to be a relatively brief commitment. Nearly twenty years on, the challenge of PIRA remains, and because of Libyan backing for the Republican movement, its guerilla fighters are better armed than ever before. Thus, in late 1988 army resources were heavily committed to seeking out hidden caches of weapons, some of them highly sophisticated. The old Russian RPG 7 rocket was still in use, but PIRA was thought to have stockpiled American SAM-7 ground-to-air missiles which posed a special threat to army helicopters which, it was disclosed in September 1988, were permitted to make limited overflights of the border. Special measures were taken to protect the Wessex, Lynx and Scout 'choppers', flown by the Army Air Corps, which were vital in surveillance and transport, as well as the occasionally used RAF Chinooks. Helicopters provided the 'eye in the sky' in the shape of binocular observation, photographic techniques, and video cameras. 'Heli-tele' came of age in 1988 when video material shot from a helicopter was admitted in evidence in a Belfast court, where men faced charges of murder of two soldiers attacked at a funeral in Andersonstown (*see* Andersonstown).

The scale of the arms finds in 1988 (up to 21 November) showed the potential of the terrorist groups: 56 machine guns, 195 rifles, 139 pistols, 47 shotguns, 12 rocket-launchers, 46 rockets, 37 mortars, 15 mortar bombs, 90,166 rounds of ammunition (more than in the previous four years combined), 18,029 pounds of explosives, and one napalm flame-thrower. Some 470 bombs were defused during the same period and there were 223 explosions. Most of these caches were attributed to PIRA, but substantial loyalist arms were also uncovered in 1988, some of them not far from the border in S. Armagh, and suspected of being held for cross-border raids. However, PIRA posed the major threat because it was believed to be gearing up for the use of its most deadly weapons by organising training camps in remote parts of Ireland and possibly in Libya. It might have only five hundred members in ASUs, and no more than £4 million a year to keep its campaign going, but intelligence sources accepted that it had a core of hardened killers, and that, despite a series of blunders in 1987 and 1988, it had shown increased sophistication in mounting attacks. In 1970, for example, it had to make an average 191 attacks to kill a single member of the security forces; by 1984 the figure was 18 attacks. However, the army's losses have been greatly inflated by a small number of serious incidents; the deaths of eighteen soldiers at Warrenpoint, Co. Down, in August 1979; eleven deaths in the Ballykelly pub bombing, Co. Derry, in December 1982; eight killed when a bus was blown up near Ballygawley, Co. Tyrone, in August 1988; and six killed by a bomb in Lisburn, Co. Down, after taking part in a 'fun run' in June 1988. (*See* Security Statistics section, p. 411 for detailed casualties.) PIRA has improved on its initially poor performance with mortars, and has introduced a highly dangerous weapon in the 'drogue bomb', known to the army as IAAG (improvised anti-armour grenade), which consists of an explosive charge in a baked beans tin, carried by a small parachute and exploding on impact. And a flame-thrower of the type uncovered in W. Belfast in 1988 could have devastating effects if fired at a security forces' vehicle. Despite intensive searches, PIRA was also believed to hold a few Russian heavy machine guns; this is believed to be the weapon which brought down an army helicopter in S. Armagh in June 1988.

Shields and Saracens

Much special equipment has been employed by the army to cope with the varied situations encountered in NI. For the handling of street disturbances, soldiers have been issued with plastic visors fitted to their steel helmets which protect the face against bricks, stones or other missiles. On occasions, plastic shields have also been carried, sometimes with leg-guards. Flak jackets, giving protection against low-velocity weapons, are normally worn. In the early days of the violence troops were permitted to shoot at identified petrol-bombers, but political considerations forced the authorities to look for weapons which fitted in with the 'minimum force' commitment. Water cannon were frequently deployed in the 1969 riots, but the main weapons in serious street disturbances have been the rubber bullet, later replaced by the plastic bullet, and CS gas.

The rubber bullet, 14 centimetres long and 4 centimetres in diameter, weighed 142 grams. It was designed to bounce off the ground and strike at about knee level. In practice it proved highly unpredictable and there were three deaths from rubber bullets and many severe injuries. Between 1972 and 1975 it was employed extensively to break up crowds engaged in stoning or petrol-bombing and finally gave way to the plastic bullet, which was first used in 1973.

The Ministry of Defence said the plastic bullet had been introduced because it was more effective and accurate. But the new baton round – as both rubber and plastic bullets are officially termed – was developed, according to *Jane's Infantry Weapons* (1976), because the disability and injury rates of the rubber bullet were not acceptable. The plastic bullet, made of PVC, is 10 centimetres long and 4 centimetres in diameter, and also weighs 142 grams. Unlike the rubber bullet, it is fired directly at its target. In the 1981 disturbances during the H-Block hunger strike, many thousands of plastic bullets were fired by the army and the RUC, and four deaths resulted in two months. By the end of 1982 the plastic bullet had caused eleven deaths and many of its critics argued that it was proving even more dangerous than the rubber bullet. These critics have included many Nationalist spokespersons and all NI Catholic Bishops. The British Labour conference has also opposed their use, and the European Parliament has called for a ban throughout the EC. But in October 1984 the European Commission of Human Rights held that they could be used in riot situations. The security forces, supported by Government Ministers, have always argued that they cannot face rioters, who are prepared to cause death and injury, without making some effective retort. In the late 1980s the plastic bullet was still being employed, although more sparingly. (During riots involving loyalists in Portadown in April 1986, a twenty-year-old Protestant man was fatally injured by a plastic bullet.) Batons, 0.6 metres long, are also available to the army for street troubles.

The main army weapons in 1988 were the SA80 5.56 mm. rifle (replacing the 7.6 mm. self-loading rifle), the Sterling 9 mm. sub-machine-gun, and the general purpose machine gun, which is un-suitable for use in urban conditions. Special rifle night-sights have been developed to counter snipers operating in darkness.

On average two army technical officers engaged in bomb-disposal work were killed each year in the early years of violence. Robot devices serve to reduce the risk of examining suspect objects. From the beginning of 1970 to the end of 1987 nearly 4,000 bombs were defused.

Four vehicles have been employed in the NI campaign. The land-rover, usually protected with steel sheeting and sometimes with asbestos, has been the workhorse of the mobile patrol. The Saracen armoured personnel carrier, capable of carrying ten soldiers and their equipment, has been used generally in the cities. The Ferret scout car has been a popular escort vehicle, used sometimes for patrols. The Saladin armoured car, with a 75 mm. gun and two Brownings, has been largely confined to border patrols.

Although in the armed forces the army has provided the bulk of the manpower in support of the police, the Royal Marines have also served in an infantry role, and together with the Royal Navy, they have mounted coastal and lough patrols to prevent the smuggling of arms into NI. The RAF has been involved in transport and in reconnaissance, and the RAF regiment has guarded the airfield at Aldergrove and the radar facilities at Bishop's Court.

Ulster Defence Regiment

The Ulster Defence Regiment, a locally raised and mainly part-time force within the army structure, derived from the proposals of the Hunt committee. It became operational on 1 April 1970, and was designed to replace the former USC, or B Specials, which, as a wholly Protestant force, did not fit in with the Government's bid to develop security forces with cross-community support. Early on, it did attract up to 18 per cent Catholic membership, but by 1978 Catholics accounted for only 3 per cent of the force, a percentage which still applied in 1988.

Its early recruiting policy was criticised from both sides of the community, with some Unionists protesting that vetting procedures were keeping out many experienced ex-'Specials', while Nationalists complained that it was too loyalist-oriented. Certainly, its popularity rating has never been high in the minority community. From time to time, SDLP and leading Dublin politicians have urged its disbandment and in 1985 the independent Kilbrandon committee of politicians and academics suggested that it should be phased out. The Government and successive UDR commanders have insisted on its value and impartiality. However, convictions of members, or ex-members, on sectarian murder charges and occasional convictions for offences linked with loyalist paramilitaries have created an image problem. But it has been defended in the loyalist community with as much vigour as the former USC.

The Government, in its 1986 Defence White Paper, hit out at Nationalists who discouraged Catholics from joining the regiment. It accepted that, with terrorist activity often concentrated in Nationalist areas, UDR operations were likely to make a greater impact there, but it argued that the UDR's impartiality had been clearly demonstrated during the 1977 loyalist strike. In 1985 more extended training was introduced for part-time members, and full-time officers were permitted to attend standard Sandhurst courses. In the late 1980s it has been the back-up for the RUC over 85 per cent of NI, but it was still not meeting the demand of the Irish Government that all its patrols should be accompanied by police.

In its early years there was talk of a recruitment target of 10,000, and its peak strength of 9,000 was reached in 1972. And while it is thought of as largely part time, its full-time element in November 1988 stood at 46 per cent, with overall strength at 6,300. This makes it the largest regiment in the army, and it is said to have been operational for a longer period than any other unit since the Napoleonic Wars. Since 1973 it has had women members, dubbed 'Greenfinches' after their original radio code name, and although they are unarmed, four have been killed on duty. (There were about seven hundred 'Greenfinches' in 1988.) Members of the UDR have been PIRA targets since the mid-1970s and 146 of the 178 killed up to November 1988 died from attacks while off duty.

The Government's long-term commitment to the UDR was underlined in June 1988, when it was announced that the Queen had approved the granting of colours to all its nine battalions. The first would be presented in 1991 to mark its twenty-first birthday, and the remainder before 1995, its silver jubilee.

ANTI-TERRORIST LAWS

There are two main pieces of anti-terrorist legislation – Prevention of Terrorism and Emergency Provisions. Prevention of Terrorism legislation, which dates from the Birmingham pub bombings in 1974, applies largely in NI, but since 1984 it is directed also at international terrorism. Emergency Provisions legislation, limited to NI, dates from 1973 and replaced the Special Powers Act and the Detention of Terrorists Order.

The 1974 PTA gave two main powers:

1   to exclude from GB, from NI, or the UK as a whole, persons involved in terrorism associated with NI;
2   to arrest suspected terrorists and detain them for forty-eight hours, with the possibility of extending detention for a further five days on authority of Home Secretary or NI Secretary of State.

The powers have been criticised as providing a form of 'internal exile'. Under (1) the NI Secretary of State excluded thirty-one people from NI between November 1974 and the end of 1987; eleven of these orders were made in 1981, the year of the hunger strike; there were no exclusions in 1985 and 1986, and one in 1987. In 1988 twenty-three of the exclusion orders were still in operation. A new

PTA took effect in 1976, which retained the powers granted by the 1974 Act, but also made it an offence to contribute or solicit money for terrorism, or to withhold information on terrorism. The 1984 PTA extended the detention power to international terrorists, and it also put a three-year limit on the life of an exclusion order, although the Secretary of State could make a new order if there was fresh intelligence. The PTA gives power to proscribe organisations in GB; only PIRA was outlawed in 1974, but INLA was added after the murder of Airey Neave MP in 1979. Between 1974 and 1987, 103 people were charged in NI with offences specifically listed in the PTAs, 71 for withholding information. In the same period 2,577 people were charged following detention under the PTAS (1,830 after extensions had been granted) and tried in criminal courts.

Following a recommendation by Lord Jellicoe, who inquired into the operation of the legislation, the 1984 PTA had a life limited to five years; that is, expiring in March 1989. Margaret Thatcher disclosed in August 1988 that the replacement Bill would include measures to tackle paramilitary racketeering and to combat fund-raising by illegal groups. Powers would be modelled broadly on existing legislation which allowed the seizure of assets of convicted drug smugglers. There would also be a 'purpose-designed, administrative anti-racketeering body'. Defending the move against terrorist funding, Home Secretary Douglas Hurd said that terrorists sometimes ran otherwise legitimate businesses to finance their murders.

In the event, the Bill brought forward in November 1988, to become operative in March 1989, was designed as a permanent measure, subject to annual renewal. It also cut from 50 per cent to 33 per cent the maximum remission allowed to terrorist convicts. But almost as soon as it was published the European Court of Human Rights ruled, in a separate legal action, that seven-day detention for questioning was excessive. In December 1988 Hurd indicated that he required time to consider how to introduce a judicial element into the detention process and that in the meantime a temporary derogation was being sought from the ECHR. The decision was attacked by the Labour Party as a snub to the Strasbourg court. Shadow Home Secretary Roy Hattersley said powers to deal with terrorist funding should have been taken earlier, but he renewed Labour's objections to the rest of the Bill, saying that the general powers were more likely to assist terrorists than to harm them.

In 1978 the new EPA consolidated emergency powers in NI, giving wide powers of search, arrest and even internment without trial if the Government decided to reintroduce it. It listed the organisations proscribed in NI – IRA, Cumann na mBan, Fianna na hÉireann, Red Hand Commandos, Saor Éire, UFF, UVF and INLA. It provided that bail could be granted only by the Supreme Court or trial judge. A court was given power to exclude a statement by an accused person if it was satisfied that the statement was obtained by torture or by inhuman or degrading treatment. The wearing of a hood or mask or paramilitary dress in a public place was outlawed. It listed scheduled terrorist offences to which the Act applied, going back to the Offences Against the Person Act of 1861 and Explosive Substances Act of 1883. It also provided, together with the Republic's reciprocal legislation and the Criminal Law Jurisdiction Act, 1975, that a terrorist could be tried on whichever side of the border he was arrested. (This provision was used in fourteen cases up to October 1988, when the Republic urged its increased use as an alternative to extradition.) In 1985 the Government withdrew derogations under the ECHR, thus declaring that NI's emergency laws did not violate minimum international standards.

Non-jury Courts

The Diplock report in 1972 recommended that non-jury trials should be introduced for a wide range of terrorist offences because of the intimidation of jurors and witnesses. In 1973, under the EPA, the Government adopted its proposals and Diplock courts came into existence.

Following the late Sir George Baker's report in 1984 on the working of the EPA, an amending Act was passed in 1987 and the Government gave information about the operation of Diplock courts. It was shown that in 1986, 596 defendants appeared before Diplock courts, with 567 convicted. Of the total number of defendants, 89 per cent had pleaded guilty and 11 per cent not guilty; 43 per cent of those who pleaded not guilty were acquitted. It was also reported that only 17 per cent of arrests under the 1978 Act led to charges. The Government rejected a move by the Labour opposition to drop internment powers through the 1987 Act. The amending measure, which represented the first major change in

emergency legislation since 1975, shifted the onus in bail applications towards the prosecution instead of the defendant. It also
allowed magistrates to remand for up to twenty-eight days instead of
seven, so as to reduce pressure on court accommodation in Belfast.
The Secretary of State was empowered to set time limits to reduce
delays in bringing terrorist-type cases to trial. (This change arose
from an amendment originally tabled by Seamus Mallon, SDLP MP.)
The Lord Chancellor was given power to direct that particular cases
should be heard in courts outside Belfast.

The amended EPA also provided that the use or threat of violence
would become an additional ground for declaring a statement inad-
missible. It repealed the arrest powers in the 1978 EPA, so as to avoid
duplicating PTA powers of arrest; the effect of this was to allow arrest
on 'reasonable suspicion' rather than simply 'suspicion', a change
widely welcomed by lawyers. The offence of collecting information
likely to be of use to terrorists was extended to include former
members of the security services, the judiciary, courts' service, and
the prison service. A new system of registration of private security
firms was introduced to prevent paramilitary groups operating such
services. The new Act was scheduled to expire in June 1992.

Widening Net

In 1988, when PIRA stepped up its campaign and was clearly seen to
have accumulated large supplies of arms, the Government's attention
turned to extra legal powers to use against terrorist suspects. In July
it brought in 'genetic fingerprinting'. The technique entails taking
mouth swabs from suspects for 'DNA profiling' and the authorities
claimed that samples could provide conclusive proof of guilt or
innocence. The SACHR said it was 'firmly opposed' to the provision,
since it differed from that in England and Wales, where mouth
samples could only be taken with the written consent of the suspect
and by a doctor, not a police officer. Up to October 1988 the
technique had been used in one case.

After an in-depth review of security in September–October 1988,
the ending of the 'right to silence' for terrorist suspects was also
introduced. It had been recommended by Lord Colville, when he
reviewed anti-terrorist laws in 1987, and Secretary of State Tom
King argued that it was necessary to counter the practice of suspects
refusing to answer any questions during interrogation. (Paramilitaries

were told in their news-sheets: 'Whatever you say, say nothing.') Labour's NI spokesman, Kevin McNamara, protested that the change meant the over-turning of 'one of the pillars of the British system of justice'. The SDLP was also critical of the change and the NI Law Society complained that it had not been consulted about a legal change 'of such a fundamental nature', which also meant 'a drift towards an inquisitorial system'.

A further move by the Government in the autumn of 1988 was to order the broadcasting organisations not to allow direct broadcasts by members of proscribed organisations or supporters of violence. The ban applied to PSF and UDA as well as all outlawed para-militaries. Home Secretary Douglas Hurd claimed that such appearances caused offence and also fear, but critics included the Labour opposition, SDLP, most of the press, the broadcasting organisations, and the National Union of Journalists. Towards the end of 1988 it became clear that the NUJ would challenge the ban in the courts; PSF also launched a legal challenge in February 1989.

The restriction was less onerous than the 'section thirty-one' legislation in the Irish Republic, since it did not apply to elections and permitted a PSF councillor, for example, to be interviewed on some social issue in his council role. But the Government also moved, at the end of 1988, to make it more difficult for supporters of violence to be elected to councils. The Elected Authorities (NI) Bill provided that a candidate on nomination would have to make a declaration renouncing violence. It also changed the disqualification rule for those seeking election to councils. A five-year ban on ex-prisoners would date from release rather than sentencing. Tom King said that the introduction of the declaration occurred against a background of 'very real concern' at the way groups like PSF exploited the democratic process. (PSF had already indicated that its candidates would sign the declaration to ensure that its supporters were not disenfranchised.) The legislation provided that breach of the anti-violence declaration could be pursued through the civil courts by individuals or councils. It would not apply to Westminster elections.

Internment Without Trial

The introduction of internment without trial by the NI Government on 9 August 1971 proved to be one of the most controversial moves of the authorities to combat violence. This was partly because it was followed by an escalation of violence, and partly because it led to the serious alienation of the Catholic community from the Stormont system. The swoop in Republican areas to arrest IRA suspects came at 4 a.m. on 9 August, four days after the NI Government had decided to use the Special Powers Act for this purpose and after talks with the British Conservative Government. The action of Brian Faulkner's Government was approved by Home Secretary Reginald Maudling, who was reputed to be unenthusiastic about the move but who said later that he had feared a Protestant backlash had internment not been used. The operation, code-named 'Demetrius', came after weeks of probing activity by the army and police to finalise the list of suspects. In the event, there were 452 names thought to be members of the IRA, or associated with it, but some of them had fled in anticipation of internment, and the actual arrests totalled 350. Of these, 104 were released within forty-eight hours, which indicated the poor intelligence involved. Brian Faulkner, in announcing the introduction of internment, said the main aim was to smash the IRA, but the Government would not hesitate to take similar action against any individual or organisation which might pose a similar threat in the future.

The decision to intern was backed by most Unionists, although the Rev. Ian Paisley was against it on the grounds that it was also likely to be employed against loyalists. The swoop was followed quickly by serious rioting and shooting in Belfast and many other places. Twenty-three people died on 9 and 10 August, and a massive civil disobedience campaign, involving the withholding of rent and rates, was launched in the Catholic community, with the backing of opposition MPs and NICRA. The Nationalist and SDLP MPs had already withdrawn from Stormont, and the SDLP now said that they would not take part in dialogue with either a British or NI Government until internment was ended.

Internees were held in a new camp at Long Kesh, near Lisburn (later to be known as the Maze Prison), Magilligan army camp in Co. Derry, and the ship *Maidstone* in Belfast harbour. A small number of those arrested were subjected to 'interrogation in depth', which eventually gave rise to a finding in 1978 by the European Court of Human Rights that they had been subjected to inhuman and degrading treatment, but not to torture. A month after the start of internment, a three-man advisory committee, headed by Judge James

Brown QC, was set up to advise the Government on individual internees. Where they recommended a release, they required the individual to take the following oath: 'I swear that for the remainder of my life, I will not join or assist any illegal organisation or engage in any violence or counsel or encourage others to do so.' In the wake of intense violence and reports of intimidation, the Republic's Government set up five camps to accommodate refugees and dependants of internees.

Between the introduction of internment in August and the end of the year, 146 people were killed, including 47 members of the security forces, and 99 civilians, and there were 729 explosions and 1,437 shooting incidents. And immediately before direct rule was imposed in March 1972, the number of internees reached a peak of 924. When William Whitelaw took over as Secretary of State, he declared his intention to review personally the cases of all internees. On 7 April 1972 he announced the release of forty-seven internees, and said they had not been asked to give any assurance about future behaviour. He also stated that no further use would be made of the prison ship *Maidstone*. In May 1972 a new advisory committee was set up under the chairmanship of Judge Leonard, from Oxfordshire, which was empowered to consider only applications for release from internees. By mid-August the number of men held under the Special Powers Act had been cut to 243. Whitelaw was engaged in a drive to phase out internment, and was looking for a response from the PIRA in terms of reduced violence and possibly some switch to political activity. But in this he was disappointed, and after the re-entry of security forces to the no-go areas in the summer of 1972, there was a further slow build-up in the total of those detained.

Under the Detention of Terrorists Order, the Government introduced a new system of internment in November 1972. This involved an initial 'interim custody' order, and after twenty-eight days the person must be either released or referred to a commissioner, who would decide whether he should be detained. At this point the term 'internee' was replaced by 'detainee' in official language. Meantime, the Diplock committee reported in favour of some form of continued detention without trial. Between November 1972 and September 1973, the commissioners authorised 453 detention orders and directed release in 126 cases. In answer to the suggestion that ex-internees frequently became involved again in violence, a

Government spokesman said in March 1973 that of the more than 800 persons released from internment or detention since direct rule, only 10 had been subsequently charged with offences. With rising loyalist violence, two loyalists were served with interim custody orders on 5 February 1973, the first to be so treated. Two months later, the number of loyalists held had gone up to twenty-two. In August 1973 the Emergency Provisions Act replaced the Special Powers Act and the Detention of Terrorists Order as the legal basis of detention, but it kept the arrangements for interim custody and commissioners' hearings, and brought in a new power to hold suspects for seventy-two hours for questioning. Between 1 February 1973 and 30 October 1974 interim custody orders were served on 626 Catholics and 99 Protestants. Shortly before Christmas 1973, 63 Catholics and 2 Protestants were released.

In January 1975 the Gardiner committee said that detention without trial could only be tolerated in a democratic society in the most extreme circumstances. 'We would like to be able to recommend that the time has come to abolish detention, but the present level of violence, the risks of increased violence, and the difficulty of predicting events even a few months ahead, make it impossible for us to put foward a precise recommendation on timing. We think that this grave decision can only be made by the Government.' In August 1975 the Secretary of State (under the Emergency Provisions Amendment Act) took back the power to make detention orders, and ended the commissioner system. The Secretary of State would, however, consider reports on detainees from legally qualified advisers. But the then Secretary of State, Merlyn Rees, was committed to ending internment quickly, and on 5 December 1975 he signed orders for the release of the last seventy-five detainees. The SACHR suggested in 1979 that the power to intern without trial should be abandoned, but Secretary of State Humphrey Atkins argued that it would be premature to drop it. He apparently supported repeal in 1980, however, but in the event the power was retained, most recently through the EPA.

With a big surge in PIRA violence in the summer of 1988, the OUP was demanding 'selective internment', and the DUP called for the introduction of internment against Republicans only. There were also some Conservative voices in favour of the former. But the SDLP was firmly against both demands, and so were leading Catholic

Churchmen. The Republic was also believed to be opposing internment generally within the Anglo-Irish Conference. Margaret Thatcher said she would be 'very reluctant' to see its return, but Secretary of State Tom King talked of it as an option. And the wide range of anti-terrorist measures which came in the autumn of 1988 was probably considered to be the alternative to internment which was being increasingly regarded as a last resort.

THE SECRET ARM

It was only in November 1988 that the role of MI5 in NI was officially acknowledged. The NI Secretary of State was then empowered through the Security Service Bill to authorise specific burglaries or bugging by MI5 agents and the service was put on a statutory basis for the first time. The alignment of Secretary of State powers with those of the Home Secretary in this way was a clear indication of the growing importance of MI5 in anti-PIRA operations. Although a special tribunal was to be set up to deal with complaints about MI5 behaviour, the Bill stated that 'no entry on, or interference with, property shall be unlawful if it is authorised by a warrant issued by the Secretary of State'. The Bill also made it clear that such break-ins would be directed to securing information 'likely to be of substantial value' in helping MI5 to discharge any of its functions. Media critics of the legislation concentrated on the point that it would be difficult for any individual to lodge a complaint about the service because it would be an offence under new Official Secrets legislation for any MI5 officer or Government official to reveal anything about operations of the service, or for the media to report on them.

The Bill had the effect of highlighting the significance of MI5 in local security operations, although it appears that it has been active in NI at least since direct rule was imposed in 1972, and probably for some years before that. Most likely, MI5 took a serious interest in NI in 1970, when PIRA began to gather strength and to cast about for sources of weapons and ammunition. At that period, the focus was strongly on contacts between extreme Republicans and their Irish-American sympathisers, and MI5 was in regular contact with the FBI. It was close collaboration of this kind which led to the interception of a cargo of arms and ammunition intended for PIRA which was carried across the Atlantic in 1984 by the US vessel *Valhalla*, and then transferred to the *Marita Ann* off the Irish coast. But satellite tracking could also have figured in this operation. The FBI was also engaged in several other moves to frustrate US arms dealers seeking to provide materials for PIRA, although Armalite rifles and even machine guns have in fact reached PIRA from across the Atlantic.

MI5 is, of course, only one of the elements in the NI intelligence picture, but it does seem to have a central co-ordinating task. Obviously, its precise *modus operandi* is a closely guarded secret but the key figure is believed to be a senior officer based at Stormont, who maintains close contact with the Secretary of State. He is thought to have the task of overseeing actual operations within NI, in close consultation with army intelligence (which draws on SAS surveillance), and the RUC's Special Branch. Incidentally, Sir Howard Smith, who was appointed head of MI5 in the late 1970s by Merlyn Rees, had been the last UK Government representative in NI (the office disappeared after direct rule). Sir Howard was thus able to bring useful local knowledge to the MI5's anti-terrorist operations at a time when army–RUC co-operation was not at its best. It was this situation which led to Sir Maurice Oldfield (ex-head of the Secret Intelligence Service, or MI6) becoming Security Co-ordinator in NI in 1979, an initiative which apparently sprang directly from Margaret Thatcher's own observations on the ground. MI5 officer Michael Bettaney, who in 1984 was sentenced to twenty-three years' imprisonment at the Old Bailey for spying for the Russians, was based at army HQ in Lisburn for a period in the early 1980s.

In *Spycatcher* Peter Wright provides some curious observations on MI5's attitude to NI in 1973. He claims that he was invited to produce 'bright ideas' to deal with what he himself termed a situation very like that in Cyprus, with a 'fierce, insoluble conflict made worse by a vacillating British policy'. But Wright admits that he fared badly with those suggestions he did put forward. The Foreign Office, he says, vetoed the idea of monitoring (via equipment in the attic of the British Embassy in Dublin) PIRA telephone communications between Dublin and the west of Ireland, and neither MI5 nor MI6 would countenance his proposal to put booby-trapped detonators on Provisionals.

It is hardly surprising that Wright's ideas found no favour in Whitehall, since he was advancing them during the run-up period to the crucial Sunningdale Conference upon which both the British and Irish Governments placed high hopes. With the well-known suspicion in Irish political circles of British intelligence services, and even occasionally of the British Embassy in Dublin, the Foreign Office and the NIO have always been anxious to avoid any incidents in this field which could set back cross-border security co-operation. There was considerable embarrassment at Stormont when, in May 1976, eight members of the SAS were arrested by the Garda when they crossed the S. Armagh border while engaged on covert observation. Even the intervention of PM James Callaghan with the Irish Government failed to stop the prosecutions of the SAS men, who were eventually fined £100 each for having unlicensed guns. It appears that while the Irish Cabinet did not favour the charges, they had no power to stop the DPP bringing them.

The SAS, and units trained by it, have remained a key factor in collecting information about PIRA. This has frequently entailed groups of four or five soldiers digging themselves in for several days at a time, often in extremely uncomfortable conditions, to observe locations such as disused houses in remote areas. Many seizures are attributed to such unromantic spying. This time-consuming observation is more suited to the working conditions of the army than those of the RUC, who are, however, better placed to penetrate the loyalist paramilitaries. The failure of the loyalist organisations to maintain the same degree of secrecy as PIRA has been one of their major weaknesses.

The RUC, however, does have a large central intelligence effort, backed by computer records since the mid-1970s, and its E4A covert operators are said to have had considerable successes in tracking both PIRA and loyalist suspects, and in countering the PIRA's own intelligence agents, some of them women, who are known to operate in pubs and other public places, ready to profit from any 'loose talk' by off-duty members of the security forces. To defeat such PIRA efforts, local army units maintain lists of establishments which are at any moment out of bounds to soldiers. The permanent border checks, with records of movements of vehicles, are also a valuable part of the intelligence network. The more secure radio systems of both police and army in recent times have also removed a source of information for paramilitaries who, in the early years of the Troubles, were known to listen in on VHF communications between security-force bases and mobile patrols. Telephone tapping is a long-established means of uncovering terrorist contacts. In the old Stormont Parliament there were regular questions about the alleged activities of monitoring agents based in room twenty-two of the old Post Office HQ in Royal Avenue, Belfast, and under direct rule there has been evidence that some journalists' conversations have been intercepted. But no official statistics are available on the practice, which has to be authorised by the Secretary of State or the Home Secretary, and which has been subject to review by a High Court judge since 1985.

The Army Air Corps helicopter operation is a further important source of information, and the use of airborne infra-red photography is believed to have helped greatly in finding buried caches of weapons in the widespread searches of 1987 and 1988. How far such operations have led to finds on the Republic's side of the border is not known, but it emerged in late 1988 that an agreement had existed between the British and Irish Governments since early 1987, allowing short overflights of the border to investigate suspect devices. The Republic's authorities were still denying such an arrangement in late 1988 although it had been confirmed to journalists by Security Minister Ian Stewart.

Clearly, MI6 has had a heavy involvement in identifying foreign agents of PIRA and tracing sources of funds and arms outside the UK. The Libyan shipments of arms to Ireland in the late 1980s have presented a special challenge to MI6, and its task is likely to be widened as the new legislation to prevent 'laundering' of terrorist funds becomes effective, as there is obviously a strong international aspect to such operations.

SECURITY STATISTICS

TABLE 1
Deaths, August 1969–December 1988

	RUC	RUCR	Army	UDR	Civilians	Annual death toll
1969	1	0	0	0	12	13
1970	2	0	0	0	23	25
1971	11	0	43	5	115	174
1972	14	3	103	26	321	467
1973	10	3	58	8	171	250
1974	12	3	28	7	166	216
1975	7	4	14	5	217	247
1976	13	10	14	15	245	297
1977	8	6	15	14	69	112
1978	4	6	14	7	50	81
1979	9	5	38	10	51	113
1980	3	6	8	9	50	76
1981	13	8	10	13	57	101
1982	8	4	21	7	57	97
1983	9	9	5	10	44	77
1984	7	2	9	10	36	64
1985	14	9	2	4	25	54
1986	10	2	4	8	37	61
1987	9	7	3	8	66	93
1988	4	2	21	12	54	93
Total	168	89	410	178	1,866	2,711

Note   Figures for civilians include terrorist suspects and prison officers.

TABLE 2

Monthly record of deaths, 1972–88

	1972	1973	1974	1975	1976	1977	1978	1979	1980
Jan.	26	17	19	8	48	13	2	2	15
Feb.	22	37	15	19	27	13	21	6	8
Mar.	39	30	26	13	17	14	7	2	4
Apr.	22	16	14	36	20	17	4	16	9
May	40	30	25	11	26	13	2	7	4
June	35	30	14	21	37	9	13	11	4
July	95	17	12	15	28	10	5	7	4
Aug.	55	21	14	29	20	7	6	25	11
Sept.	40	10	12	23	12	3	7	6	3
Oct.	39	8	19	31	28	6	4	11	3
Nov.	20	20	35	24	23	4	5	9	5
Dec.	34	14	11	17	11	3	5	11	6
Total	467	250	216	247	297	112	81	113	76

	1981	1982	1983	1984	1985	1986	1987	1988
Jan.	7	8	6	8	1	4	2	6
Feb.	5	1	5	4	20	5	4	5
Mar.	4	8	5	6	3	3	13	10
Apr.	9	11	5	7	4	4	14	3
May	22	4	5	9	6	10	14	5
June	5	4	3	5	3	1	9	9
July	11	2	9	5	0	12	6	11
Aug.	5	3	5	4	5	5	4	26
Sept.	11	9	4	3	3	6	6	4
Oct.	8	12	8	5	1	6	5	8
Nov.	14	13	14	2	6	2	13	4
Dec.	0	22	8	6	2	3	3	2
Total	101	97	77	64	54	61	93	93

Note   Consolidated figures for 1969–71 unavailable.

TABLE 3

Murders by paramilitaries, 1981–7

	Republican		Loyalist	
	Murders	Attempted murders	Murders	Attempted murders
1981	69	461	12	26
1982	71	401	13	12
1983	54	286	7	13
1984	40	185	7	22
1985	42	140	5	11
1986	41	87	14	31
1987	69	176	11	23
Total	386	1,736	69	138

Note Consolidated figures for 1969–80 unavailable; figures for 1988 not yet available.

TABLE 4

Injuries, 1968–87

	RUC/ RUCR	Army/ UDR	Civilians	Punishment shootings etc.	Annual injuries total
1968	379	0	u/a	u/a	379
1969	711	22	u/a	u/a	733
1970	191	620	u/a	u/a	811
1971	315	390	1,838	u/a	2,543
1972	485	578	3,813	u/a	4,876
1973	291	548	1,812	74	2,725
1974	235	483	1,680	127	2,525
1975	263	167	2,044	189	2,663
1976	303	264	2,162	98	2,827
1977	183	187	1,027	126	1,523
1978	302	135	548	67	1,052
1979	155	135	557	76	914
1980	194	77	530	77	878
1981	332	149	877	80	1,438
1982	99	99	328	89	615
1983	142	88	280	34	544
1984	267	86	513	70	936
1985	415	33	468	62	978
1986	622	55	773	82	1,532
1987	246	104	780	184	1,314
Total	6,130	4,220	20,030	1,435	31,806

Note Figures for 1988 not yet available; 'u/a' means 'unavailable'. Figures for civilians include terrorist suspects and prison officers.

TABLE 5
Record of violence, 1969–87

	Shooting incidents	Explosions	Bombs defused	Malicious fires	Armed robberies	Amounts stolen
						£
1969	u/a	8	u/a	u/a	u/a	u/a
1970	213	153	17	u/a	u/a	u/a
1971	1,756	1,022	493	u/a	437	303,787
1972	10,628	1,382	471	u/a	1,931	790,687
1973	5,018	978	542	587	1,215	612,015
1974	3,206	685	428	636	1,231	572,951
1975	1,803	399	236	248	1,201	572,105
1976	1,908	766	426	453	813	545,340
1977	1,181	366	169	432	591	446,898
1978	755	455	178	269	439	230,750
1979	728	422	142	315	434	568,359
1980	642	280	120	275	412	496,829
1981	815	398	132	536*	587	894,929
1982	382	219	113	499	580	1,392,202
1983	290	266	101	528	622	830,258
1984	230	193	155	840	627	701,903
1985	196	148	67	740	459	655,690
1986	285	172	82	906	724	1,207,152
1987	489	236	148	506	858	1,900,098
Total	30,525	8,548	4,020	7,770	13,161	£12,721,953

Note Figures for 1988 not yet available.
*No figures available for April–June 1981.

415

TABLE 6
Arms finds and house searches, 1970–87

	Firearms found	Explosives found (lb)	Ammunition found (rounds)	Number of house searches
1970	324	798	43,095	3,107
1971	717	2,748	157,944	17,262
1972	1,264	41,488	183,410	36,617
1973	1,595	38,418	187,399	74,556
1974	1,260	26,120	147,202	74,914
1975	825	11,565	73,604	30,002
1976	837	21,714	70,306	34,919
1977	590	3,819	52,091	20,724
1978	400	2,108	43,512	15,462
1979	301	1,996	46,280	6,452
1980	203	1,810	28,078	4,106
1981	398	7,536	47,070	4,104
1982	321	5,066	41,453	4,045
1983	200	3,762	32,451	1,497
1984	197	8,534	27,211	1,282
1985	238	7,373	13,748	812
1986	215	5,386	29,061	1,273
1987	267	12,974	19,796	1,523
Total	10,152	203,215	1,243,711	332,657

Note   Arms finds figures indicate totals from all sources, including house searches.
Consolidated figures for 1968–9 unavailable; figures for 1988 not yet
available.

TABLE 7
Persons charged with terrorist-type offences, July 1972–December 1987

	Murder	Attempted murder	Firearms	Explosives	Theft	Other
1972*	13	16	242	86	111	63
1973	71	85	631	236	186	205
1974	75	75	544	161	232	275
1975	138	88	460	100	314	97
1976	120	211	353	215	188	279
1977	131	135	301	146	203	392
1978	60	79	225	79	151	249
1979	45	39	177	40	152	210
1980	63	59	112	39	128	149
1981	48	72	155	39	158	446
1982	51	96	173	41	130	196
1983	75	60	150	48	119	161
1984	41	68	155	21	94	149
1985	24	52	105	37	65	239
1986	12	28	128	31	70	386
1987	28	21	132	22	109	156
Total	995	1,184	4,043	1,341	2,410	3,652

Note *Consolidated figures for January 1968–June 1972 unavailable; figures for 1988 not yet available.

OTHER TITLES
from
BLACKSTAFF PRESS

THE WIDENING GULF

NORTHERN ATTITUDES TO THE INDEPENDENT
IRISH STATE 1919–49

DENNIS KENNEDY

'The rights of the minority must be sacred to the majority. . . it will only be by broad views, tolerant ideas and a real desire for liberty of conscience that we here can make an ideal of the Parliament and the executive.'

Thus Sir James Craig, shortly to become the first Prime Minister of Northern Ireland, speaking in Belfast in February 1921. For good measure he went on to say that Unionists in the North were very much bound up in the rest of Ireland. They must hope not only for a brilliant prospect for Ulster, but a brilliant future for Ireland.

What went wrong? This penetrating study by Dennis Kennedy, former deputy editor of the *Irish Times,* examines the evolution of Unionist attitudes towards nationalist Ireland in the three decades after partition. As well as exploring the gulf that inexorably widened between Unionism and nationalism and between the two perceptions of Irish events, the book looks at the strains which developed between Belfast and London as Unionists became increasingly nervous about the security of their position within the UK.

Using as its main sources the *Belfast News-Letter,* the *Northern Whig* and the *Belfast Telegraph,* all Unionist-controlled and, through proprietors, editors and staff, closely integrated into the Unionist community, *The Widening Gulf* makes an important and original contribution to the debate on the roots of the continuing instability in Ireland.

198 x 129 mm; 272 pp; 0 85640 396 2; hb
£11.95

HELL OR CONNAUGHT!

THE CROMWELLIAN COLONISATION OF IRELAND
1652–1660

PETER BERRESFORD ELLIS

Cromwell's ruthless colonisation of Ireland is a story of cruelty and terror which still reverberates after more than three hundred years. Peter Berresford Ellis's acclaimed account of the period chillingly re-creates 'the curse of Cromwell' – the executions and mass transportations, the confiscation of lands and the banishment of Irish landowners 'to Hell or Connaught'.

'*Hell or Connaught!* covers the 1650s in more detail, and more readably, than any earlier work.'
Ruth Dudley Edwards, *Irish Independent*

'. . . full of Celtic virtues: sad, vivid, full of suppressed emotion'
Tom Pakenham, *Sunday Times*

'The Englishman who says that he cannot understand the Irish mind should first read this book.'
Lord O'Neill, *Books and Bookmen*

'fluently written. . . Cromwell's curse still lies on Ireland'
T.C. Barnard, *Times Literary Supplement*

First paperback edition

198 x 129 mm; 288 pp; illus; 0 85640 404 7; pb
£5.95

THE BOYNE WATER
THE BATTLE OF THE BOYNE 1690
PETER BERRESFORD ELLIS

In the year 1690 Ireland, still suffering from the effects of
Cromwell's colonisation, found itself the pivot of a wider
European crisis, with the battle eventually fought at the River
Boyne proving decisive of both international and Irish issues.
Peter Berresford Ellis's masterly account of the battle and of its
causes and consequences makes it plain why, after almost three
hundred years, the Boyne remains one of the most potent
symbols in Irish politics.

'It throws new light on that encounter and on the men who
fought on either side on that scorching July day. . . Well told,
the account is enlivened by vivid eye-witness descriptions of the
battle and its aftermath.'
Evening Herald

'an admirably impartial account'
Sunday Telegraph

'Although this is a history, it has the readability of a well-
written suspense novel, without losing any of the complexity of
life.'
Irish Democrat

'Thoroughly researched, competently put together and fluently
written. It can be recommended without reserve.'
British Book News

First paperback edition

198 x 129 mm; 176 pp; illus; 0 85640 419 5; pb
£5.95

BELFAST
An Illustrated History
Jonathan Bardon

Soundly established as the definitive book on the subject, this
bestselling history of Belfast – from its beginnings as a river-
crossing, through its centuries of radical politics and thrusting
commercial enterprise to its present state of violent conflict – has
now reached its fourth printing and features a new
full-colour jacket.

'Belfast has had to wait a long time for a history as good as this – lively,
objective, full of fascinating detail. The reader will be gripped by this fresh
and scholarly account long before he reaches the tumultuous years of our
present discontents.'
A.T.Q. Stewart

'Belfast is a place of superlatives: the finest setting of any large city in the
British Isles; the most explosive growth of any industrial centre in the
nineteenth century; arguably the most miserable architectural heritage of
any provincial capital, and definitely the least sought-after urban address
in the UK. Now it has a history to match its puzzling combination of
achievements. . . Jonathan Bardon is a Dubliner who has for twenty years
taught in Belfast and learned from it. . . and what an exciting story he has
to tell.'
Guardian

290 x 214 mm; 332 pp; illus; 0 85640 272 9; hb
£16.95

The Book of
ULSTER SURNAMES
Robert Bell

What's your name? What was your mother called? And her mother? What was your father's mother's name? Most of us know at least a few of the surnames that make up the heritage of our own families. But what do these names mean and where did they come from?

The Book of Ulster Surnames has entries for over five hundred of the most common family names of the province, with references to thousands more, and is packed with unexpected insights into the complex, turbulent origins of the Ulster people.

'. . . the most interesting book I have come across in a long time. . . Fascinating, fascinating, fascinating: buy yourself a late Christmas present, and have hours of entertainment.'
Kevin Myers, *Irish Times*

198 x 129 mm; 304 pp; 0 85640 416 0; hb
£12.95
0 85640 405 5; pb
£6.95

ORDERING
BLACKSTAFF BOOKS

All Blackstaff Press books are available through bookshops. In the case of difficulty, however, orders can be made directly to the publisher. Indicate clearly the title and number of copies required and send order with your name and address to:

Cash Sales
Blackstaff Press Limited
3 Galway Park
Dundonald
Belfast BT16 0AN
Northern Ireland

Please enclose a remittance to the value of the cover price plus: 60p for the first book plus 30p per copy for each additional book ordered to cover postage and packing. Payment should be made in sterling by UK personal cheque, postal order, sterling draft or international money order, made payable to Blackstaff Press Limited.

Applicable only in the UK and Republic of Ireland